Contents

◀◀ Canalside, Damme ◀ Brabo Fountain, Antwerp Grote Markt

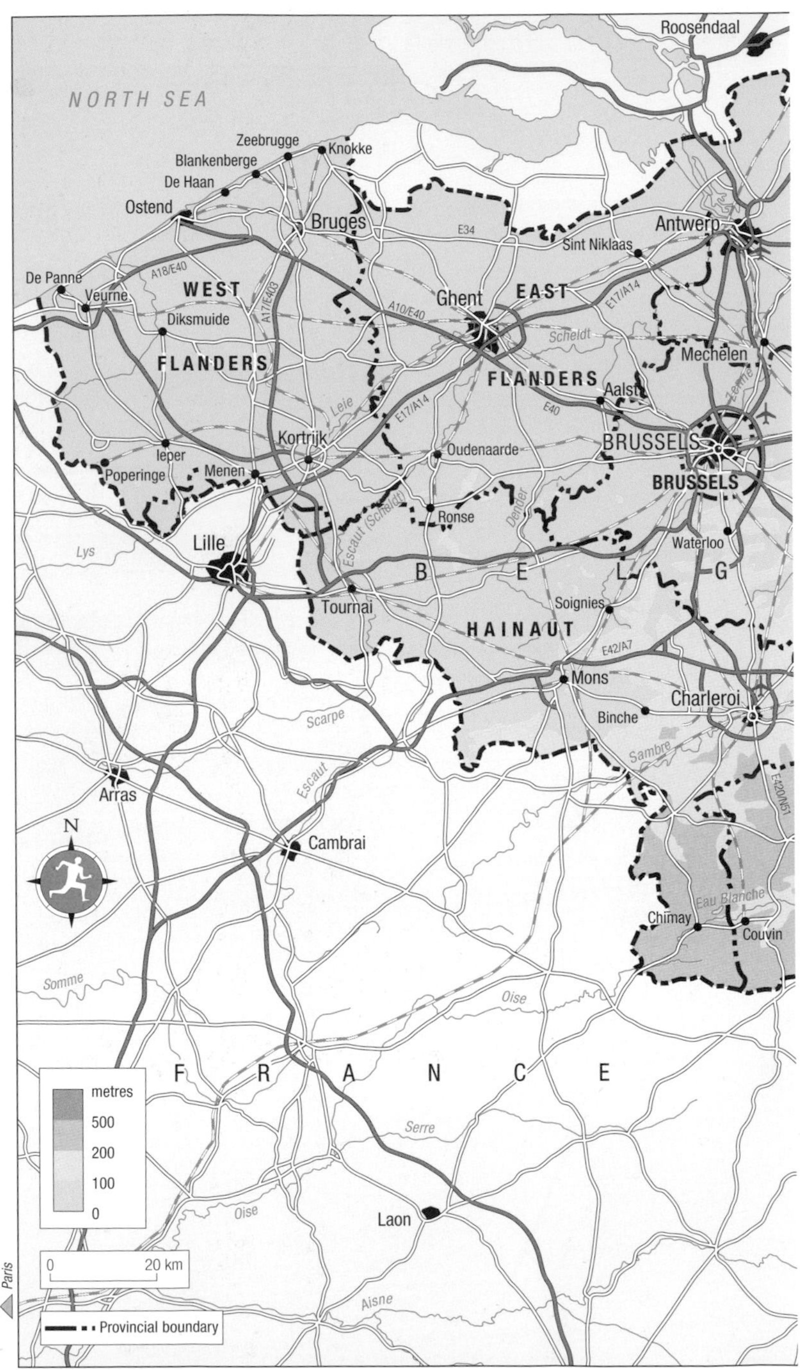
NORTH SEA
Roosendaal
Zeebrugge
Knokke
Blankenberge
De Haan
Ostend
Bruges
Antwerp
Sint Niklaas
E34
De Panne
A18/E40
Veurne
WEST
Diksmuide
A17/E403
FLANDERS
A10/E40
Ghent
EAST
E17/A14
Scheldt
Mechelen
FLANDERS
Aalst
Leie
E40
E17/A14
Kortrijk
BRUSSELS
BRUSSELS
Ieper
Poperinge
Menen
Oudenaarde
Ronse
Escaut (Scheldt)
Dender
Lys
Lille
Waterloo
B
E
L
G
Tournai
Soignies
HAINAUT
E42/A7
Mons
Charleroi
Binche
Scarpe
Sambre
Escaut
E420/N51
Arras
N
Cambrai
Eau Blanche
Chimay
Couvin
Somme
Oise
F
R
A
N
C
E
metres
500
200
100
0
Serre
Oise
Laon
0
20 km
Paris
Aisne
Provincial boundary

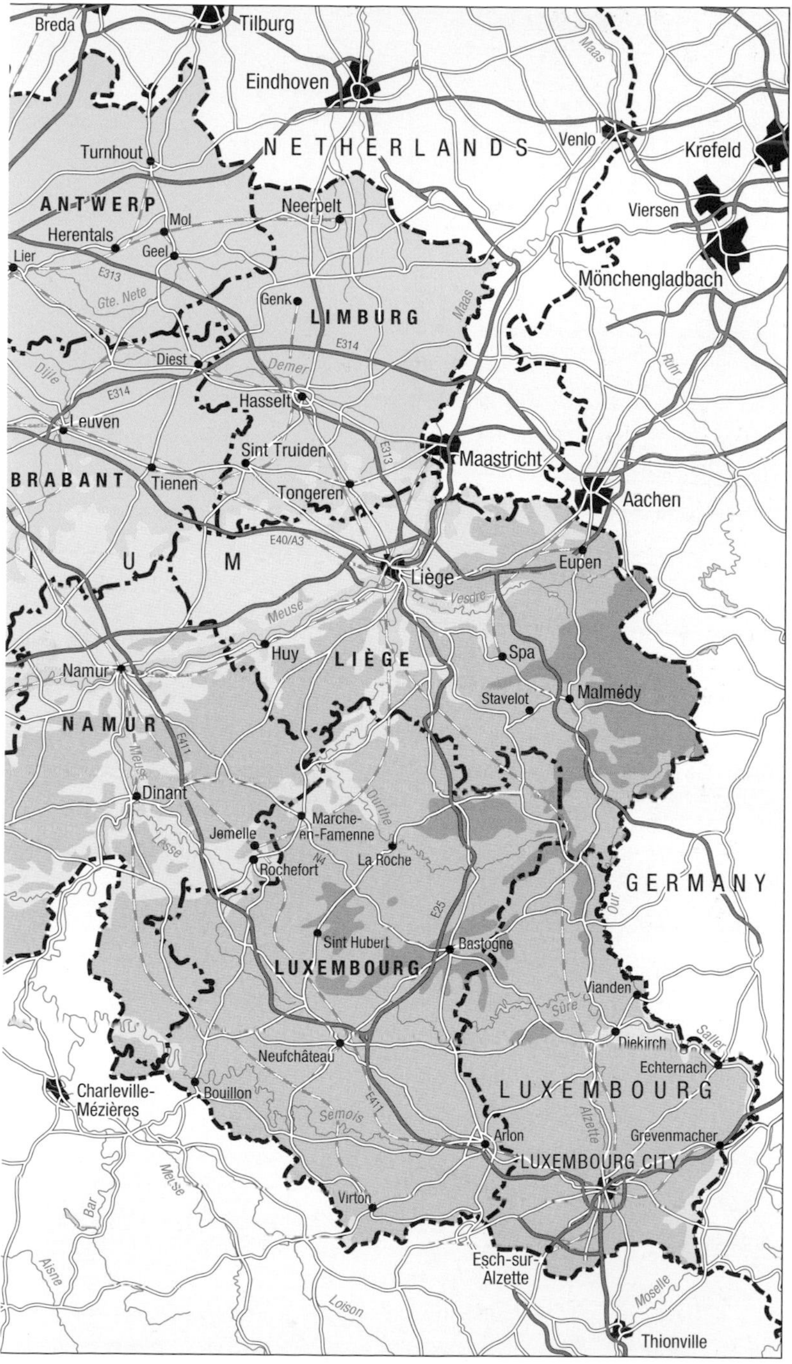
Breda
Tilburg
Eindhoven
NETHERLANDS
Venlo
Krefeld
Viersen
Mönchengladbach
Maas
Turnhout
ANTWERP
Neerpelt
Mol
Herentals
Geel
Lier
E313
Gte. Nete
Genk
LIMBURG
E314
Diest
Demer
Dijle
Hasselt
Ruhr
Leuven
Sint Truiden
E313
Maastricht
BRABANT
Tienen
Tongeren
Aachen
E40/A3
U
M
Eupen
Liège
Vesdre
Meuse
Huy
LIÈGE
Spa
Namur
Stavelot
Malmédy
NAMUR
E411
Meuse
Dinant
Marche-en-Famenne
Ourthe
Jemelle
Lesse
Rochefort
N4
La Roche
GERMANY
E25
Our
Sint Hubert
Bastogne
LUXEMBOURG
Vianden
Sûre
Diekirch
Sauer
Echternach
Neufchâteau
LUXEMBOURG
Charleville-Mézières
Bouillon
Alzette
Semois
E411
Arlon
Grevenmacher
LUXEMBOURG CITY
Meuse
Bar
Virton
Esch-sur-Alzette
Aisne
Moselle
Loison
Thionville

Introduction to

Belgium & Luxembourg

Belgium is perhaps the world's most misunderstood nation, but also one of its most fascinating, punching far above its weight in all sorts of ways. With three official languages, and an intense regional rivalry between the Flemish-speaking north and the French-speaking south that perpetually threatens to split the country in two, it's actually a miracle that Belgium exists at all. But its historic cities – most famously Brussels, Bruges, Antwerp and Ghent – are the equal of any in Europe; and its cuisine is reason alone to justify a visit, with a host of wonderful regional specialities. Belgium also boasts some pockets of truly beautiful countryside in its hilly, wooded south and the flatter north – and, perhaps most famously, it produces the most diverse range of beers of any country on the planet. Commonly regarded as a refuge of bankers and diplomats, neighbouring Luxembourg is perhaps more modest in its appeal, but it too has surprises in store. The capital, Luxembourg City, has an especially handsome setting, perched on a plateau above deep green gorges, with alluring landscapes of steep wooded hills and plunging valleys beyond.

Many outsiders view Belgium and Luxembourg as good weekend-break material, but not much else – which is a pity, as this is historically one of the most complex and intriguing parts of Europe. Squeezed in between France, Germany and the Netherlands, Belgium and Luxembourg occupy a spot that has often decided the European balance of power. It was

▲ Manneken Pis chocolates, Brussels

here that the Romans shared an important border with the Germanic tribes to the north; here that the Spanish Habsburgs finally met their match in the Protestant rebels of the Netherlands; here that Napoleon was finally defeated at the Battle of Waterloo; and – most famously – here, too, that the British and Belgians slugged it out with the Germans in World War I. Indeed so many powers have had an interest in this region that it was only in 1830 that Belgium and Luxembourg became separate, independent states.

Where to go

Belgium divides between the Flemish (Dutch-speaking) north of the country, known as **Flanders**, and French-speaking **Wallonia** in the south. There's more to this divide than just language, though: the north and south

Fact file

- **Belgium** is one of the smallest nations in Europe, with a population of around 10 million. Of these, around 5.5 million live in Flemish-speaking Flanders, while 3.5 million dwell in French-speaking Wallonia; there's also a small German-speaking community in the east. The tenacity of regional (and linguistic) feeling is such that Belgium is a federal state: both Flanders and Wallonia have their own regional administrations, as does the capital, Brussels, which is officially bilingual and has a population of around one million. A constitutional monarchy, Belgium has a bicameral parliament, comprising the Senate and Chamber of Deputies.
- The tiny Grand Duchy of **Luxembourg** has a population of around 480,000, a sixth of which lives in the capital, Luxembourg City. Luxembourgers switch comfortably between French, German and their own official spoken language, Lëzeburgesch (Luxembourgish), a dialect of German – all without so much as an intercommunal ripple. French and German are the official languages for all written purposes except governmental administration, which is conducted in French. The Duchy is a constitutional monarchy governed by the Chamber of Deputies, working in tandem with the Council of State.
- The vast majority of Belgians and Luxembourgers classify themselves as Roman Catholics.

▲ Ghent

of the country are visually very different. The **north**, made up of the provinces of West and East Flanders, Antwerp, Limburg and the top half of Brabant, is mainly flat, with a landscape and architecture not unlike the Netherlands. **Antwerp** is the largest city here, a sprawling, bustling old port with doses of high fashion and high art in roughly equal measure. Further west, in the two provinces of **Flanders**, are the great Belgian medieval cloth towns of **Bruges and Ghent**, with a stunning concentration of Flemish art and architecture. Bruges in particular is the country's biggest tourist pull, and although this inevitably means it gets very crowded, you shouldn't miss it on any account. Beyond lies the **Belgian coast**, which makes valiant attempts to compete with the seaside resorts of the rest of Europe but is ultimately let down by the coldness of the North Sea. Nonetheless, there are a couple of appealing seaside resorts, most notably **De Haan**, and the beaches and duney interludes along the coast are delightful. Nonetheless, you might be better off spending time in some of the other inland Flanders towns, not least **Ieper**, formerly and better known as Ypres, where every year visitors come to reflect on the stark sights of the nearby World War I battlefields and vast, sad acreages of cemeteries.

Marking the meeting of the Flemish and Walloon parts of Belgium, **Brussels**, the capital, is more exciting and varied than its reputation as a bland Euro-capital would suggest. Central enough to be pretty much unavoidable, it's moreover useful as a base for day-trips, especially given that Belgium isn't a large country and has an excellent public transport system. Bruges and Ghent are easily accessible from here, as is the old university city of **Leuven** to the east, and the cathedral city of **Mechelen**, halfway to Antwerp.

Flemish Brabant encircles Brussels, but to the south of the capital it narrows into a slender corridor beyond which lies Wallonian Brabant, distinguished by the splendid church at **Nivelles** and the elegaic abbey ruins at nearby **Villers-**

la-Ville. To the west of Brussels, the Walloon province of Hainaut is dotted with industrial centres like **Charleroi** and more appealing **Mons**, but also home to the handsome old town of **Tournai**; while to the east lies Belgium's most scenically rewarding region, the **Ardennes**, spread across the three provinces of **Namur**, **Liège** and **Luxembourg**. This is an area of deep, wooded valleys and heathy plateaux, often very wild and excellent for hiking, cycling and canoeing. Use either Namur or Luxembourg City as a jumping-off point for the heart of the region, at **Bouillon** or **La Roche-en-Ardenne**.

The Ardennes reaches across the Belgian border into the northern part of the **Grand Duchy** of Luxembourg, a green landscape of high hills and wooded ravines topped with crumbling castles overlooking rushing rivers. The two best centres for touring the countryside are the quiet little towns of **Vianden** and **Echternach**, featuring an extravagantly picturesque castle and a splendid abbey respectively. Indeed, despite its feeble reputation, the Duchy – or rather its northern reaches – packs more scenic highlights into its tight borders than many other more renowned

Chocolate

Belgians get through a lot of chocolate – several kilograms per person every year – but thereagain, considering how good it is here, it's a wonder it isn't more. The Belgians picked up their love of chocolate via the most circuitous of historical routes. The Aztecs of Mexico were drinking chocolate, which they believed gave them wisdom and power, when Hernando Cortéz's Spanish conquistadors turned up in 1519. Cortéz took a liking to the stuff and, after butchering the locals, brought cocoa beans back to Spain as a novelty gift for the Emperor Charles V in 1528. Within a few years its consumption had spread across Charles's empire, including today's Belgium and Luxembourg. At first the making of chocolate was confined to a few Spanish monasteries, but eventually Belgians got into the act and they now produce what are generally regarded as the best chocolates in the world. There are around two thousand chocolate shops around the country and even the smallest town or village will have at least one. Some brands are everywhere – Leonidas is perhaps the most ubiquitous; others include Godiva, Neuhaus and Moeder Babelutte – and you won't go far wrong buying from one of these places (it's worth remembering that Belgian chocolates are cheaper in Belgium!). But try also to seek out the independent producers, for example Wittamer or Pierre Marcolini in Brussels (see p.108), or Chocolate Line in Bruges (see p.172), which may be a little more expensive but will often be higher quality and more interesting.

Sandcastles

The Belgian coast may be crowded and short, the weather unreliable and the North Sea decidedly chilly, but it does boast a superb sandy beach, stretching – with very few interruptions – from Knokke-Heist in the north to De Panne, 70km to the south. The Belgians make the most of it, descending in their thousands every summer weekend to play beach sports and build sandcastles – but not just any old sandcastle. Right along the coast, ardent enthusiasts (helped by JCBs and tractors) apply themselves with industrial zeal, creating enormous, imaginative edifices from spaceships to sculpted tableaux of Belgians in some metaphysical mess or another, all cheered on by an appreciative crowd. Almost every resort has at least one sandcastle-building competition each summer, with one of the best held in the tiny resort of Zeebrugge in late August.

holiday spots, and is perfect for hiking and, at a pinch, mountain-biking. The Ardennes fizzles out as you reach the plainer scenery of the south, where the rolling agricultural terrain of the **Gutland** is a pleasant preamble to **Luxembourg City**, whose bastions and bulwarks recall the days when this was one of the strongest fortresses in Europe.

▲ Luxembourg City

When to go

Belgium enjoys a fairly standard temperate **climate**, with warm – if mild – summers and moderately cold winters. Generally speaking, temperatures rise the further south you go, with Wallonia a couple of degrees warmer than Flanders for most of the year, though in the east this is offset by the more severe climate of continental Europe, and

▶ Ostend beach

emphasized by the increase in altitude of the Ardennes. Luxembourg, too, has more extreme temperatures and harsher winters, often accompanied by snow. In both countries rain is always a possibility, though you can expect a greater degree of precipitation in the Ardennes and upland regions than on the northern plains.

The cities of Belgium and Luxembourg are all-year tourist destinations, though you might think twice about visiting Bruges, the region's most popular spot, during August, when things get mighty crowded. Flanders as a whole is best visited any time between early spring and late autumn, though winter has its advantages too – iced canals and hoarfrost polders – if you don't mind the short hours of daylight. Wallonia, especially the Ardennes, is more seasonal, with many things closing down in the winter, so try to visit between April and October.

Monthly temperatures and rainfall

	Jan	Feb	Mar	Apr	May	Jun	Jul	Aug	Sep	Oct	Nov	Dec
Brussels												
max/min (ºC)	4/-1	7/0	10/2	14/5	18/8	22/11	23/12	22/12	21/11	15/7	9/3	6/0
rainfall (mm)	66	61	53	60	55	76	95	80	63	83	75	88
Luxembourg City												
max/min (ºC)	3/-1	4/-1	10/1	14/4	18/8	21/11	23/13	22/12	19/10	13/6	7/3	4/0
rainfall (mm)	61	65	42	47	64	64	60	84	72	53	67	81

16 things not to miss

It's not possible to see everything that Belgium and Luxembourg have to offer in one trip – and we don't suggest you try. What follows, in no particular order, is a selective and subjective taste of the two countries' highlights, from wonderful food and striking Gothic architecture to handsome forested hills. They're all arranged in five colour-coded categories to help you find the very best things to see, do and experience. All entries have a page reference to take you straight into the Guide, where you can find out more.

01 Grand-Place, Brussels Page **60** • There are beautiful, delicately carved guildhouses in many Belgian towns, but none quite reaches the heights of those in the capital's main square.

02 The beach Page **119** • The Like many of the resorts along Belgium's coast, Ostend boasts a glorious stretch of beach.

03 Kayaking and hiking in the Ardennes Page **292** • The Ardennes' beautiful hills and valleys are perfect for a range of outdoor activities, and you don't have to be a well-equipped expert to have a go.

04 St-Baafskathedraal, Ghent Page **182** • Ghent's centre is a joy to discover, and its cathedral is home to Jan van Eyck's *Adoration of the Mystic Lamb* – one of the medieval world's most astonishing paintings.

05 Museeés Royaux des Beaux Arts, Brussels Page **76** • You'd have to go an awfully long way to beat Belgium's best art museum, with superb collections ranging from Jan van Eyck, Bosch and Bruegel to Ensor and beyond.

06 Moules Page **32** • Belgian cuisine is second to none, but has none of the pretentiousness of French food – and the national dish, mussels and fries, proves the point.

07 Luxembourg City Page **329** • Luxembourg's diminutive capital is one of the most dramatically situated in Europe, built astride two valleys and with a green, almost rural heart.

08 Musée Hergé Page **269** • Everyone knows Tintin, and this is an appropriately thoughtful homage to his creator, housed in a magnificent purpose-built structure.

09 Antwerp's Cathedral Page **212** • Perhaps the most beautiful Gothic structure in Belgium, with an interior graced by four fine paintings by Rubens.

10 Beer See ***Belgian beer* colour section** • With over seven hundred different brews to choose from, picking your way through the beer menus of Belgium's many cosy cafés is one of the country's real pleasures.

11 Bruges Page **148** • With its canals, museums and gorgeous medieval architecture, Bruges is without question one of Europe's most beguiling cities.

12 The Hautes Fagnes Page **321** • This high plateau in the Ardennes provides some fabulous hiking territory amid a windswept expanse of moorland and woodland.

13 Carnival Page 33 • Nowhere else in Europe celebrates carnival with the vim and gusto of Belgium. For originality, the pick of the carnival crop is at Binche, Malmedy – and Stavelot, where hooded Blancs Moussis take over the streets.

14 Brussels' Art Nouveau Page 91 • The capital's middle class took to this style of architecture like ducks to water; Victor Horta and Paul Hankar are the names to conjure with.

15 Menin Gate Page 136 • World War I was decided on the plain of Flanders, a point hammered home by the interminable names on the hulking mass of the Menin Gate in Ieper – perhaps the world's saddest war monument.

16 Musée Magritte Page 79 • One of Brussels' unmissable sights, the Musé Magritte displays the definitive collection of works by Belgium's most famous modern artist.

Basics

Basics

Getting there

UK travellers are spoilt for choice when it comes to deciding how to get to Belgium. There are flights to Brussels from London and a string of regional airports; Eurostar trains direct from London to Brussels; ferries from Rosyth and Hull to Zeebrugge, near Bruges, and from Ramsgate to Ostend; Eurotunnel services from Folkestone to Calais, a short drive from the Belgian coast; and frequent international buses from London to Brussels and Antwerp. Buses are usually the least expensive means of transportation, but the train is faster and often not that much more expensive, and there are all sorts of great deals on flights too. Luxembourg is also easy to get to: there are flights from London and Manchester but, perhaps most tempting of all, it's just three hours from Brussels to Luxembourg City by train.

For travellers arriving from North America, the main decision is whether to fly direct to Brussels – though the options are limited – or via another European city, probably London. Australians, New Zealanders and South Africans have to fly via another city – there are no nonstop flights.

Flights from the UK and Ireland

From the UK, Belgium's major airport – Brussels – is readily reached from London and a large number of regional airports. There's also Brussels-Charleroi airport, whose name is somewhat deceptive – it's actually on the edge of Charleroi, about 50km south of the capital. Luxembourg City airport, the third choice, is just a short bus ride from Luxembourg City. **Airlines** flying from the UK to Belgium include British Airways, bmi, Brussels Airlines, easyJet, Flybe, Lufthansa, KLM and Ryanair. Luxair and CityJet have flights to Luxembourg City from London City, British Airways flies there from Gatwick, and Lufthansa from Manchester. **Flying times** are insignificant: no more than 1.5hr from London or regional airports to Brussels and Luxembourg.

Flying **from Ireland**, there's much less choice, but Ryanair charges very reasonable rates for flights from Dublin to Brussels-Charleroi, while Aer Lingus links Dublin with Brussels airport, and Scandinavian Airlines flies from Dublin to both Brussels and Luxembourg City.

Whichever route and carrier you choose, it's hard to say precisely what you'll **pay** at any given time – there are just too many variables. That said, flying to Brussels from the UK with one of the low-cost airlines, a reasonable average **fare** would be about £100 return (including taxes), though you can pay as little as £50 and as much as £400.

From the US and Canada

From the **US**, you can fly direct to Brussels **from New York City** (American, Delta or Continental from Newark), Philadelphia (US Airways), Atlanta (Delta), Washington (United) and Chicago (American), but you'll often find cheaper deals if you're prepared to stop once, either in the US or mainland Europe. **Return fares** to Brussels from New York can be found for as little as $800, but $1200–1500 is a more normal fare. **From Chicago**, fares can cost as little as $1000, but $1500 is more the average. There are no direct flights **from the West Coast**, but plenty of carriers will get you to Brussels with one stop, for as little as $1200 return. There are no direct flights from the US to Luxembourg.

From Canada, Air Canada flies nonstop to London Heathrow, with onward connections to Brussels. **From Toronto** to Brussels,

Six steps to a better kind of travel

At Rough Guides we are passionately committed to travel. We feel strongly that only through travelling do we truly come to understand the world we live in and the people we share it with – plus tourism has brought a great deal of **benefit** to developing economies around the world over the last few decades. But the extraordinary growth in tourism has also damaged some places irreparably, and of course **climate change** is exacerbated by most forms of transport, especially flying. This means that now more than ever it's important to **travel thoughtfully** and **responsibly**, with respect for the cultures you're visiting – not only to derive the most benefit from your trip but also to preserve the best bits of the planet for everyone to enjoy. At Rough Guides we feel there are six main areas in which you can make a difference:

- Consider what you're contributing to the local economy, and how much the services you use do the same, whether it's through employing local workers and guides or sourcing locally grown produce and local services.
- Consider the environment on holiday as well as at home. Water is scarce in many developing destinations, and the biodiversity of local flora and fauna can be adversely affected by tourism. Try to patronize businesses that take account of this.
- Travel with a purpose, not just to tick off experiences. Consider spending longer in a place, and getting to know it and its people.
- Give thought to how often you fly. Try to avoid short hops by air and more harmful night flights.
- Consider alternatives to flying, travelling instead by bus, train, boat and even by bike or on foot where possible.
- Make your trips "climate neutral" via a reputable carbon offset scheme. All Rough Guide flights are offset, and every year we donate money to a variety of charities devoted to combating the effects of climate change.

return fares range from Can$700 to Can$2000, and about twenty percent more (Can$850–2400) from **Vancouver**.

From Australia and New Zealand

There are no direct flights **from Australia or New Zealand** to Brussels or Luxembourg City. Most itineraries will involve two changes, one in the Far East – Singapore, Bangkok or Kuala Lumpur – and then another in the gateway city of the airline you're flying with (most commonly Paris, Amsterdam or London). You can get tickets to Brussels **from Sydney** or **Melbourne** for Aus$1500–2000 if you shop around, and **from Auckland** for slightly more.

From South Africa

There are no direct flights **from South Africa** to Belgium or Luxembourg City, but KLM does offer direct flights to Amsterdam, a short train ride away from Belgium, from both Cape Town and Johannesburg. Alternatively, South African Airways flies direct to London, Munich and Frankfurt, from where it's a short hop onto Belgium and Luxembourg. **Return fares** with KLM from both cities direct to Amsterdam cost ZAR9000–10000.

By train from the UK

Eurostar trains running through the Channel Tunnel put Belgium within easy striking distance of London's St Pancras plus two stations in Kent – Ashford and Ebbsfleet. Indeed, considering the time it takes to check into any of London's airports, Eurostar is often faster than a flight – if, that is, you live in or near London. Eurostar operates around ten services a day from London St Pancras to Bruxelles-Midi, and the **journey time** is a very competitive two hours. **Fares** are largely defined by ticket flexibility, with the least flexible returns costing around £150, the most flexible, whose times and dates can be changed at will, working out at about £400. However, **advance booking** – at least three

Eurostar's monopoly

Eurostar has had a monopoly of train travel in the Channel Tunnel ever since it opened in 1994, but this monopoly ended in January 2010. Since then – and at time of writing – several rail companies have expressed an interest in running services through the tunnel, but the only one to have made significant progress is Germany's **Deutsche Bahn**, who are looking at the feasibility of operating services direct from London to Brussels, Cologne, Frankfurt and Amsterdam in 2013.

weeks ahead – halves the cost of the cheapest return ticket, and Eurostar also offers myriad special deals and discounts. Eurostar tickets from London to Brussels are also **common rated** for Belgium as a whole, which means, for example, that you can travel on to and return from Bruges via Brussels at no extra cost; this common rating system may come to an end if and when other train companies start using the Channel Tunnel (see box above).

If you're visiting Belgium and/or Luxembourg as part of a longer European trip, it may be worth considering a **pan-European rail pass**. There are lots to choose from and **Rail Europe** (Ⓦwww.raileurope.com), the umbrella company for all national and international passes, operates a comprehensive website detailing all the options with prices. Note in particular that some passes have to be bought before leaving home, others can only be bought in specific countries. For train travel within Belgium and Luxembourg, see p.23.

Driving from the UK

To reach Belgium **by car or motorbike**, you can either take one of the car ferries mentioned below or use **Eurotunnel**'s shuttle train through the Channel Tunnel. Note that Eurotunnel only carries cars (including occupants) and motorbikes, not foot passengers. From the Eurotunnel exit in Calais, it's just 50km or so to De Panne, on the Belgian coast, 120km to Bruges and 200km to Brussels.

Eurotunnel

There are up to four **Eurotunnel shuttle trains** per hour (only one per hour midnight–6am), taking 35 minutes (45min for some night departure times), you must check in at Folkestone at least thirty minutes before departure. It's possible to turn up and buy your ticket at the toll booths (exit the M20 at junction 11a), though advance booking is advisable and usually much less expensive. **Fares**, which are levied on the vehicle (not the number of passengers), depend on the time of year, time of day and length of stay; it's usually cheaper to travel between 10pm and 6am, and advance booking attracts substantial discounts. Book well ahead, and a week-long return ticket in June will cost £100–140 without any flexibility, £200 with flexibility.

By ferry from the UK

Three operators currently run **car ferries** from the UK direct to two ports in Belgium. They are **Transeuropa**, whose vessels link Ramsgate with Ostend (4hr); **P&O** from Hull to Zeebrugge (13hr); and **Norfolkline** from Rosyth to Zeebrugge (20hr). Zeebrugge is a few kilometres from Bruges. **Tariffs** vary enormously, depending on when you leave, how long you stay, what size your vehicle is and how many passengers are in it; on the two longer routes, there is also the cost of a cabin to consider. As a sample fare, Transeuropa Ferries charges about £50 to transport a car and four passengers from Ramsgate to Ostend – and the return costs about the same, though special deals can lower the price even further. On the two longer routes, booking ahead is strongly recommended – indeed it's essential in summer.

By train from continental Europe

Belgium and Luxembourg have borders with France, Germany and the Netherlands. A veritable raft of rail lines runs into Belgium from its neighbours – and Luxembourg has good international connections too. Ordinary trains link many cities and towns and there are also the express trains of **Thalys**, a combined project of the Belgian, Dutch, French and German railways. The hub of the

Thalys network is Brussels, from where there are trains to – among many destinations – Rotterdam, Amsterdam, Paris and Cologne.

By bus from the UK

Given the low cost of budget-airline airfares, travelling by long-distance **bus** from the UK to Belgium may not seem too attractive a proposition, but it is still likely to be the cheapest way of getting there. **Eurolines**, part of National Express, has four daily departures from London's Victoria coach station to Antwerp and Brussels, with a journey time of around eight hours to both destinations. **Return tickets** cost £40–60, and there are small discounts for travellers under 25 and over 60. There are also less frequent Eurolines buses to several other Belgian cities, including Ghent.

Airlines, agents and operators

Airlines

Air Canada Ⓦ www.aircanada.com.
Aer Lingus Ⓦ www.aerlingus.com.

Air New Zealand Ⓦ www.airnz.co.nz.
American Airlines Ⓦ www.aa.com.
bmi Ⓦ www.flybmi.com.
bmibaby Ⓦ www.bmibaby.com.
British Airways Ⓦ www.ba.com.
Brussels Airlines Ⓦ www.brusselsairlines.com.
CityJet Ⓦ www.cityjet.com.
Continental Airlines Ⓦ www.continental.com.
Delta Ⓦ www.delta.com.
easyJet Ⓦ www.easyjet.com.
Flybe Ⓦ www.flybe.com.
KLM Ⓦ www.klm.com.
Lufthansa Ⓦ www.lufthansa.com.
Luxair Ⓦ www.luxair.lu.
Qantas Airways Ⓦ www.qantas.com.
Ryanair Ⓦ www.ryanair.com.
Singapore Airlines Ⓦ www.singaporeair.com.
South African Airways Ⓦ www.flysaa.com.
United Airlines Ⓦ www.united.com.
US Airways Ⓦ www.usairways.com.

Agents and operators

North South Travel UK Ⓣ 01245/608 291, Ⓦ www.northsouthtravel.co.uk. Friendly, competitive travel agency, offering discounted fares worldwide. Profits are used to support projects in the developing world, especially the promotion of sustainable tourism.
STA Travel UK Ⓣ 0871/2300 040, US Ⓣ 1-800/781-4040, Australia Ⓣ 134 782, New Zealand Ⓣ 0800/474 400, South Africa Ⓣ 0861/781 781; Ⓦ www.statravel.co.uk. Worldwide specialists in independent travel; also student IDs, travel insurance, car rental, rail passes, and more. Good discounts for students and under-26s.
Trailfinders UK Ⓣ 0845/058 5858, Ireland Ⓣ 01/677 7888, Australia Ⓣ 1300/780 212; Ⓦ www.trailfinders.com. One of the best-informed and most efficient agents for independent travellers.
Travel CUTS Canada Ⓣ 1-866/246-9762, US Ⓣ 1-800/592-2887; Ⓦ www.travelcuts.com. Canadian youth and student travel firm.
USIT Ireland Ⓣ 01/602 1906, Northern Ireland Ⓣ 028/9032 7111; Ⓦ www.usit.ie. Ireland's main student and youth travel specialists.

Train contacts

Belgian Railways Ⓦ www.b-rail.be.
Eurostar Ⓦ www.eurostar.com.
French Railways (SNCF) Ⓦ www.sncf.fr.
German Rail Ⓦ www.bahn.de.
Netherlands Rail Ⓦ www.ns.nl.
Rail Europe Ⓦ www.raileurope.com.
Thalys Ⓦ www.thalys.com.

Bus contact

Eurolines ⓦ www.eurolines.co.uk.

Ferry contacts

Norfolkline ⓦ www.norfolkline.com.
P&O Ferries ⓦ www.poferries.com.
Transeuropa Ferries ⓦ www.transeuropaferries.com.

Eurotunnel contact

Eurotunnel ⓦ www.eurotunnel.com.

Getting around

Travelling around Belgium is almost always easy: it's a small country, and there's an extremely well-organized – and reasonably priced – public transport system in which an extensive train network is supplemented by (and tied in with) a plethora of local bus services. Luxembourg is, of course, even smaller, but here matters are not quite so straightforward: the train network is limited, and the public transport system is largely based around buses, whose timetables can demand careful scrutiny.

Travel **between Belgium and Luxembourg** is a seamless affair – with no border controls and with routine through-ticketing by train and bus. Two main rail lines link the two countries: the first runs from Brussels to Luxembourg City via Namur and Arlon, the second links Liège with Luxembourg City. Journey times are insignificant – Brussels to Luxembourg City takes under three hours – and services are frequent. Note also that in addition to the domestic deals and discounts described below, there are a host of **pan-European rail passes**. Some have to be bought before leaving home while others are available only in specific countries; for further details, see p.21.

Belgium by train

The best way of getting around **Belgium** is by **train**. The system, operated by the Société Nationale des Chemins de Fer Belges/Belgische Spoorwegen (Belgian Railways; ⓦ www.b-rail.be), is one of the best in Europe: trains are fast, frequent and very punctual; the network of lines is comprehensive; and **fares** are relatively low. For example, a standard, second-class ticket (*billet ordinaire/gewone biljet*) from Bruges to Arlon, one of the longest domestic train journeys you can make, costs just €19.40 one-way, whilst the forty-minute trip from Ghent to Brussels cost €7.50. Standard return tickets are twice the cost of a single, but same-day return tickets knock about ten percent off the price. First-class fares cost about fifty percent on top of the regular fare. There are substantial discounts for children and seniors (65+). With any ticket, you're free to stop off anywhere en route and continue your journey later that day, but you're not allowed to backtrack. Belgian Railways publishes a comprehensive and easy-to-use **timetable** (*indicateur/spoorboekje*), which is available for €11 at all major stations, as well as mounds of information on its various services, passes and fares. Note, however, that you are not allowed to buy a ticket with a foreign debit card and neither do automatic ticket machines accept foreign credit or debit cards.

Discount train tickets and deals

Belgian Railways offers a variety of **discount tickets and deals**. Some reward off-peak travelling, others offer substantial discounts if you are making the same journey on several occasions, but perhaps the most useful are the **special weekend returns**, which can knock up to fifty percent off the cost of regular travel. For further information, consult Belgian Railways' website.

Luxembourg by train

In **Luxembourg**, the trains are run by the Société Nationale des Chemins de Fer Luxembourgeois (CFL; Ⓦwww.cfl.lu in French, details in English at Ⓦwww.luxembourg.co.uk). The network comprises just a handful of lines, with the principal route cutting north–south down the middle of the country from Belgium's Liège to Luxembourg City via Clervaux and Ettelbruck. Trains are fast and efficient, and most operate hourly. A free diagrammatic **plan** of the country's bus and train network is available at most train stations, as are individual train and bus timetables, or you can purchase a countrywide bus and train timetable from all major train stations at minimal cost. A **network ticket** (*billet réseau*), valid for train and bus travel across the whole of the Grand Duchy, is very reasonably priced, with a one-day pass costing €4, or €16 for a pack of five. These are valid from the first time you use them (you must punch them in the machines provided to record the time) until 8am the following day. Another option, available between Easter and October, is the **Luxembourg Card**, which permits free travel on the country's buses and trains and also gives discounted admission to many tourist attractions (see p.325).

Belgium by bus

With so much of the country covered by the rail network, **Belgian buses** are mainly of use for travelling short distances, and wherever there's a choice of transportation the train is quicker and not that much more expensive. Indeed, in most of Belgium buses essentially supplement the trains, with services radiating out from the train station and/or connecting different rail lines. That said, local buses are invaluable in some parts of rural Belgium, like the Botte de Hainaut and the Ardennes, where the train network fizzles out. Three **bus companies** provide nationwide coverage: De Lijn (Ⓦwww.delijn.be) in the Flemish-speaking areas; STIB (Ⓦwww.stib.be) in Brussels; and TEC (Ⓦwww.infotec.be) in Wallonia.

Luxembourg by bus

In **Luxembourg**, the sparseness of the rail system means that **buses** are much more important than in Belgium, though again bus and train services are fully integrated. A free diagrammatic **plan** of the Grand Duchy's bus and train network is available at major bus and train stations, as are individual bus **timetables**; alternatively, for a few euros, you can purchase a countrywide bus and train timetable from all major train stations. For details of tickets and fares, see "Luxembourg by train", above.

By car

For the most part, **driving** around Belgium and Luxembourg is pretty much what you would hope: smooth, easy and quick. Both countries have a good road network, with most of the major towns linked by some kind of motorway or dual carriageway, though snarl-ups are far from rare, especially in Belgium. That said, big-city driving, where congestion and one-way systems are the norm, is almost always problematic, particularly as drivers in Belgium are generally considered some of the most pugnacious in Europe. One problem peculiar to Belgium, however, is **signage**. In most cases the French and Flemish names are similar – or at least mutually recognizable – but in others they do not resemble each other at all (see box, p.26, for some of the trickier examples). In Brussels and its environs, all the road signs are bilingual, but elsewhere it's either French or Flemish and, as you cross **Belgium's language divide** (see p.370), the name you've been following on the road signs can simply disappear, with, for example, "Liège" suddenly transformed into "Luik". Whatever you do, make sure you've got a good road map (see p.40).

Rules of the road are straightforward: you drive on the right, and **speed limits** are 50kph in built-up areas, 90kph outside, 120kph on motorways; note that speed cameras are commonplace. Drivers and front-seat passengers are required by law to wear seatbelts, and penalties for drunk driving are always severe. Remember also

French and Flemish place names

The list below provides the **French and Flemish names** of some of the more important towns in Belgium where the difference may cause confusion. The official name comes first, the alternative afterwards, except in the case of Brussels where both languages are of equal standing.

French–Flemish
Bruxelles – Brussel
Ath – Aat
Liège – Luik
Mons – Bergen
Namur – Namen
Nivelles – Nijvel
Soignies – Zinnik
Tournai – Doornik

Flemish–French
Antwerpen – Anvers
Brugge – Bruges
De Haan – Le Coq
Gent – Gand
Ieper – Ypres
Kortrijk – Courtrai
Leuven – Louvain
Mechelen – Malines
Oostende – Ostende
Oudenaarde – Audenarde
Ronse – Renaix
Sint Truiden – St-Trond
Tienen – Tirlemont
Tongeren – Tongres
Veurne – Furnes
Zoutleeuw – Léau

that trams have right of way over any other vehicle, and that, unless indicated otherwise, motorists must give way to traffic merging from the right. There are no toll roads, and although **fuel** is expensive, at €1.40–1.50 per litre (diesel €1.17) in Belgium, slightly less in Luxembourg, the short distances involved mean this isn't too much of an issue.

Most **foreign driving licences** are honoured in Belgium and Luxembourg, including all EU, Australian, New Zealand, US, Canadian and South African ones. If you're **bringing your own car**, you must have adequate insurance, preferably including coverage for legal costs, and it's advisable to have an appropriate breakdown policy from your home motoring organization too.

Renting a car

All the major **international car rental agencies** are represented in Belgium and Luxembourg and a scattering of contact details are given in the "Listings" section at the end of the Guide accounts of major towns. To rent a car, you'll have to be 21 or over (and have been driving for at least a year), and you'll need a credit card – though some local agencies will accept a hefty cash deposit instead. **Rental charges** are fairly high, beginning around €300 per week for unlimited mileage in the smallest vehicle, but include collision damage waiver and vehicle (but not personal) insurance. To cut costs, book in advance and online. If you go to a smaller, local company (of which there are many), you should proceed with care: in particular, check the policy for the excess applied to claims and ensure that it includes a collision damage waiver (applicable if an accident is your fault) as well as adequate levels of financial cover.

If you **break down** in a rented car, you'll get roadside assistance from the particular repair company the rental firm has contracted. The same principle works with your own vehicle's breakdown policy providing you have coverage abroad.

Car rental agencies

Auto Europe ⓦ www.autoeurope.com.
Avis ⓦ www.avis.com.
Budget ⓦ www.budget.com.
Europcar ⓦ www.europcar.com.
Hertz ⓦ www.hertz.com.
National ⓦ www.nationalcar.com.
Skycars ⓦ www.skycars.com.

Cycling

Cycling is something of a national passion **in Belgium**, and it's also – given the short distances and largely flat terrain – a viable and fairly effortless way of getting around. That said, you do have to be selective:

cycling in most of the big cities and on the majority of trunk roads – where separate cycle lanes are far from ubiquitous – is precarious, verging on the suicidal. On the other hand, once you've reached the countryside, there are dozens of clearly **signposted cycle routes** to follow – and local tourist offices will invariably have maps and route descriptions, which you can supplement with the relevant IGN (NGI) map (see p.40). The logic of all this means that most Belgian cyclists – from Eddy Merckx lookalikes to families on an afternoon's pedal – carry their bikes to their chosen cycling location by car or train (though not by bus – it's not usually allowed). To aid the process, **Belgian Railways** transports bicycles with the minimum of fuss and at minimal cost.

If you haven't brought your own bicycle, you can **rent bikes** from ten train stations nationwide (mostly in Flanders) and from a veritable host of local bike rental shops. **Prices** start at around €12 per day. There's also the **Train & Bike** (Train & Vélo/Trein & Fiets) package, in which the price of a day-long excursion includes both a return train ticket and cycle rental. For a full list of train stations offering bike rental, consult the "useful tips" section of ⓦwww.b-rail.be. It's a good idea to reserve your bike ahead of time during the summer.

Cycling in Luxembourg

Luxembourg is popular with cyclists and has over 500km of **cycle tracks**, many of them following old railway lines. You can **rent bikes** at an assortment of campsites, hostels, hotels and tourist offices for around €12 a day (€20–30 for a mountain bike); tourist offices also have comprehensive lists of local bike rental outlets. Bear in mind also that you can take your bike on trains (but not buses) anywhere in the country at minimal cost. For further details, consult the website of the Luxembourg National Tourist Office (see p.44).

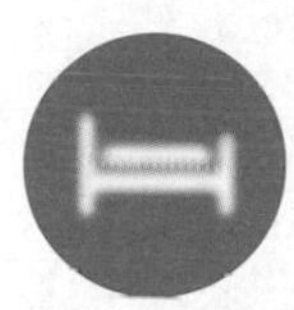

Accommodation

Inevitably, hotel accommodation is one of the major expenses you'll incur on a trip to Belgium and Luxembourg – indeed, if you're after a degree of comfort, it's going to be the costliest item by far. There are budget alternatives, however, beginning with the no-frills end of the hotel market and B&Bs – though note these are effectively rented rooms in private houses rather than the British-style bed-and-breakfast. Even more of a bargain are the youth hostels, be they Hostelling International-affiliated or "unofficial" (private) ones, which are located in the larger cities and/or main tourist spots of both countries.

Advance booking is recommended everywhere, but most tourist offices do operate an on-the-spot reservation service for same-night accommodation, either free or at minimal charge. Alternatively, consult Belgium Hospitality (ⓦwww.belgium-hospitality.com), which operates an efficient hotel reservation service, seeking out the best deals and discounts.

Hotels

Across Belgium, Luxembourg and the Netherlands, a common **Benelux standard** is used to classify all those hotels, guesthouses (*auberges/gasthofs*) and motels that are recognized and licensed by the appropriate government agency. In Belgium, there are three such licensing agencies – one each for Brussels and the French- and

Accommodation price codes

All the accommodation listed in this Guide has been graded according to the following price codes, which indicate the price for the least expensive double room available during high season excluding special deals and discounts. **Single rooms** generally cost between sixty and eighty percent of the double-room rate. These codes are above all a guide to price, and aren't intended to indicate the level of facilities available. You'll also find that many hotels have a wide range of rooms, some with en-suite facilities, some without, some large and luxurious, some small; thus, an establishment graded, for example, as a ❸ may also have plenty of more comfortable rooms at ❹. Most hotels only charge the full quoted rates at the very busiest times, which means that you'll often pay less than the price quoted in this book; it's certainly always worth asking if there is any discount available either by phone or **online**, where most of the best deals are posted. In the case of hostels we've given the code if they have double rooms; otherwise, we've stated the price per dorm bed.

❶ €60 and under
❷ €61–80
❸ €81–100
❹ €101–120
❺ €121–150
❻ €151–180
❼ €181–210
❽ €211–250
❾ €251 and over

Flemish-speaking regions; Luxembourg has just one. The Benelux standard grades establishments within general categories – from **one-star** to **five-star** – and the appropriate number of stars is displayed outside all licensed premises on a blue permit shield; places that fail to obtain a licence are not allowed a shield. The classification system is, by necessity, measured against easily identifiable criteria – lifts, toilets, room service, etc – rather than aesthetics, specific location or even cost. Consequently, they only provide a general guide to both quality and prices: a poky room in a three-star hotel in a mediocre part of Bruges may, for instance, cost more than a comfortable room in a four-star hotel in the centre of a less popular town. That said, one- and two-star places are frequently rudimentary (incidentally, hotel foyers can be deceptively plush compared with the rooms beyond) and, in general, you only begin to hit the real comfort zone at three stars. **Prices** fluctuate wildly with demand and not necessarily with the season – indeed summertime is bargain time in Brussels. Typically, the stated price includes **breakfast**.

B&Bs

In recent years, the number of **Belgian B&Bs** (*chambres d'hôtes/gastenkamers*) has increased rapidly, though "B&B" is perhaps something of a misnomer as guests rarely have much contact with their hosts – it's more like a rented room in a private house. The average B&B in both Belgium and Luxembourg works out at €50–80 per double per night, a tad more in Brussels and Bruges. The only common snag is that many B&Bs are inconveniently situated far from the respective town or city centre – be sure to check out the location before you accept a room. Note too that as the owners don't usually live on the premises, access often has to be arranged beforehand. In most places, the tourist office has a list of local B&Bs, which it will issue to visitors, but in the more popular destinations – for instance Bruges and Ghent – B&Bs are publicized alongside hotels. In **Luxembourg**, B&Bs are less of a feature, though again local tourist offices have the details.

Wherever the arrangements are more formalized – again as in Bruges – the B&B premises are inspected and awarded stars in accordance with the Benelux standard (see p.27).

Hostels

If you're travelling on a tight budget, a **hostel** is likely to be your accommodation of choice, whether you're youthful or not. They can often be extremely good value, and offer clean and comfortable dorm beds as well as a choice of rooms (doubles and sometimes singles) at rock-bottom prices. Both city and country locations can get very full between

June and September, when you should book in advance. If you're planning on spending some nights in HI-affiliate hostels, it makes sense to **join your home HI organization** (see below) before you leave in order to avoid paying surcharges.

Belgian hostels

Belgium has around thirty HI-affiliated **hostels** (*auberges de jeunesse/jeugdherbergen*) operated by two separate organizations, **Vlaamse Jeugdherbergen** (Ⓦwww.vjh.be), covering the Flemish region, and **Les Auberges de Jeunesse de Wallonie** (Ⓦwww.laj.be) for Wallonia. Both run hostels in Brussels. **Dorm beds** cost about €16 per person per night including breakfast; there are no age restrictions. Accommodation is usually in small **dormitories**, though most hostels have single- and double-bedded rooms in which prices rise to €18–20 per person per night. **Meals** are often available and in some hostels there are **self-catering facilities** too. Most Belgian hostels accept online bookings.

Luxembourg hostels

In addition to the HI-affiliated hostels, some of Belgium's larger cities – primarily Antwerp, Bruges and Brussels – have several **private hostels**, sometimes referred to as *logements pour jeunes/jeugdlogies*, offering dormitory accommodation (and invariably double- and triple-bedded rooms, too) at broadly similar prices, though standards vary enormously; we've given detailed reviews in the Guide.

Luxembourg has ten youth hostels, all members of the Centrale des Auberges de Jeunesse Luxembourgeoises (CAJL; Ⓦwww.youthhostels.lu). **Prices** for HI members are €16–20 per person for a dorm bed, €23–25 per person in a double room, both with breakfast included; some places also serve meals.

Youth hostel associations

US and Canada

Hostelling International–American Youth Hostels Ⓦwww.hiusa.org.
Hostelling International Canada Ⓦwww.hihostels.ca.

UK and Ireland

Youth Hostel Association (YHA; England & Wales) Ⓦwww.yha.org.uk.
Scottish Youth Hostel Association Ⓦwww.syha.org.uk.
Irish Youth Hostel Association Ⓦwww.anoige.ie.
Hostelling International Northern Ireland Ⓦwww.hini.org.uk.

Australia, New Zealand and South Africa

Australian Youth Hostels Association Ⓦwww.yha.com.au.
Youth Hostelling Association New Zealand Ⓦwww.yha.co.nz.
South African Youth Hostel Association Ⓦwww.hisa.org.za.

Camping

Camping is a popular pastime in both Belgium and Luxembourg. In **Belgium**, there are literally hundreds of campsites to choose from, anything from a field with a few pitches through to extensive complexes with all mod

Campsite classifications in Belgium

Campsites in Belgium are graded within the following general categories. They provide a guide as to facilities, but not necessarily to cost.
1-star Must comply with minimum camping regulations by having drinking-water facilities, cold showers, flush toilets, washbasins and power points.
2-star As for previous grade, but must have daytime supervision and more electrical facilities.
3-star Must have hot showers, sports facilities and a shop.
4-star As for previous grade, but must also possess a restaurant, children's playing area and electrical fixtures throughout the site.
5-star As for previous grade, but more facilities per person and a higher level of supervision.

cons. The country's campsites are regulated by two governmental agencies – one for Flanders and one for Wallonia – and each produces its own camping booklets and operates a **website**: Ⓦwww.camping.be for Flanders, Ⓦwww.campingbelgique.be for Wallonia. Many Belgian campsites are situated with the motorist in mind, occupying key locations beside main roads, and they are all classified within the **Benelux one- to five-star matrix** (see box, p.27). The majority are one- and two-star establishments, for which a family of two adults, two children, a car and a tent can expect to pay between €15 and €30 per night. Prices are comparable in **Luxembourg**, which has around ninety registered campsites, all detailed on Ⓦwww.camping.lu. Luxembourg does not now enforce the Benelux star system (though individual campsites can register if they wish) and the best campsites are now awarded the **Luxembourg Quality Label**; environmentally friendly sites can opt for the **Luxembourg EcoLabel** instead.

Farm and rural holidays

In both Belgium and Luxembourg, the tourist authorities coordinate **farm and rural holidays**, ranging from family accommodation in a farmhouse to the renting of rural apartments and country dwellings. In Wallonia and Luxembourg, there are also **gîtes d'étapes** – dormitory-style lodgings situated in relatively remote parts of the country – which can house anywhere between ten and one hundred people per establishment. You can often choose to rent just part of the *gîte d'étape* or stay on a bed-and-breakfast basis. Some of the larger *gîtes d'étapes* (or *gîtes de groupes*) cater for large groups only, accepting bookings for a minimum of 25 people.

In all cases, advance booking is essential and **prices**, naturally enough, vary widely depending on the quality of accommodation, the length of stay and the season. As examples, a high-season (mid-June to Aug), week-long booking of a pleasantly situated and comfortable farmhouse for four adults and three children might cost you in the region of €350–450, whereas a ten-person *gîte d'étape* might cost €300–400. For further details, check out Ⓦwww.hoevetoerisme.be for Flanders, Ⓦwww.gitesdewallonie.net for Wallonia, and Ⓦwww.gites.lu for Luxembourg.

Food and drink

Belgian cuisine, particularly that of Brussels and Wallonia, is held in high regard worldwide, and in most of Europe is seen as second only to French in quality – indeed many feel it's of equal standing. For such a small country, there's a surprising amount of provincial diversity, but it's generally true to say that pork, beef, game, fish and seafood – especially mussels – are staple items, often cooked with butter, cream and herbs, or sometimes beer – which is, after all, Belgium's national drink. Soup is also common, a hearty stew-like affair offered in a huge tureen from which you can help yourself – a satisfying and reasonably priced meal in itself. The better Belgian chefs are often eclectic, dipping into many other cuisines, especially those of the Mediterranean, and also borrowing freely from across their own country's cultural/linguistic divide.

Luxembourg cuisine doesn't rise to quite such giddy heights, though it's still of an excellent standard. The food here borrows extensively from the **Ardennes** but, as you might expect, has more Germanic influences, with sausages and sauerkraut

For a menu reader for both French and Flemish (Dutch) terms, see pp.388–390 & pp.392–394.

featuring on menus alongside pork, game and river fish. As for **drink**, **beer** is one of the real delights of Belgium, and Luxembourg produces some very drinkable **white wines** from the vineyards along the west bank of the River Moselle.

Food

In both countries, the least expensive places to eat are **cafés** and **bars** – though the distinction between the two is typically blurred, hence the large number of **café-bars**. A number of these establishments flank every main square in every small and medium-sized town, offering basic dishes, such as pasta, soups, croque-monsieur (a toasted ham and cheese sandwich with salad) and chicken or steak with chips. Prices are usually very reasonable – reckon on about €12 for the more modest dishes, €17 for the more substantial – though of course you will often pay more in the most popular tourist destinations. In general, and especially in Wallonia, the quality of these dishes will regularly be excellent and portions characteristically substantial. In the big cities, these café-bars play second fiddle to more specialist – and equally inexpensive – places, primarily pasta and pizza joints, cafés that cater for the shopper – and specialize in cakes and pastries – ethnic café-restaurants and so forth.

Though there's often a thin dividing line between the café and the **restaurant**, the latter are mostly a little more formal and, not surprisingly, rather more expensive. Even in the cheapest restaurant a main course will rarely cost under €15, with a more usual figure being between €20 and €27. Restaurants are usually open at lunchtime (noon–2pm), but the main focus is in the evening. In addition, many restaurants close one day a week, usually Monday or Tuesday, and in the smaller towns kitchens start to wind down around 9.30/10pm. One final point is that many bars, cafés and restaurants offer a good-value *plat du jour/dagschotel*, usually for around €15, and frequently including a drink.

Wallonian cuisine

Wallonian cuisine is broadly similar to French, based upon a fondness for rich sauces and the freshest of ingredients. From the Walloons come *truite à l'Ardennaise*, trout cooked in a wine sauce; *chicorées gratinées au four*, chicory with ham and cheese; *fricassée Liègeois*, basically, fried eggs, bacon and sausage or blood pudding; *fricadelles à la bière*, meatballs in beer; and *carbonnades de porc Bruxelloise*, pork with a tarragon and tomato sauce.

The **Ardennes**, in particular, is well known for its cured **ham** (similar to Italian Parma ham) and, of course, its **pâté**, made from pork, beef, liver and kidney – though it often takes a particular name from an additional ingredient, for example *pâté de faisan* (pheasant) or *pâté de lièvre* (hare). Unsurprisingly, game (*gibier*) features heavily on most Ardennes menus. Among the many salads you'll find are *salade de Liège*, made from beans and potatoes, and *salade wallonio*, a warm salad of lettuce, fried potatoes and bits of bacon.

Flemish cuisine

In **Flanders**, the food is more akin to that of the Netherlands, characteristically plainer and simpler. Indeed, for decades traditional Flemish cuisine was regarded with much disdain as crude and unsubtle, but in recent years there's been a dramatic revival of its

Vegetarians

Traditional Belgian and Luxembourg cuisine is largely fish- and meat-based, which means **vegetarians** can be in for a difficult time, though all of the larger towns do have at least a couple of vegetarian places, even if these tend to operate limited opening hours. Antwerp and Ghent are the vegetarian high points, not only because of the number of vegetarian places, but also because non-meat options are available on many regular menus.

fortunes, and nowadays Flemish specialities appear on most menus in the north and there are dozens of speciality Flemish restaurants too.

Commonplace **dishes** include *waterzooi*, a soup-cum-stew consisting of chicken or fish boiled with fresh vegetables; *konijn met pruimen*, an old Flemish standby of rabbit with prunes; *paling in 't groen*, eel braised in a green (spinach) sauce with herbs; *stoofvlees*, beef marinated in beer and cooked with herbs and onions; *stoemp*, mashed potato mixed with vegetable and/or meat purée; and *hutsepot*, literally hotchpotch, a mixed stew of mutton, beef and pork.

Luxembourg cuisine

Favourite dishes in **Luxembourg** include pike in green sauce (*hiecht mat kraïderzooss*); jugged hare (*huesenziwwi*); black pudding (*boudin*) served with apple sauce and mashed potatoes; tripe (*kuddelfleck*); nettle soup (*brennesselszopp*); buckwheat dumplings (*stäerzelen*) and smoked collar of pork with broad beans (*judd mat gaardebou'nen*), which is virtually the national dish. On the Moselle many restaurants serve *friture de la Moselle*, small fried fish. At many annual celebrations and fairs, lots of restaurants serve *fesch* – whole fish fried in batter.

Breakfast and snacks

In most parts of Belgium and Luxembourg you'll **breakfast** in routine fashion with a cup of coffee and a roll or croissant, though the more expensive hotels usually offer sumptuous banquet-like breakfasts with cereals, fruit, hams and cheeses. Everywhere, **coffee** is almost always first-rate – aromatic and strong, but rarely bitter; in Brussels and the south it's often accompanied by hot milk (*café au lait*), but throughout Belgium there's a tendency to serve it in the Dutch fashion, with a small tub of evaporated rather than fresh milk.

Later in the day, the most common **snack** is *frites* (chips) – served everywhere in Belgium from *friture/frituur* stands or parked vans, with salt or mayonnaise, or more exotic dressings. **Mussels** – *moules/mosselen* – cooked in a variety of ways and served with chips, is akin to Belgium's national dish, and makes a good fast lunch. Just as wholesome are the filled **baguettes** (*broodjes*) that many bakeries and cafés prepare on the spot – imaginative, tasty creations that make a meal in themselves. Many fish shops, especially on the coast, also do an appetizing line in seafood baguettes, while **street vendors** in the north sell various sorts of toxic-looking sausage (*worst*), especially black pudding (*bloedworst*).

Everywhere there are stands selling **waffles** (*gaufres/wafels*), served up steaming hot with jam, honey, whipped cream, ice cream, chocolate or fruit. There are two main types of waffle – the more common Liège version, sweet, caramelized and with the corners squared off; and the Brussels waffle, larger, fluffier and needing a topping to give added flavour.

Cakes, pastries and chocolate

Belgium and Luxembourg heave with **patisseries**, where you can pick up freshly baked bread and choose from a mouthwatering range of cakes and pastries – from mousse slices through to raspberry tarts and beyond.

As almost everyone knows, Belgium is famous for its **chocolate** and on average each Belgian eats a prodigious 12.5kg of the stuff annually; chocolates are also the favoured gift when visiting friends. The big Belgian **chocolatiers**, for example Neuhaus, Godiva and Leonidas, have stores in all the main towns and cities, but many consider their products too sugary, one of the reasons why all of Belgium's cities now boast at least a couple of small, independent chocolate makers. These almost invariably charge more than their bigger rivals, but few would deny the difference in taste.

Drink

No trip to **Belgium** would be complete without sampling its **beer**, which is always good, almost always reasonably priced and comes in an amazing variety of brews. There's a **bar** on almost every corner and most serve at least twenty types of beer; in some the beer list runs into the hundreds. Traditionally, Belgian bars are cosy, unpretentious places, the walls stained brown by years of tobacco smoke, but in recent years many have been decorated in anything from a sort of potty medievalism (wooden beams etc) through to Art Nouveau and a frugal post-modernist style, which is especially fashionable in the big cities. Many bars serve simple food too, while a significant percentage pride themselves on first-rate food served from a small but well-conceived menu.

Luxembourg also has a good supply of bars, with imported Belgian beers commonplace alongside the fairly modest lagers of the country's three dominant breweries – Diekirch, Mousel and Bofferding – and the white wines from the west bank of the River Moselle. For more on beer, see the *Belgian beer* colour insert.

Wines and spirits

In **Belgium**, beer very much overshadows **wine**, but the latter is widely available with French vintages being the most popular. In **Luxembourg**, the duchy's domestic wines are very popular, being pleasant whites, fruitier and drier than the average French wine and more akin to the vintages of Germany. A Luxembourg speciality is its sparkling **méthode champenoise wine** – very palatable and reasonably priced: try the St-Martin brand, which is excellent and dry. To guarantee quality, all the premium Luxembourg wines are marked with the appellation "Marque Nationale".

There's no one national Belgian **spirit**, but the Flemings have a penchant – like their Dutch neighbours – for **jenever**, which is similar to gin, made from grain spirit and flavoured by juniper berries. It's available in most ordinary as well as specialist bars, the latter selling as many as several hundred varieties. Broadly speaking, jenever comes in two types, young (*jonge*) and old (*oude*), the latter characteristically pale yellow and smoother than the former; both are served ice-cold. In Luxembourg, you'll come across locally produced bottles of **eau de vie** – distilled from various fruits and around fifty percent alcohol by volume – head-thumping stuff. Finally, all the usual spirits – gin, whisky, etc – are widely available.

Festivals and events

Belgium and Luxembourg are big on festivals and special events – everything from religious processions through to cinema, fairs and contemporary music binges. These are spread right throughout the year, though as you might expect, most tourist-oriented events and festivals take place in the summer. Information on upcoming festivals and events is easily obtained from local tourist offices and on the internet.

Belgian festivals

Belgium's annual **carnivals** (*carnavals*), held in February and early March, are original, colourful and boisterous in equal measure. One of the most renowned is held in February at Binche, in Hainaut, when there's a procession involving some 1500 extravagantly dressed dancers called Gilles. There are also carnivals in Ostend and Aalst, and in Eupen, where the action lasts over the weekend before Shrove Tuesday and culminates with **Rosenmontag** on the Monday – a pageant of costumed groups and floats parading through the town centre. And, most uniquely, there is Stavelot's carnival, where the streets are overtaken by so-called **Blancs Moussis**, townsfolk clothed in white hooded costumes and equipped with long red noses.

Festival van Vlaanderen (June–Dec)

The extraordinarily ambitious **Festival van Vlaanderen** (Flanders Festival; Ⓦwww.festival.be) offers over 500 concerts of classical music in churches, castles and other historic venues in over eighty Flemish towns, cities and villages. Each of the big Flemish-speaking cities – Antwerp, Mechelen, Ghent and Bruges – gets a fair crack of the cultural whip, as does Brussels, with the festival celebrated for about two weeks in each city before it moves on to the next.

Nominally commemorating the arrival by boat of a miraculous statue of the Virgin Mary from Antwerp in the fourteenth century, the **Brussels Ommegang** is the best known of the festivals with a religious inspiration; a largely secular event these days, it's held on the first Tuesday and Thursday of July. If you want to see anything on the Grand-Place, however, where most of the action is, you have to reserve seats months in advance. Among the other religious events perhaps the most notable is the **Heilig-Bloedprocessie** (Procession of the Holy Blood) held in Bruges on Ascension Day, when the shrine encasing the medieval phial, which supposedly contains a few drops of the blood of Christ, is carried solemnly through the streets.

Among any number of folkloric events and fairs, one of the biggest is the **Gentse Feesten**, a big nine-day knees-up held in Ghent in late July, with all sorts of events from music and theatre through to fireworks and fairs.

Festivals in Luxembourg

Carnival is a big deal in Luxembourg, too, with most communities having some kind of celebration – if nothing else, almost every patisserie sells small doughnut-like cakes, *knudd*, during the days beforehand. On Ash Wednesday, a great straw doll is set alight and then dropped off the Moselle bridge in **Remich** with much whooping-it-up, while on the first Sunday after Carnival bonfires are lit on hilltops all over the country on **Buurgbrennen**. Mid-Lent Sunday sees **Bretzelsonndeg** (Pretzel Sunday), when pretzels are sold in all the duchy's bakeries and there are lots of processions. At **Easter**, no church bells are rung in the whole of the country between Maundy Thursday and Easter Saturday – folklore asserts that the bells fly off to Rome for confession – and their place is taken by children, who walk the streets with rattles announcing the Masses from about 6am onwards. On Easter Monday morning, with the bells "back", the children call on every house to collect their reward – brightly coloured Easter eggs.

Every village in Luxembourg has an annual fair – **kermess** – which varies in scale and duration according to the size of the village, ranging from a stand selling fries and hot dogs to a full-scale funfair. The **Schueberfouer** in Luxembourg City – over the first three weeks of September – is one of the biggest mobile fairs in Europe, held since 1340 (it started life as a sheep market) and traditionally opened by the royal family. On the middle Sunday, in the **Hammelsmarsch**, shepherds bring their sheep to town, accompanied by a band, and then proceed to work their way round the bars.

Luxembourg's National Day is on June 23, and on the previous evening, at 11pm or so, there is an enormous fireworks display off the Pont Adolphe in the capital and all the bars and cafés are open through most of the night. On June 23 itself there are parades and celebrations across most of the country.

Selected festivals and events

February

Luxembourg: Carnival Sunday preceding Shrove Tues; Ⓦwww.visitluxembourg.com. Carnival parades take place in several Luxembourg towns, including Diekirch and Remich.

Eupen: Carnival Shrove Tuesday and the preceding four or five days; Ⓦwww.opt.be. Eupen Carnaval kicks off with the appearance of His Madness the Prince and climaxes with the Rosenmontag (Rose Monday) procession.

Malmédy: Carnival Shrove Tuesday and the preceding four or five days; Ⓦwww.opt.be. In Malmédy carnival is called Cwarme, and on the

Sunday groups of Haguètes, masked figures in red robes and plumed hats, wander around seizing passers-by with wooden pincers.

Aalst: Carnival Shrove Tuesday and the preceding two days; ⓦ www.opt.be. Aalst Carnaval begins on the Sunday with a parade of the giants – locals on stilts hidden by elaborate costumes – and floats, often with a contemporary/satirical theme.

Binche: Carnival Shrove Tuesday and the preceding two days; ⓦ www.opt.be. Binche Carnaval builds up to the parade of the Gilles, locals dressed in fancy gear complete with ostrich-feather hats. See p.266.

Luxembourg: Buurgbrennen (Bonfire Day) First Sunday after Carnival (between late Feb and early March); ⓦ www.visitluxembourg.lu. Bonfires plus hot-food stalls all over Luxembourg, but especially in Luxembourg City.

March

Brussels: Ars Musica All month; ⓣ 02 219 26 60, ⓦ www.arsmusica.be. This contemporary classical music festival has an impressive international reputation and regularly features world-renowned composers. Performances are held in numerous venues around the city – and there are concerts in Bruges, Antwerp, Mons and Liège too.

Brussels: Anima, the International Animation Film Festival Ten days in early March; ⓦ www.animatv.be. First-rate animation festival, which screens over 100 new and old cartoons from around the world at the Flagey Centre in Ixelles.

Ostend: Bal Rat Mort (Dead Rat Ball) First Saturday of March; ⓦ www.ratmort.be. Held in the kursaal, this is a lavish, fancy-dress carnival ball with a different theme each year. The casino holds two and a half thousand revellers, but you still need to book early.

Stavelot: Carnival Refreshment Sun (fourth Sun in Lent); ⓦ www.opt.be. Stavelot Carnaval features the famous parade of the Blancs Moussis, all hoods and long red noses.

April

Brussels: International Fantastic Film Festival Two weeks in the middle of April; ⓦ www.bifff.org. This well-established festival is a favourite with cult-film lovers, and has become the place to see all those entertainingly dreadful B-movies, as well as more modern sci-fi classics, thrillers and fantasy epics. Held at the Tour & Taxis exhibition centre.

Sint-Truiden: Bloesemfeesten (Blossom festival) Late April; ⓦ www.bloesemfeesten-haspengouw.be. Blessing of the blossoms and other such rural fruitery in Sint-Truiden, at the heart of the Haspengouw fruit-growing region.

May

Brussels: Concours Musical International Reine Elisabeth de Belgique Early to late May; ⓣ 02 213 40 50, ⓦ www.cmireb.be. A world-famous classical music competition. Founded over fifty years ago by Belgium's violin-playing Queen Elisabeth. The categories change annually, rotating piano, voice and violin, and the winners perform live in the Grand-Place in July. Tickets can be difficult to get hold of and can cost as much as €50, but the venues do include the splendid Palais des Beaux Arts and the Conservatoire Royal de Musique.

Mechelen: Hanswijkprocessie (Procession of our Lady of Hanswijck) Sun before Ascension Day; ⓦ www.hanswijkprocessie.org. Large and ancient procession held in the centre of Mechelen. Traditionally focused on the veneration of the Virgin Mary, but more a historical pageant today.

Bruges: Heilig Bloedprocessie (Procession of the Holy Blood) Ascension Day, forty days after Easter; ⓦ www.holyblood.org. One of medieval Christendom's holiest relics, the phial of the Holy Blood, is carried through the centre of Bruges once every year. Nowadays, the procession is as much a tourist attraction as a religious ceremony, but it remains a prominent event for many Bruggelingen (citizens of Bruges).

Echternach, Luxembourg: Springprozession Whit Tues; ⓦ www.springprozession.com. Ancient and rather eccentric dancing procession commemorating the eighth-century English missionary St Willibrord.

Brussels: Jazz Marathon Three days in May; ⓦ www.brusselsjazzmarathon.be. Hip jazz cats can listen to nonstop groove around the city for three whole days (which change each year – check the website), and although most of the seventy-plus bands are perhaps less familiar names, the quality of the music is usually very high. Entrance fees vary depending on the venue, but you can buy a three-day pass from the tourist office and there are a number of free jazz concerts too.

June

Tournai: Les journées des quatre cortèges (Days of the Four Processions) Second Sat & Sun; ⓦ www.opt.be. Lively carnival mixing modern and traditional themes, from fifteen folkloric giants representing historic figures with local connections, such as Louis XIV and the Merovingian king Childeric, to flower-decked floats, fireworks and military bands.

Luxembourg: Luxembourg National Day June 23. Fireworks in the capital and celebrations – including much flag-waving – all over the Grand Duchy.

Brussels: Brussels Festival of European Film Eight days in late June; ⓦ www.fffb.be. Something of a moveable feast – it's previously been held in April and June – this festival promotes the work of young film directors from the 47 countries of the Council of Europe. It's not one of Europe's better-known film festivals, but the organizers have worked hard to establish a solid reputation and it's a great opportunity to catch up on some of the latest European (and Belgian) films. The festival takes place in the capital's Flagey arts centre, in Ixelles.

July

Knokke-Heist: Internationaal Cartoonfestival Early July to mid-Sept; ⓦ www.cartoonfestival.be. Established in the 1960s, this summer-season festival in the seaside resort of Knokke-Heist showcases several hundred world-class cartoons drawn from every corner of the globe.

Brussels: Ommegang First Tues & Thurs of July; ⓦ www.ommegang.be. This grand procession, cutting a colourful course from place du Grand Sablon to the Grand-Place, began in the fourteenth century as a religious event, celebrating the arrival of a miracle-working statue of the Virgin from Antwerp; nowadays it's almost entirely secular with a whole gaggle of locals dressed up in period costume. It all finishes up with a traditional dance on the Grand-Place and has proved so popular that it's now held twice a year, when originally it was just once. To secure a seat on the Grand-Place for the finale, you'll need to reserve at the Brussels tourist office (see p.54) at least six months ahead.

Werchter, near Leuven: Rock Werchter Festival Four days in early July; ⓦ www.rockwerchter.be. Belgium's premier rock and pop festival and one of the largest open-air music events in Europe. In recent years the all-star line-up has included Arcade Fire, Pink, Delphic, Sweet Coffee, Crookers and Midlake. There are special festival buses from Leuven train station to the festival site.

Bruges: Cactusfestival Three days over the second weekend of July; ⓦ www.cactusmusic.be. Going strong for over twenty years, the Cactusfestival is something of a classic. Known for its amiable atmosphere, it proudly pushes against the musical mainstream with rock, reggae, rap, roots and R&B all rolling along together, from both domestic and foreign artists. It's held in Bruges' city centre, in the park beside the Minnewater.

Ghent: Gentse Feesten (Ghent Festival) Mid- to late July, but always including July 21; ⓦ www.gentsefeesten.be. For ten days every July, Ghent gets stuck into partying, pretty much round the clock. Local bands perform free open-air gigs throughout the city and street performers turn up all over the place – fire-eaters, buskers, comedians, actors, puppeteers and so forth. There's also an outdoor market selling everything from jenever (gin) to handmade crafts.

Bruges: Klinkers Two weeks, usually from the last weekend of July; ⓦ www.klinkers-brugge.be. Bruges' biggest musical knees-up devoted to just about every type of music you can think of. There are big-time concerts on the Markt and the Burg, the city's two main squares, plus more intimate performances in various bars and cafés. It's Bruges at its best – and most of the events are free.

Veurne: Boetprocessie (Penitents' Procession) Last Sun in July; ⓦ www.boetprocessie.be. Although this event is now a good deal cheerier, with lots of townsfolk dressed up in fancy historical gear, it's still got a gloomy heart with a couple of hundred participants dressed in the brown cowls of the Capuchins, some dragging heavy crosses behind them. See p.130.

Boechout, Antwerp: Sfinks Last weekend in July; ⓦ www.sfinks.be. Sfinks is Belgium's best world-music festival, held outdoors in the suburb of Boechout, about 10km southeast of downtown Antwerp.

August

Bruges: Musica Antiqua Ten days in early Aug; ⓦ www.musica-antiqua.be. Part of the Festival van Vlaanderen (see box p.34), this well-established and well-regarded festival of medieval music offers an extensive programme of live performances at a variety of historic venues in Bruges. Tickets go on sale in February and are snapped up fast.

Zeebrugge and the coast: Sand sculpture Aug to late Sept. All sorts of sand sculpture competitions are popular along the Belgian coast throughout the summer – and Zeebrugge features some of the best. Amazing creations – everything from the bizarre to the surreal and beyond – but there again participants are allowed to use heavy-plant diggers and bulldozers.

Kiewit, just outside Hasselt: Pukkelpop Three days in the middle of Aug; ⓦ www.pukkelpop.be. Large-scale progressive music festival running the gamut from indie through R&B to house.

Ath: La Ducasse Four days at the end of Aug; ⓦ www.ath.be. Dating back to the thirteenth century, this festival has all sorts of parades and parties, but the star turn is the giant figures – or goliaths – that make their ungainly way round town, representing historical and folkloric characters.

Luxembourg City: Schueberfouer Three weeks from the last week of August; ⓦ www.fouer.lu. A former shepherds' market, this is now the capital's largest funfair.

September

Nivelles: Le Tour Sainte-Gertrude de Nivelles Last Sun in Sept or first Sun in Oct; Ⓦwww.toursaintegertrude.be. Beginning in the centre of Nivelles, this is a religious procession in which the reliquary of St Gertrude is escorted on a circular, 15km route out into the countryside surrounding the town. The jollity gets going when locals dressed in historical gear and several goliaths join the last leg of the procession.

Tournai: La Grande Procession de Tournai Second Sun in Sept. Part secular shindig in historical costume, part religious ceremony involving the carrying of the reliquary of St Eleuthère through the city's streets, this procession dates back to the eleventh century.

October

Ghent: Ghent Film Festival Twelve days in Oct; Ⓦwww.filmfestival.be. The Ghent Film Festival is one of Europe's foremost cinematic events. Every year, the city's cinemas combine to present a total of around two hundred feature films and a hundred shorts from all over the world, screening Belgian films and the best of world cinema well before they hit the international circuit. There's also a special focus on music in film.

November

Vianden, Luxembourg: Miertchen (St Martin's Fire) Mid-Nov. A celebration of the end of the harvest (and formerly the payment of the levy to the feudal lord), with bonfires and a big open-air market.

December

Nationwide: The Arrival of St Nicholas (aka Santa Klaus) Dec 6. The arrival of St Nicholas from his long sojourn abroad is celebrated by processions and the giving of sweets to children right across Belgium and Luxembourg. In Luxembourg, he's traditionally accompanied by "Père Fouettard" (the bogey-man), dressed in black and carrying a whip to punish naughty children.

Travel essentials

Children

In general terms at least, Belgian/Luxembourg society is sympathetic to its **children** and the tourist industry follows suit. Extra beds in hotel rooms are usually easy to arrange; many restaurants (but not the smartest) have children's menus; concessions for children are the rule, from public transport to museums; and baby-changing stations are commonplace. Pharmacists carry all the kiddie stuff you would expect – nappies, baby food and so forth. Certain hotels, particularly the better ones on the coast, offer a **babysitting** service, and a few resorts operate a municipal service of registered babysitters.

Costs

Travelling by bicycle, eating picnics bought from supermarkets and cooking your own food at campsites, it's possible to keep **costs** down to €25 a day per person. Moving up a notch, if you picnic at lunch, stick to less expensive bars and restaurants, and stay in cheap hotels or hostels, you could get by on around €50–60 a day. Staying in two-star hotels, eating out in medium-range restaurants and going to bars, you should reckon on about €120 a day, the main variable being the cost of your room. On €150 a day and upwards, you'll be limited only by time, though if you're planning to stay in a five-star hotel and have a big night out, this still won't be enough. For further information on accommodation costs, see pp.27–30.

Crime and personal safety

By comparison with other parts of Europe, both Belgium and (even more so) Luxembourg are relatively free of **crime**, so there's little reason why you should ever come into contact with either country's police force. However, there is more street crime in Belgium than there used to be, especially in Brussels and Antwerp, and it's advisable to be on your guard against petty theft. If you are robbed, you'll need to go to a **police station** to report it, not least because your insurance company will require a police report; remember to make a note of the report number – or, better still, ask for a copy of the statement itself. Don't expect a great deal of concern if your loss is relatively small – and don't be surprised if the process of completing forms and formalities takes ages.

As for **personal safety**, it's generally possible to walk around without fear of harassment or assault, but certain parts of all the big cities – especially Brussels, around the Gare du Midi – are decidedly dodgy, and wherever you go at night it's always better to err on the side of caution. Using public transport, even late at night, isn't usually a problem, but if in doubt take a taxi.

Electricity

The **electric current** is 220 volts AC, with standard European-style two-pin plugs. British equipment needs only a plug adaptor; American apparatus requires a transformer and an adaptor.

Entry requirements

Citizens of **EU** and **EEA** countries only need a valid **passport** or **national identity card** to enter Belgium and Luxembourg, where – with some limitations – they also have the right to work, live and study. US, Australian, Canadian, South African and New Zealand citizens need only a valid passport for visits of up to **ninety days**, but are not allowed to work. Passports must be valid for at least three months beyond the period of intended stay.

Non-EU citizens who wish to visit Belgium and Luxembourg for longer than ninety days must get a special **visa** from a Belgian/Luxembourg consulate or embassy before departure (see below for details). Visa requirements do change and it is always advisable to check the current situation before leaving home.

Belgian embassies and consulates abroad

For further information, consult Ⓦwww.diplomatie.belgium.be.

Australia Embassy: 19 Arkana St, Yarralumla, ACT 2600, Canberra ⓣ02/6273 2501, Ⓦwww.diplomatie.be/canberra. Also consular representation in Adelaide, Brisbane, Darwin, Hobart, Melbourne, Perth and Sydney.

Canada Embassy: 360 Albert St, Suite 820, Ottawa, Ontario K1R 7X7 ⓣ613/236 7267, Ⓦwww.diplomatie.be/ottawa. Also consular representation in Edmonton, Halifax, Montréal, Québec City, Toronto, Vancouver and Winnipeg.

Ireland 2 Shrewsbury Rd, Ballsbridge, Dublin 4 ⓣ01/205 71 00, Ⓦwww.diplomatie.be/dublin. Also consuls in Cork and Limerick.

Luxembourg Embassy: rue des Girondins 4, 1626 Luxembourg ⓣ25 43 25 1, Ⓦwww.diplomatie.be/luxemburg.

Netherlands Embassy: Alexanderveld 97, 2585 DB Den Haag ⓣ070/312 3456, Ⓦwww.diplomatie.be/thehague. Consulates in eight other Dutch cities, including Amsterdam, Maastricht and Rotterdam.

New Zealand No embassy, but consular representation at 13 Entrican Ave, Remuera 1050 Auckland ⓣ09/524 2154. Also consular representation in Wellington and Christchurch.

South Africa Embassy: Leyds St 625 Muckleneuk, 0002 Pretoria ⓣ012/440 32 01, Ⓦwww.diplomatie.be/pretoria. Also consular representation in Cape Town, Johannesburg, Durban and Port Elizabeth.

UK Embassy: 17 Grosvenor Crescent, London SW1X 7EE ⓣ020/7470 3700, Ⓦwww.diplomatie.be/London. Also consular representation in nine other UK cities.

US Embassy: 3330 Garfield St NW, Washington DC 20008 ⓣ202/333 6900, Ⓦwww.diplobel.us. Also consular representation in 34 other US cities.

Luxembourg embassies and consulates abroad

Belgium Embassy: ave de Cortenbergh 75, B-1000 Brussels ⓣ02/737 57 00.

UK Embassy: 27 Wilton Crescent, London SW1X 8SD ⓣ020/7235 6961.

US Embassy: 2200 Massachusetts Ave NW, Washington DC 20008 ⓣ202/265 4171. Also consulates in New York and San Francisco.

Gay and lesbian travellers

Gay and **lesbian** life in both Belgium and Luxembourg does not have a high international profile, especially in comparison with the Netherlands next door. Nonetheless, there's still a vibrant gay scene in Brussels (see p.106) and Antwerp (see p.227) and at least a couple of gay bars and clubs in every major town. In both countries the gay/lesbian scene is left largely unmolested by the rest of society, a pragmatic tolerance – or intolerance soaked in indifference – that has provided opportunities for legislative change. In 1998 Belgium passed a law granting certain rights to cohabiting couples irrespective of their sex, and civil unions for same-sex couples were legalized, after much huffing and puffing by the political right, in 2003; Luxembourg legalized same-sex civil unions in 2004. The legal **age of consent** for men and women is 16 in both Belgium and Luxembourg.

Health

Under reciprocal health care arrangements, all citizens of the **EU** (European Union) and **EEA** (European Economic Area) are entitled to free, or at least subsidized, **medical treatment** within the public health care system of both Belgium and Luxembourg. With the exception of Australians, whose government has a reciprocal health agreement with Belgium, **non-EU/EEA** nationals are not entitled to any free treatment and should, therefore, take out their own medical insurance. However, EU/EEA citizens may also want to consider **private health insurance**, both to cover the cost of items not within the EU/EEA scheme, such as dental treatment and repatriation on medical grounds, and to enable them to seek treatment within the private sector. Note also that the more worthwhile insurance policies promise to sort matters out before you pay (rather than after) in the case of major expense; if you do have to pay upfront, get and keep the receipts. For more on insurance, see below. No **inoculations** are currently required for either Belgium or Luxembourg.

Emergency number

In both Belgium and Luxembourg, for police, fire brigade & emergency medical assistance, call ⓣ112.

The **public health care system** in Belgium and Luxembourg is of a good standard. If you're seeking treatment under EU/EEA reciprocal health arrangements, it may be necessary to double-check that the medic you see is working within (and seeing you as) a patient of the public system. That being the case, you'll receive subsidized treatment just as the locals do. Technically you should have your passport and your **European Health Insurance Card (EHIC)** to hand to prove that you are eligible for EU/EEA health care, but often no one bothers to check. **English-speaking medical staff** are commonplace in Brussels, Luxembourg City and the Flemish-speaking parts of Belgium, but elsewhere, you'll be struggling unless you have some rudimentary grasp of French. Your hotel will usually be able to arrange – or help to arrange – an appointment with a doctor, but note that he/she will almost certainly see you as a private patient.

Minor complaints can often be remedied at a **pharmacy** (French *pharmacie*, Flemish *apotheek*): pharmacists are highly trained, willing to give advice (often in English), and able to dispense many drugs which would only be available on prescription in many other countries. Pharmacies are ubiquitous.

Insurance

Prior to travelling, you'd do well to take out an **insurance policy** to cover against theft, loss and illness or injury. Before paying for a new policy, however, it's worth checking whether you already have some degree of cover: for instance, EU health care privileges apply in both Belgium and Luxembourg (see above) and some all-risks home insurance policies may cover your possessions when overseas.

After exhausting the possibilities above, you might want to contact a **travel insurance company**. A typical travel insurance policy usually provides cover for loss of baggage, tickets and – up to a certain limit – cash or cheques, as well as cancellation or curtailment of your journey and medical costs. Most of them exclude so-called **dangerous sports** – climbing, horseriding, rafting, skiing, windsurfing and so forth – unless an extra premium is paid. Many policies can be chopped and changed

Rough Guides travel insurance

Rough Guides has teamed up with WorldNomads.com to offer great **travel insurance** deals. Policies are available to residents of over 150 countries, with cover for a wide range of **adventure sports**, 24hr emergency assistance, high levels of medical and evacuation cover and a stream of **travel safety information**. Roughguides.com users can take advantage of their policies online 24/7, from anywhere in the world – even if you're already travelling. And since plans often change when you're on the road, you can extend your policy and even claim online. Roughguides.com users who buy travel insurance with WorldNomads.com can also leave a positive footprint and donate to a community development project. For more information go to ⓦ**www.roughguides.com/shop**.

to exclude coverage you don't need – for example, sickness and accident benefits can often be excluded or included at will. If you do take medical coverage, ascertain whether benefits will be paid as treatment proceeds or only after your return home, and whether there is a 24-hour medical emergency number. If you need to make a claim, keep **receipts** for medicines and medical treatment and, in the event of you have anything stolen, you should obtain a **crime report** statement or number from the police.

The internet

Belgium and Luxembourg are well geared up for **internet access** and almost all hotels, B&Bs and hostels provide it for their guests either free or at minimal charge.

Mail

Both Belgium and Luxembourg have an efficient postal system. **Post offices** are fairly plentiful and mostly open Monday to Friday 9am to 4pm or 5pm, though some big-city branches also open on Saturday from 9am to 3pm. **Stamps** are sold at a wide range of outlets including many shops and hotels. Mail to the US takes seven days or so, within Europe two to three days. **Mail boxes** are painted red in Belgium and yellow in Luxembourg.

Maps

The **maps** provided in this guide should be sufficient for most purposes, but drivers will need to buy a good road map and prospective hikers will need specialist hiking maps. One very good-value **national road map** is the clear and easy-to-use Michelin (ⓦwww.michelintravel.com) *Belgium and Luxembourg* (1:350,000) map, which comes complete with an index. Michelin also publishes an excellent **Benelux road map** in book form at 1:150,000; this comes with 74 city maps, though the **free city maps** issued by the tourist offices in all the major towns are even better and have more detail.

Belgium's Institut Géographique National/Nationaal Geografisch Instituut (IGN/NGI; ⓦwww.ngi.be) produces the most authoritative **hiking maps** (1:10,000, 1:20,000, 1:50,000) covering the whole of the country. The equivalent organization in Luxembourg, Luxembourg Survey (ⓦwww.act.public.lu), does a similarly thorough job in Luxembourg with two series of Ordnance Survey maps, one at 1:50,000 (2 sheets), the other at 1:20,000 (30 sheets).

All the maps mentioned above should be easy enough to track down in Belgium or Luxembourg, but to be sure (and to check what's currently on the market) you might consider ordering from a leading **bookseller** before departure – ⓦwww.stanfords.co.uk is hard to beat.

Media

British **newspapers** and **magazines** are easy to get hold of in both Belgium and Luxembourg and neither is there much difficulty in finding American publications. British **radio stations** can also be picked up in much of Belgium and Luxembourg: you'll find BBC Radio 4 on 198kHz long wave; the World Service on 648kHz (463m) medium wave; and BBC Radio 5 Live on 909am and 693am. Short-wave frequencies and schedules for BBC World Service (ⓦwww.bbc.co.uk/worldservice), Radio Canada (ⓦwww.rcinet.ca) and Voice of America (ⓦwww.voa.gov) are listed on their respective websites.

As far as **British TV** is concerned, BBC1 and BBC2 television channels are on most hotel-room TVs in Belgium and on some in Luxembourg too. Access to cable and satellite channels is commonplace in hotels and bars across both countries. **Domestic TV** is largely uninspiring, though the Flemish-language TV1 and Kanaal 2 usually run English-language films with subtitles, whereas the main Wallonian channels – RTBF 1 and ARTE – mostly dub and Luxembourg's RTL channel does both.

Money and exchange

In both Luxembourg and Belgium, the currency is the **euro** (€). Each euro is made up of 100 cents. There are seven euro **notes** – in denominations of €500, €200, €100, €50, €20, €10 and €5, each a different colour and size – and eight different **coins**, specifically €2 and €1, then 50, 20, 10, 5, 2 and 1 cents. Euro notes and coins feature a common EU design on one face, but different country-specific designs on the other. All euro notes and coins can be used in any of the sixteen euro-zone states. At the time of writing the **rate of exchange for €1** is £0.88; US$1.40; Can$1.43; Aus$1.41; NZ$1.86; ZAR9.6. For the most up-to-date rates, check the currency converter website ⓦwww.oanda.com.

ATMs are liberally dotted around every major city and town in both Belgium and Luxembourg, and they accept a host of **debit cards**, though note that every transaction attracts a small fee. **Credit cards** can be used in ATMs too, but in this case transactions are treated as loans, with interest accruing daily from the date of withdrawal. All major credit cards, including American Express, Visa and MasterCard, are widely accepted in both countries. Typically, ATMs give instructions in a variety of languages.

All well-known brands of **travellers' cheque** in all major currencies are widely accepted in both countries, and you can change these, as well as foreign currency, into euros at most **banks** and **savings banks**, which are ubiquitous; **banking hours** are usually Monday to Friday from 9am to 3.30/4pm, with a few banks also open on Saturday mornings.

Mosquitoes

These pesky blighters thrive in the watery environment of northern Belgium and can be particularly irritating at campsites. If you are bitten, an antihistamine cream such as Phenergan is the best antidote, although these can be difficult to find in Belgium, so best advice is to take it with you if camping – and use insect repellants to keep the bugs at bay in the first place.

Opening hours and public holidays

Business hours (ie office hours) normally run from Monday to Friday 9.30/10am to 4.30/5pm. Normal **shopping hours** are Monday through Saturday 10am to 6pm, though many smaller shops open late on Monday morning and/or close a tad earlier on Saturdays. In addition, in some of the smaller towns and villages many places

Public holidays in Belgium and Luxembourg

New Year's Day
Easter Monday
Labour Day (May 1)
Ascension Day (forty days after Easter)
Whit Monday
Luxembourg National Day (June 23)
Flemish Day (Flemish-speaking Belgium only; July 11)
Belgium National Day (July 21)
Assumption (mid-August)
Walloon Day (French-speaking Belgium only; Sept 27)
All Saints' Day (November 1)
Armistice Day – Belgium only (November 11)
Christmas Day
St Stephen's Day (Boxing Day, Dec 26, but only an official holiday in Luxembourg)

(Note that if any of the above falls on a Sunday, the next day becomes a holiday.)

International calls

Phoning home from Belgium and Luxembourg

To make an international phone call from Belgium or Luxembourg, dial the appropriate international access code as below, then the number you require, omitting the initial zero where there is one.

Australia ⓣ0061
Canada ⓣ001
Republic of Ireland ⓣ00353
New Zealand ⓣ0064
South Africa ⓣ0027
UK ⓣ0044
US ⓣ001

Phoning Belgium and Luxembourg from abroad

To call a number in Belgium or Luxembourg, dial the local international access code, then ⓣ32 for Belgium or ⓣ352 for Luxembourg, followed by the number you require, omitting the initial zero where there is one.

close at lunchtime (noon–2pm) and for the half-day on Wednesdays or Thursdays. At the other extreme, larger establishments – primarily supermarkets and department stores – are increasingly likely to have extended hours, often on Fridays when many remain open till 9pm. In the big cities, a smattering of **convenience stores** (*magasins de nuit/avondwinkels*) stay open either all night or until 1am or 2am daily; other than these, only die-hard money-makers – including some **souvenir shops** – are open late or on Sunday.

In Belgium, there are ten national **public holidays** per year and two regional holidays, one each for Wallonia and Flanders. Luxembourg has pretty much the same public holidays with a couple of exceptions. For the most part, these holidays are keenly observed, with most businesses and many attractions closed and public transport reduced to a Sunday service.

Phones

All but the remotest parts of Belgium and Luxembourg are on the **mobile phone** (**cell phone**) network at GSM900/1800, the band common to the rest of Europe, Australia and New Zealand. Mobile/cell phones bought in North America need to be of the **triband** variety to access this GSM band. If you intend to use your own phone in Belgium and Luxembourg, note that despite recent legislation, **roaming call charges** can be excruciating – particularly irritating is the supplementary charge that you often have to pay on incoming calls – so check with your supplier before you depart. **Similarly, text messages**, sent overseas can cost more, too; check with your provider if in doubt. To cut costs, consider buying a local pre-paid SIM card.

In both Belgium and Luxembourg, domestic and international phonecards – **télécards** – for use in public phones can be bought at many outlets, including post offices, some supermarkets, railway stations and newsagents. They come in several specified denominations, beginning at €5. To make a **reverse-charge** or collect call, phone the international operator (they almost all speak English). Remember also that although virtually all hotel rooms have phones, there is almost always an exorbitant surcharge for their use.

There are **no area codes** in either Belgium or Luxembourg, but Belgian numbers mostly begin with a zero, a relic of former area codes, which have now been incorporated into the numbers themselves. Telephone numbers beginning ⓣ0900 or 070 are premium-rated, ⓣ0800 are toll-free. Within both countries, there's no distinction between local and long-distance calls – in other words calling Ostend from Brussels costs the same as calling a number in Brussels.

Useful telephone numbers

Operator numbers

Belgium Domestic directory enquiries Flemish ⓣ1207; French ⓣ1307.

International directory enquiries & operator assistance

Flemish ⓣ1204; French ⓣ1304.
Luxembourg Domestic, International directory enquiries & International operator assistance ⓣ12410.

Shopping

Both Belgium and Luxembourg have flourishing retail sectors and all the large towns and cities are jammed with department stores and international chains. More distinctively, the big cities in general, and Brussels in particular, play host to scores of specialist shops selling everything from comics to secondhand clothes. There are certain obvious Belgian goods – chocolates and beer to name the big two – but it's the Belgian flair for design that is the most striking feature, whether reflected in clothes, fine art or interior design.

Regular **shopping hours** are Monday through Saturday 10am to 6pm. However, many smaller shops open late on Monday morning and/or close a little earlier on Saturdays, most supermarkets and department stores are likely to have extended hours with late-night opening on Fridays (till 8 or 9pm) especially popular, and tourist-oriented shops everywhere generally open seven days a week until the early evening.

Sports and outdoor activities

Most visitors to Belgium confine their exercise to **cycling** (see pp.26–27) and **walking**, both of which are ideally suited to the flatness of the terrain and, for that matter, the excellence of the public transport system. The same applies to Luxembourg, except that the land is much hillier and often more scenic. Both also offer all the sporting facilities you would expect of prosperous, European countries, from golf to gymnasia, swimming pools to horseriding. More distinctive offerings include **Korfbal** (Ⓦwww.korfbal.be), a home-grown sport popular in the Netherlands and Flemish-speaking Belgium, cobbled together from netball, basketball and volleyball, and played with mixed teams and a high basket; **canal ice skating**, again in the Flemish-speaking areas, though this is of course dependent on the weather being cold enough; and, in the Ardennes, **canoeing**, **kayaking** and **mountaineering**. Belgium also possesses some great **sandy beaches** on its western seaboard, although it has to be admitted that the weather is notoriously unreliable and the North Sea distinctly murky. There are a number of fully fledged seaside resorts – like Knokke-Heist – but there are nicer, quieter stretches of coast, most notably among the wild dunes and long beaches around the pretty little resort of De Haan (see p.25).

The chief spectator sport is **football** and the 34 teams that make up the two leading divisions of the country's national league attract a fiercely loyal following. Big-deal clubs include RSC Anderlecht of Brussels (Ⓦwww.rsca.be), Club Brugge (Ⓦwww.clubbrugge.be), and Standard Liège (Ⓦwww.standard.be). The football season runs from early August to May with a break over the Christmas period.

Time

Both Belgium and Luxembourg are on **Central European Time** (CET) – one hour ahead of Greenwich Mean Time, six hours ahead of US Eastern Standard Time, nine hours ahead of US Pacific Standard Time, nine hours behind Australian Eastern Standard Time and eleven hours behind New Zealand. There are, however, variations during the changeover periods involved in **daylight saving**. Both Belgium and Luxembourg operate daylight saving time, moving their clocks forward one hour in the spring and one hour back in the autumn.

Tipping

There's no need to **tip** when there's a service charge – as there often is – but when there isn't, restaurant waiters will anticipate a ten to fifteen percent tip. In taxis, tipping is neither necessary nor expected, but often people will simply round up the fare.

Toilets

Public toilets remain comparatively rare in both Belgium and Luxembourg, but a few big-city cafés and bars operate what amounts to an ablutionary sideline, charging a €0.20–0.50 fee for the use of their toilets whether you're a customer or not; you'll spot the plate for the money as you enter.

Tourist information

Belgium has two official tourist boards, one covering the French-speaking areas, the

Tourist-office websites

Toerisme Vlaanderen (Visit Flanders) Ⓦwww.visitflanders.com. Also Ⓦwww.visitflanders.us and Ⓦwww.visitflanders.co.uk.

Office de Promotion du Tourisme de Wallonie et Bruxelles Ⓦwww.belgiumtheplaceto.be or Ⓦwww.opt.be.

Office National du Tourisme Luxembourg Ⓦwww.ont.lu. Also Ⓦwww.luxembourg.co.uk and Ⓦwww.visitluxembourg.com.

other the Flemish-speaking regions; they share responsibility for Brussels. These boards are respectively the **Office de Promotion du Tourisme de Wallonie et Bruxelles** (OPT), and **Toerisme Vlaanderen** (Visit Flanders). Both operate all-encompassing websites (see above) covering everything from hotels and campsites to forthcoming events. Both also publish a wide range of glossy, free booklets of both a general and specific nature, available at tourist offices throughout Belgium. A similarly excellent set of services is provided by the **Office National du Tourisme Luxembourg** (Luxembourg National Tourist Office) – for website details see above.

In both Belgium and Luxembourg, there are **tourist offices** in every large village, town and city and most are located on or near the main square.

Travellers with disabilities

In all the major cities, the most obvious difficulty facing people with **mobility problems** is in negotiating the cobbled streets and narrow, often broken pavements of the older districts, where the key sights are mostly located. Similarly, provision for people with disabilities on the **public transport** system is only average, although improving – many new buses, for instance, are now wheelchair accessible. And yet, while it can be difficult simply to get around, practically all **public buildings**, including museums, theatres, cinemas, concert halls and hotels, are obliged to provide access, and do. Hotels, hostels and campsites that have been certified wheelchair-accessible carry the **International Symbol of Accessibility** (ISA). Bear in mind, however, that a lot of the older, narrower **hotels** are not allowed to install lifts for reasons of conservation, so check first.

Guide

Guide

Brussels

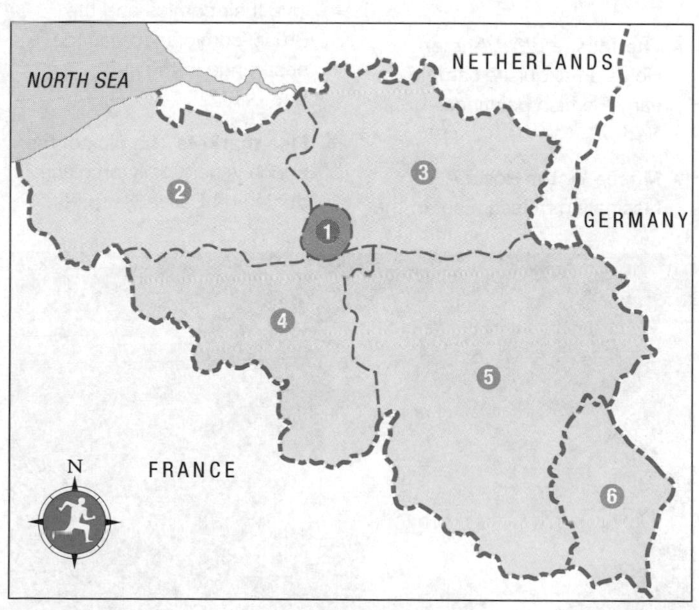

CHAPTER 1

Highlights

* **The Grand-Place** Extraordinarily beautiful, this is one of Europe's most perfectly preserved Gothic-Baroque squares. See p.60

* **Éditions Jacques Brel** Devotees of *chanson* should make a beeline for the Éditions to hear Brel in full, very anguished voice. See p.71

* **The Musée d'Art Ancien** Holds an exquisite sample of early Flemish paintings. See p.76

* **Musée Victor Horta** A fascinating museum set in the old house and studio of Victor Horta, the leading exponent of Art Nouveau. See p.90

* **Bars** Brussels has some wonderful bars; two of the oldest and most atmospheric are *À l'Imaige de Nostre-Dame* and *Au Bon Vieux Temps*. See p.100

* **Comic strips** The Belgians love their comics and the Brüsel comic shop has the best range in the city. See p.107

* **Flea markets** The pick of the bunch is held daily on place du Jeu de Balle. See p.108

▲ Jacques Brel

1 Brussels

Wherever else you go in Belgium, allow at least a little time for **BRUSSELS**, which is undoubtedly one of Europe's premier cities. Certainly, don't let its unjustified reputation as a dull, faceless centre of EU bureaucracy deter you: in postwar years, the city has become a thriving, cosmopolitan metropolis, with top-flight museums and architecture (including a well-preserved late seventeenth-century centre), a superb restaurant scene and an energetic nightlife. Moreover, most of the key attractions are crowded into a centre that is small enough to be absorbed over a few long days, its boundaries largely defined by a ring of boulevards – the "petit ring", or less colloquially, the "petite ceinture".

First-time visitors to Brussels are often surprised by the raw vitality of the **city centre**. It isn't neat and tidy, and many of the old tenement houses are shabby and ill-used, but there's a buzz about the place that's hard to resist. The city centre is divided into two main areas. The larger westerly portion comprises the **Lower Town**, fanning out from the marvellous **Grand-Place**, with its exquisite guild-houses and town hall, while up above, on a ridge to the east, lies the much smaller **Upper Town**, home to the finest art collection in the country in the Musées Royaux des Beaux Arts.

Since the eleventh century, the ruling elite has lived in the Upper Town, keeping a beady eye on the workers and shopkeepers down below – a state of affairs that still – in part – remains. In recent times, this fundamental class division, so obvious in the layout of the centre, has been further complicated by discord between Belgium's two main linguistic groups, the **Walloons** (the French-speakers) and the **Flemings** (the Dutch- or Flemish-speakers), and to add to the communal stew, these two groups now share their city with many others, including EU civil servants and immigrants from North and Central Africa, Turkey and the Mediterranean. Each of these communities tends to live a very separate, distinct existence, and Brussels' compact nature heightens the contrasts: in five minutes you can walk

Bilingual Brussels

As a cumbersome compromise between Belgium's French- and Flemish-speaking communities, Brussels is the country's only officially **bilingual region**. This means that every instance of the written word, from road signs and street names to the *Yellow Pages*, has by law to appear in both languages. Visitors soon adjust – though on arrival the names of the main train stations can be confusing (see box, p.53) – but for simplicity we've used the French version of street names, sights etc throughout this chapter.

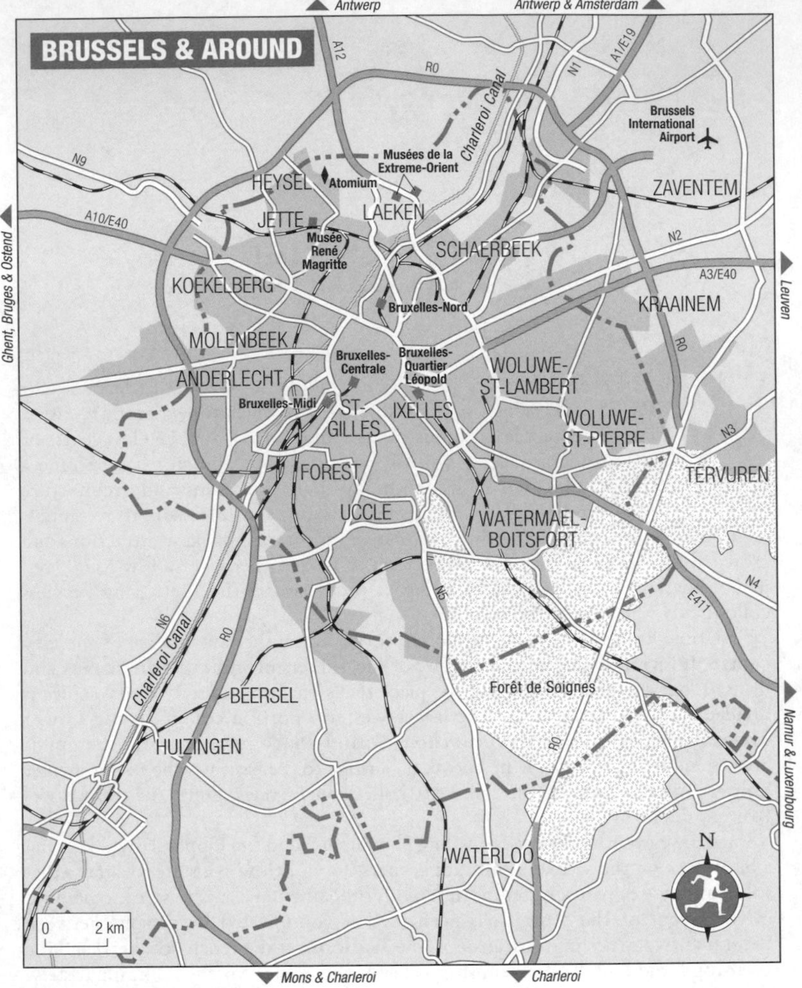

from a chichi shopping mall into an African bazaar, or from a depressed slum quarter to a resplendent square of antique shops and exclusive cafés. This is something that increases the city's allure, not least by way of the sheer variety of affordable **cafés** and **restaurants** – Brussels is a wonderful place to eat, its gastronomic reputation rivalling that of Paris. It's also a great place to drink, with **bars** ranging from designer chic to rough and ready with everything in between.

The city's **specialist shops** are another pleasure. Everyone knows about Belgian chocolates, but here in the capital there are also huge open-air markets, contemporary art galleries and establishments devoted to anything from comic books to costume jewellery and clubland fashion. Furthermore, Belgium is such a small country, and the rail network so fast and efficient, that Brussels also makes the perfect base for a wide range of **day-trips**. An obvious target is the battlefield of **Waterloo**, one of the region's most visited attractions.

Some history

Brussels takes its name from Broekzele, or "village of the marsh", the community which grew up beside the wide and shallow River Senne in the sixth century, allegedly around a chapel built here by St Géry, a French bishop turned missionary. A tiny and insignificant part of Charlemagne's empire at the end of the eighth century, it was subsequently inherited by the dukes of **Lower Lorraine** (or Lotharingia – roughly Wallonia and northeast France), who constructed a fortress here in 979. Protected, the village benefited from its position on the trade route between Cologne and the burgeoning towns of Bruges and Ghent to become a significant trading centre in its own right. The surrounding marshes were drained to allow for further expansion, and in 1229 the city was granted its first charter by the **dukes of Brabant**, the new feudal overlords who controlled things here, on and off, for around two hundred years. In the early fifteenth century, marriage merged the interests of the Duchy of Brabant with that of Burgundy, whose territories passed to the **Habsburgs** in 1482 when Mary, the last of the Burgundian line, died; she was succeeded by her husband, Maximilian I, who was anointed Holy Roman Emperor in 1494.

The first Habsburg rulers had close ties with Brussels, and the **Emperor Charles V** (1519–55) ran his vast kingdom from the city for over a decade, making it wealthy and politically important in equal measure. By contrast, his successor **Philip II** (1527–98) lived in Spain and ruled through a governor (for the whole of the Low Countries) resident in Brussels. It could have been a perfectly reasonable arrangement, but Philip's fanatical Catholicism soon unpicked the equilibrium. Horrified by the Protestant leanings of many of his Low Country subjects, the king imposed a series of anti-Protestant edicts, and when these provoked extensive **rioting**, he dispatched an army of ten thousand men – led by a hardline reactionary, the Duke of Albe – to crush his opponents in Brussels absolutely. Albe quickly restored order and then, with the help of the Inquisition, set about the rioters with gusto, his Commission of Civil Unrest soon nicknamed the "**Council of Blood**" after its habit of executing those it examined. Goaded into rebellion by Albe's brutality, Brussels, along with much of the Low Countries, exploded in revolt, and in 1577, the one-time protégé of the Habsburgs, **William the Silent**, made a triumphant entry into the city and installed a Calvinist government. Protestant control lasted for just eight years, before Philip's armies recaptured Brussels – and the king wasn't a man to forgive and forget. Seeing which way the religious wind was blowing, hundreds of Protestants left the city and the economy slumped, though complete catastrophe was averted by the conspicuous consumption of the (Brussels-based) Habsburg elite, whose high spending kept hundreds of workers in employment. Brussels also benefited from the digging of the Willebroek Canal, which linked it to the sea for the first time in its history in 1561.

By the 1580s, the Habsburgs had lost control of the northern part of the Low Countries (now the Netherlands) and Brussels was confirmed as the capital of the remainder, the **Spanish Netherlands** (broadly modern Belgium). Brussels prospered more than the rest of the country, but it was always prey to the dynastic squabbling between France and Spain: in 1695, for example, **Louis XIV** bombarded Brussels for 36 hours merely to teach his rivals a lesson, though the **guilds**, those associations of skilled merchants and workers who were crucial to the economy of Brussels, rebuilt their devastated city in double time, and it's this version of the Grand-Place that survives today.

In 1700 Charles II, the last of the Spanish Habsburgs, died without issue. The ensuing **War of the Spanish Succession** dragged on for over a decade, but eventually the Spanish Netherlands were passed to the Austrian Habsburgs, who ruled – as had their predecessors – through a governor based in Brussels. It was during this period as capital of the **Austrian Netherlands** (1713–94) that most of the monumental buildings of the Upper Town were constructed and its Neoclassical avenues and boulevards laid out – grand extravagance in the context of an increasingly industrialized city crammed with a desperately poor working class.

The **French Revolutionary army** brushed the Austrians aside at the Battle of Fleurus in 1794, and the Austrian Netherlands promptly became a *département* of France. This lasted until the defeat of Napoleon when, under the terms of the Congress of Vienna which ended hostilities, the great powers decided to absorb the country into the new **Kingdom of the Netherlands**, ruled by the Dutch King William I. Brussels took turns with The Hague as the capital, but the experiment was short-lived, and in 1830 a Brussels-led rebellion removed the Dutch and led to the creation of an **independent Belgium** with Brussels as capital.

The **nineteenth century** was a period of modernization and expansion, during which the city achieved all the attributes of a modern European capital under the guidance of Burgomaster Anspach and **King Léopold II**. New boulevards were built; the free university was founded; the Senne – which by then had become an open sewer – was covered over in the city centre; many slum areas were cleared; and a series of grand buildings were erected. The whole enterprise culminated in the golden jubilee exhibition celebrating the founding of the Belgium state in the newly inaugurated Parc du Cinquantenaire.

Following the German occupation of Belgium in World War II, the modernization of Brussels has proceeded inexorably, with many major development projects – not least the new métro system – refashioning the city and reflecting its elevated status as the headquarters of both NATO and the EU.

Arrival

Brussels has Belgium's busiest international **airport** and is on the main routes heading inland from the Channel **ports** via Flanders. **Eurostar trains** arrive here direct from London via the Channel Tunnel and, in addition, the city is a convenient stop on the train line between France and Holland. Brussels itself has an excellent public transport system which puts all the main **points of arrival** – its airport, train and bus stations – within easy reach of the city centre.

By air

Most flights to Brussels land at the city's **international airport** in the satellite suburb of Zaventem, 14km northeast of the city centre. You'll find a **Brussels International tourist information desk** (daily 8am–9pm) in the arrivals hall, with a reasonable range of blurb on the city, including free maps. It shares its space with **Espace Wallonie**, representing OPT, the Wallonian tourist board.

From the airport, trains run every ten to twenty minutes to the city's three main stations. The journey to Bruxelles-Centrale, the nearest station to the Grand-Place, takes about twenty minutes and costs €5.10 each way. Trains run from around 5.30am until midnight, after which you'll need to take a **taxi** to get to the city centre – reckon on paying €40/45. The airport also has its own **bus station** with a number of services to the capital, most usefully hourly **#12** running to Métro Schuman in the EU quarter, though note that on Saturdays and Sundays and during the week after 8pm, this becomes **bus #21**.

Train station names

When you first arrive, the city's bilingual signage can be very confusing, especially with regard to the names of the **three main train stations**: Bruxelles-Nord (in Flemish Brussel-Noord), Bruxelles-Centrale (Brussel-Centraal) and, most bewildering of the lot, Bruxelles-Midi (Brussel-Zuid). To add to the puzzle, each of the three adjoins a métro station – respectively the Gare du Nord (Noordstation), Gare Centrale (Centraal Station) and Gare du Midi (Zuidstation).

Some airlines – principally Ryanair – fly to **Brussels (Charleroi) airport**, which is also sometimes called Brussels South, though it is in fact some 50km south of central Brussels. This secondary airport is rapidly expanding and has a reasonable range of facilities, including an **Espace Wallonie tourist information desk** (daily 9am–9pm). From the airport, there is a twice-hourly bus service (8.30am–11.30pm) to Brussels departing from outside the terminal building. In Brussels, passengers are dropped at the bus stop on the west side of Bruxelles-Midi train station at the junction of rue de France and rue de l'Instruction; double-check pick-up arrangements, as several of our readers have missed the bus back to the airport. Depending on traffic, the journey takes about an hour and costs €13 one-way, €22 return. Alternatively, you can take a local bus (every 30min; 20min) from the airport to **Charleroi Sud train station**, from where there are regular services to all three of Brussels' main stations (every 30min, hourly on Sat & Sun; 50min); the combined train and bus fare is €11.30 each way.

By train

Brussels has **three main train stations** – Bruxelles-Nord, Bruxelles-Centrale and Bruxelles-Midi. Almost all **domestic** trains stop at all three, but the majority of **international** services only stop at Bruxelles-Midi, including Eurostar trains from London and Thalys express trains from Amsterdam, Paris, Cologne and Aachen.

Bruxelles-Centrale is, as its name suggests, the most central of the stations, a five-minute walk from the Grand-Place; **Bruxelles-Nord** lies among the bristling tower blocks of the business area just north of the main ring road; and **Bruxelles-Midi** is located in a depressed area to the south of the city centre. Note that on bus timetables and on maps of the city transit system (and on this book's maps), Bruxelles-Nord usually appears as "Gare du Nord", Bruxelles-Centrale as "Gare Centrale" and Bruxelles-Midi as "Gare du Midi", taking the names of their respective métro stops. If you arrive late at night, it's best to take a taxi to your hotel or hostel – and you should certainly avoid the streets around Bruxelles-Midi. If you need to **transfer** from one of the three main train stations to another, simply jump on the next available main-line train; there are services between the three stations every ten minutes or so, the journey only takes minutes and all you'll have to do (at most) is swap platforms.

By bus

Most **international bus** services to Brussels, including Eurolines from Britain, use the Bruxelles-Nord station complex as their terminus. Belgium's comprehensive rail network means that it's unlikely that you'll arrive in the city by long-distance domestic bus, but if you do, Bruxelles-Nord is the main terminal for these services too.

Information

In addition to the tourist information desks at the airports (see p.52 & p.53), there are two **Brussels International tourist offices** in the centre. One is in the Hôtel de Ville, on the Grand-Place (Jan to Easter Mon–Sat 9am–6pm; Easter to Sept daily 9am–6pm; Oct–Dec Mon–Sat 9am–6pm & Sun 10am–2pm; ⓣ02 513 89 40, ⓦwww.brusselsinternational.be); the other is on place Royale (daily 10am–6pm; same phone & website). Both issue free city and transit maps, have details of forthcoming events and concerts, make reservations on guided tours (see p.56) and sell the **Brussels Card** (see box below). The most useful of their many leaflets is the compendious *Brussels Guide and Map* (€4). They also issue a free booklet detailing all the city's (recognized) hotels and can make **last-minute hotel reservations**. Supplementing these two offices is a **tourist information desk** in the main concourse at Bruxelles-Midi train station (May–Sept daily 8am–8pm; Oct–April Mon–Thurs 8am–5pm, Fri 8am–8pm, Sat 9am–6pm & Sun 9am–2pm).

If you're heading off into Flemish-speaking Belgium (see Chapters 2 & 3), you can pick up oodles of information at **Tourism Flanders**, metres from the Grand-Place at rue du Marché aux Herbes 61 (April & Sept Mon–Sat 9am–6pm, Sun 10am–5pm; July & Aug daily 9am–7pm; Oct–March Mon–Sat 10am–5pm, Sun 10am–4pm; ⓣ02 504 03 90, ⓦwww.visitflanders.com).

City transport

The easiest way to get around the city centre is to **walk**, but to reach some of the more widely dispersed attractions you'll need to use **public transport**. Operated by **STIB** (information line ⓣ070 23 2000, ⓦwww.stib.be), the system comprises an integrated mixture of bus, tram, underground tram and métro lines that covers the city comprehensively. It's a user-friendly network, with every métro station carrying métro system diagrams, **route maps** available free from the tourist office and from most major métro stations, and timetables posted or signed at most bus and tram stops.

Tickets and MOBIB cards

Tickets, which can be used on any part of the STIB system, are available from métro kiosks, automatic machines at métro stations and from newsagents displaying the STIB sign; tram and bus drivers will only issue single-journey tickets. Prices are very reasonable: a single ticket costs €1.70 if pre-paid, €2 from the driver; five tickets (a *carte jump de 5 voyages*) €7.30, and ten (a *carte jump de 10 voyages*) €12.30. A go-as-you-please **carte d'un jour**, for €4.50, allows for

The Brussels Card

The good-value **Brussels Card** (ⓦwww.brusselscard.be) provides free access to most of the city's key museums, unlimited travel on the STIB public transport network, and discounts of up to 25 percent at specified restaurants and bars. There are three versions – 24hr (€24), 48hr (€34), and 72hr (€40) – and each is valid from the first time it is used, rather than the day of issue. The card is on sale online via the website and at both main tourist offices (see above); there are no concessionary rates for seniors or children. It's issued with a booklet detailing all the concessions and discounts.

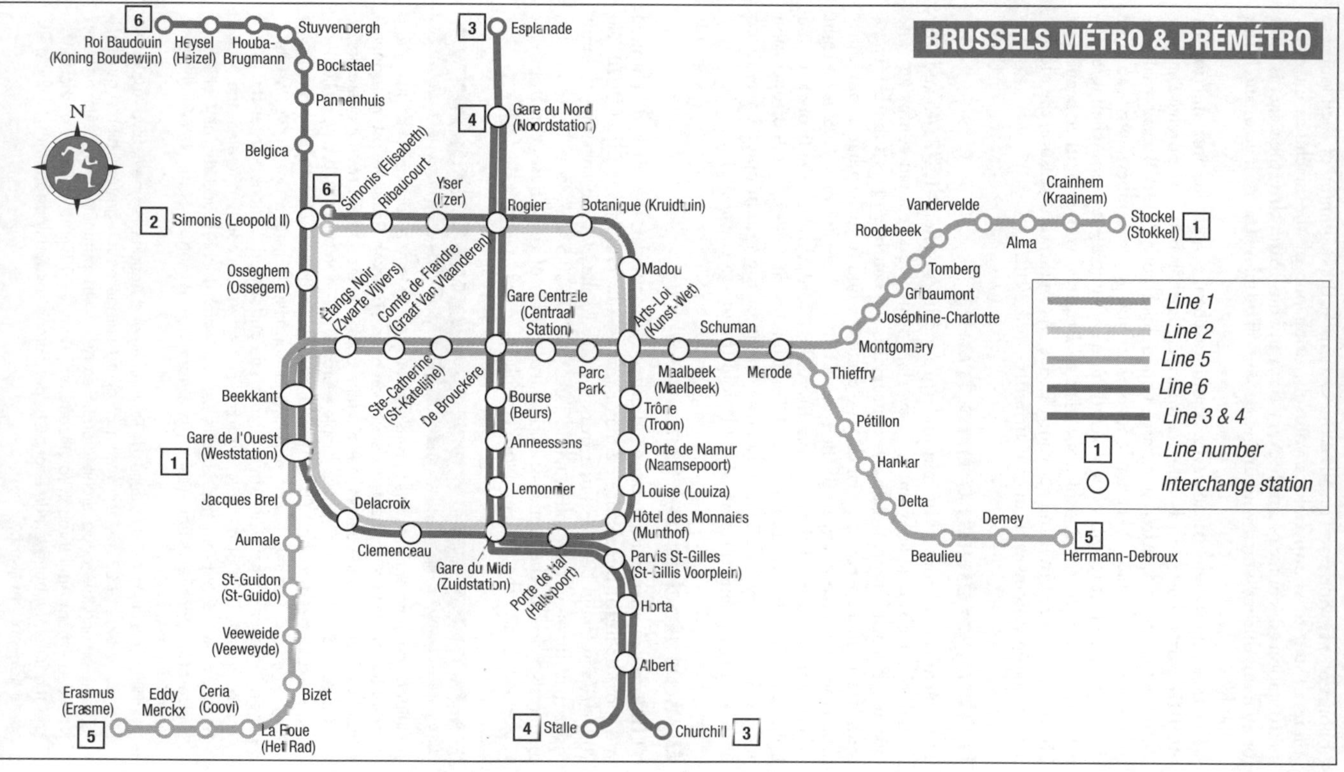
BRUSSELS MÉTRO & PRÉMÉTRO
N
Line 1
Line 2
Line 5
Line 6
Line 3 & 4
Line number
Interchange station
Roi Baudouin (Koning Boudewijn)
Heysel (Heizel)
Houba-Brugmann
Stuyvenbergh
Bockstael
Pannenhuis
Belgica
Simonis (Leopold II)
Simonis (Elisabeth)
Ribaucourt
Yser (Ijzer)
Osseghem (Ossegem)
Etangs Noir (Zwarte Vijvers)
Comte de Flandre (Graaf Van Vlaanderen)
Ste-Catherine (St-Katelijne)
De Brouckère
Beekkant
Gare de l'Ouest (Weststation)
Jacques Brel
Aumale
St-Guidon (St-Guido)
Veeweide (Veeweyde)
Bizet
La Foue (Het Rad)
Ceria (Coovi)
Eddy Merckx
Erasmus (Erasme)
Delacroix
Clemenceau
Gare du Midi (Zuidstation)
Porte de Hal (Hallepoort)
Esplanade
Gare du Nord (Noordstation)
Rogier
Botanique (Kruidtuin)
Gare Centrale (Centraal Station)
Parc Park
Bourse (Beurs)
Anneessens
Lemonnier
Madou
Arts-Loi (Kunst-Wet)
Maalbeek (Maelbeek)
Trône (Troon)
Porte de Namur (Naamsepoort)
Louise (Louiza)
Hôtel des Monnaies (Munthof)
Parvis St-Gilles (St-Gillis Voorplein)
Horta
Albert
Stalle
Churchill
Schuman
Merode
Montgomery
Joséphine-Charlotte
Gribaumont
Tomberg
Roodebeek
Vandervelde
Alma
Crainhem (Kraainem)
Stockel (Stokkel)
Thieffry
Pétillon
Hankar
Delta
Beaulieu
Demey
Herrmann-Debroux

24 hours of citywide travel on all of the system. At the beginning of each journey, you're trusted to **stamp tickets** yourself, using one of the machines on every métro station concourse or inside every tram and bus. After that, the ticket is valid for an hour, during which you can get on and off as many trams, métros and buses as you like.

The ticketing system is, however, about to change with the introduction of **MOBIB cards**, credit-card-style transport cards that you can purchase at any métro station for €5. After purchase, you upload your MOBIB card with the tickets you want at GO ticket machines and off you go, remembering to scan your card against the first red ticketing machine you encounter – it beeps when it recognizes your card. At the end of your visit to Brussels, you can either keep your MOBIB card or return it and get your €5 back. As an interim measure, the old and new ticketing systems will run concurrently until 2012.

Métro, prémétro and trams

The **métro** system consists of four underground lines (Lines #1, #2, #5 and #6), though to a considerable extent they overlap, which can be a tad confusing. The city also has a substantial **tram** system serving the centre and its suburbs. These trams are at their speediest when they go underground to form what is sometimes called the **prémétro**, that part of the system which runs – as Lines #3 & #4 – right underneath the heart of the city from Bruxelles-Nord, through De Brouckère and Bourse, to Bruxelles-Midi, Porte de Hal and on into St-Gilles. Times of operation and frequency vary considerably, but key parts of the system operate from 6am until midnight. Lone travellers should avoid the métro late at night.

Buses and local trains

STIB buses supplement the trams and métro. In particular, they provide a limited and sporadic **night bus** service on major routes. In addition, **De Lijn** (Ⓣ070 220 200, Ⓦwww.delijn.be) runs buses from the city to the Flemish-speaking communities that surround the capital, while **TEC** (Ⓣ010 230 53 53, Ⓦwww.infotec.be) operates services to the French-speaking areas. Most of these buses run from – or at least call in at – the Gare du Nord complex.

Guided tours

Guided tours are big business in Brussels; everything from a quick stroll or bus ride round the city centre to themed visits is on offer, and both **Brussels International** tourist offices have the details of – and take bookings for – about twenty operators. As a general rule, the more predictable tours can be booked on the day, while the more exotic need to be booked ahead of time, either direct with the company concerned or with the tourist office, who normally require at least two weeks' advance notice. Among the many more straightforward options, **Brussels City Tours**, rue de la Colline 8 (Ⓦwww.brussels-city-tours.com), operates the Visit Brussels Line, a hop-on, hop-off bus service which loops round the city, visiting twelve of its principal sights (daily 10am–4pm, July & Aug till 5pm, Nov–March till 3pm; 24hr tickets €16).

More promising is **ARAU** (Atelier de Recherche et d'Action Urbaines), blvd Adolphe Max 55 (Ⓣ02 219 33 45, Ⓦwww.arau.org), a heritage action group which provides tours exploring the city's architectural history – with particular emphasis on Art Nouveau – from April through to December; prices vary with the length of the tour and the itinerary, but average about €10 per person for walking tours, €15 if there's some transport involved.

Supplementing the STIB network are **local trains**, run by Belgian Railways, which shuttle in and out of the city's seven train stations, connecting different parts of the inner city and the outskirts, but unless you're living and working in the city, you're unlikely to need to use them.

Bicycles

The city council operates an excellent **public bicycle scheme** (ⓣ078 05 11 10, ⓦwww.villo.be) in which bikes can be taken from stands dotted across the city centre, and returned after use to another. There are one 180 stands in total and rates are very reasonable – the bikes are free for the first thirty minutes and then cost €0.5 for the next half-hour, rising in increments to a maximum of €2 for half an hour. There's a pay machine at every bike stand with multilingual instructions.

Accommodation

With over seventy **hotels** dotted within its central ring of boulevards, Brussels has no shortage of convenient places to stay, but even so finding hotel accommodation can still prove difficult, particularly in the spring and autumn when the capital enjoys what amounts to its **high seasons** – July and August are much slacker as the business trade dips when the EU (pretty much) closes down for its summer recess. The same cautions apply to the city's **B&Bs**, though these are thin on the ground. If you do opt for a B&B, don't expect UK-style hospitality – in effect you get a self-contained room in a private house – but do expect to be on the peripheries of town, a good way from the action. The city has half a dozen **hostels**, of which we have listed the best options.

At peak times, it's prudent to **reserve a bed** at least for your first night, but if you do arrive with nowhere to stay, the city's two main tourist offices (see p.54) operate a free **same-night hotel booking service**. Hotel **prices** vary hugely. Many have both deluxe and more standard rooms, with charges adjusted accordingly, and regular **special and weekend discounts** bring prices down by about fifteen percent, with some places occasionally halving their rates.

The Grand-Place and around

The listings below are marked on the map on p.61.

Amigo rue de l'Amigo 1–3 ⓣ02 547 47 47, ⓦwww.hotelamigo.com. This lavish five-star Rocco Forte hotel is Brussels' finest, boasting impeccable service, a central location just around the corner from the Grand-Place, and supremely elegant furnishings in the public areas, from Flemish tapestries and paintings to Oriental rugs. The building itself dates back to the sixteenth century and has seen several incarnations – it was once the town prison – and only became a hotel in the 1950s. Rooms are decorated in tasteful, contemporary style, the all-natural hues enhanced with splashes of red, blue and green. It's expensive, but special deals and discounts are legion. Métro Gare Centrale or Métro Bourse. ❾

Le Dixseptième rue de la Madeleine 25 ⓣ02 517 17 17, ⓦwww.ledixseptieme.be. Just a couple of minutes' walk from the Grand-Place, this place does its best to be central Brussels' most elegant boutique hotel, with just 24 deluxe rooms and suites. Half are in the tastefully renovated seventeenth-century mansion at the front, the remainder in the contemporary extension behind. There's a lovely downstairs sitting room and bar with comfy sofas to sink into, and the rooms themselves have a grand yet homely feel – all very soothing, and a real antidote to the mayhem outside. Métro Gare Centrale. ❼, weekends ❻

La Légende rue du Lombard 35 ⓣ02 512 82 90, ⓦwww.hotellalegende.com. Very centrally located hotel, two minutes from the Grand-Place, but with a pleasant, tucked-away feel, in an old mansion set around a small courtyard. All of the 26 bedrooms have en-suite facilities, TV and telephone, and room sizes are reasonable (you pay more for the larger rooms), but the decor is pretty bare-bland and characterless. Métro Bourse. ❸

Novotel Brussels rue du Marché aux Herbes 120 ⓣ02 514 33 33, ⓦwww.novotel.com. This well-presented chain hotel off Grand-Place occupies a modern block tastefully designed to blend in with its architectural surroundings. The 138 well-appointed rooms are decorated in brisk modern style. Métro Gare Centrale. ❼

Royal Windsor rue Duquesnoy 5 ⓣ02 505 55 55, ⓦwww.royalwindsorbrussels.com. This long-established, five-star stalwart of the Brussels hotel scene has 200-odd deluxe rooms decorated in plush style, all heavy drapes and deep carpeting. If you want something a bit different you can opt for one of their "fashion rooms", each conceived by a top Belgian designer. Expensive, but expect occasional big discounts at weekends. Métro Gare Centrale. ❾

Saint-Michel Grand-Place 15 ⓣ02 511 09 56, ⓦwww.hotel-saint-michel.be. The only hotel to look out over the Grand-Place, this small, friendly establishment occupies an old guildhouse on the east side of the square. The handsome facade belies a rather humble interior, the fourteen en-suite rooms being distinctly spartan if clean and equipped with TV – but what a location. The seven front-facing rooms must be booked in advance, and they're not for light sleepers – revellers on the Grand-Place can make a real racket. Breakfast is taken downstairs at the *'t Kelderke* café or at *café La Brouette* across the square. Métro Bourse. Front rooms ❹, back rooms ❸

La Vieille Lanterne rue des Grands Carmes 29 ⓣ02 512 74 94, ⓦwww.lavieillelanterne.be. A tiny, family-run one-star pension tucked away above a souvenir shop overlooking the Manneken Pis, the briefest of strolls from the Grand-Place. There are six boxy but perfectly adequate rooms, simply furnished and each with shower and TV; breakfast (included in the price) is brought up to your room. Métro Bourse. ❸

The Lower Town and Upper Town

The listings below are marked on the map on pp.66–67.

Atlas rue du Vieux Marché-aux-Grains 30 ⓣ02 502 60 06, ⓦwww.atlas.be. Modern three-star hotel behind the handsome stone facade of a nineteenth-century mansion in the heart of the Ste-Catherine district, a five-minute walk or so from the Grand-Place. The 88 rooms are a (slight) cut above those of the average chain, and the building is wheelchair accessible. Métro Ste-Catherine. ❺, weekends ❸

Bruegel rue du Saint-Esprit 2 ⓣ02 511 04 36, ⓦwww.vjh.be. This official HI hostel, which occupies a functional modern building, has 135 beds in one- to four-berth rooms. A basic breakfast is included in the overnight fee – €36 singles, €26 per person in a double room, €21 in a room for four – and there is a curfew. Good location, by the church of Notre-Dame de la Chapelle. Métro Gare Centrale. ❶

Brussels Welcome Hotel quai au Bois à Brûler 23 ⓣ02 219 95 46, ⓦwww.hotelwelcome.com. Extremely friendly, family-run two-star well positioned in the heart of the Ste-Catherine district. Each of the seventeen themed rooms is decorated in the style of a particular country, from Bali to Japan and Tibet. The Silk Road suite is a particularly sumptuous affair, and there's an attractive wood-panelled breakfast room too. Métro Ste-Catherine. ❺, weekends ❹

Le Centre Vincent Van Gogh – CHAB rue Traversière 8 ⓣ02 217 01 58, ⓦwww.chab.be. A rambling and spacious hostel with friendly staff, though things can seem a bit chaotic. Sinks in all rooms, but showers and toilets are shared, as are launderette and kitchen facilities. No curfew, but there are age restrictions – you have to be between 18 and 35 years old. Breakfast is included in the price – singles €33, doubles €26 per person, quads €21. Métro Botanique. ❶

The Dominican rue Léopold 9 ⓣ02 203 08 08, ⓦwww.thedominican.be. This deluxe four-star boasts a prime location close to the Grand-Place, and a claim to fame as the place where the painter Jacques-Louis David (see p.79) drew his last breath in 1825 – hence the plaque on the facade. The spacious foyer sets the funky, stylish tone, as do the generous banquettes in the courtyard-style breakfast/restaurant area behind. Beyond, all 150 rooms are well appointed and stylishly kitted out with wooden floors and earthy tones. Prices fluctuate enormously, but weekend deals abound. Midway between Métro De Brouckère and Métro Bourse. ❻

Du Congrès rue du Congrès 42 ⓣ02 217 18 90, ⓦwww.hotelducongres.be. Pleasant three-star hotel occupying a set of attractive late nineteenth-century town houses in an especially appealing corner of the Upper Town. Each of the seventy-odd en-suite rooms is spacious, airy and decorated in plain, modern style. Métro Madou. ❺

A La Grande Cloche place Rouppe 10 ⓣ02 512 61 40, ⓦwww.hotelgrandecloche.com. In a lively little area, ten minutes' walk from the Grand-Place – and not much more from the Gare du Midi – this hotel has 37 well-priced double rooms, all en suite and decorated in a brisk and functional modern style. Métro Anneessens. ❸

Jacques Brel rue de la Sablonnière 30 ⓣ02 218 01 87, ⓦwww.laj.be. This official HI hostel, arguably the best in the city, is modern and comfortable, and has a hotel-like atmosphere. All the one- to six-berth rooms have showers and breakfast is included in the price: singles €34, doubles €24.80 per person, €20.50 for quads. There's no curfew and inexpensive meals can be bought at the café. Reservations advised. Métro Madou or Botanique. ❶

Métropole place de Brouckère 31 ⓣ02 217 23 00, ⓦwww.metropolehotel.be. Dating from 1895, this grand five-star, one of Brussels' finest, boasts exquisite Empire and Art Nouveau decor in its public areas, and although some of the rooms beyond are comparatively routine, albeit very spacious, others retain their original fittings. Doubles start at €390, but substantial discounts are commonplace. Métro De Brouckère. ❾

NH Atlanta blvd Adolphe Max 7 ⓣ02 217 01 20, ⓦwww.nh-hotels.com. The NH chain has moved in on Brussels big time and it now operates six hotels in and around the city centre. This is the pick of the bunch, decorated in the chain's trademark style of sleek modern furnishings and fittings matched by pastel-painted walls – very IKEA. All 241 rooms are pleasantly comfortable and similarly well appointed, though those on the front, overlooking the boulevard, can be a tad noisy. Otherwise, it's a good location, immediately to the north of place de Brouckère. Métro De Brouckère. ❹

Noga rue du Béguinage 38 ⓣ02 218 67 63, ⓦwww.nogahotel.com. Not the grandest of the city's hotels by a long chalk, but this pleasant two-star offers nineteen comfortable en-suite guest rooms decorated in a mild form of country-house style. Competitive rates plus a library for guests' use and a handy location, close to Métro Ste-Catherine. ❹, weekends ❸

Orts rue Auguste Orts 38–40 ⓣ02 450 22 00, ⓦwww.hotelorts.com. Situated above its café-restaurant, the *Orts* is a relative newcomer to the city's hotel scene, and it's a welcome one, with fourteen impeccably furnished rooms decked out in soothing neutrals with vinyl floors. It can get a bit noisy at night, but the location, between the Bourse and Ste-Catherine, is excellent. Métro Bourse. ❺

Sleep Well rue du Damier 23 ⓣ02 218 50 50, ⓦwww.sleepwell.be. Bright and breezy hostel close to the city centre and only a five-minute walk from place Rogier. Hotel-style facilities plus a kitchen, bike rental and internet access. Sinks in every room, and shared showers. Prices, including breakfast, are €35 for singles and €26 for doubles per person, down to €19 for a berth in an eight-bedded room. Métro Rogier. ❶

EU quarter

The listings below are marked on the map on pp.84–85.

Leopold rue du Luxembourg 35 ⓣ02 511 18 28, ⓦwww.sandton.eu. If you're staying in the EU quarter, it's easy to get stuck beside a thundering boulevard, but this smart, four-star hotel has a first-rate location on a quiet(ish) side street, a brief walk from place du Luxembourg. There are over a hundred guest rooms, all kitted out in no-nonsense, modern chain-hotel style. Métro Trône. ❺

Monty blvd Brand Whitlock 101 ⓣ02 734 56 36, ⓦwww.monty-hotel.be. Well-regarded, pocket-sized two-star boutique hotel with a commitment to modern design. The eighteen guest rooms are housed in a handsome 1930s mansion, and every fixture and fitting has been carefully chosen – no bland, chain-hotel colours here. ❺

St-Gilles, avenue Louise and Ixelles

The listings below are marked on the map on pp.92–93.

Argus rue Capitaine Crespel 6 ⓣ02 514 07 70, ⓦwww.hotel-argus.be. Not in the city centre, but a good location nonetheless, just to the south of the boulevards of the petit ring, a five-minute walk from place Louise. The hotel's forty-two modern and modest rooms can be a bit on the small side, but they're cosy enough and the service is impeccable. A nice alternative to the gargantuan – and expensive – hotels that pepper this district. Métro Louise. ❺, weekends ❷

L'Art de la Fugue rue de Suède 38 ⓣ0478 69 59 44, ⓦwww.lartdelafugue.com. At just two minutes' walk from the Eurostar terminal, it's a shame this fabulous B&B doesn't have more rooms. Each of the three has its theme – "Laurence of Arabia" with an African flavour,

"Indochina" with a collection of antique Buddhas etc – and there's plenty of space to relax and enjoy the books and art of the owners, as well as an excellent continental breakfast. Book ahead as it quickly fills up. Métro Gare du Midi. ❸

Chambres en Ville rue de Londres 19 ⓣ02 512 92 90, ⓦwww.chambresenville.be. The four large and airy, en-suite rooms in this distinguished, nineteenth-century Ixelles town house just off rue du Trône are decorated in a clever amalgam of traditional and modern styles. Each room is different, with boutique-style touches such as freestanding baths and original art on the walls, and rates include breakfast. Métro Trône. ❹

Conrad Brussels ave Louise 71 ⓣ02 542 42 42, ⓦwww.conradbrussels.com. One of the capital's top hotels, the *Conrad* was former US president Clinton's top choice when in town. Housed in an immaculate tower block, with all sorts of retro flourishes, it boasts over 250 large and lavish rooms, comprehensive facilities and impeccable service. It's situated near the north end of the avenue, a five-minute walk from Métro Louise. Prices are arm-and-a-leg stuff, from €250 and counting, but discounts are frequent. ❾

Ursule la Libellule chaussée de Vleurgat 165 ⓣ0475 715 705, ⓦwww.ursule.be. Two cosy en-suite rooms, decorated in pretty, country-cottage style, set in the garden of an old Ixelles town house. Guests are invited to help themselves to breakfast (included) from the fridge in the breakfast room, or there are plenty of cafés nearby. Two-night minimum stay. Tram #94 from Métro Louise. ❸

The Grand-Place

The obvious place to begin any tour of Brussels is the **Grand-Place**, one of Europe's most beautiful squares, which sits among a labyrinth of narrow, cobbled alleys and lanes at the heart of the Lower Town. Here, the Gothic extravagance of the Hôtel de Ville (town hall) presides over the gilded facades of a full set of late seventeenth-century **guildhouses**, whose columns, scrolled gables and dainty sculptures encapsulate Baroque ideals of balance and harmony. Inevitably, such an outstanding attraction draws tourists and expats in their droves, but there's no better place to get a taste of Brussels' past and Eurocapital present.

Originally marshland, the Grand-Place was drained in the twelfth century, and by 1350 covered markets for bread, meat and cloth had been erected, born of an economic boom that was underpinned by a flourishing cloth industry. Later, the Grand-Place's role as the commercial hub of the emergent city was cemented when the city's guilds built their headquarters on the square and, in the fifteenth century, it also assumed a civic and political function with the construction of the Hôtel de Ville. The ruling dukes visited the square to meet the people or show off in tournaments, and it was here that official decrees and pronouncements were proclaimed.

During the religious wars of the sixteenth century, the Grand-Place became as much a place of public execution as trade, but thereafter resumed its former role as a marketplace. Of the square's medieval buildings, however, only parts of the Hôtel de Ville and one or two guildhouses have survived, the consequence of an early example of the precepts of total war, a 36-hour **French artillery bombardment** which pretty much razed Brussels to the ground in 1695; the commander of the French artillery gloated, "I have never yet seen such a great fire nor so much desolation". After the French withdrew, the city's guildsmen dusted themselves down and speedily had their headquarters rebuilt, adopting the distinctive and flamboyant Baroque style that characterizes the square today.

The Hôtel de Ville

From the south side of the Grand-Place, the scrubbed and polished **Hôtel de Ville** (town hall) dominates proceedings, its 96m spire soaring high above two long series of robust windows, whose straight lines are mitigated by fancy tracery and

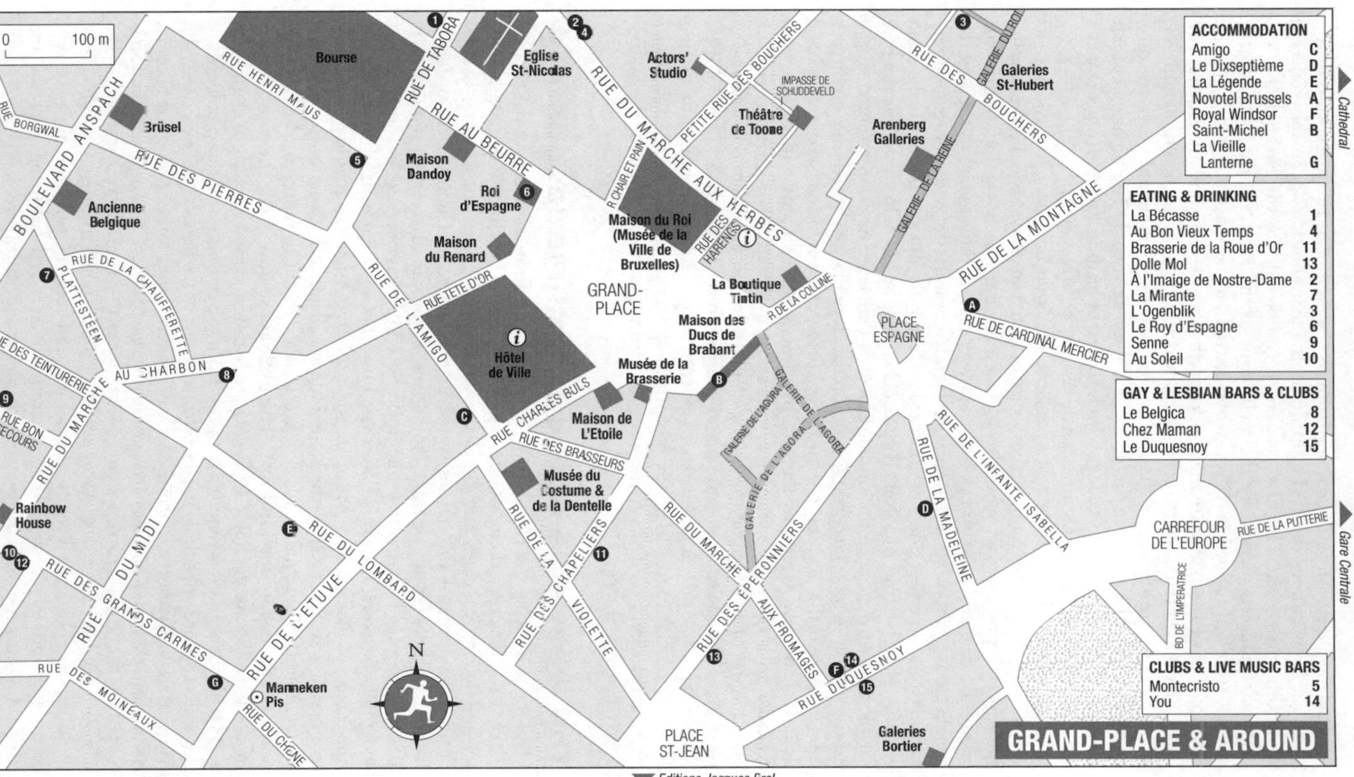
GRAND-PLACE & AROUND
ACCOMMODATION
Amigo C
Le Dixseptième D
La Légende E
Novotel Brussels A
Royal Windsor F
Saint-Michel B
La Vieille Lanterne G
EATING & DRINKING
La Bécasse 1
Au Bon Vieux Temps 4
Brasserie de la Roue d'Or 11
Dolle Mol 13
À l'Imaige de Nostre-Dame 2
La Mirante 7
L'Ogenblik 3
Le Roy d'Espagne 6
Senne 9
Au Soleil 10
GAY & LESBIAN BARS & CLUBS
Le Belgica 8
Chez Maman 12
Le Duquesnoy 15
CLUBS & LIVE MUSIC BARS
Montecristo 5
You 14
Cathedral
Gare Centrale
Editions Jacques Brel
0 100 m
Bourse
Eglise St-Nicolas
Actors' Studio
Théâtre de Toone
Arenberg Galleries
Galeries St-Hubert
Brüsel
Ancienne Belgique
Maison Dandoy
Roi d'Espagne
Maison du Renard
Maison du Roi (Musée de la Ville de Bruxelles)
GRAND-PLACE
La Boutique Tintin
Maison des Ducs de Brabant
Musée de la Brasserie
Hôtel de Ville
Maison de L'Etoile
Musée du Costume & de la Dentelle
PLACE ESPAGNE
CARREFOUR DE L'EUROPE
Rainbow House
Manneken Pis
PLACE ST-JEAN
Galeries Bortier
RUE HENRI MAUS
RUE DE TABORA
RUE AU BEURRE
RUE DU MARCHE AUX HERBES
PETITE RUE DES BOUCHERS
IMPASSE DE SCHUDDEVELD
RUE DES BOUCHERS
GALERIE DU ROI
GALERIE DE LA REINE
RUE DE LA MONTAGNE
RUE BORGWAL
BOULEVARD ANSPACH
RUE DES PIERRES
R CHAIR ET PAIN
RUE DES HARENGS
RUE DE LA CHAUFFERETTE
PLATTESTEEN
RUE TETE D'OR
RUE DE L'AMIGO
R DE LA COLLINE
RUE DE CARDINAL MERCIER
RUE DES TEINTURIERS
RUE AU CHARBON
RUE BON SECOURS
RUE DU MARCHE
RUE CHARLES BULS
RUE DES BRASSEURS
GALERIE DE L'AGORA
RUE DE LA MADELEINE
RUE DE L'INFANTE ISABELLA
RUE DE LA PUTTERIE
BD DE L'IMPERATRICE
RUE DU MIDI
RUE DU LOMBARD
RUE DE LA VIOLETTE
RUE DES CHAPELIERS
RUE DU MARCHE AUX FROMAGES
RUE DES EPERONNIERS
RUE DES GRANDS CARMES
RUE DE L'ETUVE
RUE DES MOINEAUX
RUE DU CHENE
RUE DUQUESNOY
N

an arcaded gallery. The edifice dates from the beginning of the fifteenth century, when the town council decided to build itself a mansion that adequately reflected its wealth and power. The first part to be completed was the **east wing** – the original entrance is marked by the twin lions of the Lion Staircase, though the animals were only added in 1770. Work started on the **west wing** in 1444 and continued until 1480. Despite the gap, the wings are of very similar style, and you have to look hard to notice that the later one is slightly shorter than its neighbour, allegedly at the insistence of Charles the Bold who – for some unknown reason – refused to have the adjacent rue de la Tête d'Or narrowed. The niches were left empty and the statues seen today, which represent leading figures from the city's past, were added as part of a nineteenth-century refurbishment.

By any standard, the **tower** of the Hôtel de Ville is quite extraordinary, its remarkably slender appearance the work of **Jan van Ruysbroeck**, the leading spire specialist of the day, who also played a leading role in the building of the cathedral (see p.73). Ruysbroeck had the lower section built square to support the weight above, choosing a design that blended seamlessly with the elaborately carved facade on either side – or almost: look carefully and you'll see that the main entrance is slightly out of kilter. Ruysbroeck used the old belfry porch as the base for the new tower, hence the misalignment, a deliberate decision rather than the miscalculation which, according to popular legend, prompted the architect's suicide. Above the cornice protrudes an octagonal extension where the basic design of narrow windows flanked by pencil-thin columns and pinnacles is repeated up as far as the pyramid-shaped **spire**, a delicate affair surmounted by a gilded figure of **St Michael**, protector of Christians in general and of soldiers in particular. The tower is off-limits, and **guided tours in English** (Tues 3.15pm, Wed 3.15pm & April–Sept Sun 10.45am & 12.15pm; €3) are confined to a string of lavish official rooms used for receptions and town council meetings. Tours begin at the reception desk off the interior quadrangle; be prepared for the guides' overly reverential script.

The west side of the Grand-Place: nos. 1–4

Flanking and facing the Hôtel de Ville are the **guildhouses** that give the Grand-Place its character, their slender, gilded facades swirling with exuberant, self-publicizing carvings and sculptures. Each guildhouse has a name, usually derived from one of the statues, symbols or architectural quirks decorating its facade. On the west side of the Grand-Place, at the end of the row, stands **no. 1**: **Roi d'Espagne**, a particularly fine building which was once the headquarters of the guild of bakers; it's named after the bust of King Charles II of Spain on the upper storey, flanked by a Moorish and a Native American prisoner, symbolic trophies of war. Balanced on the balustrade are allegorical statues of Energy, Fire, Water, Wind, Wheat and Prudence, presumably meant to represent the elements necessary for baking the ideal loaf. The guildhouse now holds the most famous of the square's bars, *Le Roy d'Espagne*, a surreal (but somewhat dingy) affair with animal bladders and marionettes hanging from the ceiling – and repro halberds in the toilets. More appealing is the café next door, *La Brouette*, in **nos. 2–3**: **La Maison de la Brouette**, once the tallow makers' guildhouse, though it takes its name from the wheelbarrows etched into the cartouches. The figure at the top is St Gilles, the guild's patron saint. Next door, the three lower storeys of the **Maison du Sac**, at **no. 4**, escaped the French bombardment of 1695. The building was constructed for the carpenters and coopers, with the upper storeys being appropriately designed by a cabinet-maker, and featuring pilasters and caryatids which resemble the ornate legs of Baroque furniture.

The health of Charles II

Philip IV of Spain (1605–65) had no fewer than fourteen children, but only one of his sons – **Charles II** (1661–1700) – reached his twenties. With women banned from the succession, the hapless, sickly Charles became king aged just four and, much to everyone's surprise, survived to adulthood. After his first marriage in 1679, there were great hopes that he would sire an **heir**, but none arrived, allegedly because Charles suffered from premature ejaculation. A second marriage, twenty years later, was equally fruitless and, as it became increasingly clear that Charles was unable to procreate, Europe focused on what was to happen when Charles died and the Spanish royal line died out. Every ambassador to the Spanish court wrote long missives home about the health of Charles, none more so than the English representative, **Stanhope**, who painted an especially gloomy picture: "He (Charles) has a ravenous stomach and swallows all he eats whole, for his nether jaw stands out so much that his two rows of teeth cannot meet...His weak stomach not being able to digest the food, he voids it in the same (whole) manner."

In the autumn of 1700, it was clear that Charles was dying and his doctors went to work in earnest, replacing his pillows with freshly killed pigeons and covering his chest with animal entrails. Not surprisingly, this didn't work and Charles died on November 1, an event which triggered the **War of the Spanish Succession** (see p.363).

The west side of the Grand-Place: nos. 5–7

The **Maison de la Louve**, at **no. 5**, also survived the French artillery, and was originally home to the influential archers' guild. The pilastered facade is studded with sanctimonious representations of concepts like Peace and Discord, and the medallions just beneath the pediment carry the likenesses of four Roman emperors set above allegorical motifs indicating their particular attributes. Thus, Trajan is shown above the Sun, a symbol of Truth; Tiberius with a net and cage for Falsehood; Augustus with the globe of Peace; and Julius Caesar with a bleeding heart for Disunity. Above the door, there's a charming if dusty bas-relief of the Roman she-wolf suckling Romulus and Remus, while the pediment holds a relief of Apollo firing at a python; right on top, the Phoenix rises from the ashes.

At **no. 6**, the **Maison du Cornet** was the headquarters of the boatmen's guild and is a fanciful creation of 1697, sporting a top storey resembling the stern of a ship. Charles II makes another appearance here too – it's his head in the medallion, flanked by representations of the four winds and of a pair of sailors.

The house of the haberdashers' guild, **Maison du Renard** at **no. 7**, displays animated cherubs in bas-relief playing at haberdashery on the ground floor, while a scrawny gilded fox – after which the house is named – squats above the door. Up on the second storey a statue of Justice, flanked by figures symbolizing the four continents, suggests the guild's designs on world markets – an aim to which St Nicholas, patron saint of merchants, glinting above, clearly gives his blessing.

The south side of the square

Beside the Hôtel de Ville, the arcaded **Maison de l'Étoile**, at **no. 8**, is a nineteenth-century rebuilding of the medieval home of the city magistrate. In the arcaded gallery, the exploits of one **Everard 't Serclaes** are commemorated: in 1356 the Francophile Count of Flanders attempted to seize power from the Duke of Brabant, occupying the magistrate's house and flying his standard from the roof.

'T Serclaes scaled the building, replaced the count's standard with that of the Duke of Brabant, and went on to lead the recapturing of the city, events represented in bas-relief above a reclining **statue** of 't Serclaes. His effigy is polished smooth from the long-standing superstition that good luck will come to those who stroke it – surprising really, as 't Serclaes was hunted down and hacked to death by the count's men in 1388.

Next door, the **Maison du Cygne**, at **no. 9**, takes its name from the ostentatious swan on the facade, but is more noteworthy as the place – it was once a bar – where **Karl Marx** regularly met up with Engels during his exile in Belgium. It was in Brussels in February 1848 that they wrote the *Communist Manifesto*, before they were deported as political undesirables the following month. Appropriately enough, the Belgian Workers' Party was founded here in 1885, though nowadays the building shelters one of the city's more exclusive restaurants.

The adjacent **Maison des Brasseurs**, at **no. 10**, is the only house on the Grand-Place still to be owned by a guild – the brewers' – not that the equestrian figure stuck on top gives any clues: the original effigy (of one of the city's Habsburg governors) dropped off, and the present statue, picturing the eighteenth-century aristocrat Charles of Lorraine, was moved here simply to fill the gap. Inside is a small and mundane brewery museum, the **Musée de la Brasserie** (daily 10am–5pm; €6).

The east side of the square

The seven guildhouses (**nos. 13–19**) that fill out the east side of the Grand-Place have been subsumed within one grand facade, whose slender symmetries are set off by a curved pediment and narrow pilasters, sporting nineteen busts of the dukes of Brabant. Perhaps more than any other building on the Grand-Place, this **Maison des Ducs de Brabant** has the flavour of the aristocracy – as distinct from the bourgeoisie – and, needless to say, it was much admired by the city's Habsburg governors.

The north side of the square

The guildhouses and private mansions (**nos. 20–39**) running along the north side of the Grand-Place are not as distinguished as their neighbours, though the **Maison du Pigeon** (**nos. 26–27**), the painters' guildhouse, is of interest as the house where **Victor Hugo** spent some time during his exile from France – he was expelled for his support of the French insurrection of 1848. The house also bears four unusual masks in the manner of the "green man" of Romano-Celtic folklore. The adjacent **Maison des Tailleurs** (**nos. 24–25**) is appealing too, the old headquarters of the tailors' guild, adorned by a pious bust of St Barbara, their patron saint.

Maison du Roi

Much of the northern side of the Grand-Place is taken up by the late nineteenth-century **Maison du Roi**, a fairly faithful reconstruction of the palatial Gothic structure commissioned by Charles V in 1515. The emperor had a point to make: the Hôtel de Ville was an assertion of municipal independence, and Charles wanted to emphasize imperial power by constructing his own building directly opposite. Despite its name, no sovereign ever lived here permanently, though this is where the Habsburgs installed their taxmen and law courts, and held their more important prisoners – the counts of Egmont and Hoorn (see p.82) spent their last night in the Maison du Roi before being beheaded just outside. The building now holds the **Musée de la Ville de Bruxelles** (Tues–Sun 10am–5pm; €3), comprising a wide-ranging albeit patchy collection whose best sections feature medieval fine and applied art.

Inside, the first room to the right of the entrance boasts several superb **altar-pieces**, or retables: from the end of the fourteenth century until the economic slump of the 1640s, the city produced hundreds of them, in a manner similar to a production line, with panel- and cabinet-makers, wood carvers, painters and goldsmiths (who did the gilding) working on several at any one time. The standard format was to create a series of mini-tableaux illustrating biblical scenes, with the characters wearing medieval gear in a medieval landscape. It's the extraordinary detail – a Brussels speciality – that impresses: look closely at the niche carvings on the whopping **Saluzzo** altarpiece (aka *The Life of the Virgin and the Infant Christ*) of 1505 and you'll spy the candlesticks, embroidered pillowcase and carefully draped coverlet of Mary's bedroom in the *Annunciation* scene. Up above and to the right, in a swirling, phantasmagorical landscape of what look like climbing toadstools, is the *Shepherds Hear the Good News*. Also in this room is **Pieter Bruegel the Elder**'s *Wedding Procession*, a good-natured scene with country folk walking to church to the accompaniment of bagpipes. The second room to the right is devoted to another municipal speciality, large and richly coloured **tapestries**, dating from the sixteenth and seventeenth centuries and depicting folkloric events and classical tales of derring-do.

The **upper floors** are less diverting: the first floor has scale models of the city and various sections on aspects of its history, the second continues in the same vein. Also on the second floor is a goodly sample of the **Manneken Pis**' (see p.71) vast wardrobe, around one hundred sickeningly saccharine costumes ranging from Mickey Mouse to a maharajah, all of them gifts from various visiting dignitaries.

The Lower Town

Cramped and populous, the **Lower Town** fans out from the Grand-Place in all directions, bisected by one major north–south boulevard, variously named Adolphe Max, Anspach and Lemonnier. Setting aside the boulevard – which was ploughed through in the nineteenth century – the **layout** of the Lower Town remains essentially medieval, a skein of narrow, cobbled lanes and alleys in which almost every street is crimped by tall and angular town houses. There's nothing neat and tidy about all of this, but that's what gives it its appeal – dilapidated terraces stand next to prestigious mansions and the whole district is dotted with superb buildings, everything from beautiful Baroque churches through to Art Nouveau department stores.

The Lower Town is at its most beguiling to the **northwest** of the Grand-Place, where the churches of Ste-Catherine and Ste-Jean-Baptiste au Béguinage stand amid a cobweb of quaint streets and tiny squares. The streets to the **north** of the Grand-Place are of less immediate appeal, with particularly dreary rue Neuve, a pedestrianized main drag that's home to the city's mainstream shops and stores, leading up to the clumping skyscrapers that surround the place Rogier and the Gare du Nord. This is an uninviting part of the city, but relief is at hand in the precise Habsburg symmetries of the place des Martyrs and at the Belgian Comic Strip Centre, the Centre Belge de la Bande Dessinée. To the **south** of the Grand-Place, almost everyone makes a beeline for the city's mascot, the **Manneken Pis**, but much more enjoyable is the museum dedicated to Belgium's most celebrated chansonnier, **Jacques Brel**.

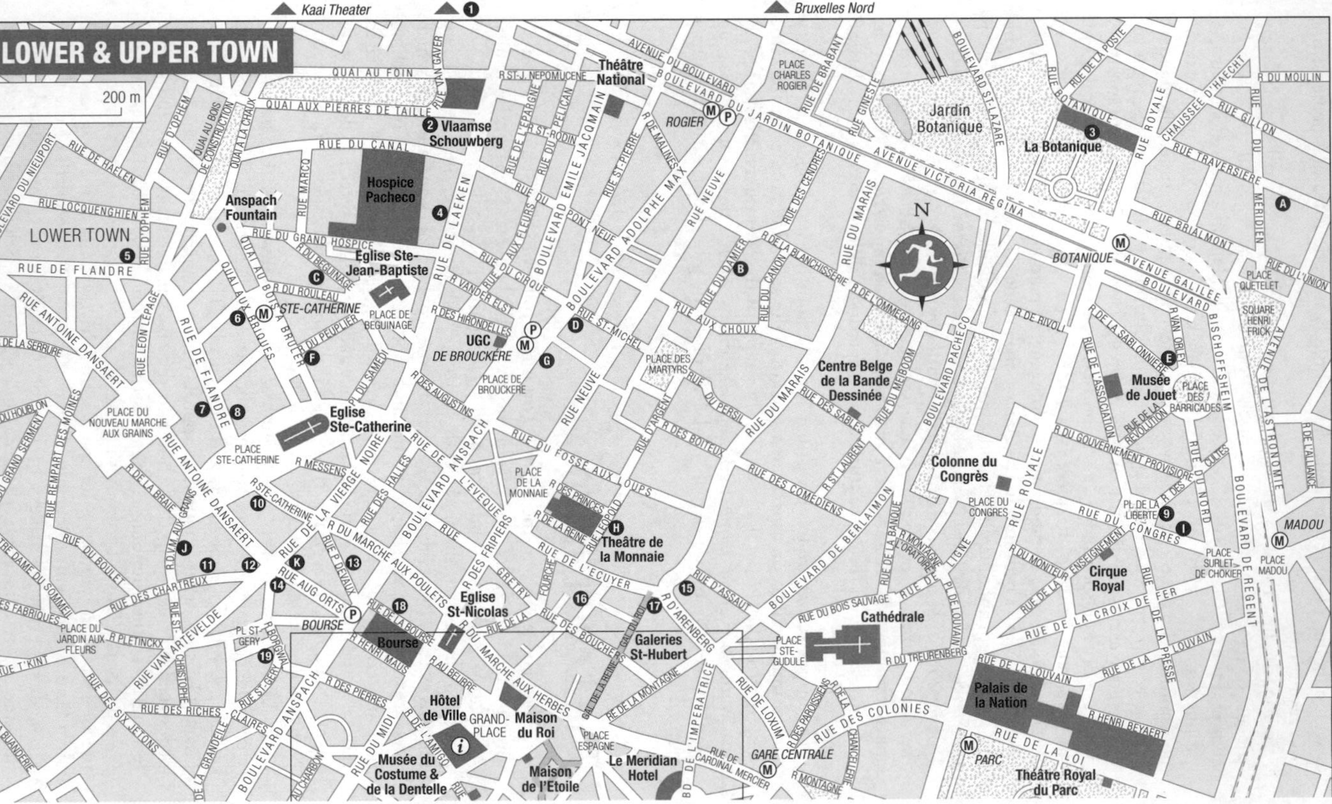
LOWER & UPPER TOWN
0 200 m
Kaai Theater
1
Bruxelles Nord
LOWER TOWN
Anspach Fountain
Hospice Pacheco
2 Vlaamse Schouwberg
Théâtre National
Jardin Botanique
La Botanique
Eglise Ste-Jean-Baptiste
STE-CATHERINE
Eglise Ste-Catherine
UGC
DE BROUCKERE
ROGIER
BOTANIQUE
Centre Belge de la Bande Dessinée
Musée de Jouet
Colonne du Congrès
Théâtre de la Monnaie
Eglise St-Nicolas
Galeries St-Hubert
Cathédrale
Cirque Royal
Bourse
BOURSE
Hôtel de Ville
GRAND-PLACE
Maison du Roi
Musée du Costume & de la Dentelle
Maison de l'Etoile
Le Meridian Hotel
GARE CENTRALE
Palais de la Nation
PARC
Théâtre Royal du Parc
MADOU
QUAI AU FOIN
QUAI AUX PIERRES DE TAILLE
RUE DU CANAL
RUE DE FLANDRE
RUE ANTOINE DANSAERT
BOULEVARD ANSPACH
BOULEVARD ADOLPHE MAX
BOULEVARD EMILE JACQMAIN
RUE NEUVE
RUE DU MARAIS
RUE ROYALE
BOULEVARD DE BERLAIMONT
BOULEVARD PACHECO
AVENUE VICTORIA REGINA
BOULEVARD DE REGENT
BOULEVARD BISCHOFFSHEIM
AVENUE DE L'ASTRONOMIE
RUE DE LA LOI
RUE DES COLONIES
RUE DU MARCHE AUX HERBES
RUE DU MARCHE AUX POULETS
RUE DE LAEKEN
BOULEVARD DU JARDIN BOTANIQUE
RUE DE LOXUM
RUE DE LA CROIX DE FER
RUE DU FOSSE AUX LOUPS

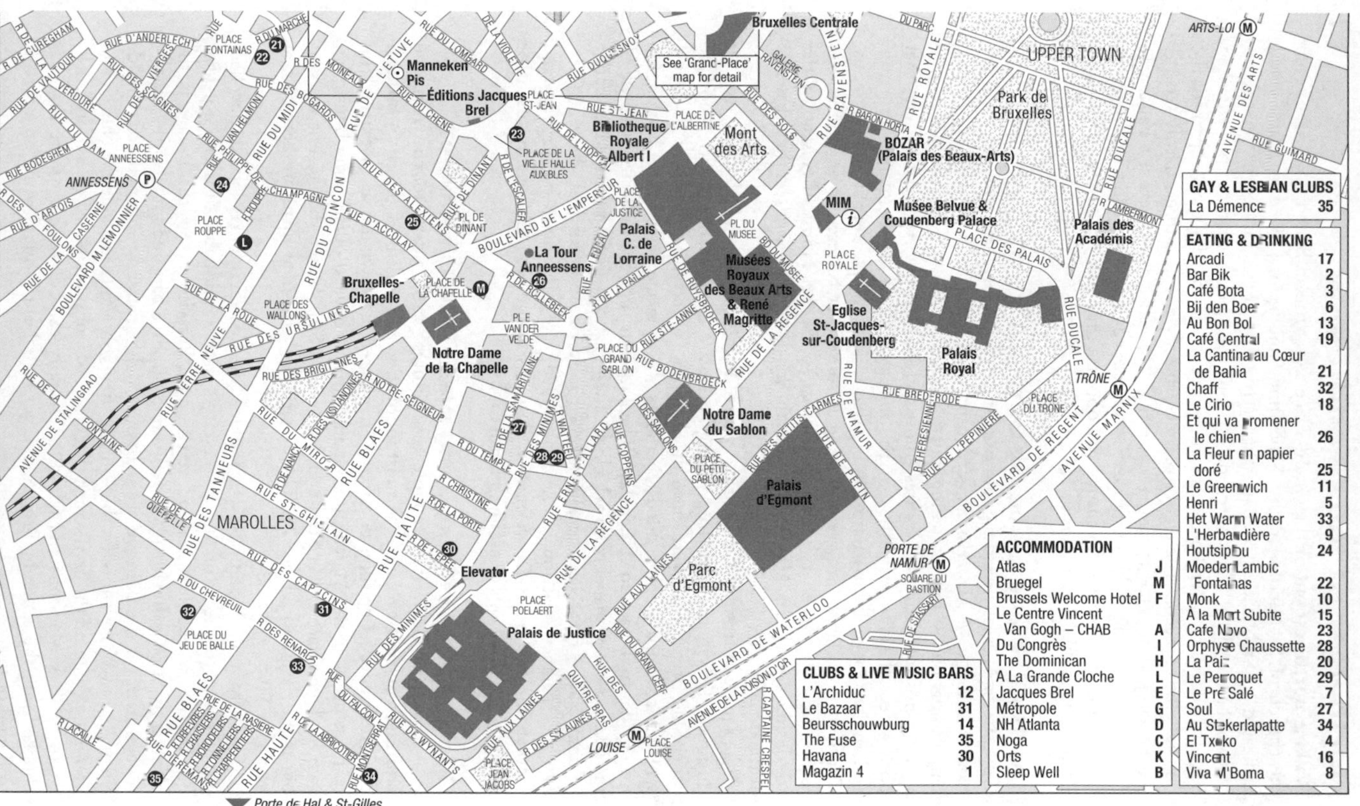

UPPER TOWN
Park de Bruxelles
MAROLLES
Bruxelles Centrale
See 'Grand-Place' map for detail
Manneken Pis
Éditions Jacques Brel
Bibliotheque Royale Albert I
Mont des Arts
BOZAR (Palais des Beaux-Arts)
MIM
Musée Belvue & Coudenberg Palace
Palais des Académis
Palais C. de Lorraine
Musées Royaux des Beaux Arts & René Magritte
Eglise St-Jacques-sur-Coudenberg
Palais Royal
La Tour Anneessens
Bruxelles-Chapelle
Notre Dame de la Chapelle
Notre Dame du Sablon
Palais d'Egmont
Parc d'Egmont
Elevator
Palais de Justice
ANNESSENS
ARTS-LOI
TRÔNE
PORTE DE NAMUR
LOUISE
Bruxelles Midi
Porte de Hal & St-Gilles
GAY & LESBIAN CLUBS
La Démence 35
EATING & DRINKING
Arcadi 17
Bar Bik 2
Café Bota 3
Bij den Boer 6
Au Bon Bol 13
Café Central 19
La Cantina au Cœur de Bahia 21
Chaff 32
Le Cirio 18
Et qui va promener le chien? 26
La Fleur en papier doré 25
Le Greenwich 11
Henri 5
Het Warm Water 33
L'Herbaudière 9
Houtsiplou 24
Moeder Lambic Fontainas 22
Monk 10
À la Mort Subite 15
Cafe Novo 23
Orphyse Chaussette 28
La Paix 20
Le Perroquet 29
Le Pré Salé 7
Soul 27
Au Stekerlapatte 34
El Txoko 4
Vincent 16
Viva M'Boma 8
ACCOMMODATION
Atlas J
Bruegel M
Brussels Welcome Hotel F
Le Centre Vincent Van Gogh – CHAB A
Du Congrès I
The Dominican H
A La Grande Cloche L
Jacques Brel E
Métropole G
NH Atlanta D
Noga C
Orts K
Sleep Well B
CLUBS & LIVE MUSIC BARS
L'Archiduc 12
Le Bazaar 31
Beursschouwburg 14
The Fuse 35
Havana 30
Magazin 4 1

Northwest of the Grand-Place

Walking **northwest** out of the Grand-Place along rue au Beurre, you soon reach the church of **St-Nicolas** (daily: Sept–June 9am–6pm; July–Aug 10am–6pm), dedicated to St Nicholas of Bari, the patron saint of sailors or, as he's better known, Santa Claus. The church dates from the twelfth century, but has been heavily restored on several occasions, most recently in the 1950s when parts of the outer shell were reconstructed in a plain Gothic style. The interior hardly sets the pulse racing, although – among a scattering of objets d'art – there is a handsome reliquary shrine near the entrance. Of gilded copper, the shrine was made in Germany in the nineteenth century to honour a group of Catholics martyred by Protestants in the Netherlands in 1572.

The Bourse and place St-Géry

Opposite St Nicolas rises the grandiose **Bourse**, formerly the home of the city's stock exchange, a Neoclassical structure of 1873 caked with fruit, fronds, languishing nudes and frolicking putti. This breezily self-confident structure sports a host of allegorical figures (Industry, Navigation, Asia, Africa, etc) that both reflect the preoccupations of the nineteenth-century Belgian bourgeoisie and, in their easy self-satisfaction, imply that wealth and pleasure are synonymous. The Bourse is flanked by good-looking if somewhat battered town houses, the setting for two of the city's more famous cafés, the Art Nouveau *Falstaff*, on the south side at rue Henri Maus 17–23, and the *fin-de-siècle Le Cirio*, on the other side at rue de la Bourse 18.

The square in front of the Bourse – **place de la Bourse** – is little more than an unsightly, heavily trafficked pause along boulevard Anspach, but the streets on the other side of the boulevard have more appeal, especially tiny **place St-Géry**, which is crowded by high-sided tenements whose stone balconies and wrought-iron grilles hark back to ritzier days. The square is thought to occupy the site of the sixth-century chapel from which the medieval city grew, but this is a matter of conjecture – no archeological evidence has ever been unearthed. Place St-Géry has one specific attraction in the refurbished, late nineteenth-century covered market, the **Halles St-Géry**, an airy glass, brick and iron edifice now used for temporary exhibitions of art and photography.

Rue Antoine Dansaert and place Ste-Catherine

From place St-Géry, it's a couple of minutes' stroll north to **rue Antoine Dansaert**, where several of the most innovative and stylish of the city's **fashion designers** have set up shop among the dilapidated old town houses that stretch up to place du Nouveau Marché aux Grains. Among several outstanding boutiques, two of the best are Oliver Strelli, at no. 46, and Stijl, which showcases a bevy of big-name designers, at no. 74. There's strikingly original furniture here too, at Max, no. 90.

Metres from rue Antoine Dansaert, **place Ste-Catherine** may look dishevelled, but it lies at the heart of one of the city's most fashionable districts, not least because of its excellent seafood restaurants. Presiding over the square is the **church of Ste-Catherine** (daily 8.30am–5.30pm) a battered nineteenth-century replacement for the Baroque original, of which the creamy, curvy **belfry** beside the west end of the church is the solitary survivor. Venture inside the church and you'll spy – behind the glass screen that closes off most of the nave – a fourteenth-century Black Madonna and Child, a sensually carved stone statuette that was chucked into the Senne by Protestants, but fished out while floating on a fortuitous clod of peat.

Quai aux Briques

Quai aux Briques and the parallel quai au Bois à Brûler extend northwest from place Ste-Catherine on either side of a wide and open area that was – until it was filled in – the most central part of the city's main **dock**. Strolling along this open area, you'll pass a motley assortment of old houses, warehouses, shops and restaurants which together maintain an appealing canalside feel – an impression heightened in the early morning when the streets are choked with lorries bearing trays of fish for local restaurants. The fanciful **Anspach water fountain** at the end of the old quays, with its lizards and dolphins, honours Burgomaster Anspach, a driving force in the move to modernize the city during the 1880s.

Ste-Jean-Baptiste au Béguinage

Place du Béguinage, just to the east of quai au Bois à Brûler, is an attractive piazza dominated by **St-Jean-Baptiste au Béguinage** (Tues–Sat 10am–5pm), a supple, billowing structure dating from the second half of the seventeenth century, and the only building left from the Béguine convent founded here in the thirteenth century. The convent once crowded in on the church and only since its demolition – and the creation of the star-shaped place du Béguinage in 1855 – has it been possible to view the exterior with any degree of ease. There's a sense of movement in each and every feature, a dynamism of design culminating in three soaring gables where the upper portion of the central tower is decorated with pinnacles that echo those of the Hôtel de Ville. The light and spacious interior is lavishly decorated, the white stone columns and arches dripping with solemn-faced cherubs intent on reminding the congregation of their mortality. The nave and aisles are wide and open, offering unobstructed views of the high altar, but you can't fail to notice the enormous wooden **pulpit** featuring St Dominic preaching against heresy – and trampling a heretic underfoot for good measure.

North of the Grand-Place

Take rue des Harengs north from the Grand-Place and at the end, across the street, you'll see the (signed) ancient alley that leads through to the **Théâtre Royal de Toone**, a long-established puppet theatre at Impasse Schuddeveld 6 (see p.105). From the Toone, another little alley leads west into pedestrianized **petite rue des Bouchers** which, along with **rue des Bouchers**, is the city's best-known restaurant ghetto, where the narrow cobblestone lanes are transformed at night into fairy-lit tunnels flanked by elaborate displays of dull-eyed fish and glistening molluscs; it's all very tempting, but these restaurants have a reputation for charging way over the odds.

Galeries St-Hubert, Théâtre de la Monnaie and place des Martyrs

Cutting across rue des Bouchers are the **Galeries St-Hubert**, whose handsome glass-vaulted galleries – du Roi, de la Reine and the smaller des Princes – were opened in 1847, making this one of Europe's first shopping arcades. Even today, it's a grand place to escape the weather or have a coffee, and the pastel-painted walls, classical pilasters and cameo sculptures retain an air of genteel sophistication. The *galeries* are close to **place de la Monnaie**, a drab and dreary modern square that's overshadowed by the huge **centre Monnaie**, housing offices and shops. The only building of interest here is the **Théâtre de la Monnaie**, Brussels' opera house, a Neoclassical structure built in 1819 and with an interior added in 1856 to a design by Poelaert, the architect of the Palais de Justice (see p.83). The theatre's real claim to fame, however, is as the starting point of the revolution against the Dutch in 1830: a nationalistic libretto in Auber's *The Mute Girl of Portici* sent the audience wild, and they poured out into the streets to raise the flag of Brabant, signalling the start of the rebellion. The opera told the tale of an Italian uprising against the Spanish, and with such lines as "To my country I owe my life, to me it will owe its liberty", one of the Dutch censors – of whom there were many – should really have seen what was coming, as a furious King William I pointed out.

From place de la Monnaie, pedestrianized **rue Neuve** forges north, flanked by a string of chain stores. About halfway up, turn right along rue St-Michel for the **place des Martyrs**, a cool, rational square superimposed on the city by the Habsburgs in the 1770s. There's no mistaking the architectural elegance of the ensemble, though the imposing centrepiece was added later: it comprises a stone plinth surmounted by a representation of the Fatherland Crowned and rising from an arcaded gallery inscribed with the names of those 445 rebels who died in the Belgian revolution of 1830.

Centre Belge de la Bande Dessinée

From place des Martyrs, it's a five-minute walk through offices and warehouses to the city's only surviving **Horta**-designed department store, the **Grand Magasin Waucquez**, at rue des Sables 20. Recently restored after lying empty for thirty years, it's a wonderfully airy, summery construction, with light filtering down from the glass ceiling above the expansive entrance hall. Completed in 1906, it was built for a textile tycoon, and exhibits all the classic features of Victor Horta's work (see p.91), from the soft lines of the ornamentation to the metal grilles, exposed girders and balustrades. The building now holds the **Centre Belge de la Bande Dessinée** (Belgian Comic Strip Centre) with a café, reference library and bookshop downstairs and the enjoyable **comic-strip museum** (Tues–Sun 10am–6pm; €7.50; ⓦwww.cbbd.be) on the floors above. The labelling of the displays is almost exclusively in French and Dutch, but a free and very thorough English guidebook is available at the ticket desk. Amongst much else, there are examples of the work of all the leading practitioners, including Tintin creator Georges Remi (see below), Jijé, Peyo, Marc Steen and Edgar-Pierre Jacobs, whose theatrical compositions and

Tintin

Tintin was the creation of Brussels-born **Georges Remi**, aka **Hergé** (1907–83). Remi's first efforts (pre-Tintin) were sponsored by a right-wing Catholic journal, *Le XXième Siècle*, and in 1929 when this same paper produced a kids' supplement – *Le Petit Vingtième* – Remi was given his first major break. He was asked to produce a two-page comic strip and the result was *Tintin in the Land of the Soviets*, a didactic tale about the evils of Bolshevism. Tintin's Soviet adventure lasted until May 1930, and to round it all off the director of *Le XXième Siècle* decided to stage a PR-stunt reception to celebrate Tintin's return from the USSR. Remi – along with a Tintin lookalike – hopped on a train just east of Brussels and when they pulled into the capital they were mobbed by scores of excited children. Remi and Tintin never looked back. Remi decided on the famous **quiff** straight away, but other features – the mouth and expressive eyebrows – only came later. His popularity was – and remains – quite phenomenal: *Tintin* has been translated into sixty languages and over twenty million copies of the comic *Le Journal de Tintin*, Remi's own independent creation first published in 1946, have been sold – and that's not mentioning all the *Tintin* TV cartoon series. Remi's life and work are also celebrated at the Musée Hergé in Louvain-la-Neuve (see p.269).

fluent combination of genres – science fiction, fantasy and crime – are seen to good effect in his *Blake and Mortimer* series.

South of the Grand-Place

In the 1890s, burgomaster **Charles Buls** spearheaded a campaign to preserve Brussels' ancient buildings. One of his rewards was to have a street named after him, and this runs south from the Grand-Place to the corner of **rue des Brasseurs**, the scene of a bizarre incident in 1873 when the French Symbolist poet Paul Verlaine shot and wounded his fellow poet and lover **Arthur Rimbaud**. This rash act earned him a two-year prison sentence – and all because Rimbaud had dashed from Paris to dissuade him from joining the Spanish army. The next turn on the left is rue de la Violette, and here, at nos. 4–12, the **Musée du Costume et de la Dentelle** (Mon, Tues, Thurs & Fri 10am–12.30pm & 1.30–5pm; Sat & Sun 2–5pm; €3) has many examples of antique and contemporary lace mixed in with various temporary displays on costume.

Manneken Pis

From the foot of rue de la Violette, it's the briefest of walks south along rue de l'Etuve to the **Manneken Pis**, a diminutive statue of a pissing urchin stuck high up in a shrine-like affair that's protected from the crowds by an iron fence. There are all sorts of folkloric tales about the origins of the lad, from lost aristocratic children recovered when they were taking a pee to peasant boys putting out dangerous fires and – least likely of the lot – kids slashing on the city's enemies from the trees and putting them to flight. More reliably, it seems that Jerome Duquesnoy, who cast the original bronze statue in the 1600s, intended the Manneken to embody the "irreverent spirit" of the city; certainly, its popularity blossomed during the sombre, priest-dominated years following the Thirty Years' War. The statue may have been Duquesnoy's idea, or it may have replaced an earlier stone version of ancient provenance, but whatever the truth it has certainly attracted the attention of thieves, notably in 1817 when a French ex-convict swiped it before breaking it into pieces. The thief and the smashed Manneken were apprehended, the former publicly branded on the Grand-Place and sentenced to a life of forced labour, while the fragments of the latter were used to create the mould in which the present-day Manneken was cast. It's long been the custom for visiting VIPs to donate a **costume**, and the little chap is regularly kitted out in different tackle – often military or folkloric gear, but occasionally stetsons and chaps, golfers' plus fours and Mickey Mouse outfits.

Éditions Jacques Brel

From the Manneken Pis, it's a short stroll to place de la Vieille Halle aux Blés, where the **Éditions Jacques Brel** (Tues–Fri 10am–6pm, Sat & Sun noon–6pm, plus July & Aug Mon 10am–6pm; €5; Ⓦwww.jacquesbrel.be) is a small but inventive museum celebrating the life and times of the Belgian singer Jacques Brel (1933–78), who was born and raised in Schaarbeek, a suburb of Brussels, though he lived most of his life in France. A legend in his own musical lifetime, Brel became famous in the 1960s as a gravelly voiced singer of mournful *chansons* about death, loss, desire and love, all of which he wrote himself. Inside the museum, a sequence of life-size tableaux give the impression that you have just missed Brel – a cigarette still burns in the replica bar – and you can watch films of the man in concert in the small and cosy theatre-cum-cinema. Brel's performances were famous for their intensity and if you watch a show you can't fail to be affected, though actually liking the music is another thing altogether.

Jacques Brel playlist

If you like what you hear at the Éditions Jacques Brel, you might want to check out some songs from the **playlist** below, which covers the very best of Brel's work.

Amsterdam Brel's deliberately repetitive, climactic tale of sailors in seedy ports is a fantastically evocative song, and was one of his most intense live numbers.

Les Bonbons This is Brel at his wittiest and most unforgiving, poking fun at 1960s hippies.

Le chanson de Jackie Brel in autobiographical mode, looking back in fantastically rumbustious fashion on his career and forward into his future.

Mathilde One of Brel's greatest love songs, brilliantly covered by Scott Walker.

Le Moribond The tormented and yet curiously upbeat lament of a dying man that gave rise to the Terry Jacks hit of 1974.

Ne me quitte pas Brel's most anguished love song, and perhaps one of the most affecting ever written, memorably covered by Nina Simone.

Quand on n'a que l'amour One of Brel's earliest songs, *When we have only Love* was his first hit single.

La Quete *The Impossible Dream* has been covered by just about everyone and is quite rightly one of Brel's best-known songs, but his version stands out.

Je suis un soir d'été This late and very atmospheric study of summer ennui in small-town Belgium is one of Brel's most beautiful songs.

Au Suivant Brel is typically satirical in this biting rant against war, militarism and middle-class bourgeois values.

Notre Dame de la Chapelle

Heading south from the Éditions Jacques Brel, it's a short walk up the slope to boulevard de l'Empereur, a wide carriageway that slices through this part of the centre. Turn right along the boulevard and you'll soon spy **Notre Dame de la Chapelle** (daily 9am–6pm), a sprawling, broadly Gothic structure founded in 1134, which makes it the city's oldest church, though the attractive Baroque bell tower was only added after the French artillery bombardment of 1695 had damaged the original. Inside, heavyweight columns with curly-kale capitals support the well-proportioned **nave**, whose central aisle is bathed in light from the soaring clerestory windows. Amongst the assorted furniture and fittings, the **pulpit** is the most arresting, an intricately carved hunk of wood featuring the Old Testament prophet Elijah stuck out in the wilderness. The prophet looks mightily fed up, but then he hasn't realized that there's an angel beside him with a loaf of bread (manna). The church's main claim to fame, however, is the **memorial to Pieter Bruegel the Elder**, located high up on the wall of the south side-aisle's fourth chapel. The plaque was the work of Pieter's son Jan and the painting is a copy of a Rubens showing St Peter being given the keys to heaven; the other plaque and bronze effigy in the chapel were added in the 1930s. Pieter is supposed to have lived and died just down the street at rue Haute 132.

The Quartier Marolles

South of Notre Dame de la Chapelle, rue Blaes, together with the less appealing rue Haute, form the double spine of the **Quartier Marolles**, which grew up in the seventeenth century as a centre for artisans working on the nearby mansions of the Sablon. Industrialized in the eighteenth century, it remained a thriving working-class district until the 1870s, when the paving-over of the Senne led to the riverside factories closing down and moving to the suburbs. The workers and their

Moving on from the Quartier Marolles

If you've ventured as far south as the place du Jeu de Balle, then you're within easy striking distance of St-Gilles (see p.90), a five- to ten-minute walk to the south. Alternatively, a free **public elevator** (daily 7am–midnight), just off rue Haute on rue Notre-Dame de Graces, will whisk you up to the Palais de Justice in the Upper Town – a useful short cut.

families followed, initiating a long process of decline, which turned the district into an impoverished slum. Things finally started to change in the late 1980s, when outsiders began to snaffle up property here, and although the *quartier* still has its rougher moments, rue Blaes – or at least that part of it from Notre Dame de la Chapelle to place du Jeu de Balle – is now lined with antique and interior-design shops. It's an appropriate location as **place du Jeu de Balle**, the square at the heart of Marolles, has long been home to the city's best **flea market** (daily 7am–2pm), which is at its hectic best on Sunday mornings.

The Upper Town

From the heights of the **Upper Town**, the Francophile ruling class long kept a beady eye on the proletarians down below, and it was here they built their palaces and mansions, churches and parks. Political power is no longer concentrated hereabouts, but the wide avenues and grand architecture of this aristocratic quarter – the bulk of which dates from the late eighteenth and nineteenth centuries – have survived pretty much intact, lending a stately, dignified feel that's markedly different from the bustle of the Lower Town.

The Lower Town ends and the Upper Town begins at the foot of the **sharp slope** which runs north to south from one end of the city centre to the other, its course marked – in general terms at least – by a wide **boulevard** that's variously named Berlaimont, L'Impératrice and L'Empereur. This slope is home to the city's **cathedral**, but otherwise is little more than an obstacle to be climbed by a series of stairways. Among the latter, the most frequently used are the covered walkway running through the **Galerie Ravenstein** shopping arcade behind the Gare Centrale, and the open-air stairway that climbs up through the stodgy, modern buildings of the so-called **Mont des Arts**. Léopold II gave the area its name in anticipation of a fine art museum he intended to build, but the project was never completed, and the land was only properly built upon in the 1950s.

Above the rigorous layout of the Mont des Arts lie the **rue Royale** and **rue de la Régence**, which together make up the Upper Town's spine, a suitably smart location for the outstanding **Musées Royaux des Beaux Arts**, the pick of Belgium's many fine art collections, the surprisingly low-key **Palais Royal**, and the entertaining **Musée des Instruments de Musique** (**MIM**). Further south, rue de la Régence soon leads to the well-heeled **Sablon** neighbourhood, whose antique shops and chic bars and cafés fan out from the medieval church of **Notre Dame du Sablon**. Beyond this is the monstrous **Palais de Justice**, traditionally one of the city's most disliked buildings.

The Cathedral

It only takes a couple of minutes to walk from the Grand-Place to the east end of rue de la Montagne, where a short slope climbs up to the **Cathedral** (daily

8.30am–6pm), a splendid Gothic edifice whose commanding position has been sorely compromised by a rash of modern office blocks. Begun in 1215, and three hundred years in the making, the cathedral is dedicated jointly to the patron and patroness of Brussels, respectively St Michael the Archangel and St Gudule, the latter a vague seventh-century figure whose reputation was based on her gentle determination: despite all sorts of shenanigans, the devil could never make her think an uncharitable thought.

The cathedral sports a striking, twin-towered, white stone **facade**, with the central double doorway trimmed by fanciful tracery as well as statues of the Apostles and – on the central column – the Three Wise Men. The facade was erected in the fifteenth century in High Gothic style, but the intensity of the decoration fades away inside with the cavernous triple-aisled **nave**, completed a century before. Other parts of the interior illustrate several phases of Gothic design, the chancel being the oldest part of the church, built in stages between 1215 and 1280 in the Early Gothic style.

The interior is short on **furnishings and fittings**, reflecting the combined efforts of the Protestants, who ransacked the church (and stole the shrine of St Gudule) in the middle of the seventeenth century, and the French Republican army, who wrecked the place a century later. One survivor is the massive oak **pulpit**, an extravagant chunk of frippery by the Antwerp sculptor Hendrik Verbruggen. Among several vignettes, the pulpit features Adam and Eve, dressed in rustic gear, being chased from the Garden of Eden, while up above the Virgin Mary and some helpful cherubs stamp on the head of the serpent-dragon.

The stained-glass windows

The cathedral also boasts some superb sixteenth-century **stained-glass windows**, beginning above the main doors with the hurly-burly of the Last Judgement. Look closely and you'll spy the donor in the lower foreground with an angel on one side and a woman with long blonde hair (symbolizing Faith) on the other. Each of the main colours has a symbolic meaning, green representing hope, yellow eternal glory and light blue heaven. There's more remarkable work in the **transepts**, where the stained glass is distinguished by the extraordinary clarity of the blue backgrounds. These windows are eulogies to the Habsburgs – in the north transept, Charles V kneels alongside his wife beneath a vast triumphal arch as their patron saints present them to God the Father, and in the south transept Charles V's sister, Marie, and her husband, King Louis of Hungary, play out a similar scenario. Both windows were designed by Bernard van Orley (1490–1541), long-time favourite of the royal family and the leading Brussels artist of his day.

Chapelle du Saint Sacrement de Miracle

Just beyond the north transept, flanking the choir, the cathedral treasury (see opposite) is displayed in the Flamboyant Gothic **Chapelle du Saint Sacrement de Miracle**, named after a shameful anti-Semitic legend whose key components were repeated again and again across medieval Christendom. Dating back to the 1360s, this particular version begins with a Jew from a small Flemish town stealing the consecrated Host from his local church. On Good Friday, he presents the Host at the synagogue; his fellow Jews stab it with daggers, whereupon it starts to bleed and they disperse, terrified. Shortly afterwards, the thief is murdered in a brawl and his fearful wife moves to Brussels, taking the Host with her. The woman then decides to try to save her soul by giving the Host to the city's cathedral – hence this chapel, which was built to display the retrieved Host in the 1530s. The four **stained-glass windows** of the chapel retell the tale, a strip cartoon that unfolds above representations of the aristocrats who paid for the windows. The workmanship is delightful – based on designs by van Orley and his one-time apprentice Michiel van Coxie (1499–1592) – but the effects of this unsavoury legend on the congregation are not hard to imagine.

The treasury

Inside the Chapelle du Saint Sacrement de Miracle, the cathedral **treasury** (Le trésor; Mon–Fri 10am–12.30pm & 2–5pm, Sat 10am–12.30pm & 2–3pm, Sun 2–5pm; €1) is smartly turned out, but the exhibits themselves, for the most part at least, are a fairly plodding assortment of monstrances, vestments and reliquaries. The main exception is a splendid Anglo-Saxon reliquary of the **True Cross** (Item 5), recently winkled out of the ornate, seventeenth-century gilded silver reliquary Cross (Item 4) that was made to hold it. There's also a flowing altar painting, *The Legend of Ste Gudule* (Item 2), by Michiel van Coxie, who spent much of his long life churning out religious paintings in the High Renaissance style he picked up when visiting Italy early in his career. Behind the chapel's high altar, look out also for the more-than-usually ghoulish **skull** of St Elizabeth of Hungary (1207–31), a faithful wife, a devoted mother and a loyal servant of the church – hence her beatification.

Galerie Ravenstein and BOZAR (the Palais des Beaux Arts)

From the cathedral, it's a brief walk south along boulevard de l'Impératrice to **Gare Centrale**, a bleak and somewhat surly Art Deco creation, one of Victor Horta's last, that is seemingly dug deep into the slope where the Lower and Upper Town meet. Behind the station, on the far side of rue Cantersteen, is the **Galerie Ravenstein** shopping arcade, which is traversed by a pleasant covered walkway that clambers up to rue Ravenstein. A classic piece of 1950s design, the arcade sports bright and cheerful tiling and has an airy atrium equipped with a (defunct) water fountain. At the far end of the walkway, on rue Ravenstein, stands the **Palais des Beaux Arts** (now called **BOZAR**), a severe, low-lying edifice designed by Horta during the 1920s. The building holds a theatre and concert hall and hosts numerous temporary exhibitions, mostly of contemporary art and photography. From here, you can either climb the steps up to rue Royale and the Musées Royaux des Beaux Arts (see pp.76–81), or stroll south to the top of the Mont des Arts and the Musée des Instruments de Musique.

The Mont des Arts and the Musée des Instruments de Musique

The wide stone **stairway** that clambers up through the chunky 1940s and 1950s government buildings of the **Mont des Arts** also climbs the slope marking the start of the Upper Town, and serves as an alternative to the Galerie Ravenstein. The stairs begin on **place de l'Albertine**, which is itself overlooked by a large and imposing statue of Belgium's most popular king, **Albert I** (1875–1934). They then proceed up to a wide **piazza**, equipped with water fountains, footpaths and carefully manicured shrubbery, and then it's on up again, with splendid **views** over the Lower Town with the tower of the Hôtel de Ville soaring high above its surroundings.

Across from the top of the stairway, at rue Montagne de la Cour 2, the **Old England building** is a whimsical Art Nouveau confection – all glass and wrought iron – that started life as a store built by the eponymous British company as its Brussels headquarters in 1899. Cleverly recycled, it now houses the entertaining **Musée des Instruments de Musique** (Tues–Fri 9.30am–4.45pm, Sat & Sun 10am–4.45pm; €5; Ⓦ www.mim.fgov.be), whose permanent collection, featuring several hundred musical instruments, spreads over four main floors. The special feature here is the **infrared headphones**, which are cued to play music to match the type of instrument you're looking at. This is really good fun, especially in the folk-music section on **Floor 1**, where you can listen, for example, to a Tibetan temple trumpet, Congolese drums, a veritable battery of bagpipes and a medieval Cornemuse, as featured in the paintings of Pieter Bruegel the Younger. One word of caution, however: middle-aged parents will no doubt spot the dreaded ocarina, a slug-shaped instrument that was once popular with children and drove many an adult to despair.

Place Royale

Composed and self-assured, **place Royale** forms a fitting climax to rue Royale, the dead straight backbone of the Upper Town, which runs the 2km north to the Turkish inner-city suburb of St-Josse. Precisely symmetrical, the square is framed by late eighteenth-century mansions, each an exercise in architectural restraint, though there's no mistaking their size or the probable cost of their construction. Pushing into this understated opulence is the facade of the church of **St-Jacques-sur-Coudenberg** (Tues–Sat 1–5.30pm, Sun 9am–5.30pm), a fanciful 1780s version of a Roman temple, with a colourfully frescoed pediment representing Our Lady as Comforter of the Depressed. Indeed, the building was so secular in appearance that the French Revolutionary army had no hesitation in renaming it a Temple of Reason. The French also destroyed the statue of a Habsburg governor that once stood in front of the church; its replacement – a dashing equestrian representation of **Godfrey de Bouillon**, one of the leaders of the First Crusade – dates from the 1840s. It was an appropriate choice, as this was the spot where Godfrey is supposed to have exhorted his subjects to enlist for the Crusade, rounding off his appeal with a thunderous "*Dieu li volt*" (God wills it).

Musées Royaux des Beaux Arts

On the edge of place Royale, the **Musées Royaux des Beaux Arts** (Tues–Sun 10am–5pm; €8, €13 with Musée Magritte; Ⓦwww.fine-arts-museum.be) holds Belgium's most satisfying all-round collection of fine art, a vast hoard that is exhibited in three interconnected museums, one displaying modern art from the nineteenth century onwards, a second devoted to René Magritte, and a third to older works. Finding your way around is made easy by the English-language, **colour-coded museum plan** issued at the information desk behind the entrance. The museum also hosts a prestigious programme of **temporary exhibitions** (colour-coded red on the museum plan) for which a supplementary admission fee is usually required.

Musée d'Art Ancien

In the **Musée d'Art Ancien**, the **blue area** displays paintings of the fifteenth and sixteenth centuries, including the Flemish primitives and the Bruegels, and the **brown area** concentrates on paintings of the seventeenth and eighteenth centuries, with the collection of Rubens (for which the museum is internationally famous) as a particular highlight.

Rogier van der Weyden and Dieric Bouts

The museum owns several paintings by **Rogier van der Weyden** (1399–1464), who moved to Brussels from his home town of Tournai (in today's southern Belgium) in the 1430s, becoming the city's official painter shortly afterwards. When it came to portraiture, Weyden's favourite technique was to highlight the features of his subject – and tokens of rank – against a black background. His *Portrait of Antoine de Bourgogne* is a case in point, with Anthony, the illegitimate son of Philip the Good, casting a haughty, tight-lipped stare to his right while wearing the chain of the Order of the Golden Fleece and clasping an arrow, the emblem of the guild of archers.

Weyden's contemporary, Leuven-based **Dieric Bouts** (1410–75) is well represented by the two panels of his *Justice of the Emperor Otto*. The story was well known: in revenge for refusing her advances, the empress accuses a nobleman of attempting to seduce her. He is executed, but the man's wife remains convinced of his innocence and subsequently proves her point by means of an ordeal by fire – hence the red-hot iron bar she's holding. The empress then receives her just desserts, being burnt on the hill in the background.

Master of the Legend of St Lucy and Hans Memling

Moving on, the anonymous artist known as the **Master of the Legend of St Lucy** weighs in with a finely detailed, richly allegorical *Madonna with Saints* where, with the city of Bruges in the background, the Madonna presents the infant Jesus for the adoration of eleven holy women. Decked out in elaborate medieval attire, the women have blank, almost expressionless faces, but each bears a token of her sainthood, which would have been easily recognized by a medieval congregation: St Lucy, whose assistance was sought by those with sight problems, holds two eyeballs in a dish.

The museum has several fine portraits by **Hans Memling** (1430–94) as well as his softly hued *Martyrdom of St Sebastian*. Legend asserts that Sebastian was an officer in Diocletian's bodyguard until his Christian faith was discovered, at which point he was sentenced to be shot to death by the imperial archers. Left for dead by the bowmen, Sebastian recovered and Diocletian had to send a bunch of assassins to finish him off with cudgels. The tale made Sebastian popular with archers across Western Europe, and Memling's picture, which shows the trussed-up saint serenely indifferent to the arrows of the firing squad, was commissioned by the guild of archers in Bruges around 1470.

School of Hieronymus Bosch and Quinten Matsys

One of the museum's most interesting paintings is a copy of *Temptations of St Anthony* by **Hieronymus Bosch** (1450–1516); the original is in Lisbon's Museu Nacional. No one is quite sure who painted this triptych – it may or may not have been one of Bosch's apprentices – but it was certainly produced in Holland in the late fifteenth or early sixteenth century. The painting refers to St Anthony, a third-century nobleman who withdrew into the desert, where he endured fifteen years of temptation before settling down into his long stint as a hermit. It was the temptations that interested Bosch – rather than the ascetic steeliness of Anthony – and the central panel has an inconspicuous saint sticking desperately to his prayers surrounded by all manner of fiendish phantoms. The side panels develop the theme – to the right Anthony is tempted by lust and greed, and on the left Anthony's companions help him back to his shelter after he's been transported through the skies by weird-looking demons.

Another leading Flemish artist, **Quinten Matsys** (1465–1530) is well represented by the *Triptych of the Holy Kindred*. Matsys' work illustrates a turning point in the development of Low Country painting, and in this triptych, completed in 1509, he abandons the realistic interiors and landscapes of his Flemish predecessors in favour of the grand columns and porticoes of the Renaissance. Each scene is rigorously structured, its characters – all relations of Jesus – assuming lofty, idealized poses.

The Bruegels

The museum's collection of works by the Bruegel family, notably **Pieter the Elder** (1527–69), is simply superb. Little is known for certain of Pieter the Elder's life, but it's likely he was apprenticed in Antwerp, and he certainly moved to Brussels in the early 1560s. He also made at least one long trip to Italy, but judging by his oeuvre, he was – unlike most of his "Belgian" contemporaries – decidedly unimpressed by Italian art. He preferred instead to paint in the Netherlandish tradition and his works often depict crowded Flemish scenes in which are embedded religious or mythical stories. This sympathetic portrayal of everyday life revelled in the seasons and was worked in muted browns, greys and bluey greens with red or yellow highlights. Typifying this approach are two particularly absorbing works, the *Adoration of the Magi* and the *Census at Bethlehem* – a scene that **Pieter** (1564–1638), his son, repeated on several occasions – in which the traditionally momentous events happen, almost incidentally, among the bustle of everyday life. The versatile Pieter the Elder also dabbled with the lurid imagery of Bosch, whose influence is seen most clearly in the *Fall of the Rebel Angels*, a frantic panel painting which had actually been attributed to Bosch until Bruegel's signature was discovered hidden under the frame. The *Fall of Icarus* is, however, his most haunting work, its mood perfectly captured by Auden in his poem *Musée des Beaux Arts*:

In Bruegel's Icarus, for instance: how everything turns away
Quite leisurely from the disaster; the ploughman may
Have heard the splash, the forsaken cry,
But for him it was not an important failure; the sun shone
As it had to on the white legs disappearing into the green
Water; and the expensive delicate ship that must have seen
Something amazing, a boy falling out of the sky,
Had somewhere to get to and sailed calmly on.

Rubens and his contemporaries

Apprenticed in Antwerp, **Rubens** (1577–1640) spent eight years in Italy studying the Renaissance masters before returning home, where he quickly completed a stunning series of paintings for Antwerp Cathedral (see p.212). His fame spread far and wide, and for the rest of his days he was inundated with work, receiving commissions from all over Europe. The museum holds a wide sample of Rubens' work, including a sequence of exquisite **portraits**, each drawn with great care and attention, which soon dispel the popular misconception that he painted nothing but chubby nude women and muscular men. In particular, note the exquisite ruffs adorning the Archdukes Albert and Isabella and the wonderfully observed *Studies of a Negro's Head*, a preparation for the black magus in the *Adoration of the Magi*, a luminous work that's one of several huge canvases in the museum's possession. Other giant works include the *Ascent to Calvary*, an intensely physical painting, capturing the confusion, agony and strain as Christ struggles on hands and knees under the weight of the cross; and the bloodcurdling *Martyrdom of St Lieven*, whose cruel torture – his tongue has just been ripped out and fed to a dog – is watched from on high by cherubs and angels.

Two of Rubens' pupils, **Anthony van Dyck** (1599–1641) and **Jacob Jordaens** (1593–1678), are also well represented, notably the studied portraits of the former and the big and brassy canvases of the latter. Like Rubens, Jordaens had a bulging order book, and for years he and his apprentices churned out paintings by the cartload. His best work is generally agreed to have been completed early on – between about 1620 and 1640 – and there's evidence here in the two versions of the *Satyr and the Peasant*, the earlier work clever and inventive, the second a hastily cobbled-together piece that verges on buffoonery.

Jacques-Louis David

One obvious highlight of the brown area is the much celebrated *Death of Marat* by **Jacques-Louis David** (1748–1825), a propagandist piece of 1793 showing Jean-Paul Marat, the French Revolutionary hero, dying in his bath after being stabbed by Charlotte Corday. David has given Marat a perfectly proportioned, classical torso and a face which, with its large hooded eyes, looks almost Christ-like, the effect heightened by the flatness of the composition and the emptiness of the background. The dead man clasps a quill in one hand and the letter given him by Corday in the other, inscribed "my deepest grief is all it takes to be entitled to your benevolence". As a counterpoint, to emphasize the depth of Corday's betrayal, David has added another note, on the wooden chest, written by Marat and beginning, "You will give this warrant to that mother with the five children, whose husband died for his country". The painting was David's paean to a fellow revolutionary for, like Marat, he was a Jacobin – the deadly rivals of the Girondins, who were supported by Corday. David was also a leading light of the Neoclassical movement and became the new regime's Superintendent of the Fine Arts. He did well under Napoleon, too, but after Waterloo David, along with all the other regicides, was exiled, ending his days in Brussels.

Musée Magritte

From the ground floor of the Musée d'Art Ancien, an underground passageway leads through to Level -2 of the **Musée Magritte** (Tues–Sun 10am–5pm; €8, €13 with Musées d'Art Ancien & d'Art Moderne), whose five small floors – two underground and three above – are devoted to the life, times and work of **René Magritte** (see box, p.80). The museum trawls through his life chronologically, beginning on the top floor, Level +3, its detailed texts illuminated by original documents, old photos and a superb sample of the great man's paintings. These works are often perplexing pieces, whose weird, almost photographically realized images and bizarre juxtapositions aim to disconcert. Magritte was the prime mover in Belgian Surrealism, developing (by the time he was 30) an individualistic style that remained fairly constant throughout his entire career. It was not, however, a style that brought him much initial success and, surprising as it may seem today, he remained relatively unknown until the 1950s. Three of the more intriguing canvases on display here are the baffling *Secret Player*, the subtly discordant *Empire of Lights*, and the threatening, frightening *L'Homme du Large*, which may well have been inspired by the novels of Joseph Conrad.

Musée d'Art Moderne

From Level -2 of the Musée Magritte, a second stairway proceeds down to the six subterranean half-floors of the **Musée d'Art Moderne** (Tues–Sun 10am–5pm; €8 including Musée d'Art Ancien, €13 with Musée Magritte). Two of these half-floors are used for temporary exhibitions, and the other four – the **green area** – feature nineteenth- and twentieth-century works with the former concentrated on Levels -5 and -6, the latter on -7 and -8.

Social Realists

The museum is strong on Belgium's **Social Realists**, whose paintings and sculptures championed the working class. One of the early figures in this movement was **Charles de Groux** (1825–70), whose paternalistic *Poor People's Pew* and *Benediction* are typical of his work. Look out also for the stirring canvases of **Eugene Laermans**

René Magritte

René Magritte (1898–1967) is easily the most famous of Belgium's modern artists, his disconcerting, strangely haunting images a familiar part of popular culture. Born in a small town just outside Charleroi, he entered the Royal Academy of Fine Arts in Brussels in 1915, and was a student there until 1920. His appearances were, however, few and far between as he preferred the company of a group of artists and friends fascinated with the **Surrealist movement** of the 1920s. Their antics were supposed to incorporate a serious intent – the undermining of bourgeois convention – but the surviving home movies of Magritte and his chums fooling around don't appear very revolutionary today.

Initially, Magritte worked in a broadly Cubist manner, but in 1925, influenced by the Italian painter Giorgio de Chirico, he switched over to Surrealism and almost immediately stumbled upon the themes and images that would preoccupy him for decades to come. His work incorporated startling comparisons between the ordinary and the extraordinary, with the occasional erotic element thrown in. **Favourite images** included men in bowler hats, metamorphic figures, enormous rocks floating in the sky, tubas, fishes with human legs, bilboquets (the cup and ball game), and juxtapositions of night and day – one part of the canvas lit by artificial light, the other basking in full sunlight. He also dabbled in word paintings, mislabelling familiar forms to illustrate (or expose) the arbitrariness of linguistic signs. His canvases were devoid of emotion, deadpan images that were easy to recognize but perplexing because of their setting – perhaps most famously, the man in the suit with a bowler hat and an apple for a face.

He broke with this characteristic style on two occasions, once during the war – in despair over the Nazi occupation – and again in 1948, to revenge long years of neglect by the French artistic establishment. Hundreds had turned up to see Magritte's first **Paris exhibition**, but were confronted with crass and crude paintings of childlike simplicity. These so-called **Vache** paintings created a furore, and Magritte beat a hasty artistic retreat behind a smokescreen of self-justification. These two experiments alienated Magritte from most of the other Surrealists, but this was of little consequence as he was picked up and popularized by an American art dealer, Alexander Iolas, who made him very rich and very famous.

Magritte and his family lived in Jette, a suburb of Brussels, until the late 1950s, and the house is now the **Musée René Magritte** (see p.95). He died in 1967, shortly after a major retrospective of his work at the Museum of Modern Art in New York confirmed his reputation as one of the great artists of the twentieth century.

(1864–1940), who shifted from the Realist style into more Expressionistic works, as in the overtly political *Red Flag* and *The Corpse*, a sorrowful vision which is perhaps Laermans' most successful painting. Much more talented was their mutual friend **Constantin Meunier** (1831–1905; see also p.94), who is well represented here by one particularly forceful bronze, the *Iron Worker*.

Impressionism and Post-Impressionism

French Impressionists and Post-Impressionists – Monet, Seurat, Gauguin – also make an appearance in the green area, along with their Belgian imitators, one of the most talented of whom was **Émile Claus** (1849–1924), who produced the charmingly rustic *Cows Crossing the River Leie*. From the same period comes **Théo van Rysselberghe** (1862–1926), a versatile Brussels artist whose most interesting canvases exhibit a studied pointillism – as in his *The Promenade*. **Henry van de Velde** (1863–1957) changed his painting style as often as Rysselberghe, but in the late 1880s he was under the influence of Seurat – hence *The Mender*.

Symbolists and Expressionists

Amongst the **Symbolists**, look out for the disconcerting canvases of **Fernand Khnopff** (1858–1921), who painted his sister, Marguerite, again and again, using her refined, almost plastic beauty to stir a vague sense of passion – for she's desirable and utterly unobtainable in equal measure. His haunting *Memories of Lawn Tennis* is typical of his oeuvre, a work without narrative, a dream-like scene with each of the seven women bearing the likeness of Marguerite. In *Caresses* Marguerite pops up once more, this time with the body of a cheetah pawing sensually at an androgynous youth. **Antoine Wiertz**, who has a museum all to himself near the EU Parliament building (see p.86), pops up too, his *La Belle Rosme* a typically disagreeable painting in which the woman concerned faces a skeleton.

There is also a superb sample of the work of **James Ensor** (1860–1949). Ensor, the son of a Flemish mother and an English father, spent nearly all of his long life working in Ostend, his home town. His first paintings were demure portraits and landscapes, but in the early 1880s he switched to a more Impressionistic style, delicately picking out his colours as in *La Dame Sombre*. It is, however, Ensor's use of masks which sets his work apart – ambiguous carnival masks with the sniff of death or perversity. His *Scandalized Masks* of 1883 was his first mask painting, a typically unnerving canvas that works on several levels, while his *Skeletons Quarrelling for a Kipper* (1891) is one of the most savage and macabre paintings you're ever likely to see.

Contemporary art

The museum holds a diverse, sometimes challenging collection of contemporary art and sculpture from an international range of artists. The exhibits are regularly rotated, but you're likely to see an eerie **Francis Bacon**, *The Pope with Owls*, as well as the tongue-in-cheek work of **Marcel Broodthaers** (1924–76), famously his *Red Mussels Casserole*, and the swirling abstracts of Brussels-born and Paris-based **Pierre Alechinsky** (b. 1927). A painter and graphic artist, Alechinsky was briefly a member of the CoBrA group, but left in 1951. Thereafter, his work picked up on all sorts of international themes and movements, from Japanese calligraphy through to Nordic Expressionism, with a good dose of Surrealism (and Ensor) thrown in. Look out also for the work of the Surrealist **Paul Delvaux** (1897–1994; see p.127), whose trademark themes of trains and stations or ice-cool nudes set against a disintegrating backdrop are displayed in the *Evening Train* and in the ghoulish *Nocturnes*.

The Palais Royal

Around the corner from place Royale, the long and rather cumbersome **Palais Royal** (late July to mid-Sept Tues–Sun 10.30am–4.30pm; free) is something of a disappointment, consisting of a stodgy nineteenth-century conversion of late eighteenth-century town houses, begun by King William I, the Dutch royal who ruled both Belgium and the Netherlands from 1815 to 1830. The Belgian rebellion of 1830 polished off the joint kingdom, and since then the kings of independent Belgium haven't spent much time here. Indeed, although it remains their official residence, the royals have lived elsewhere (in Laeken; see p.96) for decades and it's hardly surprising, therefore, that the **palace interior** is formal and unwelcoming. It comprises little more than a predictable sequence of opulent rooms, all gilt trimmings, parquet floors and endless royal portraits, though three features make a visit (just about) worthwhile: the tapestries designed by Goya; the magnificent chandeliers of the Throne Room; and the Mirror Room's *Heaven of Delight* iridescent ceiling, which is made up of more than a million wing cases of the Thai jewel beetle, the work of Belgium's own Jan Fabre.

Le Musée Belvue and the Coudenberg Palace

The **Hôtel Bellevue**, at the corner of place des Palais and rue Royale, was once part of the palace, but has been turned into **Le Musée Belvue** (Tues–Fri 10am–5pm, Sat–Sun 10am–6pm; museum €3, Coudenberg Palace €6; combined ticket €8; Ⓦwww.belvue.be), which tracks through the brief history of independent Belgium. It's all very professionally done, with the corridor displays concentrating on the country's kings, the rooms on Belgium as a whole. Juicing up the displays is a wide range of original artefacts – documents, letters and so forth – but it's the old photographs that really catch the eye. One particularly interesting display focuses on those Flemish nationalists who collaborated with the Germans during the occupation of World War II; another is devoted to the protracted conflict between the Catholics and the anticlericalists that convulsed the country for much of the nineteenth century. It's an appropriate location for the museum too, as it was in this building that the rebellious Belgians fired at the Dutch army, which was trying to reach the city centre across the Parc de Bruxelles (see below) in 1830.

Dating from the 1770s, the Hôtel Bellevue was built on top of the subterranean remains of the **Coudenberg Palace** (same times as museum), which stretched right across to what is now place Royale. A castle was first built on this site in the eleventh century and was enlarged on several subsequent occasions, but it was badly damaged by fire in 1731 and the site was cleared forty years later, leaving only the foundations. These have recently been cleared of debris, revealing a labyrinth of tunnels that can only be reached from the Hôtel Bellevue. Visitors can wander round these foundations, the most notable feature of which is the massive **Magna Aula**, or great hall, built by Philip the Good in the 1450s. A small display of excavated items, including a pair of helmets, does put some flesh on the historical bones and a map of the layout of the palace is provided at reception, but you still need a vivid imagination to get much out of a visit.

Parc de Bruxelles and place du Trône

Opposite the Palais Royal, the **Parc de Bruxelles** is the most central of the city's main parks, along whose tree-shaded footpaths civil servants and office workers stroll at lunchtime, or race to catch the métro in the evenings. They might well wish the greenery was a bit more interesting. Laid out in the formal French style in 1780, the park undoubtedly suited the courtly – and courting – rituals of the times, but today the straight footpaths and long lines of trees merely seem tedious, though the classical statues and large water fountain do cheer things up a tad.

From the east side of the royal palace, rue Ducale leads to **place du Trône**, where the conspicuous equestrian statue of Léopold II was the work of Thomas Vinçotte, whose skills were much used by the king – look out for Vinçotte's chariot on top of the Parc du Cinquantenaire's triumphal arch (see p.87). Place du Trône is a short walk from the EU Parliament building (see p.85).

Sablon

Anchoring the southern end of the Upper Town, the **Sablon** neighbourhood incorporates **place du Petit Sablon**, a small rectangular area which was laid out as a public garden in 1890 after previous use as a horse market. The wrought-iron fence surrounding the garden is decorated with 48 statuettes representing the medieval guilds while inside, near the top of the slope, are ten slightly larger statues honouring some of the country's leading sixteenth-century figures. The ten are hardly household names in Belgium, never mind anywhere else, but one or two may ring a few bells – Mercator, the geographer and cartographer responsible for Mercator's projection of the earth's surface; and William the Silent (see p.360), to all intents and purposes the founder of the Netherlands. Here also, on top of the fountain, are the figures of the counts **Egmont and Hoorn**, beheaded on the Grand-Place for their opposition to the Habsburgs in 1568.

The fifteenth-century church of **Notre Dame du Sablon** (daily 9am–6pm), opposite place du Petit Sablon, began life as a chapel for the guild of archers in 1304. Its fortunes were, however, transformed when a **statue of Mary**, purportedly with healing powers, was brought here from Antwerp in 1348. The chapel soon became a centre of pilgrimage and a proper church – in High Gothic style – was built to accommodate its visitors. The church endured some inappropriate tinkering at the end of the nineteenth century, but remains a handsome structure, the sandy hues of its exterior stonework enhanced by slender buttresses and a forest of prickly pinnacles. The **interior** no longer holds the statue of Mary – the Protestants chopped it up in 1565 – but two carvings of a boat with its passengers and holy cargo recall its story, one located in the nave, the other above the inside of the rue de la Régence door. The woman in the boat is one Béatrice Sodkens, the pious creature whose visions prompted her to procure the statue and bring it here. The occasion of its arrival in Brussels is still celebrated annually in July by the **Ommegang** historic-heritage procession from the Sablon to the Grand-Place.

Behind the church, the sloping wedge of the **place du Grand Sablon** serves as the centre of one of the city's wealthiest districts, and is busiest at weekends, when it hosts an **antiques market**. Many of the shops hereabouts are devoted to antiques and art, and you could easily spend an hour or so browsing – or you can soak up the atmosphere in one of Sablon's several cafés.

Palais de Justice and place Louise

From place du Grand Sablon, it's a brief walk south up to place Poelaert, named after the architect who designed the immense **Palais de Justice**, a monstrous Greco-Roman wedding cake of a building, dwarfing the square and everything around it. It's possible to wander into the building's sepulchral main hall, but it's the size alone that impresses – not that it pleased the several thousand townsfolk who were forcibly evicted so that the place could be built. Poelaert became one of the most hated men in the capital and, when he went insane and died in 1879, it was widely believed a *steekes* (witch) from the Marolles had been sticking pins into an effigy of him. A stone's throw from the Palais de Justice, **place Louise**, part square, part traffic junction, heralds the start of the city's most exclusive shopping district. Here and in the immediate vicinity you'll find designer boutiques, jewellers and glossy shopping malls. The glitz spreads east along boulevard de Waterloo and south down the first part of avenue Louise.

East of the centre: the EU quarter and Le Cinquantenaire

Brussels by no means ends at the **petit ring**. King Léopold II pushed the city limits out beyond the course of the old walls, grabbing land from the surrounding *communes* to create the irregular boundaries that survive today. To the **east**, he sequestered a rough rectangle of land across which he ploughed two wide boulevards to link the city centre with **Le Cinquantenaire**, a

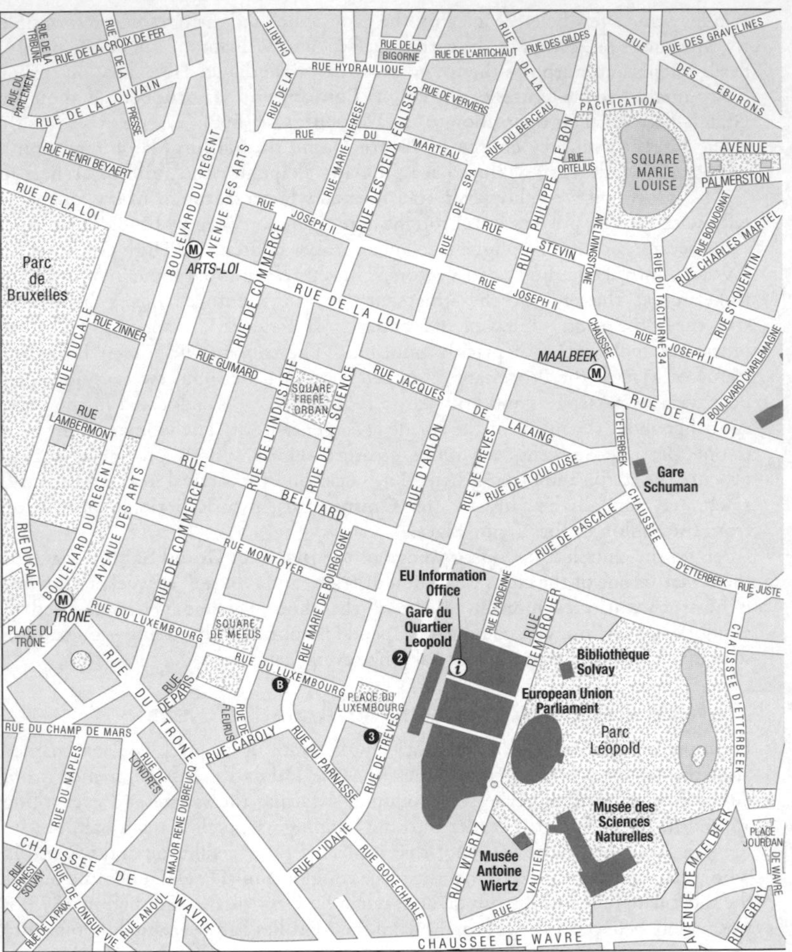

self-glorifying and markedly grandiose monument erected to celebrate the golden jubilee of Belgian independence, and one that now houses three sprawling museums, two specialists and the more general **Musées Royaux d'Art et d'Histoire**. There's no disputing the grandness of Léopold's design, but in recent decades it has been overlaid with the uncompromising office blocks of the EU. These high-rises coalesce hereabouts to form the loosely defined **EU quarter**, not a particularly enjoyable area to explore, though the strikingly flashy **European Parliament building** is of passing interest, especially as it is just footsteps from the fascinating – and fascinatingly eccentric – paintings of the **Musée Antoine Wiertz**. If, however, you've an insatiable appetite for the monuments of Léopold, then you should venture further east to **Tervuren**, where the king built the massive Musée Royal de L'Afrique Centrale on the edge of the woods of the Forêt de Soignes.

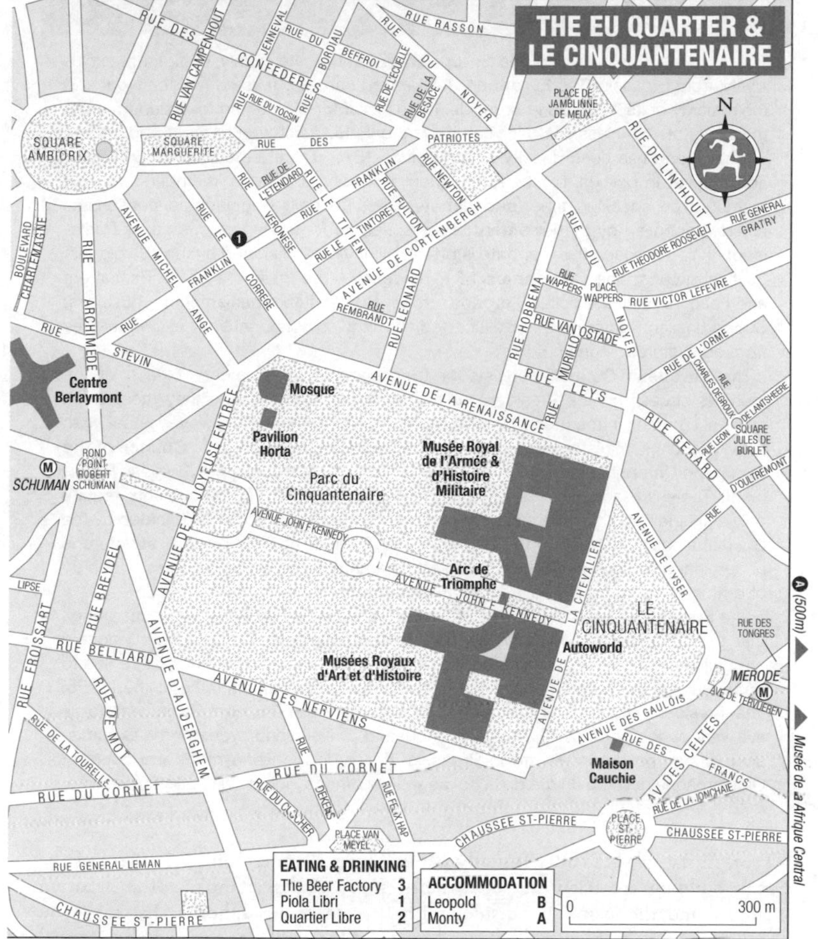

Place du Trône to the EU Parliament building

From place du Trône (see p.82), it's a five-minute walk east to **place du Luxembourg**, a wide and attractive square framed on three sides by late nineteenth-century town houses and on the fourth by the old **Gare du Quartier Léopold** train station, now dwarfed by a gargantuan EU office block. Fortunately, there are two breaches in this edifice right behind the station and both passageways lead through to the striking **European Union Parliament building**, a glass, stone and steel behemoth equipped with a horseshoe-shaped debating chamber and a curved glass roof that rises to a height of 70m. Completed in 1997, this **Spaak building** has its admirers, but is known locally as the "*caprice des dieux*", a wry comment on the EU's sense of its own importance.

The EU in Brussels

The three main institutions of the **European Union** operate mainly, though not exclusively, from Brussels. The **European Parliament** carries out its committee work and the majority of its business in Brussels, heading off for Strasbourg for around twelve, three-day plenary sessions per year. It's the only EU institution to meet and debate in public, and has been directly elected since 1979. There are currently 736 MEPs, and they sit in political blocks rather than national delegations; members are very restricted on speaking time, and debates tend to be well-mannered consensual affairs, controlled by the **President**, who is elected for a five-year period by Parliament itself – although this mandate is often split in two and shared by the two biggest political groups. The **Conference of Presidents** – the President of the Parliament and Leaders of all the political groups – meet to plan future parliamentary business. Supporting and advising this political edifice is a complex network of committees from agriculture to human rights.

The **European Council** consists of the heads of government of each of the member states and the President of the European Commission; they meet twice every six months in the much-publicized "European Summits". However, in between these meetings, ministers responsible for different issues meet in the **Council of the European Union**, the main decision-making structure alongside the European Parliament. There are complex rules regarding decision-making: some subjects require only a simple majority, others need unanimous support, some can be decided by the Council alone, others need the agreement of Parliament. This political structure is underpinned by scores of Brussels-based committees and working parties, made up of both civil servants and political appointees.

The **European Commission** acts as the EU's executive arm and board of control, managing funds and monitoring all manner of agreements. The 27 Commissioners are political appointees, nominated by their home countries, but their tenure has to be agreed by the European Parliament and they remain accountable to the MEPs. The president of the Commission is elected by the European Parliament for a five-year period of office. Over twenty thousand civil servants work for the Commission, whose headquarters are in Brussels, mainly in the Berlaymont and adjacent Charlemagne building on rue de la Loi as well as other buildings in the Schuman area.

Free, thirty-minute **tours** (usually Mon–Thurs 10am & 3pm, Fri 10am) of the Spaak building are fairly cursory affairs, more or less a look at the debating chamber and the stairwell outside, with the aid of headphones that take you through the whole thing and explain how the EU works. It's not exactly essential viewing, but you do learn something of the purpose of the building – which, amazingly enough, is here mainly to house the Parliament's various committees. To take the tour, report to the visitors' entrance fifteen minutes in advance and be sure to take photo ID. If you're fired with EU enthusiasm before or after the tour, pop into the **information office** at the Gare du Quartier Léopold end of one of the office passageways to pick up all sorts of free gubbins (Mon–Thurs 9am–5pm, Fri 9am–1pm).

Musée Antoine Wiertz

From the EU Parliament building, it's a couple of minutes' walk up the slope to the **Musée Antoine Wiertz**, rue Vautier 62 (Tues–Fri 10am–noon & 1–5pm; free), a small museum devoted to the works of one of the city's most distinctive, if disagreeable, nineteenth-century artists. Once immensely popular – so much so that in *Tess of the d'Urbervilles* Thomas Hardy could write of "the staring and ghastly attitudes of a Wiertz museum" – **Antoine-Joseph Wiertz** (1806–65) painted religious and mythological canvases, featuring gory hells and strapping nudes, as well as fearsome scenes of human madness and suffering.

The core of the museum is housed in his **studio**, a large, airy gallery that was built for him by the Belgian state on the understanding that he bequeath his oeuvre to the nation. Pictures include *The Burnt Child* and a small but especially gruesome *Suicide* – not for the squeamish. There are also a number of quite elegantly painted quasi-erotic pieces featuring coy nudes, and a colossal *Triumph of Christ*, a melodramatic painting of which Wiertz was inordinately proud. Three adjoining **rooms** contain further macabre works, such as *The Thoughts and Visions of a Severed Head* and (the most appalling of them all) his *Hunger, Folly, Crime* – in which a madwoman is pictured shortly after hacking off her child's leg and throwing it into the cooking pot. Mercifully, there is some more restrained stuff here too, including several portraits and more saucy girls in various states of undress. Wiertz eventually came to believe that he was a better painter than his artistic forebears, Rubens and Michelangelo; judge for yourself.

Muséum des Sciences Naturelles

Follow rue Vautier up the hill from the Wiertz museum and you soon reach the **Musée des Sciences Naturelles**, at rue Vautier 29 (Tues–Fri 9.30am–5pm, Sat & Sun 10am–6pm; €7; Ⓦwww.naturalsciences.be), which holds the city's natural history collection. It's a large, sprawling and somewhat disorientating museum, whose wide-ranging displays are lodged in a mixture of late nineteenth-century and 1960s galleries. There are sections devoted to crystals and rocks; rodents and mammals; insects and crustaceans; a whale gallery featuring the enormous remains of a blue whale and, most impressive of the lot, a capacious **dinosaur gallery** with a superb selection of dinosaur fossils discovered in the coal mines of Hainaut in the late nineteenth century. The most striking are those of a whole herd of **iguanodons**, whose skeletons are raised on two legs, though in fact these herbivores may well have been four-legged; an excellent multilingual text explains it all.

Parc Léopold

On rue Vautier, almost opposite the Musée Wiertz, a back entrance leads into the rear of **Parc Léopold**, a green and hilly enclave landscaped around a lake. The park is pleasant enough, but its open spaces were encroached upon years ago when the industrialist Ernest Solvay began constructing the educational and research facilities of a prototype science centre here. The end result is a string of big, old buildings that spread along the park's western periphery. The most interesting – and one of the first you'll come to – is the **Bibliothèque Solvay** (no set opening times), a splendid barrel-vaulted structure with magnificent mahogany panelling overlaying a cast-iron frame. The northern edge of the park abuts rue Belliard, which runs east to the Parc du Cinquantenaire.

Parc du Cinquantenaire

The wide and leafy lawns of the **Parc du Cinquantenaire** slope up towards a gargantuan triumphal arch surmounted by a huge and bombastic bronze entitled *Brabant Raising the National Flag*. The arch, along with the two heavyweight stone buildings it connects, comprise **Le Cinquantenaire**, which was erected by Léopold II for an exhibition to mark the golden jubilee of the Belgian state in 1880. By all accounts the exhibition of all things made in Belgium and its colonies was a great success in an imperialist sort of way, while the buildings themselves – a brief walk from Métro Merode and Métro Schuman – contain extensive collections of art and applied art, weapons and cars, displayed in three separate museums.

Musées Royaux d'Art et d'Histoire

The **Musées Royaux d'Art et d'Histoire**, on the south side of the south wing of the Cinquantenaire complex (Tues–Fri 9.30am–5pm, Sat & Sun 10am–5pm; €5; Ⓦwww.mrah.be), is made up of a maddening and badly labelled maze of pottery, carvings, furniture, tapestries, glassware and paintings from all over the world. There's almost too much to absorb in even a couple of visits, and there's no plan, which makes it even harder to select the bits that interest you most. There are enormous galleries of early Greek, Egyptian and Roman artefacts, an assortment of Far Eastern art and textiles, medieval and Renaissance carving and religious artefacts, and a decent collection of glasswork from all eras. But perhaps the best thing to do with a large, disorganized museum of this nature is to wander freely and stop when something catches your eye.

To the right of the entrance hall, the **European decorative arts** galleries have perhaps the most immediacy, featuring everything from Delft ceramics, altarpieces, porcelain and silverware through to tapestries and Art Deco and Art Nouveau furnishings. It's all a little bewildering, however, with little to link one set of objects to another. Highlights include some striking fifteenth- and sixteenth-century **altarpieces**; a prime collection of Brussels **tapestries** dating from the middle of the sixteenth century, the heyday of the city's tapestry industry; and an intriguing **Art Nouveau** section, where the display cases, which were designed by Victor Horta for a firm of jewellers, now accommodate the celebrated *Mysterious Sphinx*, a ceramic bust of archetypal Art Nouveau design. It was the work of Charles van der Stappen in 1897.

Autoworld

Housed in a vast hangar-like building in the south wing of Le Cinquantenaire, **Autoworld** (daily: April–Sept 10am–6pm; Oct–March 10am–5pm; €6; Ⓦwww.autoworld.be) is a chronological stroll through the short history of the automobile, with a huge display of **vintage vehicles**, beginning with turn-of-the-century motorized cycles and Model Ts. Perhaps inevitably, European varieties predominate: there are lots of vehicles from Peugeot, Renault and Benz, and homegrown examples, too, including a Minerva from 1925 which once belonged to the Belgian monarch. American vehicles include early Cadillacs, a Lincoln from 1965 that was also owned by the Belgian royals, and some great gangster-style Oldsmobiles; among the British brands, there's a mint-condition Rolls-Royce Silver Ghost from 1921, one of the first Austins and, from the modern era, the short-lived De Lorean sports car. Upstairs is a collection of assorted vehicles that don't fit into the main exhibition. It's a bit of a mishmash, but worth a brief look for some early Porsches and Volvos, classic 1960s Jags and even a tuk-tuk from Thailand.

Musée Royal de l'Armée et d'Histoire Militaire

In the north wing of Le Cinquantenaire, on the other side of the triumphal arch from the other two museums, the **Musée Royal de l'Armée et d'Histoire Militaire** (Tues–Sun 9am–noon & 1–4.45pm; free; Ⓦwww.klm-mra.be) traces the history of the "Belgian" army from the late eighteenth century to the present day by means of a vast hoard of weapons, armaments and uniforms. The first part of the collection is enjoyably old-fashioned with a long series of glass cases holding a small army of life-sized model soldiers, with assorted rifles, swords and muskets nailed to the walls above. Of particular interest here are the sections dealing with "Belgian" regiments in the Austrian and Napoleonic armies, and the volunteers who formed the nucleus of the 1830 revolution. Moving on, the hall devoted to World War I is excellent, displaying uniforms and kit from every nationality involved in the conflict, together with a fearsome array of field guns, artillery pieces and early, very primitive tanks. A second, even larger hall covers World War II, depicting the build-up to the war and including the Belgian experience of collaboration and resistance, all illustrated by a superb selection of blown-up period photographs. The courtyard outside has a large collection of World War II tanks, armoured cars and artillery pieces – British, American and German – and there's a third large hall dedicated to military aviation. A welcome bonus to a visit is that you can access the **triumphal arch** from the museum and enjoy extensive views over the city from its terrace.

Tervuren's Musée Royal de L'Afrique Centrale

Personally presented with the vast **Congo River basin** by a conference of the European Powers in 1885, **King Léopold II** of Belgium made the most of his colonial assets, becoming one of the world's richest men. His initial attempts to secure control of the area were abetted by the explorer – and ex-Confederate soldier – **Henry Stanley**, who went to the Congo on a five-year fact-finding mission in 1879, just a few years after he had famously found the missionary David Livingstone. Even by the standards of the colonial powers, Léopold's regime was too chaotic and too extraordinarily cruel to countenance, and the Belgian government was finally shamed into taking over the territory in 1908: a British diplomat by the name of **Roger Casement** (1864–1916) played a leading role in exposing the barbarity and banditry of Léopold's regime – the same Casement who was hung by the British for his involvement in the Dublin Easter Rising of 1916. After the 1908 takeover, the Belgian government installed a marginally more efficient state bureaucracy, but when the Belgian Congo gained independence as the Republic of Congo in 1960, it was poorly prepared and its subsequent history (as both Zaire and the Republic of Congo) has been one of the most bloodstained in Africa.

Léopold II was proud of his African possessions and to show them off he built the grandiose **Musée Royal de L'Afrique Centrale** (Tues–Fri 10am–5pm, Sat & Sun 10am–6pm; €4; Ⓦwww.africamuseum.be), out in the suburb of Tervuren, some 10km east of the Parc du Cinquantenaire along avenue de Tervueren – a journey is best completed on tram #44 (1–2 hourly; 25min) from place (and Métro) Montgomery; the museum is a couple of minutes' walk from the tram terminus. The museum's origins may be colonialist and racist, but the collection, which occupies the whole of the **ground floor**, is undeniably rich, and is in fact part ethnographic and part natural history museum. Off to the left of the entrance hall, various cases cover many aspects of domestic Congolese life – clothing, furniture, tools and musical instruments, an impressive array of dope pipes, and a superb 60m-long dugout canoe that is some 300 hundred years old. The galleries beyond, filling the left-hand wing of the museum, hold an army of stuffed mammals, birds, fish and insects, but things pick up opposite, on the right side of the building, which gets to grips with Congolese culture and ritual, with nail sculptures, masks, sculptures and busts. Beyond, the museum tells the sad and bitter story of colonization by means of photos, maps and other documents. There are ancient shots of Stanley, and later ones of Baudouin, the Belgian king, visiting Leopoldville for the independence celebrations, when his ill-conceived speech infuriated several Congolese leaders. Here also Room 8 is of interest for its old – and thoroughly unreconstructed – tributes to those "noble" Belgians who died in the Congo and for the PR display (of 1934) claiming that Belgium's main concern in the Congo was the extirpation of the Arab-run slave trade.

The museum's **grounds** are also well worth a stroll, with the formal gardens set around a series of geometric lakes flanked by wanderable woods.

South of the centre: St-Gilles, avenue Louise and Ixelles

Cobwebbed by tiny squares and narrow streets, home to a plethora of local bars and many of the capital's finest Art Nouveau houses, the neighbouring areas of St-Gilles and Ixelles, just south of the petit ring, make a great escape from the razzmatazz of the city centre. **St-Gilles**, the smaller of the two *communes*, does have patches of inner-city decay, but it gets more beautiful the further east it spreads, its run-down streets soon left behind for attractive avenues interspersed with dignified squares. **Ixelles**, for its part, is one of the capital's most interesting and exciting outer areas, with a diverse street-life and café scene. Historically something of a cultural crossroads, Ixelles has long drawn artists, writers and intellectuals – Karl Marx, Auguste Rodin and Alexandre Dumas all lived here – and today it retains an arty, sometimes Bohemian feel. Ixelles is cut into two by **avenue Louise**, a prosperous corridor that is actually part of the city – a territorial anomaly inherited from Léopold II, who laid it out and named it after his eldest daughter in the 1840s. Some of Brussels' premier hotels, shops and boutiques flank the northern reaches of the avenue and further along is the enjoyable **Musée Constantin Meunier**, sited in the sculptor's old house.

More than anything else, however, it's the superb range of **Art Nouveau buildings** clustering the streets of St-Gilles and Ixelles that really grab the attention. Many of the finest examples are concentrated on and around the boundary between the two *communes* – in between chaussée de Charleroi and avenue Louise – and it's here you'll find Horta's own house and studio, now the glorious **Musée Victor Horta**, one of the few Art Nouveau buildings in the country fully open to the public. Access to most of the city's Art Nouveau buildings is restricted, so you can either settle for the view from outside, or enrol on one of ARAU's specialist Art Nouveau tours (see p.56).

Musée Victor Horta

The best place to start a visit to **St-Gilles** is the delightful **Musée Victor Horta** (Tues–Sun 2–5.30pm; €7; Ⓦwww.hortamuseum.be), just off the chaussée de Charleroi at rue Américaine 25 and reachable by tram #92 from place Louise. The museum occupies the two houses Horta designed as his home and studio at the end of the nineteenth century, and was where he lived until 1919. The exterior sets the tone, a striking re-working and re-ordering of what was originally a modest terraced structure, the fluidity of the design incorporating almost casually knotted and twisted ironwork. Yet it is for his interiors that Horta is particularly famous. Inside is a sunny, sensuous dwelling exhibiting all the architect's favourite flourishes – wrought iron, stained glass, ornate furniture and panelling made from several different types of timber. The main unifying feature is the **staircase**, a dainty spiralling affair, which runs through the centre of the house illuminated by a large skylight. Decorated with painted motifs and surrounded by mirrors, it remains one of Horta's most magnificent and ingenious creations, giving access to a sequence of wide, bright rooms. Also of interest is the modest but enjoyable

Horta's progress

The son of a shoemaker, **Victor Horta** (1861–1947) was born in Ghent, where he failed in his first career, being unceremoniously expelled from the city's music conservatory for indiscipline. He promptly moved to Paris to study architecture, returning to Belgium in 1880 to complete his internship in Brussels with Alphonse Balat, architect to King Léopold II. Balat was a traditionalist, partly responsible for the classical facades of the Palais Royal – among many other prestigious projects – and Horta looked elsewhere for inspiration. He found it in the work of William Morris, the leading figure of the English Arts and Crafts movement, whose designs were key to the development of **Art Nouveau**. Taking its name from the Maison de l'Art Nouveau, a Parisian shop which sold items of modern design, Art Nouveau rejected the imitative architectures which were popular at the time – Neoclassical and neo-Gothic – in favour of an innovatory style characterized by sinuous, flowing lines. In England, Morris and his colleagues had focused on book illustrations and furnishings, but in Belgium Horta extrapolated the new style into architecture, experimenting with new building materials – steel and concrete – as well as traditional stone, glass and wood.

In 1893, Horta completed the curvaceous **Hôtel Tassel**, Brussels' first Art Nouveau building ("hôtel" meaning town house; see p.94). Inevitably, there were howls of protest from the traditionalists, but no matter what his opponents said, Horta never lacked work again. The following years – roughly 1893 to 1905 – were Horta's most inventive and prolific. He designed over forty buildings, including the **Hôtel Solvay** (see p.94), the **Hôtel Max Hallet** (see p.94), and his own beautifully decorated house and studio, now the **Musée Victor Horta** (see p.90). The delight Horta took in his work is obvious, especially when employed on private houses, and his enthusiasm was all-encompassing – he almost always designed everything from the blueprints to the wallpaper and carpets. He never kept a straight line or sharp angle where he could deploy a curve, and his use of light was revolutionary, often filtering through from above, with skylights and as many windows as possible. Horta felt that the architect was as much an artist as the painter or sculptor, and so he insisted on complete stylistic freedom; curiously, he also believed that originality was born of frustration, so he deliberately created architectural difficulties, pushing himself to find harmonious solutions. It was part of a well-thought-out value system that allied him with the political Left; as he wrote, "My friends and I were reds, without however having thought about Marx or his theories".

Completed in 1906, the **Grand Magasin Waucquez** (see p.70) department store was a transitional building signalling the end of Horta's Art Nouveau period. His later works were more Modernist constructions, whose understated lines were a far cry from the ornateness of his earlier work. In Brussels, the best example of his later work is the Palais des Beaux Arts (BOZAR) of 1928 (see p.75).

selection of paintings, many of which were given to Horta by friends and colleagues, including works by Félicien Rops and Joseph Heymans.

Art Nouveau in western Ixelles and avenue Louise

From the Musée Victor Horta, it's a five-minute walk north to **rue Defacqz**, the site of several charming Art Nouveau houses. Three of them were designed by **Paul Hankar** (1859–1901), a classically trained architect and contemporary of Horta, who developed a real penchant for **sgraffiti** – akin to frescoes – and multi-coloured brickwork. Hankar was regarded as one of the most distinguished exponents of Art Nouveau and his old home, at **no. 71**, is marked by its skeletal metalwork, appealing bay windows and four sgraffiti beneath the cornice – one

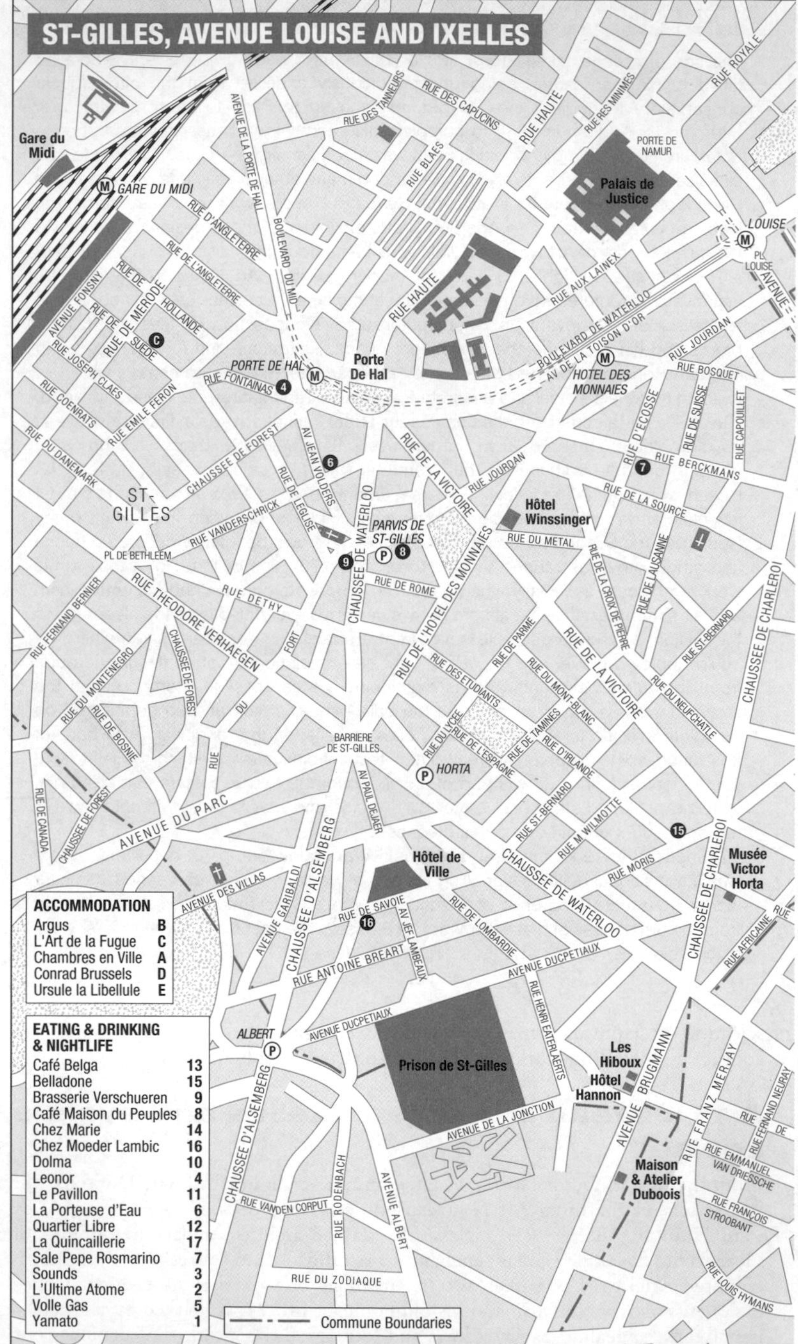
ST-GILLES, AVENUE LOUISE AND IXELLES
Gare du Midi
GARE DU MIDI
Palais de Justice
PORTE DE NAMUR
LOUISE
PL. LOUISE
Porte De Hal
PORTE DE HAL
HOTEL DES MONNAIES
Hôtel Winssinger
PARVIS DE ST-GILLES
ST-GILLES
BARRIERE DE ST-GILLES
HORTA
Hôtel de Ville
Musée Victor Horta
ALBERT
Prison de St-Gilles
Les Hiboux
Hôtel Hannon
Maison & Atelier Dubois
RUE DES TANNEURS
RUE DES CAPUCINS
RUE HAUTE
RUE DES MINIMES
RUE ROYALE
AVENUE DE LA PORTE DE HAL
RUE BLAES
BOULEVARD DU MIDI
RUE D'ANGLETERRE
RUE DE L'ANGLETERRE
AVENUE FONSNY
RUE DE MERODE
RUE DE HOLLANDE
RUE DE SUEDE
RUE JOSEPH CLAES
RUE COENRAETS
RUE EMILE FERON
RUE FONTAINAS
RUE DU DANEMARK
CHAUSSEE DE FOREST
AV JEAN VOLDERS
RUE DE L'EGLISE
RUE VANDERSCHRICK
PL DE BETHLEEM
RUE AUX LAINES
BOULEVARD DE WATERLOO
AV DE LA TOISON D'OR
RUE JOURDAN
RUE BOSQUET
RUE D'ECOSSE
RUE DE SUISSE
RUE CAPOUILLET
RUE BERCKMANS
RUE DE LA SOURCE
AVENUE LOUISE
RUE DE LA VICTOIRE
RUE DU METAL
RUE DE LA CROIX DE PIERRE
RUE DE LAUSANNE
CHAUSSEE DE CHARLEROI
CHAUSSEE DE WATERLOO
RUE DE ROME
RUE DETHY
RUE THEODORE VERHAEGEN
RUE FERNAND BERNIER
RUE DU FORT
RUE DE L'HOTEL DES MONNAIES
RUE DE PARME
RUE ST-BERNARD
RUE DES ETUDIANTS
RUE DU MONT-BLANC
RUE DU NEUFCHATEL
RUE DU MONTENEGRO
RUE DE BOSNIE
RUE DU LYCEE
RUE DE L'ESPAGNE
RUE DE TAMINES
RUE D'IRLANDE
RUE DE CANADA
AVENUE DU PARC
AV PAUL DEJAER
RUE M WILMOTTE
RUE MORIS
AVENUE DES VILLAS
AVENUE GARIBALDI
CHAUSSEE D'ALSEMBERG
RUE DE SAVOIE
AV JEF LAMBEAUX
RUE DE LOMBARDIE
RUE ANTOINE BREART
AVENUE DUCPETIAUX
RUE HENRI EATERLAERTS
RUE AFRICAINE
AVENUE BRUGMANN
RUE FRANZ MERJAY
RUE FERNAND NEURAY
RUE EMMANUEL VAN DRIESSCHE
RUE FRANÇOIS STROOBANT
RUE LOUIS HYMANS
AVENUE DE LA JONCTION
RUE VANDEN CORPUT
RUE RODENBACH
AVENUE ALBERT
RUE DU ZODIAQUE
ACCOMMODATION
Argus B
L'Art de la Fugue C
Chambres en Ville A
Conrad Brussels D
Ursule la Libellule E
EATING & DRINKING & NIGHTLIFE
Café Belga 13
Belladone 15
Brasserie Verschueren 9
Café Maison du Peuples 8
Chez Marie 14
Chez Moeder Lambic 16
Dolma 10
Leonor 4
Le Pavillon 11
La Porteuse d'Eau 6
Quartier Libre 12
La Quincaillerie 17
Sale Pepe Rosmarino 7
Sounds 3
L'Ultime Atome 2
Volle Gas 5
Yamato 1
Commune Boundaries

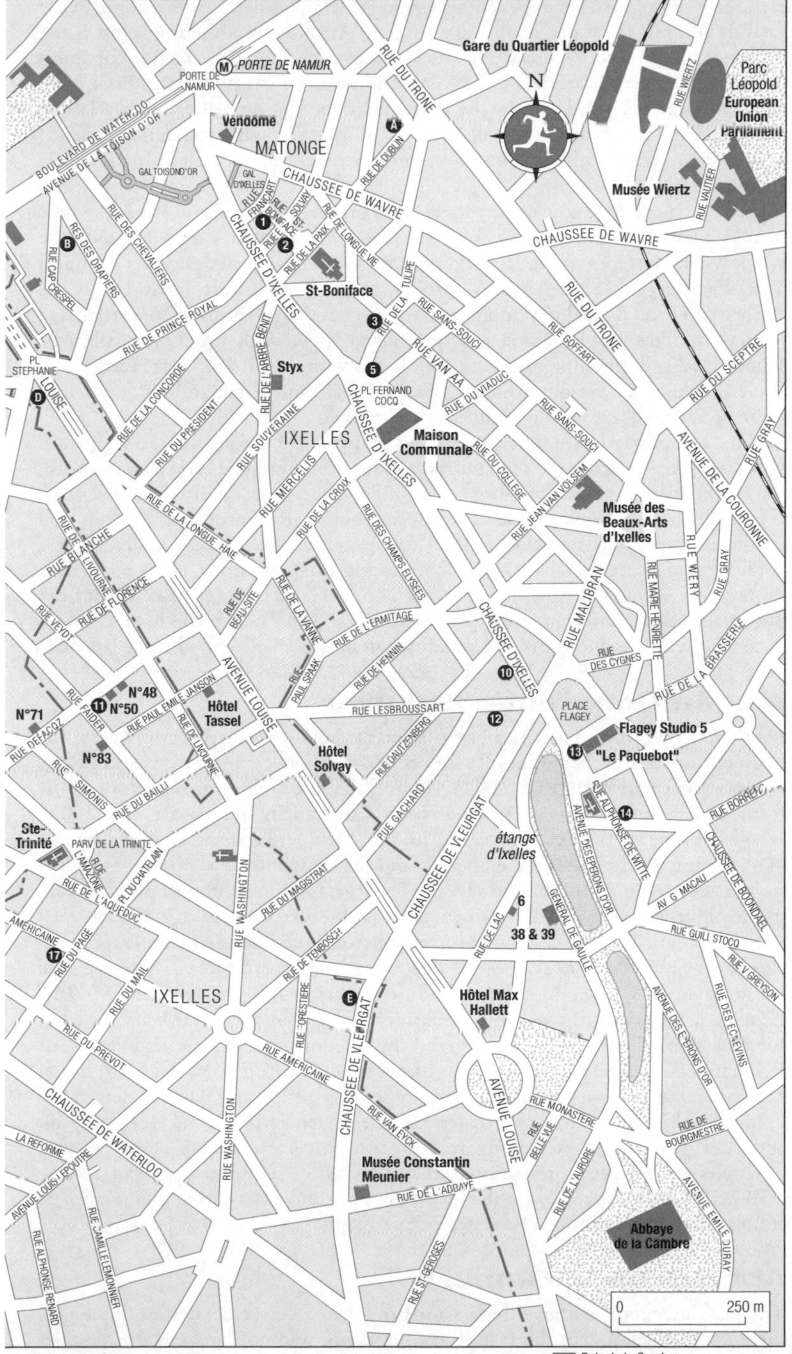

Gare du Quartier Léopold
PORTE DE NAMUR
Parc Léopold
European Union Parliament
Vendome
MATONGE
Musée Wiertz
CHAUSSEE DE WAVRE
RUE DU TRONE
BOULEVARD DE WATERLOO
AVENUE DE LA TOISON D'OR
GAL TOISON D'OR
GAL D'IXELLES
RUE FRANCART
RUE ST-BONIFACE
RUE SOLVAY
RUE DE LA PAIX
RUE DE LONGUE VIE
RUE DE DUBLIN
RUE WIERTZ
RUE VAUTIER
RUE DES CHEVALIERS
RES DES DRAPIERS
RUE CAPITAINE CRESPEL
CHAUSSEE D'IXELLES
St-Boniface
RUE DE LA TULIPE
RUE SANS-SOUCI
RUE GOFFART
RUE DU SCEPTRE
RUE DE PRINCE ROYAL
RUE DE L'ARBRE BENIT
Styx
PL STEPHANIE
LOUISE
RUE VAN AA
PL FERNAND COCQ
RUE DU VIADUC
RUE DE LA CONCORDE
RUE DU PRESIDENT
RUE SOUVERAINE
IXELLES
Maison Communale
RUE DU COLLEGE
AVENUE DE LA COURONNE
RUE GRAY
RUE MERCELIS
RUE DE LA CROIX
RUE DES CHAMPS ELYSEES
RUE JEAN VAN VOLSEM
Musée des Beaux-Arts d'Ixelles
RUE DE LA LONGUE HAIE
RUE BLANCHE
RUE DE LIVOURNE
RUE DE FLORENCE
RUE DE BEAU-SITE
RUE DE LA VANNE
RUE DE L'ERMITAGE
RUE MALIBRAN
RUE MARIE HENRIETTE
RUE WERY
RUE VEYDT
RUE PAUL SPAAK
RUE DE HENNIN
RUE DES CYGNES
RUE DE LA BRASSERIE
AVENUE LOUISE
N°48
N°50
N°71
RUE FAIDER
RUE PAUL EMILE JANSON
Hôtel Tassel
RUE LESBROUSSART
PLACE FLAGEY
Flagey Studio 5
"Le Paquebot"
RUE DEFACQZ
N°83
RUE SIMONIS
RUE DU BAILLI
Hôtel Solvay
RUE DAUTZENBERG
RUE GACHARD
CHAUSSEE DE VLEURGAT
étangs d'Ixelles
RUE ALPHONSE DE WITTE
AVENUE DES EPERONS D'OR
RUE BORRENS
CHAUSSEE DE BOONDAEL
Ste-Trinité
PARV DE LA TRINITE
R DE L'AMAZONE
PL DU CHATELAIN
RUE DE L'AQUEDUC
RUE WASHINGTON
RUE DU MAGISTRAT
AV G MACAU
RUE GUILI STOCQ
AMERICAINE
RUE DU PAGE
RUE DE TENBOSCH
RUE DE LAC
GENERAL DE GAULLE
38 & 39
RUE V GREYSON
RUE DU MAIL
IXELLES
RUE ORESTIERE
Hôtel Max Hallett
AVENUE DES ECUYERS
RUE DES ECHEVINS
RUE DU PREVOT
RUE AMERICAINE
CHAUSSEE DE WATERLOO
RUE VAN EYCK
RUE MONASTERE
RUE BELLE VUE
RUE DE BOURGMESTRE
LA REFORME
AVENUE LOUIS LEPOUTRE
Musée Constantin Meunier
RUE DE L'ABBAYE
RUE DE L'AURORE
AVENUE EMILE DURAY
Abbaye de la Cambre
RUE CAMILLE LEMONNIER
RUE ALPHONSE RENARD
RUE ST-GEORGES
0
250 m
Bois de la Cambre

each for morning, afternoon, evening and night. Hankar designed his home in the early 1890s, making it one of the city's earliest Art Nouveau buildings. Just along the street, over in **Ixelles**, attractive **rue Defacqz 50** is a Hankar creation too, built for the painter René Janssens in 1898 and noteworthy for its fanciful brickwork and handsome bay window. Yet the house next door, at **no. 48**, is where Hanker really let rip, covering almost all of the 1897 facade with romantic, "poetic" sgraffiti as much to please himself as his customer, the Italian painter Albert Ciamberlani.

There are more Art Nouveau treats in store on neighbouring **rue Faider**, where **no. 83** boasts a splendidly flamboyant façade, with ironwork crawling over the windows and frescoes of pert Pre-Raphaelite women, all to a design by **Armand Van Waesberghe** (1879–1949). Close by, at **rue Paul Émile Janson 6**, is the celebrated **Hôtel Tassel** (no public access), the building that made Victor Horta's reputation. The supple facade is appealing enough, with its clawed columns, stained glass and spiralling ironwork, but it was with the interior that Horta really made a splash, an uncompromising fantasy featuring a fanciful wrought-iron staircase and walls covered with linear decoration.

At the end of rue Paul Emile Janson you hit **avenue Louise**, where a right turn will take you – in a couple of hundred metres – to another Horta extravagance, the **Hôtel Solvay** (no public access), at no. 224. The Solvay family, who had made a fortune in soft drinks, gave the 33-year-old Horta complete freedom and unlimited funds to design this opulent town house, whose facade is graced by a confetti of delicate metalwork and contrasting types of stone. Also on avenue Louise, five minutes further along at no. 346, is Horta's **Hôtel Max Hallet** (no public access), a comparatively plain structure of 1904 where the long facade is decorated with elegant doors and windows alongside an elongated stone balcony.

Musée Constantin Meunier

South of Hôtel Max Hallet and just off avenue Louise at rue de l'Abbaye 59, the **Musée Constantin Meunier** (Tues–Fri 10am–noon & 1–5pm; weekends by advance request only on ⓣ02 648 44 49; free) is housed on the ground floor of the former home and studio of Brussels-born **Constantin Meunier** (1831–1905), who lived here for the last six years of his life. Meunier began as a painter, but it's as a sculptor that he's best remembered, and the museum has a substantial collection of his dark and brooding bronzes. The largest and most important pieces are in the old studio at the back, where a series of life-size bronzes of muscular men with purposeful faces stand around looking heroic – *Le Faucheur* (The Reaper), *Un Semeur* (A Sower) and *Le Marteleur* (The Metalworker) are typical. There are oil paintings in this room too, gritty industrial scenes like the coalfield of *Black Country Borinage* and the gloomy dockside of *The Port*, one of Meunier's most forceful works. Meunier was angered by the dreadful living conditions of Belgium's working class, particularly (like Van Gogh before him) the harsh life of the coal miners of the Borinage. This anger fuelled his art, which asserted the dignity of the worker in a style that was to be copied by the Social Realists of his and later generations. According to historian Eric Hobsbawm's *Age of Empire*, "Meunier invented the international stereotype of the sculptured proletarian".

To get to the museum by public transport from the city centre, take **tram** #94 from place Louise, rue de la Régence or rue Royale.

Abbaye de la Cambre

The postcard-pretty **Abbaye de la Cambre** (open access; free) nestles in a lovely little wooded dell just to the east of avenue Louise and not far from the Meunier

Museum. Of medieval foundation, the French Revolutionary army suppressed the abbey at the beginning of the nineteenth century, but its eighteenth-century brick buildings survived pretty much untouched and, after many toings and froings, have ended up as government offices. An extensive complex, the main courtyard is especially attractive and it serves as the main entrance to the charming **abbey church** (9am–noon & 2–5pm), whose nave, with its barrel vaulting and rough stone walls, is an exercise in simplicity. The church is an amalgamation of styles, but Gothic predominates except in the furnishings of the nave, where carefully carved Art Deco wooden panelling frames a set of religious paintings of the Stations of the Cross. The church also holds one marvellous **painting**, Albert Bouts' *The Mocking of Christ*, an early sixteenth-century work showing a mournful, blood-spattered Jesus. Around the abbey's buildings are walled and terraced **gardens** plus the old abbatical pond, altogether an oasis of peace away from the hubbub of avenue Louise. To **get to** the abbey, take tram #94 along avenue Louise.

North of the centre: Jette, Laeken and Heysel

To the north of the city centre lies **Jette**, a well-heeled suburb that wouldn't merit a second glance if it weren't for the former home of René Magritte, now turned into the engaging **Musée René Magritte**, which pays detailed tribute to the artist, his family and friends. East of here is leafy **Laeken**, where the Belgian royal family hunker down, and next door again is **Heysel**, with its trademark **Atomium**, a hand-me-down from the 1958 World's Fair.

Musée René Magritte

The enthralling **Musée René Magritte**, on rue Esseghem 135 in Jette (Wed–Sun 10am–6pm; €7, on weekends includes guided tour; Ⓦ www.magrittemuseum.be), holds a plethora of the Surrealist's paraphernalia as well as a limited collection of his early paintings and sketches. Magritte lived with his wife Georgette on the ground floor of this modest house for twenty-four years, from 1930 to the mid-1950s, an odd location for what was effectively the headquarters of the Surrealist movement in Belgium, most of whose leading lights met here every Saturday to concoct a battery of subversive books, magazines and images.

The **ground floor** has been faithfully restored to recreate the artist's studio and living quarters, using mostly original ornaments and furniture, with the remainder carefully replicated from photographs; the famous bowler hat which crops up in several of Magritte's paintings is hung near the indoor studio. Many features of the house itself also appear in a number of his works: the sash window, for instance, framed the painting entitled *The Human Condition*, while the glass doors to the sitting room and bedroom appeared in *The Invisible World*. Magritte built himself a studio – which he named **Dongo** – in the garden, and it was here he produced his bread-and-butter work, such as graphics and posters, though he was usually unhappy when working on such mundane projects, and his real passions were painted in the **dining-room studio**, where he displayed just one work by another artist – a photo by Man Ray – which is there again today.

You have to don shoe covers to visit the **first and second floors** of the house, which were separate apartments when the Magrittes lived here, but are now taken up by letters, photos, telegrams, lithographs, posters and sketches pertaining to the artist, all displayed in chronological order. There are two fine posters announcing the world film and fine arts festivals which took place in Brussels in 1947 and 1949, as well as Magritte's first painting, a naive landscape which he produced at the tender age of 12, the blue rug he had made for the bedroom, work by other Surrealists. Finally, there are a number of personal objects displayed in the **attic**, which he rented, including the easel he used at the end of his life. Overall, it's a fascinating glimpse into the life of one of the most important artists of the twentieth century.

To get to the museum, take the **métro** to Belgica and then **tram** #51.

Laeken

Beginning some 4km north of the Grand-Place, leafy **Laeken** is home of the Belgian royal family, who occupy a large, out-of-bounds palace here and have colonized the surrounding parkland with their monuments and memorials. Approaching Laeken from the south on métro/tram #3, get off at the Araucaria tram stop and you're a stone's throw from the **Musées de la Extrême-Orient** (Tues–Fri 9.30am–5pm, Sat & Sun 10am–5pm; €5), which is made up of a decent collection of Far Eastern artefacts displayed in some wonderfully fake Oriental buildings erected at the behest of Léopold II. First up is the **Pavillon Chinois**, an elegant and attractive replica of a Chinese pavilion built in a gaudy mix of Rococo European and oriental styles, and housing a first-rate collection of Chinese and Japanese porcelain and furniture. A glorious turn-of-the-century fantasy, it's all deftly done and beautifully restored – much like the matching **Tour Japonaise** across the road, reached by a tunnel from the ticket office. This is another of Léopold's follies, this time a copy of a Buddhist pagoda with parts made in Paris, Brussels and Yokohama. You can't actually visit the pagoda itself, but the lower floors of the adjacent building contain beautiful displays of Japanese porcelain. Finally, back on the other side of the road, behind the Chinese pavilion, the **Musée d'Art Japonais** holds an excellent display of samurai armour, swords, textiles and lacquerwork.

From the Chinese pavilion, it's a brief walk to avenue du Parc Royal, a busy boulevard that runs past the sedate **Château Royal** (no entry), the principal home of the Belgian royal family. Built in 1790, its most famous occupant was Napoleon, who stayed here on a number of occasions and signed the declaration of war on Russia here in 1812. Opposite the front of the royal palace, a wide footpath leads up to the fanciful neo-Gothic monument erected in honour of Léopold I, the focal point of the pretty **Parc de Laeken**, whose lawns and wooded thickets extend northwest for a couple of kilometres towards Heysel.

Heysel and the Atomium

Most easily reached by métro, **Heysel** comprises a 500-acre estate bequeathed to the city by Léopold II in 1909, but is best described as a theme park without a theme. Nevertheless, its assorted attractions do include the famous **Atomium** (daily 10am–6pm; €11; Ⓦwww.atomium.be), a curious model of a molecule expanded 165 billion times, built for the 1958 World Fair in Brussels. Gleaming from its recent renovation, the structure is something of a symbol of the city, and it's looking better than it has for some time. Visits are in two parts: the lift whizzes you up to the top sphere for the views, after which you descend and then come back up again to take in the other three spheres, reached by a mixture of escalators and stairs. It's all pleasingly retro – the Atomium was quite a feat of technology in its time (its elevator was the world's fastest, the escalator connecting the spheres the world's longest), and its construction is remembered by apposite photos. However, the thoroughness of the restoration can't disguise the fact that there's not really that much to see – the spheres are mainly given over to temporary exhibition space and a rather feeble café, and trudging up and down the stairs and escalators can turn into a bit of a slog. There again, it's undeniably impressive from the bottom and the views from the top are as spectacular as you would expect (enhanced by computer screens pointing out what you're looking at).

Eating and drinking

Brussels can hold its own with any international city when it comes to **eating out**, and whatever your taste, price range or preferred type of cuisine there is almost always something that will suit. Look out particularly for traditional Bruxellois dishes, canny amalgamations of Walloon and Flemish ingredients and cooking styles, whether rabbit cooked in beer, steamed pigs' feet or *waterzooi* (for more on Belgian specialities, see p.389 & p.394). As for where to eat, the distinction between the city's **cafés**, **café-bars** and **restaurants** is fairly elastic, and there are great places over the city, with particular concentrations on place Ste-Catherine and rue du Flandre in the Lower Town and place Boniface and place du Châtelain in Ixelles.

Drinking in Brussels, as in the rest of the country, is a joy. The city boasts an enormous variety of **café-bars** and **bars**: sumptuous Art Nouveau establishments, traditional bars with ceilings stained brown by a century's smoke, speciality beer bars with literally hundreds of different varieties of ale and, of course, more modern hangouts. Many of the more distinctive bars are handily located within a few minutes' walk of the Grand-Place and also in Ixelles, but really you'll be spoiled for choice.

There's **no smoking** in any establishment that sells food, and in 2012 this will be extended to all bars and clubs. Note also that we've given métro stations for all places that have a stop nearby.

Restaurants

Restaurant opening times are pretty standard – a couple of hours at lunchtime, usually noon to 2pm or 2.30pm, and again in the evening from 7pm to around 10pm; precise hours are given with the reviews below. At all but the cheapest restaurants, advance reservations are recommended, especially on Friday and Saturday evenings.

The Grand-Place and around

The listings below are marked on the map on p.61.

Brasserie de la Roue d'Or rue des Chapeliers 26 ⓣ02 514 25 54. Just south of the Grand-Place, this eminently appealing old brasserie, with wood panelling, stained glass and brass fittings, serves generous portions of Belgian regional specialities, such as *poulet à la Bruxelles*. Also recommended, if you can face it, is the pig's trotter and snails. Main courses hover at €20–30. Daily noon–midnight, but closed for one month in summer, usually July. Métro Gare Centrale.

La Mirante Plattesteen 13 ⓣ02 511 15 80. Arguably the best pizza in the city, cooked in the wood-fired oven at the back of this very popular restaurant. Whether yours is a "Pavarotti" with spinach and ricotta or a "Dante" with aubergine and fennel seeds, the pizzas are imaginative and generous. Pizzas and pastas at around €10; seafood risotto for €15, but double-check your bill – mathematics is not their forte. Mon–Sat noon–2.30pm & 6–11.30pm; Sun 6–11.30pm. Closed Aug and last week of Dec. Métro Bourse.

L'Ogenblik galerie des Princes 1 ⓣ02 511 61 51. In the Galeries St-Hubert, this outstanding restaurant is kitted out in antique bistro style, right down to the ancient cash till. The well-judged, wide-ranging menu begins with the basics – steak and chips with wild mushrooms – but soon climbs to greater gastronomic heights, such as pigeon in truffle jus. Main courses are €25–35; look out for daily specials. Mon–Sat noon–2.30pm & 7–11.30pm. Métro Gare Centrale.

Lower Town

The listings below are marked on the map on pp.66–67.

Bar Bik quai aux Pierres de Taille 3 ☎02 219 75 00. This trendy Flemish restaurant, next to the KVS theatre (see p.105), is a colourful oasis of freshly prepared, imaginative dishes. No fixed menu but daily specials from rabbit with endive salad (around €10) to red tuna with noodles, mango and coconut for around €20. Vegetarian preparations are never a problem, even if not listed on the menu. Mon–Fri 11am–10.30pm. Métro Rogier.

Bij den Boer quai aux Briques 60 ☎02 512 61 22. Atmospheric bistro-style place with tiled floors and old posters and photos on the wall. The menu features a wide range of delicious seafood with main courses averaging €25–35, though excellent daily specials are a less expensive option. Mussels are a house speciality. Mon–Sat noon–2.30pm & 6–10.30pm. Métro Ste-Catherine.

Au Bon Bol rue Paul Devaux 9 ☎02 513 16 88. In a functional and spotless setting close to the Bourse, this Chinese place (with a hint of Thai spice) is as cheap as it gets – yet the vegetables are as fresh as they come and the long noodles are made in front of you. A huge bowl of noodle soup with beef, duck or seafood will set you back €7.50. Daily noon–2.30pm & 7–10.30pm. Métro Bourse.

La Cantina au Cœur de Bahia rue du Jardin des Olives 13–15 ☎02 513 42 76. All the warmth and exuberance of Brazil awaits in this colourful restaurant just west of the Grand-Place. The menu is short but awash with exotic ingredients, and naturally there are one or two cocktails to wash everything down. Buffet available at lunchtimes when you pay by weight, otherwise main courses around €14. Mon–Fri noon–3pm, Mon–Sat 7–11pm. Métro Anneessens.

Henri rue de Flandre 113–115 ☎02 218 00 08. Belgo-French fusion with everything made on site, right down to the stock cubes. The menu changes regularly, dishes are always seasonal and the ingredients top-notch. There's a lunch menu for €12, while the evening is à la carte – or rather from the blackboard – with mains such as sole with cheese croquettes for €11.50. Reservations recommended at all times. Tues–Fri noon–2.30pm & 6–10pm, Sat 6–10pm. Métro Ste-Catherine.

Houtsiplou place Rouppe 9 ☎02 511 38 16. A short walk west of the Grand-Place, this is an ode to Belgium, with walls covered in cartoons depicting the country's history in true Surrealistic style. An equally colourful menu offers home-made burgers with a plant pot of chips, some Belgian classics such as *stoemp* and *chicons au gratin* and generous delicious salads (€8–14 a dish). Large terrace in the summer – for which you should book early. Mon–Sun 11am–midnight. Métro Anneessens.

Orphyse Chaussette rue Charles Hanssens 5 ☎02 502 75 81. Chef and owner Philippe Renoux prides himself on original dishes with quality ingredients: spiced tuna tartare (€12.50) is a house speciality. Despite the predominantly French inspiration, vegetarians are not neglected – there's always one non-meat dish on the small menu. The setting is candlelit and intimate, and the staff are willing to help you navigate your way around the extensive Tour de France wine menu. Main dishes €12–25. Tues–Sat noon–2.30pm & 7–10.30pm.

La Paix rue Ropsy-Chaudron 49 ☎02 523 09 58. Much lauded restaurant featuring the creative cuisine of young chef David Martin, who is known for his dedication to pigs' trotters and all things offal. Try the Basque hot black pudding (€16) or Belgian pork cheek with Colonnata bacon, vegetables and truffles (€25.50). Strategically placed opposite the Brussels abattoir, a short walk from the city centre toward Gare du Midi. Mon–Fri noon–2.30pm, Fri & Sat 7–11.30pm. Métro Clemenceau.

Le Pré Salé rue de Flandre 20 ☎02 513 65 45. Agreeable, typically Bruxellois neighbourhood restaurant, just off place Ste-Catherine, providing an appealing alternative to the swankier places nearby. The plain-cream tiled interior dates from the days it used to be a chip shop, but now the menu offers great mussels (€21), fish dishes (*anguilles au vert* €13) and other Belgian specialities. Wed–Sun noon–2.30pm & 6.30–10.30pm. Métro Ste-Catherine.

Soul rue de la Samaritaine 20 ☎02 513 52 13. An evening at *Soul*, on the edge of the Marolles, is both a gastronomic delight and an education. The underpinning philosophy is that we are what we eat – but there's nothing ascetic about the mainly organic food, with delights such as beef and shiitake mushroom kebab or nut and bean burger with chilli salsa and yoghurt. Choose between the various menu options – pregnancy, energy, aphrodisiac to name a few – at €25–35 for two courses. Open Wed–Sun 7–11pm.

El Txoko rue de Laeken 122 ☎02 203 10 22. Basque tapas, with hot dishes listed on the menu and cold ones to choose from at the counter. Combining goat's cheese with aubergine (€3), lamb cutlets with chorizo purée (€5), and a scallop with *chicon* salad for the Belgian twist (€5) makes for a reasonably priced and tasty dinner in a warm and convivial atmosphere. Wash it all down with a glass of cava and leave a space for the *churros con chocolate*. Mon–Sat noon–2.30pm & 6–10pm, Sat 6–10.30pm. Métro De Brouckère.

Vincent rue des Dominicains 8–10 ⓣ02 511 26 07. The entrance to this lively restaurant is through the kitchen, which gives customers a good view of the action. Keep going for the restaurant beyond, which specializes in Belgo-French cuisine, with meat and seafood dishes both prominent. The waiters in their long aprons will flambé a steak at your table – entertainment in itself. Main dishes €12–25. Daily noon–3pm, 6.30–11pm; closed early Jan and first two weeks in Aug. Métro Bourse.

Viva M'Boma rue de Flandre 17 ⓣ02 512 15 93. The name means "long live grandma" in the Brussels dialect, and this is one of the best stops in the city for tasting local cuisine prepared in the traditional manner. Minimalist decor in an old tripe shop, and nothing is over €18 a dish; the food – such as large portions of beef with home-made chips – is a carnivore's delight. Mon–Sat noon–2pm & Thurs–Sat 7.30–10.30pm. Métro Ste-Catherine.

Upper Town

The listings below are marked on the map on pp.66–67.

Café Bota rue Royale 236 ⓣ02 219 20 65. Part of the Botanique arts centre (see p.105), this is perfect for a bite to eat before a concert or to enjoy the terrace overlooking the city's skyscrapers as the sun sets. Basic but tasty Italian cuisine with antipasti, pasta and meat dishes on offer, including a good selection for vegetarians. Pasta at around €10, *saltimbocca alla Romana* or escalope Milanese for around €12. Excellent value. Daily 11am–11pm. Métro Botanique.

Et qui va promener le chien? rue de Rollebeek 2 ⓣ02 503 23 04. Situated on the pedestrianized street at the base of the Sablon, this curiously named restaurant – "And who is going to walk the dog?" – offers Belgian classics with a contemporary twist. All the old favourites are on offer: *waterzooi*, *carbonnade*, *boulettes*, and at lunch the menu of starter, main course and coffee is just €14. In the evening dessert is added to the €32 menu, or you can go a la carte. Tues–Sun noon–3pm & 6–11pm. Métro Gare Centrale.

Au Stekerlapatte rue des Prêtres 4 ⓣ02 512 86 81. This long-established brasserie, on a side street tucked away behind the Palais de Justice, serves Franco-Belgian cuisine in a bustling atmosphere. Try the roasted pork (€19.50) or *poulet à la Bruxelles* (€16.50). There's also a daily vegetarian option. For lunch during the week a three-course menu will set you back €12.50. The smoking bar on the first floor evades anti-smoking legislation. Tues–Wed noon–3pm & 7–11pm, Thurs–Sat noon–3pm & 7–midnight. Métro Hôtel des Monnaies.

St-Gilles and Ixelles

The listings below are marked on the map on pp.92–93.

Chez Marie rue Alphonse de Witte 40 ⓣ02 644 30 31. Just south of place Flagey, this well-known Ixelles haunt serves impressive, mostly French cuisine in lavish but never snobbish surroundings. There's also an extensive wine list. You can get a lovely two-course lunch for a very reasonable €16.50, but in the evenings prices are considerably inflated (main dishes €24–30). Tues–Fri noon–2pm & 7.30–10.30pm, Sat 7.30–10.30pm.

Dolma chaussée d'Ixelles 329–331 ⓣ02 649 89 81. New-agey, veggie and organic joint, popular with the locals for the all-you-can-eat buffet lunch (€15) and dinner (€18). Offers an army of quiches, soups and salads and, although it's not the most refined vegetarian cuisine, for a very pleasant carb-feast it's a good address and excellent value. Organic shop next door. Mon–Sat noon–2pm & 7–9.30pm.

Leonor ave de la Porte de Hal 19 ⓣ02 537 51 56. Something of a city institution, this popular tapas restaurant has been going strong for over thirty years. The ground floor doubles up as a bar, while upstairs the wooden tables and dimmer lighting make for more intimate dining. Tapas are mainly fish-based and include plenty of octopus and coquilles Saint-Jacques (between €6 and €15). Main dishes include pork with chickpeas and rosemary (€10.50). A two-course lunch is a very reasonable €8. No credit cards. Mon & Tues, Thurs–Sat noon–3pm & 6.30–10pm. Métro Porte de Hal.

Le Pavillon rue Defacqz 64 ⓣ02 538 02 15. This appealing restaurant, with the atmosphere of a cosy bistro, offers straightforward cuisine such as roast shoulder of lamb (€12) and sausage with lentils (€12.90). The menu is strictly seasonal and is sourced locally. No credit cards. Mon–Fri noon–11.30pm, closed Wed lunchtime.

Quartier Libre rue Lesbroussart 16 ⓣ02 644 94 00. Just off place Flagey, this bright and quirky restaurant offers a choice of four small dishes served together on your personalized tray. Each table has paper and pencils: you make your choice from the list on the blackboards, put your name on the top and hey presto! €14 for the four dishes, which include the likes of marinated salmon with soya shoots or a shiitake pastry with truffle cream. Mon noon–2pm, Tues–Fri noon–2pm & 7–10.30pm, Sat 7–10.30pm. There's also another branch at rue de Treves 44 in the EU quarter (Mon–Fri noon–2pm; see map, pp.84–85).

La Quincaillerie rue du Page 45 ⓣ02 533 98 33. Mouthwatering Belgian and French cuisine in this delightful restaurant, one of the longest established in the ultra-cool Chatelain area. Occupying an imaginatively converted old hardware shop with splendid Art Nouveau flourishes, it's a good spot for fish and fowl. There's a decent choice of "business lunch" dishes at a very reasonable €13, but the evening à la carte is more pricey, with mains weighing in at €22. Reservations advised, especially on Wednesday when the local market is on. Mon–Fri noon–2.30pm & 7pm–midnight, Sat & Sun 7pm–midnight.

Sale Pepe Rosmarino rue Berckmans 98 ⓣ02 538 90 63. Authentic, delicious Italian cuisine, with good pizzas overshadowed by the pastas and meat dishes, which change regularly according to the creative influence of owners Aurelio and Antonio. Linguine à la Botarga (pasta with Italian sausage and leek) or *orechiette aux cime di rape* (pasta with a little-known, very tasty green vegetable) are mouthwateringly good. Reservations essential. Main dishes around €10. Mon–Fri noon–3pm & 7–11pm, Sat 7–11pm. Métro Hôtel des Monnaies.

Volle Gas place Fernand Cocq 21 ⓣ02 502 89 17. This traditional, wood-panelled bar-brasserie serves classic Belgian cuisine in a friendly, family atmosphere. The Brussels specialities on offer include the delicious *carbonnades de boeuf à la Gueuze* and *lapin à la kriek* – beef or rabbit cooked in beer – but there is also regular pasta and salads. Main dishes €12–20. Mon–Sat noon–3pm & 6pm–midnight.

Yamato rue Francart 11 ⓣ02 502 28 93. Authentic Japanese food at this tiny, very modern place just round the corner from place St-Boniface. Affordable prices, with mains for as little as €8, but vegetarians mustn't be fooled by the noodles with vegetables – there's a big bone simmering in the pot. Not the place for a leisurely lunch: it's eat and go Tokyo-style. Tues–Sat noon–2pm & 7–10pm, closed Thurs lunchtime. Métro Porte de Namur.

Bars and cafés

Belgians make little – or no – distinction between their **bars** and **cafés**: both serve alcohol, many stay open late (until 2am or even 3am) and most sell food as well. What you won't find (thank goodness) are lots of the coffee house chains which beleaguer so many big cities.

The Grand-Place and around

The listings below are marked on the map on p.61.

La Bécasse rue de Tabora 11. Just to the northwest of the Grand-Place and metres from St-Nicolas, this is an old-fashioned bar with neo-baronial decor: long wooden benches, ancient blue-and-white wall tiles and beer served in earthenware jugs. The beer menu is excellent – this is one of the few places in the country you can drink authentic Lambic and Gueuze. Métro Bourse.

Au Bon Vieux Temps rue du Marché aux Herbes 12. Ancient, idiosyncratic little place, dating back to 1695 and tucked away down an alley just a minute's walk from the Grand-Place. The building has all sorts of ancient bric-a-brac, including a stained-glass window depicting the Virgin Mary and St Michael, which was originally in the local parish church. Popular with British servicemen just after the end of World War II, the bar still has comforting old-fashioned signs advertising Mackenzie's port and Bass pale ale. Métro Bourse.

Dolle Mol rue des Éperonniers 52. In the 1960s *Dolle Mol* was home to a band of anarcho-artistic regulars. It was closed down and the building abandoned until Jan Bucquoy – artist and political activist – came along and squatted the building until he could convince the Flemish community to buy it as part of the local heritage. Now reopened, the walls tell the tale, the beer is cheap and there is occasional (anarchic) entertainment. Métro Gare Centrale.

À l'Imaige de Nostre-Dame Impasse des Cadeaux, rue du Marché aux Herbes 6. A welcoming, very quirky little bar, decorated like an old Dutch kitchen and situated at the end of a long, narrow alley. Good range of speciality beers – including seven on tap. Métro Bourse.

Le Roy d'Espagne Grand-Place 1. Supremely touristy café-bar in a seventeenth-century guild-house with a collection of marionettes and inflated animal bladders suspended from the ceiling, and naff pikes in the boys' toilet. You get a fine view of the Grand-Place from the rooms upstairs, as well as from the pavement terrace, and the drinks aren't too expensive. Métro Bourse.

Senne rue du Bon Secours 4. Named after the river that once ran through the centre of Brussels, this café-épicerie serves reasonably priced, fresh and healthy food amid the tall shelves filled with gastronomic delights. The tempting menu includes home-made quiches, pastas, soups and cakes, either takeaway or stay-in, and it's also open for breakfast. Mon–Sat 9am–6pm. Métro Anneessens.

Au Soleil rue Marché au Charbon 86. A short walk west from the Grand-Place, this popular bar, formerly a men's clothing shop, quenches the thirst of a young and arty Brussels clientele. Inexpensive bar snacks are on offer and there's a pavement terrace where you can while away the day over a coffee or something stronger. A laidback atmosphere, but it's often difficult to get a seat come nightfall. Métro Anneessens.

The Lower Town

The listings below are marked on the map on pp.66–67.

Arcadi rue d'Arenberg 1B. At the north end of the Galeries St-Hubert, this busy café is a perfect spot for lunch, afternoon tea or a bite before the cinema. The menu offers lots of choices, but the salads, quiches and fruit tarts are particularly delicious and cost only a few euros each. Can get a little too crowded for comfort at lunchtimes. Mon–Fri 7am–11pm, Sat–Sun 10am–11pm. Métro Gare Centrale.

Café Central rue Borgval 14 ⓣ0486 72 26 24, ⓦwww.lecafecentral.com. Cool bar just off place St-Géry, with DJs, concerts and film showings packing the agenda. You have to battle at the bar for a drink but there's a great atmosphere and clientele. Worth checking the website for details of upcoming events. Métro Bourse.

Chaff place du Jeu de Balle 21, Marolles ⓣ02 502 58 48. There's no better place to take in the hustle and bustle of the city's biggest and best flea market than this amenable café-bar. There are some real bargains at lunchtime from the black-board menu, and it's also open in the evening for drinks only.

Le Cirio rue de la Bourse 18. On the north side of the Bourse, this is one of Brussels' oldest bars, originally opened in 1886 as a shop-cum-eatery by Francesco Cirio, a pioneer of canned fruit and vegetables. Sumptuously decorated in *fin-de-siècle* style, though now somewhat frayed round the edges, it was once frequented, they say, by Jacques Brel. The speciality is "half and half", a mix of Italian spumante and white wine. Métro Bourse.

La Fleur en papier doré rue des Alexiens 53. Cosy, smoke-free bar recently reopened by a group of enthusiasts keen to preserve this slice of Brussels heritage: *La Fleur* was one of the preferred watering holes of René Magritte, and the novelist Hugo Claus apparently held his wedding reception here. Idiosyncratic antique decor and serves beers (including several Gueuzes), excellent house wine and strong coffee with exclusive chocolates. Food also available. Métro Gare Centrale.

Le Greenwich rue des Chartreux 7. A short walk west of the Bourse, this is the city's traditional chess café, with a lovely old wood-panelled, mirrored interior and, in the men's, a fabulous antique ceramic urinal. Métro Bourse.

Moeder Lambic Fontainas place Fontainas 8. Beer enthusiasts Jean Hummler and Nassim Dessicy have given a new lease of life to the small square off blvd Anspach, opening a sister bar to the original behind the St Gilles town hall (see p.102). Forty beers on tap and trained staff to give guidance and recommendations are enough temptation – particularly as these are not your run-of-the-mill beers, with small Belgian brewers such as Dupont, Val-Dieu and Cantillon from across the way in Anderlecht all on offer. Métro Anneessens.

Monk rue Ste Catherine 42. Just off place Ste-Catherine, this dark and deep bar, with its high ceilings and wood panelling, attracts a young and largely Flemish-speaking crew. It's named after the jazz musician Thelonious Monk – hence the grand piano. Service is at the bar, so don't be bashful. Métro Ste-Catherine.

À la Mort Subite rue Montagne aux Herbes Potagères 7. Notorious 1920s bar that loaned its name to a popular bottled beer, occupying a long narrow room with nicotine-stained walls, long tables and lots of mirrors. On a good night it's inhabited by a dissolute arty clientele, but by large groups of teenage tourists. Sp or just order a plate of cheese cubes to accompany your beer. Just northeast of the Grand-Place opposite the far end of the Galeries St-Hubert. Métro Gare Centrale.

Cafe Novo place de la Vieille Halle aux Blés 37. Bright, quirky café with lots of original touches, from the menus in old books to the colourful selection of chairs both out on the square in front and in the back garden. Food is available at lunchtime and in the evening, and to while away the in-between-time, there's a wide selection of newspapers and books – *Novo* is part of a "book travelling" scheme. Métro Anneessens.

Het Warm Water rue des Renards 25, Marolles. At the top of this cobbled street filled with galleries and shops, *Warm Water* is a very typical Marolles café. One evening a week there is also a political debate when you're bound to hear a spot of Brusseleir, the local lingo. Food is simple and it's one of the few Belgian originals that's great for veggies. Mon, Tues & Sun 8am–7pm, Thurs–Sat 8am–10pm.

Upper Town

The listings below are marked on the map on pp.66–67.

L'Herbaudière place de la Liberté 9 ⓣ02 218 77 13. Well-established Breton crêperie in a lovely little square up near the Cirque Royale (see p.105). Long list of tasty sweet or savoury fillings to lip-smack the pancakes (€7–10), which are prepared on the restaurant counter. The prim and proper decor is a good fit for this low-key, family-run café. Mon–Fri 11am–7pm. Métro Madou.

Le Perroquet rue Watteeu 31. Busy, semi-circular café-bar occupying attractive Art Nouveau premises close to the place du Grand Sablon. Imaginative range of stuffed pittas, salads and other tasty snacks – though you'll find it difficult to get a seat on Fri or Sat night. Excellent beer menu.

St-Gilles and Ixelles

The listings below are marked on the map on pp.92–93.

Café Belga place Flagey 18. This is a bar for any time of day: coffee and croissants on the terrace after visiting the market, buffet lunches or a bite to eat in the evening before a film or concert at the cultural centre next door, and boozing into the early hours with the mixed crowd who flock here from all over the city.

Belladone rue Moris 17A. East European bar whose menu sports all kinds of interesting bits of information – "Belladone" is, for instance, the plant used by women to bring about success in love or business, or bad luck to an enemy. Pilsner Urquell on tap and available by the litre, plus flavoured vodkas, specialist teas (including Hot Attila – tea with schnapps) and many tasty sweet and savoury bites to eat. Off the chaussée de Charleroi.

Brasserie Verschueren parvis de St-Gilles 11–13. Art Deco neighbourhood bar with a laidback atmosphere and football league results on the wall – essential in the days before television. You can buy your croissant in the bakery opposite and just come here for the coffee to dip it in. A good range of Belgian beers too. Not far from the petit ring, off the chaussée de Waterloo. Métro Parvis de St-Gilles.

Chez Moeder Lambic rue de Savoie 68. This small and very popular bar, just behind the Hôtel de Ville in St-Gilles, has over a thousand beers available, including 500 Belgian varieties, mostly bottled. For a wider selection on draft, check out its sister bar in the Lower Town (see p.101). Métro Albert.

Café Maison du Peuples parvis de St-Gilles 39 ⓦwww.maison-du-peuple.be. Built in 1907 for the education and entertainment of the workers, the "People's House" of St-Gilles got a new lease of life in 2008 when the ground floor opened as a spacious café hosting DJs and concerts, exhibiting local artists and providing a perfect spot for breakfast or lunch while visiting the market on the *parvis*. Worth checking the website for what's on. Métro Parvis de St-Gilles.

La Porteuse d'Eau ave Jean Volders 48a. Refurbished Art Nouveau café on the corner of rue Vanderschrick, near the Porte de Hal. The food isn't up to much, but the ornate interior is well worth the price of a beer. Métro Porte de Hal.

L'Ultime Atome rue St-Boniface 14. The large selection of beers and wines, simple but tasty food (kitchen opens till 12.30am) and late opening hours make this funky café-bar a hit with the trendy Ixelles crowd on weekdays and weekends alike. Its location, on the appealing place St-Boniface, also makes it a great place to sit outside with a newspaper in the summer. Métro Porte de Namur.

The EU quarter

The listings below are marked on the map on pp.84–85.

The Beer Factory place du Luxembourg 6. A recent addition to the bevy of bars on this appealing square, metres from the European Parliament, and the chosen haunt of Eurocrats for after-work hobnobbing. Impressive building, with the centrepiece bar made out of an old beer vat, and as the name suggests, there's a good range of beers alongside some pretty decent food.

Piola Libri rue Franklin 66–68. Aperitif Italian-style with a glass of wine or prosecco and a selection of the tasty antipasti on the counter – just help yourself. Popular with the EU workers, in particular the Italians, since this bar doubles up as a bookshop and organizes a number of literary events, all in Italian. Métro Trône.

Nightlife and entertainment

As far as **nightlife** goes, it's likely you'll be happy to while away the evenings in one of the city's bars or café-bars – there are plenty in which you can drink until sunrise. If that isn't enough, Brussels also has a clutch of established **clubs**, though most of the action revolves around club nights with moveable locations. It's a fast-moving scene, so the best bet is to check out local websites to see what's on – see box below. Brussels is a good place to catch **live bands**, with a number of especially appealing smaller venues such as *Ancienne Belgique* and *Botanique*. Along with Antwerp, the city is also a regular stop on the European tours of major artists, the big venue being *Forest Nationale*. **Jazz** is well catered for too, with several bars playing host to local and international acts, as well as the internationally acclaimed Jazz Marathon held every May (Ⓦwww.brusselsjazzmarathon.be).

The **classical musical scene** is excellent. The Orchestre National de Belgique (Ⓦwww.nob.be) enjoys an international reputation and the city showcases a number of excellent classical music festivals. Cream of the crop are the Ars Musica festival of contemporary music held in March (Ⓦwww.arsmusica.be), and May's prestigious Concours Musical Reine Elisabeth (Ⓦwww.concours-reine-elisabeth.be), a competition for piano, violin and voice. **Opera lovers** should make a beeline for the Théâtre Royal de la Monnaie, which is much praised for staging contemporary interpretations of classic operas, as well as offering a more eclectic repertoire of music and dance. Indeed, the city's **dance** scene has been impressing visitors ever since Maurice Béjart brought his classical Twentieth Century Ballet here in 1959. Now the main dance venues are the Koninklijke Vlaamse Schouwberg and the Kaaitheatre, but the innovative legacy of Béjart lives on, with his old company (now called Rosas and led by Anne Theresa de Keersmaeker) regularly performing at Théâtre Royal de la Monnaie.

The big players in the Brussels **theatre** scene are the Francophone Théâtre National and the Flemish Koninklijke Vlaamse Schouwberg, but the city also has an abundance of small theatres providing an eclectic programme from experimental theatre to political pieces and comedy. Most productions are performed in French and Flemish, but several American, Irish and British theatre groups put on high-quality amateur productions too.

Club-night websites

Check out Ⓦwww.readytomove.be for an updated list of **club nights** around Brussels. Some regulars include Ⓦwww.anarchic.be and Ⓦwww.losninos.be.

The free, trilingual *Agenda* has the most comprehensive **listings** of concerts and events. Published every Thursday, it can be picked up in all main métro stations, plus some bars and cafés. **Tickets** for most concerts are available at Caroline Music (passage St-Honoré 20 in the city centre), Fnac in the City 2 shopping complex on rue Neuve, or from the venue websites listed below. **Last-minute tickets** are available at reduced prices at Arsène50, Galerie de la Reine 13–15, or at Flagey arts centre, place Flagey, Ixelles (Tues–Sat 2–5.30pm; Ⓦwww.arsene50.be).

Clubs

Le Bazaar rue des Capucins 63, Marolles Ⓣ02 511 26 00, Ⓦwww.bazaarresto.be. Try out the delicious international cuisine in the upstairs bar-restaurant before picking up your drinks and descending to the cellar-like club below for a mixture of funk, soul, rock and indie. Good choice for a combination of chatting and dancing. Tues–Thurs & Sun 7.30pm–midnight, Fri & Sat 7.30pm–4am. Free. See map, pp.66–67.

The Fuse rue Blaes 208, Marolles Ⓦwww.fuse.be. Widely recognized as the finest techno club in Belgium, this pulsating venue has played host to some of Europe's best DJs, including Dave Clark, Miss Kittin, Carl Cox, Ken Ishii and Laurent Garnier. Three floors of techno, house, jungle and occasional hip-hop, as well as the usual chill-out rooms and visuals. Entrance is €5 before midnight, €10 after. The price goes up if there's a big-name DJ. Sat 11pm–7am. See map, pp.66–67.

Havana rue de l'Epée 4, Marolles Ⓦwww.havana-brussels.com. Latin club that's very popular with a thirty-something expat crowd. Punters mostly start early with a bite to eat, then schmooze the night away on mojitos and margaritas, dancing till dawn to the hot Latino tunes. Off – and about halfway down – rue Haute. Free admission. Thurs 7pm–2am, Fri 7pm–5am, Sat 7pm–7am. See map, pp.66–67.

Montecristo rue Henri Maus 25. Beside the Bourse, the *Montecristo* is well known as a salsa venue. Wednesday night is pure salsa night, whilst on the weekend Latin beats are mixed up with more mainstream stuff. Attracts a mixed crowd. Entrance up to €5. Wed 10.30pm–2am, Thurs–Sat 10.30pm–5am. Métro Bourse. See map, p.61.

You rue du Duquesnoy 18 Ⓦwww.leyou.be. A short walk southeast of the Grand-Place, *You* boasts an interior design by Miguel Cancio Martins, the man behind the *Buddha Bar* in Paris, and considers itself not only a club but a design concept – and the doormen expect the punters to match. Set over two levels, with comfy couches in the bar-lounge, visiting DJs playing everything from funk and disco to electro and house, plus gay tea dances on Sun. Admission €10, including two drinks. Thurs–Sun 11pm–late. Métro Gare Centrale. See map, p.61.

Live music bars

L'Archiduc rue Antoine Dansaert 6 Ⓣ02 512 06 52, Ⓦwww.archiduc.net. Art Deco cigar and jazz bar with live jazz on Mondays and at the weekend, including a free concert every Sat and Sun afternoon (from 5pm). Daily 4pm–5am. Métro Bourse. See map, pp.66–67.

Beursschouwburg rue Auguste Orts 20–28, Ⓦwww.beursschouwburg.be. Occupying a handsomely restored building from 1885, this is a fine venue that makes the most of its different spaces, from the cellar to the stairs, the theatre to the café. Features DJs of all genres, plus an eclectic live music programme catering for a wide range of tastes. Thurs–Sat 7pm–late. Métro Bourse. See map, pp.66–67.

Magazin 4 rue du Magasin 4 Ⓣ02 223 34 74, Ⓦwww.magasin4.be. In an old warehouse off blvd d'Anvers, this is a favourite venue for up-and-coming Belgian indie bands, as well as a smattering of punk, rap and hip-hop. Only open when there's a gig, and entrance is usually around €10. Métro Yser. See map, pp.66–67.

Sounds rue de la Tulipe 28, Ixelles Ⓣ02 512 92 50, Ⓦwww.soundsjazzclub.be. Off place Ferdinand Cocq, this atmospheric café has showcased both local and internationally acclaimed jazz acts for over twenty years. Live music most nights, but the biggies usually appear Sat. Mon–Sat 8pm–4am. See map, pp.92–93.

Concert halls and large performance venues

AB (Ancienne Belgique) blvd Anspach 110 Ⓣ02 548 24 24, Ⓦwww.abconcerts.be. The capital's leading rock and indie venue; artists perform either in the main auditorium or the smaller space on the first floor. Usually around four gigs a week. Closed July & Aug. Métro Bourse. See map, p.61.

BOZAR rue Ravenstein 23 Ⓣ02 507 82 00, Ⓦwww.bozar.be. An innovative programme of events including theatre, world music and themed cultural nights in a 2000-seater, Art Deco concert

hall as well as several smaller auditoria. Hosts the Orchestre National de Belgique and the Rideau de Bruxelles theatre company. Métro Gare Centrale. See map, pp.66–67.
Botanique and Cirque Royal rue Royale 236 and rue de l'Enseignement 81 ⓣ02 218 20 15, ⓦwww.botanique.be. Two venues working together to provide a selection of intimate venues for a wide range of bands. Cirque Royal, formerly an indoor circus, is the larger. Look out for Les Nuits Botanique in May to hear lots of new bands in a festival atmosphere. Métro Botanique for Botanique, Métro Madou for Cirque Royal. See map, pp.66–67.
Forest National ave du Globe 36 ⓣ0900 00 991, ⓦwww.forestnational.be. Brussels' main arena for big-name international concerts, holding around 11,000 people. Tram #32 from the city centre, #82 from Gare du Midi or #97 from Louise; get off at stop Zaman.
Théâtre Royal de la Monnaie place de la Monnaie ⓣ02 229 12 11, ⓦwww.lamonnaie.be. Belgium's premier opera house, consistently earning glowing reviews and much lauded for its adventurous repertoire. It has a policy of nurturing promising singers rather than casting the more established stars, so it's a good place to spot up-and-coming talent. Book in advance as tickets are often difficult to come by. Métro De Brouckère. See map, pp.66–67.

Theatres

Kaai Theater place Sainctelette 20 ⓣ02 201 59 59, ⓦwww.kaaitheater.be. This Flemish-language theatre, lodged in an Art Deco building on the banks of the canal to the west of place Rogier, offers a lively programme, featuring local and visiting companies with occasional performances in English; plenty of dance and music too. Tickets cost around €12.50. Métro Yser. See map, pp.66–67.
Koninklijke Vlaamse Schouwberg rue de Laeken 146 and quai aux Pierres de Taille 7 ⓣ02 210 11 00, ⓦwww.kvs.be. Two adjacent venues comprise this Flemish-language theatre – the original neo-Renaissance building (BOL) and the studio (BOX), which has an excellent reputation for showcasing the works of up-and-coming young playwrights as well as some innovative dance. Métro Yser. See map, pp.66–67.
Théâtre National blvd Emile Jacqmain 111–115 ⓣ02 203 41 55, ⓦwww.theatrenational.be. Performances, mainly theatre and invariably in French, are highly polished productions of everything from the classics – Molière and so forth – to cabaret. *Le Café Nationale*, situated on the 1st floor, offers a buffet at lunch times and before performances for €14. Métro Rogier. See map, pp.66–67.
Théâtre Royal de Toone Impasse Schuddeveld 6 ⓣ02 511 71 37, ⓦwww.toone.be. Puppet theatre with a long and distinguished pedigree offering one performance every evening, two on Saturdays, mostly in French but sometimes in the traditional Bruxellois dialect known as Brusselse Sproek or Marollien, a colourful, ribald brand of Flemish which is in danger of dying out. Entry €10, no cards. Métro Bourse or Gare Centrale. See map, p.61.
The Warehouse rue Waelham 73 ⓣ02 203 53 03, ⓦatc.theatreinbrussels.com. In 1994, the American Theatre Company, the English Comedy Club and the Irish Theatre Group purchased a complex now known as The Warehouse. If you want English language theatre, this is where you'll find it, but it's a short trek north from the centre in the suburb of Schaerbeek. Tram #92 from Louise or #55 from place Rogier.

Cinema

In Brussels, the vast majority of **films** are shown in the original language and subtitled in French and/or Flemish (coded "VO", *version originale*). The main exception is in some of the multi-screen cinemas, where some films, especially kids' movies, are likely to be dubbed into French (look out for "VF", *version française*). Brussels has an excellent range of small cinemas and these consistently undercut prices at the multi-screens, though you are expected to tip the usher who checks your ticket – 50 cents will do. The city's annual **film festivals** are highly recommended. They include the Brussels Festival of European Film (ⓦwww.fffb.be) held in June and the utterly fantastical Brussels Festival of Fantasy Film, Science Fiction and Thrillers (ⓦwww.bifff.org) in April. Cinemas usually change their programmes on Wednesday.

Actors' Studio petite rue des Bouchers 16 ⓣ02 512 16 96. This small cinema is a good place to catch art-house or independent films. It's cheaper than its more commercial rivals and has the added advantage that you can buy a beer or a coffee and take it in with you. Métro Bourse or Gare Centrale. See map, p.61.

Arenberg Galleries Galerie de la Reine 26, in Galeries St-Hubert, close to the Grand-Place ⓣ02 512 80 63, ⓦwww.arenberg.be. Set in a handsome Art Deco converted theatre, the Arenberg Galleries is best known for its "Ecran Total", a programme of classic and art-house films over the summer months. An adventurous variety of world films is also screened throughout the year. Métro Bourse or Gare Centrale. See map, p.61.

Flagey Studio 5 place Sainte-Croix, Ixelles ⓣ02 641 10 20, ⓦwww.flagey.be. Part of place Flagey's Art Deco cultural centre, this studio cinema showcases an impressive range of films, usually focusing on a particular genre or director, and hosts the Brussels Festival of European Film in the first two weeks of June (ⓦwww.fffb.be). See map, pp.92–93.

UGC De Brouckère place de Brouckère 38 ⓣ0900 10 440, ⓦwww.ugc.be. A ten-screen cinema showing the usual Hollywood stuff. Take care to go to the right screen as they sometimes show two versions of the same film, one in the original language, the other dubbed. Métro De Brouckère. See map, pp.66–67.

Styx rue de l'Arbre Bénit 72, Ixelles ⓣ02 512 21 02. Two small theatres showing a choice selection of films just after they finish at the bigger cinemas. Ten minutes' walk from Métro Porte de Namur or bus #71. See map, p.93.

Vendôme chaussée de Wavre 18, Ixelles ⓣ02 502 37 00, ⓦwww.cinema-vendome.be. Five-screen cinema that's well known for its wide selection of art films as well as more mainstream flicks. Also hosts a number of film festivals including shorts, Brazilian and Arab film festivals and the gay and lesbian film festival. Loyalty card offer is a multiple ticket – six films for €30.30 – which is pretty good value. Métro Porte de Namur. See map, p.93.

Gay and lesbian scene

The focus of the city's **gay and lesbian scene** is the Rainbow House, rue Marché au Charbon 42 (ⓣ02 503 59 90, ⓦwww.rainbowhouse.be); you can pick up the latest information either in person or on the website. Three highlights are the Gay and Lesbian Film Festival held every January at the Vendôme (ⓦwww.fglb.org); Gay Pride in May (ⓦwww.thepride.be); and the Sunday afternoon gay-friendly tea dance at *You* (4–11pm; see p.104).

Bars and clubs

Le Belgica rue Marché au Charbon 32 ⓦwww.lebelgica.be. A popular fixture of the Brussels gay scene, *Le Belgica* is arguably the capital's most popular gay bar and pick-up joint. It's a tad run-down, with formica tables and dilapidated chairs that have seen better days, but if you're out for a lively, friendly atmosphere, you could do a lot worse. Come at the weekend when the place is heaving – all are welcome, whether male, female, gay or straight – and be sure to slam back a few of the house speciality lemon-vodka "Belgica" shots. Thurs–Sat 10pm–3am. Métro Bourse. See map, p.61.

Chez Maman rue des Grands Carmes 7 ⓦwww.chezmaman.be. Not a lesbian place per se, but this tiny bar has achieved cult-like status for the transvestite cabaret of the proprietor, Maman, with crowds flocking in from all corners of Brussels to see him and his protégés strut up and down. Jam-packed every weekend. Occasional lesbian nights on Thursdays, otherwise Fri & Sat midnight until dawn. Métro Anneessens. See map, p.61.

La Démence at *the Fuse*, rue Blaes 208, Marolles ⓣ02 538 99 31, ⓦwww.lademence.com. The city's most popular gay club, held on two floors in *the Fuse* (see p.104) and playing cutting edge techno. Bus-loads of guys from Amsterdam, Cologne and Paris muster here, making the crowd a bit difficult to pigeonhole – expect to find a hybrid mix of muscle men, transsexuals and out-and-out ravers. Usually last Friday of the month, but check website for dates. 11pm–7am. See map, p.67.

Le Duquesnoy rue Duquesnoy 12. Simply "Le Duq" to the regulars, this gay bar/club is open every night and on Sunday afternoons from 3–6pm, when there's a themed party. Dress code is leather, rubber, latex, uniform or naked – no suits or ties. Mon–Thurs 9pm–3am, Fri & Sat 9pm–5am & Sun 3pm–3am. Métro Gare Centrale. See map, p.61.

Shopping

Brussels has a supreme selection of small, independent **shops**, a smashing range of open-air **markets** and a number of charming **galeries**, covered shopping "streets" dating back to the nineteenth century. The main downtown shopping street is **rue Neuve**, but this is dominated by chain stores; the **Galeries St-Hubert**, near the Grand-Place, are much more distinctive, accommodating a smattering of upmarket shops and stores, while the nearby **Galerie Agora** peddles bargain-basement leather jackets, incense, jewellery and ethnic goods. Behind the Bourse, **rue Antoine Dansaert** caters for the young and fashionable, housing the stores of upcoming designers as well as big Belgian names like Strelli, and in neighbouring **St-Géry**, rue des Riches Claires and rue du Marché au Charbon are good for streetwear. More than anything else, however, Brussels is famous for three things: **comic strips, beer** and **chocolate**.

Generally speaking, shops and stores are **open** from 10am to 6pm or 7pm Monday through Saturday. On Fridays, most department stores stay open till 8pm, and some tourist-oriented shops open on Sundays too.

Antiques and art

Alice rue du pays de Liege 4 ⓣ02 513 33 07, ⓦwww.alicebxl.com. Contemporary gallery specializing in graphic design and textiles. Up-and-coming artists exhibit, and a shop sells books and affordable designer T-shirts. Métro Ste-Catherine. Wed–Sat noon–6pm.

L'Instant Présent rue Blaes 136, Marolles, ⓣ02 513 28 91. Photographer Nicolas Springael opens his shop on Thursdays and weekends to sell his stunning black-and-white photos of Brussels, framed as per requirements. Thurs, Sat & Sun 10.30am–4pm.

Passage 125 Blaes rue Blaes 125, Marolles ⓣ02 503 10 27. Thirty antique dealers occupy the four floors of this labyrinthine shop, with retro, Art Deco and vintage all well represented. Mon, Wed & Fri 10am–5pm, Tues, Thurs & Sat 10am–6pm, Sun 10am–5.30pm.

Books and comics

La Boutique Tintin rue de la Colline 13 ⓣ02 514 51 52. Tintinarama, from comics to all sorts of branded goods – postcards, stationery, figurines, T-shirts and sweaters. Geared up for the tourist trade, it's located just off the Grand-Place. Mon–Sat 10am–6pm, Sun 11am–5pm. Métro Gare Centrale.

Brüsel blvd Anspach 100 ⓣ02 511 08 09. This well-known comic shop stocks more than eight thousand new issues and specializes in French underground editions – Association, Amok and Bill to name but three. You'll also find the complete works of Belgian comic-book artist Schuiten, most popularly known for his controversial comic *Brüsel*, which depicts the architectural destruction of a city (guess which one) in the 1960s. Mega Tintin collection and small English section too. Métro Bourse. Mon–Sat 10am–6.30pm, Sun noon–6.30pm.

Passa Porta rue Antoine Dansaert 46 ⓣ02 502 94 60, ⓦwww.passaportabookshop.be. Haven for book-lovers where manager practises his theory that you wouldn't buy clothes without first trying them on – and the same goes for books. Regular events in all languages with guest authors and readings, and a literary festival in March. About ten percent of the total stock is in English. Métro Ste-Catherine. Mon–Sat 11am–7pm, Sun noon–6pm.

Sterling Books rue du Fossé aux Loups 38 ⓣ02 223 78 35. The largest independent English-language bookshop in Belgium, with more than 40,000 UK and US titles, including a decent selection of magazines. There's a children's corner with a small play area too. Métro De Brouckère. Mon–Sat 10am–7pm, Sun noon–6.30pm.

Chocolates

Frederic Blondeel Chocolatier quai aux Briques 24 ⓣ02 502 21 31. Frederic is a renowned chocolatier from Flanders who has opened up a Brussels café-cum-shop which is simply paradise for chocolate connoisseurs. All the chocolate is made on site, beautifully displayed and reasonably priced, while the café's Madagascan chocolate and Tahitian vanilla ice cream in a chocolate-filled cone are heaven on earth. Métro Ste-Catherine. Mon–Fri 10.30am–6.30pm, Sat 10.30am–10.30pm, Sun 1–6.30pm.

Galler rue au Beurre 44 ⓣ02 502 02 66. Galler is the chocolatier to the King – and therefore the holder of the Royal Warrant – but is still less well known than many of its rivals and rarely seen outside Belgium, so a good choice for a special present. Excellent dark chocolate – 250g will set you back €13.90. Métro Bourse. Daily 10am–9.30pm.

Pierre Marcolini place du Grand Sablon 1 ⓣ02 514 12 06. Considered by many to be the best chocolatier in the world, Pierre Marcolini is a true master of his art – try his spice- and tea-filled chocolates to get the point. Classy service, beautiful packaging and a mouthwatering choice of chocolate cakes. Expect to pay extra for the quality (€17.50 for 250g). On a winter weekend you can have a glass of wonderful hot chocolate at the shop's small bar. Métro Louise. Wed–Fri & Sun 10am–7pm, Sat 10am–6pm.

Wittamer place du Grand Sablon 6 ⓣ02 512 37 42. Brussels' most famous patisserie and chocolate shop, established in 1910 and still run by the Wittamer family, who sell gorgeous (if expensive) light pastries, cakes, mousses and chocolates. They also serve speciality teas and coffees in their tearoom along the street at no. 12. Métro Louise. Mon 8am–6pm, Tues–Sat 7am–7pm, Sun 7am–6pm.

Food and drink

Beer Mania chaussée de Wavre 174–176, Ixelles ⓣ02 512 17 88, ⓦwww.beermania.be. A drinker's heaven, this store stocks more than 400 different types of beer, and you can even buy the correct glass to match your favourite. It's one of the few places where you can get hold of the elusive Trappist beer from Westvleteren (€12 per bottle), usually only for sale at the abbey gates, and there's a small bar, where you can taste before you buy. The owner's own brew, Mea Culpa, includes ten different herbs and is served in an impressive Bohemian glass. Mon–Sat 11am–9pm.

Dandoy rue au Beurre 31 ⓣ02 511 03 26. Biscuits have been made at this famous shop just off the Grand-Place since 1829, so it's no surprise they have it down to a fine art. The main speciality is known locally as "speculoos", a kind of hard gingerbread which comes in every size and shape imaginable – the largest are the size of a small child and cost as much as €50. Mon–Sun 10am–7pm.

La Maison du Miel rue du Midi 121 ⓣ02 512 32 50. As the name suggests, this tiny family-run shop is stacked high with jar upon jar of honey and its multifarious by-products, from soap and candles to sweets and face creams, plus a number of curious honeypots and receptacles. It's a short walk southwest of the Grand-Place, and there's another branch on the north side of the Grand-Place at rue Marché aux Herbes 11. Métro Bourse. Mon–Sat 9.30am–6pm.

La Maison du Thés Plattesteen 11 ⓣ02 512 32 26. A shop dedicated to the good old cuppa, but a far cry from the average English brew. Floor-to-ceiling tins harbour a vast range of teas to smell, read about, taste and buy. Lots of tea-related paraphernalia too. Métro Bourse. Tues–Sat 9am–6pm.

Markets

Ateliers des Tanneurs rue de Tanneurs 58–62, Marolles. Indoor organic food market in a good-looking Art Nouveau building on the west side of the Marolles quarter. Good prices for high-quality products, mostly from local producers, plus a café that serves an excellent brunch buffet at weekends. Fri, Sat and Sun 10am–3pm.

Gare du Midi One of Brussels' largest and most colourful food markets is held here outside the main station every Sunday, with traders crammed under the railway bridge and spilling out into the surrounding streets. Among the vegetables and cheap clothes, numerous stands sell pitta, olives, North African raï tapes, spices and herbs. There's a first-rate flower and plant section too. Métro Gare du Midi. Sun 6am–1.30pm.

Place du Châtelain Ixelles. A weekly food and general market at this busy Ixelles square, packed with stalls selling fresh vegetables, cheeses, cakes, pastries, plants, flowers and home-made wines. Wed 2–7pm.

Place du Grand Sablon The swankiest antiques and collectables market in town; and plenty of pricey antique shops in the surrounding streets too. Métro Louise. Sat 9am–6pm, Sun 9am–2pm.

Place du Jeu de Balle Marolles. This sprawling flea market opens up every morning, but it's at its biggest and best on the weekend, when an eccentric muddle of colonial spoils, quirky odds and ends and domestic and ecclesiastical bric-a-brac give an impression of a century's fads and fashions. Daily 7am–2pm.

Listings

Airport information For flight information at Brussels' international airport, call ⓣ0900 70 000 or go to ⓦwww.brusselsairport.be.

Banks and exchange There are ATMs dotted right across the city centre, including one at Grand-Place 7 and another at rue Marché-aux-Herbes 6.

There are also bureaux de change with extended opening hours at Gare du Midi (Mon–Sat 7am–8.30pm & Sun 9am–5pm) and Gare du Nord (Mon–Fri 8am–6pm, Sat 9am–3pm).
Bus enquiries Within the city, STIB ⓣ070 23 2000, ⓦwww.stib.be; for the Walloon communities south of the city, TEC ⓣ010 23 53 53, ⓦwww.infotec.be; for the Flemish communities near the city, De Lijn ⓣ070 220 200, ⓦwww.delijn.be.
Car rental All main companies have a desk at the airport and at Gare du Midi train station. Contact numbers for the airport are Avis ⓣ02 720 09 44; Budget ⓣ02 753 21 70; Europcar ⓣ02 721 05 92 and Sixt ⓣ070 225 800.
Dentists Standby municipal dentist ⓣ02 426 10 26.
Doctors Standby municipal doctor ⓣ02 479 18 18.
Embassies Australia, rue Guimard 6–8 ⓣ02 286 05 00; Canada, ave de Tervuren 2 ⓣ02 741 06 11; Ireland, chaussée d'Etterbeek 180 ⓣ02 235 66 76; New Zealand, square de Meeus 1 ⓣ02 512 10 40; UK, ave d'Auderghem 10 ⓣ02 287 62 11; USA, blvd du Régent 27 ⓣ02 508 21 11.
Emergencies Phone ⓣ112.
Football Brussels has several soccer teams, of which Royal Sporting Club (RSC) Anderlecht (ⓣ02 529 40 67, ⓦwww.rsca.be) is by far the best known. Their stadium is the Stade Constant Vanden Stock, at ave Théo Verbeeck 2, within comfortable walking distance of Métro St Guidon. The season runs from August to May, but tickets can be hard to get hold of.
Internet access Most hotels and hostels provide internet access for their guests either free or at minimal charge. There are also wi-fi zones in many cafés and public spaces.
Left luggage There are coin-operated lockers at all three main train stations.
Lost property For the métro, buses and trams, the lost property office is at ave de la Toison d'Or 15 (Mon, Wed & Fri noon–5.30pm & Wed–Thurs noon–7pm; ⓣ02 515 23 94).
Post The main post office is at Gare du Midi, exit rue Fosny (Mon–Fri 8am–7.30pm & Sat 10.30am–4.30pm). Post office counters are located in many supermarkets.
Pharmacies Multipharma, near the Grand-Place at rue du Marché aux Poulets 37 (ⓣ02 511 35 90). Details of 24hr pharmacies are available on ⓣ070 66 01 60 or ⓦwww.servicedegarde.be, and details of duty pharmacies are usually posted on the front door of every pharmacy.
Police Brussels Central Police Station, rue du Marché au Charbon 30 ⓣ02 279 79 79.
Taxis Taxis don't cruise the streets, but can be picked up at stands around the city, notably on De Brouckère and outside the main train stations. There is a fixed tariff consisting of two main elements – a fixed charge of €2.40 (€4.40 at night) and the price per kilometre (€1.35 inside the city). If you can't find a taxi, phone Taxis Verts on ⓣ02 349 49 49 or Taxis Orange on ⓣ02 349 43 43.
Train enquiries SNCB, for Belgian Rail/domestic journeys ⓣ02 528 28 28, ⓦwww.b-rail.be; for international journeys Eurostar & Thalys ⓣ070 79 79 79 (premium line).

Around Brussels: Waterloo

Brussels lies at the centre of **Brabant**, one of Belgium's nine provinces. The Flemings claim the lion's share of the province with their **Vlaams Brabant** (Flemish Brabant) actually encircling the capital – a noticeably narrow corridor of Flemish-speaking communities runs round the southern edge of Brussels. The highlights of Vlaams Brabant are covered in Chapter 3, but **WATERLOO**, easily the most popular attraction in **Brabant Wallon** (French speaking Brabant), is best seen on a day-trip from the capital. A run-of-the-mill suburb about 18km south of the centre of Brussels, the town has a resonance far beyond its size. On June 18, 1815, at this small crossroads town on what was once the main route to Brussels from France, Wellington masterminded the battle that put an end to the imperial ambitions of Napoleon. The battle turned out to have far more significance than even its generals realized, for not only was this the last throw of the dice for the formidable army born of the French Revolution, but it also marked the end of France's prolonged attempts to dominate Europe militarily.

Nevertheless, the historic importance of Waterloo has not saved the **battlefield** from interference – a motorway cuts right across it – and if you do visit you'll need

The Battle of Waterloo

Napoleon escaped from imprisonment on the Italian island of Elba on February 26, 1815. He landed in Cannes three days later and moved swiftly north, entering Paris on March 20 just as his unpopular replacement – the slothful **King Louis XVIII** – high-tailed it to Ghent (see p.191). Thousands of Frenchmen rallied to Napoleon's colours and, with little delay, Napoleon marched northeast to fight the two armies that threatened his future. Both were in Belgium. One, an assortment of British, Dutch and German soldiers, was commanded by the **Duke of Wellington**, the other was a Prussian army led by **Marshal Blücher**. At the start of the campaign, Napoleon's army was about 130,000 strong, larger than each of the opposing armies but not big enough to fight them both at the same time. Napoleon's strategy was, therefore, quite straightforward: he had to stop Wellington and Blücher from joining together – and to this end he crossed the Belgian frontier near Charleroi to launch a quick attack. On June 16, the French hit the Prussians hard, forcing them to retreat and giving Napoleon the opportunity he was looking for. Napoleon detached a force of 30,000 soldiers to harry the retreating Prussians, while he concentrated his main army against Wellington, hoping to deliver a knockout blow. Meanwhile, Wellington had assembled his troops at **Waterloo**, on the main road to Brussels.

At **dawn on Sunday June 18**, the two armies faced each other. Wellington had some 68,000 men, about one third of whom were British, and Napoleon around five thousand more. The armies were deployed just 1500m apart with Wellington on the ridge north of – and uphill from – the enemy. It had rained heavily during the night, so Napoleon delayed his first attack to give the ground a chance to dry. At **11.30am**, the battle began when the French assaulted the fortified farm of Hougoumont, which was crucial for the defence of Wellington's right. The assault failed and at approximately **1pm** there was more bad news for Napoleon when he heard that the Prussians had eluded their pursuers and were closing fast. To gain time he sent 14,000 troops off to impede their progress and at **2pm** he tried to regain the initiative by launching a large-scale infantry attack against Wellington's left. This second French attack also proved inconclusive and so at **4pm** Napoleon's cavalry charged Wellington's centre, where the British infantry formed into squares and just managed to keep the French at bay – a desperate engagement that cost hundreds of lives. By **5.30pm**, the Prussians had begun to reach the battlefield in numbers to the right of the French lines and, at **7.30pm**, with the odds getting longer and longer, Napoleon made a final bid to break Wellington's centre, sending in his Imperial Guard. These were the best soldiers Napoleon had, but slowed down by the mud churned up by their own cavalry, the veterans proved easy targets for the British infantry, and they were beaten back with great loss of life. At **8.15pm**, Wellington, who knew victory was within his grasp, rode down the ranks to encourage his soldiers before ordering the large-scale counterattack that proved decisive.

The French were vanquished and Napoleon subsequently **abdicated**, ending his days in exile on St Helena, where he died in 1821. Popular memory, however, refused to vilify Napoleon as the aggressor – and not just in France, but right across Europe, where the Emperor's bust was a common feature of the nineteenth-century drawing room. In part, this was to do with Napoleon's obvious all-round brilliance, but more crucially, he soon became a symbol of opportunity: in him the emergent middle classes of western Europe saw a common man becoming greater than the crowned heads of Europe, an almost unique event at the time.

a lively imagination to picture what happened and where – unless, that is, you're around to see the large-scale re-enactment which takes place every five years in June; the next one is scheduled for 2015. Scattered round the **battlefield** are

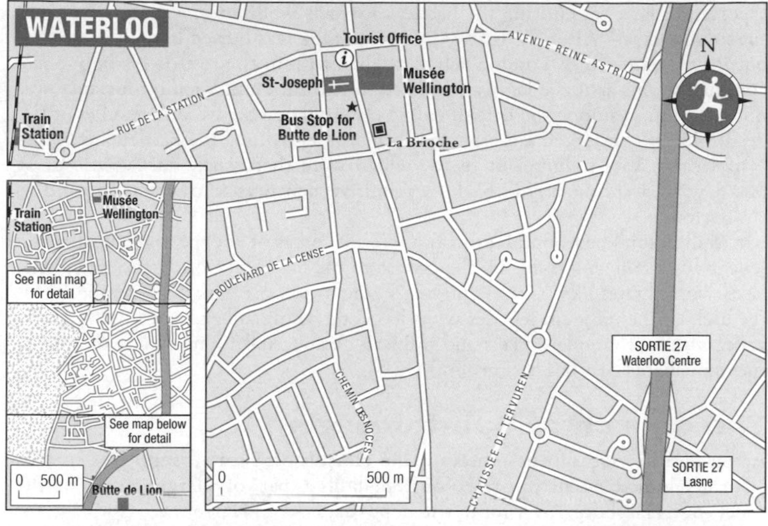

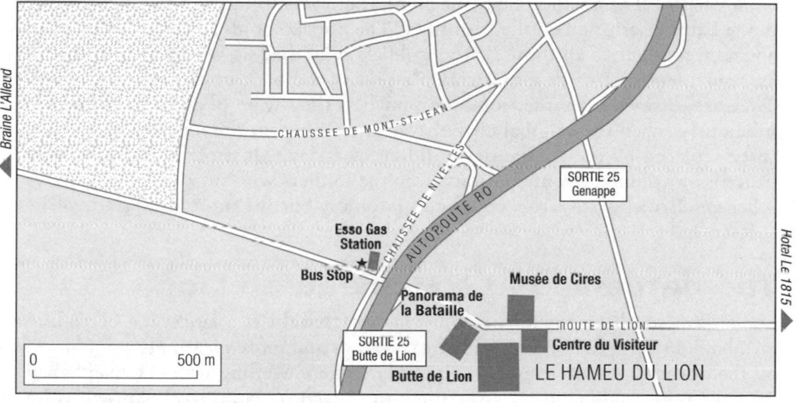

several monuments and memorials, the most satisfying of which is the **Butte de Lion**, a huge earth mound that's part viewpoint and part commemoration. The battlefield is 3km south of the centre of Waterloo, where the **Musée Wellington** is easily the pick of several Waterloo museums.

The Musée Wellington

The **Musée Wellington**, chaussée de Bruxelles 147 (daily: April–Sept 9.30am–6.30pm; Oct–March 10am–5pm; €5; Ⓦwww.museewellington.com), occupies the old inn where Wellington slept the nights before and after the battle. It's an enjoyable affair, whose displays detail the build-up to – and the course of – the battle via plans and models, alongside an engaging hotchpotch of personal effects. **Room 4** holds the bed where Alexander Gordon, Wellington's principal aide-de-camp, was brought to die, and here also is the artificial leg of Lord Uxbridge, another British commander: "I say, I've lost my leg," Uxbridge is reported to have said during the battle, to which Wellington replied, "By God, sir, so you have!" After the battle, Uxbridge's leg was buried here in Waterloo, but it was returned to London when he died to join the rest of his body; as a consolation, his artificial leg was donated to the museum. Such insouciance was not uncommon among the British ruling class and neither were the bodies of the dead soldiers considered sacrosanct: tooth dealers roamed the battlefields of the Napoleonic Wars pulling out teeth, which were then stuck on two pieces of board with a spring at the back – primitive dentures known in England as "Waterloos".

In Wellington's bedroom, **Room 6**, there are copies of the messages Wellington sent to his commanders during the course of the battle, curiously formal epistles laced with phrases like "Could you be so kind as to . . .". Finally, an extension at the back of the museum reprises what has gone before, albeit on a slightly larger scale, with more models, plans and military paraphernalia plus a lucid outline of the immediate historical background.

The church of Saint Joseph

Across the street from the museum, the **church of Saint Joseph** is a curious affair, its domed, circular **portico** of 1689 built as part of a larger chapel on the orders of a Habsburg governor in the hope that it would encourage God to grant King Charles II of Spain an heir (see p.63). It didn't, but the plea to God survives in the Latin inscription on the pediment. The portico holds a bust of Wellington and a monument to all those British soldiers who died at Waterloo, and there's an assortment of British **memorial plaques** at the back of the chapel beyond. They are, however, a rather jumbled bunch as they were plonked here unceremoniously when the original chapel was demolished in the nineteenth century to be replaced by the substantial building of today. Most of the plaques were paid for by voluntary contributions from the soldiers who survived – in the days when the British state rarely coughed up for any but the most aristocratic of its veterans.

The battlefield - Le Hameau de Lion

Some 4km south of town, the Waterloo **battlefield** is a landscape of rolling farmland, interrupted by a couple of main roads and more pleasingly punctuated by the odd copse and farmstead. The ridge where Wellington once marshalled his army now holds a motley assortment of attractions collectively known as **Le Hameau du Lion** (Lion's Hamlet). This comprises four separate sites all within a few metres of each other, with the added offering of a 45-minute battlefield tour in a four-wheel-drive. Of the four sites, the worst are the **Centre du Visiteur** (daily: April–Oct 9.30am–6.30pm; Nov–March 10am–5pm), which features a dire audiovisual display on the battle, and the **Musée de Cires** (same hours), a dusty wax museum. The best is the 100m-high **Butte de Lion** (same hours), built by local women with soil from the battlefield. The Butte marks the spot where Holland's Prince William of Orange – one of Wellington's commanders and later King William II of the Netherlands – was wounded. It was only a nick, so goodness knows how high it would have been if William had been seriously injured, but even so the mound is a commanding monument, surmounted by a regal 28-tonne lion atop a stout column. From the viewing platform, there's a panoramic view over the battlefield, and a plan identifies which army was where. Also enjoyable is the **Panorama de la Bataille** (same hours), where a circular, naturalistic painting of the battle, on a canvas no less than 110m in circumference, is displayed in a purpose-built, rotunda-like gallery

– to a thundering soundtrack of bugles, snorting horses and cannon fire. Panorama painting is extremely difficult – controlling perspective is always a real problem – but it was very much in vogue when the Parisian artist Louis Dumoulin began this effort in 1912. Precious few panoramas have survived and this one is a bit past its best, but it does at least give a sense of the battle. You can also venture out onto the battlefield under your own steam by following the old **track** that cuts south across the fields from beside the Panorama.

Tickets – and ticketing combinations – are confusing and are only available at the **Centre du Visiteur**. There are four options: a pass for everything, including the battlefield tour, costs €12, or €8.70 without the tour; the Butte de Lion and the Panorama only cost €6; and the battlefield tour on its own costs €5.50.

Practicalities

There are several ways of getting to Waterloo and its scattering of sights, but the most effective is to make a circular loop by train, bus and train. From any of Brussels' three main stations (see p.53), **trains** take you direct to Waterloo (Mon–Fri 2 hourly, Sat & Sun 1 hourly; 25min), though you'll have to keep your wits about you to get off at the correct station as there's no on-board announcement and station signs are hard to spot. From Waterloo train station, it's an easy fifteen-minute **walk** – turn right outside the station building and then first left along rue de la Station – to Waterloo tourist office and the Musée Wellington (see p.111). After you've finished at the museum, you can take **bus #W** (every 30–40min) from across the street – the chaussée de Bruxelles – to the battlefield and the Butte de Lion (see opposite). The bus stops beside the Esso gas station about 500m from the Butte. After visiting the Butte, return to the same bus stop and catch bus #W on to **Braine-l'Alleud train station**, from where there's a fast and frequent service back to all three of Brussels' main train stations (Mon–Fri 3 hourly, Sat & Sun 2 hourly; 15min).

Waterloo **tourist office** is handily located in the centre of town, opposite the Musée Wellington at chaussée de Bruxelles 218 (daily: June–Sept 9.30am–6pm; Oct–May 10am–5pm; Ⓣ02 352 09 10, Ⓦwww.waterloo.be). They issue free town **maps** and sell a **combined ticket**, the **Pass 1815** (€12), for all the battle-related attractions, though if you're at all selective (and you'll probably want to be) this won't work out as a saving at all. The Brussels Card (see p.54) is valid for most of Waterloo's attractions too.

There's no strong reason to stay the night in Waterloo, but the tourist office does have the details of several local **hotels**. Among them, the comfortable, three-star *Hotel Le 1815*, route du Lion 367 (Ⓣ02 387 01 60, Ⓦwww.le1815.com; ❹), near the Butte de Lion, has rooms turned out in an attractive modern style. For **food**, *La Brioche* is a pleasant, modern café serving up a reasonably good line in sandwiches, pancakes and pastries; it's located just up and across the street from the Waterloo tourist office at chaussée de Bruxelles 161.

Travel details

Trains

SNCB (Belgian railways)

Almost all SNCB (Ⓣ02 528 28 28, Ⓦwww.b-rail.be) trains stop at all three of the capital's principal train stations – Bruxelles-Nord, Bruxelles-Centrale, and Bruxelles-Midi. The main exception are trains to and from Amsterdam, which only stop at Bruxelles-Centrale and Bruxelles-Midi.

Brussels to: Amsterdam Centraal Station (1 hourly; 2hr 30min); Antwerp (2–3 hourly; 40min); Bruges (2 hourly; 1hr); Charleroi (2 hourly; 50min); Ghent (2 hourly; 30min); Liège (1 hourly; 1hr 20min); Leuven (every 30 min; 25min); Luxembourg (1 hourly; 3hr); Mons (1–2 hourly; 50min); Namur (1 hourly; 1hr); Ostend (2 hourly; 1hr 10min).

Eurostar

Eurostar international trains (premium line Ⓣ070 79 79 79, Ⓦwww.eurostar.com) arrive at and depart from Bruxelles-Midi train station (see p.53).

Thalys

Thalys international trains (premium line Ⓣ070 79 79 79, Ⓦwww.thalys.com) arrive at and depart from Bruxelles-Midi train station (see p.53).

2

Flanders

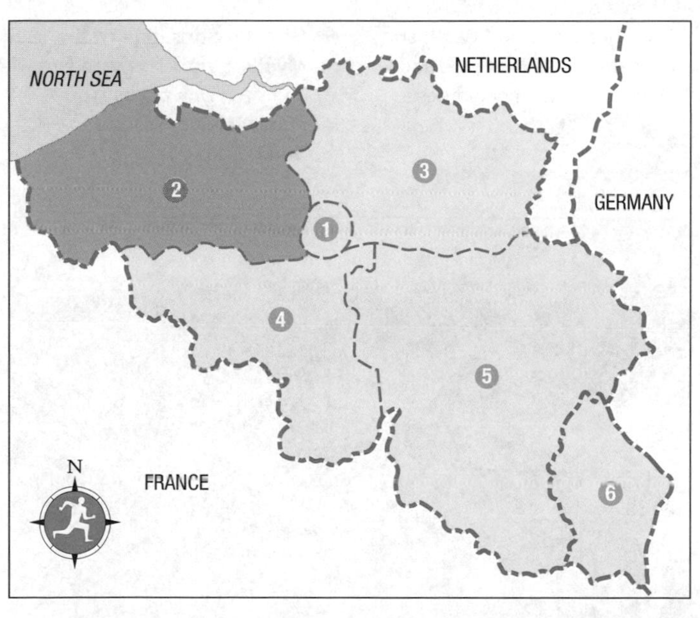

CHAPTER 2

Highlights

* **Ostend beach** The Belgian coast boasts a first-rate sandy beach for almost its entire length, and Ostend has an especially fine slice. See p.123
* **Veurne** This pretty little country town has a relaxing air and a delightful main square. See p.128
* **Ieper** Flanders witnessed some of the worst of the slaughter of World War I, and Ieper is dotted with the sad and mournful mementoes. See p.133
* **Flemish tapestries** Small-town Oudenaarde was once famous for its tapestries, and a superb selection is on display today. See pp.144–148
* **Bruges** By any measure, Bruges is one of western Europe's most beautiful cities, its jangle of ancient houses overlooking a cobweb of picturesque canals. See pp.148–173
* **Ghent's Adoration of the Mystic Lamb** This wonderful Jan van Eyck painting is absolutely unmissable. See p.183

▲ van Eyck's *Adoration of the Mystic Lamb*

2

Flanders

The Flemish-speaking provinces of **West Vlaanderen** and **Oost Vlaanderen** (West Flanders and East Flanders) roll east from the North Sea coast, stretching out towards Brussels and Antwerp. As early as the thirteenth century, Flanders was one of the most prosperous areas of Europe, with an advanced, integrated economy dependent on the **cloth trade** with England. The boom times lasted a couple of centuries, but by the sixteenth century the region was in decline as trade slipped north towards the Netherlands, and England's cloth manufacturers began to undermine its economic base. The speed of the collapse was accelerated by **religious conflict**, for though the great Flemish towns were by inclination Protestant, their kings and queens were Catholic. Indeed, once the Habsburgs had seen off the Protestant challenge in Flanders, thousands of Flemish weavers, merchants and skilled artisans poured north to escape religious persecution. The ultimate economic price of these religious wars was the closure of the River Scheldt, the main waterway to the North Sea, at the insistence of the Dutch in 1648. Thereafter, Flanders sank into poverty and decay, a static, priest-ridden and traditional society where nearly every aspect of life was controlled by decree, and only three percent of the population could read or write. As **Voltaire** quipped:

> In this sad place wherein I stay,
> Ignorance, torpidity,
> And boredom hold their lasting sway,
> With unconcerned stupidity;
> A land where old obedience sits,
> Well filled with faith, devoid of wits.

With precious little say in the matter, the Flemish peasantry of the seventeenth and eighteenth centuries saw their lands crossed and re-crossed by the armies of the Great Powers, for it was here that the relative fortunes of dynasties and nations were decided. Only with **Belgian independence** did the situation begin to change: the towns started to industrialize, tariffs protected the cloth industry, Zeebrugge was built and Ostend was modernized, all in a flurry of activity that shook Flanders from its centuries-old torpor. This steady progress was severely interrupted by the German occupations of both world wars, but Flanders has emerged prosperous, its citizens maintaining a distinctive cultural and linguistic identity, often in sharp opposition to their Walloon (French-speaking) neighbours.

With the exception of the range of low hills around Oudenaarde and the sea dunes along the coast, Flanders is unrelentingly **flat**, a somewhat monotonous landscape at its best in its quieter recesses, where poplar trees and whitewashed

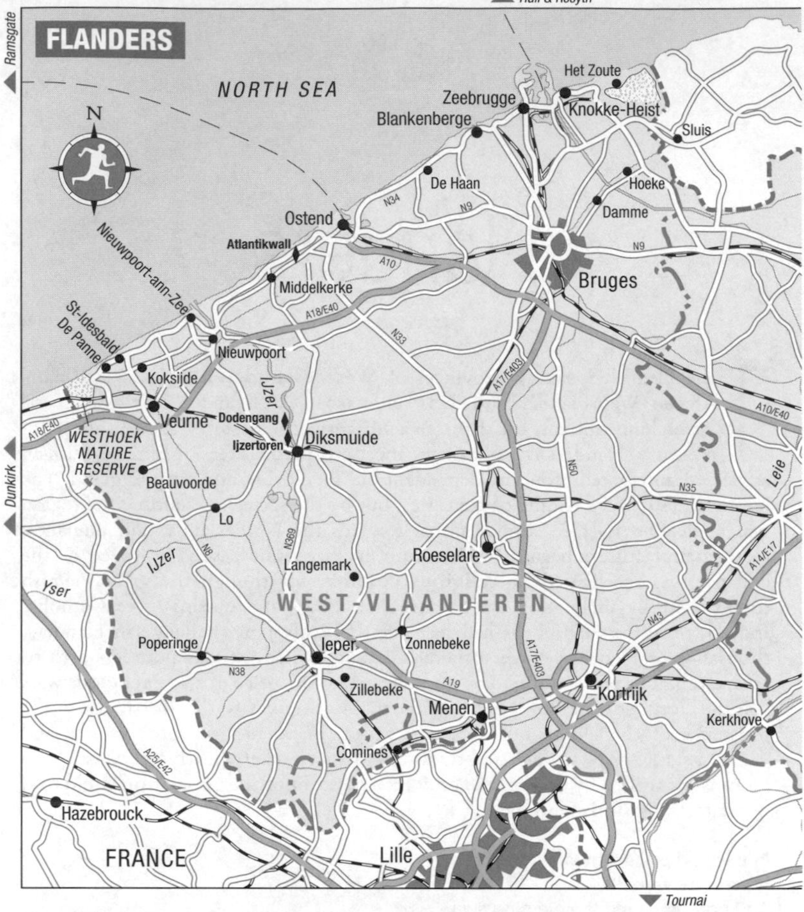

farmhouses still decorate sluggish canals. More remarkably, there are many reminders of Flanders' medieval greatness, beginning with the ancient and fascinating cloth cities of **Bruges** and **Ghent**, both of which hold marvellous collections of early Flemish art. Less familiar are a clutch of intriguing smaller towns, most memorably **Oudenaarde**, which has a delightful town hall and is famed for its tapestries; **Kortrijk**, with its classic small-town charms and fine old church; and **Veurne**, whose main square is framed by a beguiling medley of fine old buildings. There is also, of course, the legacy of **World War I**. By 1915, the trenches extended from the North Sea coast to Switzerland, cutting across West Flanders via Diksmuide and Ieper, and many of the key engagements of the war were fought here. Every year hundreds of visitors head for **Ieper** (formerly Ypres) to see the numerous cemeteries and monuments around the town – sad reminders of what proved to be a desperately pointless conflict. Not far from the battlefields, the Belgian coast is **beach** territory, an almost continuous stretch of golden sand that is filled by thousands of tourists every summer. An excellent **tram** service connects all the major resorts, and although a lot of the development has been crass, cosy **De Haan** has kept much of its late

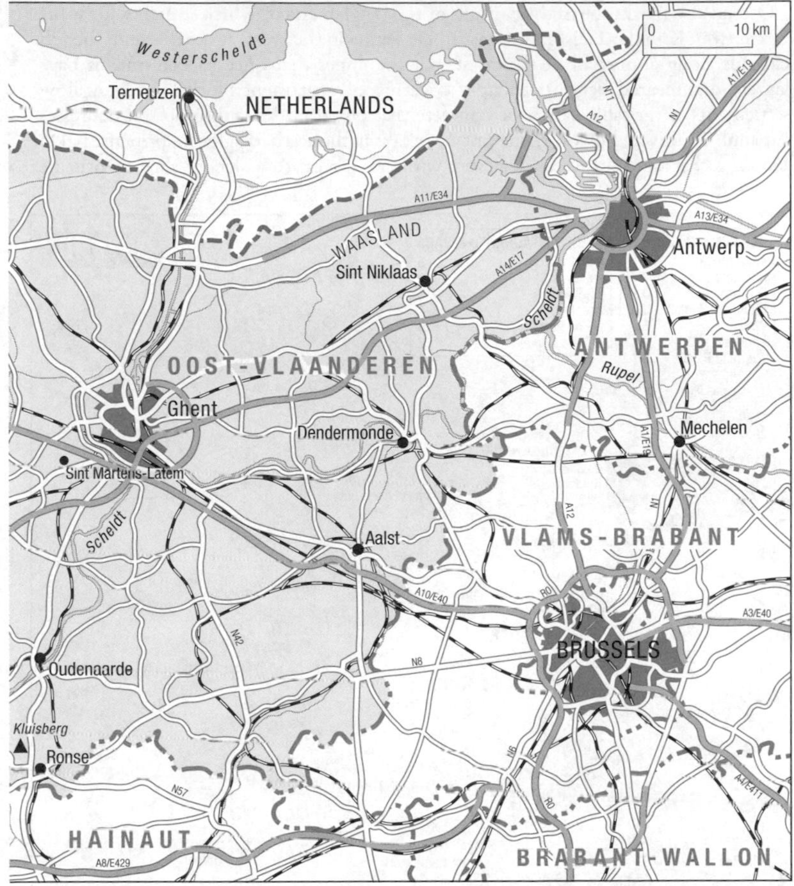

nineteenth-century charm. The largest town on the coast is **Ostend**, a lively, working seaport and resort crammed with popular bars and restaurants.

The region's public transport system is fast, efficient and inexpensive. **Trains** link all the major towns at least once an hour, **trams** shuttle up and down the coast, and where the trains and trams fizzle out, De Lijn **buses** pick up the slack.

Ostend and the coast

The *Baedeker* of 1900 distinguished **OSTEND** as "one of the most fashionable and cosmopolitan watering places in Europe". The gloss may be gone today, and the aristocratic visitors have certainly moved on to more exotic climes, but Ostend remains a likeable, liveable seaport with a clutch of first-rate seafood restaurants, a string of earthy bars, an enjoyable art museum and – easily the most popular of the lot – a long slice of sandy **beach**.

Ostend also marks the midway point of the Belgian **coast**, which stretches for some 70km from Knokke-Heist in the east to De Panne in the west. A superb sandy **beach** extends along almost all of the coast, but the dunes that once backed onto it have largely disappeared beneath an ugly covering of apartment blocks and bungalow settlements, a veritable carpet of concrete that obscures the landscape and depresses the soul. There are, however, one or two breaks in the aesthetic gloom, principally **De Haan**, a charming little seaside resort with easy access to a slender slice of pristine

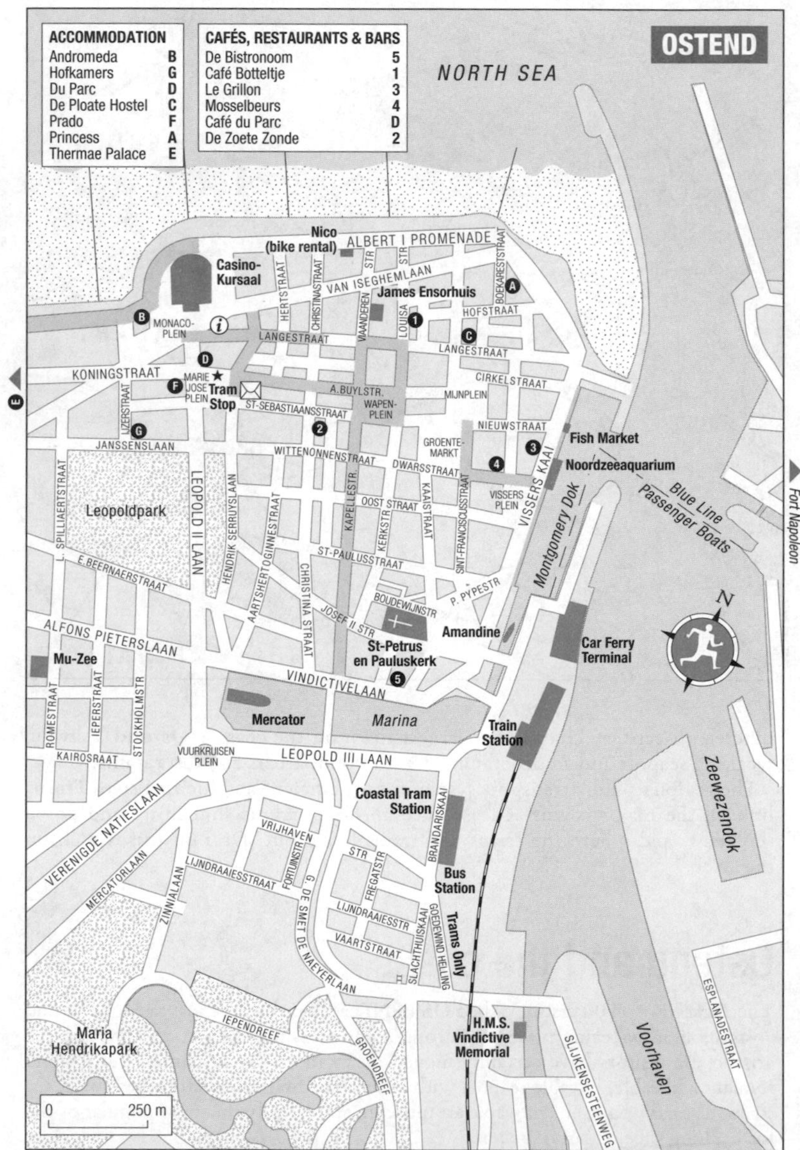

coastline; the substantial remains of **Atlantikwall** built by the Germans to repel the Allies in World War II; and the outstanding Paul Delvaux Museum in **St-Idesbald**.

Exploring the seashore by public transport could not be easier: a fast, frequent and efficient tram service – the **Kusttram** – runs from one end of the coast to the other (see box, p.125). If you're UK-bound, note that Transeuropa operates ferries from Ostend to Ramsgate, while Zeebrugge is linked to Hull by P&O Ferries and with Rosyth by Norfolkline ferries (see p.21 for more).

Some history

The old fishing village of **Ostend** was given a town charter in the thirteenth century, in recognition of its growing importance as a port for trade across the Channel. Flanked by an empty expanse of sand dune, it remained the only important coastal settlement hereabouts until the construction of Zeebrugge six centuries later – the dunes were always an inadequate protection against the sea and precious few people chose to live along the coast until a chain of massive sea walls was completed in the nineteenth century. Like so many other towns in the Spanish Netherlands, Ostend was attacked and besieged time and again, winning the admiration of Protestant Europe in resisting the Spaniards during a desperate siege that lasted from 1601 to 1604. Later, convinced of the wholesome qualities of sea air and determined to impress other European rulers with their sophistication, Belgium's first kings, Léopold I and II, turned Ostend into a chichi **resort**, demolishing the town walls and dotting the outskirts with prestigious buildings and parks. Several of these have survived, but others were destroyed during World War II, when the town's docks made it a prime bombing target. Subsequently, Ostend resumed its role as a major cross-channel port until the completion of the Channel Tunnel in 1994 undermined its position. Since then, Ostend has had to reinvent itself, emphasizing its charms as a seaside resort and centre of culture. There's a long way to go, perhaps – and parts of the centre remain resolutely miserable – but there's no denying that Ostend is on the up.

It is perhaps hard to imagine today, but for generations of Brits Ostend had a particular resonance as their first continental port of call. It also played a key role in World War II when, with the German armies closing in, thousands made a desperate dash to catch a boat to the UK; one of the escapees was the young **Ralph Miliband**, the father of the Labour politicians Ed and David. Another temporary resident was **Marvin Gaye**, who hunkered down here in 1981 until family and musical ties pulled him back to the US the year after – and just two years before he was killed by his father in bizarre circumstances in Los Angeles.

Arrival, information and getting around

Ostend's **car ferry terminal** is next to the **train station**, which is itself metres from both the **coastal tram station** (the Kusttram, see p.125) and the **bus station**. From all four, it's a ten-minute walk to the **tourist office**, on Monacoplein (June–Aug Mon–Sat 9am–7pm & Sun 10am–7pm; Sept–May Mon–Sat 10am–6pm & Sun 10am–5pm; ⓣ059 70 11 99, ⓦwww.toerisme-oostende.be). There are five **car rental** outlets in Ostend – the tourist office has the complete list – including Europcar, Kastanjelaan 3, off Torhoutsesteenweg (ⓣ059 70 01 01), as well as half a dozen **bike rental** places, including Nico, at Albert 1-Promenade 44A (ⓣ059 23 34 81, ⓦwww.nicokarts.be).

Accommodation

The tourist office will help you find accommodation in one of Ostend's many **hotels** and **guesthouses** at no extra charge. The best option is a beachside hotel, but these are few and far between – most of the seashore is given over to apartment blocks – so you might plump instead for the area round **Léopoldpark** on the west side of the centre, a pleasant district with a relaxed and easy air. There's also a decent **HI hostel**.

Hotels

Andromeda Kursaal Westhelling 5 ⓣ059 80 66 11, ⓦwww.andromedahotel.be. Smart, modern four-star high-rise next door to the casino, and overlooking the town's best beach. Many rooms have balconies and sea views, plus there are fitness facilities and an indoor pool. ❻

Hofkamers Ijzerstraat 5 ⓣ059 70 63 49, ⓦwww.dehofkamers.be. Very agreeable family-run hotel whose somewhat dour exterior belies its cosy public areas, kitted out with all sorts of local bygones, and the comfortable bedrooms beyond. The nicest room, on the top floor – Floor 6 – has its own mini-balcony with a view (admittedly a bit of a long one) of the sea. ❸

Du Parc Marie Joséplein 3 ⓣ059 70 16 80, ⓦwww.hotelduparc.be. Located in a fetching Art Deco block, this medium-sized hotel offers reasonably comfortable modern rooms at competitive prices. The ground-floor café, with its Tiffany glass trimmings, is a favourite with older locals (see p.124). Three stars. ❸

Prado Léopold II-laan 22 ⓣ059 70 53 06, ⓦwww.hotelprado.be. Very likeable three-star hotel with neatly furnished modern rooms, attentive staff, especially tasty breakfasts, and easy views over a mini-park-cum-square, Marie Joséplein. Ask for a room at the front, overlooking the square – and a few floors up from the traffic. ❹

Princess Boekareststraat 7 ⓣ059 70 68 88, ⓦwww.hotelprincess.be. Family-owned thirty-five-room hotel in a modern block on a narrow side street a couple of minutes' walk from the beach. The rooms are modestly decorated and the better ones have mini-balconies. ❸

Thermae Palace Koningin Astridlaan 7 ⓣ059 80 66 44, ⓦwww.thermaepalace.be. Four-star hotel that long enjoyed the reputation as being Ostend's best. The building is certainly striking, comprising an Art Deco extravagance with expansive public rooms and spacious bedrooms offering sea views, but the place can't but help seem a little sorry for itself – there's so much to keep in good working order. A 10min walk west of the centre. ❻

Hostel

De Ploate Hostel Langestraat 82 ⓣ059 80 52 97, ⓦwww.vjh.be. Well-maintained HI hostel right in the centre of town with 124 beds, mostly in five- to seven-bedded dorms. There's a decent café, serving inexpensive meals, internet access, a bar and no curfew. The overnight fee of €19.80 per person includes breakfast. Reservations are strongly advised in summer. The smallest rooms, which have three beds, cost ❶

The Town

There's precious little left of medieval Ostend, and today's **town centre**, which fans out from beside the train station, is a largely modern affair, whose narrow, straight streets are lined by clunky postwar apartment blocks and a scattering of older – and much more appealing – stone mansions. In front of the train station, the first specific sight is the **Amandine** (Mon 2–6pm, Tues–Sun 10am–7pm; €4), a local deep-sea fishing boat of unremarkable modern design that was decommissioned in 1995 – and then parked here, its interior turned into a museum with displays on fishing, nautical dioramas and so forth. Straight ahead from the boat rises the whopping **St-Petrus en Pauluskerk**, a church that looks old but in fact dates from the early twentieth century. Behind it, the last remnant of its predecessor is a massive sixteenth-century brick **tower** with a canopied, distinctly morbid shrine of the Crucifixion at its base. Nearby, pedestrianized **Kapellestraat**, the principal shopping street, leads north into the main square, **Wapenplein**, a pleasant open space that zeroes in on an old-fashioned bandstand. The south side of the square is dominated by the former **Feest-en Kultuurpaleis** (Festival and Culture Hall), an imposing 1950s building that has recently been turned into a shopping centre.

James Ensorhuis and the casino

From the Wapenplein, it's a couple of minutes' walk north to the **James Ensorhuis**, Vlaanderenstraat 27 (daily except Tues 10am–noon & 2–5pm; €2), which is of some specialist interest as the artist's home for the last thirty years of his life. The ground floor holds a passable re-creation of the old shop where his aunt and uncle sold shells and souvenirs, while up above the painter's living room and studio have been returned to something like their appearance at the time of his death, though the works on display aren't originals. From here, it's a brief stroll west to the **casino** (gaming daily from 9am–5am), an expansive structure dating from 1953 and attached to the **Kursaal** exhibition and concert centre.

The seafront west of the casino

To the west of the casino lies Ostend's main attraction, its **sandy beach**, which extends as far as the eye can see. On summer days, thousands drive into town to soak up the sun, swim and amble along the seafront **promenade**, which runs along the top of the sea wall. Part sea defence and part royal ostentation, the promenade was built to link the town centre with the Wellington racecourse, 2km to the west. It was – and remains – an intentionally grand walkway that pandered to the grandiose tastes of King Léopold II. To hammer home the royal point, the king's **statue**, with fawning Belgians and Congolese at its base, still stands in the middle of a long line of columns towards the promenade's west end. These columns now abut the **Thermae Palace Hotel**, which was the epitome of luxury when it was added in the 1930s.

Léopoldpark and Mu-Zee

The casino sits at the top of **Léopold II-laan**, a dead-straight boulevard that soon leads to the little lakes and mini-bridges of the verdant **Léopoldpark**. On the other side of the park, at Romestraat 11, is Ostend's premier fine-art museum, **Mu-Zee** (Kunstmuseum aan Zee; Tues–Sun 10am–6pm; €7), which displays a wide selection of modern Belgian paintings drawn from its permanent collection alongside temporary exhibitions, mostly of contemporary works. The paintings are regularly rotated, but highlights of the permanent collection include the harsh Surrealism of **Paul Delvaux**'s (1897–1994) *The Ijzer Time* and several piercing canvases by **Leon Spilliaert** (1881–1946). A native of Ostend, Spilliaert was smitten by the land and seascapes of his home town, using them in his work time and again: as in *De Windstoot* (*Gust of Wind*), with its dark, forbidding colours and screaming woman, and the comparable *Melancholie*. There's also an excellent sample of the work of **James Ensor** (1860–1949), who was born in Ostend, the son of an English father and Flemish mother. Barely noticed until the 1920s, Ensor spent nearly all his 89 years working in his home town, and is nowadays considered a pioneer of Expressionism. His first paintings were rather sombre portraits and landscapes, but in the early 1880s he switched to brilliantly contrasting colours, most familiarly in his *Self-portrait with Flowered Hat*, a deliberate variation on Rubens' famous self-portraits. Less well known is *The Artist's Mother in Death*, a fine, penetrating example of his preoccupation with the grim and macabre.

Mercator, Visserskaai and Fort Napoleon

From Mu-Zee, it's a brief stroll east to the **marina**, where the sailing ship **Mercator** (May–June & Sept–Oct daily 10am–12.30pm & 2–5.30pm; July & Aug daily 10am–5.30pm; Nov–April 10am–12.30pm & 2–4.30pm; €4), the old training vessel of the Belgian merchant navy, has been converted into a marine museum holding a hotchpotch of items accumulated during her world voyages.

Take Vindictivelaan along the north side of the marina and you'll soon reach Visserskaai, which cuts up beside the harbour passing both the **Noordzee-aquarium** (North Sea Aquarium; daily: April & May 10am–noon & 2–5pm; June–Sept 10am–12.30pm & 2–6pm; €2) and the **Vistrap** (Fish Market; daily from 8am). En route, you may well spot the little **Blue Link passenger ferry** (July & Aug daily 10.30am–6pm, every 30min; April–June & Sept–Oct Sat & Sun 10.30am–6pm, hourly; €1.50 each way; ⓣ059 50 26 76), which leaves the Montgomery Dok to bob across the harbour. The ferry drops passengers on Maritiemplein, a ten-minute walk from **Fort Napoleon**, an impressive star-shaped structure built on the dunes immediately behind the seashore (April–June & Sept–Oct Tues–Sun 10am–6pm; July–Aug daily 10am–6pm; Nov–March Wed–Fri 1–5pm; €5; ⓦwww.fortnapoleon.be). Completed in 1812, this is one of the best preserved Napoleonic fortresses in Europe, its brick walls the work of Spanish prisoners of war. It had a garrison of 260 men and was defended by no less than 46 cannon, but although it's in good condition, there's nothing much to see and you'll soon end up at the café.

Eating and drinking

Ostend has scores of **cafés**, **café-bars** and **restaurants**, with a string of seafood places – and seafood stalls – lining up along Visserskaai. The town is a particularly great spot to sample what amounts to the country's national dish, North Sea mussels and French fries – and hundreds of Belgians come here to do just that. The city centre's **bars** are, on the other hand, rather harder to warm to, and although there are one or two exceptions, most are rough and ready or at least dark and gloomy.

De Bistronoom Vindictivelaan 22 ⓣ0473 73 48 01. This well-regarded restaurant is particularly strong on seafood, with the likes of hand-peeled grey shrimps, Ostend oysters and Norwegian king crab featuring on the menu. Emphasis is also given to local ingredients cooked in the traditional Flemish manner, often in beer. Main courses €22–30. Daily except Tues & Wed 11.30am–10pm.

Café Botteltje Louisastraat 19. Erzatz brown café with a bit more character than most of the bars in downtown Ostend – plus a formidable selection of bottled and draft beers. Mon 4.30pm–1am, Tues–Sun 11.30am–1am.

Le Grillon Visserskaai 31 ⓣ059 70 60 63. Among the string of seafood restaurants on Visserskaai, this is arguably the best, a smart but nonetheless relaxed little place with an excellent range of fresh fish served in delicious sauces. Mains hover around €25. Daily except Wed & Thurs noon–3pm & 6–10pm.

Mosselbeurs Dwarsstraat 10 ⓣ059 80 73 10. One of the liveliest restaurants in town, with cheerfully naff nautical fittings and top-notch fishy dishes, especially eels and mussels. Reasonable prices, too, with mains from €20. Wed–Sun noon–2pm & 6–10pm.

Café du Parc Marie Joséplein 3. Old-fashioned café, part of the *Hotel du Parc* (see p.122), whose main claim to fame is its Art Deco decor. Avoid the food. Daily from 10am.

De Zoete Zonde Christinastraat 54. Modest little café that's extremely popular with the locals for its light meals and pancakes, which are quite simply the best in town – and a snip at €3–6. Mon, Tues & Thurs–Sat 8am–6pm, Sun 1.30–6pm.

The coast east of Ostend

Heading east along the coast from Ostend, the undoubted highlight is **De Haan**, the prettiest and the most appealing seaside resort of them all. Beyond lie kiss-me-quick **Blankenberge** and the heavily industrialized port of **Zeebrugge**, both of which are best avoided – as is sprawling **Knokke-Heist**, though you might be drawn here by one of its many **festivals**, most notably the Internationaal Cartoonfestival (ⓦwww.cartoonfestival.be), which runs from the end of June to the middle of September.

The Kusttram – the coastal tram

Fast and efficient, the **Kusttram** (coastal tram; Ⓦwww.delijn.be/dekusttram) travels the length of the Belgian coast from Knokke-Heist in the east to De Panne in the west, putting all the Belgian resorts within easy striking distance of each other. There are numerous stops and one tram station, in Ostend beside the train station. Services in both directions depart every ten or fifteen minutes in summer, every half-hour in winter. There are **multilingual ticket machines** at most tram stops and there's a De Lijn **ticket office** at Ostend tram station. Tickets can also be bought from the driver, but in this case you pay a premium of around twenty percent. **Fares** are relatively inexpensive – Ostend to either Knokke-Heist or De Panne, for instance, costs €2 (€3 from the driver). You can also buy multiple journey tickets (Lijnkaart) at a discount on the regular price and tickets for unlimited tram travel, valid for either one day (*dagpas*; €5, €6 from the driver) or three days (*driedagenpas*; €10, €12).

De Haan

Established at the end of the nineteenth century, **DE HAAN** was conceived as an exclusive seaside village in a rustic Gothic Revival style known as *Style Normand*. The building plots were irregularly dispersed between the tram station and the sea, with the whole caboodle set around a pattern of winding streets reminiscent of – and influenced by – contemporaneous English suburbs such as Liverpool's Sefton Park. The only formality was provided by a central circus with a casino plonked in the middle, though this was demolished in 1929. Casino apart, De Haan has survived pretty much intact, a welcome relief from the surrounding high-rise development. Flanked by empty sand dunes, it's become a popular family resort, with an excellent **beach** and pleasant seafront promenade.

Practicalities

De Haan aan Zee **tram stop** is next to the **tourist office** (April–Oct daily 9.30am–noon & 1.30–5pm; Nov–March Sat & Sun 10am–noon & 2–5pm; Ⓣ059 24 21 35, Ⓦwww.dehaan.be), which is itself a five-minute walk from the beach. They have the details of local accommodation, including a number of **B&Bs** (❷), and issue a useful English-language leaflet describing walking and cycling routes in the vicinity of De Haan; **cycle hire** is available close by at André Fietsen, Leopoldlaan 9 (Ⓣ059 23 37 89, Ⓦwww.fietsenandre.be).

De Haan is chock-a-block with **cafés** and **restaurants**, which line up along the seafront and dot the streets on and around the central circus. One of the most popular spots for a snack or a light meal is *Brasserie Beaufort* (daily from 9am), a tearoom-cum-brasserie in one of the attractive Gothic Revival piles close to the tram stop at Koninklijk Plein 6. Much more upmarket is the *Restaurant Rabelais*, Van Eycklaan 2 (Ⓣ059 43 33 99; Wed–Sun 7–9pm, plus Sun noon–1.30pm), a smart, pricey and fairly formal restaurant, which focuses on set meals, with three courses from around €40. The food is nouvelle with the likes of Iberian pork in a pear sauce getting the taste buds working overtime. As for drinking, the **bar** of the *Hotel des Brasseurs*, just across from the tram stop, has the resort's widest range of beers.

Hotels

Auberge des Rois Zeedijk 1 Ⓣ059 23 30 18, Ⓦwww.beachhotel.be. This smart, modern, medium-sized hotel has a splendid location, overlooking the beach and a few metres from an undeveloped tract of sand dune. The guest rooms are decoratively uninspiring, but the best ones have wide sea views. ❻ with sea view, ❺ without.

Manoir Carpe Diem Prins Karellaan 12 Ⓣ059 23 32 20, Ⓦwww.manoircarpediem.com. Chichi, four-star hotel in a handsome *Style Normand* villa, which perches on a grassy knoll about 400m from

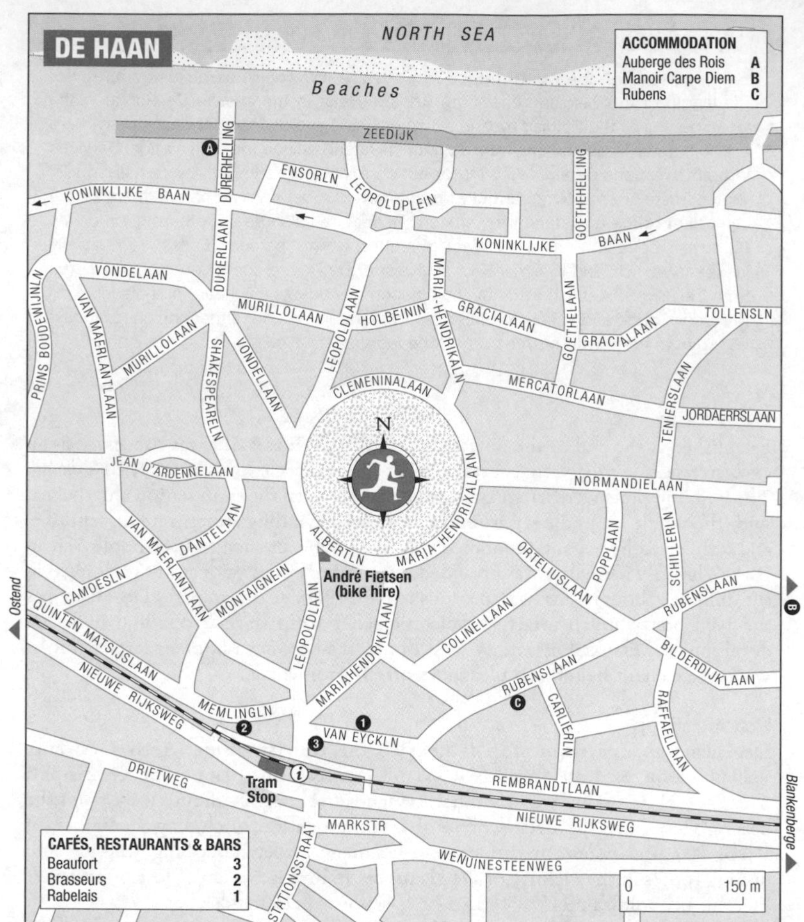

the beach. It's all very period – from the Dutch gables, open fires and heavy drapes through to the fifteen guest rooms, which are decorated in an attractive version of country-house style. There's an immaculate garden and an outside pool too. ❻

Hotel Rubens Rubenslaan 3 ⓣ059 24 22 00, ⓦwww.hotel-rubens.be. In a tastefully decorated modern house, the guest rooms at this three-star hotel are spotless and cosy in equal measure. The hotel prides itself on its banquet breakfasts, which can be taken outside in the garden when the weather is good. There's also an outside pool. ❸

The coast west of Ostend

Travelling west from Ostend, the Kusttram (coastal tram) skirts the sand dunes of a long and almost entirely undeveloped stretch of coast dotted with the substantial military remains of the **Atlantikwall** (Atlantic Wall), built during the German occupation of World War II to guard the coast from Allied invasion. Beyond, the tram cuts inland to round the estuary of the River Ijzer, scuttling through the small town of **Nieuwpoort**, scene of some of the bloodiest fighting in World War I, before proceeding onto **St-Idesbald**, home to the impressive Paul Delvaux Museum. After St-Idesbald comes **De Panne**, an uninspiring resort at the west end of the Belgian coast that is partly redeemed by its proximity to a pristine slice of beach and dune, **De Westhoekreservaat**.

The Atlantikwall

A chunk of the coast just to the west of Ostend has managed to dodge development and it's here you'll find the **Domein Raversijde**, a protected area whose most interesting attraction is the open-air **Atlantikwall** (April to mid-Nov Mon–Fri 2–5pm, Sat & Sun 10.30am–6pm; €6.50), a series of well-preserved gun emplacements, bunkers, pillboxes, tunnels, trenches and artillery pieces that line up along the dunes just behind the beach and the coastal tram line. The Germans had these elaborate fortifications constructed in World War II to forestall an Allied invasion, though in the event the Allies landed much further to the west in France.

To reach the Atlantikwall, get off the tram at the Domein Raversijde tram stop (not to be confused with the Raversijde stop), take the conspicuous wooden stairway over the dunes and then follow the signs. It takes between five and ten minutes to get there from the tram stop and you should allow about two hours more to walk the Atlantikwall itself.

Nieuwpoort

NIEUWPOORT (tram stop Nieuwpoort Stad) hasn't had much luck. Founded in the twelfth century, it was besieged nine times in the following six hundred years, but this was nothing compared to its misfortune in World War I. In 1914, the first German campaign reached the River Ijzer, prompting the Belgians to open the sluices along the Noordvaart Canal, just to the east of the town. The water stopped the invaders in their tracks and permanently separated the armies, but it also put Nieuwpoort on the front line, where it remained for the rest of the war. Every day volunteers had to abandon the safety of their bunkers to operate the ring of sluice gates, without which the water would either have drained away or risen to flood the Belgian trenches. Those grim days are recalled by the assorted **war memorials** placed round the ring of sluice gates that lies beside the bridge just to the east of the Nieuwpoort Stad tram stop. The largest monument consists of a sombre, Art Deco rotunda with King Albert I at the centre. Rather more cheerfully, Nieuwpoort is also home to one of the best fish shops on the coast, **Vishandel Albert**, just opposite the Nieuwpoort Stad tram stop at Kaai 27.

St-Idesbald: the Paul Delvaux Museum

ST-IDESBALD, one hour by tram from Ostend, is a well-heeled seaside town and resort that would be of no particular interest were it not for the artist **Paul Delvaux** (1897–1994), who stumbled across what was then an empty stretch of coast at the end of World War II and stayed here – despite the development that went on all around him – for the rest of his life. Delvaux's old home and studio have been turned into the **Paul Delvaux Museum**, Paul Delvauxlaan 42 (April–Sept Tues–Sun 10.30am–5.30pm; Oct–Dec Thurs–Sun 10.30am–5.30pm; €8; Ⓦwww.delvauxmuseum.com), which holds a comprehensive collection of his work, following his development from early Expressionist days through to the Surrealism that defined his oeuvre from the 1930s onwards. Two of his pet motifs were train stations, in one guise or another, and nude or semi-nude women set against some sort of classical backdrop. His intention was to usher the viewer into the unconscious with dreamlike images where every perspective is exact, but, despite the impeccable craftsmanship, there's something very cold about his vision.

At their best, his paintings achieve an almost palpable sense of foreboding, good examples being *The Garden* of 1971 and *The Procession* dated to 1963, while *The Station in the Forest* of 1960 has the most wonderful trees.

Finding the museum is a bit tricky. From the St-Idesbald tram stop, walk 100m or so west towards De Panne, turn left (away from the coast) down the resort's main street, Strandlaan, and keep going until you reach Albert Nazylaan, where you go right to follow the signs to the museum; the walk takes about fifteen minutes.

De Panne and De Westhoekreservaat

From St-Idesbald, it only takes the tram a couple of minutes to slide into **DE PANNE**, sitting close to the French border and now one of the largest settlements on the Belgian coast – though as late as the 1880s it was a tiny fishing village of low white cottages, nestling in the wooded hollow (*panne*) from which it takes its name. The town achieved ephemeral fame in World War I, when it was part of the tiny triangle of Belgian territory that the German army failed to occupy, becoming the home of King Albert's government from 1914 to 1918. A generation later, the retreating British army managed to reach the sand dunes between De Panne and Dunkirk, 15km to the west, just in time for their miraculous evacuation back to England – in eight days, an armada of vessels of all sizes and shapes rescued over three hundred thousand Allied soldiers.

On the western edge of De Panne, a small segment of these same sand dunes has been protected by the creation of **De Westhoekreservaat**, an expanse of wild, unspoiled coastline whose dunes, grasslands and scrub are crisscrossed by a network of marked footpaths. The main access point is about 2km west of the town centre: follow Duinkerkelaan, the main east–west street, to the traffic island, turn right down Dynastielaan and keep going as far as the T-junction at the end, where you make a left turn along Schuilhavenlaan. The walk is a bore, but the tram does go as far as the traffic island.

Veurne

Rural Flanders at its prettiest, **VEURNE** is a charming market town just 7km inland by road and rail from De Panne. Founded in the ninth century, Veurne was originally one of a chain of fortresses built to defend the region from the raids of the Vikings, but without much success. The town failed to flourish and two centuries later it was small, poor and insignificant. All that changed when Robert II of Flanders returned from the Crusades in 1099 with a piece of the **True Cross**. His ship was caught in a gale, and in desperation he vowed to offer the relic to the first church he saw if he survived. He did, and the lucky church was Veurne's St-Walburgakerk, which became an important centre of medieval pilgrimage for some two hundred years, a real fillip to the local economy. These days Veurne is one of the more popular day-trip destinations in West Flanders, a neat and very amenable backwater whose one real attraction is its **Grote Markt**, one of the best-preserved town squares in Belgium.

Arrival, information and accommodation

Veurne's **train station** and main **bus stops** are located a five-minute stroll from the **tourist office**, which is right in the centre at Grote Markt 29 (April–Sept daily 10am–noon & 1.30–5.30pm; Oct to mid-Nov daily 10am–noon & 2–4pm; mid-Nov to March Mon–Sat 10am–noon & 2–4pm; Ⓣ058 33 55 31, Ⓦwww.vvvveurne.be). There are three **bicycle rental** outlets in town, the most central

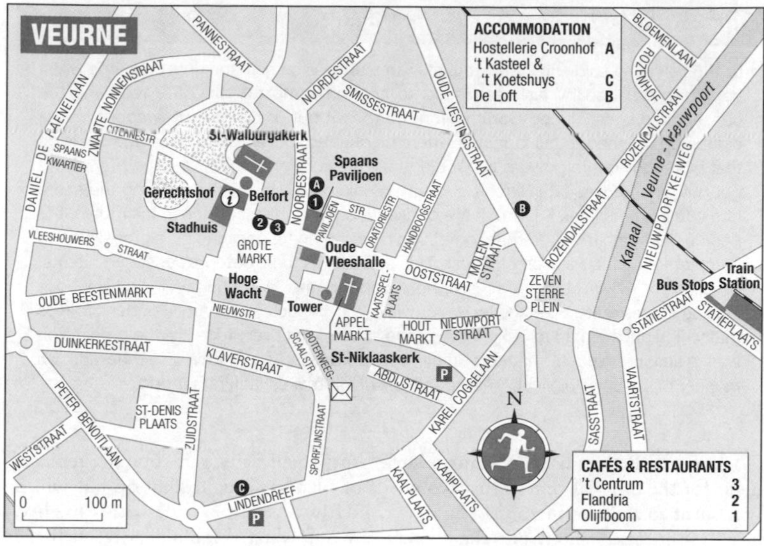

of which is at *Hotel De Loft* (see below). As regards **accommodation**, there are lots of B&Bs (❶–❷) in and around town – the tourist office has the details – and three central hotels.

Hotels

Hostellerie Croonhof Noordstraat 9 ⓣ058 31 31 28, ⓦwww.croonhof.be. This smart and well-cared-for three-star hotel, in an attractively converted old house just off the Grote Markt, has fourteen spotless rooms of modern demeanour. Advance reservations are advised in the summer. ❸

't Kasteel & 't Koetshuys Lindendreef 5 ⓣ058 31 53 72, ⓦwww.kasteelenkoetshuys.be. Family-run hotel in a sympathetically renovated Edwardian mansion which now comes complete with a sauna. The large and well-appointed guest rooms are decorated in relaxing pastel shades and have high ceilings and marble fireplaces. ❹

De Loft Oude Vestingstraat 36 ⓣ058 31 59 49, ⓦwww.deloft.be. In a cleverly recycled industrial building, this eight-room hotel is an inventive affair, with a café, a kids' play area and a small art gallery. The guest rooms are kitted out in the full flush of modern style with lots of greys, creams and blues. ❸

The Town

All of Veurne's leading sights are on or around the **Grote Markt**, beginning in the northwest corner with the **Stadhuis** (guided tours daily: April–Sept 10am–noon & 2–5pm; Oct to mid-Nov 10am–noon & 2–4pm; €3), an engaging mix of Gothic and Renaissance styles built between 1596 and 1612 and equipped with a fine blue-and-gold decorated stone loggia projecting from the original brick facade. The interior displays items of unexceptional interest, the best of which is a set of leather wall coverings made in Córdoba. The Stadhuis connects with the more austere classicism of the **Gerechtshof** (Law Courts), whose symmetrical pillars and long, rectangular windows now hold the tourist office, but once sheltered the Inquisition as it set about the Flemish peasantry with gusto. The attached tiered and balconied **Belfort** (belfry; no public access) was completed in 1628, its Gothic lines culminating in a dainty Baroque tower, from where carillon concerts ring out over the town throughout the summer.

Boeteprocessie (Penitents' Procession)

In 1650 a young soldier by the name of Mannaert was on garrison duty in Veurne when he was persuaded by his best friend to commit a **mortal sin**. After receiving the consecrated wafer during Communion, he took it out of his mouth, wrapped it in a cloth, and returned to his lodgings where he charred it over a fire, under the delusion that by reducing it to powder he would make himself invulnerable to injury. The news got out, and he was later arrested, tried and executed, his friend suffering the same fate a few weeks later. Fearful of the consequences of this sacrilege in their town, the people of Veurne resolved that something must be done, deciding on a procession to commemorate the Passion of Christ. This survives as the **Boeteprocessie** (Penitents' Procession; Ⓦwww.boeteprocessie.be), held on the last Sunday in July, whose leading figures dress up in the brown cowls of the Capuchins to carry wooden crosses that weigh anything up to 50kg through the streets. Until very recently, the procession was a serious-minded, macabre affair, but nowadays lots of locals clamber into all manner of vaguely "biblical" gear to join in, which makes it all rather odd.

Behind the Belfort is **St-Walburgakerk** (April–Sept daily 9am–6pm), a replacement for the original church that Robert II of Flanders caught sight of, but which was burnt to a cinder in 1353. The new church was begun in style with a mighty, heavily buttressed choir, but the money ran out when the builders reached the transepts and the nave – a truncated affair if ever there was one – was only finished off in 1904. The interior has three virtues: the ornately carved Flemish Renaissance choir stalls; a handsome set of stained-glass windows, some Gothic, some neo-Gothic; and the superb stonework of the tubular, composite columns at the central crossing.

At the northeast corner of the Grote Markt, the **Spaans Paviljoen** (Spanish Pavilion) was built as the town hall in the middle of the fifteenth century, but takes its name from its later adaptation as the officers' quarters of the Habsburg garrison. It's a self-confident structure, the initial square brick tower, with its castellated parapet, extended by a facade of long, slender windows and flowing stone tracery in the true Gothic manner – an obvious contrast to the Flemish shutters and gables of the **Oude Vleeshalle** (Old Meat Hall) standing directly opposite.

Crossing over to the southeast side of the square, the **Hoge Wacht**, which originally housed the town watch, displays a fetching amalgam of styles, its brick gable decorated with a small arcaded gallery. The east side of this building edges the Appelmarkt, home to the low-slung medieval brickwork of **St-Niklaaskerk**, whose detached tower gives spectacular views over the surrounding countryside (mid-June to mid-Sept 10–11.45am & 2–5.15pm; €1.50).

Eating and drinking

To cater for all the day-trippers, Veurne has a small army of **cafés** and **bars** – by and large nothing fancy, but reliable places serving large portions of traditional Flemish food. Given its proximity to the coast, Veurne is also a good spot to try the classic Flemish treat, mussels and chips.

't Centrum Grote Markt 33. Popular café-bar, with a large pavement terrace, offering reasonably priced snacks and meals from a straightforward Flemish menu; pancakes are a house speciality. Tues–Sun 8am to midnight.

Flandria Grote Markt 30. Cosy café-bar next door to the tourist office where the Flemish snacks and meals are best washed down with a Trappist ale, of which they have a wide range. Daily except Thurs 9am till late.

Olijfboom Noordstraat 3 Ⓣ058 31 70 77. The best restaurant in town, this chic and modern place has a well-considered French menu where the lobster (*kreeft*) and bouillabaisse are hard to beat; mains average €25. Tues–Sat noon–2pm & 7–9.30pm.

Around Veurne: Lo and Diksmuide

Veurne is the capital of the **Veurne-Ambacht**, a pancake-flat agricultural region of quiet villages and narrow country lanes that stretches south of the town, encircled by the French border and the canalized River Ijzer. Of all the villages, **Lo** is the prettiest, but the district also holds a sprinkling of World War I sights that lie dotted along the line of the **River Ijzer**, which formed the front line for most of the war; the most interesting of these are in the vicinity of the small town of **Diksmuide**.

The best way to see the district is by **bike** – cycles can be rented in Veurne (see p.128), where maps of routes are available from the tourist office (see p.128). Alternatively, De Lijn (Ⓣ070 220 200, Ⓦwww.delijn.be) operates a patchy **bus** service from both Veurne and Ieper to Lo (for details see p.198), and there are hourly trains from Veurne to Diksmuide.

Lo

The agreeable little hamlet of **LO**, off the N8 some 15km southeast of Veurne, has one claim to fame. It was here that Julius Caesar tethered his horse to a yew on his way across Gaul, an event recalled by a plaque and a battered old tree by what is now the **Westpoort**, whose twin turrets and gateway are all that remains of Lo's medieval ramparts. Less apocryphally, the village once prospered under the patronage of its Augustinian **abbey**, founded in the twelfth century and suppressed by the French Revolutionary army. Of the abbey, only the **dovecote** survives, a flashy affair hidden away beside the *Hotel Oude Abdij*, which is itself tucked in behind the village **church**, whose graceful spire soars high above the Markt. Lo's old stone houses fan out from the square – nothing remarkable, it's the peace and quiet that appeals.

From September to June only, Lo is on the Veurne–Ieper **bus** route and buses pull in near the Markt, where the *Hotel Stadhuis* (Ⓣ058 28 80 16, Ⓦwww.stadhuis-lo.be; ❷) offers a handful of clean, simple, en-suite rooms inside the old town hall, a much-modified sixteenth-century structure made appealing by a slender tower. The ground-floor **restaurant** (closed Tues & Wed) serves good quality Flemish food in pleasant surroundings; mains cost around €20.

Diksmuide

From Lo, it's a short hop of about 12km northeast past the Ijzertoren (see below) to **DIKSMUIDE**, a modest little town on the east bank of the River Ijzer – which turned out to be a particularly unfortunate location in World War I. In 1914, the German offensive across Belgium came to a grinding halt when it reached the river, which then formed the front line for the next four years. As a result, Diksmuide was literally shelled to pieces, so much so that by 1918 its location could only be identified from a map. Painstakingly rebuilt in the 1920s, the reconstruction works best in the **Grote Markt**, a pleasant, spacious square flanked by an attractive set of brick gables in traditional Flemish style. There's nothing outstanding to see, but it's an enjoyable spot to nurse a coffee and you can't help but notice the large and heroic-looking statue of **Colonel Jacques** (1858–1928), the commander of the Belgian 12th Line Regiment, which did so much to delay the German advance in 1914.

The Ijzertoren

A ten-minute walk from the Grote Markt via Reuzemolenstraat and Ijzerlaan, the domineering **Ijzertoren** (April–Sept Mon–Fri 9am–6pm, Sat & Sun 10am–6pm; Oct–March Mon–Fri 9am–5pm, Sat & Sun 10am–5pm; €7; Ⓦwww.ijzertoren.org) is a massive war memorial and museum which, at 84m, rises high above the

River Ijzer. The present structure, a broody affair dating from the 1950s, bears the letters **AVV-VVK** – Alles voor Vlaanderen ("All for Flanders") and Vlaanderen voor Kristus ("Flanders for Christ") – in a heady mix of religion and nationalism. The tower is actually the second version – the original, erected in 1930, was blown up in mysterious circumstances in 1946: Belgium's French-speakers usually blame Flemish Fascists disappointed at the defeat of Hitler, whilst the Flemings accuse French-speaking leftists, who allegedly took offence at the avowedly Flemish character of the memorial.

In front of the Ijzertoren are a few incidental memorials, principally the **Pax gateway** of 1950, built of rubble from the original tower, and a **crypt** holding the gravestones of a number of Belgian soldiers. **Lifts** inside the Ijzertoren whisk visitors up to the top, from where there are grand views out across West Flanders, and this is also where you start a visit to the **war museum**, which has about twenty floors, each getting larger as you descend the tapering tower. The displays start with a bitter little section on the unequal treatment dished out to the Flemings by Belgium's French-speakers in general and the Belgian army's Francophone officer class in particular – and the subsequent rise of the Flemish Movement. Thereafter, the museum hits a more assured tone, tracking through World War I from its beginnings to the invasion of Belgium and continuing on to World War II. Included are a couple of **re-created trenches** – and very convincing they are too – as well as a number of mini-sections on the likes of gas and gas masks, trench art (featuring all manner of carved and decorated shell casings), and **animals at war**, with a couple of very odd photos of dogs wearing gas masks. There are also several sections describing how part of the Flemish Nationalist Movement collaborated with the Germans during both world wars; several of its leaders, most notably August Borms, were shot for their treachery at the end of World War II.

The Dodengang

There's a second reminder of World War I about 1.5km to the north of the Ijzertoren along the west bank of the river. The **Dodengang** (Trench of Death; April to mid-Nov daily 10am–5pm; mid-Nov to March Tues & Fri 9.30am–4pm; free) was an especially dangerous slice of trench that was held by the Belgians throughout the war. Around 400m of trench are viewable and although the original sandbags have, of necessity, been replaced by concrete imitations, it's all very well done – and the attached museum fills in the military background.

Practicalities

From Diksmuide's **train** and adjacent **bus station**, it's a five-minute walk along L-shaped Stationsstraat to the Grote Markt, where the **tourist office** is at no. 28 (Easter to mid-Nov daily 10am–noon & 2–5pm; mid-Nov to March Mon–Fri 10am–noon & 2–5pm; ⓣ051 51 91 46, ⓦwww.diksmuide.be). Easily the best **accommodation** hereabouts is *De Groote Waere*, Vladslostraat 21 (ⓣ0477 24 19 38, ⓦwww.degrootewaere.be; ❷), a top-notch B&B on a farm about 4.5km from Diksmuide. Breakfast is served in the attractively modernized farmhouse, and the barnlike annexe behind holds several comfortable, modern rooms with all mod cons. To get there, drive east from Diksmuide on the N35, take the Vladslo turning and it's beside the road on the left.

For **food**, the neat and trim café-restaurant of the *Polderbloem*, Grote Markt 8 (ⓣ051 50 29 05; daily except Tues from 8am), offers a lively, creative menu with the emphasis on local, seasonal ingredients; main courses here average about €20. Also on the Grote Markt, at no.17, is *Fijnbakkerij*, a modern café where the coffee is good and the cakes are better (Sun & Mon 7am–4pm, Wed–Sat 7am–6.30pm).

Ieper and around

At heart, **IEPER**, about 30km southeast of Veurne, is a pleasant, middling sort of place, a typical Flemish small town with a bright and breezy main square overlooked by the haughty reminders of its medieval heyday as a centre of the cloth trade. Initial appearances are, however, deceptive, for all the old buildings of the town centre were built from scratch after World War I, when Ieper – or **Ypres** as it was then known – was shelled to smithereens, the reconstruction a tribute to the remarkable determination of the town's citizens. Today, with its clutch of good-quality restaurants and hotels, Ieper is an enjoyable place to spend a couple of nights, especially if you're after exploring the assorted **World War I** cemeteries, monuments and memorials that speckle both the town and its environs, the most famous of which are the **Menin Gate** and **Tyne Cot**.

Some history

Ieper's long and troubled history dates back to the tenth century, when it was founded at the point where the Bruges–Paris trade route crossed the River Ieperlee. Success came quickly and the town became a major player in the **cloth trade**, its thirteenth-century population of two hundred thousand sharing economic control of the region with rivals Ghent and Bruges. The most precariously sited of the great Flemish cities, Ypres was too near the French frontier for comfort, and too strategically important to be ignored by any of the armies whose campaigns crisscrossed the town's surroundings with depressing frequency. The city governors kept disaster at bay by reinforcing their defences and switching alliances whenever necessary, fighting against the French at the Battle of the Golden Spurs in 1302 (see p.143), and with them forty years later at Roosebeke. The first **major misjudgement** came in 1383 after Henry Spencer, bishop of Norwich, landed at Calais under the pretext of supporting the armies of Pope Urban VI, who occupied the Vatican, against his rival Clement VII, who was installed in Avignon. The burghers of Ghent and Bruges flocked to Spencer's standard, and the allies had little difficulty in agreeing on an attack against Ypres, which had decided to champion Clement and trust the French for support. The ensuing siege lasted two months before a French army appeared to save the day, and all of Ypres celebrated the victory. In fact, the town was ruined, its trade never recovered and, unable to challenge its two main competitors again, many of the weavers upped sticks and migrated. The process of depopulation proved irreversible, and by the sixteenth century the town had shrunk to a mere five thousand inhabitants.

In **World War I**, the first German thrust of 1914 left a bulge in the Allied line to the immediate east of Ypres. This **Salient** (see pp.137–141) preoccupied the generals of both sides and during the next four years a series of bloody and particularly futile offensives attempted to break the stalemate – with disastrous consequences for Ypres, which served as the Allied communications centre. Comfortably within range of the German artillery, Ypres was rapidly reduced to rubble and its inhabitants had to be evacuated in 1915. After the war, the returning population decided to rebuild their town, a remarkable twenty-year project in which the most prominent medieval buildings – the old cloth hall, the **Lakenhalle**, and the **cathedral** – were meticulously reconstructed. The end result must once have seemed strangely antiseptic – old-style edifices with no signs of decay or erosion – but now, after eighty-odd years, the brickwork has mellowed and the centre looks authentically antique and rather handsome.

Arrival and information

Ieper's **train** and **bus stations** stand on the western edge of the centre, a ten-minute walk from the Grote Markt. The **tourist office**, in the Lakenhalle on the Grote Markt (April to mid-Nov Mon–Fri 9am–6pm, Sat & Sun 10am–6pm; mid-Nov to March Mon–Fri 9am–5pm, Sat & Sun 10am–5pm; ⓣ 057 23 92 20, ⓦ www.ieper.be), has details of car and cycle routes around the Salient and sells a first-rate range of books on World War I. **Bike rental** is available at the train station from April to September and all year from the *Hotel Ambrosia*, D'Hondtstraat 54 (ⓣ 057 36 63 66). There are no major **car rental** companies – ask at the tourist office for local suppliers – but several **taxi** firms, try *Taxi Leo* (ⓣ 057 20 04 13).

Accommodation

Ieper tourist office has the details of around twenty **B&Bs** (❶–❷), though the majority are either out in the sticks or on the peripheries of town. Most of Ieper's **hotels** are, by comparison, much more central and there's a handily located **campsite** too.

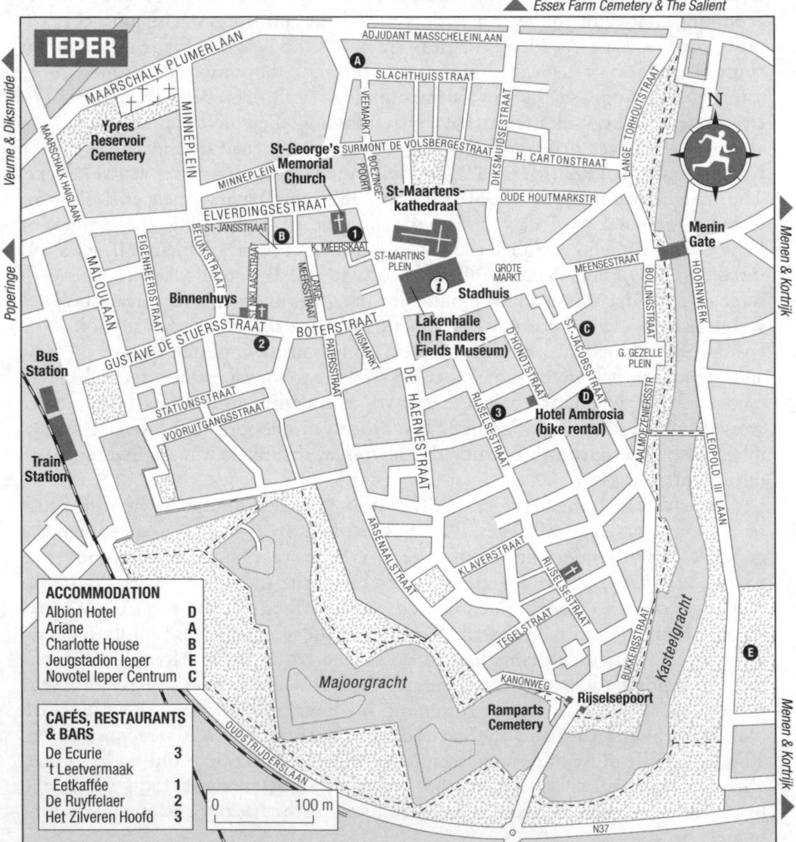

Hotels

Albion Hotel St-Jacobsstraat 28 ⓣ057 20 02 20, ⓦwww.albionhotel.be. Very appealing three-star hotel with eighteen large and well-appointed en-suite guest rooms decorated in an easy going modern style. The public areas are commodious, the breakfasts are good, and it's in a handy location, a brief stroll from the Grote Markt. ❹

Ariane Slachthuisstraat 58 ⓣ057 21 82 18, ⓦwww.ariane.be. A prim and proper garden flanks this ultramodern four-star, a 5min walk north of the Grote Markt. Presumably it was built with the passing business trade in mind, but somehow it looks a little marooned rather than secluded, despite the water fountain and mature trees. Nevertheless, the fifty en-suite rooms are large, well appointed and very comfortable. ❺

Charlotte House St Jansstraat 14 ⓣ0477 33 91 83, ⓦwww.charlotteshouse.be. A stone's throw from the town centre, this 1920s terrace house has been pleasantly re-equipped to accommodate a three-bedroom B&B (though the owners don't actually live here). The rooms are all en suite and are decorated in a no-frills modern manner with wooden floors and simple furnishings. Guests also have use of the kitchen and lounge. ❷

Novotel Ieper Centrum St-Jacobsstraat 15 ⓣ057 42 90 00, ⓦwww.novotel.com. Lovers of chain hotels will be pleased to find this here in Ieper. The building is a bit of a modern bruiser, but the hundred-odd rooms are all comfortably modern in true *Novotel* style, and there are fitness facilities and a sauna. ❹

Campsite

Jeugstadion Ieper Bolwerkstraat 1, off Karel Steverlyncklaan ⓣ057 21 72 82, ⓦwww.jeugdstadion.be. Pocket-sized campsite in a leafy location across the canal from the southeast tip of town. You can walk there via Leopold III-laan – it takes about twenty-five minutes from the train station – but drivers have to use the ring road, the N37. Tent pitches, car and tent pitches, bike hire and four hikers' huts (❶). March to mid-Nov.

The Town

A monument to the power and wealth of the medieval guilds, the **Lakenhalle**, on the Grote Markt, is a copy of the thirteenth-century original that stood beside the River Ieperlee, which now flows underground. Too long to be pretty and too square to be elegant, it's nonetheless an impressive edifice, one that was built with practical considerations uppermost: no fewer than 48 doors once gave access from the street to the old selling halls, while boats sailed in and out of the jetty on the west wing, under the watchful eyes of the mighty turreted belfry. During winter, wool was stored on the upper floor and **cats** were brought in to keep the mice down. The cats may have had a good time in winter, but they couldn't have relished the prospect of spring, when they were thrown out of the windows to a hostile crowd below as part of the **Kattestoet** or Cats' Festival, the slaughter intended to symbolize the killing of evil spirits. The festival ran right up until 1817, and was revived in 1938, when the cats were (mercifully) replaced by cloth imitations. Since then it's developed into Ieper's principal shindig, held every three years on the second Sunday in May – the next one is in 2012. The main event is the parade of cats, a large-scale celebration of all things feline, complete with processions, dancers and bands, and some of the biggest models and puppets imaginable.

The interior of the Lakenhalle holds the ambitious **In Flanders Fields Museum** (April to mid-Nov daily 10am–6pm; mid-Nov to March Tues–Sun 10am–5pm; €8; ⓦwww.inflandersfields.be), which focuses on the experiences of those caught up in the war rather than the ebb and flow of the military campaigns, though these are sketched in too. The exhibits are wide-ranging and thoughtful, and the multilingual quotations well chosen, but above all it's the photographs that steal the show: soldiers grimly digging trenches, the pathetic casualties of a gas attack, flyblown corpses in the mud and panoramas of a blasted landscape.

The Stadhuis, the cathedral and St George's

The east end of the Lakenhalle is attached to the dinky little **Stadhuis**, whose fancy Renaissance facade rises above an elegant arcaded gallery. Round the back rises **St-Maartenskathedraal**, a 1930 copy of the thirteenth-century Gothic original. The church's cavernous nave is a formal, rather bland affair, but the rose window above the south transept door is a fine tribute to King Albert I of Belgium, its yellow, green, red and blue stained glass the gift of the British armed forces. Just to the northwest of the cathedral, at the end of Elverdingsestraat, is **St George's Memorial Church** (daily 9.30am–8pm), a modest brick building finished in 1929. The interior is crowded with brass plaques honouring the dead of many British regiments, and the chairs carry individual and regimental tributes. It's hard not to be moved, for there's nothing vainglorious in this public space, so consumed as it is with private grief.

The Ypres Reservoir Cemetery and onto the Vismarkt

From St George's, it's a brief walk to the silent graves of the **Ypres Reservoir Cemetery**, laid out to a pre-ordained plan (see p.138) and one of two British Commonwealth graveyards in the town centre. Doubling back from the cemetery to Boterstraat, take a look at the **Binnenhuys**, an elegant eighteenth-century mansion in the French style that was, remarkably enough, the only Ieper building to survive World War I intact. Close by, also on Boterstraat, watch out for the fancy Baroque portal that leads through to the old **Vismarkt** (fish market), another 1920s reconstruction, complete with canopied stone stalls and a dinky little toll house.

The Menin Gate and the Ramparts Cemetery

East of the Grote Markt, the massive **Menin Gate** war memorial was built on the site of the old Menenpoort, which served as the main route for British soldiers heading for the front. It's a simple, brooding monument, towering over the edge of the town, its walls covered with the names of those fifty thousand British and Commonwealth troops who died in the Ypres Salient but have no grave. The simple inscription above the lists of the dead has none of the arrogance of the victor, but rather a sense of great loss. The self-justifying formality of the memorial did, however, offend many veterans and prompted a bitter verse from Siegfried Sassoon:

Was ever an immolation so belied
As these intolerably nameless names?
Well might the Dead who struggled in slime
Rise and deride this sepulchre of crime.

Volunteers from the local fire brigade sound the **Last Post** beneath the gate each and every evening at 8pm. Sometimes it's an extremely moving ceremony, especially when the fire brigade is joined by other bands, but at other times it's noisy and really rather crass with scores of school kids milling around.

Curiously, the seventeenth-century brick and earthen **ramparts** on either side of the Menin Gate were strong enough to survive World War I in good condition – the vaults even served as some of the safest bunkers on the front. These massive ramparts and their protective moat still extend right round the east and south of the town centre, and a pleasant **footpath** runs along the top amid scores of mature horse-chestnut trees to a second British Commonwealth graveyard, the **Ramparts Cemetery**.

Eating and drinking

A string of **cafés** and **restaurants** flanks Ieper's Grote Markt, but there are several better – and cheaper – places close by. Almost all of Ieper's **bars** are on the main square too, and though the action could hardly be described as frenetic, there's enough to keep most visitors happy.

Cafés and restaurants

Restaurant De Ecurie Arthur Merghelynckstraat 1A ⓣ057 36 03 67. Smooth and polished restaurant serving upmarket Flemish cuisine with an international twist – the guinea fowl and the scallops are especially tasty. Mains average €23. Tues–Sat 11.30am–2pm & 6.30–10pm.

't Leetvermaak Eetkaffée Korte Meersstraat 2 ⓣ057 21 63 85. Excellent café-restaurant, with tastefully upgraded premises and a smooth, jazzy soundtrack. The food hits all the Flemish buttons and then some, but it's the Mediterranean dishes which catch the eye, with superb Spanish/Portuguese concoctions for as little as €19, less if you stick to the daily specials. Cultural events are staged here too. Wed–Fri & Sun 11.30am–1.30pm & 6–11pm, plus Tues & Sat 6–11pm.

De Ruyffelaer Gustave de Stuersstraat 9 ⓣ057 36 60 06. Especially cosy restaurant kitted out with all sorts of local bygones and offering delicious home-made food, with Flemish dishes uppermost – the stews are outstanding. Mains average €18. Wash it down with Hommel, the tangy local ale from the neighbouring town of Poperinge. Thurs & Fri 5.30–10pm, Sat & Sun from 11.30am.

Het Zilveren Hoofd Rijselsestraat 49. Amenable café-cum-snack bar offering filling and reasonably tasty dishes from as little as €10. The pastas are the best bet. Next door to – and run by the same people as – the *Restaurant De Ecurie* (see above). Tues–Sat 11am–10pm.

The Ypres Salient

Immediately to the east of Ieper, the **Ypres Salient** occupies a basin-shaped parcel of land about 25km long, and never more than 15km deep. For the

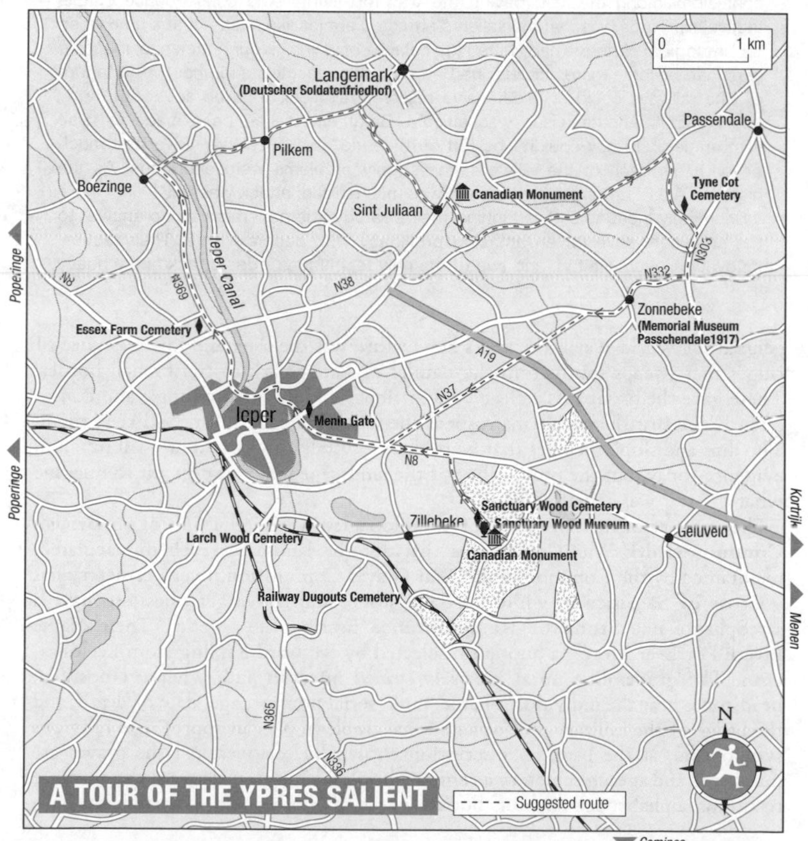

The Ypres Salient

The creation of the **Ypres Salient** was entirely **accidental**. When the German army launched the war in the west by invading Belgium, they were following the principles – if not the details – laid down by a chief of the German General Staff, Alfred von Schlieffen, who had died eight years earlier. The idea was simple: to avoid fighting a war on two fronts, the German army would outflank the French and capture Paris by attacking through Belgium, well before the Russians had assembled on the eastern frontier. It didn't work, with the result that as the initial German offensive ground to a halt, so two lines of opposing **trenches** were dug, which soon stretched from the North Sea down to Switzerland.

No one knew quite what to do next, but attention focused on the two main bulges – or **salients** – in the line, one at Ieper, the other at Verdun, on the Franco-German frontier just to the south of Luxembourg. To the Allied generals, the bulge at Ieper – the **Ypres Salient** – was a good place to break through the German lines and roll up their front; to the Germans it represented an ideal opportunity to break the deadlock by attacking enemy positions from several sides at the same time. To make matters worse, contemporary **military doctrine** on both sides held that the way to win a war was to destroy the enemy's strongest forces first. In retrospect this may seem strange, but the generals of the day were schooled in cavalry tactics, where a charge that broke the enemy's key formations was guaranteed to spread disorder and confusion among the rest, paving the way for victory. The consequence of this tactical similitude was that the salients attracted armies like magnets at a time when **technological changes** had shifted the balance of war in favour of defence: machine guns had become more efficient, barbed wire more effective and, most important of all, the railways could shift defensive reserves far faster than an advancing army could march. Another issue was **supply**. Great efforts had been made to raise vast armies but they couldn't be fed off the land, and once they advanced much beyond the reach of the railways, the supply problems were enormous. As the historian A.J.P. Taylor put it, "Defence was mechanized; attack was not".

Seemingly incapable of rethinking their strategy, the generals had no answer to the stalemate save for an amazing profligacy with people's lives. Their tactical innovations were limited, and two of the new techniques – gas attack and a heavy

generals of World War I, the area's key feature was the long and low sequence of ridges that sweeps south from the hamlet of Langemark to the French border. These gave the occupants a clear view of Ieper and its surroundings, and consequently the British and Germans spent the war trying to capture and keep them. The dips and sloping ridges that were then so vitally important are still much in evidence today, but the tranquillity of the landscape makes it difficult to imagine what the war was actually like.

The most resonant reminders of the blood-letting are the 160 or so **British Commonwealth War Cemeteries** that dot the landscape, each immaculately maintained by the Commonwealth War Graves Commission. Every cemetery has a **Cross of Sacrifice** in white Portland stone, and the larger ones also have a sarcophagus-like **Stone of Remembrance** bearing the legend "Their Name Liveth For Ever More", a quotation selected by Rudyard Kipling from Ecclesiasticus. The **graves** line up at precisely spaced intervals and, wherever possible, headstones bear the individual's name, rank, serial number, age, date of death, and the badge of the military unit or a national emblem, plus an appropriate religious symbol and, at the base, an inscription chosen by relatives. All the graves are numbered and at each cemetery a **registry book** is kept in an alcove at the entrance recording alphabetically who is buried where, if – of course – the remains have preliminary bombardment – actually made matters worse. The **shells** forewarned the enemy of an offensive and churned the trenches into a muddy maelstrom where men, horses and machinery were simply engulfed; the **gas** was as dangerous to the advancing soldiers as it was to the retreating enemy. **Tanks** could have broken the impasse, but their development was never prioritized.

Naturally enough, soldiers of all armies involved lost confidence in their generals, and by 1917, despite court martials and firing squads, the sheer futility of the endless round of failed offensives made **desertion** commonplace and threatened to bring mass mutiny to the western front. Yet, although it is undeniably true that few of the military commanders of the day showed much understanding of how to break the deadlock – and they have been savagely criticized for their failures – some of the blame must be apportioned to the politicians. They demanded attack rather than defence, and continued to call for a general "victory" even after it had become obvious that this was beyond reach and that each assault cost thousands of lives. In the event, none of the governments concerned was able to adjust to the **military impasse**. There were no moves toward a negotiated settlement, because no one was quite sure what they would settle for – a lack of clarity that contrasted starkly with the jingoistic sentiments stirred up to help sustain the conflict in the first place. In this context, how could a general recommend a defensive strategy or a politician propose a compromise? Those who did were dismissed.

This was the background to the four years of war that raged in and around the Ypres Salient, the scene of **four major battles**. The first, in October and November of 1914, settled the lines of the bulge as both armies tried to outflank each other; and the second was a German attack the following spring that moved the trenches a couple of kilometres west. The third, launched by British Empire soldiers in July 1917, was even more pointless, with thousands of men dying for an advance of only a few kilometres. It's frequently called the Battle of Passchendaele, but Lloyd George more accurately referred to it as the "battle of the mud", a disaster that cost 250,000 British lives. The fourth and final battle, in April 1918, was another German attack inspired by General Ludendorff's desire to break the British army. Instead it broke his own, and led to the **Armistice** of November 11.

been identified: thousands of gravestones do not carry any or all of these tags as the bodies were buried without proper identification. If you are looking for the grave of someone in particular, consult the **Commonwealth War Graves Commission**'s excellent website (Ⓦ www.cwgc.org).

Visiting the Ypres Salient

If you're undertaking a detailed exploration of the Ypres Salient, then the best place to start is *Major & Mrs Holt's Pocket Battlefield Guide to the Ypres Salient*, a well-written and thoroughly researched book that details all its nooks and crannies, both in the full version and in a shorter edition. Both are on sale at Ieper tourist office, but note that the **maps** in the book are insufficient and you're best off supplementing them with the detailed Westhoek Zuid map, again available at the tourist office. With less time, we've also described a short **driving tour** below and this can be completed comfortably in half a day, a day if you dilly and dally. Alternatively, **guided tours** beginning in Ieper are provided by both Flanders Battlefield Tours (Ⓣ 057 36 04 60, Ⓦ www.ypres-fbt.com), which offers four-hour and two-and-a-half-hour trips for €35 and €30 respectively, and Salient Tours (Ⓣ 057 21 46 57, Ⓦ www.salienttours.be), with a similar programme at about the same prices. For both operators, advance reservations are strongly advised. For those staying in Bruges, Quasimodo operates excellent all-inclusive battlefield tours from Bruges to Ieper and back (see p.152).

A short tour of the Salient

Ieper's one-way system initially makes things a little confusing, but leave the town to the north along the **N369**, the road to Diksmuide. About 3km from the centre of Ieper, just beyond the flyover, keep an eye out for **Essex Farm Cemetery** on the right, where the dead were brought from the neighbouring battlefield. In the bank behind – and to the left of – the cemetery's Cross of Sacrifice are the remains of several British bunkers, part of a combined forward position and first-aid post, where the Canadian **John McCrae** wrote the war's best-known poem, *In Flanders Fields*:

. . . We are the Dead. Short days ago
We lived, felt dawn, saw sunsets glow,
Loved and were loved, and now we lie
In Flanders fields . . .

Back on the N369, proceed north for another 3km and you'll reach the next bridge over the canal. Turn right over the bridge and drive the 4.5km east to **LANGEMARK**, a largish village just beyond which (follow the signs) is a German war cemetery, the **Deutscher Soldatenfriedhof**. Nearly forty-five thousand German soldiers are buried here, mostly in communal graves, but others are interred in groups of eight with stone plaques above each tomb carrying the names of the dead where known. The entrance gate is a squat neo-Romanesque structure, whose style is continued by the basalt crosses dotting the rest of the site, and overlooking it all is a sad and moving **bronze** of four mourning soldiers by the Munich sculptor Emil Krieger.

Doubling back to Langemark, take the Zonnebeke road southeast and, after 2km, you'll reach a T-junction. Turn right, left and then left again at the little roadside shrine to get onto the country lane leading the 4km east to Tyne Cot (see below). These manoeuvres take you round the **Canadian Monument**, a 10m-high granite statue topped by the bust of a Canadian soldier, which was raised in honour of those men who endured the first German chlorine gas attacks in April 1915.

Tyne Cot

Tyne Cot is the largest British Commonwealth war cemetery in the world, containing no fewer than 11,956 graves as well as the so-called **Memorial to the Missing**, a semicircular wall inscribed with the names of a further thirty-five thousand men whose bodies were never recovered. The soldiers of a Northumbrian division gave the place its name, observing, as they tried to fight their way up the ridge, that the Flemish house on the horizon looked like a Tyneside cottage. The house disappeared during the war, but the largest of the concrete **pillboxes** the Germans built to defend the ridge has survived, incorporated within the mound beneath the **Cross of Sacrifice** at the suggestion of George V – you can still see a piece of it where a slab of stone has been deliberately omitted. The scattered graves behind the cross were dug during the final weeks of the war and have remained in their original positions, adding a further poignancy to the seemingly endless lines of tombstones below. Strangely, the Memorial to the Missing at the back of the cemetery wasn't part of the original design: the intention was that these names be recorded on the Menin Gate, but there was not enough room. Beside the car park, the **visitor centre** (daily 10am–6pm; free) gives further background information and has a fascinating selection of World War I photos.

Tyne Cot cemetery overlooks the shallow valley that gently shelves up to **PASSENDALE**, known then as **Passchendaele**. This village was the British objective in the **Third Battle of Ypres**, but torrential rain and intensive shelling turned the valley into a giant quagmire. The whole affair came to symbolize the futility of the war and the incompetence of its generals: when Field-Marshal Haig's Chief of Staff ventured out of his HQ to inspect progress, he allegedly said, "Good God, did we really send men to fight in that?"

To Zonnebeke

Double back from the Tyne Cot car park, turn left when you reach the country lane you originally approached on, and after about 400m you reach a wider road, the **N303**, which runs along the top of the Passendale ridge. Turn right onto it and shortly afterwards, after 800m, turn right again, down the N332 into **ZONNEBEKE**. Here, beside the main road in the middle of the village – and occupying a nineteenth-century chateau and its grounds – is the **Memorial Museum Passchendaele 1917** (Feb–Nov daily 9am–5pm; €5; ⓦwww.passchendaele.be), with the region's largest collection of World War I artefacts. Displays are focused on the Third Battle of Ypres, illustrating this desperately futile conflict with photos, military hardware and reconstructions of a trench and a dugout.

To Sanctuary Wood Museum

At the far end of Zonnebeke, fork left onto the **N37**, keep straight over the motorway and you'll soon reach the **N8**, once the infamous "Menin Road" which cut across the back of the Salient, crowded with marching armies at night and peppered by German shrapnel during the day. Go round the island onto the N8 heading east (in the direction of Menen), and after 1.2km turn right up Canadalaan for the 1.3km trip to **Sanctuary Wood Cemetery**, holding two thousand British and Commonwealth dead.

Just beyond the cemetery, the **Sanctuary Wood Museum** (daily 10am–6pm or dusk; €7.50) holds a ragbag of shells, rifles, bayonets, billycans and other incidental artefacts. Outside, things have been left pretty much as they were the day the war ended, and though the original tackle rotted away ages ago, a zigzag of sandbagged trenches with accompanying shell craters really do convey the flavour of the fighting. The woods beside the museum and on the adjacent Hill 62 were bitterly contested, and there's a modest **Canadian monument** on the brow of the hill 300m up the road from the museum. From the monument, you can see Ieper – just 5km away, across the rolling ridges of the countryside and reached along the N8.

Kortrijk

KORTRIJK (Courtrai in French), just 8km from the French border, is the largest town in this part of West Flanders, a lively, busy sort of place with a couple of excellent hotels, several good places to eat and a smattering of distinguished medieval buildings. The town traces its origins back to a Roman settlement called Cortoriacum, but its salad days were in the Middle Ages when its burghers made a fortune producing linen and flax. The problem was its location: Kortrijk was just too close to France for comfort and time and again the town was embroiled in the wars that swept across Flanders, right up to the two German occupations of the last century.

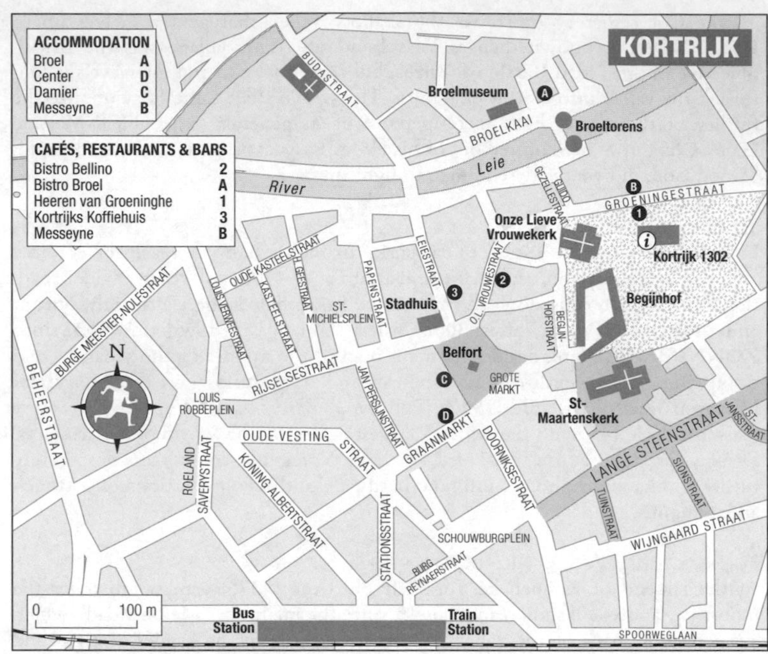

Arrival, information and accommodation

Kortrijk **train and bus stations** are a five-minute walk from the Grote Markt, itself a five-minute stroll from the **tourist office**, a part of the town's cultural-cum-visitor centre in the Begijnhofpark (April–Sept Mon–Fri 9am–6pm, Sat & Sun 10am–5pm; Oct–March Mon–Fri 9am–5pm, Sat & Sun 10am–4pm, but closed Sun Nov–Feb; ⓣ056 27 78 40, ⓦwww.tourismkortrijk.be). They issue a free and comprehensive town brochure, which includes details of around twenty **B&Bs** (❶–❷).

Hotels

Hotel Broel Broelkaai 8 ⓣ056 21 83 51, ⓦwww.hotelbroel.be. The plain exterior of this four-star hotel on the north bank of the River Leie is deceptive, for the inside of the building, which was once a tobacco factory, has a mock-monastic theme, its tunnels and stone-trimmed arches entirely bogus but great fun. Each of the seventy en-suite rooms is spacious and relaxing, and decorated in a tasteful version of country-house style. There's a pool, sauna and solarium too. ❺

Center Hotel Graanmarkt 6 ⓣ056 21 97 21, ⓦwww.centerhotel.be. Medium-sized three-star in a handy location near the Grote Markt. There's nothing fancy about the rooms, but they're comfortable enough and each is kitted out in a sharp modern-minimalist manner. ❸

Hotel Damier Grote Markt 41 ⓣ056 22 15 47, ⓦwww.hoteldamier.be. Popular with visiting business folk, this four-star hotel has fifty commodious rooms decorated in a modern rather functional country-house manner. Set behind an imperious Neoclassical facade, complete with its old carriage archway. ❺

Hotel Messeyne Groeningestraat 17 ⓣ056 21 21 66, ⓦwww.hotelmesseyne.be. Excellent, four-star hotel in a creatively modernized eighteenth-century mansion. There's a sauna and a health centre, and twenty-eight large and well-appointed rooms, most of which are decorated in fetching creams and browns; the pick have retained their timber-beam ceilings. ❺

The Town

Heavily bombed during World War II, Kortrijk's **Grote Markt** is a comely but architecturally incoherent mixture of bits of the old and a lot of the new, surrounding the forlorn, turreted **Belfort** – all that remains of what was once a splendid medieval cloth hall. At the northwest corner of the Grote Markt stands the **Stadhuis** (Mon–Fri 9am–noon & 2–5pm; free), a sedate edifice with modern statues of the counts of Flanders on the facade, above and beside two lines of ugly windows. Inside, through the side entrance on the left, things improve with two fine sixteenth-century **chimneypieces**. The first is in the old **Schepenzaal** (Aldermen's Room) on the ground floor, a proud, intricate work decorated with municipal coats of arms and carvings of bishops, saints and the Archdukes Albert and Isabella of Spain; the other, upstairs in the **Raadzaal** (Council Chamber), is a more didactic affair, ornamented by three rows of precise statuettes representing, from top to bottom, the virtues, the vices (to either side of the Emperor Charles V), and the torments of hell.

On the other side of the Grote Markt rises the heavyweight tower of **St-Maartenskerk** (Mon–Fri 9am–5pm, Sat & Sun 10am–5pm), whose gleaming white-stone exterior, dating from the fifteenth century, has recently been cleaned of decades of grime. The outside of the church may be handsome, but the cavernous interior is a yawn and it won't be long before you're moving onto the neighbouring **Begijnhof**, founded in 1238 by a certain Joanna of Constantinople and preserving the cosy informality of its seventeenth-century houses (for more on Begijnhofs, see box, p.357).

The Onze Lieve Vrouwekerk

On the north side of the Begijnhof, pushing into Groeningestraat, is the **Onze Lieve Vrouwekerk** (Church of Our Lady; Mon–Sat 7am–7pm & Sun 7am–6pm), a hulking grey structure that formerly doubled as part of the city's fortifications. In July 1302, the nave of the church was crammed with hundreds of spurs, ripped off the feet of dead and dying French knights at what has become known as the **Battle of the Golden Spurs**. These plundered spurs were the pathetic remains of the army Philip the Fair had sent to avenge the slaughter of the Bruges Matins earlier that year (see p.149). The two armies, Philip's heavily armoured cavalry and the lightly armed Flemish weavers, had met outside Kortrijk on marshy ground, strategic parts of which the Flemish had disguised with brushwood. Despising their lowly born adversaries, the French knights made no reconnaissance and fell into the trap, milling around in the mud like cumbersome dinosaurs. They were massacred, the first time an amateur civilian army had defeated professional mail-clad knights. The spurs disappeared long ago and today the church's **interior** is a riot of styles, from the Gothic and the Baroque to the Neoclassical. However, the gloomy and truncated north transept does hold one splendid painting, **Anthony van Dyck**'s *Raising of the Cross*, a muscular, sweeping work with a pale, almost vague-looking Christ, completed just before the artist went to England. Across the church, the **Counts' Chapel** has an unusual series of somewhat crude nineteenth-century portraits painted into the wall niches, but the highlight is a sensuous medieval alabaster **statue of St Catherine**, her left hand clutching a representation of the spiked wheel on which her enemies tried to break her (hence the "Catherine wheel" firework).

The rest of the centre

From opposite the Onze Lieve Vrouwekerk, Guido Gezellestraat cuts through to the **River Leie**, which is guarded by a pair of enormously strong and conical towers, the **Broeltorens**, all that remains of the old town walls. Over the bridge is the town's best museum, the **Broelmuseum**, at Broelkaai 6 (Tues–Fri 10am–noon & 2–5pm, Sat & Sun 11am–5pm; €3), where pride of place goes to the paintings of Kortrijk's own **Roelandt Savery** (1576–1639). Trained in Amsterdam, Savery worked for the Habsburgs in Prague and Vienna before returning to the Low Countries. To suit the tastes of his German patrons, he infused many of his landscapes with the romantic classicism that they preferred – Orpheus and the Garden of Eden were two favourite subjects – but the finely observed detail of his paintings was always in the true Flemish tradition. Among the works on display is the striking *Plundering of a Village*, where there's a palpable sense of outrage in contrast to *The Drinking-Place*, depicting a romanticized, arboreal idyll. The museum also possesses a passable collection of nineteenth-century land- and seascapes plus local scenes by another native artist **Emmanuel Viérin** (1869–1954). From the Broelmuseum, it's a short stroll to the leafy **Begijnhofpark**, where the tourist office shares its premises with **Kortrijk 1302**, a multimedia exploration of the Battle of the Golden Spurs (Tues–Sun 10am–5pm; €6).

Eating and drinking

Kortrijk may be a Flemish-speaking city, but its proximity to France has given its **cafés** and **restaurants** a decidedly French influence, which adds a good helping of gastronomic gusto. Local specialities include *kalletaart* (apple-cake with calvados) and the beers and ales of the Picobrouwerij Alvinne brewery – try the Podge Belgian stout for starters.

Bistro Bellino Onze Lieve Vrouwestraat 18 ⓣ056 25 43 54. A cosy little Italian place serving up all the classics, with main courses starting at a very affordable €13. Closed Wed.

Bistro Broel Broelkaai 8 ⓣ056 21 83 51. Expansive, stone-flagged restaurant on the ground floor of the *Hotel Broel* (see p.142), though it doesn't look or feel like the usual hotel restaurant at all. The emphasis is very much on Flemish cuisine, with one particular recommendation being river eel in spinach sauce (*rivierpaling in 't groen*). Mains average €23. Mon–Fri 11am–1am, Sat 5pm–2am.

Heeren van Groeninghe Groeningestraat 36 ⓣ056 25 40 25. Large, smart and popular, this bistro-style bar and restaurant in a cleverly revamped eighteenth-century mansion does a very good line in Flemish and Italian dishes and is also strong on salads. Eat inside or outside on the terrace. Mains from a very reasonable €18. Daily except Tues & Wed 10am–10pm.

Kortrijks Koffiehuis Leiestraat 20. With its charming Art Deco facade, this unusual little place – part shop, part cafe – sells the best coffee in town, and there's a good selection of coffee beans to choose from too. Mon–Sat 9am–5pm.

Restaurant Messeyne Groeningestraat 17 ⓣ056 21 21 66. Small and deluxe-meets-bijou restaurant in the *Hotel Messeyne* (see p.142). The menu is extremely well chosen and the cuisine French – the *jus* are particularly delicious. Mains hover around €28. Mon–Fri noon–2pm & 7–9.30pm & Sat 7–9.30pm.

Oudenaarde

Situated some 25km east of Kortrijk, the attractive and gently old-fashioned town of **OUDENAARDE**, literally "old landing place", hugs the banks of the River Scheldt as it twists its way north towards Ghent. The town has a long and chequered history. Granted a charter in 1193, it concentrated on cloth manufacture until the early fifteenth century, when its weavers cleverly switched to **tapestry making**, an industry that made its burghers rich and the town famous, with the best tapestries becoming the prized possessions of the kings of France and Spain. So far so good, but Oudenaarde became a key military objective during the religious and dynastic wars of the sixteenth to the eighteenth centuries, perhaps most famously in July 1708, when the **Duke of Marlborough** came to its rescue and won a spectacular victory here

Belgian beer

No other country in the world produces more beers than Belgium – around seven hundred and counting. There are strong, dark brews from a handful of Trappist monasteries, light wheat beers perfect for a hot summer's day, fruit beers bottled and corked like champagne, and unusual concoctions that date back to medieval times. We've listed a selection of the best and most common to get you started, but really the joy is in experimenting with new brews. Any decent establishment will have a beer menu that includes at least a few of the brews covered here, as well as the glasses to go with them – no Belgian bar worth its salt would dare to serve a beer in anything other than its proper glass.

Brugse Zot ▲

Abbaye Notre-Dame de Scourmont, Chimay ▼

Kwak drinkers ▼

Brugse Zot (Blond 6%, Brugse Zot Dubbel 7.5%) Huisbrouwerij De Halve Mann, a small brewery located in the centre of Bruges, produces zippy, refreshing ales with a dry, crisp aftertaste. Their Blond is a light and tangy pale ale, whereas the Bruin – Brugse Zot Dubbel – is a classic brown ale with a full body.

Bush Beer (7.5% and 12%) A Walloon speciality. At 12%, it's claimed that the original version is the strongest beer in Belgium, and it's actually more like a barley wine, with a lovely golden colour and an earthy aroma. The 7.5% Bush is a tasty pale ale with a hint of coriander.

Chimay (red top 7%, blue top 9%) Made by the Trappist monks of Forges-les-Chimay, in southern Belgium, Chimay beers are widely regarded as among the best in the world. Of the several brews they produce, these two are the most readily available, fruity and strong, deep in body, and somewhat spicy with a hint of nutmeg and thyme.

La Chouffe (8%) Produced in the Ardennes, this distinctive beer is instantly recognisable by the red-hooded gnome (*chouffe*) that adorns its label. It's a refreshing pale ale with a peachy aftertaste – very palatable indeed, but also very strong.

De Koninck (5%) Antwerp's leading brewery, De Koninck, is something of a Flemish institution. Its standard beer is a smooth pale ale that's very drinkable, with a sharp aftertaste; better on draught than in the bottle.

Kriek (Cantillon Kriek Lambic 5%, Belle Vue Kriek 5.2%, Mort Subite Kriek 4.3%) A type of beer rather than a particular brew, Kriek is made from a base lambic beer to which are added cherries or, in the case of the more commercial brands, cherry juice and perhaps even sugar. Other against the French in the War of the Spanish Succession. Attacked and besieged time and again, Oudenaarde found it impossible to sustain any growth, and the demise of the tapestry industry pauperized the town, rendering it an insignificant backwater in one of the poorest parts of Flanders. In the last few years, however, things have improved considerably due to its canny use of regional development funds, and today's town – with its fascinating old buildings – makes an enjoyable and pleasant day out.

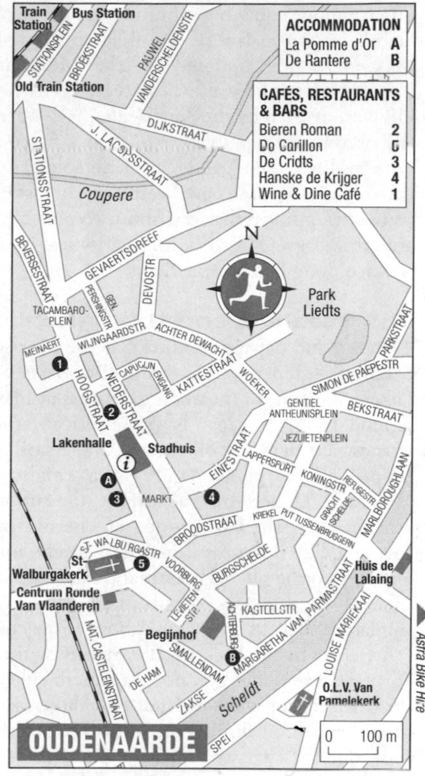

Arrival, information and accommodation

Next door to the **bus station**, Oudenaarde's modern **train station** has usurped its neo-Gothic predecessor, which stands lonely and forlorn next door. From the stations, it's a ten-minute walk to the town centre, where the **tourist office** is located in a glassy extension added to the side of the old Lakenhalle, just off the Markt (April–Oct Mon–Fri 9am–5.30pm, Sat & Sun 10am–5.30pm; Nov–March Mon–Fri 9.30am–noon & 1.30–4pm, Sat 2–5pm; ⓣ055 31 72 51, ⓦwww.oudenaarde.be). They issue free town brochures and sell cycling maps of the **Vlaamse Ardennen** (Flemish Ardennes), the ridge of low, wooded hills that rises from the Flanders plain a few kilometres to the south of town. **Bike rental** is available from Asfra, a short walk southeast of the centre at Bergstraat 75 (ⓣ055 31 57 40, ⓦwww.asfra.be).

Hotels

La Pomme d'Or Markt 62 ⓣ055 31 19 00, ⓦwww.pommedor.be. In a large and really rather good-looking old building on the main square, this three-star hotel offers ten plain but perfectly adequate, modern rooms. ④

De Rantere Jan Zonder Vreeslaan 8 ⓣ055 31 89 88, ⓦwww.derantere.be. In a brisk modern building overlooking the River Scheldt, this three-star hotel has thirty-odd comfortable rooms decorated in a straightforward (some would say frugal) style, but the rooms are large and the beds comfy. There's also a less well-appointed annexe just a couple of minutes' walk away. ④

The Town

On the way into town from the train station, the only surprise is the romantic war memorial occupying the middle of **Tacambaroplein**. For once it's nothing to do with either world war, but instead it commemorates those who were daft or unscrupulous enough to volunteer to go to Mexico and fight for Maximilian, the Habsburg son-in-law of the Belgian king, Leopold I. Unwanted and unloved, Maximilian was imposed on the Mexicans by a French army provided by Napoleon III, who wanted to create his own western empire while the eyes of the US were averted by the American Civil War. It was, however, all too fanciful and the occupation rapidly turned into a fiasco. Maximilian paid for the adventure with his life in 1867, and few of his soldiers made the return trip. The reasons for this calamity seem to have been entirely lost on Maximilian, who declared, in front of the firing squad that was about to polish him off, "Men of my class and lineage are created by God to be the happiness of nations or their martyrs…Long live Mexico, long live independence".

The Stadhuis and the Lakenhalle

The airy and expansive **Markt** at the heart of Oudenaarde is overlooked by the **Stadhuis** (guided tours: April–Oct Tues–Sun at 11am & 3pm; €5, including Lakenhalle), one of the finest examples of Flamboyant Gothic in the country. Built around 1525, its elegantly symmetrical facade spreads out on either side of the extravagant tiers, balconies and parapets of a slender central tower, which is itself topped by the gilded figure of a knight, *Hanske de Krijger* ("Little John the Warrior"). Underneath the knight, the cupola is in the shape of a crown, a theme reinforced by the two groups of cherubs on the dormer windows below, who lovingly clutch the royal insignia. Inside, a magnificent oak **doorway** forms the entrance to the old Schepenzaal (Aldermen's Hall). A stylistically influential piece of 1531, the doorway consists of an intricate sequence of carvings, surmounted by miniature cherubs who frolic above three coats of arms and a 28-panel door.

Attached to the back of the Stadhuis, the thirteenth-century **Lakenhalle** is a Romanesque edifice that holds a superb collection of **tapestries** – or at least it will do when it reopens in 2012 after a thorough refurbishment (in the meantime key tapestries are on display in St-Walburgakerk, see below). Among the tapestries, look out for two wonderful eighteenth-century pieces, *Nymphs in a Landscape*, showing four nymphs picking and arranging flowers, and *Return from Market*, featuring trees in shades of blue and green, edged by sky and bare earth – a composition reminiscent of Dutch landscape paintings. There are also several excellent examples of the classical tapestries that were all the rage in the sixteenth century, such as *Hercules and the Stymphalian Birds*, a scene set among what appear to be cabbage leaves. Equally impressive is *Scipio and Hannibal*, in which the border is decorated with medallions depicting the Seven Wonders of the World – though the Hanging Gardens of Babylon appear twice to create the symmetry. Glamorized pastoral scenes were perennially popular: the seventeenth-century *Landscape with Two Pheasants* frames a distant castle with an intricate design of trees and plants, while *La Main Chaude* depicts a game of blind man's buff.

St-Walburgakerk and the rest of town

Soaring high above the town, **St-Walburgakerk** (Easter to May & Oct Tues, Thurs & Sat 2.30–5pm, plus Thurs 10–11am; June–Aug Tues–Sun 2.30–5pm) is a hulking, rambling mass of Gothic masonry which took a real hammering from the Protestants, who trashed almost all the original furnishings and fittings. Nowadays, gaudy Baroque altarpieces dot the cavernous interior, but the church does possess several fine tapestries and these are currently augmented by a dozen more, which are on loan from the Lakenhalle whilst it's being refurbished (see above).

From the church, it's a brief stroll down to the river past the elaborate seventeenth-century **portal of the Begijnhof**, whose huddle of whitewashed

Cantillon barrel ▲

Cantillon Geuze production ▼

Drinkers at *À la Mort Subite*, Brussels ▼

Rodenbach **(Rodenbach 5% and Rodenbach Grand Cru 6.5%)** Located in the Flemish town of Roeselare, the Rodenbach brewery produces a reddish-brown ale in several forms, with the best brews aged in oak containers. Their widely available Rodenbach is a tangy brown ale with a hint of sourness. The much fuller – and sourer – Rodenbach Grand Cru is more difficult to get hold of, but delicious.

Westmalle **(Westmalle Dubbel 7%, Tripel 9%)** The Trappist monks of Westmalle, just north of Antwerp, claim their beers not only cure loss of appetite and insomnia, but reduce stress by half. Whatever the truth, the prescription certainly tastes good. Their most famous beer, Westmalle Tripel, is deliciously creamy and aromatic, while the popular Westmalle Dubbel is dark and supremely malty.

Lambic beers

One of the world's oldest styles of beer manufacture, Brussels' **lambic** beers are tart brews made with at least thirty percent raw wheat as well as the more usual malted barley. Their key feature, however, is the use of wild yeast in their production, a process of spontaneous fermentation in which the yeasts – which are specific to the air of the Brussels area – gravitate down into open wooden casks over a period of between two and three years. Draught lambic is extremely rare, but the bottled varieties are more commonplace; **Cantillon Lambik** is perhaps the most authentic, an excellent drink with a lemony zip. **Gueuze** is a blend of old and new lambics in a bottle, a little sweeter and fuller bodied than straight lambic, with an almost cidery aftertaste; again Cantillon's is the best you'll find (5%), although you may have to settle for Belle Vue Gueuze (5.2%), Timmermans Gueuze (5.5%) or Lindemans Gueuze (5.2%).

Oudenaarde tapestries

Tapestry manufacture in Oudenaarde began in the middle of the fifteenth century, an embryonic industry that soon came to be based on a dual system of **workshop** and **outworker**, the one with paid employees, the other with workers paid on a piecework basis. From the beginning, the town authorities took a keen interest in the business, ensuring its success by a rigorous system of quality control, which soon gave Oudenaarde an international reputation for consistently well-made tapestries. The other side of this interventionist policy was less palatable: wages were kept down and the Guild of the Masters cunningly took over the running of the Guild of Weavers in 1501. To make matters worse, tapestries were by definition a luxury item, and workers were hardly ever able to accumulate enough capital to buy either their own looms or even raw materials.

The first great period of Oudenaarde tapestry making lasted until the middle of the sixteenth century, when religious conflict overwhelmed the town and many of its Protestant-inclined weavers, who had come into direct conflict with their Catholic masters, migrated north to the rival workshops of Antwerp and Ghent. In 1582 Oudenaarde was finally incorporated into the Spanish Netherlands, precipitating a revival of tapestry production fostered by the king and queen of Spain, who were keen to support the industry and passed draconian laws banning the movement of weavers. Later, however, French occupation and the shrinking of the Spanish market led to diminishing production, the industry finally fizzling out in the late eighteenth century.

There were only two significant types of tapestry: **decorative**, principally *verdures*, showing scenes of foliage in an almost abstract way (the Oudenaarde speciality), and **pictorial** – usually variations on the same basic themes, particularly rural life, knights, hunting parties and religious scenes. Over the centuries, changes in style were strictly limited, though the early part of the seventeenth century saw an increased use of elaborate woven borders, an appreciation of perspective and the use of a far brighter, more varied range of colours.

The **technique** of producing tapestries was a cross between embroidery and ordinary weaving. It consisted of interlacing a wool weft above and below the strings of a vertical linen "chain", a process similar to weaving; the appearance of a tapestry was entirely determined by the weft, the design being taken from a painting to which the weaver made constant reference. However, the weaver had to stop to change colour, requiring as many shuttles for the weft as he had colours, as in embroidery.

Standard-size Oudenaarde tapestries took six months to make and were produced exclusively for the very wealthy. The tapestries were normally in yellow, brown, pale blue and shades of green, with an occasional splash of red, though the most important clients would, on occasion, insist on the use of gold and silver thread. Some also insisted on the employment of the most famous **artists** of the day for the preparatory painting – Pieter Paul Rubens, Jacob Jordaens and David Teniers all completed tapestry commissions.

cottages has recently been repaired and revamped. From here, it's another stroll over the river to the **Huis de Lalaing**, a grand old mansion at Bourgondiestraat 9 (April–Oct Tues–Fri 1.30–4.30pm; €3), where they specialize in repairing old tapestries. They don't make a big thing out of showing visitors round, but everyone is quite friendly and you can spend time looking at the various restorative processes.

Oudenaarde is also home to a noteworthy special interest museum, the **Centrum Ronde Van Vlaanderen**, Markt 43 (Tour of Flanders Museum; Tues–Sun 10am–6pm, closed Jan; €7; ⓦ www.rvv.be), with everything you could ever want to know about Belgium's premier professional cycling competition.

Eating and drinking

Oudenaarde may only have a population of 28,000, but it punches above its weight in terms of **cafés** and **bars**, the pick of which are either on or close to the Markt.

Bieren Roman Hoogstraat 21. The local Roman brewery rules the Oudenaarde roost, and this traditional neighbourhood bar is devoted to its products – try, for example, the Tripel Ename, a strong blond beer, or the Roman Dobbelen Bruinen, a snappy filtered stout.

De Carillon Markt 49. Old-fashioned café-bar that occupies an ancient brick-gabled building in the shadow of St-Walburgakerk. Its at its best in the summertime, when large pavement terrace heaves with drinkers (rather than eaters). Tues–Sun 9am till late.

De Cridts Markt 58. Friendly, traditional and family-owned café-restaurant serving standard-issue but tasty Flemish dishes at very reasonable prices – main courses average €18. Mon–Wed, Sat & Sun 9.30am–10pm, Thurs 7am–2pm.

Hanske de Krijger Einestraat 3. Youthful bar painted in deep, dark shades and with a good selection of ales. Just off the east side of the Grote Markt.

Wine & Dine Café Hoogstraat 34 ⓣ055 23 96 97. Arguably the best and certainly the nattiest café-restaurant in town, offering a choice selection of Franco-Flemish food served with style and panache. Fish and meat dishes here cost around €22, salads €18. Tues–Sat 11.30am–2.30pm & 6–10.30pm.

Bruges

"Somewhere within the dingy casing lay the ancient city," wrote Graham Greene of **BRUGES**, "like a notorious jewel, too stared at, talked of, and trafficked over". And it's true that Bruges's reputation as one of the most perfectly preserved medieval cities in western Europe has made it the most popular tourist destination in Belgium, packed with visitors throughout the season. Inevitably, the crowds tend to overwhelm the city, but you'd be mad to come to Flanders and miss the place: its museums hold some of the country's finest collections of Flemish art, and its intimate, winding streets, woven around a skein of narrow canals and lined with gorgeous ancient buildings, live up to even the most inflated tourist hype. See it out of season, or in the early morning before the hordes have descended, and it can be memorable – though not so much on **Mondays**, when many of the sights are closed.

Some history

Bruges started out as a ninth-century fortress built by the warlike first count of Flanders, **Baldwin Iron Arm**, who was intent on defending the Flemish coast from Viking attack. The settlement prospered, and by the fourteenth century it shared effective control of the **cloth trade** with its two great rivals, Ghent and Ypres (now Ieper), turning high-quality English wool into clothing that was exported all over the known world. An immensely profitable business, it made the city a focus of international trade, and at its peak the town was a key member of – and showcase for the products of – the **Hanseatic League**, the most powerful economic alliance in medieval Europe. Through the harbours and docks of Bruges, Flemish cloth and Hansa goods were exchanged for hogs from Denmark, spices from Venice, hides from Ireland, wax from Russia, gold and silver from Poland and furs from Bulgaria. The business of these foreign traders was protected by no fewer than 21 consulates, and the city developed a wide range of support services, including banking, money-changing, maritime insurance and an elementary shipping code, known as the *Roles de Damme*.

Despite (or perhaps because of) this lucrative state of affairs, Bruges was dogged by **war**. Its weavers and merchants were dependent on the goodwill of the **kings**

of England for the proper functioning of the wool trade, but their feudal overlords, the counts of Flanders, and their successors, the dukes of Burgundy (from 1384), were vassals of the rival **king of France**. Although some of the dukes and counts were strong enough to defy their king, most felt obliged to obey his orders and thus take his side against the English when the two countries were at war. This conflict of interests was compounded by the designs the French monarchy had on the independence of Bruges itself. Time and again, the French sought to assert control over the cities of West Flanders, but more often than not they encountered armed rebellion. In Bruges, **Philip the Fair** precipitated the most famous insurrection at the beginning of the fourteenth century. Philip and his wife, Joanna of Navarre, had held a grand reception in Bruges, but it had only served to feed their envy. In the face of the city's splendour, Joanna moaned, "I thought that I alone was Queen, but here in this place I have six hundred rivals". The opportunity to flex royal muscles came shortly afterwards when the city's guildsmen flatly refused to pay a new round of taxes. Enraged, Philip dispatched an army to restore order and garrison the town, but at dawn on Friday May 18, 1302, a rebellious force of Flemings crept into the city and massacred Philip's sleepy army – an occasion later known as the **Bruges Matins**: anyone who couldn't correctly pronounce the Flemish shibboleth *schild en vriend* ("shield and friend") was put to the sword. There is a statue celebrating the leaders of the insurrection – Jan Breydel and Pieter de Coninck – in the Markt (see p.156).

The **Habsburgs**, who inherited Flanders – as well as the rest of present-day Belgium and Holland in 1482 – whittled away at the power of the Flemish cities, no one more so than **Charles V**, the ruler of a vast kingdom that included the Low Countries and Spain. As part of his policy, Charles favoured Antwerp at the expense of Flanders, and to make matters worse, the Flemish cloth industry began its long decline in the 1480s. Bruges was especially badly hit and, as a sign of its decline, failed to dredge the silted-up **River Zwin**, the town's trading lifeline to the North Sea. By the 1510s, the stretch of water between Sluis and Damme was only navigable by smaller ships, and by the 1530s the city's sea trade had collapsed completely. Bruges simply withered away, its houses deserted, its canals empty and its money spirited north with the merchants.

Some four centuries later, **Georges Rodenbach**'s novel *Bruges-la-Mort*e alerted well-heeled Europeans to the town's aged, quiet charms, and Bruges – frozen in time – escaped damage in both world wars to emerge as the perfect tourist attraction.

Arrival

Bruges **train station** adjoins the **bus station** about 2km southwest of the town centre. Operated by De Lijn, **local buses** depart for the town centre from in front of the train station every few minutes; most services stop on the Markt, the main square, others in the surrounding side streets. All local buses have destination signs at the front, but if in doubt check with the driver. Single **tickets** cost €2 from the driver, €1.20 in advance from the De Lijn ticket machines, also outside the train station. A **taxi** from the train station to the centre costs about €8.

Most **motorists** arrive via the **E40**, which runs west from Brussels to Ostend, skirting Bruges on the way. Bruges is clearly signed from the E40 and its oval-shaped centre is encircled by the **R30** ring road following the course of the old city walls. **Parking** in the centre can be a real tribulation and easily the best and most economical option is to use the massive 24/7 car park by the train station, particularly as the price – €2.50 per day – includes the cost of the bus ride to and from the centre.

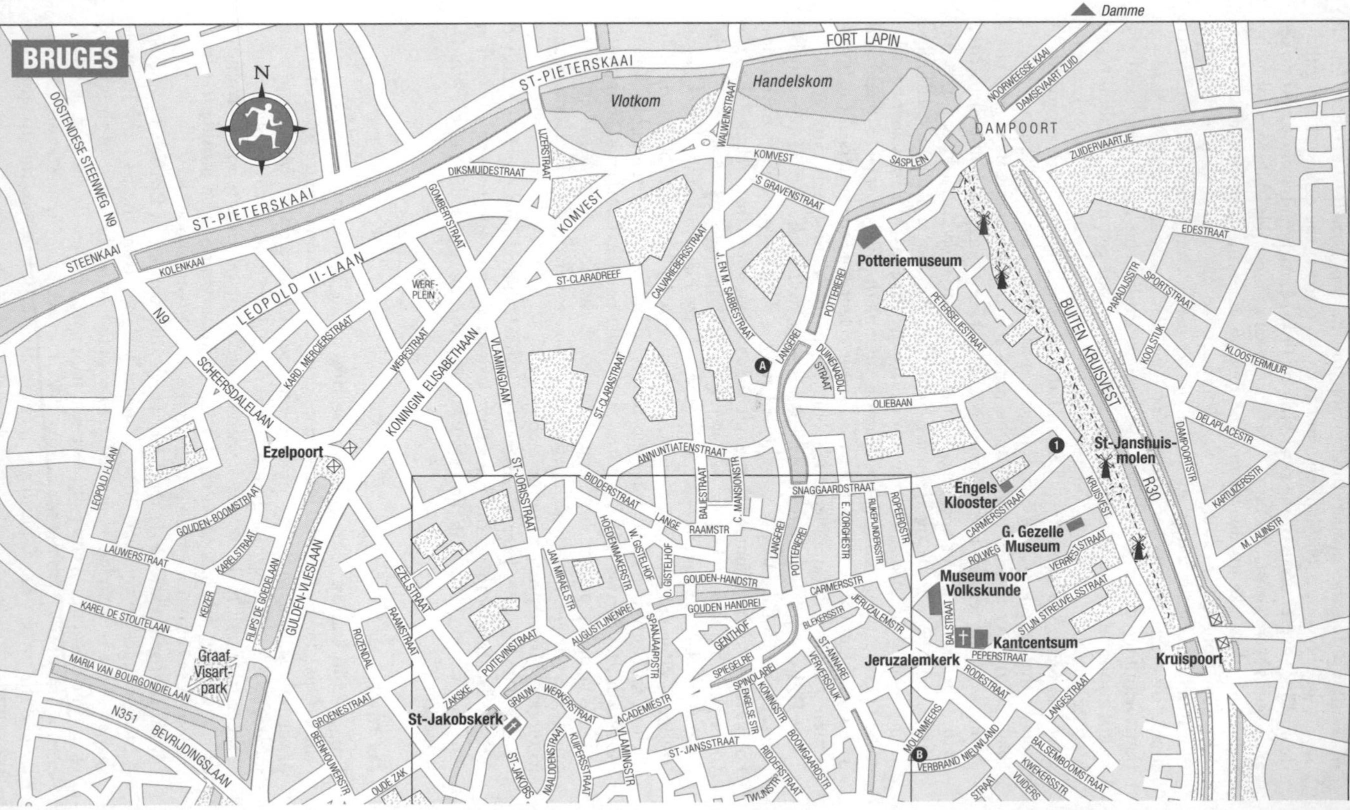
BRUGES
Potteriemuseum
St-Janshuis-molen
Engels Klooster
G. Gezelle Museum
Museum voor Volkskunde
Kantcentsum
Jeruzalemkerk
Kruispoort
St-Jakobskerk
Ezelpoort
Graaf Visart-park
Handelskom
Vlotkom
DAMPOORT
Damme
N9
BUITEN KRUISVEST
R30
KRUISVEST
DAMPOORTSTR
FORT LAPIN
ST-PIETERSKAAI
LEOPOLD II-LAAN
KONINGIN ELISABETHLAAN
GULDEN-VLIESLAAN
SCHEERSDALELAAN
OOSTENDSE STEENWEG N9
STEENKAAI
KOLENKAAI
VLAMINGDAM
ST-JORISSTRAAT
KOMVEST
POTTERIEREI
LANGEREI
ST-ANNAREI
PEPERSTRAAT
BALSTRAAT
CARMERSSTRAAT
SNAGGAARDSTRAAT
EZELSTRAAT
BEVRIJDINGSLAAN
N351
MARIA VAN BOURGONDIELAAN
KAREL DE STOUTELAAN
LAUWERSTRAAT

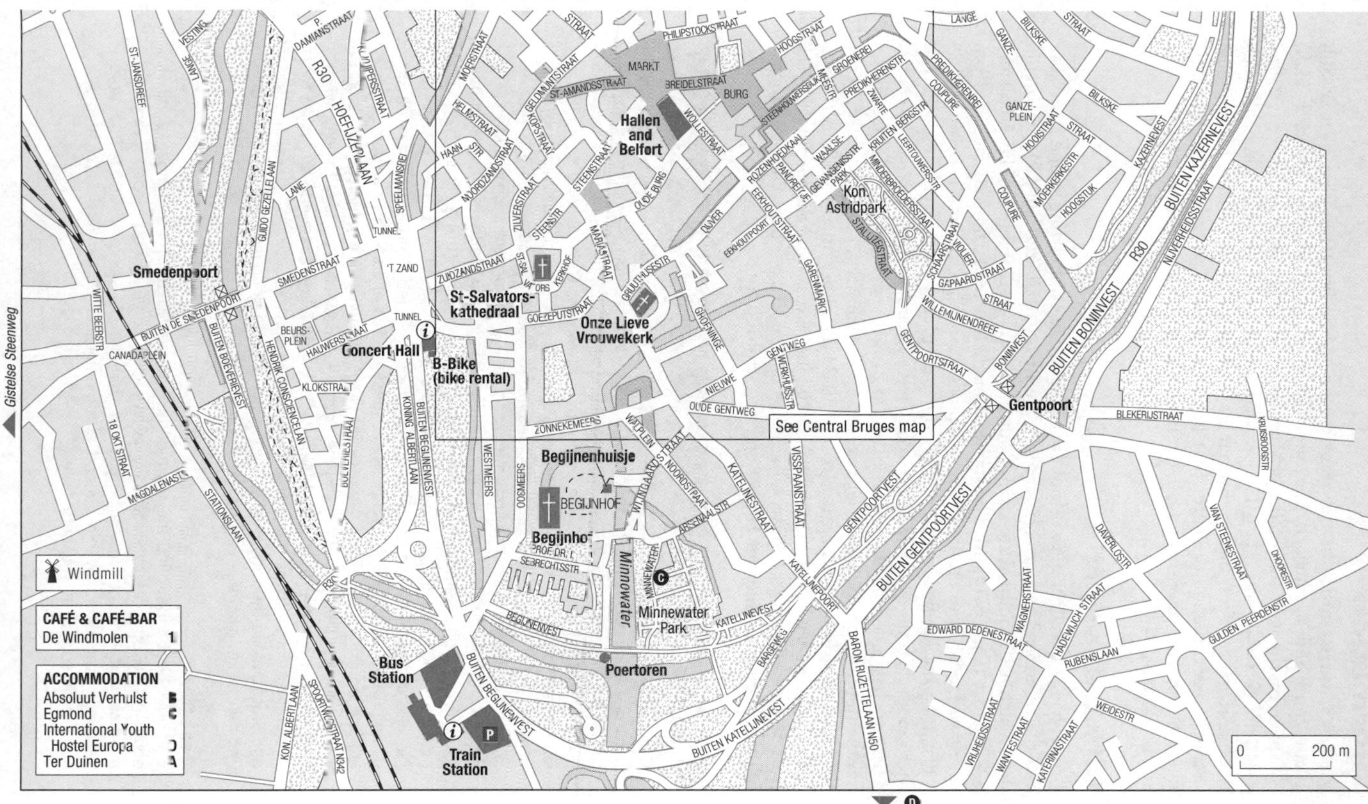
Smedenpoort
Hallen and Belfort
Markt
Burg
Kon. Astridpark
St-Salvators-kathedraal
Onze Lieve Vrouwekerk
Concert Hall
B-Bike (bike rental)
Gentpoort
See Central Bruges map
Begijnenhuisje
Begijnhof
Minnewater
Minnewater Park
Poertoren
Bus Station
Train Station
'T Zand
Gistelse Steenweg
Windmill
CAFÉ & CAFÉ-BAR
De Windmolen 1
ACCOMMODATION
Absoluut Verhulst
Egmond
International Youth Hostel Europa
Ter Duinen
0 200 m

Information

There's a **tourist office** at the train station (Mon–Fri 10am–5pm, Sat & Sun 10am–2pm) and a much larger one in the Concertgebouw (Concert Hall) complex, on the west side of the city centre on 't Zand (daily 10am–6pm; ⓣ050 44 46 46, ⓦwww.brugge.be). They both have local bus and train timetables, sell tickets for many events and performances, and supply a bimonthly, multilingual events booklet, though the latter isn't nearly as detailed as **Exit**, a free monthly, Flemish-language newssheet available here and at many town-centre bars, cafés and bookshops.

City transport

Bruges has an excellent network of **local bus** services, shuttling round the centre and the suburbs. These are operated by **De Lijn** (ⓣ070 220 200, ⓦwww.delijn.be), which has an information kiosk outside the train station (Mon–Fri 10.30am–5.45pm, Sat 10am–5.15pm). The standard single **fare** is €1.20 in advance (€2 from the driver); a 24-hour city bus pass, a Dagpas, costs €5 (€6 from the driver).

Flat as a pancake, Bruges and its environs are a great place to **cycle**, especially as there are cycle lanes on many of the roads and cycle racks dotted across the centre. There are half a dozen **bike rental** places in Bruges – the tourist office (see above) has the full list – but Belgian Railways sets the benchmark, hiring out bikes at the railway station for €9.50 per day (ⓣ050 30 23 29). One other option is B-Bike, 't Zand (daily 10am–7pm; ⓣ0479 97 12 80), just across from the tourist office on the side of the Concertgebouw, where they charge €12 per day. The main tourist office sells **cycling maps** of Bruges and its surroundings.

Guided tours and boat trips

Guided tours are big business in Bruges. The tourist office (see above) has comprehensive details, but among the many options, one long-standing favourite is a **horse-drawn carriage ride** (daily 10am–10pm). Carriages hold a maximum of five, and line up on the Markt to offer a 30min canter round town for €36; demand can outstrip supply, so expect to queue at the weekend. Bruges has a small army of tour operators, but one of the best is **Quasimodo Tours** (ⓣ050 37 04 70, ⓦwww.quasimodo.be), which runs a first-rate programme of excursions both in and around Bruges and out into Flanders. Highly recommended is their **Flanders Fields minibus tour** of the World War I battlefields near Ieper (see pp.137–141). Tours cost €60 (under 26 €50), including picnic lunch, and last about eight hours. Reservations are required and hotel or train station pick-up can be arranged. Their sister organization, **Quasimundo** (ⓣ050 33 07 75, ⓦwww.quasimundo.be) runs several **bike tours**, starting from the Burg. Their "Bruges by Bike" excursion (daily March–Oct; 2.5hr; €24) zips round the main sights and then explores less visited parts of the city, while their "Border by Bike" tour (daily March–Oct; 4hr; €24) is a 25km ride out along the poplar-lined canals to the north of Bruges, visiting Damme and Oostkerke with stops and stories along the way. Both are good fun and the price includes mountain bike and rain-jacket hire; reservations are required.

Boat trips

Half-hour **boat trips** round the city's central canals leave from a number of jetties south of the Burg (March–Nov daily 10am–6pm; €6.90). Boats depart every few minutes, but long queues still build up during high season, with few visitors seemingly concerned by the canned commentary. In winter (Dec–Feb), there's a spasmodic service at weekends only.

Accommodation

Bruges has over one hundred hotels, dozens of B&Bs and several youth hostels, but still can't accommodate all its visitors at the height of the season, when you'd be well advised to **book ahead** (though the tourist office – see opposite – does operate a last-minute accommodation booking service). At other times of the year, things are usually much less pressing, but it's still a good idea to make an advance reservation especially if you're picky about where you want to stay. Twenty-odd establishments are reviewed below, but if you need a more general view of what's on offer either consult the city's official website (ⓦwww.brugge.be) or pick up a free accommodation booklet at the tourist office. Most of the city's **hotels** are small – twenty rooms, often less – and few are owned by a chain. Standards are generally high, but note that hoteliers are wont to deck out their foyers rather grandly, often in contrast to the spartan rooms beyond, while many places offer rooms of widely divergent size and comfort. The city's **hostels** are a patchy bunch: don't expect too much in the way of comfort.

Unless otherwise stated, the places below are marked on the central Bruges map, p.154.

Hotels

Adornes St Annarei 26 ⓣ050 34 13 36, ⓦwww.adornes.be. Medium-sized, three-star in a tastefully converted old Flemish town house with a plain, high-gabled facade. Both the public areas and the comfortable bedrooms are decorated in attractive pastel shades which emphasize the antique charm of the place. Great location, at the junction of two canals near the east end of Spiegelrei, and delicious breakfasts. Also very child-friendly: high chairs for the dining room are no problem, for example. ❺

Alegria St-Jakobsstraat 34 ⓣ050 33 09 37, ⓦwww.alegria-hotel.com. Formerly a B&B, this appealing, family-run three-star has a dozen or so large and well-appointed rooms, each decorated in attractive shades of brown, cream and white. The rooms at the back, overlooking the garden, are quieter than those at the front. The owner is a goldmine of information about where and what to eat, and a central location, just a brief stroll from the Markt. ❸

Cordoeanier Cordoeaniersstraat 18 ⓣ050 33 90 51, ⓦwww.cordoeanier.be. Medium-sized, family-run two-star hotel handily located in a narrow side street a couple of minutes' walk north of the Burg. Mosquitoes can be a problem here, but the twenty-two rooms are clean and pleasant. ❸

Egmond Minnewater 15 ⓣ050 34 14 45, ⓦwww.egmond.be. Set in a neo-Gothic manor house, this rambling three-star stands in a quiet location in its own gardens just metres from the Minnewater. The public rooms have wooden beamed ceilings and fine eighteenth-century chimneypieces, while the eight guest rooms are comfortable-traditional and surprisingly affordable. See map, pp.150–151. ❹

Europ Augustijnenrei 18 ⓣ050 33 79 75, ⓦwww.hoteleurop.com. Two-star hotel in a late nineteenth-century town house overlooking a canal about 5min walk north of the Burg. The public areas are somewhat frumpy and the modern bedrooms distinctly spartan, but the prices are very competitive. ❷

Jacobs Baliestraat 1 ⓣ050 33 98 31, ⓦwww.hoteljacobs.be. Pleasant three-star set in a creatively modernized old brick building complete with a precipitous crow-step gable. The twenty-odd rooms are decorated in brisk modern style, though some are a little small. In a quiet location in an attractive part of the centre, a 10min walk to the northeast of the Markt. ❸

Montanus Nieuwe Gentweg 78 ⓣ050 33 11 76, ⓦwww.montanus.be. Smart four-star occupying a substantial seventeenth-century mansion kitted out in crisp modern style – though most of the rooms are at the back, in chalet-like accommodation at the far end of a large and attractive garden. There's also an especially appealing room in what amounts to a (cosy and luxurious) garden shed. ❺

Passage Hotel Dweersstraat 28 ⓣ050 34 02 32, ⓦwww.passagebruges.com. A ten-minute stroll west of the Markt, this bargain-basement hotel is a real steal, with simple and straightforward en-suite doubles for just €65, plus doubles with shared facilities from €50. It's a very popular spot and there are only ten rooms (four en suite) so advance reservations are essential. The busy bar serves inexpensive meals and is a favourite with backpackers. ❶

Die Swaene Steenhouwersdijk 1 ⓣ050 34 27 98, ⓦwww.dieswaene.com. The

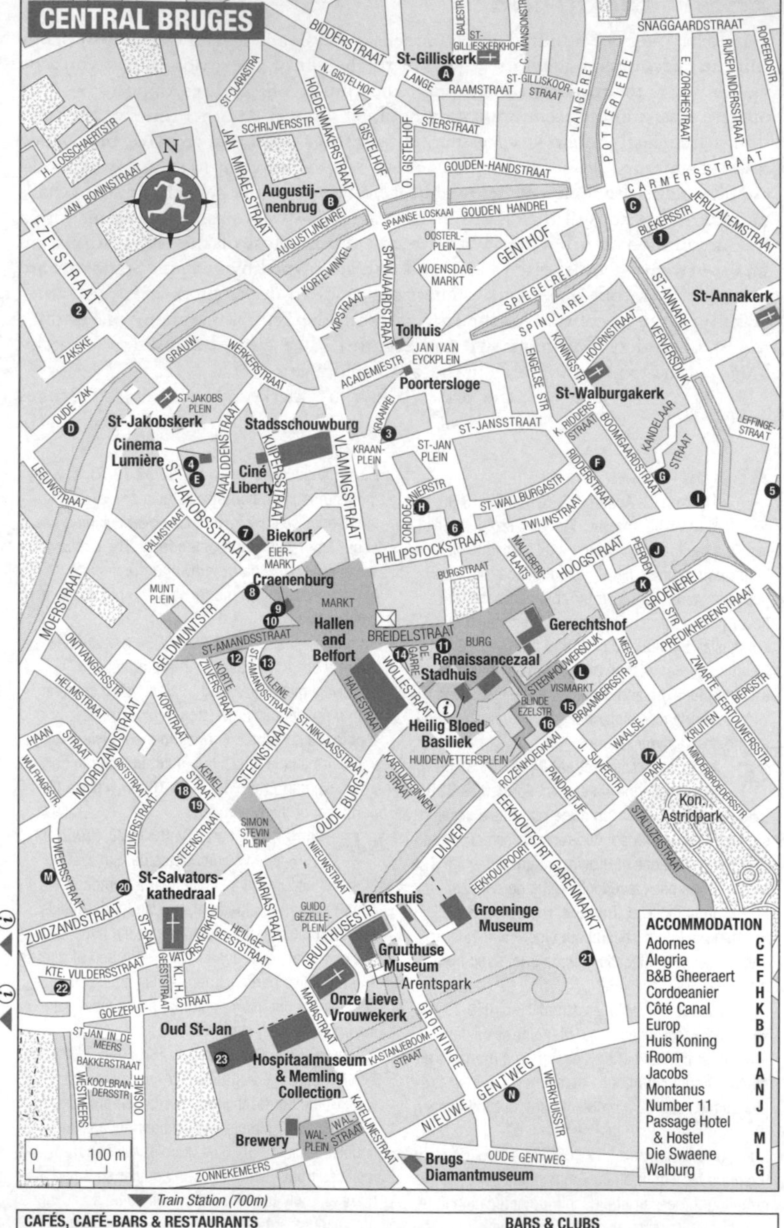

Train Station (700m)

CAFÉS, CAFÉ-BARS & RESTAURANTS

- Den Amand 10
- De Belegde Boterham 13
- Breydel De Coninc 11
- Café Craenenburg 9
- Cafedraal 20
- Christophe 21
- Het Dagelijks Brood 6
- Gran Kaffee de Passage M
- Herberghe Vlissinghe 1
- Kok au Vin 2
- Lokkedize 22
- Café de Medici 8
- De Refter 5
- De Stove 12
- De Visscherie 15
- In Den Wittenkop 7

BARS & CLUBS

- B-in 23
- Het Brugs Beertje 19
- Dreupelhuisje 18
- L'Estaminet 17
- De Garre 14
- De Republiek 4
- De Vuurmolen 3
- Wijnbar Est 16

unassuming brick exterior of this long-established four-star is deceptive, as each of the large rooms beyond is luxuriously furnished in an individual antique style; a new annexe has ten sumptuously decorated "Pergola" suites complete with marble bathrooms and lavish soft furnishings. The location is perfect too, beside a particularly pretty and peaceful section of canal close to the Burg – which partly accounts for its reputation as one of the city's most "romantic" hotels. There's a heated pool and sauna. The breakfast will set you up for the best part of a day. 7

Ter Duinen Langerei 52 ⓣ050 33 04 37, ⓦwww.hotelterduinen.eu. Charming, three-star hotel in a lovely part of the city, beside the Langerei canal about ten minutes' walk from the Markt. Occupies a beautifully maintained eighteenth-century villa, where the public areas are decidedly period and the rooms very modern. Superb breakfasts, too. See map, pp.150–151. 5

Walburg Boomgaardstraat 13 ⓣ050 34 94 14, ⓦwww.hotelwalburg.be. Engaging four-star in an elegant nineteenth-century mansion – with splendidly large doors – a short walk east of the Burg along Hoogstraat. The rooms are smart and comfortable without being overly fussy, and there are also capacious suites. 5

Bed & breakfasts

Absoluut Verhulst Verbrand Nieuwland 1 ⓣ050 33 45 15, ⓦwww.b-bverhulst.com. Immaculate B&B with a handful of en-suite rooms in a tastefully modernized seventeenth-century house with its own walled garden. The Loft Suite is larger (and slightly more expensive) than the other rooms. See map, pp.150–151. 3

B&B Gheeraert Riddersstraat 9 ⓣ050 33 56 27, ⓦwww.bb-bruges.be. The three en-suite guest rooms here are bright and smart, and occupy the top floor of a creatively modernized old house a short walk east from the Burg. No credit cards. 2

Côté Canal Hertsbergestraat 10 ⓣ0475 45 77 07, ⓦwww.bruges-bedandbreakfast.be. Deluxe B&B in a handsome – and handsomely restored – eighteenth-century mansion, with two large guest rooms kitted out in grand period style down to the huge, flowing drapes. Central location. 5

Huis Koning Oude Zak 25 ⓣ0476 25 08 12, ⓦwww.huiskoning.be. A plushly renovated B&B in a seventeenth-century terrace house with a pleasant canalside garden. The three en-suite guest rooms are decorated in a crisp modern style and two have canal views. 4

iRoom Verversdijk 1 ⓣ050 33 73 53, ⓦwww.iroom.be. Three well-equipped and well-appointed modern rooms, all en suite, in a sympathetically updated old town house within easy walking distance of the centre. Competitively priced. 3

Number 11 Peerdenstraat 11 ⓣ050 33 06 75, ⓦwww.number11.be. In the heart of Bruges, on a traffic-free side street, this first-rate B&B has just three lavish guest rooms, all wooden floors, beamed ceilings and expensive wallpaper. Every comfort – and smashing breakfasts too. 6

Hostels

International Youth Hostel Europa Baron Ruzettelaan 143 ⓣ050 35 26 79, ⓦwww.vjh.be. Big and institutional HI-affiliated hostel in its own grounds, a (dreary) 2km south of the centre in the suburb of Assebroek. There are over 200 beds in a mixture of rooms from singles through to six-bed dorms, some en suite. Breakfast is included in the price. Security lockers, internet access and no curfew. City bus #2 from the train station goes within 150m – ask the driver to let you off at the Wantestraat bus stop. See map, pp.150–151. Dorm beds from €15.70, doubles 1

Passage Dweersstraat 26 ⓣ050 34 02 32, ⓦwww.passagebruges.com. Next to the bargain-basement hotel of the same name (see p.153), this hostel can accommodate fifty people in ten comparatively comfortable dormitories, all with shared bathrooms. Free wi-fi and no curfew. Rates from €15 for a dorm bed, sheets included, €5 extra for breakfast. 1

The City

Passing through Bruges in 1820, William Wordsworth declared that this was where he discovered "a deeper peace than in deserts found". He was neither the first nor the last Victorian to fall in love with the place; by the 1840s there was a substantial **British colony** here, its members enraptured by the city's medieval architecture and air of lost splendour. Neither were the expatriates slow to exercise their economic muscle, applying an architectural **Gothic Revival** brush to parts of the city that weren't "medieval" enough. Time and again, they intervened in municipal planning decisions, allying themselves to like-minded Flemings in a movement that changed, or at least modified, the face of the city – and ultimately proved highly profitable with the arrival of mass tourism in the 1960s. Thus,

The tourist office and the major museums sell a variety of **passes**, with the most economic being the **3-Dagenkaart**, a three-day pass covering all the major sights and costing €15.

Bruges is not the perfectly preserved medieval city of much tourist literature, but rather a clever, frequently seamless combination of medieval original and nineteenth- and sometimes twentieth-century additions.

The obvious place to start an exploration of the city is in the two principal squares: the **Markt**, overlooked by the mighty **belfry**, and the **Burg**, flanked by the city's most impressive architectural ensemble. Almost within shouting distance, along the Dijver, are the three main museums, among which the **Groeninge** offers a wonderful sample of early Flemish art. Another short hop brings you to **St Janshospitaal** and the important paintings of the fifteenth-century artist **Hans Memling**, as well as Bruges's most impressive churches, the **Onze Lieve Vrouwekerk** and **St-Salvatorskathedraal**.

Further afield, the gentle canals and maze-like cobbled streets of eastern Bruges – stretching out from **Jan van Eyckplein** – are extraordinarily pretty. The most characteristic architectural feature is the crow-step gable, popular from the fourteenth to the eighteenth century and revived by the restorers of the 1880s and later, but there are also expansive Georgian-style mansions and humble, homely cottages. There are one or two obvious targets here, principally the **Kantcentrum** (Lace Centre), where you can buy locally made lace and watch its manufacture, and the city's most unusual church, the adjacent **Jeruzalemkerk**. Above all, however, eastern Bruges excels in the detail, surprising the eye again and again with its sober and subtle variety, featuring everything from intimate arched doorways and bendy tiled roofs to wonky chimneys and a bevy of discrete shrines and miniature statues.

The Markt

At the heart of Bruges is the **Markt**, an airy open space edged on three sides by rows of gabled buildings and with horse-drawn buggies clattering over the cobbles. The burghers of nineteenth-century Bruges were keen to put something suitably civic in the middle of the square and the result was the conspicuous **monument** to the leaders of the Bruges Matins (see p.149), Pieter de Coninck, of the guild of weavers, and Jan Breydel, dean of the guild of butchers. Standing close together, they clutch the hilt of the same sword, their faces turned to the south in slightly absurd poses of heroic determination.

The biscuit-tin buildings flanking most of the Markt form a charming architectural chorus, their mellow ruddy-brown brick shaped into a long string of pointed gables, each gable of which is compatible with but slightly different from its neighbour. Most are late nineteenth- or even twentieth-century re-creations – or re-inventions – of older buildings, though the old **post office**, which hogs the east side of the square, is a thunderous neo-Gothic edifice that refuses to camouflage its modern construction. The **Craenenburg Café**, on the corner of St Amandsstraat at Markt 16, occupies a modern building too, but it marks the site of the eponymous medieval mansion in which the guildsmen of Bruges imprisoned the Habsburg heir, Archduke Maximilian, for three months in 1488. The reason for their difference of opinion was the archduke's efforts to limit the city's privileges, but whatever the justice of their cause, the guildsmen made a big mistake. Maximilian made all sorts of promises to escape their clutches, but a few weeks after his release his father, the Emperor Frederick III, turned up with an army to take imperial revenge. Maximilian became emperor in 1493 and he never forgave Bruges, doing his considerable best to push trade north to its great rival, Antwerp.

The Belfort and the Hallen

Filling out the south side of the Markt, but entered via the Hallen (see below), the mighty **Belfort** (daily 9.30am–5pm; €8) was long a potent symbol of civic pride and municipal independence, its distinctive octagonal lantern visible for miles across the surrounding polders. The Belfort was begun in the thirteenth century, when the town was at its richest and most extravagant, but has had a blighted history. The original wooden version was struck by lightning and burned to the ground in 1280. Its brick replacement received its octagonal stone lantern and a second wooden spire in the 1480s, but the new spire was lost to a thunderstorm a few years later. Undeterred, the Flemings promptly added a third spire, though when this went up in smoke in 1741 the locals gave up, settling for the present structure, with the addition of a stone parapet in 1822. Few would say the Belfort is good-looking – it's large and really rather clumsy – but it does have a certain ungainly charm, though this was lost on G.K. Chesterton, who described it as "an unnaturally long-necked animal, like a giraffe".

Entry to the belfry is via the quadrangular **Hallen** at its base. Now used for temporary exhibitions, the Hallen is a much-restored edifice also dating from the thirteenth century, its style and structure modelled on the Lakenhalle in Ieper (see p.135). In the middle, overlooked by a long line of galleries, is a rectangular courtyard which originally served as the city's principal market, its cobblestones once crammed with merchants and their wares. On the north side of the courtyard, up a flight of steps, is the **entrance to the belfry**. Inside, the **belfry staircase** begins innocuously enough, but it gets steeper and much narrower as it nears the top. On the way up, it passes several mildly interesting chambers, beginning with the **Treasury Room**, where the town charters and money chest were locked for safe keeping. Here also is an iron trumpet with which a watchman could warn the town of a fire outbreak – though given the size of the instrument, it's hard to believe this was very effective. Further up is the **Carillon Chamber**, where you can observe the slow turning of the large spiked drum that controls the 47 bells of the municipal carillon (for more on the carillon see p.234). The city still employs a full-time bell ringer – you're likely to see him fiddling around in the Carillon Chamber – who puts on regular **carillon concerts** (mid-June to mid-Sept Mon, Wed & Sat at 9pm, plus Sun at 2pm; mid-Sept to mid-June Wed at 11am, Sat & Sun at 2pm; free). A few stairs up from here and you emerge onto the belfry **roof**, which offers fabulous views over the city, especially in the late afternoon when the warm colours of the city are at their deepest.

The Burg

From the east side of the Markt, Breidelstraat leads through to the city's other main square, the **Burg**, named after the fortress built here by the first count of Flanders, Baldwin Iron Arm, in the ninth century. The fortress disappeared centuries ago, but the Burg long remained the centre of political and ecclesiastical power with the Stadhuis (which has survived) on one side and **St-Donaaskathedraal** (which hasn't) on the other. The French army destroyed the cathedral in 1799 and although the foundations were laid bare in the 1950s, they were promptly re-interred – they lie in front of and underneath the *Crowne Plaza Hotel*.

Heilig Bloed Basiliek

The southern half of the Burg is fringed by the city's finest group of buildings, beginning on the right with the **Heilig Bloed Basiliek** (Basilica of the Holy Blood; April–Sept daily 9.30am–noon & 2–6pm; Oct–March Mon–Tues & Thurs–Sun 10am–noon & 2–4pm, Wed 10am–noon), named after the holy relic that found its way here in the Middle Ages. The church divides into two parts.

Tucked away in the corner, the **lower chapel** is a shadowy, crypt-like affair, originally built at the beginning of the twelfth century to shelter another relic, that of St Basil, one of the great figures of the early Greek Church. The chapel's heavy and simple Romanesque lines are decorated with just one relief, carved above an interior doorway and showing the baptism of Basil in which a strange giant bird, representing the Holy Spirit, plunges into a pool of water.

Next door, approached up a wide, low-vaulted curving staircase, the **upper chapel** was built a few years later, but has been renovated so frequently that it's impossible to make out the original structure; it also suffers from excessively rich nineteenth-century decoration. The building may be disappointing, but the large silver **tabernacle** that holds the rock-crystal phial of the Holy Blood is simply magnificent, being the gift of Albert and Isabella of Spain in 1611. One of the holiest relics in medieval Europe, the **phial of the Holy Blood** purports to contain a few drops of blood and water washed from the body of Christ by Joseph of Arimathea. Local legend asserts that it was the gift of Diederik d'Alsace, a Flemish knight who distinguished himself by his bravery during the Second Crusade and was given the phial by a grateful patriarch of Jerusalem in 1150. It is, however, rather more likely that the relic was acquired during the sacking of Constantinople in 1204, when the Crusaders simply ignored their collective job description and robbed and slaughtered the Byzantines instead – hence the historical invention. Whatever the truth, after several weeks in Bruges, the relic was found to be dry, but thereafter it proceeded to liquefy every Friday at 6pm until 1325, a miracle attested to by all sorts of church dignitaries, including Pope Clement V.

The phial of the Holy Blood is still venerated and, despite modern scepticism, reverence for it remains strong. It's sometimes available for visitors to touch under the supervision of a priest inside the chapel, and on Ascension Day (mid-May). it's carried through the town centre in a colourful but solemn procession, the **Heilig-Bloedprocessie**, a popular event for which grandstand tickets are sold at the main tourist office (see p.152) from March 1.

The **shrine** that holds the phial during the procession is displayed in the tiny **Schatkamer** (treasury; same times as basilica; €1.50), next to the upper chapel. Dating to 1617, it's a superb piece of work, the gold and silver superstructure encrusted with jewels and decorated with tiny religious figures. The treasury also contains an incidental collection of ecclesiastical bric-a-brac plus a handful of old paintings. Look out also, above the treasury door, for the faded strands of a locally woven seventeenth-century tapestry depicting St Augustine's funeral, the sea of helmeted heads, torches and pikes that surround the monks and abbots very much a Catholic view of a muscular State supporting a holy Church.

The Stadhuis

Immediately to the left of the basilica, the **Stadhuis** (daily 9.30am–5pm; €2 including the Renaissancezaal, see opposite) has a beautiful fourteenth-century sandstone facade, though its statues, mostly of the counts and countesses of Flanders, are modern replacements for those destroyed by the occupying French army in 1792. Inside, a flight of stairs climbs up to the magnificent **Gothic Hall**, dating from 1400 and the setting for the first meeting of the States General (parliamentary assembly) in 1464. The ceiling has been restored in a vibrant mixture of maroon, dark brown, black and gold, dripping pendant arches like decorated stalactites. The ribs of the arches converge in twelve circular **vault-keys**, picturing scenes from the New Testament. These are hard to see without binoculars, but down below – and much easier to view – are the sixteen gilded **corbels** that support them, representing the months and the four elements. The **frescoes** around the walls were commissioned in 1895 to illustrate the history of the town – or rather history as the council wanted to recall it. The largest scene, commemorating the victory over the French at the Battle of the Golden Spurs in 1302, has lots of noble knights hurrah-ing, though it's hard to take this seriously when you look at the dogs, one of which clearly has a mismatch between its body and head.

Renaissancezaal 't Brugse Vrije and Gerechtshof

Next door to the Stadhuis, above and beside the archway, is the bright and cheery **Civiele Griffie** (no admission), which was built to house the municipal records office in 1537, its elegant facade decorated with Renaissance columns and friezes superimposed on the Gothic lines of the gable below. The adjacent **Paleis van het Brugse Vrije** (Mansion of the Liberty of Bruges) is demure by comparison, but pop inside to look at the only room to have survived from the original fifteenth-century building, the Schepenkamer (Aldermen's Room), now known as the **Renaissancezaal 't Brugse Vrije** (Renaissance Hall of the Liberty of Bruges; daily 9.30am–12.30pm & 1.30–5pm; €2 including Stadhuis). Dominating the room is an enormous marble and oak **chimneypiece**, a superb example of Renaissance carving completed in 1531 to celebrate the defeat of the French at Pavia six years earlier and the advantageous Treaty of Cambrai that followed. A paean of praise to the Habsburgs, the work features the Emperor Charles V and his Austrian and Spanish relatives, each person identified by the audio-guide, though it's the trio of bulbous **codpieces** that really catch the eye. The **alabaster frieze** running below the carvings was a caution for the Liberty's magistrates, who held their courts here. In four panels, it relates the then-familiar biblical story of **Susanna**, in which – in the first panel – two old men surprise her bathing in her garden and threaten to accuse her of adultery if she resists their advances. Susanna does just that and the second panel shows her in court. In the third panel, Susanna is about to be put to death, but the magistrate, Daniel, interrogates the two men and uncovers their perjury. Susanna is acquitted and, in the final scene, the two men are stoned to death.

Adjoining the Brugse Vrije is the plodding courtyard complex of the **Gerechtshof** (Law Courts), dating from 1722 and now home to municipal offices.

To the Dijver

From the arch beside the Stadhuis, **Blinde Ezelstraat** (Blind Donkey Street) leads south across the canal to the sombre eighteenth-century Doric colonnades of the **Vismarkt** (fish market), which is still in use by a handful of traders today. The fish sellers have done rather better than the tanners and dyers who used to work in neighbouring **Huidenvettersplein**. Both disappeared long ago and nowadays tourists converge on this picturesque square in their droves, holing up in its bars and restaurants and snapping away at the postcard-perfect views of the belfry from the adjacent **Rozenhoedkaai**. From here, it's footsteps to both the Wollestraat bridge, whose sturdy stonework is overlooked by **St John Nepomuk**, the patron saint of bridges, and the **Dijver**, which tracks along the canal passing the path to the first of the city's main museums, the Groeninge, just before reaching the Arentshuis (see p.163).

The Groeninge Museum

The **Groeninge Museum** (Tues–Sun 9.30am–5pm; €8) possesses one of the world's finest samples of early Flemish paintings, from Jan van Eyck through to Hieronymus Bosch and Jan Provoost. These paintings make up the kernel of the museum's permanent collection, but there are later (albeit lesser) pieces on display too, reaching into the twentieth century, with works by the likes of Constant

Permeke and Paul Delvaux. The description below details some of the most important works and, although the collection is regularly rotated, you can expect most if not all of the ones described to be on display.

Jan van Eyck

Arguably the greatest of the early Flemish masters, **Jan van Eyck** (1385–1441) lived and worked in Bruges from 1430 until his death eleven years later. He was a key figure in the development of oil painting, modulating its tones to create paintings of extraordinary clarity and realism. The Groeninge has two gorgeous examples of his work, beginning with the miniature portrait of his wife, *Margareta van Eyck*, painted in 1439 and bearing his motto, "als ich can" (the best I can do). The painting is very much a private picture and one that had no commercial value, marking a small step away from the sponsored art – and religious preoccupations – of previous Flemish artists. The second Eyck painting is the remarkable *Madonna and Child with Canon George van der Paele*, a glowing and richly symbolic work with three figures surrounding the Madonna: the kneeling canon, St George (his patron saint) and St Donatian, to whom he is being presented. St George doffs his helmet to salute the infant Christ and speaks by means of the Hebrew word "*Adonai*" (Lord) inscribed on his chin strap, while Jesus replies through the green parrot in his left hand: folklore asserted that this type of parrot was fond of saying "*Ave*", the Latin for welcome. The canon's face is exquisitely executed, down to the sagging jowls and the bulging blood vessels at his temple, while the glasses and book in his hand add to his air of deep contemplation. Audaciously, van Eyck has broken with tradition by painting the canon among the saints rather than as a lesser figure – a distinct nod to the humanism that was gathering pace in contemporary Bruges.

Rogier van der Weyden

The Groeninge possesses two fine and roughly contemporaneous copies of paintings by **Rogier van der Weyden** (1399–1464), one-time official city painter to Brussels. The first is a tiny *Portrait of Philip the Good*, in which the pallor of the duke's aquiline features, along with the brightness of his hatpin and chain of office, are skilfully balanced by the sombre cloak and hat. The second and much larger painting, *St Luke painting the Portrait of Our Lady*, is a rendering of a popular if highly improbable legend that Luke painted Mary – thereby becoming the patron saint of painters. The painting is notable for the detail of its Flemish background and the cheeky-chappie smile of the baby Christ.

Hugo van der Goes

One of the most gifted of the early Flemish artists, **Hugo van der Goes** (d.1482) is a shadowy figure, though it is known that he became master of the painters' guild in Ghent in 1467. Eight years later, he entered a Ghent priory as a lay-brother, perhaps related to the prolonged bouts of depression that afflicted him. Few of his paintings have survived, but these exhibit a superb compositional balance and a keen observational eye – as in his last work, the luminescent *Death of Our Lady*. Sticking to religious legend, the Apostles have been miraculously transported to Mary's deathbed, where, in a state of agitation, they surround the prostrate woman. Mary is dressed in blue, but there are no signs of luxury, reflecting both der Goes's asceticism and his polemic – the artist may well have been appalled by the church's love of glitter and gold.

Hans Memling

Hans Memling (1430–1494) is represented by a pair of *Annunciation* panels from a triptych – gentle, romantic representations of an angel and Mary in contrasting shades of grey, a monochrome technique known as *grisaille*. Here also is Memling's *Moreel Triptych*, in which the formality of the design is offset by the warm colours and the gentleness of the detail – St Giles strokes the fawn and the knight's hand lies on the donor's shoulder. The central panel depicts saints Giles and Maurus to either side of St Christopher with a backdrop of mountains, clouds and sea. St Christopher, the patron saint of travellers, carries Jesus on his shoulders in an abbreviated reference to the original story which has the saint, who made his living lugging travellers across a river, carrying a child who becomes impossibly heavy. In the way of such things, it turns out that the child is Jesus and the realization turns Christopher into a Christian. The side panels show the donors and their sixteen children along with their patron saints – the knight St William for Willem Moreel, a wealthy spice trader and financier, and St Barbara for his wife. There are more Memling paintings at St-Janshospitaal (see p.165).

Gerard David and Hieronymus Bosch

Born near Gouda in the Netherlands, **Gerard David** (c.1460–1523) moved to Bruges in his early twenties. Soon admitted into the local painters' guild, he quickly rose through the ranks, becoming the city's leading artistic light after the death of Memling. Official commissions rained in on David, mostly for religious paintings, which he approached in a formal manner but with a fine eye for detail. The Groeninge holds two excellent examples of his work, starting with the *Baptism of Christ Triptych*, in which a boyish, lightly bearded Christ is depicted as part of the Holy Trinity in the central panel. There's also one of David's few secular ventures, the intriguing *Judgement of Cambyses*, painted on two oak panels. Based on a Persian legend related by Herodotus, the first panel's background shows the corrupt judge Sisamnes accepting a bribe, with his subsequent arrest by grim-faced aldermen filling the rest of the panel. The aldermen crowd in on Sisamnes with a palpable sense of menace and, as the king sentences him to be flayed alive, a sweaty look of fear sweeps over the judge's face. In the gruesome second panel the king's servants carry out the judgement, applying themselves to the task with clinical detachment. Behind, in the top right corner, the fable is completed with the judge's son dispensing justice from his father's old chair, which is now draped with the flayed skin. Completed in 1498, the painting was hung in the council chamber by the city burghers to encourage honesty amongst its magistrates.

The Groeninge also holds **Hieronymus Bosch**'s (1450–1516) *Last Judgement*, a trio of oak panels crammed with mysterious beasts, microscopic mutants and scenes of awful cruelty – men boiled in a pit or cut in half by a giant knife. It looks like unbridled fantasy, but in fact the scenes were read as symbols, a sort of strip cartoon of legend, proverb and tradition. Indeed Bosch's religious orthodoxy is confirmed by the appeal his work had for that most Catholic of Spanish kings, Philip II.

Jan Provoost and Adriaen Isenbrandt

There's more grim symbolism in **Jan Provoost**'s (1465–1529) crowded and melodramatic *Last Judgement*, painted for the Stadhuis in 1525, and his striking *The Miser and Death*, which portrays the merchant with his money in one panel, trying desperately to pass a promissory note to the grinning skeleton in the next. Provoost's career was typical of many of the Flemish artists of the early sixteenth century. Initially he worked in the Flemish manner, his style greatly influenced by Gerard David, but from about 1521 his work was reinvigorated by contact with the German painter and engraver Albrecht Dürer, who had himself been inspired by the artists of the early Italian Renaissance. Provoost moved around too, working in Valenciennes and Antwerp, before settling in Bruges in 1494. One of his Bruges contemporaries was **Adriaen Isenbrandt** (died 1551), whose speciality was small, precisely executed panels. His *Virgin and Child* triptych is a good example of his technically proficient work.

Pieter Pourbus, Frans the Elder and Frans the Younger

The Groeninge's collection of late sixteenth- and seventeenth-century paintings isn't especially strong, but there's enough to discern the period's watering down of religious themes in favour of more secular preoccupations. **Pieter Pourbus** (1523–1584) is well represented by a series of austere and often surprisingly unflattering portraits of the movers and shakers of his day. There's also his *Last Judgement*, a much larger but atypical work, crammed with muscular men and fleshy women; completed in 1551, its inspiration came from Michelangelo's Sistine Chapel. Born in Gouda, Pourbus moved to Bruges in his early twenties, becoming the leading local portraitist of his day as well as squeezing in work as a civil engineer and cartographer. Pieter was the first of an artistic dynasty with his son, **Frans the Elder** (1545–1581), jumping municipal ship to move to Antwerp as Bruges slipped into the economic doldrums. Frans was a noted portraitist too, but his success was trifling in comparison with that of his son, **Frans the Younger** (1569–1622), who became one of Europe's most celebrated portraitists, working for the Habsburgs and the Medicis amongst a bevy of powerful families. In the collection is a fine example of his work, an exquisite double portrait of the Archdukes Albert and Isabella.

The Symbolists

There is a substantial collection of nineteenth- and early twentieth-century Belgian art at the Groeninge. One obvious highlight is the work of the Symbolist **Fernand Khnopff** (1858–1921), who is represented by *Secret Reflections*, not perhaps one of his better paintings, but interesting in so far as its lower panel – showing St Janshospitaal reflected in a canal – confirms one of the movement's favourite conceits, "Bruges the dead city". This was inspired by Georges Rodenbach's novel *Bruges-la-Morte*, a highly stylized muse on love and obsession first published in 1892. The book started the craze for visiting Bruges, the so-called "dead city" where the action unfolds. The upper panel of Khnopff's painting is a play on appearance and desire, but it's pretty feeble, unlike his later attempts, in which he painted his sister, Marguerite, again and again, using her refined, almost plastic beauty to stir a vague sense of passion – for him she was desirable and unobtainable in equal measure.

The Expressionists and Surrealists

The museum has a healthy sample of the work of the talented **Constant Permeke** (1886–1952). Wounded in World War I, Permeke's grim wartime experiences helped him develop a distinctive **Expressionist** style in which his subjects – usually agricultural workers, fishermen and so forth – were monumental in form, but invested with sombre, sometimes threatening emotion. His charcoal drawing the *Angelus* is a typically dark and earthy representation of Belgian peasant life dated to 1934. In similar vein is the enormous *Last Supper* by **Gustave van de Woestijne** (1881–1947), another excellent example of Belgian Expressionism, with Jesus and the disciples, all elliptical eyes and restrained movement, trapped within prison-like walls.

Also noteworthy is the spookily stark Surrealism of **Paul Delvaux**'s (1897–1994) *Serenity*. One of the most interesting of Belgium's modern artists, Delvaux started out as an Expressionist but came to – and stayed with – **Surrealism** in the 1930s. This painting is a classic example of his oeuvre and, if it whets your artistic appetite, you might consider visiting Delvaux's old home, in St-Idesbald, which has been turned into a museum with a comprehensive selection of his paintings (see p.127).

The Groeninge also owns a couple of minor oils and a number of etchings and drawings by **James Ensor** (1860–1949), one of Belgium's most innovative painters, and **Magritte**'s (1898–1967) characteristically unnerving *The Assault*; for more on Magritte, see p.80.

The Arentshuis

The **Arentshuis**, at Dijver 16 (Tues–Sun 9.30am–5pm; €2), occupies an attractive eighteenth-century mansion with a stately porticoed entrance. Now a museum, the interior is divided into two separate sections: the ground floor is given over to temporary exhibitions, usually of fine art, while the **Brangwyn Museum** upstairs displays the moody sketches, etchings, lithographs, studies and paintings of the much-travelled artist Sir Frank Brangwyn (1867–1956). Born in Bruges of Welsh parents, Brangwyn flitted between Britain and Belgium, donating this sample of his work to his native town in 1936. Apprenticed to William Morris in the early 1880s and an official UK war artist in World War I, Brangwyn was nothing if not versatile, turning his hand to several different mediums, though his forceful drawings and sketches are much more appealing than his paintings, which often slide into sentimentality. In particular, look out for the sequence of line drawings exploring industrial themes – powerful, almost melodramatic scenes of shipbuilding, docks, construction and the like.

The Arentspark

The Arentshuis stands in the north corner of the pocket-sized **Arentspark**, whose pair of forlorn stone columns are all that remains of the Waterhalle, a large trading hall which once straddled the most central of the city's canals but was demolished in 1787 after the canal was covered over. Also in the Arentspark is the tiniest of humpbacked bridges – **St Bonifaciusbrug** – whose stonework is framed against a tumble of antique brick houses. One of Bruges's most picturesque (and photographed) spots, the bridge looks like the epitome of everything medieval, but in fact it was built only in 1910. St Bonifaciusbrug spans the canal behind and between two of the city's main museums – the Arentshuis and the Gruuthuse.

The Gruuthuse Museum

The **Gruuthuse Museum**, at Dijver 17 (Tues–Sun 9.30am–5pm; €6), is located inside a rambling mansion that dates back to the fifteenth century. The building is a fine example of civil Gothic architecture and it takes its name from the house-owners' historical right to tax the *gruit*, the dried herb and flower mixture once added to barley during the beer-brewing process to improve the flavour. The last lord of the *gruit* died in 1492 and, after many twists and turns, the mansion was turned into a museum to hold a hotchpotch of Flemish fine, applied and decorative arts, mostly from the medieval and early modern periods. The museum's strongest suit is its superb collection of **tapestries**, mostly woven in Brussels or Bruges during the sixteenth and seventeenth centuries, but the most famous artefact is a much-reproduced polychromatic terracotta **bust** of a youthful Emperor Charles V. An unusual feature is the oak-panelled **oratory** that juts out from the first floor to overlook the altar of the Onze Lieve Vrouwekerk next door. A curiously intimate room, the oratory allowed the lords of the *gruit* to worship without leaving home – a real social coup.

Onze Lieve Vrouwekerk

Next door to the Gruuthuse, the **Onze Lieve Vrouwekerk** (Church of Our Lady; Mon–Fri 9.30am–5pm, Sat 9am–4.45pm & Sun 1.30–5pm) is a rambling shambles of a building, a clamour of different dates and styles whose brick spire is – at 122m – one of the tallest in Belgium. Entered from the south, the **nave** was three hundred years in the making, an architecturally discordant affair, whose thirteenth-century grey-stone central aisle is the oldest part of the church. The central aisle blends in with the south aisle, but the later, fourteenth-century north aisle doesn't mesh at all – even the columns aren't aligned. This was the result of changing fashions, not slapdash work: the High Gothic north aisle was intended to be the start of a complete remodelling of the church, but the money ran out before the work was finished.

In the south aisle is the church's most acclaimed objet d'art, a delicate marble *Madonna and Child* by **Michelangelo**. Purchased by a Bruges merchant, this was the only one of Michelangelo's works to leave Italy during the artist's lifetime and it had a significant influence on the painters then working in Bruges, though its present setting – beneath gloomy stone walls and set within a gaudy Baroque altar – is hardly prepossessing.

The chancel

Michelangelo apart, the most interesting part of the church is the **chancel** (Tues–Sat 9.30am–5pm, Sun 1.30–5pm; €2), beyond the black and white marble rood screen. Here you'll find the **mausoleums** of Charles the Bold and his daughter Mary of Burgundy (see box below), two exquisite examples of Renaissance carving, their side panels decorated with coats of arms connected by the most intricate of floral designs. The royal figures are enhanced in the detail, from the helmet and gauntlets placed gracefully by Charles's side to the pair of watchful dogs nestled at Mary's feet. Oddly enough, the **hole** dug by archeologists beneath

The earthly remains of Mary of Burgundy and Charles the Bold

The last independent rulers of Flanders were **Charles the Bold**, the Duke of Burgundy, and his daughter **Mary of Burgundy**, both of whom died in unfortunate circumstances, Charles during the siege of the French city of Nancy in 1477, she after a riding accident in 1482, when she was only 25. Mary was married to **Maximilian**, a Habsburg prince and future Holy Roman Emperor, who inherited her territories on her death – thus, at a dynastic stroke, Flanders was incorporated into the Habsburg empire.

In the sixteenth century, the Habsburgs relocated to Spain, but they were keen to emphasize their connections with – and historical authority over – Flanders, one of the richest parts of their expanding empire. Nothing did this quite as well as the ceremonial burial – or reburial – of bits of royal body. Mary was safely ensconced in Bruges's Onze Lieve Vrouwekerk, but the body of Charles was in a makeshift grave in **Nancy**. The Emperor Charles V, the great grandson of Charles the Bold, had – or thought he had – this body exhumed and carried to Bruges, where it was reinterred next to Mary. There were, however, persistent rumours that the French, the traditional enemies of the Habsburgs, had deliberately handed over a dud skeleton, specifically one of the knights who died in the same engagement. In the 1970s, **archeologists** had a bash at solving the mystery. They dug beneath Charles and Mary's mausoleums in the Onze Lieve Vrouwekerk, but, among the assorted tombs, they failed to authoritatively identify either the body or even the tomb of Charles; Mary proved more tractable, with her skeleton confirming the known details of her hunting accident. Buried alongside her also was the **urn** which contained the heart of her son, Philip the Fair, placed here in 1506.

the mausoleums during the 1970s to discover who was actually buried here was never filled in, so you can see Mary's coffin, the urn containing the heart of her son and the burial vaults of several unknown medieval dignitaries, three of which have now been moved across to the Lanchals Chapel.

Just across the ambulatory from the mausoleums is the **Lanchals Chapel**, which holds the imposing Baroque gravestone of Pieter Lanchals, a one-time Habsburg official who had his head lopped off by the citizens of Bruges for corruption in 1488. In front of the Lanchals gravestone are three relocated **medieval burial vaults**, each plastered with lime mortar. The inside walls of the vaults sport brightly coloured **grave frescoes**, a type of art which flourished hereabouts from the late thirteenth to the middle of the fifteenth century. The iconography is fairly consistent, with the long sides mostly bearing one, sometimes two, angels apiece, and most of the angels are shown swinging thuribles (the vessels in which incense is burnt during religious ceremonies). Typically, the short sides show the Crucifixion and a Virgin and Child. The background decoration is more varied with crosses, stars and dots all making appearances as well as two main sorts of flower – roses and bluebells. The frescoes were painted freehand and executed at great speed – Flemings were then buried on the day they died – hence the delightful immediacy of the work.

The Hospitaalmuseum and the Memling Collection

Opposite the entrance to the Onze Lieve Vrouwekerk is **St-Janshospitaal**, a sprawling complex that sheltered the sick of mind and body until well into the nineteenth century. The oldest part – at the front on Mariastraat, behind two church-like gable ends – has been turned into the slick Hospitaalmuseum, while the nineteenth-century annexe, reached along a narrow passageway on the north side of the museum, has been converted into a really rather tatty exhibition-cum-shopping centre called – rather confusingly – **Oud St-Jan**.

The **Hospitaalmuseum** (Tues–Sun 9.30am–5pm; €8) divides into two, with one large section – in the former hospital ward – exploring the historical background to the hospital through documents, paintings and religious objets d'art. Highlights include a pair of sedan chairs used to carry the infirm to the hospital in emergencies, and Jan Beerblock's *The Wards of St Janshospitaal*, a minutely detailed painting of the hospital ward as it was in the late eighteenth century, the patients tucked away in row upon row of tiny, cupboard-like beds. Other noteworthy paintings include an exquisite *Deposition of Christ*, a late fifteenth-century version of an original by Rogier van der Weyden, and a stylish, intimately observed diptych by Jan Provoost, with portraits of Christ and the donor – a friar - on the front and a skull on the back.

The old chapel inside the Hospitaalmuseum displays six wonderful paintings by **Hans Memling** (1433–1494). Born near Frankfurt, Memling spent most of his working life in Bruges, where Rogier van der Weyden (see p.373) instructed him. He adopted much of his tutor's style and stuck to the detailed symbolism of his contemporaries, but his painterly manner was distinctly restrained, often pious and grave. Graceful and warmly coloured, his figures also had a velvet-like quality that greatly appealed to the city's burghers, whose enthusiasm made Memling a rich man – in 1480 he was listed among the town's major moneylenders.

Of the six works on display, the most unusual is the **Reliquary of St Ursula**, comprising a miniature wooden Gothic church painted with the story of St Ursula. Memling condensed the legend into six panels with Ursula and her ten companions landing at Cologne and Basle before reaching Rome at the end of their pilgrimage. Things go badly wrong on the way back: they leave Basle in good order, but are then – in the last two panels – massacred by Huns as they pass through Germany. Memling had a religious point to make, but today it's the mass of incidental detail that makes the reliquary so enchanting, providing an intriguing evocation of the late medieval world. Equally delightful is the **Mystical Marriage of St Catherine**, the middle panel of a large triptych depicting St Catherine, who represents contemplation, receiving a ring from the baby Jesus to seal their spiritual union. The complementary side panels depict the beheading of St John the Baptist and a visionary St John writing the Book of Revelation on the bare and rocky island of Patmos. Again, it's the detail that impresses: between the inner and outer rainbows above St John, for instance, the prophets play music on tiny instruments – look closely and you'll spy a lute, a flute, a harp and a hurdy-gurdy. Across the chapel are two more Memling triptychs, a *Lamentation* and an *Adoration of the Magi*, in which there's a gentle nervousness in the approach of the Magi, here shown as the kings of Spain, Arabia and Ethiopia.

Memling's skill as a portraitist is demonstrated to exquisite effect in his **Portrait of a Young Woman**, where the richly dressed subject stares dreamily into the middle distance, her hands – in a superb optical illusion – seeming to clasp the picture frame. The lighting is subtle and sensuous, with the woman set against a dark background, her gauze veil dappling the side of her face. A high forehead was then considered a sign of great womanly beauty, so her hair is pulled right back and was probably plucked – as are her eyebrows. There's no knowing who the woman was, but in the seventeenth century her fancy headgear convinced observers that she was one of the legendary Persian sibyls who predicted Christ's birth; so convinced were they that they added the cartouche in the top left-hand corner, describing her as *Sibylla Sambetha* – and the painting is often referred to by this name.

The sixth and final painting, the **Virgin and Martin van Nieuwenhove** diptych, is exhibited in the adjoining side chapel. Here, the eponymous merchant has the flush of youth and a hint of arrogance: his lips pout, his hair cascades down to his shoulders and he is dressed in the most fashionable of doublets – by the middle of the 1480s, when the portrait was commissioned, no Bruges merchant wanted to appear too pious. Opposite, the Virgin gets the full stereotypical treatment from the oval face and the almond-shaped eyes through to full cheeks, thin nose and bunched lower lip.

St-Salvatorskathedraal

From St Janshospitaal, it's a couple of minutes' walk north to **St-Salvatorskathedraal** (Holy Saviour Cathedral; Mon 2–5.30pm, Tues–Fri 9am–noon & 2–5.30pm, Sat 9am–noon & 2–3.30pm, Sun 9–10am & 2–5pm), a bulky Gothic edifice that mostly dates from the late thirteenth century, though the ambulatory was added some two centuries later. A parish church for most of its history, it was only made a cathedral in 1834 following the destruction of St Donatian's (see p.157) by the French. This change of status prompted lots of ecclesiastical rumblings – nearby Onze Lieve Vrouwekerk (see p.164) was bigger and its spire higher – and when part of St Salvators went up in smoke in 1839, the opportunity was taken to make its tower higher and grander in a romantic rendition of the Romanesque style.

Recently cleaned, the cathedral's **nave** has emerged from centuries of accumulated grime, but it remains a cheerless, cavernous affair. The star turn is the **set of eight paintings** by Jan van Orley displayed in the transepts. Commissioned in the 1730s, the paintings were used for the manufacture of a matching set of **tapestries** from a Brussels workshop and, remarkably enough, these have survived too and hang in sequence in the choir and nave. Each of the eight scenes is a fluent, dramatic composition featuring a familiar episode from the life of Christ – from the Nativity to the Resurrection – complete with a handful of animals, including a remarkably determined Palm Sunday donkey. The tapestries are actually mirror images of the paintings as the weavers worked with the rear of the tapestries uppermost on their looms; the weavers also had sight of the tapestry paintings – or rather cartoon copies, as the originals were too valuable to be kept beside the looms.

Entered from the nave, the cathedral **Schatkamer** (treasury; daily except Sat 2–5pm; €2.50) occupies the adjoining neo-Gothic chapter house, whose nine rooms are packed with ecclesiastical tackle, from religious paintings and statues through to an assortment of reliquaries, vestments and croziers. The labelling is poor, however, so it's a good idea to pick up the English-language mini-guide at the entrance. **Room B** holds the treasury's finest painting, a gruesome, oak-panel triptych, *The Martyrdom of St Hippolytus*, by Dieric Bouts (1410–1475) and Hugo van der Goes (d. 1482). The right panel depicts the Roman Emperor Decius, a notorious persecutor of Christians, trying to persuade the priest Hippolytus to abjure his faith. He fails, and in the central panel Hippolytus is pulled to pieces by four horses.

The Begijnhof

Heading south from St-Janshospitaal (see p.165), it's a short stroll to **Wijngaardstraat**, whose antique terrace houses have been turned into souvenir shops, cafés and restaurants. This is one of the most visited corners of Bruges, not least because it's metres from the **Begijnhof** (daily 6.30am–6.30pm or sunset; free), where a rough circle of old and infinitely pretty whitewashed houses surrounds a central green; the best time to visit is in spring, when a carpet of daffodils pushes up between the wispy elms. There were once *begijnhofs* all over Belgium, and this is one of the few to have survived in good nick. They date back to the twelfth century, when a Liège priest, a certain Lambert le Bègue, encouraged widows and unmarried women to live in communities, the better to do pious acts, especially caring for the sick. These communities were different from convents in so far as the inhabitants – the **beguines** (*begijns*) – did not have to take conventual vows and had the right to return to the secular world if they wished. Margaret, Countess of Flanders, founded Bruges's *begijnhof* in 1245 and, although most of the houses now standing date from the eighteenth century, the medieval layout has survived intact, preserving the impression of the *begijnhof* as a self-contained village, with access controlled through two large gates.

The houses of the *begijnhof* are still in private hands, but, with the beguines long gone, they are now occupied by Benedictine nuns, who you'll see flitting around in their habits, mostly on their way to and from the **Begijnhofkerk**, an appropriately simple place of worship. Only one house is open to the public – the **Begijnenhuisje** (Mon–Sat 10am–5pm, Sun 2.30–5pm; €2), a pint-sized celebration of the simple life of the beguines. The prime exhibit is the *schapraai*, a traditional beguine's cupboard, which was a frugal combination of dining table, cutlery cabinet and larder.

The Minnewater

Facing the more southerly of the *begijnhof*'s two gates is the **Minnewater**, often hyped as the city's "Lake of Love". The tag certainly gets the canoodlers going, but in fact the lake – more a large pond – started life as a city harbour. The distinctive stone **lock house** at the head of the Minnewater recalls its earlier function, though it's actually a very fanciful nineteenth-century reconstruction of the medieval original. The **Poertoren**, on the west bank at the far end of the lake, is more authentic, its brown brickwork dating from 1398 and once part of the city wall. This is where the city kept its gunpowder – hence the name, "powder tower".

Beside the Poertoren, a footbridge spans the southern end of the Minnewater to reach the leafy expanse of **Minnewaterpark**, which trails north back towards the *begijnhof*.

North and east of the Markt

Jan van Eyckplein, a five-minute walk north of the Markt, is one of the prettiest squares in Bruges, its cobbles backdropped by the easy sweep of the Spiegelrei canal. The centrepiece of the square is an earnest **statue of Van Eyck**, erected in 1878, whilst on the north side is the **Tolhuis**, whose fancy Renaissance entrance is decorated with the coat of arms of the dukes of Luxembourg, who long levied tolls here. The Tolhuis dates from the late fifteenth century, but was extensively remodelled in medieval style in the 1870s, as was the **Poortersloge** (Merchants' Lodge), whose slender tower pokes up above the rooftops on the west side of the square. Theoretically, any city merchant was entitled to be a member of the Poortersloge, but in fact membership was restricted to the richest and the most powerful. An informal alternative to the Town Hall, it was here that key political and economic decisions were taken – and this was also where local bigwigs could drink and gamble discreetly.

The Spiegelrei canal and the Augustijnenbrug

Running east from Jan van Eyckplein, the **Spiegelrei canal** was once the heart of the foreign merchants' quarter, its frenetic quays overlooked by the trade missions of many of the city's trading partners. The medieval buildings were demolished long ago but they have been replaced by an exquisite medley of architectural styles, from expansive Georgian mansions to pirouetting crow-step gables.

At the far end of Spiegelrei, turn left onto one of the city's prettiest streets, **Gouden-Handrei**, which – along with its continuation, **Spaanse Loskaai** – was once the focus of the Spanish merchants' quarter. The west end of Spaanse Loskaai is marked by the **Augustijnenbrug**, the city's oldest surviving bridge, a sturdy three-arched structure dating from 1391. The bridge was built to help the monks of a nearby (and long demolished) Augustinian monastery get into the city centre speedily; the benches set into the parapet were cut to allow itinerant tradesmen to display their goods here.

Running south from the bridge is **Spanjaardstraat**, also part of the Spanish enclave. It was here, at no. 9, in a house formerly known as **De Pijnappel** (The Fir Cone), that the founder of the Jesuits, Ignatius Loyola (1491–1556), spent his holidays while he was a student in Paris, but unfortunately the town's liberality failed to dent Loyola's nascent fanaticism. Spanjaardstraat leads back to Jan van Eyckplein.

Kantcentrum

Beyond the east end of the Spiegelrei canal is an old working-class district, whose low brick cottages surround a substantial complex of buildings that originally belonged to the wealthy Adornes family, who migrated here from Genoa in the thirteenth century. Inside the complex, the **Kantcentrum** (Lace Centre; Mon–Sat 10am–5pm; €2.50), on the right-hand side of the entrance, has a busy workshop and offers very informal demonstrations of traditional lacemaking in the afternoon (no set times). They sell the stuff too – both here and in the shop at the ticket kiosk – but it isn't cheap: a smallish Bruges table mat, with two swans, for example, costs €20–25; if you fancy having a go yourself, the shop sells all the gubbins.

Jeruzalemkerk

Across the passageway from the Kantcentrum is one of the city's real oddities, the **Jeruzalemkerk** (Jerusalem Church; same times & ticket as the Kantcentrum), which was built by the Adornes family in the fifteenth century as an approximate copy of the Church of the Holy Sepulchre in Jerusalem after one of their number, Pieter, had returned from a pilgrimage to the Holy Land. The interior is on two levels: the lower one is dominated by a large and ghoulish altarpiece, decorated with skulls and ladders, in front of which is the black marble tomb of Anselm Adornes, the son of the church's founder, and his wife Margaretha. There's more grisliness at the back of the church, where the small vaulted **chapel** holds a replica of Christ's tomb – you can glimpse the imitation body down the tunnel behind the iron grating. To either side of the main altar, steps ascend to the choir, which is situated right below the eccentric, onion-domed lantern tower.

Kantmuseum

Behind the Jeruzalemkerk, the tiny **Kantmuseum** (Lace Museum; same times & ticket as the Kantcentrum) is of passing interest for its samples of antique lace. Renowned for the fineness of its thread and beautiful motifs, Belgian lace – or **Flanders lace** as it was formerly known – was once worn in the courts of Brussels, Paris, Madrid and London, with Bruges the centre of its production. Handmade lace reached the peak of its popularity in the early nineteenth century, when hundreds of Bruges women and girls worked as home-based lacemakers. The industry was, however, transformed by the arrival of **machine-made lace** in the 1840s and, by the end of the century, handmade lace had been largely supplanted, with the lacemakers obliged to work in factories. This highly mechanized industry collapsed after World War I when lace, a symbol of an old and discredited order, suddenly had no place in the wardrobe of most women. The Kantmuseum holds fifty or so examples of old, handmade lace, the most elaborate of which is its sample of late nineteenth-century Chantilly lace. Incidentally, most **lace shops in Bruges** – and there are lots – sell lace manufactured in the Far East, especially China. For details of the best lace shop in town, see p.172.

Museum voor Volkskunde and St Janshuismolen

From the Kantcentrum, it's a brief walk north to the **Museum voor Volkskunde** (Folklore Museum; Tues–Sun 9.30am–5pm; €2), which occupies a long line of low-ceilinged almshouses set beside a trim courtyard. It's a varied collection, comprising a string of period rooms and workshops with the emphasis on the nineteenth and early twentieth centuries, but the labelling is patchy so it's best to pick up an English guidebook at reception. Beside the entrance, *In De Zwarte Kat* – the Black Cat – is a small tavern done out in traditional style and serving ales and snacks.

Rolweg leads east from the Museum voor Volkskunde to the long and wide earthen **bank** that marks the path of the old town walls. Perched on top are a quartet of **windmills** – two clearly visible close by and another two beyond eyeshot, about 300m and 500m to the north. You'd have to be something of a windmill fanatic to want to visit them all, but the nearest two are mildly diverting – and the closest, **St-Janshuismolen**, is in good working order (May–Aug Tues–Sun 9.30am–12.30pm & 1.30–5pm; €2).

From the **St Janshuismolen,** it's a ten- to fifteen-minute stroll back to the Markt.

Eating

There are literally scores of **cafés** and **restaurants** in Bruges, and thankfully precious few of them are owned by chains. Many are geared up for the day-trippers, with variable results, but the city also boasts lots of first-rate, reasonably priced places as well as a slew of prestige restaurants, where standards (and prices) are high. Here, as elsewhere in Belgium, the distinction between the city's cafés and bars (see p.171) is blurred with both selling a wide range of beers and food – and we've listed some of these as **café-bars**. Across the city, most waiters speak at least a modicum of English – many are fluent – and **multilingual menus** are the norm.

Unless otherwise stated, the places below are marked on the Central Bruges map, p.154.

Cafés and café-bars

De Belegde Boterham Kleine St-Amandsstraat 5. Most of the cafés in and around the Markt are firmly tourist-orientated, but this bright and breezy little place, in attractively renovated old premises down a narrow lane, has a strong local following on account of its fresh sandwiches (€7–10) and tasty salads (€12–14). Mon–Sat noon–4pm.

Café Craenenburg Markt 16. Unlike the Markt's other tourist-dominated café-restaurants, this old-fashioned place still attracts a loyal, local clientele. With its leather and wood panelling, wooden benches and mullion windows, the *Craenenburg* has the flavour of old Flanders, and although the daytime-only food is routine (mains from €16), it has a good range of beers, including a locally produced, tangy brown ale called Brugse Tripel. Daily 10am until late.

Het Dagelijks Brood Philipstockstraat 21. This first-rate bread shop doubles as a wholefood café, with one long wooden table – enforced communalism, which can be good fun – and a few smaller side tables too. The home-made soup and bread makes a meal in itself for just €9, or you can chomp away on a range of snacks and cakes. Mon & Wed–Sun 8am–6pm.

Gran Kaffee de Passage Dweersstraat 26. This lively café-bar is extremely popular with backpackers, many of whom have bunked down in the adjacent *Passage Hostel* (see p.155). Serves up a good and filling line in Flemish food, with many dishes cooked in beer, as well as mussels and vegetarian options. Not much in the way of frills, but then main courses only cost around €10. Daily 6pm–midnight, kitchen closes 10.30pm.

Herberghe Vlissinghe Blekersstraat 2. With its wood panelling, antique paintings and long wooden tables, this is one of the oldest and most distinctive bars in Bruges, thought to date from 1515. The atmosphere is relaxed and easy-going, with the emphasis on quiet conversation – there are certainly no jukeboxes here – and the café-style food is very Flemish. There's a pleasant garden terrace too. Wed–Sat 11am–midnight, Sun 11am–7pm.

Lokkedize Korte Vuldersstraat 33. This sympathetic café-bar – all subdued lighting and jazz-meets-chanson music – serves up a good line in Mediterranean food, with main courses averaging around €12, bar snacks from €7. Wed–Sun 6pm to midnight.

Café de Medici Geldmuntstraat 9. An enjoyable antidote to the plain modernism of many of its rivals, this attractive café boasts an extravagantly ornate interior, complete with a huge mirror and spindly curving staircase. The best range of coffees in town, not to mention mouthwatering cakes and tarts, plus sandwiches and salads too, from as little as €5. Mon–Sat 9am–6pm.

De Windmolen Carmersstraat 135. This amiable neighbourhood café-bar in an old brick house at the east end of Carmersstraat dishes up a decent line in inexpensive snacks and light meals – *croque monsieur*, spaghetti, lasagne and so forth – and possesses a competent beer menu. A pleasant outside terrace and an interior dotted with folksy knick-knacks. Mon–Thurs 10am–10pm, Fri & Sun 10am–3pm. See map, pp.150–151.

Restaurants

Den Amand St-Amandstraat 4 ☎050 34 01 22. Decorated in pleasant modern style, this cosy and informal family-run restaurant offers an inventive range of dishes combining French and Flemish cuisines. Mains from the limited but well-chosen menu – for instance, turbot or seafood *waterzooi* (soup) – average a very reasonable €20. It's a small place, so best to book a few hours in advance. Daily except Wed & Sun noon–2.15pm & 6–9.15pm.

Breydel De Coninc Breidelstrat 24 ☎050 33 97 46. In the heart of the tourist scrum, perhaps, but this well-regarded, modern restaurant is strong on seafood with mussels and eels the house specialities and a lobster tank too. Mains average €26. Daily except Wed noon–2pm & 6–10pm.

Cafedraal Zilverstraat 38 ☎050 34 08 45, ⓦwww.cafedraal.be. Fashionable and popular restaurant decked out in ersatz medieval style, with oodles of wood panelling, a big open fire in winter and an outside garden terrace in summer. The menu runs the gamut of French and Flemish dishes, but it's hard to beat the North Sea bouillabaisse or the lobster and veal cooked in mustard. The only fly in the ointment is the patchy service. Main courses €20–25. Mon–Sat noon–3pm & 6–11pm.

Christophe Garenmarkt 34 ⓣ050 34 48 92. Particularly attractive little bistro, where a small but well-chosen menu features the likes of scampi in an almond sauce. The steaks are especially good. Mains average €24. Daily except Tues & Wed 7–11pm.

Kok au Vin Ezelstraat 19 ⓣ050 33 95 21. Chic restaurant in tastefully modernized old premises on the north side of the city centre. An ambitious menu covers all the Franco-Belgian bases and then some, with mains averaging around €25, though lunch is half that. Try the signature dish – coq au vin. Reservations essential. Daily except Sun & Mon noon–2pm & 6.30–10pm.

De Refter Molenmeers 2 ⓣ050 44 49 00. Fashionable bistro-restaurant with über-cool decor where the emphasis is on local, seasonal ingredients cooked up into all the classic Flemish dishes – try the meatballs in a tarragon sauce. Competitively priced too, with a two-course set meal costing just €25. Outside terrace for summertime dining. Tues–Sat noon–2pm & 6.30–10pm.

De Stove Kleine St-Amandsstraat 4 ⓣ050 33 78 35. Noticeably small and extraordinarily cosy Franco-Belgian restaurant that's recommended by just about everyone, including Michelin. The menu is carefully constructed with both fish and meat dishes given equal prominence. A la carte mains around €26, but the big deal is the three-course set menu for €45, €60 with wine. Reservations essential. Daily except Wed & Thurs 7–10pm, plus Sat & Sun noon–2pm.

De Visscherie Vismarkt 8 ⓣ050 33 02 12, ⓦwww.visscherie.be. One of the city's smartest restaurants, *De Visscherie* specializes in seafood, its well-presented and imaginative menu featuring such delights as a spectacularly tasty fish soup (€14) and cod cooked in traditional Flemish style with leeks (€32). The restaurant occupies a spacious nineteenth-century mansion, but the decor has some intriguing modern touches – small sculptures and so on – and the chairs are supremely comfortable. Love it or hate it, the bill is served up underneath a large sea shell. Daily except Tues noon–2pm & 7–10pm.

In Den Wittenkop St-Jakobstraat 14 ⓣ050 33 20 59. This small and intimate split-level restaurant is one of the most appealing in town, its interior a fetching mixture of the tasteful and the kitsch. There's smooth jazz as background music plus good Flemish food, including the local speciality of pork and beef stewed in Trappist beer. Mains average around €18. Tues–Sat noon–2pm & 6–9.30pm.

Drinking

Few would say Bruges's **bars** are cutting edge, but neither are they staid and dull – far from it if you know where to go. Indeed, drinking in the city can be a real pleasure and one of the potential highlights of any visit. As for the **club scene**, Bruges struggles to make a real fist of it, though a couple of places are enjoyable enough.

All the places below are marked on the Central Bruges map, p.154.

Bars and clubs

B-in Mariastraat 38 ⓣ050 31 13 00, ⓦwww.b-in.be. The coolest place in town, this slick bar, club and restaurant is kitted out in attractive modern style with low sofa-seats and an eye-grabbing mix of coloured fluorescent tubes and soft ceiling lights. Guest DJs play funky, uplifting house and the drinks and cocktails are reasonably priced. Attracts a relaxed and friendly crowd; the club side of things gets going about 11pm. Free entry. Daily except Sun & Mon 11am–3am, sometimes later.

Het Brugs Beertje Kemelstraat 5. This small and friendly speciality beer bar claims a stock of three hundred beers, which aficionados reckon is one of the best selections in Belgium, plus five guest brews on draft. There are tasty snacks too, such as cheeses and salad, but note that the place is very much on the (backpacker) tourist trail. Daily except Wed 4pm–1am.

Dreupelhuisje Kemelstraat 9. Traditional, likeable little bar where the big deal is the Dutch gin (jenever), served ice cold and with over twenty-five varieties to choose from. Smokers can puff away here too. Fri & Sat 5.30pm till late.

L'Estaminet Park 5. Groovy café-bar with a relaxed neighbourhood feel and (for Bruges) a diverse and cosmopolitan clientele. Rickety furniture both inside and on the large outside terrace adds to the flavour of the place, as does the world music backing track, while the first-rate beer menu skilfully picks its way through Belgium's vast offering. Daily 11am–1am or later, Thurs from 4pm.

De Garre De Garre 1. Down a narrow alley off Breidelstraat, in between the Markt and the Burg, this cramped but charming tavern has an outstanding range of Belgian beers and tasty snacks, while classical music adds to the relaxed

Shopping in Bruges: a top five

Chocolate

The Chocolate Line Simon Stevinplein 19 ⓣ050 34 10 90, ⓦwww.thechocolateline.be. The best chocolate shop in town – no mean boast – serving up quality chocolates, handmade on the premises using natural ingredients. Truffles and figurines are a speciality. Boxes of mixed chocolates are sold in various sizes: a 250g box costs €12. Tues–Sat 9.30am–6pm, Mon & Sun 10.30am–6pm.

Comics

De Striep Katelijnestraat 42 ⓣ050 33 71 12, ⓦwww.striepclub.be. Comics are a Belgian speciality (as per Tintin), but this is the only comic-strip specialist in Bruges, stocking everything from run-of-the-mill cheapies to collector items in Flemish, French and even English. Mon 1.30–7pm, Tues–Sat 10am–12.30pm & 1.30–7pm, Sun 2–6pm.

Food

Diksmuids Boterhuis Geldmuntstraat 23 ⓣ050 33 32 43. One of the few traditional food shops to have survived in central Bruges, this Aladdin's cave of a place specializes in cooked meats, breads, butters and Belgian cheeses. Mon–Sat 9.30am–12.30pm & 2–6.30pm.

Interior design

Callebert Wollestraat 25 ⓣ050 33 50 61, ⓦwww.callebert.be. Bruges' top contemporary homeware, ceramics and furniture store, featuring leading brands such as Alessi and Bodum, as well as less familiar names. They also stock everything from bags, watches and jewellery to household utensils, textiles and tableware, and the art gallery presents the best of contemporary design, primarily in glass and ceramics. Mon 2–6pm, Tues–Sat 10am–noon & 2–6pm, Sun 3–6pm.

Lace

Claeys Katelijnestraat 54 ⓣ050 33 98 19, ⓦwww.claeysantique.com. Diane Claeys studied lace history and design in various parts of Europe before opening this shop in 1980. She now sells handmade antique-style lace, from handkerchiefs to edging and tablecloths, plus handmade jewellery. Daily 9am–6pm.

and relaxing air. Mon–Fri noon–midnight, Sat & Sun 5pm–1am.

De Republiek St-Jacobsstraat 36 ⓣ050 34 02 29, ⓦwww.derepubliek.be. One of the most fashionable and popular spots in town, this large and darkly lit café-bar attracts an arty, mostly youthful crew. Groovy soundtrack and very reasonably priced snacks, including vegetarian and pasta dishes, plus the occasional gig. Terrace at the back for summertime drinking. Daily from 11am until 3/4am.

De Vuurmolen Kraanplein 5 ⓦwww.vuurmolen.be. This crowded, student-meets-local bar has a reasonably wide range of beers, a large front terrace and some of the best DJs in town playing a good mix of music – techno through to house and beyond. Daily 11am–3am.

Wijnbar Est Braambergstraat 7 ⓣ050 33 38 39, ⓦwww.wijnbarest.be. The best wine bar in town, with a friendly and relaxed atmosphere, an extensive cellar and over twenty wines available by the glass every day. It's especially strong on New World vintages, and also serves a selection of cheeses in the evening. There's live (and free) jazz, blues and folk music every Sunday from 8pm and the premises are smallish – so expect a crush. Wed–Sun 4pm–1am.

Performing arts, festivals and cinema

Keen to entertain its many visitors, Bruges puts on a varied programme of **performing arts**, mostly as part of its annual schedule of festivals and special events. In particular, look out for the **Musica Antiqua** festival of medieval music at the beginning of August (ⓦwww.musica-antiqua.be), though this is but one small part of the more generalized **Festival van Vlaanderen** (Flanders Festival; June–Dec; ⓦwww.festival.be), which comprises more than one hundred classical concerts distributed among the big Flemish-speaking cities, including Bruges. The two principal **venues** are the municipal theatre, the Stadsschouwburg, and the concert hall, the Concertgebouw. Bruges also hosts two big-deal music festivals, the **Cactus-festival** (ⓦwww.cactusmusic.be) of rock, reggae, rap, roots and R&B spread over three days on the second weekend of July; and **Klinkers** (same website), two and a half weeks (usually from the last weekend of July) devoted to just about every type of music you can think of, with bands and artists drawn from every corner of the globe. As for film, Bruges has two excellent **art-house cinemas**; films are normally shown in the original language, with Dutch subtitles as required.

There are several ways to find out about upcoming concerts and performances. The main tourist office on 't Zand (see p.152) posts information on its website and publishes a free, monthly and multilingual **events calendar** called *events@brugge*. Much more detailed is *Exit*, a local **listings magazine**, also published monthly, which has in-depth reviews and a calendar. It's widely available in bookshops and assorted outlets, including the tourist office, but is (almost entirely) in Dutch.

Major venues

Concertgebouw 't Zand ⓣ070 22 33 02, ⓦwww.concertgebouw.be. Built to celebrate Bruges's year as a cultural capital of Europe in 2002, and hosts all the performing arts, from opera and classical music through to big-name bands.

Stadsschouwburg Vlamingstraat 29 ⓣ050 44 30 60, ⓦwww.cultuurcentrumbrugge.be. Occupying a big and breezy, neo-Renaissance building from 1869, and with a wide-ranging programme, including theatre, dance, musicals, concerts and opera.

Art-house cinemas

Ciné Liberty Kuipersstraat 23 ⓣ050 33 20 11, ⓦwww.cinebel.be. Right in the centre of town, this cinema offers a choice selection of English and American mainstream and cult films.

Cinema Lumière Sint Jacobstraat 36 ⓣ050 34 34 65, ⓦwww.lumiere.be. Bruges's premier venue for alternative, cult, foreign and art-house movies, with three screens.

Listings

ATMs ATMs in central Bruges include ones at the post office, Markt 5; KBC, Steenstraat 38; Fortis Bank, Simon Stevinplein 3; the Europabank, Vlamingstraat 13; and at the train station.

Books and maps A reasonable selection of English paperbacks and Belgian walking maps are available at Standaard Boekhandel, Steenstraat 88 (Mon–Sat 8.30am–6pm & Sun 2–6pm).

Car rental Europcar, St Pieterskaai 48 (ⓣ050 31 45 44); Hertz, at Pathoekewg 25 (ⓣ050 37 72 34).

Doctors A list of doctors is available from the tourist office; for night-time doctors (7pm–8am) call ⓣ078 15 15 90.

Emergencies Phone ⓣ112.

Football Club Brugge (ⓦwww.clubbrugge.be) is one of Belgium's premier soccer clubs and they play in the Jan Breydelstadion, about 3km southwest from the centre along Gistelse Steenweg; on match days there are special buses to the ground from the train station.

Internet access Most hotels and hostels provide internet access either free or at minimal charge.

Left luggage There are luggage lockers and a luggage office at the train station.

Pharmacies Pharmacies are liberally distributed across the city centre and late-night duty rotas are usually displayed in pharmacists' windows; for late-night and weekend pharmacies, you can also call ⓣ0900 10 500.

Post office Markt 5 (Mon–Fri 9am–6pm, Sat 10am–3pm).

Supermarkets Ordinary shops have all but disappeared from central Bruges, but there is one sizeable supermarket, Louis Delhaize, Noordzandstraat 7 (Mon–Sat 9am–7pm).

Taxis There's a taxi rank on the Markt (ⓣ050 33 44 44) and outside the train station on Stationsplein (ⓣ050 38 46 60).

Train enquiries For domestic and international services, drop by the train station or the tourist office or consult ⓦwww.b-rail.be. Alternatively, for domestic journeys call ⓣ02 528 28 28, international routes ⓣ070 79 79 79 (premium line).

Damme

Now a popular day-trippers' destination, well known for its easy-going atmosphere and classy restaurants, the quaint little village of **DAMME**, 7km northeast of Bruges, was in medieval times the town's main seaport. At its height, it boasted a population of ten thousand and its garrison guarded the banks of the **River Zwin**, which gave Bruges direct access to the sea. But the river silted up in the late fifteenth century and Damme slipped into a long decline, its old brick buildings crumbling away until the tourists and second-homers arrived to create the pretty and genteel village of today.

Damme's main street, **Kerkstraat**, is edged by what remains of the medieval town, most memorably the Stadhuis, and it also lies at right angles to the pretty, tree-lined **canal** that links Bruges with Damme and ultimately Sluis, a tiny village over the border in Holland. The Sluis canal intersects with the wider **Leopoldkanaal** just 2km to the northeast of Damme, and together they frame a delightfully scenic sliver of countryside dotted with whitewashed farmhouses and patterned by old causeways – perfect for **cycling** (see box opposite).

The Village

Funded by a special tax on barrels of herrings, the fifteenth-century **Stadhuis** (no public access), just a few steps down Kerkstraat from the Sluis canal, is easily the best-looking building in the village, its elegant, symmetrical facade balanced by the graceful lines of its exterior stairway. In one of the niches you'll spy Charles the Bold offering a wedding ring to Margaret of York, who stands in the next niche along – appropriately, as the couple got spliced here, a prestige event that attracted aristocratic bigwigs from all over western Europe.

Across from the Stadhuis, in the same premises as the tourist office, is the **Tijl Ulenspiegel Museum** (mid-April to mid-Oct Mon–Fri 9am–noon & 1–6pm, Sat & Sun 10am–noon & 2–6pm; mid-Oct to mid-April Mon–Fri 9am–noon & 1–5pm, Sat & Sun 2–5pm; €2.50), whose various displays are devoted to the eponymous folkloric figure who started out as a fool-cum-prankster in Germany in the fourteenth century. As Ulenspiegel stories spread into Flanders, so he became more of a scoundrel than a joker until, that is, the Belgian Charles de Coster (1827–79) subverted the legend, turning Ulenspiegel into the enemy of King Philip II of Spain and the embodiment of the Belgian hankering for freedom. The most interesting displays outline some of the tall stories associated with Ulenspiegel, most of which have an anti-authoritarian edge. All the captions are in Dutch, but an English guide is available at reception.

The old **St Janshospitaal** (April–Sept Mon & Fri 2–6pm, Tues–Thurs, Sat & Sun 11am–noon & 2–6pm; €1.50), just down Kerkstraat from the tourist office, accommodates a small museum of five rooms and a dainty little chapel. Room 1 displays a couple of curiously crude parchment-and-straw peasants' pictures of St Peter and St Magdalena, while Room 4 has an enjoyable sample of Delft and pewterware, though it's the chimneypiece that grabs the attention, a Baroque extravagance with a cast-iron backplate representing the penance of King David for the murder of Bathsheba's husband.

From St Janshospitaal, it's a couple of minutes' walk further down Kerkstraat to the **Onze Lieve Vrouwekerk** (May–Sept Tues–Sun 2–5pm), a sturdy Gothic structure dating from the fourteenth century. The church is attached to a ruined segment of the original **nave** (open access) which speaks volumes about Damme's decline: when the population shrank, the church was just too big and so the inhabitants abandoned part of the nave and the remnants are now stuck between the

Cycling around Damme

Damme lies at the start of a pretty little parcel of land, a rural backwater criss-crossed by drowsy canals and causeways, each of which is shadowed by two long lines of slender poplar trees which quiver and rustle in the prevailing westerly winds. This is ideal **cycling country** and it extends as far as the E34 motorway, about 6km from Damme. There are lots of possible cycling **routes** and, if you want to explore the area in detail, you should buy the detailed **Fietsnetwerk Brugse Ommeland Noord** (cycling map; 1:50,000) from any major bookstore or Bruges tourist office before you set out.

One especially delightful itinerary is a 15km round trip that begins by leaving Damme to the northeast along the Brugge–Sluis canal, which you follow as far as the tiny hamlet of **Hoeke**, crossing over the wider **Leopoldkanaal** on the way. At Hoeke, just over the bridge, turn hard left for the narrow causeway – the **Krinkeldijk** – that wanders straight back in the direction of Damme, running to the north of the Brugge–Sluis canal. Just over 3km long, the Krinkeldijk drifts across a beguiling landscape of whitewashed farmhouses and deep-green grassy fields before reaching an intersection where you turn left to regain the Brugge–Sluis waterway.

present church and its clumpy tower. Climb the **tower** (€2) for panoramic views over the surrounding polders. Incidentally, the large and enigmatic, three-headed modern **statue** beside the tower is the work of the contemporary Belgian painter and sculptor Charles Delporte (b.1928), who has a studio here.

Practicalities

There are several ways of reaching Damme from Bruges, the most rewarding being the 7km **cycle ride** out along the tree-lined Brugge–Sluis canal, which begins at the Dampoort, on the northeast edge of the city centre (for cycle hire in Bruges, see p.152). You can also get from Bruges to Damme on the **Lamme Goedzak canal boat**, with excursions starting about 500m east of the Dampoort on the Noorweegse Kaai (April to mid-Oct; five daily each way; single 40min €6, return €7.50); tickets are purchased on board. Connecting buses #4 and #43 from the Markt and the bus station run to the Noorweegse Kaai to meet most departures – but check the connection with the De Lijn information kiosk, outside the train station, before you set out. Finally, during the summertime you can reach Damme on **city bus** #43 from the bus station and the Markt (April–Sept 6 daily each way; 20min). Out of season, there are only a couple of buses daily and you'll probably have to hang around in Damme for longer than you want – if, indeed, you can make the return journey at all.

Damme has its own **tourist office**, right in the centre of the village across the street from the Stadhuis (mid April to mid Oct Mon–Fri 9am–noon & 1–6pm, Sat & Sun 10am–noon & 2–6pm; mid-Oct to mid-April Mon–Fri 9am–noon & 1–5pm, Sat & Sun 2–5pm; Ⓣ050 28 86 10, Ⓦwww.toerismedamme.be). With Bruges so near, there's no strong reason to **overnight** here, but if you do decide to stay the tourist office can help you find a bed – Damme has a reasonable range of **B&Bs** (❷–❸). The village's real forte is its **restaurants**, with a string of first-class places lining up along Kerkstraat and the surrounding side streets. One of the best is the excellent *De Lieve*, just behind the Stadhuis at Jacob van Maerlantstraat 10 (Ⓣ050 35 66 30; Wed–Sun 6–10pm). This smart and fairly formal restaurant, with a large pavement terrace, offers the best of Flemish and French cuisine with mains from €26. A more economical alternative is *Tante Marie*, Kerkstraat 38 (daily 10am–7pm, mid-June to mid-Sept till 10pm), a smart and modern café-cum-patisserie where they serve a tasty range of salads plus mouth-watering cakes. A little further afield, *Le Siphon*, north along the canal towards Hoeke at Damse Vaart-Oost 1 (☎050 62 02 02; Sat–Wed 11am–3pm & 5–11pm), is a particular favourite with well-heeled locals, who are attracted by the canalside setting, the prettiness of the old, whitewashed premises and the freshness of the Flemish food; eels are the house speciality.

Ghent

Of all the cities in Belgium, it's hard to trump **GHENT**, a vital, vibrant metropolis whose booming restaurant and bar scene wends its way across a charming cityscape, a network of narrow canals overseen by dozens of antique brick houses. If Bruges is a tourist industry with a town attached, Ghent is the reverse – a proudly Flemish city which, with a population of 240,000, is now Belgium's third largest conurbation. Evidence of Ghent's medieval pomp is to be found in a string of superb Gothic buildings including **St-Baafskathedraal**, whose principal treasure is Jan van Eyck's remarkable *Adoration of the Mystic Lamb*, one of the world's most important paintings. Supporting the cathedral are the likes of **St-Niklaaskerk**, with its soaring arches and pencil-thin turrets; the forbidding castle of the counts of Flanders, **Het Gravensteen**; and the delightful medieval guildhouses of the Graslei. These central attractions are supplemented by a trio of outlying museums: **S.M.A.K**, a Museum of Contemporary Art; **STAM**, which explores the city's history; and the fine art of the **Museum voor Schone Kunsten**.

Some history

The principal seat of the counts of Flanders and one of the largest towns in western Europe during the thirteenth and fourteenth centuries, **Ghent** was once at the heart of the **Flemish cloth trade**. By 1350, the city boasted a population of fifty thousand, of whom no fewer than five thousand were directly involved in the industry, a prodigious concentration of labour in a predominantly rural Europe. Like Bruges, Ghent prospered throughout the Middle Ages, but it also suffered from endemic disputes between the count and his nobles (who supported France) and the cloth-reliant citizens (to whom friendship with England was vital).

The relative decline of the cloth trade in the early sixteenth century did little to ease the underlying tension, as the people of Ghent were still resentful of their ruling class, from whom they were now separated by **language** – French against Flemish – and **religion** – Catholic against Protestant. Adapting to the new economic situation, the town's merchants switched from industry to trade, exporting surplus grain from France, only to find their efforts frustrated by an interminable series of wars in which their rulers were involved. The catalyst for conflict was usually taxation: long before the Revolt of the Netherlands (see p.359), Ghent's merchants and artisans found it hard to stomach the financial dictates of their rulers – the Habsburgs after 1482 – and time and again they rose in revolt only to be crushed and punished. In 1540, for example, the Holy Roman Emperor **Charles V** lost patience and stormed the town, abolishing its privileges, filling in the moat and building a new castle at the city's expense. Later, in 1584, with the Netherlands well on the way to independence from Habsburg Spain, Philip II's armies captured Ghent. It was a crucial engagement: thereafter Ghent proved to be too far south to be included in the United Provinces and was reluctantly pressed into the **Spanish Netherlands**. Many of its citizens fled north, and those who didn't may well have regretted their decision when the Inquisition arrived and the Dutch forced the Habsburgs to close the River Scheldt, Ghent's economic lifeline, as the price of peace in 1648.

In the centuries that followed, Ghent slipped into a slow decline from which it only emerged during the **industrial boom** of the nineteenth century. In optimistic mood, the medieval merchants had built the city's walls a fair distance from the town centre to allow Ghent to expand, but the expected growth had never taken place until now. Within the space of twenty years, these empty districts filled up with factories, whose belching chimneys encrusted the old city with soot and grime, a disagreeable measure of the city's economic revival. Indeed, its entrepreneurial mayor, Emille Braun, even managed to get the **Great Exhibition**, showing the best in contemporary design and goods, staged here in 1913.

Ghent remains an industrial city, but in the last twenty years it has benefited from an extraordinarily ambitious programme of **restoration and refurbishment**, thanks to which the string of fine Gothic buildings that dot the ancient centre have been returned to their original glory.

Arrival and information

Ghent has two **train stations**, but the one you're almost bound to arrive at is **Ghent St-Pieters**, which adjoins the **bus station** about 2km south of the city centre. From the tunnel on the west side of St-Pieters station, **tram #1** runs up to the Korenmarkt at the heart of the city every few minutes. All trams have destination signs and numbers at the front, but if in doubt check with the driver. The **taxi** fare from the train station to the Korenmarkt is around €10.

Most motorists arrive via the **E40**, the Brussels–Ostend motorway, which clips the southern edge of the city. There are lots of city-centre **car parks** with one of the most convenient being the 24-hour one beneath the Vrijdagmarkt.

Ghent **tourist office** is currently located in the crypt of the Lakenhalle on the Botermarkt, but by November 2011 it should be ensconced in its new premises in the Oude Vismarkt, opposite the castle on St-Veerleplein (daily: mid-March to mid-Oct 9.30am–6.30pm; mid-Oct to mid-March 9.30am–4.30pm; ⓣ09 266 56 60, ⓦwww.visitgent.be). It supplies a wide range of free city information, including good-quality maps, and operates a last-minute accommodation booking service.

City transport

The city's **trams and buses** are operated by De Lijn (ⓣ070 22 02 00, ⓦwww.delijn.be). A standard one-way fare costs €1.20 in advance, €2 from the driver,

Walking tours and boat trips

Guided walking tours are particularly popular in Ghent. The standard tour, organized by the Guides' Association and bookable at the tourist office, is a two-hour jaunt round the city centre (May–Oct daily at 2.30pm; €7); advance booking – at least a few hours ahead of time – is strongly recommended. Alternatively, **horse-drawn carriages** line up outside the Lakenhalle, on St Baafsplein, offering a thirty-minute canter round town for €30 (Easter to Oct daily 10am–6pm & most winter weekends). Throughout the year, **boat trips** explore Ghent's inner waterways, departing from the Korenlei and Graslei quays, just near the Korenmarkt, as well as from the Vleeshuisbrug, metres from the Groentenmarkt (March–Oct daily 10am–6pm, Nov to Feb daily noon–4pm; €6.50). Trips last forty minutes and leave every fifteen minutes or so, though the wait can be longer as boats often delay their departure until they are reasonably full.

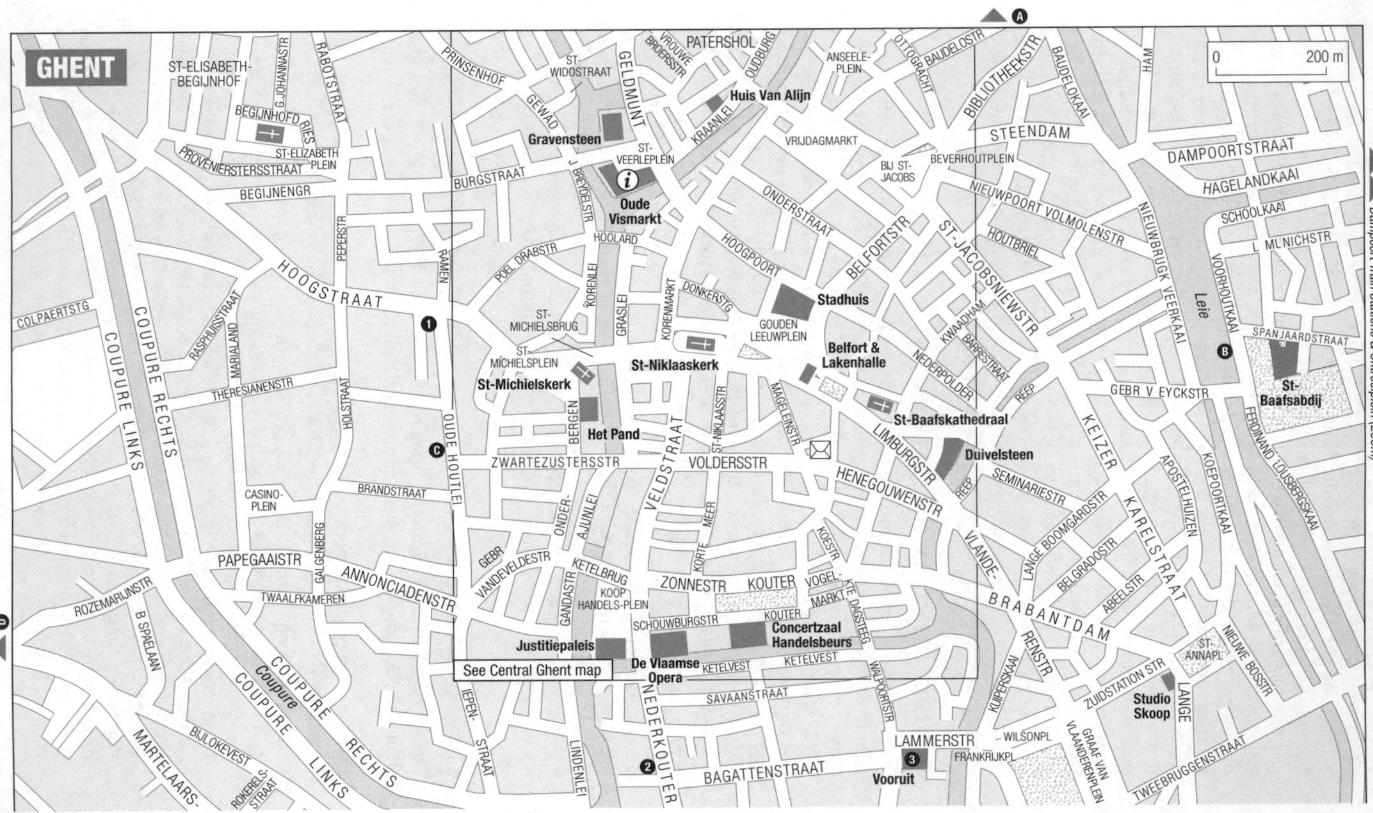
GHENT
Dampoort Train Stations & Oktrooiplein (200m)
0
200 m
St-Baafsabdij
Leie
Coupure
Gravensteen
Oude Vismarkt
Huis Van Alijn
Stadhuis
Belfort & Lakenhalle
St-Baafskathedraal
Duivelsteen
St-Niklaaskerk
St-Michielskerk
Het Pand
Concertzaal Handelsbeurs
De Vlaamse Opera
Justitiepaleis
Vooruit
Studio Skoop
See Central Ghent map
ST-ELISABETH-BEGIJNHOF
G.JOHANNASTR
RABOTSTRAAT
BEGIJNHOFD RIES
ST-ELIZABETH PLEIN
PROVENIERSTERSSTRAAT
BEGIJNENGR
PRINSENHOF
ST-WIDOSTRAAT
GEWAD
GELDMUNT
ST-VEERLEPLEIN
VROUWEBROERSSTR
PATERSHOL
OUDBURG
KRAANLEI
ANSEELE-PLEIN
OTTOGRACHT
BAUDELOSTR
BIBLIOTHEEKSTR
BAUDELOKAAI
HAM
STEENDAM
VRIJDAGMARKT
BIJ ST-JACOBS
BEVERHOUTPLEIN
DAMPOORTSTRAAT
HAGELANDKAAI
SCHOOLKAAI
L MUNICHSTR
VOORHOUTKAAI
SPANJAARDSTRAAT
NIEUWBRUGK VEERKAAI
NIEUWPOORT VOLMOLENSTR
HOUTBRIEL
ST-JACOBSNIEUWSTR
BURGSTRAAT
J BREYDELSTR
HOOLARD
ONDERSTRAAT
HOOGPOORT
BELFORTSTR
HOOGSTRAAT
PEPERSTR
RAMEN
POEL DRABSTR
KORENLEI
GRASLEI
KORENMARKT
DONKERSTG
GOUDEN LEEUWPLEIN
KWAADHAM
BARRESTRAAT
NEDERPOLDER
REEP
GEBR V EYCKSTR
FERDINAND LOUSBERGSKAAI
COLPAERTSTG
COUPURE LINKS
COUPURE RECHTS
RASPHUISSTRAAT
MARIALAND
THERESIANENSTR
HOLSTRAAT
ST-MICHIELSBRUG
ST-MICHIELSPLEIN
BERGEN
VELDSTRAAT
ST-NIKLAASSTR
MAGELEINSTR
LIMBURGSTR
KEIZER
OUDE HOUTLEI
ZWARTEZUSTERSSTR
VOLDERSSTR
HENEGOUWENSTR
SEMINARIESTR
APOSTELHUIZEN
KOEPOORTKAAI
CASINO-PLEIN
BRANDSTRAAT
ONDER-
AJUINLEI
KORTE MEER
KOESTR
LANGE BOOMGAARDSTR
KARELSTRAAT
BELGRADOSTR
ABEELSTR
PAPEGAAISTR
GALGENBERG
ANNONCIADENSTR
GEBR
VANDEVELDESTR
KETELBRUG
KOOPHANDELS-PLEIN
GANDASTR
ZONNESTR
KOUTER
VOGELMARKT
KTE DAGSTEEG
VLANDE-
BRABANTDAM
ROZEMARIJNSTR
B SPAELAAN
TWAALFKAMEREN
SCHOUWBURGSTR
KETELVEST
RENSTR
KUIPERSKAAI
ZUIDSTATION STR
ST-ANNAPL
NIEUWE BOSSTR
LANGE
IEPEN-STRAAT
SAVAANSTRAAT
WALPOORTSTR
NEDERKOUTER
LINDENLEI
LAMMERSTR
WILSONPL
FRANKRIJKPL
GRAAF VAN VLAANDERENPLEIN
TWEEBRUGGENSTRAAT
BAGATTENSTRAAT
MARTELAARS-
BIJLOKEVEST
ROKERELSSTRAAT

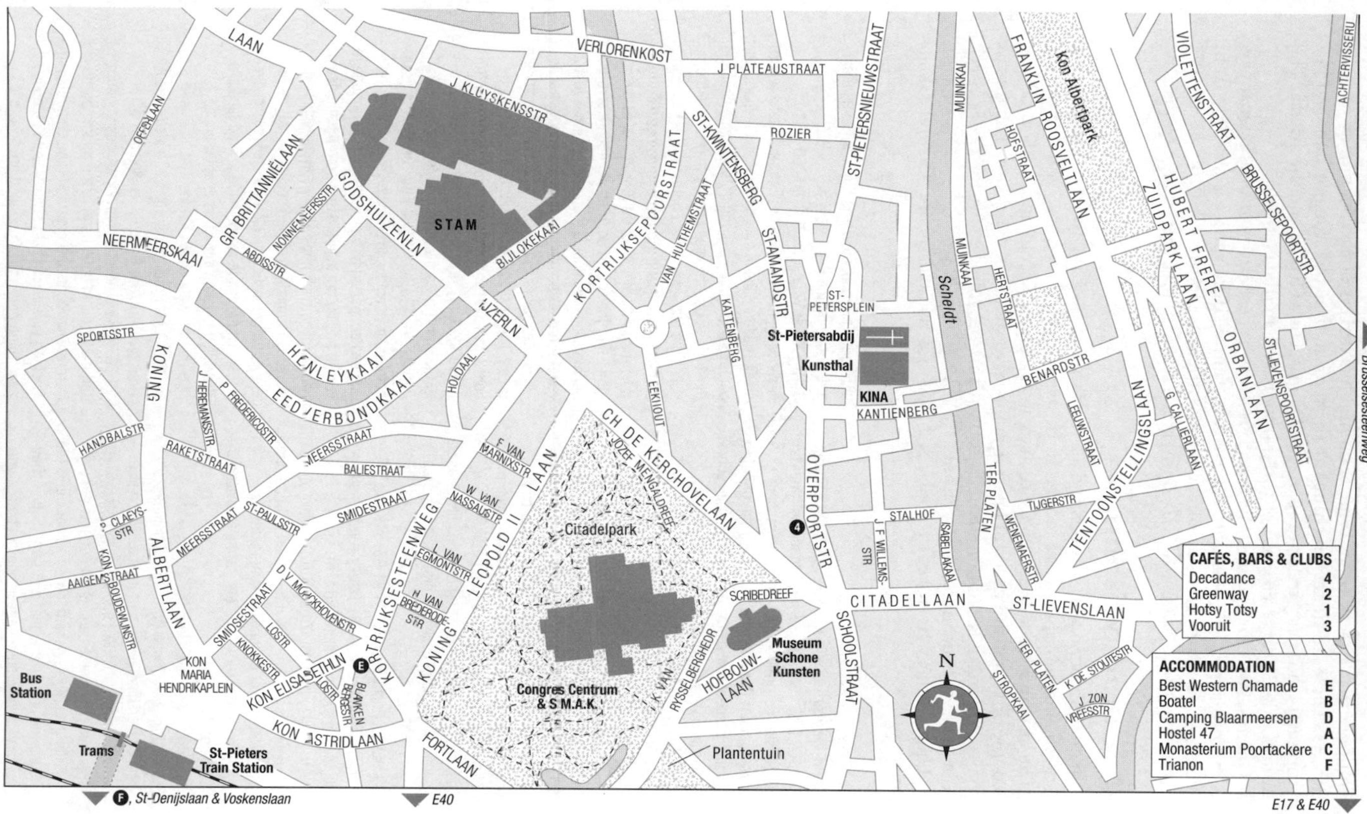
CAFÉS, BARS & CLUBS
Decadance 4
Greenway 2
Hotsy Totsy 1
Vooruit 3
ACCOMMODATION
Best Western Chamade E
Boatel B
Camping Blaarmeersen D
Hostel 47 A
Monasterium Poortackere C
Trianon F
Brusselsesteenweg
E17 & E40
E40
F, St-Denijslaan & Voskenslaan
Kon Albertpark
Scheldt
St-Pietersabdij
Kunsthal
KINA
STAM
Citadelpark
Congres Centrum & S.M.A.K.
Museum Schone Kunsten
Plantentuin
St-Pieters Train Station
Bus Station
Trams
N
VERLORENKOST
J PLATEAUSTRAAT
ST-PIETERSNIEUWSTRAAT
FRANKLIN ROOSVELTLAAN
VIOLETTENSTRAAT
BRUSSELSEPOORTSTR
HUBERT FRERE-ORBANLAAN
ZUIDPARKLAAN
ST-LIEVENSPOORTSTRAAT
ACHTERVISSERIJ
MUINKKAAI
HOFSTRAAT
HERTSTRAAT
BENARDSTR
LEEUWSTRAAT
G CALLIERLAAN
TENTOONSTELLINGSLAAN
TIJGERSTR
WENEMAERSTR
TER PLATEN
ST-LIEVENSLAAN
CITADELLAAN
SCHOOLSTRAAT
OVERPOORTSTR
STALHOF
ISABELLAKAAI
J F WILLEMS-STR
KANTIENBERG
ST-PIETERSPLEIN
ST-AMANDSTR
ROZIER
ST-KWINTENSBERG
KATTENBERG
VAN HULTHEMSTRAAT
KORTRIJKSEPOORTSTRAAT
EEKHOUT
CH DE KERCHOVELAAN
JOZEF MENGALDREEF
SCRIBEDREEF
HOFBOUW-LAAN
RYSSELBERGHEDR
K VAN
K DE STOUTESTR
J ZON VREESSTR
STROPKAAI
J KLUYSKENSSTR
GODSHUIZENLN
BIJLOKEKAAI
NONNEMEERSSTR
ABDISSTR
GR BRITTANNIËLAAN
OFFERLAAN
LAAN
NEERMEERSKAAI
IJZERLN
HENLEYKAAI
EEDVERBONDKAAI
HOLDAAL
F VAN MARNIXSTR
W VAN NASSAUSTR
L VAN EGMONTSTR
H VAN BREDERODE-STR
LEOPOLD II LAAN
KONING
KORTRIJKSESTEENWEG
FORTLAAN
KON ASTRIDLAAN
BLANKENBERGESTR
LOSTR
KON ELISABETHLN
D V MOOCKHOVENSTR
SMIDSESTRAAT
KNOKKESTR
SMIDESTRAAT
ST-PAULSSTR
BALIESTRAAT
MEERSSTRAAT
RAKETSTRAAT
P FREDERICOSTR
J HEREMANSSTR
KONING ALBERTLAAN
HANDBALSTR
SPORTSSTR
P CLAEYS-STR
KON BOUDEWIJNSTR
AAIGEMSTRAAT
KON MARIA HENDRIKAPLEIN

but note that at peak times some tram and bus drivers don't take money or issue tickets. There are **ticket machines** at the train station and at major tram and bus stops. A 24-hour city transport pass, the Dagpas, costs €5 (€6 from the driver). The tourist office issues free maps of the transport system (the Netplan).

Ghent is good for **cycling**: the terrain is flat and there are cycle lanes on many of the roads and cycle racks dotted across the centre. **Bike rental** is available from Biker, on the northeast side of the city centre at Steendam 16 (ⓣ09 224 29 03; Mon–Sat 9am–12.30pm & 1.30–6pm); for a standard bike they charge €9 per day.

Accommodation

Ghent has around thirty **hotels** and a small army of **B&Bs** with several of the most stylish and enjoyable places located in the centre, which is where you want to be. The city also has a good supply of bargain-basement accommodation, notably a couple of bright and cheerful **hostels** and a large suburban **campsite**. The tourist office will make last-minute hotel **reservations** on your behalf; for B&Bs check out ⓦwww.bedandbreakfast-gent.be.

Unless otherwise stated, the places below are marked on the Central Ghent map, p.181.

Hotels

Best Western Chamade Koningin Elisabethlaan 3 ⓣ09 220 15 15, ⓦwww.chamade.be. Standard three-star accommodation in bright, modern bedrooms at this chain hotel, though the building itself – a six-storey block – is a bit of an eyesore. A five-minute walk north of the train station. Significant weekend discounts. See map, pp.178–179. ❹

Boatel Voorhoutkaai 44 ⓣ09 267 10 30, ⓦwww.theboatel.com. Arguably the most distinctive of the city's hotels, the two-star *Boatel* is an imaginatively and immaculately refurbished 1950s canal barge moored in one of the city's outer canals, a pleasant ten- to fifteen-minute walk east from the centre. The seven bedrooms are decked out in crisp, modern style, and breakfasts, taken on the poop deck, are first-rate. See map, pp.178–179. ❺

Erasmus Poel 25 ⓣ09 224 21 95, ⓦwww.erasmushotel.be. Friendly, family-run two-star located in a commodious old town house a few metres away from the Korenlei. Each room is thoughtfully decorated and furnished in traditional style with lots of antiques. The breakfast is excellent and reservations are strongly advised in summer. ❹

Flandre Poel 1 ⓣ09 266 06 00, ⓦwww.hoteldeflandre.be. Four-star hotel in an imaginatively refashioned nineteenth-century mansion with a modern, portacabin-like annexe at the back. The spacious public areas are kitted out in sharp style, with original floorings and low sofa seats, and the bedrooms beyond are neat and trim, though they do vary considerably – check one out before you shell out. The rooms towards the rear are quieter than those on the Poel. ❻

Ghent River Waaistraat 5 ⓣ09 266 10 10, ⓦwww.ghent-river-hotel.be. Four-star hotel whose bleak modern facade doesn't do it any favours, but persevere: the interior is much more appealing and most of the guest rooms occupy that part of the building which was once a cotton mill – hence the bare-brick walls and industrial trappings. ❺

Harmony Kraanlei 37 ⓣ09 324 26 80, ⓦwww.hotel-harmony.be. In an immaculately renovated old mansion, this deluxe four-star hotel has just 24 guest rooms decorated in attractive modern style, all wooden floors and shades of brown, cream and green. The best rooms are on the top floor and come complete with their own mini-terrace from where there are grand views over the city. ❺

Monasterium Poortackere Oude Houtlei 56 ⓣ09 269 22 10, ⓦwww.monasterium.be. This unusual hotel-cum-guesthouse occupies a rambling and somewhat spartan former nunnery and orphanage, whose ageing brickwork dates from the nineteenth century. There's a choice between unassuming, en-suite rooms in the hotel section or the more authentic monastic-cell experience in the guest-house, where some rooms have shared facilities. Breakfast is taken in the old chapter house. A five-minute walk west of Veldstraat. See map, pp.178–179. Hotel rooms ❹–❻, guesthouse ❸

Novotel Centrum Goudenleeuwplein 5 ⓣ09 224 22 30, ⓦwww.novotel.com. First-class, modern three-star chain hotel bang in the middle of the city centre. The rooms are neat and trim, decorated in a fetching version of chain style. Has an outdoor swimming pool and offers good breakfasts. ❹

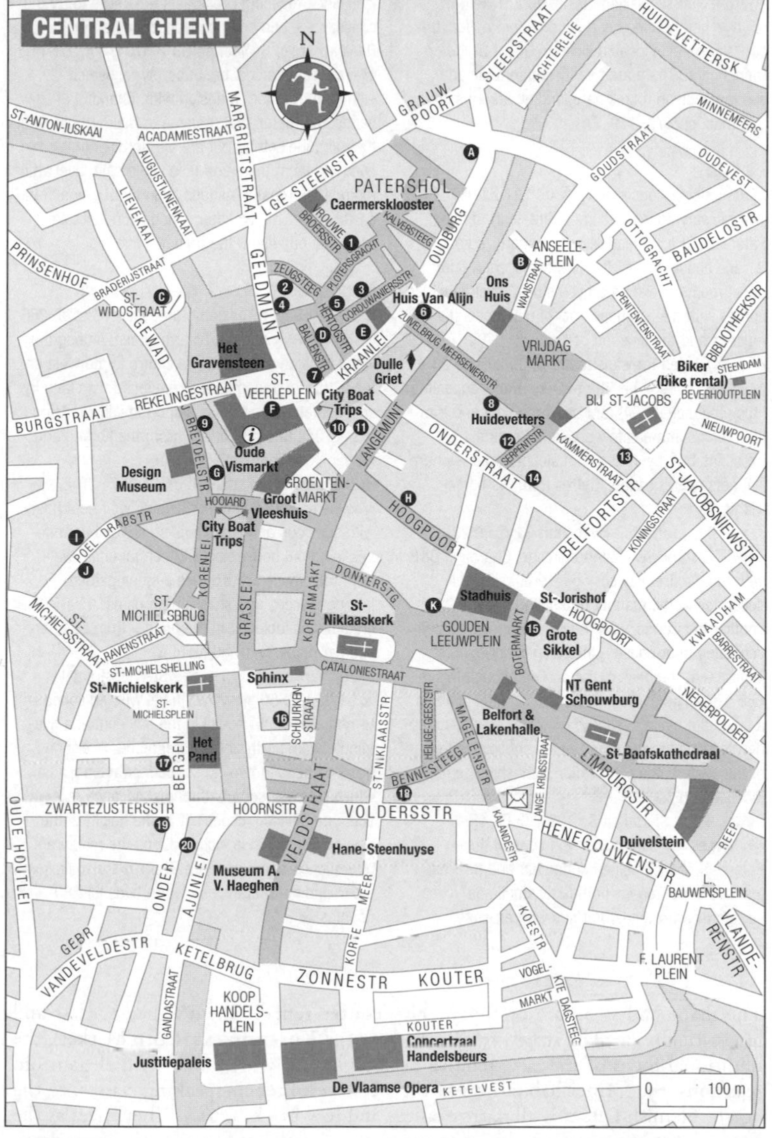

ACCOMMODATION

Atgenesis	D
Brooderie	G
Chambreplus	H
Erasmus	I
Flandre	J
Ghent River	B
Harmony	E
Jeugdherberg De Draecke	C
Novotel Centrum	K
Simon Says	A
De Waterzooi	F

CAFÉS & RESTAURANTS

Avalon	4
Bij den wijzen en den zot	5
De Blauwe Zalm	1
Brooderie	G
Coeur d'Artichaut	17
Domestica	20
Gwenola	18
House of Eliott	9
Julie's House	7
Lepelblad	19
Marco Polo Trattoria	12
Pakhuis	16
Souplounge	6
De 3 Biggetjes	2

BARS, CAFÉ-BARS & CLUBS

't Dreupelkot	11
Dulle Griet	8
Pink Flamingos	14
Rococo	3
De Trollekelder	13
Den Turk	15
Het Waterhuis aan de Bierkant	10

Trianon Sint Denijslaan 203 T 09 221 39 44, W www.hoteltrianon.be. A good budget option, this two-star hotel is located close to Ghent St-Pieters train station. There are twenty comfortable and spotlessly clean rooms here, and all are en suite. See map, pp.178–179. ❷

B&Bs

Atgenesis Hertogstraat 15 T 09 224 21 08, W www.stayatgenesis.com. In the heart of the Patershol, in a sympathetically modernized old terrace house, this B&B offers two second-floor guest rooms above an artist's studio, each of which comes with a kitchenette, lots of nice decorative touches and the beamed ceilings. ❸

Brooderie Jan Breydelstraat 8 T 09 225 06 23, W www.brooderie.be. The owners of this appealing little café (see p.194) rent out three neat and trim little rooms immediately above it. Breakfast is excellent, but if you're a light sleeper go elsewhere – it gets noisy outside. Metres from the Korenmarkt. ❷

Chambreplus Hoogpoort 31 T 09 225 37 75, W www.chambreplus.be. Charming B&B with three extremely cosy guest rooms: one is decorated in the manner of a sultan's room, another the Congo, with the third occupying a self-contained mini-house – including a sky-light jacuzzi – at the back of the garden, though this is €60 extra. The garden, with its dinky little pond, is a delightful place to sit and read and breakfasts are delicious, as are the home-made chocolates (one of the owners is a chocolatier). Smashing central location, too. ❹

Simon Says Sluizeken 8 T 09 233 03 43, W www.simon-says.be. On the edge of the Patershol, this combined coffee bar and B&B has just two guest rooms, both fairly small and straightforward modern affairs with en-suite facilities. Smashing breakfasts – be sure to try the croissants – and competitively priced at ❸

De Waterzooi St-Veerleplein 2 T 0475 43 61 11, W www.dewaterzooi.be. Superbly renovated eighteenth-century mansion with a handful of handsome rooms that manage to make the most of their antique setting but are extraordinarily comfortable at the same time – the split-level attic room is the most ambitious. Wonderful views of the castle, and if the weather is good you can take breakfast outside in the garden-patio. ❻

Hostels and camping

Camping Blaarmeersen Zuiderlaan 12 T 09 266 81 60, W www.gent.be/blaarmeersen. Among the woods beside a watersports centre to the west of town, this large campsite is equipped with laundry, shop, cafeteria and various sports facilities. March to mid-Oct. Bus #38 or #39 from the Korenmarkt (10min). See map, pp.178–179.

Hostel 47 Blekerijstraat 47 T 0478 71 28 27, W www.hostel47.com. Particularly well-kept hostel with spacious and clean two- to six-bed dormitories in an old house about fifteen minutes' walk from the city centre. There's a small garden, internet access and shared bathrooms. A basic breakfast is included in the price – from €24 per bed per night. Two-bed room ❷

Jeugdherberg De Draecke St-Widostraat 11 T 09 233 70 50, W www.vjh.be. Well-equipped, HI-affiliated youth hostel in the city centre, a five-minute walk north of the Korenmarkt. Over one hundred beds in two- to six-bedded rooms, all of which have en-suite bathrooms. Advance reservations are advised, especially in the height of the season. Breakfast is included, and the restaurant offers lunch and dinner too. There are also lockers, a bar, and internet access. Dorm beds €17.80, doubles ❶

The City Centre

The shape and structure of today's **city centre** reflect Ghent's ancient class and linguistic divide. The streets to the south of the **Korenmarkt** (Corn Market), the traditional focus of the city, tend to be straight and wide, lined with elegant old mansions, the former habitations of the wealthier, French-speaking classes; to the north, Flemish Ghent is all narrow alleys and low brick houses. They meet at the somewhat confusing sequence of **squares** that spread east from the Korenmarkt to St-Baafskathedraal.

St-Baafskathedraal

The best place to start an exploration of the city is the mainly Gothic **St-Baafskathedraal** (St Bavo's Cathedral; April–Oct Mon–Sat 8.30am–6pm & Sun 1–6pm; Nov–March Mon–Sat 8.30am–5pm & Sun 1–5pm), squeezed into the eastern corner of St-Baafsplein. The third church on this site, and 250 years

A **museum pass**, valid for three days and covering fourteen of the city's sights and museums, as well as free and unlimited use of the city's buses and trams. It costs €20 and is available at any of the fourteen sights as well as the tourist office.

in the making, the cathedral is a tad lop-sided, but there's no gainsaying the imposing beauty of the **west tower**, with its long, elegant windows and perky corner turrets. Some 82m high, the tower was the last major part of the church to be completed, topped off in 1554 – just before the outbreak of the religious wars that were to wrack the country for the next one hundred years.

The Adoration of the Mystic Lamb

Inside the cathedral, in a small **chapel** to the left of the entrance (April–Oct Mon–Sat 9.30am–5pm, Sun 1–5pm; Nov–March Mon–Sat 10.30am–4pm, Sun 1–4pm; €4), is Ghent's greatest treasure, a **winged altarpiece** known as *The Adoration of the Mystic Lamb* (*De Aanbidding van het Lam Gods*), a seminal work of the early 1430s, though of dubious provenance. Since the discovery of a Latin verse on its frame in the nineteenth century, academics have been arguing about who actually painted it. The inscription reads that **Hubert van Eyck** "than whom none was greater" began, and **Jan van Eyck**, "second in art", completed the work, but as nothing else is known of Hubert, some art historians doubt his existence. They argue that Jan, who lived and worked in several cities (including Ghent) was entirely responsible for the painting and that only later, after Jan had firmly rooted himself in the rival city of Bruges, did the citizens of Ghent invent "Hubert" to counter his fame. No one knows the altarpiece's authorship for sure, but what is certain is that in his manipulation of the technique of **oil painting** the artist – or artists – was able to capture a needle-sharp, luminous realism that must have stunned his contemporaries.

The altarpiece is now displayed with its panels open, though originally these were kept closed and the painting only revealed on high days and holidays. Consequently, it's actually best to begin round the back with the **cover screens**, which hold a beautiful Annunciation scene with the Archangel Gabriel's wings reaching up to the timbered ceiling of a Flemish house, the streets of a town visible through the windows. In a brilliant coup of lighting, the shadows of the angel dapple the room, emphasizing the reality of the apparition – a technique repeated on the opposite cover panel around the figure of Mary. Below, the donor and his wife, a certain Joos Vydt and Isabella Borluut, kneel piously alongside statues of the saints.

By design, the restrained exterior was but a foretaste of what lies within – a striking, visionary work of art whose brilliant colours and precise draughtsmanship still take the breath away. On the **upper level** sit God the Father (some say Christ Triumphant), the Virgin and John the Baptist in gleaming clarity; to the right are musician-angels and a nude, pregnant Eve; and on the left is Adam plus a group of singing angels, who strain to read their music. The celebrated sixteenth-century Flemish art critic Karel van Mander argued that the singers were so artfully painted that he could discern the different pitches of their voices – and true or not, it is the detail that impresses, especially the richly embroidered trimmings on the cloaks. In the **lower central panel** the Lamb, the symbol of Christ's sacrifice, is depicted in a heavenly paradise – "the first evolved landscape in European painting", suggested Kenneth Clark – seen as a sort of idealized Low Countries. The Lamb stands on an altar whose rim is minutely inscribed with a quotation from the Gospel of St John, "Behold the Lamb of God, which taketh away the sins of the world". Four groups converge on the Lamb from the corners of the central panel. In the bottom right are a group of male saints and up above them are their female equivalents; the bottom left shows the patriarchs of the Old Testament and above them are an assortment of bishops, dressed in blue vestments and carrying palm branches.

On the **side panels**, approaching the Lamb across symbolically rough and stony ground, are more saintly figures. On the right-hand side are two groups, the first being St Anthony and his hermits, the second St Christopher, shown here as a giant with a band of pilgrims. On the left side panel come the horsemen, the inner group symbolizing the Warriors of Christ – including St George bearing a shield with a red cross – and the outer group showing the Just Judges, each of whom is dressed in fancy Flemish attire. The **Just Judges panel** is not, however, authentic. It was added during the 1950s to replace the original, which was stolen in 1934 and never recovered. The lost panel features in **Albert Camus**'s novel *The Fall*, whose protagonist keeps it in a cupboard, declining to return it for a complex of reasons, one of which is "because those judges are on their way to meet the Lamb ...[but]...there is no lamb or innocence any longer". Naturally enough, there has been endless speculation as to who stole the panel and why with suspicion ultimately resting on a certain Arsène Goedertier, a stockbroker and conservative politician from just outside of Ghent, who made a deathbed confession in 1934. Whether he was acting alone or as an agent for others is still hotly contested – some argue that the Knights Templar orchestrated the theft, others accuse the Nazis, but no one really knows.

The theft was just one of many **dramatic events** to befall the painting – indeed it's remarkable that the altarpiece has survived at all. The Calvinists wanted to destroy it; Philip II of Spain tried to acquire it; the Emperor Joseph II disapproved of the painting so violently that he replaced the nude Adam and Eve with a clothed version of 1784 (exhibited today on a column at the start of the nave just inside the church entrance); and near the end of World War II the Germans hid it in an Austrian salt mine, where it remained until American soldiers rescued it in 1945.

The rest of the cathedral

The chapel displaying the *Adoration of the Mystic Lamb* is at the beginning of the cathedral's mighty, fifteenth-century **nave**, whose tall, slender columns give the whole interior a cheerful sense of lightness, though the Baroque marble screen spoils the effect by darkening the choir. In the nave, the principal item of interest is the Rococo **pulpit**, a whopping oak and marble affair, where the main timber represents the Tree of Life with an allegorical representation of Time and Truth at its base. Beyond is the **high altar**, a marble extravaganza featuring St Baaf (aka St Bavo) ascending to heaven on an untidy heap of clouds, while the neighbouring **north transept** holds a characteristically energetic painting by **Rubens** (1577–1640) entitled *St Baaf entering the Abbey of Ghent*. Dating to 1624, it includes a self-portrait – he's the bearded head. Also in the north transept is the entrance to the dank and capacious vaulted **crypt**, a survivor from the earlier Romanesque church. The crypt is stuffed with religious bric-a-brac of only limited interest with the exception of a superb triptych, *The Crucifixion of Christ*, by **Justus van Gent** (1410–1480). The painting depicts the crucified Christ flanked, on the left, by Moses purifying the waters of Mara with wood, and to the right by Moses and the bronze serpent which cured poisoned Israelites on sight. As the Bible has it: "So Moses made a bronze serpent [as the Lord had commanded] and set it on a pole; and if a serpent bit any man, he would look at the bronze serpent and live".

The Lakenhalle and the Belfort

Across from the cathedral, on the west side of St Baafsplein, stands the **Lakenhalle** (Cloth Hall), a sombre hunk of a building with an unhappy history. Work began on the hall in the early fifteenth century, but the cloth trade slumped before it was finished and it was only grudgingly completed in 1903. Since then, no one has ever worked out what to do with the building and today it's little more than an empty shell, though its basement did once serve as the town prison. The entrance to the prison was round on the west side of the Lakenhalle through the **Mammelokker** (The Suckling), a grandiose Louis XIV-style portal of 1741 that stands propped up against the main body of the building. Part gateway, part warder's lodging, the Mammelokker is adorned by a bas-relief sculpture illustrating the classical legend of Cimon, who the Romans condemned to death by starvation. Pero, his daughter, saved him by turning up daily to feed him from her breasts – hence the name.

The first-floor entrance on the south side of the Lakenhalle is the only way to reach the adjoining **Belfort** (Belfry; daily 10am–6pm; €5), a much-amended medieval edifice whose soaring spire is topped by a comically corpulent gilded copper dragon. Once a watchtower and storehouse for civic documents, the interior is now little more than an empty shell displaying a few old bells and statues alongside the rusting remains of an antique dragon, which formerly perched on top of the spire. The belfry is equipped with a glass-sided lift that climbs up to the roof, where consolation is provided in the form of excellent views over the city centre.

The Stadhuis

Stretching along the west side of the Botermarkt, just to the north of the Lakenhalle, is the **Stadhuis** (City Hall), whose discordant facade comprises two distinct sections. Dating from the 1580s, the later section, which frames the central stairway, is a fine example of Italian Renaissance architecture, its crisp symmetries faced by a multitude of black-painted columns. In stark contrast are the wild, curling patterns of the section to the immediate north, carved in Flamboyant Gothic style at the beginning of the sixteenth century to a design by one of the era's most celebrated architects, **Rombout Keldermans** (1460–1531). The whole of the Stadhuis was originally to have been built by Keldermans, but the money ran out when the wool trade collapsed and the city couldn't afford to finish it off until much later – hence today's mixture of styles.

Guided tours of the Stadhuis (May–Oct Mon–Thurs daily at 2.30pm as the first 45min of the 2hr walking tour organized by the Guides' Association, see p.177; full 2hr tour €7, Stadhuis only €4) amble round a series of halls and chambers, the most interesting being the old Court of Justice or **Pacificatiezaal** (Pacification Hall), where the Pacification of Ghent was signed in 1576. A plaque commemorates this treaty, which momentarily bound the rebel armies of the Low Countries (today's Belgium and The Netherlands) together against their rulers, the Spanish Habsburgs. The carrot offered by the dominant Protestants was the promise of religious freedom, but they failed to deliver and much of the south (present-day Belgium) soon returned to the Spanish fold. The hall's charcoal and cream tiled **floor** is designed in the form of a maze. No one's quite certain why, but it's thought that more privileged felons (or sinners) had to struggle round the maze on their knees as a substitute punishment for a pilgrimage to Jerusalem – a good deal if ever there was one.

St-Niklaaskerk

The cobbled square to the west of the Belfort is **Emile Braunplein**, named after the reforming burgomaster who cleared many of the city's slums at the beginning of the twentieth century. The west edge of the square abuts **St-Niklaaskerk** (Mon 2–5pm, Tues–Sun 10am–5pm), an architectural hybrid dating from the thirteenth century that was once the favourite church of the city's principal merchants. It's the shape and structure that pleases most, especially the arching buttresses and pencil-thin turrets which, in a classic example of the early Scheldt Gothic style, elegantly attenuate the lines of the nave. Inside, many of the original Baroque furnishings and fittings have been removed and the windows un-bricked, thus returning the church to its early appearance. One feature you can't miss is the giant-sized Baroque **high altar** with its mammoth representation of God the Father glowering down its back, blowing the hot wind of the Last Judgement from his mouth and surrounded by a flock of cherubic angels. The church is sometimes used for temporary art exhibitions, which can attract an admission fee.

The Korenmarkt and St-Michielsbrug

St-Niklaaskerk marks the southern end of the **Korenmarkt** (Corn Market), a long and wide cobbled area where the grain which once kept the city fed was traded after it was unloaded from the boats that anchored on the Graslei dock nearby (see below). The one noteworthy building here is the former **post office**, whose combination of Gothic Revival and neo-Renaissance styles illustrates the eclecticism popular in Belgium at the beginning of the twentieth century. The carved heads encircling the building represent the great and the good who came to the city in numbers for the Great Exhibition of 1913 – among them was Florence Nightingale. Unfortunately, the grand interior of the post office has been turned into a shopping mall.

Behind the old post office, **St-Michielsbrug** (St Michael's bridge) offers fine views back over the towers and turrets that pierce the Ghent skyline – just as it was meant to: the bridge was built in 1913 to provide visitors to the Great Exhibition with a vantage point from which to admire the city centre. As such, it was one of several schemes dreamed up to enhance Ghent's medieval appearance, one of the others being the demolition of the scrabbly buildings that had sprung up in the lee of the Lakenhalle. The bridge also overlooks the city's oldest harbour, the **Tussen Bruggen** (Between the Bridges), from whose quays – the **Korenlei** and the **Graslei** – boats leave for trips around the city's canals (see box, p.177).

The guildhouses of the Graslei

Ghent's boatmen and grainweighers were crucial to the functioning of the medieval city, and they built a row of splendid **guildhouses** along the **Graslei**, each gable decorated with an appropriate sign or symbol. Working your way north from St Michielsbrug, the first building of distinction is the **Gildehuis van de Vrije Schippers** (Guildhouse of the Free Boatmen), at no. 14, where the badly weathered sandstone is decorated with scenes of boatmen weighing anchor plus a delicate carving of a caravel – the type of Mediterranean sailing ship used by Columbus – located above the door. Medieval Ghent had two boatmen guilds: the Free, who could discharge their cargoes within the city, and the Unfree, who could not. The Unfree Boatmen were obliged to unload their goods into the vessels of the Free Boatmen at the edge of Ghent – an inefficient arrangement by any standard, though typical of the complex regulations governing the guilds.

Next door, the seventeenth-century **Cooremetershuys** (Corn Measurers' House), at Graslei 12–13, was where city officials weighed and graded corn behind a facade graced by cartouches and garlands of fruit. Next to this, at no. 11, stands the quaint **Tolhuisje**, another delightful example of Flemish Renaissance architecture, built to house the customs officers in 1698, while the adjacent limestone **Spijker** (Staple House), at no. 10, boasts a surly Romanesque facade dating from around 1200. It was here that the city stored its grain supply for over five hundred years until a fire gutted the interior. Finally, three doors down at no. 8, the splendid **Den Enghel** takes its name from the banner-bearing angel that decorates the facade; the building was originally the stonemasons' guildhouse, as evidenced by the effigies of the four Roman martyrs who were the guild's patron saints, though they are depicted in medieval attire rather than togas and sandals.

The Groentenmarkt and the Korenlei

Just north of Graslei, on the far side of Hooiard, is the **Groentenmarkt** (Vegetable Market), whose jumble of old buildings makes for one of the city's prettiest squares. The west side of the square is flanked by a long line of sooty stone gables which were once the retaining walls of the **Groot Vleeshuis** (Great Butchers' Hall), a covered market in which meat was sold under the careful control of the city council. The gables date from the fifteenth century but are in poor condition and the interior is only of interest for its intricate wooden roof.

From the north end of Graslei, the **Grasbrug** bridge leads over to the **Korenlei**, which trips along the western side of the old city harbour. Unlike the Graslei opposite, none of the medieval buildings have survived here and instead there's a series of expansive, high-gabled Neoclassical merchants' houses, mostly dating from the eighteenth century. It's the general ensemble that appeals rather than any particular building, but the **Gildehuis van de Onvrije Schippers** (Guildhouse of the Unfree Boatmen), at no. 7, does boast a fetching eighteenth-century facade decorated with whimsical dolphins and bewigged lions, all bulging eyes and rows of teeth.

St-Michielskerk

At the south end of Korenlei, on the far side of St Michielsbrug, rises the bulky mass of **St-Michielskerk** (April–Sept Mon–Sat 2–5pm), a heavy-duty Gothic edifice begun in the 1440s. The city's Protestants seem to have taken a particularly strong dislike to the place, ransacking it twice – once in 1566 and again in 1579 – and the repairs were never quite finished, as witnessed by the forlorn and clumsily truncated tower. The interior is much more enticing, the broad sweep of the five-aisled nave punctuated by tall and slender columns that shoot up to the arching vaults of the roof. Here also is a scattering of sixteenth- and seventeenth-century paintings, most memorably a splendidly impassioned *Crucifixion* by **Anthony van Dyck** (1599–1641), which is displayed in the north transept. Trained in Antwerp, where he worked in Rubens' workshop, van Dyck made extended visits to England and Italy in the 1620s, before returning to Antwerp in 1628. He stayed there for four years – during which time he painted this *Crucifixion* – before migrating to England to become portrait painter to Charles I and his court.

The Design Museum

Doubling back from St Michielskerk, it's a short walk north along the Korenlei to the enjoyable **Design Museum**, Jan Breydelstraat 5 (Tues–Sun 10am–6pm; €5; Ⓦwww.designmuseumgent.be), which focuses on Belgian decorative and applied arts. The wide-ranging collection divides into two distinct sections. At the front, squeezed into what was once an eighteenth-century patrician's mansion, is an attractive sequence of **period rooms**, mostly illustrating the Baroque and the Rococo. The original dining room is especially fine, from its fancy painted ceiling, ornate chandelier and Chinese porcelain through to its intricately carved elm panelling.

The second section, at the back of the mansion, comprises a **modern display** area used both for temporary exhibitions and to showcase the museum's eclectic collection of applied arts, dating from 1880 to the present day. There are examples of the work of many leading designers, but the Art Nouveau material is perhaps the most visually arresting, especially the finely crafted furnishings of the Belgian **Henry van der Velde** (1863–1957).

Het Gravensteen

From the Design Museum, it's a short hop to **Het Gravensteen** (daily: April–Sept 9am–6pm; Oct–March 9am–5pm; €8), the castle of the counts of Flanders, which looks sinister enough to have been lifted from a Bosch painting. Its cold, dark walls and unyielding turrets were first raised in 1180 as much to intimidate the town's unruly citizens as to protect them and, considering the castle has been used for all sorts of purposes since then (even a cotton mill), it has survived in remarkably good nick. The imposing **gateway** comprises a deep-arched, heavily fortified tunnel leading to a large **courtyard**, which is framed by protective battlements complete with wooden flaps, ancient arrow slits and apertures for boiling oil and water.

Overlooking the courtyard are the castle's two main buildings: the **count's residence** on the left and the **keep** on the right, the latter riddled with narrow, interconnected staircases set within the thickness of the walls. A **self-guided tour** takes you through this labyrinth, the first highlight being a room full of medieval military hardware, from suits of armour, pikes, swords, daggers and early pistols through to a pair of exquisitely crafted sixteenth-century crossbows. Beyond, and also of interest, is a gruesome collection of instruments of torture; a particularly dank, underground dungeon (or *oubliette*); and the counts' vaulted council chamber. It's also possible to walk along most of the castle's encircling wall, from where there are pleasing views over the city centre.

St-Veerleplein and the Oude Vismarkt

Public punishments ordered by the counts and countesses of Flanders were carried out in front of the castle on **St-Veerleplein**, now an attractive cobbled square, but with an ersatz punishment post plonked here in 1913 and topped off by a lion carrying the banner of Flanders. At the back of the square, beside the junction of the city's two main canals, is the grandiloquent Baroque facade of the **Oude Vismarkt** (Old Fish Market), in which Neptune stands on a chariot drawn by sea horses. To either side are allegorical figures representing the River Leie (Venus) and the River Scheldt (Hercules), the two rivers that spawned the city. After years of neglect, the Oude Vismarkt has been redeveloped, and will soon be home to the tourist office (see p.177).

Huis van Alijn Museum

From St-Veerleplein, it's a brief stroll east to one of the city's more popular attractions, the **Huis van Alijn**, Kraanlei 65 (Tues–Sat 11am–5pm, Sun 10am–5pm; €5; Ⓦwww.huisvanalijn.be), a folklore museum which occupies a series of exceptionally pretty little almshouses set around a central courtyard. Dating from the fourteenth century, the almshouses were built following a major scandal reminiscent of *Romeo and Juliet*. In 1354, two members of the Rijms family murdered three of the rival Alijns when they were at Mass in St-Baafskathedraal. The immediate cause of the affray was jealousy – one man from each clan was after the same woman – but the dispute went deeper, reflecting the commercial animosity of two guilds, the weavers and the fullers. The murderers fled for their lives and were condemned to death in absentia, but were eventually – eight years later – pardoned on condition that they paid for the construction of a set of almshouses, which was to be named after the victims. The result was the Huis van Alijn, which became a hospice for elderly women and then a workers' tenement until the city council snapped it up in the 1950s.

The **museum** consists of two sets of rooms depicting local life and work in the nineteenth and twentieth centuries, one each on either side of the central courtyard. There are reconstructions of a variety of shops and workshops – a dispensary, a barber's and so forth – plus thematic displays illustrating particular aspects of traditional Flemish society such as popular entertainment, funerals and death, but unfortunately the labelling is very skimpy. One particular highlight, however, in one of the rooms on the museum's right-hand side, is a bank of miniature TV screens showing short, locally made **amateur films** in a continuous cycle. Some of these date back to the 1920s, but most are postwar, including a snippet featuring a local 1970s soccer team dressed in terrifyingly tight shorts.

The Patershol

Behind the Kraanlei are the lanes and alleys of the **Patershol**, a tight web of brick terraced houses dating from the seventeenth century. Once the heart of the Flemish working-class city, this thriving residential quarter had, by the 1970s, become a slum threatened with demolition. After much debate, the area was saved from the developers and a process of gentrification begun, the result being today's gaggle of good bars and smashing restaurants. The process is still underway and the fringes of the Patershol remain a ragbag of decay and restoration, but few Belgian cities can boast a more agreeable drinking and eating district. The only specific attraction is the grand old Carmelite Monastery on Vrouwebroersstraat, now the **Provinciaal Cultuurcentrum Caermersklooster** (Ⓦ www.caermersklooster.be), which showcases temporary exhibitions of contemporary art, photography, design and fashion.

Dulle Griet

Pushing on along the Kraanlei from the Huis van Alijn, it's footsteps to the antiquated little bridge that leads over to **Dulle Griet** (Mad Meg), a lugubrious fifteenth-century **cannon** whose failure to fire provoked a bitter row between Ghent and the nearby Flemish town of Oudenaarde, where it was cast. In the 1570s, fearful of a Habsburg attack, Ghent purchased the cannon from Oudenaarde. As the region's most powerful siege gun, able to propel a 340kg cannonball several hundred metres, it seemed a good buy, but when Ghent's gunners tried it out the barrel cracked on first firing. The useless lump was then rolled to the edge of the Vrijdagmarkt, where it has stayed ever since – and much to the chagrin of Ghent city council, Oudenaarde simply refused to offer a refund.

Vrijdagmarkt and Bij St-Jacobs

From Dulle Griet, it's metres to the **Vrijdagmarkt**, a wide and open square that was long the political centre of Ghent, the site of both public meetings and executions – sometimes both at the same time. In the middle of the square stands a nineteenth-century statue of the guild leader **Jacob van Artevelde** (see box, p.190), portrayed addressing the people in heroic style. Of the buildings flanking the Vrijdagmarkt, the most appealing is the former **Gildehuis van de**

Jacob van Artevelde comes to a sticky end

One of the shrewdest of Ghent's medieval leaders, **Jacob van Artevelde** (1290–1345) was elected captain of all the guilds in 1337. Initially, he steered a delicate course during the interminable wars between France and England, keeping the city neutral – and the textile industry going – despite the machinations of both warring countries. Ultimately, however, he was forced to take sides, plumping for England. This proved his undoing: in a burst of Anglomania, Artevelde rashly suggested that a son of Edward III of England become the new count of Flanders, an unpopular notion that prompted a mob to storm his house and hack him to death. Artevelde's demise fuelled further outbreaks of communal **violence** and, a few weeks later, the Vrijdagmarkt witnessed a riot between the fullers and the weavers that left five hundred dead. This rumbling vendetta – one of several that plagued the city – was the backdrop to the creation of the Huis van Alijn (see p.188).

Huidevetters (Tanners' Guildhouse) at no. 37, a tall Gothic structure whose pert dormer windows and stepped gables culminate in a dainty and distinctive corner turret, the Toreken. Also worth a second glance is the old headquarters of the trade unions, the whopping **Ons Huis** (Our House), a sterling edifice built in eclectic style at the beginning of the twentieth century.

Adjoining Vrijdagmarkt is **Bij St-Jacobs**, a sprawling square set around a sulky medieval church. The square hosts the city's biggest and best **flea market** (*prondelmarkt*) on Fridays, Saturdays and Sundays from 8am to 1pm. From the square, it's a couple of minutes' walk up Belfortstraat back to Hoogpoort and the Stadhuis.

East along the Hoogpoort to Geraard de Duivelsteen

St-Jorishof, the honey-coloured building facing the Stadhuis on the corner of Hoogpoort, is one of the city's oldest, its heavy-duty stonework dating from the middle of the fifteenth century. This was once the home of the Crossbowmen's Guild, and although the crossbow was a dead military duck by the time it was built, the guild was still a powerful political force – and remained so until the eighteenth century. It was here, in 1477, that Mary of Burgundy (see p.164) was pressured into signing the Great Privilege, confirming the city's commercial freedoms. She was obviously not too offended, though, as later that year this was where she chose to receive the matrimonial ambassadors of the Holy Roman Emperor, Frederick III. Frederick was pressing the suit of his son, Maximilian, whom Mary duly married, the end result being that Flanders became a Habsburg fiefdom.

Lining the **Hoogpoort** beyond St-Jorishof are some of the oldest facades in Ghent, sturdy if sooty Gothic structures dating from the fifteenth century. The third house along started out as a heavily protected aristocratic mansion called the **Grote Sikkel** and, although it is now the home of a music school, the blackened remains of an antique torch-snuffer remain fixed to the wall beside the grand double doors.

Hoogpoort leads into **Nederpolder**, from where it's a few metres to **Geraard de Duivelsteen** (no admission), a forbidding, fortified palace of splendid Romanesque design, built of grey limestone in the thirteenth century and bordered by what remains of its moat. The stronghold probably takes its name from Geraard Vilain, who earned the soubriquet "duivel" (devil) for his acts of cruelty or, according to some sources, because of his swarthy features and black hair. Vilain was not the only noble to wall himself up within a castle: well into the fourteenth century, Ghent was dotted with fortified houses (*stenen*) – such was the fear the privileged few had of the rebellious guildsmen. The last noble moved out of the Duivelsteen in about 1350 and since then the building has been put to a bewildering range of uses – at various times it served as an arsenal, a prison, a madhouse and an orphanage; nowadays it houses government archives.

Lieven Bauwensplein and the van Eyck monument

Across the street from the Duivelsteen is **Lieven Bauwensplein**, a square that takes its name from – and has a statue of – the local entrepreneur who founded the city's machine-manufactured textile industry. Born in 1769, the son of a tanner, Bauwens was an intrepid soul, who posed as an ordinary textile worker in England to learn how its (much more technologically advanced) machinery worked. In the 1790s, he managed to smuggle a spinning jenny over to the continent and soon opened cotton mills in Ghent. It didn't, however, do Bauwens much good: he over-borrowed and when there was a downturn in demand, his factories went bust and he died in poverty.

From the square, it's a short stroll north up Limburgstraat to St-Baafskathedraal (see p.182). On the way, you'll pass a **monument** to the Eyck brothers, Hubert and Jan, the painter(s) of the *Adoration of the Mystic Lamb*. The monument is a somewhat stodgy affair, knocked up for the Great Exhibition of 1913, but it's an interesting piece of art propaganda, proclaiming Hubert as co-painter of the altarpiece, when this is very speculative (see p.183). Open on Hubert's knees is the Bible's Revelation, which may or may not have given him artistic inspiration.

South of the centre

Although the majority of Ghent's key attractions are within easy strolling distance of the Korenmarkt, three of the city's principal museums are located a good walk south of the centre. These are **STAM**, the city's brand new historical museum, the well-known **Museum voor Schone Kunsten** (Fine Art Museum) and the adjacent Museum of Contemporary Art, **S.M.A.K**. All three are easy to reach by tram, but the walk down to them from the city centre can take in several less well-known sights. The route suggested below begins by heading south from the Korenmarkt along **Veldstraat**, Ghent's main shopping street.

South along Veldstraat

Leading south from the Korenmarkt, **Veldstraat** runs parallel to the River Leie. By and large, it's a very ordinary shopping strip, but the eighteenth-century mansion at no. 82 does hold the modest **Museum Arnold Vander Haeghen** (Mon–Fri 9am–noon & 2–4pm; free), where pride of place goes to the Chinese salon, whose original silk wallpaper has survived intact. The Duke of Wellington stayed here in 1815 after the Battle of Waterloo, popping across the street to the **Hôtel d'Hane-Steenhuyse**, at no. 55, to bolster the morale of the refugee King of France, **Louis XVIII**. Abandoning his throne, Louis had hot-footed it to Ghent soon after Napoleon landed in France following his escape from Elba. While others did his fighting for him, Louis waited around in Ghent gorging himself – his daily dinner lasted all of seven hours and the bloated exile was known to polish off one hundred oysters at a sitting. His fellow exile, the writer and politician François Chateaubriand, ignored the gluttony and cowardice, writing meekly, "The French alone know how to dine with method". Thanks to Wellington's ministrations, Louis was persuaded to return to his kingdom and his entourage left for Paris on June 26, 1815, one week after Waterloo. The grand eighteenth-century facade of

Louis's hideaway has survived in good condition, its elaborate pediment sporting allegorical representations of Time and History, but at present there's no access to the expansive salons beyond.

Pushing along Veldstraat, it's a couple of minutes' walk to a matching pair of grand, Neoclassical nineteenth-century buildings. On the right-hand side is the **Justitiepaleis** (Palace of Justice), whose colossal pediment sports a frieze with the figure of Justice in the middle, the accused to one side and the condemned on the other. Opposite stands the recently restored **opera house** – home to De Vlaamse Opera (see p.197) – its facade awash with playfully decorative stone panels and friezes.

STAM

Five minutes' walk further along Nederkouter, the old Cistercian **Bijlokeabdij** (Bijloke Abbey) on Godshuizenlaan, just to the west of the River Leie, was founded in the thirteenth century and savaged by Calvinists on several occasions. Much of the medieval complex survived, and the huddle of tidy brown-brick buildings have now been incorporated within **STAM** (Tues–Sun 10am–6pm; €6; Ⓦwww.stamgent.be), a lavish museum devoted to a detailed exploration of the city's turbulent history. Highlights of the permanent collection include the medieval wall paintings in the former refectory, several fine land- and cityscapes from the seventeenth century, and all manner of social paraphernalia, from freemasons' tackle and guild banners through to tapestries and clothing.

Citadelpark and S.M.A.K.

From STAM, it's a brief stroll southeast to **Citadelpark**, a large chunk of greenery which takes its name from the fortress that stood here until the 1870s, when the land was cleared and prettified with the addition of grottoes and ponds, statues and fountains, a waterfall and a bandstand. These nineteenth-century niceties survive today and, as an added bonus, the park seems refreshingly hilly after the flatness of the rest of Ghent. In the 1940s, a large brick complex was built on the east side of the park and, after many incarnations, much of this now houses **S.M.A.K**, the Stedelijk Museum voor Actuele Kunst (Municipal Museum of Contemporary Art; Tues–Sun 10am–6pm; €6; Ⓦwww.smak.be), one of Belgium's most adventurous contemporary art galleries. It's largely devoted to temporary displays of international standing, and recent exhibitions have featured the work of Simon Gush, Paul Thek and Paolo Chiasera. These exhibitions are supplemented by a regularly rotated selection of sculptures, paintings and installations taken from the museum's top-ranking **permanent collection**. S.M.A.K possesses examples of all the major artistic movements since World War II – everything from Surrealism, the CoBrA group and Pop Art through to Minimalism and conceptual art – as well as their forerunners. Perennial favourites include the installations of the influential German **Joseph Beuys** (1921–1986), who played a leading role in the European avant-garde art movement of the 1970s, a characteristically unnerving painting by **Francis Bacon** (1909–1992) entitled *Figure Seated*, and Panamarenko's eccentric polyester zeppelin entitled *Aeromodeller*.

Museum voor Schone Kunsten

Directly opposite S.M.A.K., the **Museum voor Schone Kunsten** (Fine Art Museum; Tues–Sun 10am–6pm; €5; Ⓦwww.mskgent.be) occupies an imposing Neoclassical edifice on the edge of Citadelpark. Inside, the central atrium and connecting rotunda are flanked by a sequence of rooms, with the older paintings usually exhibited to the right in Rooms 1–8, the bulk of the eighteenth- and nineteenth-century material in Rooms 14–19, and the early twentieth-century material mostly on the left in Rooms A–K, though things can get moved around during temporary exhibitions.

Early Flemish paintings

In Room 2, one highlight of the museum's small but eclectic collection of early Flemish paintings is **Rogier van der Weyden**'s (1399–1464) *Madonna with Carnation*, a charming work where the proffered flower, in all its exquisite detail, serves as a symbol of Christ's passion. Also in Room 2 are two superb works by **Hieronymus Bosch** (1450–1516), his *Bearing of the Cross* showing Christ mocked by some of the most grotesque and deformed characters Bosch ever painted. Look carefully and you'll see that Christ's head is at the centre of two diagonals, one representing evil, the other good – the latter linking the repentant thief with St Veronica, whose cloak carries the imprint of Christ's face. This struggle between good and evil is also the subject of Bosch's *St Jerome at Prayer*, in the foreground of which the saint prays, surrounded by a brooding, menacing landscape. Next door, Room 3 is notable for **Adriaen Isenbrandt**'s (d.1551) *Mary and Child*, a gentle painting showing Mary suckling Jesus on the flight to Egypt, with the artist choosing a rural Flemish landscape as the backdrop rather than the Holy Land.

Rubens and his contemporaries

Room 5 features a powerful *St Francis* by **Rubens** (1577–1640), in which a very sick-looking saint bears the marks of the stigmata, while **Jacob Jordaens** (1593–1678), who was greatly influenced by Rubens, is well represented in Room 7 by the whimsical romanticism of his *Judgement of Midas*. Jordaens was, however, capable of much greater subtlety and his *Studies of the Head of Abraham Grapheus*, also in Room 7, is an example of the high-quality preparatory paintings he completed, most of which were later recycled within larger compositions. In the same room, **Anthony van Dyck**'s (1599–1641) *Jupiter and Antiope* wins the bad taste award for its portrayal of the lecherous god with his tongue hanging out in anticipation of sex with Antiope. Next door, Room 8 holds three precise works by **Pieter Bruegel the Younger** (1564–1638), who inherited his father's interest in the landscape and those who worked and lived on it, as evidenced by his *Wedding in a Barn*, *Wedding Dance* and *Village Lawyer*.

The eighteenth to the early twentieth century

Rooms 14–19 are dedicated to the museum's eighteenth- and nineteenth-century collection with a handful of romantic historical canvases, plus – and this is a real surprise – a superbly executed portrait of a certain *Alexander Edgar* by the Scot **Henry Raeburn** (1756–1823). There are more late nineteenth-century paintings in Rooms N–S as well as some especially fine canvases from the early 1900s, most memorably **Henri Evenepoel**'s striking portrait of a bewitched-looking *Spaniard in Paris*. Room P holds several key paintings by Ostend's **James Ensor** (1860–1949), including the ghoulish *Skeleton looking at Chinoiserie* and *Pierrot and Skeleton in Yellow Robe*, as well as his much-lauded *Self-Portrait with Flower Hat*. Finally, Room F displays several characteristically unsettling works by both **Paul Delvaux** (1897–1994) and **René Magritte** (1898–1967). A case in point is Magritte's *Persepective II. Manet's Balcony*, in which wooden coffins have replaced the figures from Manet's painting.

Eating, drinking and nightlife

Ghent's multitude of **cafés**, **café-bars** and **restaurants** offer the very best of Flemish and French food alongside an international cast of other cuisines. The city has a battalion of prestige restaurants, where the food is great and prices high, but there are lots of reasonably priced places too, especially at the more informal end of the market where the distinction between café-bars and bars tends to blur. Ghent is particularly good for **vegetarians**: the tourist office has a free brochure detailing all the places where they serve vegetarian food and the city is home to **EVA** (Ethical Vegetarian Alternative; Ⓦwww.vegetarisme.be), which promotes vegetarianism in local cafés and restaurants. Across the city, most waiters speak at least a modicum of English – many are fluent – and **multilingual menus** are the norm.

The city's **bars** are a real delight and several of the most distinctive, complete with a beer list long enough to strain any liver, are within a couple of minutes' walk of Het Gravensteen. The **club** and **live music scene** is also first-rate, with Ghent's students taking the lead, congregating at the string of bars and clubs that line up along Overpoortstraat, just south of St-Pietersplein; Thursdays (rather than the weekend) is the big night out. The best **listings magazine**, though it is stuffed with ads, is the fortnightly freebie *Zone 09* (Ⓦwww.zone09.be); it's available at newspaper racks all over the city centre.

Unless otherwise stated, the places listed below are marked on the Central Ghent map, p.181.

Cafés

Avalon Geldmunt 32. This spick-and-span vegetarian restaurant offers a wide range of well-prepared dishes; the key pull is the daily specials, which cost about €12. Choose from one of the many different rooms or the terrace at the back in the summer. Mon–Sat 11.30am–2.30pm.

Brooderie Jan Breydelstraat 8. Pleasant and informal café with a healthfood slant, offering wholesome breakfasts, lunches, sandwiches and salads (from around €9), plus cakes and coffee. Also offers B&B (see p.182). Tues–Sun noon–4pm.

Greenway Nederkouter 42. Straightforward café-cum-takeaway decorated in sharp modern style, selling a wide range of eco-friendly foods, from organic burgers to pastas, noodles and baguettes, all for just a few euros each. Mon–Sat 11am–9pm. See map, pp.178–179.

Gwenola Voldersstraat 66. This long-established pancake house may be a bit over the hill decoratively, but who cares when the pancakes are so good – and inexpensive, from €2.50 and up. Mon–Fri 11am–7pm Sat 11am–5pm.

Julie's House Kraanlei 13. "Baked with love and served with joy" is the publicity tag here, a little over the top perhaps, but *Julie's* home-made cakes and patisseries are truly delicious. The premises are appealing too, occupying a tastefully revamped old house complete with original beamed ceiling, and they also serve tasty breakfasts (till 2pm) and pancakes. Wed–Sun 9am–6.30pm.

Lepelblad Onderbergen 40. Fantastically popular café, with a heaving pavement terrace, that does an especially good line in salads and pastas – and the arty decor is good fun too. Mains from €14. Tues–Fri 11am–8.30pm & Sat 11am–5pm.

Souplounge Zuivelbrug 4. Bright and cheerful modern café, where the big bowls of freshly made soup are the main event – from €6. Self-service. Daily 10am–7pm.

Restaurants

Bij den wijzen en den zot Hertogstraat 42 Ⓣ09 223 42 30. One of the better restaurants in the Patershol, serving up Flemish cuisine with more than a dash of French flair. Soft lighting and classical music set the tone, and the premises are charming – an old brick house of tiny rooms and narrow stairs with dining on two floors. Prices are bearable, with main courses averaging about €25; house specialities include eel, cooked in several different ways, and *waterzooi*. Tues–Sat noon–2pm & 6.30–10pm.

De Blauwe Zalm Vrouwebroersstraat 2 Ⓣ09 224 08 52. Outstanding seafood restaurant – the best in town – serving up everything from the more usual cod, salmon, monkfish and haddock through to the likes of seawolf, sea bass, turbot and John Dory. Tanks keep the crustacea alive and kicking, and the decor has a distinctly maritime feel – though it's all done in impeccable, ultra-cool style. Main courses from €25. Reservations essential. Tues–Fri noon–2pm, plus Mon–Sat 7–10pm.

Coeur d'Artichaut Onderbergen 6 ⓣ09 225 33 18. In a handsome eighteenth-century mansion with a lovely courtyard at the back, this smooth and polished restaurant specializes in salads – and they really are quite superb – plus innovative French, Thai and Italian dishes. Salads, as a main course, start at €16. Tues–Sat noon–2.30pm & 7–10.30pm.

Domestica Onderbergen 27 ⓣ09 223 53 00. Smart and chic brasserie-restaurant serving up an excellent range of Belgian dishes – both French and Flemish – in nouvelle cuisine style. Has a garden terrace for good-weather eating. Main courses from €25. Mon 6.30–10.30pm, Tues–Fri noon–2.30pm & 6.30–10pm, Sat 6.30–10pm.

House of Eliott Jan Breydelstraat 36 ⓣ09 225 21 28, ⓦwww.thehouseofeliott.be. Idiosyncratic split-level restaurant that's liberally sprinkled with Edwardian bric-a-brac – you'll even spot some vintage models' dummies. The menu offers a limited but well-chosen selection of freshly prepared meat and fish dishes – try, for example, the wood pigeon risotto. The window tables overlook a canal and, if the weather holds, you can eat out on the pontoon at the back. Mains average €25. Mon & Fri–Sun noon–2pm & 6–10pm, Thurs 6–10pm.

Marco Polo Trattoria Serpentstraat 11 ⓣ09 225 04 20. This simple, rustic restaurant is part of the Italian "slow food" movement in which the emphasis is on organic, seasonal ingredients prepared in a traditional manner. The menu is small, but all the dishes are freshly prepared and delicious. Mains from €15. Tues–Fri noon–2.30pm & 6–10pm, Sat & Sun 6–10pm.

Pakhuis Schuurkenstraat 4 ⓣ09 223 55 55, ⓦwww.pakhuis.be. Set in a creatively remodelled old warehouse with acres of glass and metal and a large outside area for both drinking and/or eating, this lively bistro-brasserie is one of Ghent's more fashionable options, attracting a diverse clientele. The extensive menu features Flemish and French dishes, with mains averaging €22. Down a narrow alley near St-Michielsbrug. Mon–Sat noon–11pm, bar till 1am.

Shopping in Ghent: a top five

Bric-a-brac

The Fallen Angels Jan Breydelstraat 29–31 ⓣ09 223 94 15, ⓦwww.the-fallen-angels.com. Mother and daughter run these two adjacent shops, selling all manner of antique bric-a-brac, from postcards and posters through to teddy bears and toys. Intriguing at best, twee at worst, but a useful source of unusual gifts. Wed–Sat 1.30–5.30pm.

Cheese

Kaas Mekka Koestraat 9 ⓣ09 225 83 66. Literally the "Cheese Mecca", this small specialist shop offers a remarkable range of traditional and exotic cheeses – try some of the delicious Ghent goat's cheese (*geitenkaas*). Sells a good range of wine, too. Mon–Sat 9am–6pm.

Chocolates

Van Hecke Koestraat 42 ⓣ09 225 43 57. Many locals swear that this independent chocolatier sells the best chocolates and cakes in town. Mon, Tues & Thurs–Sat 9.30am–6pm.

Mustard

Tierenteyn Groetenmarkt 3 This traditional shop, one of the city's most delightful, makes its own mustards: wonderful, tongue-tickling stuff displayed in shelf upon shelf of ceramic and glass jars. A small jar will set you back about €3. Mon–Fri 8.30am–6pm, Sat 9am–12.30pm & 1–6pm.

Wallpaper

Priem Zulvelbrugstraat 1. One of the oddest shops in Ghent, Priem has an extraordinary range of vintage wallpaper dating from the 1950s. Zuivelbrugstraat is the location of the main shop, but there are three other premises a few paces away on the Kraanlei. Mon 2–6.30pm, Tues–Fri 9.30am–12.30pm & 2–6pm, Sat 9.30am–12.30pm & 2–5.30pm.

De 3 Biggetjes Zeugsteeg 7 ⓣ09 224 46 48, ⓦwww.de3biggetjes.com. This charmingly intimate restaurant occupies an old terrace house in the heart of the Patershol. A select but well-chosen menu features the freshest of ingredients prepared with creative gusto – antelope in jenever sauce for example. Main courses from €25. Mon, Tues, Thurs & Fri noon–2pm & 7–9pm, Sat 7–9pm, Sun noon–2pm.

Bars, café-bars and clubs

Decadance Overpoortstraat 76 ⓦwww.decadance.be. This funky club near the university (hence the abundance of students) offers one of the city's best nights out, with reggae, hip-hop, drum 'n' bass and garage-techno vibes. Daily from 10pm until 8/10am, Sun until midnight. See map, pp.178–179.

't Dreupelkot Groentenmarkt 12. Cosy bar specializing in jenever (Belgian gin), of which it stocks more than 200 brands, all kept at icy temperatures – the vanilla flavour is particularly delicious. It's down a little alley leading off the Groentenmarkt, and next door to *Het Waterhuis* (see below). Daily: July & Aug 6pm until late; Sept–June 4pm until late.

Dulle Griet Vrijdagmarkt 50. Long, dark and atmospheric bar with all manner of incidental objets d'art and an especially wide range of beers. Mon 4.30pm–1am, Tues–Sat noon–1am & Sun noon–7.30pm.

Hotsy Totsy Hoogstraat 1. Long the gathering place of the city's intelligentsia – though less so today – this ornately decorated bar, with its Art Nouveau flourishes, has ranks of drinkers lining up along its long wooden bar. Live jazz too, usually on a Thursday. Mon–Fri from 6pm till late, Fri–Sun from 8pm. See map, pp.178–179.

Pink Flamingos Onderstraat 55 ⓦwww.pinkflamingos.be. Weird and wonderful place – the interior is the height of kitsch, with plastic statues of film stars, tacky religious icons and Barbie dolls. Attracts a groovy crowd, and a great place for an aperitif or cocktails. Mon–Wed noon–midnight, Thurs & Fri noon–3am, Sat 2pm–3am, Sun 2pm–midnight.

Rococo Corduwaniersstraat 57. This intimate café-cum-bar attracts a cool clientele and is a perfect place to be on a cold winter evening, with candles flickering and the fire roaring. Stocks a good range of wines and beers, and also has home-made cakes. Daily except Mon 10pm until late.

De Trollekelder Bij St-Jacobs 17. This dark and atmospheric bar offers a huge selection of beers in an ancient merchant's house – don't be deterred by the trolls stuck in the window. Mon–Thurs 5pm–2am & Fri–Sun 4pm–2am.

Den Turk Botermarkt 3. The oldest bar in the city, this tiny rabbit-warren of a place offers a good range of beers and whiskies, though a recent renovation did not do it any favours. Frequent live music, mainly jazz. Daily 11am until late.

Vooruit St Pietersnieuwstraat 23 ⓣ09 267 28 28, ⓦwww.vooruit.be. The Vooruit performing arts centre has good claim to be the cultural centre of the city (at least for the under-40s), offering a wide-ranging programme of rock and pop through to dance. It also occupies a splendid building, a twin-towered and turreted former festival hall that was built for Ghent's socialists in an eclectic rendition of Art Nouveau in 1914. The café-bar is a large barn-like affair that stays jam-packed until early in the morning. Café-bar Mon–Sat 11.30am–1am, Sun 4pm–1am. See map, pp.178–179.

Het Waterhuis aan de Bierkant Groentenmarkt 9. More than a hundred types of beer are available in this engaging canal-side bar, which is popular with tourists and locals alike. Be sure to try Stropken (literally "noose"), a delicious local brew named after the time, in 1540, when Charles V compelled the rebellious city burghers to parade outside the town gate with ropes around their necks. Daily 11am until late.

Performing arts, festivals and cinema

Ghent has invested heavily in its **performing arts** scene and now has five first-rate venues, shares a premier opera company with Antwerp and has half a dozen theatre troupes. There are literally dozens of performances of every sort during the city's two main festivals, the **Gentse Feesten**, held over ten days in mid- to late July and always including July 21 (ⓦwww.gentsefeesten.be); and the **Festival van Vlaanderen** (Flanders Festival; ⓦwww.festival.be), a classical music event which runs from June to December with concerts in all of the major cities of Flanders, including Ghent. As for **cinema**, Ghent possesses two very good art-house cinemas and also hosts the prestigious **Ghent Film Festival** (ⓦwww.filmfestival.be). Held over twelve days in October, it's one of Europe's foremost cinematic events, showcasing around two hundred feature films and a hundred shorts from all over the world, screening Belgian films and the best of world cinema well before they hit the international circuit; there's a special focus on music in film too. The best **listings magazine** is the fortnightly freebie *Zone 09* (see p.194).

Major venues

Concertzaal Handelsbeurs Kouter 29 ⓣ09 265 91 60, ⓦwww.handelsbeurs.be. The city's primary concert hall with two auditoria and hosting a diverse programme that covers all the performing arts.

Muziekcentrum De Bijloke Jozef Kluyskensstraat 2 ⓣ09 269 92 92, ⓦwww.debijloke.be. Concert Hall at STAM, the city's brand-new history museum (see p.192).

NT Gent Schouwburg Sint Baafsplein 17. Right in the centre of the city, the municipal theatre accommodates the Nederlands Toneel Gent (NTG; ⓣ09 225 01 01, ⓦwww.ntgent.be), the regional repertory company. Almost all of their performances are in Flemish, though they do play occasional host to touring English-language theatre companies.

Vlaamse Opera Gent Schouwburgstraat ⓣ09 268 10 11, ⓦwww.vlaamseopera.be. Handsomely restored nineteenth-century opera house, where the city's opera company perform when not on tour.

Vooruit Sint-Pietersnieuwstraat 23 ⓣ09 267 28 28, ⓦwww.vooruit.be. Ghent's leading venue for rock, pop and jazz concerts (see also opposite).

Art-house cinemas

Sphinx Sint-Michielshelling 3 ⓣ09 225 60 86, ⓦwww.sphinx-cinema.be. Sphinx focuses on foreign-language and art-house films (with original soundtrack intact).

Studio Skoop Sint Annaplein 63 ⓣ09 225 08 45, ⓦwww.studioskoop.be. The cosiest of the city's film venues, but still with five screens.

Listings

ATMs ATMs are liberally distributed across the city centre. ING has ATMs at most of its branches, including Belfortstraat 18 and Kouter 173.

Books FNAC, at Veldstraat 88 (Mon–Sat 10am–6.30pm; ⓣ09 223 40 80, ⓦwww.fnac.be), close to the junction with Zonnestraat, has several floors of music, books, cameras, comics and newspapers, including a good English-language section. It also sells maps, including a few Belgian hiking maps, and tickets for most mainstream cultural events.

Car rental Avis, Kortrijksesteenweg 676 (closed Sun; ⓣ09 222 00 53); Europcar, Kortrijksesteenweg 263A, Sint-Martens-Latem (closed Sun; ⓣ09 220 44 10); Hertz, at Nieuwewandeling 76 (Mon–Fri 9am–5pm; ⓣ09 224 04 06).

Internet access Almost all hotels and hostels provide internet access for their guests, either free or at minimal charge. There are also several internet cafés in the city, the most central of which is the *Coffee Lounge*, across from the Lakenhalle at Botermarkt 6 (daily 10am–7pm).

Left luggage There are luggage lockers and a luggage office at the train station.

Markets Ghent does a good line in open-air markets. There's a large and popular flea market (*prondelmarkt*) on Bij St-Jacobs and adjoining Beverhoutplein (Fri, Sat & Sun 8am–1pm); a daily flower market on the Kouter, just off Veldstraat, though this is at its best and busiest on Sundays (7am–1pm); organic foodstuffs on the Groentenmarkt (Fri 7.30am–1pm); and a bird market (not for the squeamish) on the Vrijdagmarkt on Sundays (7am–1pm).

Pharmacies Two central pharmacies are at St Michielsstraat 15 and Nederkouter 123. Duty rotas, detailing late-night opening pharmacies, should be displayed in every pharmacy window.

Post office The main post office is at Lange Kruisstraat 55 (Mon–Fri 9am–6pm, Sat 9am–3pm).

Taxi V-Tax ⓣ09 222 22 22

Train enquiries For domestic and international services, drop by the train station or consult ⓦwww.b-rail.be. Alternatively, for domestic journeys call ⓣ02 528 28 28, international routes ⓣ070 79 79 79 (premium line).

Travel details

Trains

Bruges to: Brussels (every 30min; 1hr); Ghent (3 hourly; 20min); Knokke (every 30min; 20min); Ostend (every 30min; 15min); Zeebrugge (hourly; 15min).
Ghent to: Antwerp Centraal (every 30min; 50min); Bruges (3 hourly; 20min); De Panne (hourly; 1hr 10min); Diksmuide (hourly; 50min); Kortrijk (every 30min; 20min); Mechelen (hourly; 50min); Ostend (every 30min; 40min); Oudenaarde (Mon–Fri hourly, Sat & Sun every 2hr; 25min); Veurne (hourly; 1hr 10min).
Ieper to: Kortrijk (hourly; 30min).
Kortrijk to: Ghent (every 30min; 20min); Ieper (hourly; 30min); Lille, France (hourly; 30min); Oudenaarde (hourly; 15min).
Ostend to: Bruges (every 30min; 15min); Brussels (hourly; 1hr 20min); Ghent (every 30min; 40min).
Veurne to: De Panne (hourly; 10min); Diksmuide (hourly; 10min); Ghent (hourly; 1hr).

Buses

Diksmuide to: Ieper (Mon–Sat 4–6 daily; 50min).
Ieper to: Diksmuide (Mon–Sat 4–6 daily; 50min); Lo (Sept–June Mon–Fri 6 daily; 35min); Veurne (Sept–June Mon–Fri 7 daily, Sat 4 daily, Sun 2 daily; July–Aug daily, every hour; 1hr).
Veurne to: Ieper (Sept–June Mon–Fri 7 daily, Sat 4 daily, Sun 2 daily; July–Aug daily, every hour; 1hr); Lo (Sept–June Mon–Fri 6 daily; 35min).

Coastal tram

Ostend to: De Panne (every 15min in summer, every 30min in winter; 1hr 10min); Knokke (same frequency; 1hr).

3

Antwerp and the northeast

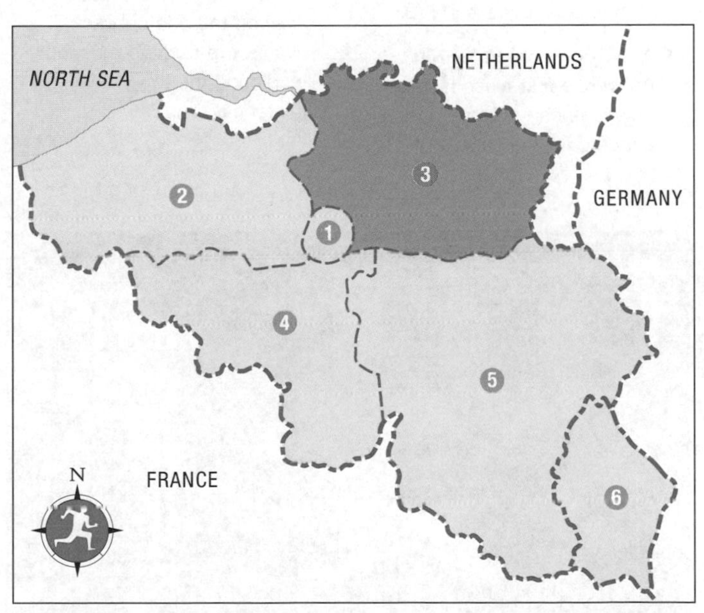

CHAPTER 3

Highlights

* **Antwerp's cathedral** This supreme example of the Gothic style is a truly magnificent, awe-inspiring structure. See p.212

* **Rubens** Don't leave Antwerp without viewing at least some of Rubens' paintings, most stirringly inside the cathedral and at the Rubenshuis, the great man's former home and studio. See p.212 & p.218

* **Antwerp Fashion MoMu**, Antwerp's first-class fashion museum, can only whet your appetite for the gaggle of designer shops in the streets that surround it. See p.221

* **Antwerp at night** The city boasts a mouthwatering selection of restaurants and bars, more than enough for the pickiest of gourmands and the strongest of livers. See pp.224–226

* **Tongeren** An amiable, traditional kind of place, well off the beaten track, with a top-ranking museum exploring the town's Roman history. See p.245

▲ Rubenshuis

Antwerp and the northeast

The **provinces** of Antwerp and Limburg, together with a chunk of Brabant, constitute the Flemish-speaking northeast rim of Belgium, stretching as far as the border with the Netherlands. The countryside is largely dull and flat, its most distinctive feature being the rivers and canals that cut across it, with the River Scheldt leading the way. Easily the main attraction hereabouts is **Antwerp**, a sprawling, intriguing city with many reminders of its sixteenth-century golden age before it was upstaged by Amsterdam as the prime commercial centre of the Low Countries. Antwerp boasts a battery of splendid medieval churches and as fine a set of museums as you'll find anywhere in Belgium, featuring in particular the stirring legacy of **Rubens**, who spent most of his career in the city and produced many of his finest works here. On a more contemporary note, Antwerp is the international centre of the diamond trade and one of Europe's biggest ports, though these roles by no means define its character – for one thing its centre has a range of bars and restaurants to rival any city in Northern Europe.

That part of **Antwerp province** lying to the south of the city isn't of much immediate appeal – it's too industrial for that – but there's compensation in a string

The Kempen – and Baarle-Hertog

Filling out the northeast corner of Belgium, just beyond Antwerp, are the flat, sandy moorlands of the **Kempen**. Once a barren wasteland dotted with the poorest of agricultural communities – and punctuated by tracts of acid heath, bog and deciduous woodland – the Kempen's more hospitable parts were first cultivated and planted with pine by pioneering Cistercian monks in the twelfth century. The monks helped develop and sustain a strong regional identity and dialect, which survives in good order today, though the area's towns and villages are in themselves uniformly drab. The Kempen was also the subject of endless territorial bickering during the creation of an independent Belgium in the 1830s, a particular point of dispute being the little town of **Baarle-Hertog**, about 35km northeast of Antwerp. The final compromise verged on the ridiculous: Baarle-Hertog was designated as being part of Belgium, but it was surrounded by Dutch territory and the international border between it and the adjoining (Dutch) town of **Baarle-Nassau** actually cut through houses, never mind dividing streets. If you're eager to have one leg in the Netherlands, another in Belgium, then here's the spot.

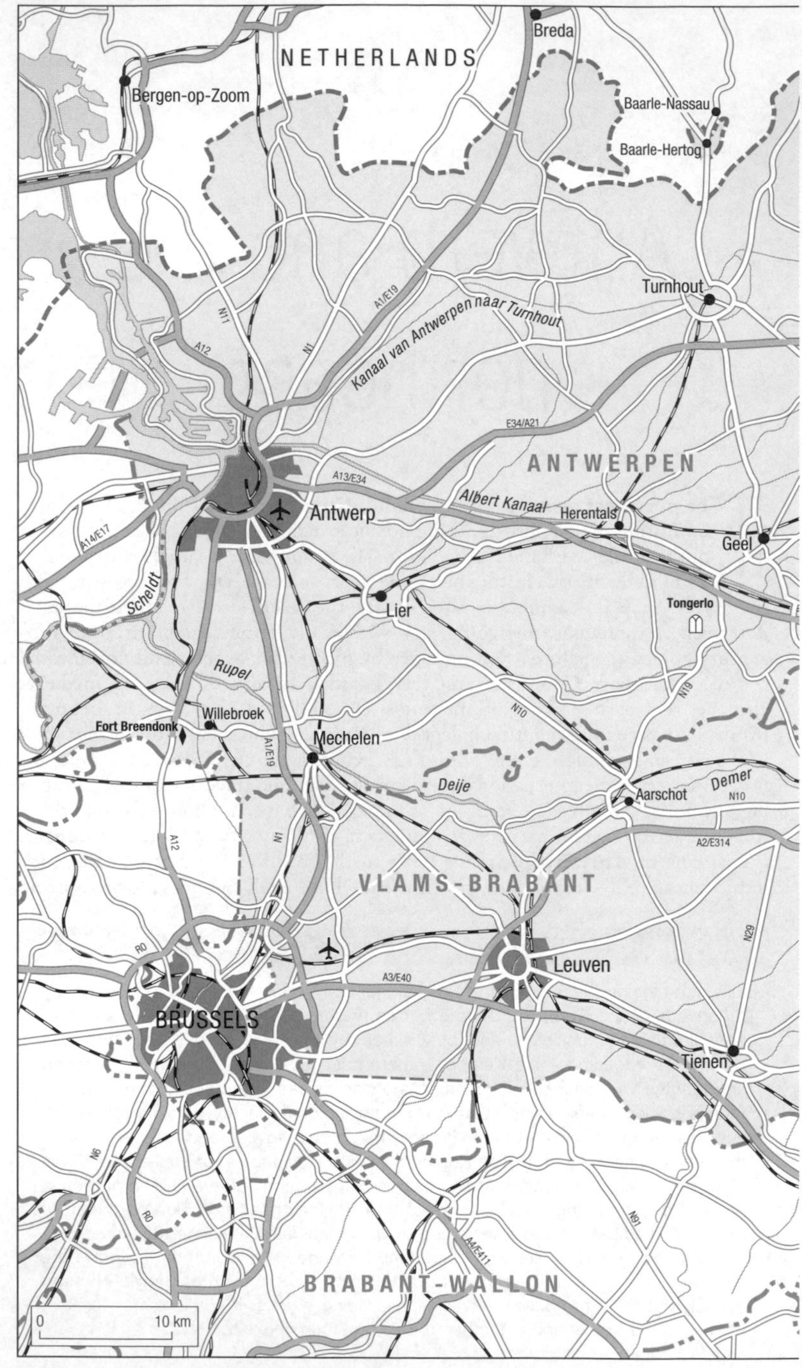

ANTWERP AND THE NORTHEAST

3

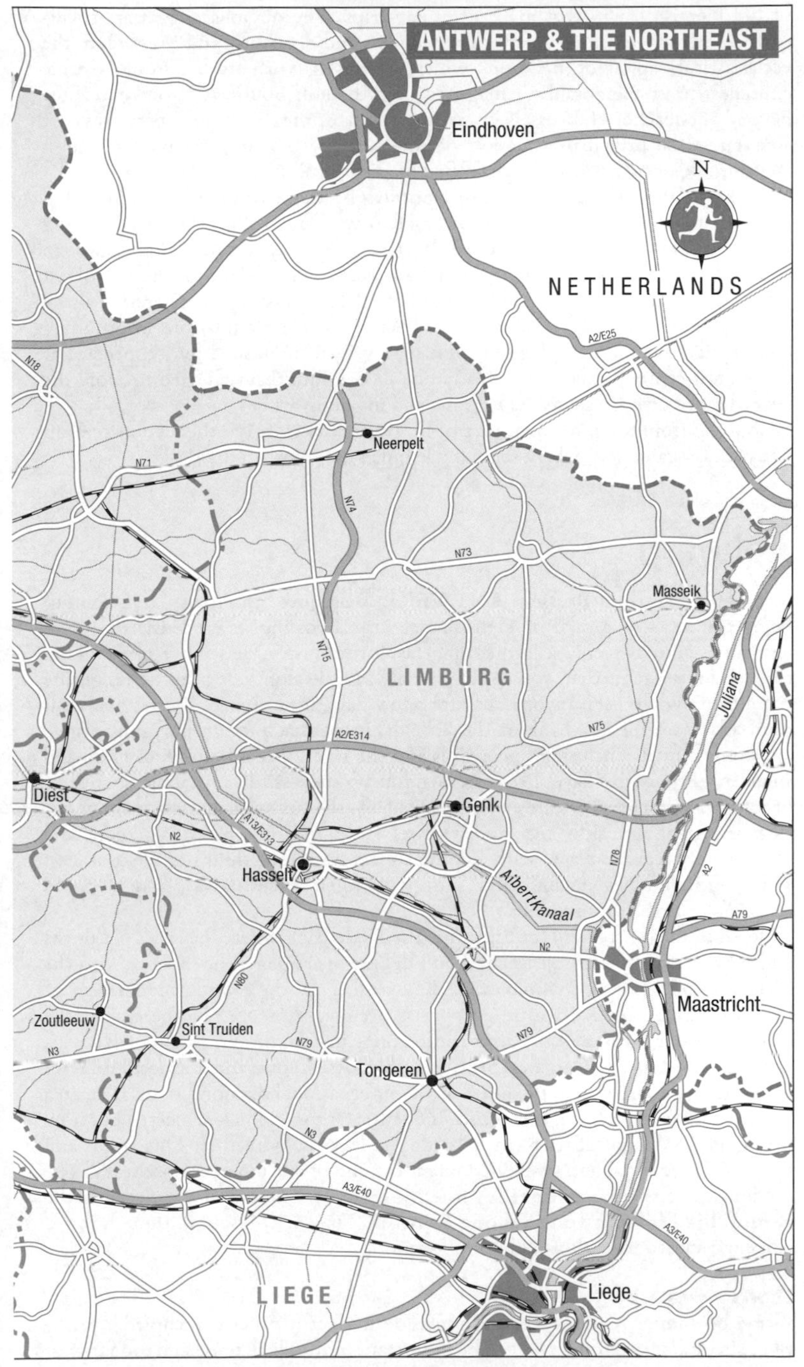

3 ANTWERP AND THE NORTHEAST

of old Flemish towns that make ideal day-trips. The obvious targets are small-town **Lier**, whose centre is particularly quaint and diverting, and **Mechelen**, the ecclesiastical capital of Belgium, which weighs in with its handsome Gothic churches, most memorably a magnificent cathedral. Southeast from here, just beyond the reaches of Brussels' sprawling suburbs, the lively university town of **Leuven** is the principal attraction of this corner of **Vlams-Brabant** (Flemish Brabant), boasting its own clutch of fine medieval buildings.

Further to the east, the province of **Limburg** is, unlike Antwerp, seldom visited by tourists, its low-key mixture of small towns and rolling farmland having limited appeal. Nevertheless, **Hasselt**, the workaday capital, does have an amenable, laidback air, and pint-sized **Tongeren**, which claims to be the oldest town in Belgium, makes a good hand of its Roman history. Tongeren is also a relaxing spot to overnight or to rent a bike and cycle off into the surrounding countryside, where the village of **Zoutleeuw** is distinguished by its spectacular fourteenth-century church – the only one in Belgium that managed to avoid the depredations of Protestants, iconoclasts and invading armies.

Hopping from town to town by **public transport** is easy – there's an excellent network of trains and, where these fizzle out, buses pick up the slack.

Antwerp

Some 50km north of Brussels, **ANTWERP**, Belgium's second city, lays claim to being the de facto capital of Flemish Belgium, boosting its credentials with an animated cultural scene, a burgeoning fashion industry, and more top-ranking cafés and restaurants than you could possibly sample alongside a spirited nightlife – quite enough to keep anyone busy for a few days, if not more. The city fans out carelessly from the east bank of the Scheldt, its **centre** a rough polygon formed and framed by its enclosing boulevards and the river. Recent efforts to clean and smarten the centre have been tremendously successful, revealing scores of beautiful buildings previously camouflaged by the accumulated grime. On the surface it's not a wealthy city, and it's rarely neat and tidy, but it is a hectic and immediately likeable place, with a dense concentration of things to see, not least some fine churches, including a simply wonderful **cathedral**, and a varied selection of excellent museums.

North of the centre lies **Het Eilandje** (the Little Isle), where the city's old docks and wharves have been rejuvenated and deluxe apartments shoehorned into the former warehouses, the whole caboodle overseen by the soaring modernism of the **Museum Aan de Stroom**, Antwerp's premier museum. To the east of the centre, the star turns are the **Rubenshuis**, one-time home and studio of Rubens, and the cathedral-like **Centraal Station**, which itself abuts the **diamond district** – the city has long been at the heart of the international diamond trade. The area to the south of the centre, **Het Zuid**, is of interest too, a long-neglected but now resurgent residential district whose wide boulevards, with their long vistas and geometrical roundabouts, were laid out at the end of the nineteenth century. The obvious targets here are **MuHKA** (the Museum of Contemporary Art) and the **Koninklijk Museum voor Schone Kunsten** (Fine Art Museum), though this is currently closed for a thoroughgoing revamp.

Some history

In the beginning **Antwerp** wasn't much desired: it may have occupied a prime river site, but it was too far east to be important in the cloth trade and too far west to be on the major trade routes connecting Germany and Holland. However, in the **late fifteenth century** it benefited from both a general movement of trade to the west and the decline of the Anglo-Flemish cloth trade. Within the space of just 25 years, many of the great trading families of western Europe had relocated here, and the tiny old fortified settlement of yesteryear was transformed by a deluge of splendid new mansions and churches, docks and harbours. In addition, the new masters of the region, the **Habsburgs**, had become frustrated with the turbulent burghers of Flanders and both the emperor Maximilian and his successor **Charles V** patronized the city at the expense of its Flemish rivals, underwriting its success as the leading port of their expanding empire.

Antwerp's golden age lasted for less than a hundred years, prematurely stifled by Charles V's son **Philip II**, who inherited Spain and the Low Countries in 1555. Fanatically Catholic, Philip viewed the reformist stirrings of the Low Countries with horror, and his sustained attempt to bring his Protestant subjects to heel brought war and pestilence to the region for decades. Protestantism had taken root in Antwerp early on and the city seethed with discontent as Philip's intentions became all too clear. The spark was the **Ommegang** of August 18, 1566, when priests carting the image of the Virgin through the city's streets insisted that all should bend the knee as it passed. The parade itself was peaceful enough, but afterwards, with the battle cry of "Long live the beggars", the city's Protestant guildsmen and their apprentices smashed the inside of the cathedral to pieces – the most extreme example of the "**iconoclastic fury**" that then swept the region. Philip responded by sending in an army of occupation, which sought to overawe and intimidate the local citizenry from a brand-new citadel built on the south side of town. Nine years later, it was this same garrison that sat unpaid and underfed in its fortress, surrounded by the wealth of what the soldiers regarded as a "heretical" city. Philip's mercenaries **mutinied**, and at dawn on November 4, 1576, they stormed Antwerp, running riot for three long days, plundering public buildings and private mansions, and slaughtering some eight thousand of its inhabitants in the "**Spanish fury**", a catastrophe that finished the city's commercial supremacy. More disasters were to follow. Philip's soldiers were driven out after the massacre, but they were back in 1585 laying siege outside the city walls for seven months, their success leading to Antwerp's ultimate incorporation within the **Spanish Netherlands**. Under the terms of the capitulation, Protestants had two years to leave town, and a flood of skilled workers poured north to the relative safety of Holland, further weakening the city's economy.

In the early seventeenth century there was a modest recovery, but the Dutch, who were now free of Spain, controlled the waterways of the **Scheldt** and were determined that no neighbouring Catholic port would threaten their trade. Consequently, in 1648, under the **Peace of Westphalia**, which finally wrapped up the Thirty Years' War, they forced the closure of the Scheldt to all non-Dutch

Mercenary mutinies

The **Spanish fury** was a disaster for Antwerp, but although the savagery of the attack was unusual, **mutinies** in the Spanish army were not. The Habsburgs often neglected to pay their soldiers for years on end and this failure, combined with harsh conditions and seemingly interminable warfare, provoked at least a couple of mutinies every year. Indeed, mutinies became so commonplace that they began to develop their own rituals, with the *tercio* (army unit) concerned refusing orders but keeping military discipline and electing representatives to haggle a financial deal with the army authorities. A deal was usually reached, outstanding wages were paid (at least in part), normal military life was resumed and, remarkably enough, punishments were rare.

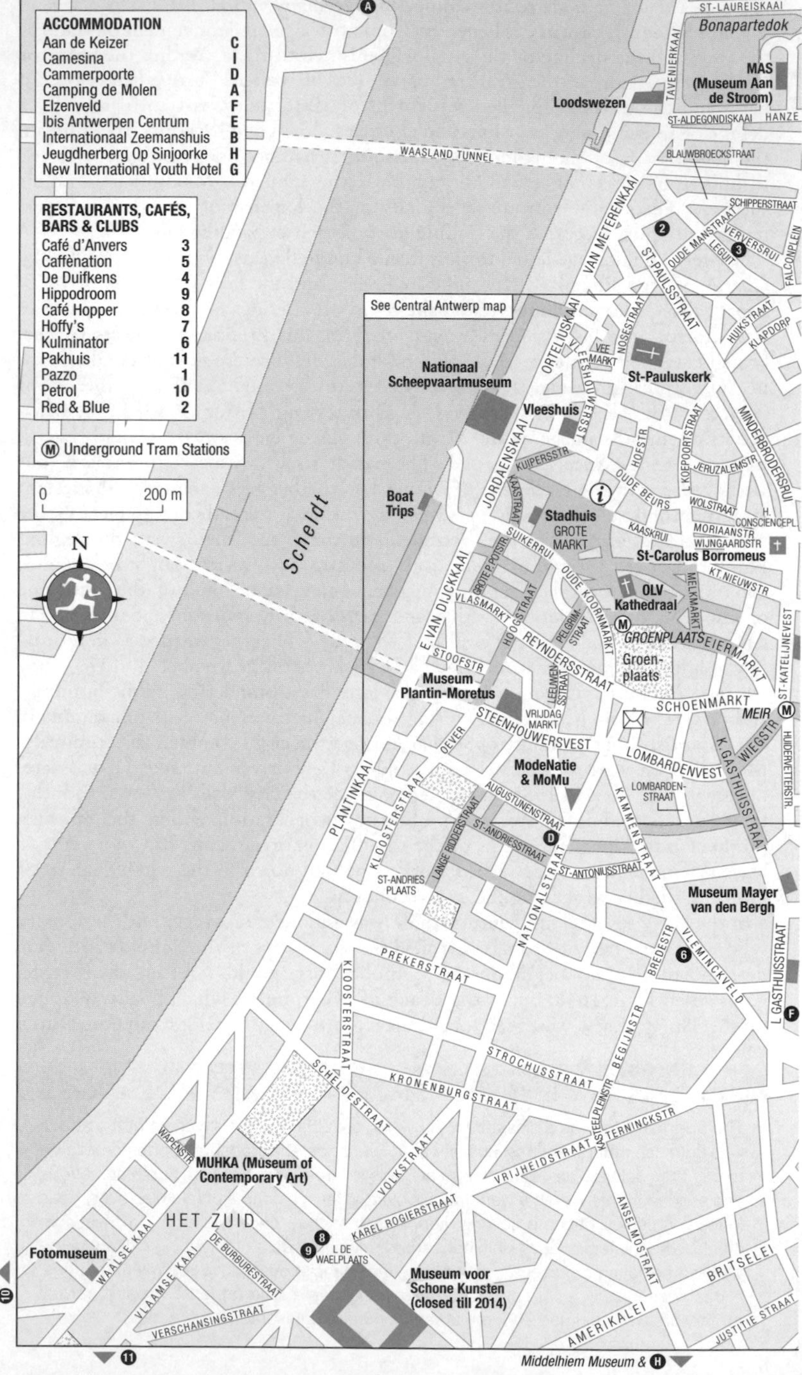
ACCOMMODATION
Aan de Keizer C
Camesina I
Cammerpoorte D
Camping de Molen A
Elzenveld F
Ibis Antwerpen Centrum E
Internationaal Zeemanshuis B
Jeugdherberg Op Sinjoorke H
New International Youth Hotel G
RESTAURANTS, CAFÉS, BARS & CLUBS
Café d'Anvers 3
Caffènation 5
De Duifkens 4
Hippodroom 9
Café Hopper 8
Hoffy's 7
Kulminator 6
Pakhuis 11
Pazzo 1
Petrol 10
Red & Blue 2
M Underground Tram Stations
0 200 m
N
Scheldt
See Central Antwerp map
Bonapartedok
MAS (Museum Aan de Stroom)
Loodswezen
WAASLAND TUNNEL
Nationaal Scheepvaartmuseum
Vleeshuis
St-Pauluskerk
Boat Trips
Stadhuis
GROTE MARKT
St-Carolus Borromeus
OLV Kathedraal
GROENPLAATS
Groenplaats
Museum Plantin-Moretus
MEIR
ModeNatie & MoMu
Museum Mayer van den Bergh
MUHKA (Museum of Contemporary Art)
HET ZUID
Fotomuseum
Museum voor Schone Kunsten (closed till 2014)
Middelhiem Museum & H

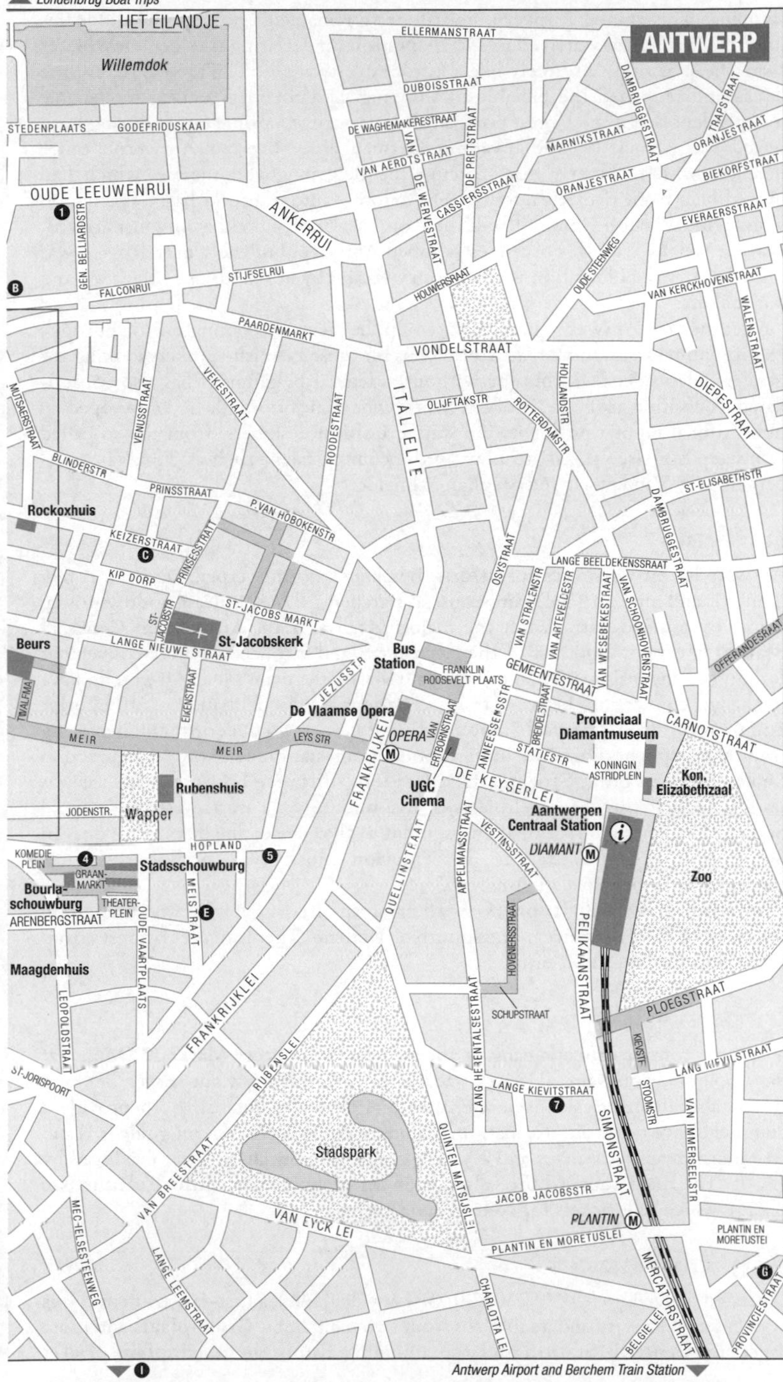
Londenbrug Boat Trips
HET EILANDJE
Willemdok
ANTWERP
ELLERMANSTRAAT
DUBOISSTRAAT
DE WAGHEMAKERESTRAAT
VAN AERDTSTRAAT
DE PRETSTRAAT
DE WERVESTRAAT
CASSIERSSTRAAT
DAMBRUGGESTRAAT
MARNIXSTRAAT
TRAPSTRAAT
ORANJESTRAAT
BIEKORFSTRAAT
EVERAERSSTRAAT
STEDENPLAATS
GODEFRIDUSKAAI
OUDE LEEUWENRUI
GEN. BELLIARDSTR
ANKERRUI
STIJFSELRUI
FALCONRUI
HOUWERSTRAAT
OUDE STEENWEG
VAN KERCKHOVENSTRAAT
WALENSTRAAT
PAARDENMARKT
VONDELSTRAAT
HOLLANDSTR
DIEPESTRAAT
MUTSAERSTRAAT
VEKESTRAAT
VENUSSTRAAT
ROODESTRAAT
ITALIELEI
OLIJFTAKSTR
ROTTERDAMSTR
BLINDERSTR
PRINSSTRAAT
ST-ELISABETHSTR
Rockoxhuis
P. VAN HOBOKENSTR
KEIZERSTRAAT
PRINSESSTRAAT
KIP DORP
OSYSTRAAT
LANGE BEELDEKENSSRAAT
VAN STRALENSTR
VAN ARTEVELDESTR
VAN WESEBEKESTRAAT
VAN SCHOONHOVENSTRAAT
ST-JACOBSTR
ST-JACOBS MARKT
Beurs
St-Jacobskerk
LANGE NIEUWE STRAAT
Bus Station
FRANKLIN ROOSEVELT PLAATS
GEMEENTESTRAAT
OFFERANDESRAAT
TWAALFMA
JEZUSSTR
EIKENSTRAAT
De Vlaamse Opera
ANNEESSENSSTR
BREIDELSTRAAT
Provinciaal Diamantmuseum
CARNOTSTRAAT
MEIR
LEYS STR
OPERA
VAN ERTBORNSTRAAT
FRANKRIJKLEI
STATIESTR
KONINGIN ASTRIDPLEIN
DE KEYSERLEI
Rubenshuis
UGC Cinema
Kon. Elizabethzaal
JODENSTR.
Wapper
Aantwerpen Centraal Station
VESTINGSTRAAT
APPELMANSSTRAAT
DIAMANT
HOPLAND
KOMEDIE PLEIN
Stadsschouwburg
GRAAN-MARKT
Bourla-schouwburg
THEATER-PLEIN
MEISTRAAT
QUELLINSTRAAT
Zoo
ARENBERGSTRAAT
OUDE VAARTPLAATS
HOVENIERSSTRAAT
PELIKAANSTRAAT
Maagdenhuis
FRANKRIJKLEI
LEOPOLDSTRAAT
SCHUPSTRAAT
PLOEGSTRAAT
RUBENSLEI
LANG HERENTALSESTRAAT
KIEVSTR
LANG KIEVITSTRAAT
ST-JORISPOORT
LANGE KIEVITSTRAAT
STOOMSTR
SIMONSTRAAT
VAN IMMERSEELSTR
QUINTEN MATSIJSLEI
Stadspark
VAN BREESTRAAT
JACOB JACOBSSTR
MEC-IELSESTEENWEG
VAN EYCK LEI
PLANTIN
PLANTIN EN MORETUSLEI
PLANTIN EN MORETUSTEI
LANGE LEEMSTRAAT
CHARLOTTA LEI
MERCATORSTRAAT
BELGIE LEI
PROVINCIESTRAAT
Antwerp Airport and Berchem Train Station

shipping. This ruined Antwerp, and the city remained firmly in the doldrums until the French army arrived in 1797 – **Napoleon** declaring it to be "little better than a heap of ruins…scarcely like a European city at all". The French rebuilt the docks and reopened the Scheldt to shipping, and the city revived to become independent Belgium's largest port, a role that made it a prime target during both world wars. In 1914, the invading German army overran Antwerp's outer defences with surprising ease, forcing the Belgian government – which had moved here from Brussels a few weeks before – into a second hasty evacuation along with Winston Churchill and the Royal Marines, who had only just arrived. During **World War II**, both sides bombed Antwerp, but the worst damage was inflicted after the Liberation when the city was hit by hundreds of Hitler's V1 and V2 **rockets**.

After the war, Antwerp quickly picked up the pieces, becoming one of Europe's major **seaports** and, more recently, a focus for those Flemish-speakers looking for greater independence within (or without) a federal Belgium. It has also consolidated its position at the heart of the worldwide **diamond** trade and developed an international reputation for its innovative **fashion** designers, from the so-called "Antwerp Six" (see p.221) to new and upcoming talent such as Tim Vansteenbergen, A.F. Vandevorst and Stephan Schneider.

Arrival

Antwerp has two main **train stations**, Berchem and Antwerpen Centraal. A few domestic and international trains pause at Berchem, 4km southeast of downtown, before bypassing Centraal, but the majority call at both. **Antwerpen Centraal Station** lies about 2km east of the city centre, and is much the more convenient for most of the major sights and the Grote Markt, the main square. If you do have to change, connections between the two stations are frequent and fast (10 hourly; 5min). **Trams** from Centraal Station to the city centre go underground, departing from the adjacent Diamant underground tram station (#2 or #15 direction Linkeroever; get off at Groenplaats). Most **long-distance buses** arrive at the bus station on Franklin Rooseveltplaats, a five-minute walk northwest of Centraal Station; Eurolines international buses pull in at the edge of the bus station on Van Stralenstraat. The bus station's **information kiosk** deals with bus services throughout the province of Antwerp.

Antwerp's pint-sized **airport** (Ⓦwww.antwerp-airport.be) is located about 6km southeast of the city centre in the suburb of **Deurne**. There are regular buses from the airport into the city centre.

Information

The main **tourist office** is bang in the city centre at Grote Markt 13 (Mon–Sat 9am–5.45pm, Sun 9am–4.45pm; Ⓣ03 232 01 03, Ⓦwww.antwerpen.be), and there's also an **infodesk** inside Centraal Station (same details). Both provide a comprehensive range of information, including a very useful pocket guide (€1) and free transit maps, city maps and a youth-oriented information sheet produced by *Use-It*. The main tourist office also shares its premises with **Info Cultuur** (see p.226), which sells tickets for concerts and events.

City transport

Operated by De Lijn (Ⓣ070 220 200, Ⓦwww.delijn.be), a first-rate **tram and bus** system serves the city and its suburbs from two main hubs, **Groenplaats** and more especially **Centraal Station** and the adjoining **Koningin Astridplein**. Ticket prices are very reasonable. A standard single fare within the city centre costs €1.20 in advance (€2 from the driver), ten rides with a "Line Card" €8 (€11); tickets are valid for one hour. Alternatively, a 24-hour unlimited citywide travel card, a **Dagpas**, costs €5 (€6 from the driver), or €10 (€12) for three days. Advance tickets are sold all over the place, but most conveniently at every tram station, where there are multilingual ticket machines.

Bike rental is available from **Freewieler**, down by the river on Steenplein at the west end of Suikerrui (Ⓣ03 213 22 51, Ⓦwww.v-zit.be). Rates are €3 for the first hour, €9 for four hours and €12 for one day.

Accommodation

Antwerp has the range of **hotels** you'd expect of Belgium's second city, an ever increasing supply of **B&B**s and several **hostels**; a large, brand-new HI hostel is also set to open in 2012 on the south side of the centre on Bogaardeplein. Consequently, finding accommodation is rarely difficult, although there are surprisingly few places in the centre, which is by far the best spot to soak up the city's atmosphere. Many medium-priced and budget places are clustered in the humdrum area around Centraal Station, where you should exercise caution at night, particularly if travelling alone.

The tourist office issues a free and comprehensive booklet detailing the city's hotels, B&Bs and hostels – and excluding the seedier establishments.

Hotels

Cammerpoorte Nationalestraat 38 Ⓣ03 231 97 36, Ⓦwww.hotelcammerpoorte.be. Modern, two-star budget place with 39 spartan en-suite rooms in a building that looks a bit like a car park. It has a mildly forlorn air, but the location is handy and the staff friendly. A couple of minutes' walk south of Groenplaats. See map, p.206. ❷

Elzenveld Lange Gasthuisstraaat 45 Ⓣ03 202 77 71, Ⓦwww.elzenveld.be. More of a conference centre than a hotel, the *Elzenveld* occupies a sympathetically modernized former monastery and its gardens. There are forty spick-and-span modern rooms, but the main pleasure is the setting rather than the decor. Breakfast included. See map, p.206. ❹

Hilton Antwerp Groenplaats 32 Ⓣ03 204 12 12, Ⓦwww.antwerp.hilton.com. Big and flashy chain hotel in a good-looking nineteenth-century building metres from the cathedral. Large, very comfortable rooms, plus a fitness centre, bars and restaurants, but still a little over-priced. See map, p.210. ❽

Ibis Antwerpen Centrum Meistraat 39 Ⓣ03 231 88 30, Ⓦwww.ibishotel.com. An *Ibis* is an *Ibis* – or so you would have thought, but several readers have written in to the Rough Guide praising this particular hotel for its friendly staff and excellent buffet breakfast. Don't expect any decorative surprises in the 150 rooms, and the building itself has a ghastly concrete exterior, but there's further compensation in its handy location, close to the Rubenshuis. See map, p.206. ❹

Internationaal Zeemanshuis (Seamen's House) Falconrui 21 Ⓣ03 227 54 33, Ⓦwww.zeemanshuis.be. In a substantial and surprisingly attractive 1950s block, perched on a hillock and in its own (mini) grounds, the *Zeemanshuis* has over one hundred brisk, modern rooms, all en suite. Despite the name, it's open to landlubbers and women as well as mariners, and is situated a 10min walk north of the Grote Markt, out towards the old docks in a lively-verging-on-the-seedy part of town. See map, p.206. ❷

Julien Korte Nieuwstraat 24 Ⓣ03 229 06 00, Ⓦwww.hotel-julien.com. Self-styled boutique hotel with just twenty-two rooms and lots of flourishes, from rain showers and flat-screen TVs to oodles of greys, creams and browns. Handy location too. See map, p.210. ❻

Matelote Haarstraat 11 Ⓣ03 201 88 00, Ⓦwww.hotel-matelote.be. Decorated in crisp, modernist style, this small and really rather stylish hotel occupies intelligently revamped and remodelled old premises on a narrow street a (long) stone's throw from the Grote Markt. The rooms are large and well appointed. See map, p.210. ❺

Rubens Grote Markt Oude Beurs 29 Ⓣ03 222 48 48, Ⓦwww.hotelrubensantwerp.be. Arguably the most agreeable hotel in town, this four-star establishment has just 36 large and well-appointed guest rooms in a real mix of styles, though the default button is set to modern. It occupies a smashing downtown location, on a quiet side street a couple of minutes' walk from the Grote Markt, and

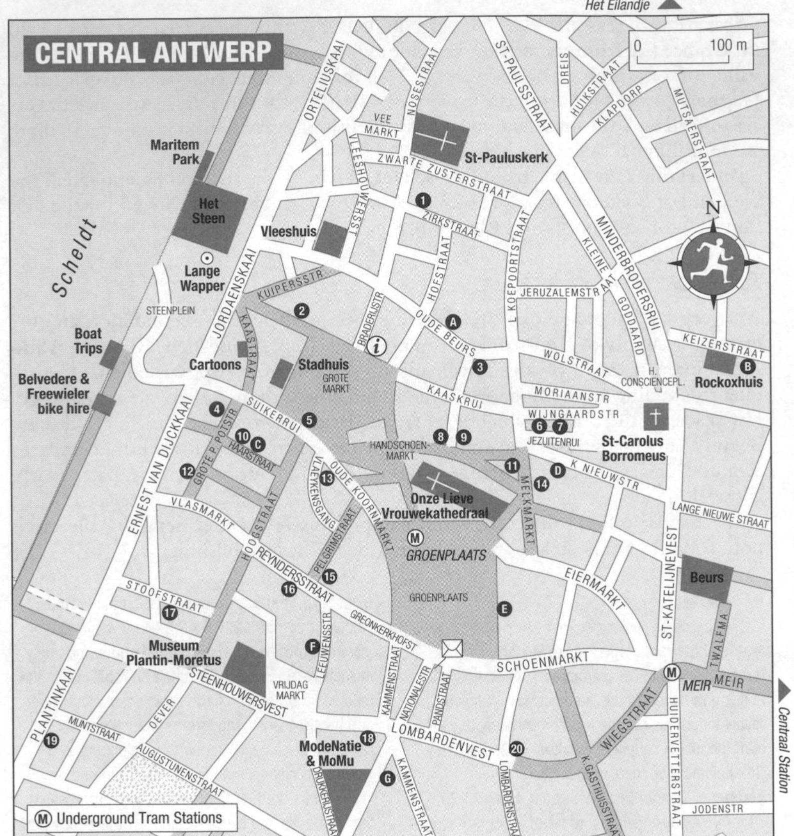

ACCOMMODATION

Enich Anders	F
Hilton Antwerp	E
Julien	D
Matelote	C
M0851	G
Rubens Grote Markt	A
De Witte Lelie	B

CAFÉS, CAFÉ-BARS & RESTAURANTS

Aurelia	7
De Groote Witte Arend	16
Hungry Henrietta	20
Invincible	10
De Kleine Zavel	17
Le Pain Quotidien	18
De Peerdestal	6
Pizzeria Da Antonio	5
Popoff	13
De Reddende Engel	9
Ulcke van Zurich	3
Varelli	19
Zoute Zoen	1

BARS & CLUBS

Het Elfde Gebod	8
Den Engel	2
De Faam	4
Den Hopsack	12
De Muze	14
Café Pelikaan	11
De Vagant	15

has a dinky little courtyard overseen by a very old brick tower, evidence that the building started out as a medieval mansion. See map, p.210. ❺

De Witte Lelie Keizerstraat 16 ⓣ03 226 19 66, ⓦwww.dewittelelie.be. Immaculate four-star hotel – the city's ritziest and most exclusive – with just ten charming rooms in a handsomely renovated seventeenth-century merchant's house, a 5min walk from the Grote Markt. See map, p.210. ❾

Bed and breakfast

Aan de Keizer Keizerstraat 62 ⓣ03 225 22 96, ⓦwww.aandekeizer.be. Deluxe B&B offering three guest rooms kitted out in plush late nineteenth-century style with four-poster beds and grand old wooden furniture. The exterior of the house is a tad dishevelled – as is this part of Keizerstraat – but don't let that deter you. See map, p.206. ❹

Camesina Mozartstraat 19 ⓣ03 257 20 38, ⓦwww.camesina.be. Smart and slick B&B with three attractive en-suite rooms in a tastefully modernized 1900s town house. A 30min walk southeast of the centre – take tram #7. See map, p.206. ❻

Enich Anders Leeuwenstraat 12 ⓣ0476 99 86 01, ⓦwww.enich-anders.be. Two furnished studios with bathroom and kitchenette above a sculptor's workshop on an old and narrow street just off the Vrijdagmark; the breakfast part of the arrangement is served up in a basket in the room itself. Minimum two nights' stay on the weekend. See map, p.210. ❷

M0851 Nationalestraat 19 ⓣ03 297 60 66, ⓦwww.m0851.be. Three, modern, self-contained suites here above the M0851 shop, each kitted out in slick modernist style – painted floor-boards and lots of blacks and whites. The top suite, right under the eaves (and with a/c), is especially cosy. All three have internet access and basic kitchen facilities; breakfast is by coupon at a nearby café. See map, p.210. ❺

Hostels and campsite

Camping de Molen Jachthavenweg z/n ⓣ03 219 81 79. This small and simple campsite is on the left-hand side of the River Scheldt – roughly opposite the Bonapartdeok – a short stroll from the slab of shingly sand that passes for the city beach. Tent pitches from €10. See map, p.206. Open mid–March to mid-Oct.

Jeugdherberg Op Sinjoorke Eric Sasselaan 2 ⓣ03 238 02 73, ⓦwww.vjh.be. HI-affiliated hostel in a park close to the ring road, about 5km south of the centre. Has 130 beds in two-, four-, six- and eight-bedded rooms with shared showers. There's a canteen serving lunch and dinner, free parking and a laundry room. To get there, take tram #2 from Centraal Station, direction Hoboken; get off at the Antwerp Expo centre, from where it's a 300-metre walk west. Breakfast included in the rate. See map, p.206. Dorm beds from €17, doubles ❶

New International Youth Hotel Provinciestraat 256 ⓣ03 230 05 22, ⓦwww.youthhotel.be. Very basic, medium-sized hostel-cum-hotel offering bargain-basement singles, doubles and dorms, some en suite. Breakfast is included. A 10min walk from Centraal Station. Dorm beds from €21, doubles ❶. See map, p.206.

The City Centre

Antwerp's bustling **centre** is the most engaging part of the city, its mazy streets and cobbled lanes studded with fine old churches, mansions and museums. The logical place to start an exploration is the **Grote Markt**, still the centre of activities and flanked by the elegant **Stadhuis**. From here, it's a couple of hundred metres south to the magnificent Gothic **Onze Lieve Vrouwekathedraal**, home to a quartet of paintings by Rubens, with the intriguing old printing house of Christopher Plantin, now the **Museum Plantin-Moretus**, just beyond. Another short hop, this time to the north, brings up the striking medieval **Vleeshuis**, one-time headquarters of the guild of butchers, with the sinuous Baroque of **St-Pauluskerk** beckoning beyond. The city centre finishes off with two other excellent attractions, the charming **Hendrik Conscienceplein** and the **Rockoxhuis**, which holds a small but superb collection of paintings.

The Grote Markt

The centre of Antwerp is the **Grote Markt**, at the heart of which stands the **Brabo Fountain**, a haphazard pile of roughly sculpted rocks created in 1887 and surmounted by a bronze of Silvius Brabo, depicted flinging the hand of the prostrate giant Antigonus into the Scheldt. Legend asserts that Antigonus extracted tolls from all passing ships, cutting off the hands of those who refused to pay. He was eventually beaten by the valiant Brabo, who tore off his hand and threw it into the river, giving the city its name, which literally means "hand-throw". There are more realistic explanations of the city's name, but this is the most colourful, and it certainly reflects Antwerp's early success at freeing the river from the innumerable taxes levied on shipping by local landowners.

The north side of the Grote Markt is lined with daintily restored **guildhouses**, their sixteenth-century facades decorated with appropriate reliefs and topped by finely cast gilded figures basking in the afterglow of the city's Renaissance lustre. No. 7, the House of the Crossbowmen, with its figures of St George and the dragon, is the tallest and most distinctive; it stands next to the Coopers' House, with its barrel motifs and statue of St Matthew.

The Stadhuis

Presiding over the Grote Markt, the **Stadhuis** was completed in 1566 to an innovative design by Cornelis Floris, though there have been several subsequent modifications. The building's pagoda-like roof gives it a faintly oriental appearance, but apart from the central gable it's quite plain, with a long pilastered facade of short and shallow Doric and Ionic columns. These, along with the windows, lend it a simple elegance, in contrast to the purely decorative **gable** (there's no roof behind it). Here, the niches at the top contribute to the self-congratulatory aspect of the building, with a statue of the Virgin Mary set above representations of *Justice* and *Wisdom*, virtues the city burghers reckoned they had in plenty.

The Handschoenmarkt

Leaving the Grote Markt by its southeast corner, you'll soon come to the triangular **Handschoenmarkt** (the former Glove Market), an appealing little square with the cathedral on one side and an attractive ensemble of antique gables on the other two. The conspicuous **stone well** in the corner of the Handschoenmarkt is adorned by a graceful iron canopy and bears the legend "It was love connubial taught the smith to paint" – a reference to the fifteenth-century painter Quinten Matsys, who learned his craft so he could woo the daughter of a local artist: at the time, marriage between families of different guilds was strongly discouraged. The Handschoenmarkt is the most westerly of a somewhat confusing cobweb of pedestrianized streets and miniature squares that laps round the edge of the cathedral.

The Onze Lieve Vrouwekathedraal

One of the finest Gothic churches in Belgium, the **Onze Lieve Vrouwekathedraal** (Cathedral of Our Lady; Mon–Fri 10am–5pm, Sat 10am–3pm, Sun 1–4pm; €5; ⓦwww.dekathedraal.be) is a forceful, self-confident structure that mostly dates from the middle of the fifteenth century. Its graceful, intricate spire dominated the skyline of the medieval city and was long a favourite with British travellers. William Beckford, for instance, fresh from spending millions on his own house in Wiltshire in the early 1800s, was particularly impressed, writing that he "longed to ascend it that instant, to stretch myself out upon its summit and calculate, from so sublime an elevation, the influence of the planets". To help guide yourself around, pick up a free diagrammatic **plan** just beyond the entry desk.

The nave and a Rubens

Inside, the seven-aisled **nave** is breathtaking, if only because of its sense of space, an impression that's reinforced by the bright, light stonework. The religious troubles of the sixteenth century – primarily the Iconoclastic Fury of 1566 – polished off the cathedral's early furnishings and fittings, so what you see today are largely Baroque embellishments, most notably four early paintings by **Pieter Paul Rubens** (1577–1640). Of these, the *Descent from the Cross*, a triptych painted after the artist's return from Italy in 1612 and hung just to the right of the central crossing, is without doubt the most beautiful, displaying an uncharacteristically moving realism derived from Caravaggio. Christ languishes in the centre in glowing white, surrounded by mourners tenderly struggling to lower him. As was normal practice at the time, students in Rubens' studio worked on the painting, among them the young **van Dyck**, who completed the face of the Virgin and the arm of Mary Magdalene. His work was so masterful that Rubens is supposed to have declared it an improvement on his own, though this story appears to originate from van Dyck himself. Oddly enough, the painting was commissioned by the guild of arquebusiers, who asked for a picture of St Christopher, their patron saint; Rubens' painting was not at all what they had in mind, and they promptly threatened him with legal action unless he added a picture of the saint to the wings. Rubens obliged, painting in the muscular giant who now dominates the outside of the left panel.

Three more Rubens and a de Vos

Above the high altar is a second Rubens painting, the *Assumption*, a swirling Baroque scene painted in 1625, full of cherubs and luxuriant drapery, while on the left-hand side of the central crossing, the same artist's *The Raising of the Cross* is a grandiloquent canvas full of straining, muscular soldiers and saints; this triptych was painted in 1610, which makes it the earliest of the four. On the right-hand side of the ambulatory in the second chapel along, there's the cathedral's fourth and final Rubens, the *Resurrection*, painted in 1612 for the tomb of his friend, the printer Jan Moretus, showing a strident, militaristic Christ carrying a red, furled banner. Among the cathedral's many other paintings, the only other highlight is **Maerten de Vos'** (1531–1603) *Marriage at Cana*, hung opposite the *Descent from the Cross*, a typically mannered work completed in 1597.

Groenplaats and Vrijdagmarkt

Flanked by some of the most popular cafés in town, **Groenplaats**, the expansive open square behind the cathedral, actually started out as the municipal graveyard, though presumably the bodies were moved long before the construction of today's underground car park. In the middle of the square stands a really rather uninspiring **statue** of Rubens, the work of the prolific Guillaume Geefs (1806–60), one of King Leopold II's favourite sculptors.

From Groenplaats, it takes a couple of minutes to thread your way southwest to the **Vrijdagmarkt**, an appealing little square that took a direct hit from a V2 rocket in World War II. It's in the middle of a one-time working-class district and hosts a browbeaten open-air **market** of old household effects on Fridays (9am–1pm).

The Museum Plantin-Moretus

One side of the Vrijdagmarkt is taken up by the **Museum Plantin-Moretus** (Tues–Sun 10am–5.30pm; €6; audioguide available), which occupies the old mansion of the printer Christopher Plantin, who rose to fame and fortune in the second half of the sixteenth century. Born in Tours in 1520, Plantin moved to Antwerp when he was 34 to set up a small bookbinding business, but in 1555 he was forced to give up all heavy work when, in a case of mistaken identity, he was wounded by revellers returning from carnival. Paid to keep quiet about his injuries, Plantin used the money to start a printing business. He was phenomenally successful, his fortune assured when King Philip II granted him the monopoly of printing missals and breviaries for the whole of the Spanish Empire. On Plantin's death, the business passed to his talented son-in-law, Jan Moerentorf, who Latinized his name, in accordance with the fashion of the day, to Moretus, as did his son, Balthasar, who was a close friend of Rubens. The family sold their mansion to the city in 1876.

From the **entrance**, a signed route takes visitors through most of the rooms of the house, which is set around a pretty central courtyard. The mansion is worth seeing in itself, its warren of small, dark rooms equipped with mullioned windows and lockable wooden window shutters, plus oodles of leather wallpaper in the Spanish style. As for the exhibits, they provide a marvellous insight into how Plantin and his offspring conducted their business. **Highlights** include several well-preserved pictorial tapestries in Room 1, a superb selection of illuminated manuscripts in

Room 3, and a delightful seventeenth-century bookshop in Room 4. Here you'll spot a list of prohibited books – the Habsburgs' Librorum Prohibitorum – along with a money-balance to help identify clipped and debased coins. Room 6 has more fine tapestries, while Room 11 displays a splendid portrait of Seneca by Rubens, and Room 14 is devoted to **Johannes Gutenberg** (1398–1468), the inventor of moveable type printing who is well represented by his famous 36-line Bible. Moving on, Room 15 displays prime examples of the work of Christopher Plantin, and Room 23 focuses on maps and atlases, most memorably examples of the work of Flanders' own **Gerardus Mercator** (1512–1594).

Throughout the museum there are lots of intriguing and intriguingly precise **woodcuts**, representing the best of an enormous number used by several centuries of print workers. In particular, look out for the superbly crafted sample in Room 18 and a splendid collection of **copper plates** next door in Room 19.

North to the waterfront

Across Vrijdagmarkt from the museum is **Leeuwenstraat**, a narrow little street flanked by some very old terraced houses. At the end, turn left and then first right for **Pelgrimstraat**, which provides one of the best views of the cathedral, with a sliver of sloping, uneven roofs set against the majestic lines of the spire behind. By no. 6, an ancient alley called **Vlaeykensgang** (Pie Lane) is a surviving fragment of the honeycomb of narrow lanes that made up medieval Antwerp. Today, it twists a quaint route through to **Oude Koornmarkt**, which soon leads west into **Suikerrui**, a wide street connecting the Grote Markt with the east bank of the Scheldt, clearly separated from the town since Napoleon razed the riverside slums and constructed proper wharves in the early 1800s. Jutting out into the river at the end of Suikerrui is an overblown **belvedere**, where the Belgian middle classes once took the air, looking out over the river before taking the ferry from the jetty next door. The latter is long gone – several roads now run under the Scheldt – and there's precious little to gaze at now except the belvedere, which can't help but seem a little eccentric. For details of the river trips that leave from here, see the box below.

Het Steen

A few metres north along the riverfront, the stalwart remains of Het Steen (castle) are approached past a statue of the giant **Lange Wapper**, a very dubious local folklore figure – part practical joker, part Peeping Tom – who, as well as being fond of children, exploited his height by spying into people's bedrooms. Beyond, all that remains of **Het Steen** (no public access), the mighty medieval fortress that once intimidated Antwerp, is the stone gatehouse and a chunk of the old curtain wall. Just behind is the **Maritiem Park** (Maritime Park; April–Oct Tues–Sun 10am–4.30pm; free), where a long line of antique tugs and barges are parked under a rickety corrugated roof.

Boat trips

From the west end of Suikerrui, Flandria (Ⓣ03 231 31 00, Ⓦwww.flandria.nu) operates enjoyable **River Scheldt cruises** that last a little under an hour (May–June & Sept Sat & Sun 4 daily; July–Aug 4 daily; €5). The same company also runs **tours of the port**, both a short version (1hr 30min; May–June & Sept–Nov Fri–Sun 1 daily; Easter holidays & July–Aug 1 daily; €10) and a longer trip (2hr 30min; same frequency; €12.50). These depart from Kaai (Quay) 14 beside Londenbrug, about 1500m north of the city centre just beyond the Willemdok. Advance reservations – at least a couple of hours ahead of time – are advised.

The Vleeshuis Museum

Opposite the Het Steen across Jordaenskaai, filling out the end of narrow Vleeshuisstraat, are the tall, turreted gables of the **Vleeshuis** (Meat Hall; Tues–Sun 10am–5pm; €5), built for the guild of butchers in 1503. This strikingly attractive building, with its alternating layers of red brick and stonework resembling rashers of bacon, was once the suitably grand headquarters of one of the most powerful of the medieval guilds. It was here in 1585, with the Spanish army approaching, that the butchers made a fateful decision: they opposed the opening of the dykes along the River Scheldt as advised by the Protestant commander, **William the Silent**, who realized that the best way to defend the city was by flooding its immediate surroundings. The butchers were, however, more worried about the safety of their sheep, which grazed the threatened meadows, and so they sent a deputation to the city magistrates to object. The magistrates yielded, and the consequences were disastrous – the Spaniards were able to close the Scheldt and eventually force the town to surrender, a defeat that placed Antwerp firmly within the Spanish Netherlands.

Inside, the cavernous brick hall that comprises the ground floor of the Vleeshuis now holds the **Klank van de Stad** (Sound of the City), an ambitious if not entirely successful exhibition on music and dance in the city over the last six hundred years. Software handed out at the reception desk enables visitors to listen to a wide range of historic instruments, but somehow it's all too fiddly and a bit tedious. More positively, the museum holds an excellent range of sixteenth- and seventeenth-century musical instruments, most memorably a platoon of primly decorated **clavichords** and **harpischords**, some of which were produced locally in the Ruckers workshop.

The Veemarkt and St-Pauluskerk

The streets around the Vleeshuis were badly damaged by wartime bombing, leaving a string of bare, open spaces edged by some of the worst of the city's slums. In the last decade, however, the area has largely been rebuilt and revamped, the prostitutes who once congregated here moved north to Verversrui, near the Willemdok, and the crumbling terraces replaced by cosy modern houses, whose pinkish brick facades imitate the style of what went before. In the middle of the area, just a couple of minutes' walk north from the Vleeshuis, is the **Veemarkt**, where an extravagant Baroque portal leads through to **St-Pauluskerk** (April–Oct daily 2–5pm), one of the city's most delightful churches, an airy, dignified late Gothic structure dating from 1517. Originally built for the Dominicans, the church was looted by the Calvinists when they expelled the monks in 1578. Restored to their property after the Spanish recaptured the city in 1585, the Dominicans refashioned St-Pauluskerk in a Baroque style that was designed to glorify the Catholic Church, grinding salt into the wounds of the defeated Protestants. To hammer home the ecclesiastical point, the Dominicans commissioned a series of **paintings** to line the wall of the nave's north aisle. Dating from 1617, this series, which depicts the "Fifteen Mysteries of the Rosary", has survived intact, a remarkable snapshot of Antwerp's artistic talent with works by the likes of Cornelis De Vos (1584–1651) – *Nativity* and *Presentation at the Temple*; David Teniers the Elder (1582–1649) – *Gethsemane*; van Dyck (1599–1641) – *The Bearing of the Cross*; and Jordaens (1593–1678) – the *Crucifixion*. But it is **Rubens**' contribution – the *Scourging at the Pillar* – which stands out, a brilliant, brutal canvas showing Jesus clad in a blood-spattered loincloth.

There's more Rubens close by – at the far end of the *Mysteries* series – in the *Adoration of the Shepherds*, an early work of 1609 which has a jaunty secular air, with a smartly dressed Mary imperiously lifting the Christ's bedsheet to the wonder of the shepherds. Across the church, in the south transept, there's the same artist's

Disputation on the Nature of the Holy Sacrament, again completed in 1609, but this time forming part of a grand marble altarpiece sprinkled with observant cherubs. The marble was crafted by **Pieter Verbruggen the Elder**, who was also responsible for the extraordinary woodcarving of the confessionals and stalls on either side of the nave, flashy work of arabesque intricacy decorated with flowers, fruit, a herd of cherubs and pious saints. Verbruggen takes some responsibility for the huge and ugly **high altar** too: he didn't fashion the black and white marble – that was the work of a certain Frans Sterbeeck – but he erected it.

Look out also for **Our Lady of the Rosary**, an early sixteenth-century polychromed wood statuette stuck to a pillar next to the nave's north aisle. It's a charming effigy, with the Virgin robed in the Spanish manner – it was the Spaniards who first introduced dressed figurines to Flemish churches. The two unusual bas-relief medallions to either side are just as folksy, telling a Faustian story of a rich woman who is gulled by the devil, shown here as a sort of lion with an extremely long tail. The first panel sees the woman entrapped by the devil's letter, the second shows the good old Dominicans coming to the rescue and the devil being carted off by an angel.

One final curiosity is the **Calvarieberg**, beside the passageway linking the Baroque portal and the church. Glued to the buttresses of the south transept in the early eighteenth century, this mound of rock and slag is decorated with statues of angels, prophets and saints beneath a crucified Christ. It was built at the behest of the Pilgrims of Jerusalem, a society keen to encourage the devout to visit the Holy Land. Writing in the nineteenth century, the traveller Charles Tennant got things about right when he described it as being "a more striking instance of religious fanaticism than good taste".

The Rockoxhuis

Southeast of St-Pauluskerk, the **Rockoxhuis**, at Keizerstraat 12 (Tues–Sun 10am–5pm; €2.50), is housed in the attractively restored seventeenth-century town house of Nicolaas Rockox, friend and patron of Rubens. Nevertheless, it's far from a re-creation of Rockox's old home, but rather a museum with a small but highly prized collection. Particular highlights include, in **Room 1**, a gentle *Holy Virgin and Child* by **Quinten Matsys** (1465–1530) as well as a *Calvary* by one of his sons, Cornelis, and a *St Christopher Bearing the Christ Child*, a typical work by Quentin's collaborator Joachim Patenier (1485–1524). Born in Dinant, Patenier moved to Antwerp, where he became the first Flemish painter to emphasize the landscape of his religious scenes at the expense of its figures – which he reduced to compositional elements within wide, sweeping vistas. Moving on, **Room 2** displays two pictures by **Rubens**, beginning with the small and romantic *Virgin in Adoration Before the Sleeping Christ Child*, which depicts the Virgin with the features of Rubens' first wife and models Jesus on the artist's son. The second work is his *Christ on the Cross*, a fascinating oil sketch made in preparation for an altarpiece he never had time to paint. Look out also for *Two Studies of a Man's Head* by **van Dyck** (1599–1641), striking portraits that the artist recycled in several later and larger commissions.

Room 6 is distinguished by two contrasting paintings by Antwerp's own Joachim Beuckelaer (1533–73), a flashy and fleshy genre painting entitled *Woman Vegetable Seller*; and the much more restrained *Flight into Egypt*, revealing a bustling riverbank where – in true Mannerist style – the Holy Family are hard to spot. In the same room, there's also **Pieter Bruegel the Younger**'s (1564–1638) *Proverbs*, an intriguing folksy work, one of several he did in direct imitation of his father, a frenetic mixture of the observed and imagined set in a Flemish village. The meaning of many of the pictured proverbs has been the subject of long debate and unfortunately the museum doesn't provide a caption – see the box on p.217 for

Bruegel's Proverbs

Pieter Bruegel the Younger's *Proverbs* illustrates over a hundred folk sayings. Some of the more diverting are explained below – to help pick them out we've divided the canvas into four squares.

Upper left

The cakes on the roof represent prosperity.
To fire one arrow after another is to throw good after bad.
The Cross hangs below the orb, which is crapped upon by the fool – it's an upside-down world.
The fool gets the trump card – luck favours the foolish.
The man with toothache behind his ear symbolizes the malingerer.

Lower left

He bangs his head against the wall – stupidity.
She carries water in one hand, fire in the other – a woman of contradictory opinions.
The pig opens the tap of the barrel – gluttony.
The knight, literally armed to the teeth, ties a bell to the cat – cowardice.
One woman holds the distaff, while the other spins – it takes two to gossip.
The hat on the post, as in to keep a secret "under your hat".
The pig shearer is a symbol of foolishness.

Upper right

The opportunist on the tower hangs his cloak according to the wind.
To fall from the ox to the ass is to go from good to bad.
He opens the door with his arse – doesn't know if he is coming or going.
The man with the fan is so miserly he even resents the sun shining on the water.

Lower right

The imprudent man fills in the well after the cow has drowned.
The poor man cannot reach from one loaf to another.
The dogs fight over a bone – hence bone of contention.
The monk giving Jesus a false beard symbolizes blasphemy.
The man trapped within the globe suggests you have to stoop low to get through life.

some pointers – but there's little doubt about the meaning of the central image depicting an old man dressed in the blue, hooded cape of the cuckold at the suggestion of his young wife.

Hendrik Conscienceplein

From the western end of Keizerstraat, it's a short stroll through to **Hendrik Conscienceplein**, which takes its name from a local nineteenth-century novelist who wrote prolifically on all things Flemish. One of the most agreeable places in central Antwerp, the square is flanked by the church of **St-Carolus Borromeus** (Mon–Sat 10am–12.30pm & 2–5pm), whose finely contrived facade may well have been based on designs by Rubens. Much of the interior was destroyed by fire at the beginning of the eighteenth century, but inside, on the right-hand side of the nave, the ornate **Onze Lieve Vrouwekapel** (Chapel of Our Lady) has survived, its ornate giltwork and luxurious mix of marbles a fancy illustration of the High Baroque. Streaky, coloured marble was a key feature of the original design and here it serves as the background for a series of tiny pictures placed to either side of the high altar.

From Hendrik Conscienceplein, it's a short walk south to Meir (see p.218).

North of the centre: Het Eilandje

Antwerp has always been reliant on its sea trade, and in the sixteenth century work began on a new network of canals, wharves and docks just to the north of the city centre, abutting the River Scheldt. The economic collapse following the Spanish Fury (see p.205) stopped the digging in its tracks and only much later, in the 1860s, did work resume and thereafter this district, **Het Eilandje** (The Little Isle), rapidly became the economic centre of the city, its docks crowded with vessels from every corner of the globe, and its quays lined by warehouses, sheds, offices, factories and terrace houses. The boom times were, however, short-lived. The docks were simply unable to accommodate the larger vessels that were built after World War II and Het Eilandje hit the skids in the late 1950s, becoming a neglected, decaying corner of the city until forty years later when – in the manner of dockside developments right across western Europe – plans were laid to rejuvenate the whole district. It's very much a work in progress, but a stroll round the area is a pleasant way to wile away a few hours, with the obvious target being the top-ranking River Museum (MAS).

To the Museum aan de Stroom

From St-Pauluskerk, it's a ten-minute walk north to **Verversrui**, the pedestrianized centre of Antwerp's **red-light district**, which is seedy and dispiriting in equal measure. Don't despair: keep on going north and you'll soon reach the cold-looking waters of the **Bonapartedok** and **Willemdok**, the first of a chain of docks that extends north to make up **Het Eilandje**. These first two docks are flanked by converted warehouses and nearby is one notable old building, the grime-spattered **Loodswezen**, a grand neo-Gothic edifice of 1885 that once housed the city's river pilots and tugboat crews. The dominant structure hereabouts, however, is the large (60m-high) and strikingly modern building on the jetty separating the two docks – a flashy home for the new **Museum aan de Stroom**, **MAS** (River Museum; Tues–Sun 10am–5pm; €6; Ⓦwww.mas.be). Bringing together several separate collections under one roof, the museum tracks through Antwerp's maritime history with both permanent and temporary exhibitions illustrating a whole range of shipping activity, from inland navigation to life on the waterfront and shipbuilding. Among the many curiosities, there's a charming British scrimshaw engraved on a whale bone and a fascinating nautical totem in the form of a snake's head that dates from the fifth century.

East of the centre

Meir, Antwerp's pedestrianized main shopping street, connects the city centre with Centraal Station, some fifteen minutes' walk away to the east. Taken as a whole this part of the city lacks any particular character – being an indeterminate medley of the old and the new – but there's no disputing the principal sight, the **Rubenshuis**, the cleverly restored former home and studio of Rubens – and the city's most popular tourist attraction by a long chalk. Rubens was buried nearby in **St-Jacobskerk**, a good-looking Gothic church that well deserves a visit, but the architectural highlight hereabouts is the neo-Baroque **Centraal Station**, a sterling edifice dating from 1905. The station presides over Koningin Astridplein, a large and very busy square that accommodates both the **Provincial Diamond Museum** and the **zoo**.

The Rubenshuis

The **Rubenshuis**, at Wapper 9 (Tues–Sun 10am–5pm; €6), attracts tourists in droves. Not so much a house as a mansion, this was where Rubens lived for most of his adult life, but it was only acquired by the city in 1937, by which time it was little more than a shell. Skilfully restored, it opened as a museum in 1946. On the right is the classical studio, where Rubens worked and taught; on the left is the gabled Flemish house where he lived, to which is attached his art gallery, an Italianate chamber where he entertained the artistic and cultural elite of Europe. Rubens had an enviably successful career, spending the first years of the seventeenth century studying the Renaissance masters in Italy, before settling in this house in 1608. Soon after, he painted two wonderful canvases for the cathedral (see p.212) and his fame spread, both as a painter and diplomat, working for Charles I in England and receiving commissions from all over Europe.

The Rubenshuis is a tad short of the great man's paintings, but the reconstruction of his old home and studio is very convincing, and a clearly arrowed **tour** begins by twisting its way through the neatly panelled and attractively furnished **domestic interiors** of the Flemish half of the building. Beyond, and in contrast to the cramped living quarters, is the elegant **art gallery**, which, with its pocket-sized sculpture gallery, was where Rubens displayed his favourite pieces to a chosen few – and in a scene comparable to that portrayed in Willem van Haecht's *The Gallery of Cornelis van der Geest*, which is displayed here. The arrows then direct you on into the **great studio**, which is overlooked by a narrow gallery and equipped with a special high door to allow the largest canvases to be brought in and out with ease. Several of Rubens' paintings are displayed here, including a playful *Adam and Eve*, an early work in which the couple flirt while the serpent slithers back up the tree. Also in the studio is a more characteristic piece, the *Annunciation*, where you can sense the drama of the angel Gabriel's appearance to Mary, who is shown in her living room complete with wicker basket and a sleeping cat.

Behind the house, the **garden** is laid out in the formal style of Rubens' day – the Baroque portico might be familiar from the artist's Medici series, on display in the Louvre.

St-Jacobskerk

Rubens died in 1640 and was buried in **St-Jacobskerk**, just to the north of the Rubenshuis on Lange Nieuwstraat (April–Oct daily 2–5pm; €2). Very much the church of the Antwerp nobility, who were interred in its multiple vaults and chapels, the church is a mighty Gothic structure begun in 1491, but not finished until 1659. This delay means that much of its Gothic splendour is hidden by an over-decorous Baroque interior, the soaring heights of the nave flattened by heavy marble altars and a huge marble rood screen.

Nine chapels radiate out from the ambulatory, including the **Rubens chapel** directly behind the high altar, where the artist and his immediate family are buried beneath the tombstones in the floor with a lengthy Latin inscription giving details of Rubens' life and honours. The chapel's altar was the gift of Helene Fourment, Rubens' second wife, and shows one of his last works, *Our Lady and the Christ Child Surrounded by Saints* (1634), in which he painted himself as St George, his wives as Martha and Mary, and his father as St Jerome. It's as if he knew this was to be his epitaph; indeed, he is said to have asked for his burial chapel to be adorned with nothing more than a painting of the Virgin Mary with Jesus in her arms, encircled by various saints.

The rest of the church is crammed with the chapels and tombs of the rich and the powerful. Most are only of moderate interest, but the **chapel** next to – and north of – the tomb of Rubens is worth a peek for its clumsily titled *St Charles Borromeo Pleading with the Virgin on Behalf of those Stricken by the Plague*, completed by Jacob Jordaens in 1655. A dark, gaudy canvas, it's not without its ironies:

Borromeo, the Archbishop of Milan, was an ardent leader of the Counter-Reformation, while the artist was a committed Protestant. Look out also for the flamboyant *St George and the Dragon* in the chapel at the far end of the south aisle: the baroness who gave the church the picture in the nineteenth century said it was a van Dyck – but it wasn't and isn't.

To Centraal Station

Heading east from the Rubenshuis, Meir leads into **Leysstraat**, which is flanked by a sweeping facade that culminates in a pair of high, turreted gables set beneath a pair of gilded cupolas. Straight ahead rises the magnificent neo-Baroque **Centraal Station**, a medley of spires and balconies, glass domes and classical pillars finished in 1905 to a design by Louis Delacenserie, who had made his reputation as a restorer of Gothic buildings in Bruges. Recently returned to its full glory, the station is an extraordinary edifice, a well-considered blend of earlier architectural styles and fashions – particularly the Gothic lines of the main body of the building and the ticket hall, which has all the darkened mystery of a medieval church – yet displaying all the self-confidence of the new age of industrial progress.

The diamond district and Antwerp zoo

The anonymous streets just to the southwest of Centraal Station, along and around **Lange Kievitstraat**, are home to the largest **diamond market** in the world. Behind these indifferent facades precious stones pour in from every continent to be cut or re-cut, polished and sold. There's no show of wealth, no grand bazaar and no tax collector could ever keep track of the myriad deals which make the business hum, the only exception being the string of diamond and gold shops that fill up the outer precincts of Centraal Station beside **Pelikaanstraat**. Playing a leading role in Antwerp's **diamond trade** are Orthodox Jews, whose ancestors arrived here from Eastern Europe towards the end of the nineteenth century, and whose presence is often the only outward indication that the business exists at all. They make most of their money by acting as middlemen in a chain that starts in the producer countries, especially South Africa, and no less than eighty-five percent of the world's rough diamonds and half the total supply of cut diamonds are traded here in the city.

In front of Centraal Station, the **Provinciaal Diamantmuseum**, Koningin Astridplein 19–23 (daily except Wed 10am–5.30pm; €6) celebrates the diamond industry with a series of clearly labelled displays on the geology, history, trading, mining and cutting of diamonds. There are regular cutting demonstrations (Mon–Fri), but the most popular exhibits are the diamonds themselves, displayed in all sorts of lavish settings, both contemporary and vintage. The problem is the PR gloss: take the museum at face value and you'd think the diamond industry has been without controversy – there's certainly precious little on the so-called "blood diamonds" that have cut a savage swathe through a fair chunk of Africa.

Also on Koningin Astridplein is Antwerp's **zoo** (daily 10am–4.45pm, later in summer; €19.50, children 3 to 11 years €14.50; Ⓦ www.zooantwerpen.be), which accommodates no fewer than six thousand animals in a range of habitats and including an aviary, a reptile house and an aquarium.

South of the centre

Cutting south from Groenplaats, **Nationalestraat** was once prime real estate, its deluxe department stores a magnet for the bustles, parasols and top hats of the bourgeoisie. It hit the skids in the 1930s, but it's now on the way back with the construction of **ModeNatie**, a large-scale celebration of the city's fashion industry – incorporating a museum, **MoMu** – and the opening of lots of designer clothes shops nearby. East of here, the **Museum Mayer van den Bergh** is another prime attraction, boasting an exquisite collection of fine and applied art, while it's south again along Nationalestraat to **Het Zuid** (The South), a residential district whose grand French-style mansions, wide avenues and symmetrical squares were laid out at the end of the nineteenth century on the site of the old Spanish citadel, of which nothing now remains. Setting aside the neighbourhood's cafés and bars, the obvious targets here are **MuHKA**, the enterprising Museum of Contemporary Art, and the **Koninklijk Museum voor Schone Kunsten**, home to an extensive collection of Belgian art, but closed for a complete refurbishment until 2014.

Het Zuid is bounded by the **Amerikalei** and **Britselei** boulevards, which mark part of the course of a circle of city fortifications finished in the early years of the twentieth century. Enormously expensive and supposedly impregnable, the design was a disaster, depending on a series of raised gun emplacements that were sitting targets for the German artillery in September 1914. The Allies had expected Antwerp to hold out for months, but in the event the city surrendered after a two-week siege, forcing Churchill and his party of marines into a hurried evacuation just two days after their arrival. In themselves, the boulevards are without much interest, but just beyond lies the outstanding **Middelheim Museum**, with three hundred sculptures spread over extensive parkland.

ModeNatie and MoMu

Spread over several floors at Nationalestraat 28, **ModeNatie** (ⓦwww.modenatie.com) is a lavish and extraordinarily ambitious fashion complex, which incorporates both the fashion department of the Royal Academy of Fine Arts and the Flanders Fashion Institute. As such, it reflects the international success of local designers, beginning in the 1980s with the so-called "**Antwerp Six**" – including Dries van Noten, Dirk Bikkembergs, Marina Yee and Martin Margiela – and continuing with younger designers like A.F. Vandevorst, Stephan Schneider and Tim Vansteenbergen; all are graduates of the academy. Part of the building contains a fashion museum, **MoMu** (Mode Museum; Tues–Sun 10am–6pm; €7; ⓦwww.momu.be), whose adventurous and thought-provoking temporary

Fashion shopping in Antwerp

The success of Antwerp's **fashion designers** has spawned dozens of excellent designer shops and stores. To help visitors get a grip on it all, the tourist office produces the **Antwerp Fashion Map** (€2), which details several city walks that take you past all the most innovative shops. There is, however, a particular concentration of **fashion shops** around the ModeNatie complex. Recommended places hereabouts kick off with the men's and women's wear of Dries van Noten's **Modepaleis**, Nationalestraat 16 – at the corner of Kammenstraat – and continue with the imported designer clothes of **Alamode**, Nationalestraat 25. Neighbouring Kammenstraat weighs in with the contemporary jewellery of **Anne Zellien**, at no. 47, and the club and streetwear of **Fish & Chips**, at no. 36, while Lombardenstraat, just to the east, is home to **Maison Anna Heylen**, at no.16, **Original**, at no. 10, and **Louis**, at no. 2, with the last two featuring the clothes of many designers, from Hilfiger to Junk de Luxe. There are a couple of **secondhand/vintage** clothes shop in the area too, with women's stuff at **Jutka & Riska**, Nationalestraat 87, and all sorts of interesting gear at **Episode**, Steenhouwersvest 34, just west of Nationalestraat. If you've wandered over onto Steenhouwersvest, then also pop into the chichi premises of the Belgian-American **Diane von Furstenberg**, at no. 44.

displays cover a lot of ground – everything from the walking stick as fashion statement through to the evolution of the trench coat.

The Museum Mayer van den Bergh

The appealing **Museum Mayer van den Bergh**, a five-minute walk east of ModeNatie at Lange Gasthuisstraat 19 (Tues–Sun 10am–5pm; €4), comprises the art collection of Frits Mayer van den Bergh, a member of a wealthy merchant family who gave his artistic hoard to the city in 1920. Very much a connoisseur's collection, it offers examples of many different branches of applied arts, from tapestries to ceramics, silver, illuminated manuscripts and furniture, all crowded into the house that the family had built in the style of a sixteenth-century mansion in 1904. There are also a number of outstanding paintings, beginning in **Room 2** with a charming portrait of a young brother and sister by the Dutchman Cornelis Ketel (1548–1616). Next door, in **Room 3**, is the earliest panel painting ever to be found in Belgium – a thirteenth-century Italian work entitled the *Virgin and Child Enthroned* by Simeone and Machilone of Spoleto – while pride of place in **Room 4** goes to a *Crucifixion* triptych by Quinten Matsys (1465–1530), with the unidentified donors painted on the wings. Intriguingly, the female donor is pictured alongside one of the family's patron saints, Mary of Egypt, a repentant prostitute who spent her final years in the desert miraculously sustained by three little loaves.

Room 5 is almost entirely devoted to the **Bruegels** and it's here you'll find the museum's most celebrated painting, **Pieter the Elder**'s (1525–69) *Dulle Griet* or "Mad Meg", one of his most Bosch-like works. Experts have written volumes on the painting's iconography, but in broad terms there's no disputing it's a misogynistic allegory in which a woman, weighed down with possessions, stalks the gates of hell in a surrealistic landscape of monsters and pervasive horror. The title refers to the archetypal shrewish woman who, according to Flemish proverb, "could plunder in front of hell and remain unscathed". Hanging next to it is the same artist's *Twelve Proverbs*, a more relaxed vision of the world, in which a sequence of miniatures illustrates popular Flemish aphorisms, including an old favourite – the man in a blue, hooded cape, symbolic of the cuckold. Moving on, **Room 6** is devoted to an exquisite collection of small-scale medieval sculptures. and **Room 10** features two tiny panels from a fifteenth-century polyptych that once adorned a travelling altar. The twin panels are beautifully decorated with informal scenes – St Christopher, the patron saint of travellers, crosses a stream full of fish, and Joseph cuts up his socks to use as swaddling clothes for the infant Jesus.

To the Bourlaschouwburg

From the Bergh Museum, you can either proceed direct to the Maagdenhuis, just along the street (see below), or make a brief detour east via Arenbergstraat to the pleasant pedestrianized streets and squares fringing the **Bourlaschouwburg** (Bourla Theatre), an elegant nineteenth-century rotunda with a handsomely restored interior. Just beyond, at the end of the Graanmarkt, lurks its modern concrete and steel equivalent, the huge and really rather brutal **Stadsschouwburg** (municipal theatre), which is now attached to a large glass roof that shelters market traders on Saturdays and Sundays (see p.227).

The Maagdenhuis

The **Maagdenhuis**, Lange Gasthuisstraat 33 (Maidens' House; Mon & Wed–Fri 10am–5pm, Sat & Sun 1–5pm; €3), was formerly a hospital and orphanage for children of the poor, but is now occupied by the city's social security offices and a small museum. Created in the middle of the sixteenth century, the **orphanage** was strictly run, its complex rules enforced by draconian punishments. On the other hand, those children who were left here were fed and taught a skill, and desperate parents felt that they could at least retrieve their children if their circumstances improved. To make sure their offspring could be identified (in an illiterate age) they were given **tokens**, usually irregularly cut playing cards or images of saints – one part was left with the child, the other kept by the parent. If the city fathers didn't actually encourage this practice, they certainly accepted it, and several municipal buildings even had specially carved alcoves on their facades where foundlings could be left under shelter, certain to be discovered in the morning.

Inside the **museum**, particular highlights in the chapel to the right of the entrance include a cabinet of foundling tokens, a petite *Adoration of the Shepherds* triptych by Jan van Scorel (1495–1562), and fifty-odd colourful, late medieval porridge bowls – the largest collection of its sort in Belgium. In the five rooms across from the chapel, three paintings are worth seeking out: at the end of the corridor is *Orphan Girl at Work* by Cornelius de Vos (1584–1651), a touching composition showing the young woman cheered by the offer of a red carnation, a symbol of fidelity; and in the end room on the right are both **van Dyck's** (1599–1641) mournful *St Jerome* and Jordaens' (1593–1678) profound study of Christ in his *Descent from the Cross*.

From the Maagdenhuis, it's a good fifteen-minute walk southwest to Het Zuid; you can also pick up **tram #8**, which runs south from Groenplaats along Nationalestraat and then Volkstraat.

Het Zuid: MuHKA and the Fotomuseum Provincie Antwerpen

The **Het Zuid** neighbourhood is at its most demure on and around **Leopold de Waelplaats**, its dead-straight streets lined with the big old mansions of the nineteenth-century bourgeoisie. The area once had its own **dock**, in between Vlaamsekaai and Waalsekaai, but this was filled in years ago, becoming the wide and dreary square of today. There are two museums on the west side of the square.

The Koninklijk Museum voor Schone Kunsten

Occupying an immense Neoclassical edifice dating from the 1880s, Antwerp's prestigious **Koninklijk Museum voor Schone Kunsten** (KMSKA; Royal Fine Art Museum), overlooking Leopold de Waelplaats, possesses a first-rate collection of Belgian art from the fifteenth century onwards, but it's closed for a long-term refurbishment until at least 2014. In the meantime, plans are afoot to display highlights of the collection elsewhere in the city – the cathedral (see p.212) and the MAS museum (see p.218) are two likely locations – and the tourist office (see p.208) will have the latest news. Key paintings in the collection include two tiny but especially delicate works by **Jan van Eyck** (1390–1441), a *Madonna at the Fountain* and a *St Barbara*, and **Quinten Matsys**' (1465–1530) triptych of the *Lamentation*, a profound and moving work portraying the Christ, his forehead flecked with blood, surrounded by grieving followers including Mary Magdalene, who tenderly wipes his feet with her hair as tears roll down her face. The museum also possesses several enormous canvases by **Rubens** (1577–1640), most notably an inventive *Last Communion of St Francis* (1619), showing a very sick-looking saint equipped with the marks of the stigmata, a faint halo and a half-smile: despite the sorrowful ministrations of his fellow monks, Francis can't wait for salvation. Also from 1619 is *Christ Crucified Between the Two Thieves* which, with its muscular thieves and belligerent Romans, possesses all the high drama you might expect, but is almost overwhelmed by its central image – you can virtually hear the tearing of Christ's flesh as the soldier's lance sinks into him.

The first, **MuHKA** (Museum of Contemporary Art; Tues–Sun 11am–6pm, Thurs till 9pm; €6; ⓦwww.muhka.be) occupies a striking functionalist building at Leuvenstraat 32 and specializes in large-scale, ambitious, avant-garde exhibitions. Nearby, the **Fotomuseum Provincie Antwerpen**, at Waalsekaai 47 (Provincial Photography Museum; Tues–Sun 10am–6pm; €6; ⓦwww.fotomuseum.be), mixes displays of all sorts of old photographic equipment, plus modern exhibitions of different photographic techniques, film showings, portfolio view days and so forth.

The Middelheim Museum

The **Middelheim Museum** (Tues–Sun: April & Sept 10am–7pm; May & Aug 10am–8pm; June & July 10am–9pm; Oct–March 10am–5pm; free; ⓦwww.middelheimmuseum.be) is one of Antwerp's most enjoyable attractions, comprising over three hundred modern sculptures spread amid the manicured lawns and trees of **Middelheim Park**, about 6km south of the city centre. The original collection was assembled here in the 1950s at the instigation of an adventurous burgomaster – one Lode Craeybeckx – and has since grown to include examples of all the major modern schools. The open-air collection is supplemented by an indoor section, in which the more delicate pieces are displayed. There is a fair sprinkling of Belgian sculptors, one of the more talented of whom was the painter-sculptor Rik Wouters (1882–1916), plus a handsome sample of the work of leading foreign practitioners like Henry Moore, Tony Cragg, Panamareko, Auguste Rodin, Alexander Calder and Ossip Zadkine.

Middelheim Park is situated just beyond the ring road on Middelheimlaan. There are several ways to get there by public transport, one of the options being to take **bus #17** from Centraal Station; ask the driver to put you off at the junction of Eglantierlaan and Beukenlaan, from where it's a ten-minute walk south via Beukenlaan.

Eating and drinking

Antwerp is an enjoyable place to eat, its busy centre liberally sprinkled with informal **cafés** and **restaurants** which excel at combining traditional Flemish dishes with Mediterranean, French and vegetarian cuisines. There is a good range of slightly more formal – and expensive – restaurants too, though generally the distinction between the city's cafés and restaurants is blurred.

Antwerp is also a fine place to **drink**. There are lots of bars in the city centre, mostly dark and tiny affairs exuding a cheerful vitality. Some of them regularly feature live music, but most don't, satisfying themselves – and their customers – with everything from taped *chanson* to house. **Bar opening hours** are elastic, with many places only closing when the last customers leave – say 2 or 3am – and, unless otherwise stated in our listings below, all are open daily. The favourite local tipple is De Koninck, a light ale drunk in a *bolleke*, or small, stemmed glass.

Restaurants

Aurelia Wijngaardstraat 22 ⓣ03 233 62 59. Smart and smooth little restaurant in an immaculately restored old merchant's house metres from Hendrik Conscienceplein. Serves delicious seafood and meat dishes in the full French style, with main courses averaging €25. Daily except Tues & Wed from 6pm. See map, p.210.

Hippodroom Leopold de Waelplaats 10 ⓣ03 248 52 52. Polished, fairly formal restaurant opposite the Koninklijk Museum voor Schone Kunsten offering a wide range of Flemish and Franco-Flemish dishes from around €23. You can eat outside in the garden in summer. Mon–Fri noon–2.30pm & 6–11pm, Sat 6–11pm. See map, p.206.

Hungry Henrietta Lombardenvest 19 ⓣ03 232 29 28. Something of a city institution, this family-owned restaurant is decorated to a modern spec and touches base with all the Flemish classics. Locals swear by the steaks. Mains average €22, but the daily specials cost half that. Mon–Fri noon–2pm & 6–9pm. See map, p.210.

Invincible Haarstraat 9 ⓣ03 231 32 07. Flashy little restaurant near the Grote Markt, where you're best off perched on a bar stool in full view of the chef. The menu is short but extremely well considered, giving due prominence to seasonal ingredients – for example spring chicken in tarragon. Three-course set menu for €35. Reservations advised. Mon–Fri noon–2pm & 6.30–10pm. See map, p.210.

De Kleine Zavel Stoofstraat 2 ⓣ03 231 96 91. Much praised bistro-style restaurant with wooden floors, old-style furniture and Franco-Belgian cuisine at its tastiest – the *jus* are simply wonderful and there's a particularly strong line in seafood. It's set on a narrow side street in between the Grote Markt and the river. Mains from €21. Reservations recommended. Tues–Fri & Sun noon–2pm & 6.30–10.30pm, Sat 6.30–10.30pm. See map, p.210.

Pazzo Oude Leeuwenrui 12 ⓣ03 232 86 82. Well-regarded cellar restaurant with a separate wine bar, set in an old warehouse to the north of the city centre near the docks. A wide-ranging menu features Italian fusion cooking and prices – with mains from around €20 – are competitive. A great selection of wine, too. Mon–Fri noon–3pm & 6–11pm. See map, p.206.

De Peerdestal Wijngaardstraat 8 ⓣ03 231 95 03. A few metres from Hendrik Conscienceplein, this popular restaurant, with its rusticated decor, is *the* place to try a traditional Belgian speciality, horsemeat – *paardenvlees*. Mains start at €21. Daily 11am–3pm & 5–10pm. See map, p.210.

Pizzeria Da Antonio Grote Markt 6 ⓣ03 232 17 07. Central Antwerp literally heaves with Italian restaurants and this is one of the better ones, serving tasty pasta and pizza from as little as €10. Very popular. Open daily from noon. See map, p.210.

De Reddende Engel Torfburg 3 ⓣ03 233 66 30. In the shadow of the cathedral, this long-established restaurant attracts an older clientele, drawn here by the antique decor and the tasty Flemish cuisine. Particularly strong on seafood – and there's a lobster tank here too. Mains from €20. Thurs, Fri, Sun & Mon noon–2pm & 6–10pm, Sat 6–10pm. See map, p.210.

Ulcke van Zurich Oude Beurs 50 ⓣ03 234 04 94. Informal, split-level café-restaurant kitted out in antique-meets-New Age style. The grilled meats are the house speciality and although there's not much in the way of finesse, the service is fast and prices are very competitive, with a two-course meal and a beer costing in the region of €30. Daily except Mon & Tues from 6pm. See map, p.210.

Varelli Plantinkaai 15 ⓣ03 485 88 82. The best Greek meze in town are served here in this arty, informal restaurant, which occupies the ground floor of an old riverside town house. Main courses €15. Mon–Sat 6–10.30pm, Sun noon–10pm. See map, p.210.

Zoute Zoen Zirkstraat 15 ⓣ03 226 92 20. A short walk north of the Grote Markt, this small and polished bistro, which is kitted out in the style of a nineteenth-century salon, offers delicious Italian, French and Flemish dishes with main courses around €20. Closed Sat lunch and all day Mon. See map, p.210.

Cafés and café-bars

Caffènation Hopland 46 Straightforward café with a student vibe and, more importantly, the best range of coffees in town. Takeaway and drink in – there's a mini-garden terrace at the back. Mon–Sat 8.30am–7.30pm; Sun noon–6pm. See map, p.206.

De Groote Witte Arend Reyndersstraat 18. Eminently appealing café-bar occupying one wing and the courtyard of an old mansion. Great range of beers – including authentic *gueuze* and *kriek* – plus delicious Flemish dishes, including *stoemp* (mashed potato with veg) and *stoofvlees* (beef cooked in beer) – all to a classical music soundtrack. Mains average €15. Sun–Thurs 10.30am–midnight, Fri & Sat 10.30am–2am; kitchen daily 11am–10pm. See map, p.210.

Hoffy's Lange Kievitstraat 52 ⓣ03 234 35 35. Outstanding, simply decorated traditional Jewish restaurant and takeaway near Centraal Station. Very reasonable prices. Try the *gefillte fisch*. Daily except Sat 11am–9pm. See map, p.206.

Le Pain Quotidien Steenhouwersvest 48. Distinctive café, where the variety of breads is the main event, served with wholesome soups and light meals at one long wooden table. Part of a chain. Daily 7am–7pm. See map, p.210.

Pakhuis Vlaamsekaai 76. Fashionable café-bar occupying an imaginatively converted two-storey warehouse. Uniformed waiters lend a brasserie air and the house beers are brewed on the premises. Mon–Sat from 11am till late, Sun from noon. See map, p.206.

Popoff Oude Koornmarkt 18. Tiny little café with the best desserts, tarts and gateaux in town, and a pavement terrace too. Tues–Thurs & Sun noon–10pm, Fri & Sat noon–midnight. See map, p.210.

Bars

De Duifkens Graanmarkt 5. Located on a pedestrianized square close to the Rubenshuis and behind the Bourlaschouwburg, this old-style Antwerp café-bar has long been a favourite haunt of the city's actors. See map, p.206.

Het Elfde Gebod Torfbrug 10. In the shadow of the cathedral, this old bar has become something of a tourist trap, but it's still worth visiting for the kitsch, nineteenth-century religious statues which cram the interior; don't bother with the food. See map, p.210.

Den Engel Grote Markt 3. Traditional bar with an easy-going, occasionally anarchic atmosphere. Occupies the ground floor of a guild-house on the northwest corner of the main square and attracts a bubbly mix of business people and locals from the residential enclave round the Vleeshuis. Late-night dancing (of no particular merit) too. See map, p.210.

De Faam Grote Pieter Potstraat 12. Cool, groovy bar in small, sparingly lit premises near the Grote Markt. An eclectic soundtrack – from *chanson* to jazz. See map, p.210.

Den Hopsack Grote Pieter Potstraat 24. Postmodern bar – all wood and spartan fittings – with highbrow conversation, an amenable, low-key atmosphere, and a thirty-something clientele. See map, p.210.

Kulminator Vleminckveld 32. A five-minute walk south of the centre, this is one of the best beer bars in Antwerp, serving over 500 varieties, with a helpful beer menu. Dark and atmospheric with New Age flourishes. Mon 8.15pm–midnight, Tues–Fri noon–midnight, Sat 5pm–midnight. See map, p.206.

Café Pelikaan Melkmarkt 14. There's nothing smart and touristy about the *Pelikaan*, a packed bar metres from the cathedral where locals get down to some serious drinking. Closed Sun. See map, p.210.

De Vagant Reyndersstraat 25. Specialist gin bar serving an extravagant range of Belgian and Dutch jenevers in comfortable, laidback surroundings. Small pavement terrace too. See map, p.210.

Entertainment and nightlife

Antwerp has a vibrant and diverse **cultural scene**, and the best way to get a handle on it is to pick up the very useful, fortnightly **Zone 03** (Ⓦ www.zone03.be), a free Dutch-language newssheet which details all up-and-coming events, exhibitions and concerts; it's available from the tourist office and at newsstands all over the city centre. The city has its own **orchestra** and **opera** companies as well as several good Flemish **theatre** troupes, and there are occasional appearances by touring English-language theatre companies too. English-language **films** are almost always subtitled – as distinct from dubbed – and Antwerp has a reliable, city-centre art-house cinema.

Antwerp's fluid **club scene** is in a rude state of health, with a handful of boisterous places dotted round the peripheries of the city centre. They get going at around midnight and admission fees are typically modest (€10 or so) except for big-name DJs. There's a flourishing **jazz** scene too, with a couple of good places in the centre.

As regards **festivals**, the city hosts a goodly portion of the **Festival van Vlaanderen** (Flanders Festival; Ⓦ www.festival.be), which runs from May to November and features more than one hundred classical concerts performed in cities across the whole of Flemish-speaking Belgium. There's also **SFINKS** (Ⓦ www.sfinks.be), Belgium's best world music festival, held outdoors over the last weekend of July in the suburb of Boechout, about 10km southeast of downtown Antwerp.

Tickets for most concerts and events are on sale at **Info Cultuur** (Tues–Fri 10am–5.45pm, Sat noon–5pm; Ⓣ 03 338 95 85, Ⓦ www.infocultuur.be), which shares its premises with the tourist office at Grote Markt 13. A comparable service is provided at the Fnac store, on the Groenplaats (see "Books" opposite).

Theatres, cinemas and concert halls

Bourlaschouwburg Komedieplaats 18 Ⓣ 03 224 88 44, Ⓦ www.toneelhuis.be. This handsomely restored nineteenth-century theatre is the city's premier venue for theatrical performances, and the home of the Het Toneelhuis repertory company.

Cartoons Kaasstraat 4, off Suikerrui Ⓣ 03 232 96 32, Ⓦ www.cartoons-cinema.be. The most distinctive downtown cinema, showing both mainstream and art-house films in several auditoria.

Koningin Elisabethzaal Koningin Astridplein 26 ⓣ0900 00 311 (premium line), ⓦwww.elisabethzaal.be. Mixed bag of a venue with opera, rock, dance and theatre. The internationally acclaimed Royal Flemish Philharmonic Orchestra (ⓦwww.defilharmonie.be) is based here, though it also performs at the Bourlaschouwburg (see p.226).

Stadsschouwburg Theaterplein 1 ⓣ0900 69 900 (premium line), ⓦwww.stadsschouwburgantwerpen.be. A big bruiser of a modern building near the Rubenshuis that mostly hosts musical concerts and theatrical performances.

UGC Antwerpen Van Ertbornstraat 17 ⓣ0900 10 440 (premium line), ⓦwww.ugc.be. A vast multi-screen complex just west of Centraal Station, off De Keyserlei – though there's an entrance on this street too.

De Vlaamse Opera Frankrijklei 3 ⓣ070 22 02 02, ⓦwww.vlaamseopera.be. The excellent Koninklijke Vlaamse Opera (Royal Flemish Opera) usually performs here at this grand, early twentieth-century building on the ring road, about halfway between the Grote Markt and Centraal Station. The **Koninklijk ballet van Vlaanderen** (Royal Ballet of Flanders; ⓦwww.koninklijkballetvanvlaanderen.be) performs here too, but also has its own small, 300-seat venue at Westkaai 16.

Live music and clubs

Café d'Anvers Verversrui 15 ⓣ03 226 38 70, ⓦwww.cafe-d-anvers.com. Youthful, fashionable, energetic club, billed as a "temple to house music", but perhaps a little too well established to be cutting edge. North of the centre in the red-light district. Thurs–Sat; free entry on Thurs.

Café Hopper Leopold De Waelstraat 2 ⓣ03 248 49 33, ⓦwww.cafehopper.be. Laidback, easy-going bar-café providing an excellent and varied programme of live jazz, sometimes with big international names.

De Muze Melkmarkt 15 ⓣ03 226 01 26. With its bare-brick walls and retro film posters, this funky café-bar is lively and popular, and regularly puts on jazz bands.

Petrol d'Herbouvillekaai 25 at General Armstrongweg ⓣ03 226 49 63, ⓦwww.petrolclub.be. One of the hottest clubs in town for both DJs and live concerts, and always open Fri and Sat nights – check the website for weekday programme. Way south out of the city centre, housed in a former waste disposal centre in an old industrial area beside the River Scheldt – take a taxi. Admission €8–10; advance tickets available from Fnac bookshop (see below).

Red & Blue Lange Schipperskapelstraat 13 ⓣ03 213 05 55, ⓦwww.redandblue.be. Other nights have other incarnations, but Saturday night here is gay night (men only) with house and techno, and a throbbing dancefloor. From 11pm, but not much happens till 1am; closes at 6/7am. €10 entry.

Listings

Antwerp airport ⓣ03 285 65 00, ⓦwww.antwerp-airport.be.

Books English books and a wide range of Belgian road and hiking maps are available from Fnac, in the Grand Bazaar shopping mall on the Groenplaats (Mon–Sat 10am–6.30pm); Fnac's main entrance is on the left hand side of the whopping *Hilton Hotel*. Standaard Boekhandel, at the corner of Huidevettersstraat and Lange Gasthuisstraat, is a good second bet (Mon–Sat 9.30am–6pm).

Buses and trams For all city and provincial bus and tram enquiries, contact De Lijn ⓣ070 220 200, ⓦwww.delijn.be.

Car rental Europcar, Plantin en Moretuslei 35 ⓣ03 206 74 44; Hertz, at Antwerp airport ⓣ03 239 29 21.

Emergencies Police ⓣ101; ambulance/fire brigade ⓣ100.

Gay scene If there is a centre to Antwerp's gay and lesbian scene it's *Café Den Draak*, Draakplaats 1 (daily from noon till late; ⓦwww.dendraak.be), a café-bar that is part of a larger gay and lesbian project, the Het Roze Huis (ⓣ03 288 00 84, ⓦwww.hetrozehuis.be). Draakplaats is a 15-minute walk south from Centraal Station: take Pelikaanstraat and its continuation Simonsstraat/Mercatorstraat, turn left down Grote Hondstraat, and it's at the end of the street. The city's biggest and best gay club is *Red & Blue* (see above).

Gin The De Vagant off-licence, opposite the bar of the same name at Reyndersstraat 21, sells a wide range of Dutch and Belgian gins. Mon & Wed–Sun 11am–6pm.

Left luggage Office and coin-operated lockers at Centraal Station.

Markets Theaterplein plays host to a food and flower market on Saturdays (8am–4pm); and a bric-a-brac, flower, plant and bird market on Sundays (8am–1pm). From Easter to October, there's also an antique and jumble market on Lijnwaadmarkt (Sat 9am–5pm), immediately to the north of Onze-Lieve-Vrouwekathedraal.

Pharmacies Apotheek Rubens is at Groenplaats 6. Details of 24hr pharmacies are available from the

tourist office; duty rotas should also be displayed on all pharmacists' windows or doors.
Post office The main post office is at Groenplaats 43 (Mon–Fri 9am–6pm, Sat 9am–3pm).
Taxis There are taxi ranks outside Centraal Station and at the top of Suikerrui, on the edge of the Grote Markt. Antwerp Taxi is on ⓣ03 238 38 38.
Train enquiries Belgian railways, NMBS ⓣ02 528 28 28, ⓦwww.b-rail.be.

Lier

Likeable **LIER**, just 17km southeast of Antwerp, has an amenable, small-town air, its pocket-sized centre boasting a particularly pretty Grote Markt and a clutch of handsome medieval buildings, especially **St-Gummaruskerk**. The town was founded in the eighth century, but despite its ancient provenance Lier has never managed to dodge the shadow of its much larger neighbour, Antwerp – even

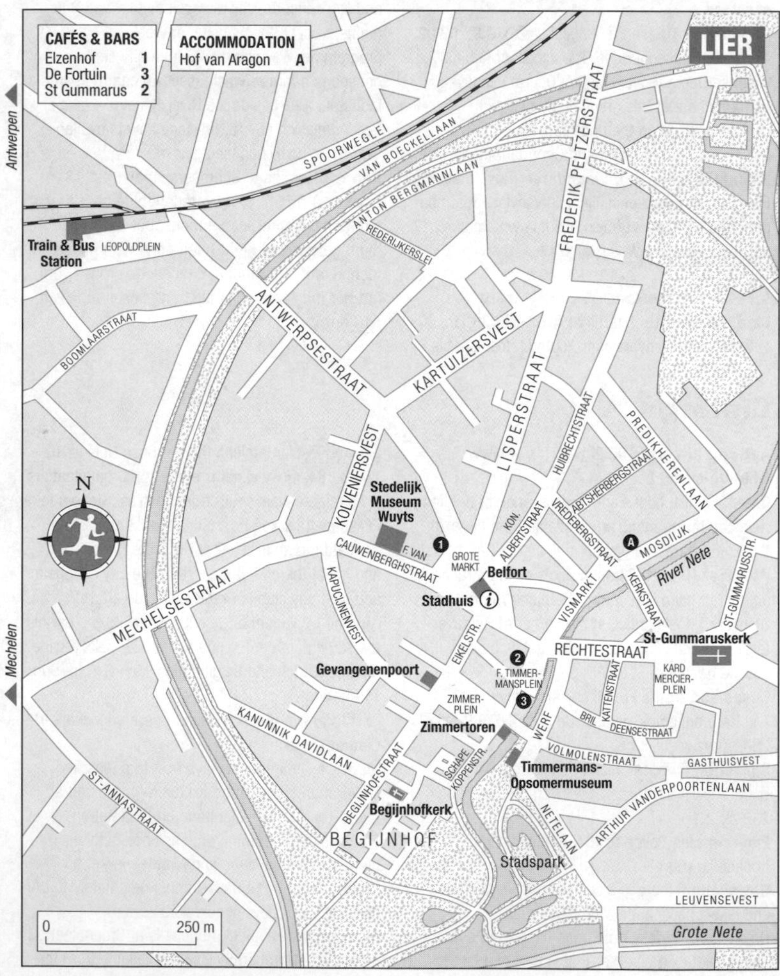

when **Felix Timmermans**, one of Belgium's best-known writers, lived here for almost all of his long life (1886–1947). All the same, Timmermans did add a certain local sparkle – and it may have been needed: other Belgians once referred to Lier's citizens as "sheepheads" (*schapenkoppen*), a reference to their reputation for stubbornness and stupidity.

Lier is an ideal day-trip from Antwerp, just a twenty-minute **train** ride away.

Arrival, information and accommodation

Lier **train station** adjoins the **bus station** on the north side of the town centre, a ten-minute walk from the Grote Markt, where the **tourist office** is in the basement of the Stadhuis (April–Oct daily 9am–12.30pm & 1.30–5pm; Nov–March Mon–Fri 9am–12.30pm & 1.30–5pm; ⓣ03 800 05 55, ⓦwww.toerismelier.be). Of the town's three **hotels**, the best is the *Hof van Aragon*, Aragonstraat 6 (ⓣ03 491 08 00, ⓦwww.hva.be/nl/hotel; ❸), a small, unpretentious place that occupies an attractively renovated old building a short walk east of the Grote Markt; the rooms are quite large, but the showers tend to be a tad poky.

The Town

Central Lier spreads out from the large, rectangular **Grote Markt**, its old streets and alleys encircled and bisected by the waterways that mark the course of its old harbours and moat. At the centre of the Grote Markt is the turreted fourteenth-century **Belfort**, an attractively spikey affair incongruously attached to the classically elegant **Stadhuis**, which was built to replace the medieval cloth hall in 1740. Otherwise, the square is an attractive medley of neos-, with neo-Gothic, Neoclassical and even neo-Romanesque buildings, mostly dating from the 1920s, jostling for space and attention.

St-Gummaruskerk

From the Grote Markt, it's a brief stroll southeast to **St-Gummaruskerk** (Easter to Oct 10am–noon & 2–5pm), which takes its name from a courtier of King Pepin of France, who, repenting of his sinful ways, settled in Lier as a hermit in the middle of the eighth century. Dating from 1425, the church is a fine illustration of the Flamboyant (or Late) Gothic style, its sturdy buttresses surmounted by a tiered and parapeted tower. Inside, chunky pillars rise up to support a vaulted roof, whose simplicity contrasts with the swirling embellishments of the **rood screen** down below. Behind, the **high altar** is topped by a second fine carving, a fourteenth-century wooden altarpiece whose inside panels are alive with a mass of finely observed detail, from the folds of the bed linen to the pile of kindling underneath Abraham's son. The church's **stained-glass windows** are reckoned to be some of the finest in Belgium. They include five stately, elongated windows above the high altar, which were presented to the town by the Emperor Maximilian in 1516, along with a more intimate sequence by Rombout Keldermans from 1475, overlooking the first section of the left-hand side of the choir. The church also owns an extremely rare and very early (1516) copy of the **Turin Shroud**, the old linen cloth that supposedly bears the image of the crucified Christ, at one tenth the size of the original; it's extremely sensitive to light, so it's only displayed a few weeks a year, usually behind the rood loft. The most interesting **painting** is the triptych in the chapel just behind and to the left of the rood screen: the two side panels are by Rubens, but the central panel is a copy – Napoleon's soldiers stole the original Rubens, and the French have never given it back.

The Timmermans-Opsomermuseum

Not far from St Gummaruskerk, beside the River Nete, the **Timmermans-Opsomermuseum** (Tues–Sun 10am–noon & 1–5pm; €2, combined ticket with Stedelijk Museum €3) celebrates the town's two most famous inhabitants, the writer Felix Timmermans (1886–1947) and the painter Isidore Opsomer (1878–1967). Timmermans and Opsomer were good friends and thought of themselves as leading custodians of Flemish culture, the one writing of traditional village life, most memorably in the earthy humour of his *Pallieter*; the other proud of his sea- and townscapes, and of his influence on contemporary Belgian painters. Inside, the ground floor has a comprehensive selection of Opsomer's work, including a whole batch of seriously bourgeois portraits along with a number of more immediately appealing rural scenes, such as the Expressionistic *Middelburg*. There's also a large and laughable, pseudo-religious painting entitled *Christ Preaches in Lier*. Another room on the ground floor is devoted to the work of their friend, the sculptor **Lodewijk van Boeckel** (1857–1944), whose old forge is surrounded by examples of his intricate, profoundly black ironwork.

Upstairs, an extensive display on Timmermans explores his life and times with the assistance of old photos and several first editions of his writings, plus paintings by and of him. During the German occupation of World War II, Timmermans edited a Flemish nationalist newspaper and had regular dealings with the governing regime, leading, with much justification, to accusations of collaboration. There is a small display on this period, but – like the rest of this floor – the labelling is only in Flemish.

The Zimmertoren

The **Zimmertoren** (daily 9am–noon & 1.30–5.30pm; €2.50), an old tower on Zimmerplein, was formerly part of the city ramparts before being equipped with the colourful **Jubelklok** (Centenary Clock), whose many dials show the phases of the moon, the zodiac, the tides of Lier and just about everything else you can think of. The clock was the work of one Lodewijk Zimmer (1888–1970), a wealthy city merchant who constructed it in 1931 in an effort to dispel local superstition and show his fellow townspeople how the cosmos worked. Inside the tower you can see the bevy of rotating dials which makes the clock tick, along with Zimmer's astronomical studio, while in the adjoining pavilion is Zimmer's no-less-detailed **Wonderklok** (Wonder Clock), which was exhibited at the World's Fairs of Brussels and New York in the 1930s. A guide explaining the internal works of the clocks and the meaning of all the dials is available in English.

The Begijnhof and the Gevangenenpoort

From the Zimmertoren, Schapekoppenstraat leads southwest past a wry modern **sculpture** of a shepherd and his metal sheep to a side-gate into the **Begijnhof**, whose lovely old seventeenth-century cottages are mixed up with the slightly grander terraced houses that were inserted later. It's one of the region's best-preserved *begijnhofs*, its narrow cobbled lanes stretching as far as the earthen bank that marks the line of the old city wall, and you can also pop into the appealingly ornate **Begijnhofkerk** (Easter to mid-Oct Sun 2–5pm). For more on *begijnhofs*, see p.357.

On the far side of the Begijnhof, Begijnhofstraat leads back to the Zimmerplein through the arches of the **Gevangenenpoort**, a strongly fortified medieval gate which served as the town's prison for many a year.

Stedelijk Museum Wuyts-Van Campen & Baron Caroly

For a small town, Lier has a surprisingly good art gallery, the **Stedelijk Museum Wuyts-Van Campen & Baron Caroly**, just off the Grote Markt at Florent van

Cauwenberghstraat 14 (Tues–Sun 10am–noon & 1–5pm; €2, combined ticket with Opsomerhuis €3). Pride of the collection, which is spread over just three rooms, are two paintings by **Pieter Bruegel the Younger** (1564–1638), namely *St John the Baptist Preaching to a Crowd*, who are dressed in an idiosyncratic mix of rural Flemish and imaginary Middle Eastern attire; and his *Flemish Proverbs* (*Vlaamse Spreekworden*), illustrating over eighty proverbs satirizing every vice and foolery imaginable. The latter is one of several almost identical proverbs' paintings completed by Bruegel – for an explanation as to who is doing what and why, see the box on p.217. The museum also possesses a small but well-chosen selection of nineteenth-century Belgian and Dutch landscapes, a pious preparatory sketch of *St Theresa* by Rubens (1577–1640), and a cruelly drawn *Brawling Peasants* by Jan Steen (1626–79). Look out also for several works by David Teniers the Younger (1610–90), who made a small fortune by churning out earthy peasant scenes such as his *Jealous Wife* and *The Backgammon Players*.

Eating and drinking

For **food**, most day-trippers head for the row of terraced cafés edging the Grote Markt and the Zimmerplein. Among them, one of the best is the *Elzenhof*, Grote Markt 41, a spick-and-span modern place where they cover all the Flemish classics from *croque-monsieur* to steaks; they also carry a wide range of ales. The most enjoyable **bar** in town is *St Gummarus*, a traditional small-town pub down by the river on tiny Felix Timmermansplein. It's next door to *De Fortuin*, a restaurant rather more than a bar that occupies lovely old premises, though you can stick to drinks on its riverside terrace.

Mechelen and around

Midway between Antwerp and Brussels, **MECHELEN** is the home of the Primate of Belgium and the country's ecclesiastical capital. It flourished during medieval times, but subsequently hit the buffers, with the *Baedeker* of 1900 witheringly describing the town as a "dull place totally destitute of the brisk traffic which enlivens most of the principal Belgian towns". Things finally picked up in the 1980s with a well-conceived municipal plan to attract new investment and gee up Mechelen's several tourist attractions. The result is the pleasant and appealing town of today, but nonetheless, considering its proximity to Antwerp and Brussels, Mechelen has a surprisingly provincial atmosphere – no bad thing. The key sights – primarily a cache of **medieval churches**, including a splendid cathedral, and a pair of superb Rubens paintings – are easily seen on a day-trip from either of its neighbours, but overnight and you'll have the time to give the place the attention it deserves. One blot on Mechelen's history was its use by the Germans as a transit camp for Jews in World War II: there's a **Deportation Museum** in town and a short train ride or drive away is **Fort Breendonk**, a one-time Gestapo interrogation centre.

Some history

Mechelen's Christian heritage dates back to **St Rombout**, an Irish evangelist who converted the locals in the seventh century. Little is known about Rombout, but legend asserts he was the son of a powerful chieftain, who gave up his worldly possessions to preach to the heathen – not that it did him much good: after publicly criticizing a stonemason for adultery, the ungrateful wretch chopped him

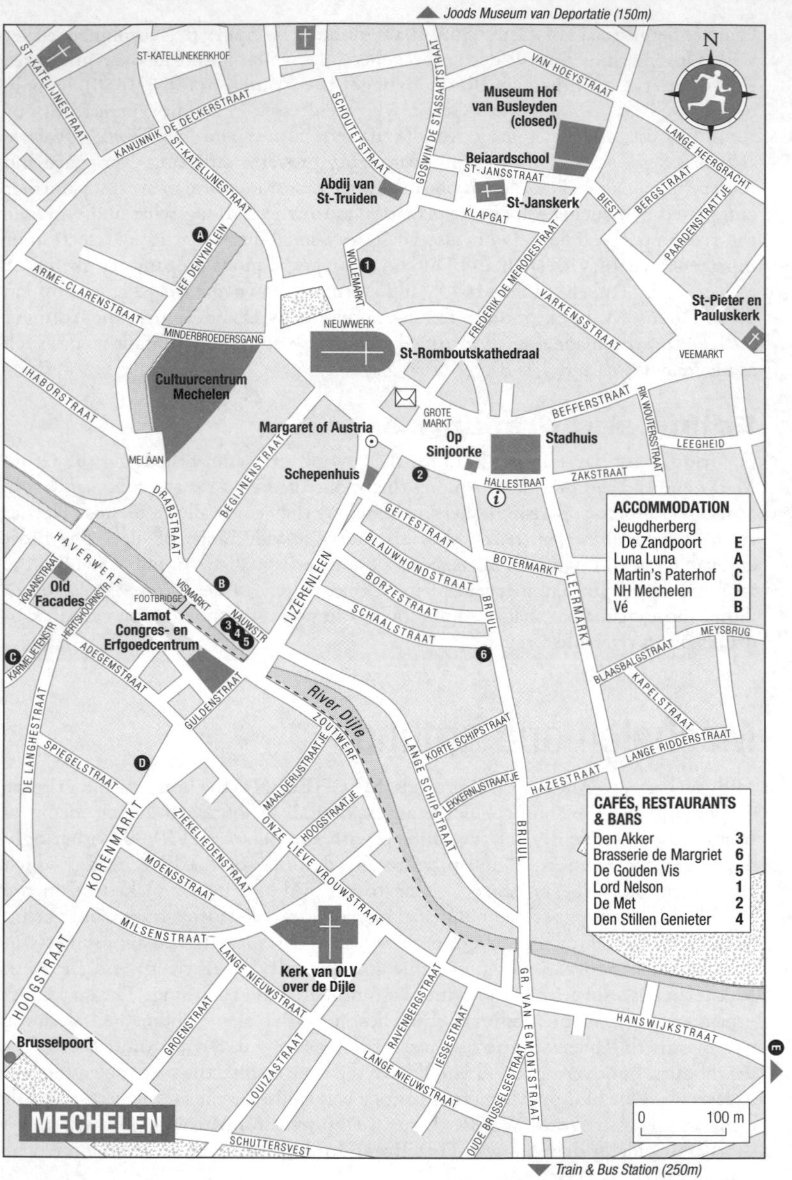

up with his axe and chucked the body into the river. In the way of such things, Rombout's remains were retrieved and showed no signs of decay, easily enough justification for the construction of a shrine in his honour. Rombout proved a popular saint and pilgrims flocked here, ensuring Mechelen a steady revenue. By the thirteenth century, Mechelen had become one of the more powerful cities of medieval Flanders and entered a brief golden age when, in 1473, the Burgundian prince, **Charles the Bold**, decided to base his administration here. Impetuous and intemperate, Charles used the wealth of the Flemish towns to fund a series of campaigns that ended with his death on the battlefield in 1477. His widow, Margaret of York, and his son's regent, the redoubtable **Margaret of Austria**, stayed in Mechelen and formed one of the most famous courts of the day. Artists and scholars were drawn here from all over Flanders, attracted by the Renaissance pomp and ceremony, with enormous feasts in fancy clothes in fancy buildings. For the men, two particular peccadilloes were **pointed shoes** (whose length – up to about 60cm – reflected social status) and bright, **two-colour hoses**. This glamorous facade camouflaged serious political intent. Surrounded by wealthy, independent merchants and powerful, well-organized guilds, the dukes and duchesses of Burgundy realized they had to impress and overawe as a condition of their survival.

Margaret of Austria died in 1530, the capital moved to Brussels and Mechelen was never quite the same, though many of its older buildings did survive the industrial boom of the nineteenth century to emerge intact today.

Arrival, information and accommodation

From Mechelen's adjoining **train** and **bus stations**, it's a fifteen-minute walk north to the town centre, straight ahead down Hendrik Consciencestraat and its continuation Graaf van Egmontstraat and then Bruul. The **tourist office** is across from the Stadhuis on the Grote Markt at Hallestraat 2–6 (April–Oct Mon–Fri 9.30am–5.30pm, Sat & Sun 9.30am–4.30pm; Nov–March Mon–Fri 9.30am–4.30pm, Sat & Sun 10.30am–3.30pm; ⓣ070 22 00 08, ⓦwww.toerismemechelen.be). They have details of – and sell tickets for – upcoming festivals and events, and will supply a list of the town's **accommodation**, among which there are about fifteen hotels and B&Bs in the centre.

Hotels, B&B and hostel

Jeugdherberg De Zandpoort Zandpoortvest 70 ⓣ015 27 85 40, ⓦwww.vjh.be. HI-affiliated hostel in an idiosyncratic modern tower block, with 112 beds in one-, two, three- and four-berth rooms. All rooms en suite, breakfast is included in the price and there's internet access, a dining room and bar. No curfew. A dull 10min walk northeast of the train station via Stationsstraat. Beds from €20, doubles. ❶

Luna Luna Jef Denynplein 4–6 ⓣ0486 29 67 98, ⓦwww.lunaluna.be. Especially pleasant B&B in a substantial old town house on a quiet side street, a brief walk from the Grote Markt. There's just one bedroom, but it's a commodious suite with a stripped-wood floor, a particularly large and comfortable bed and a view of the St-Romboutskathedraal spire. The owners work elsewhere, so arrange access before you arrive; no cards. ❹

Martin's Paterhof Karmelietenstraat 4 ⓣ015 46 46 46, ⓦwww.martinshotels.com. One of a small chain, this deluxe four-star occupies an immaculately and imaginatively renovated nineteenth-century church complete with the original stained-glass windows and neo-Gothic arches. They've shoehorned in seventy-nine rooms divided into five categories from the "Cosy" to the "Exceptional"; in terms of decor, all are über modern. Breakfasts, which are very good, are served in the former choir. ❼

NH Mechelen Korenmarkt 22 ⓣ015 42 03 03 ⓦwww.nh-hotels.com. Proficient and modern chain hotel, with three stars and forty-odd comfortable if somewhat decoratively predictable rooms, all kitted out in shades of brown and cream. ❹

Vé Vismarkt 14 ⓣ015 20 07 55, ⓦwww.hotelve.com. Enjoyable four-star hotel in an intelligently recycled former smoked-fish factory dating from the 1920s. Some thought has gone into the decor, with pride of place going to a large tubular sculpture, and the thirty-four rooms are large, well appointed and decorated in an attractive modern style. The only fly in the ointment is the night-time noise from the square in front – but get a room at the back and all is well. ❼, weekends ❺

The Town

The centre of town is, as ever, the **Grote Markt**, an especially handsome and expansive affair offering a superb view of the cathedral. It's flanked on its eastern side by the **Stadhuis**, whose bizarre and incoherent appearance was partly the responsibility of Margaret of Austria. In 1526, she had the left-hand side of the original building demolished and replaced by what you see today, an ornate arcaded loggia fronting a fluted, angular edifice, to a design by Rombout Keldermans. The plan was to demolish and rebuild the rest of the building in stages, but after her death in 1530 the work was abandoned, leaving Keldermans' extravagance firmly glued to the plain stonework and the simple gables of the fourteenth-century section on the right.

Op Sinjoorke

In front of the Stadhuis is a modern sculpture of **Op Sinjoorke**, the town's mascot, being tossed in a blanket. Once a generalized symbol of male irresponsibility, the doll and its forebears enjoyed a variety of names – *vuilen bras* (unfaithful drunkard), *sotscop* (fool) and *vuilen bruidegom* (disloyal bridegroom) – until the events of 1775 redefined its identity. Every year it was customary for the dummy to be paraded through the streets and tossed up and down in a sheet. In 1775, however, a young man from Antwerp attempted to steal it and was badly beaten for his pains: the people of Mechelen were convinced he was part of an Antwerp plot to rob them of their cherished mascot. The two cities were already fierce commercial rivals, and the incident soured relations even further. Indeed, when news of the beating reached Antwerp, there was sporadic rioting and calls for the city burghers to take some sort of revenge. Refusing to be intimidated, the people of Mechelen derisively renamed the doll after their old nickname for the people of Antwerp – "Op Sinjoorke", from "Signor", a reference to that city's favoured status under earlier Spanish kings. It was sweet revenge for an incident of 1687 that had made Mechelen a laughing stock: staggering home, a drunk had roused the town when he thought he saw a fire in the cathedral. In fact, the "fire" was moonlight, earning the Mechelaars the soubriquet "**Maneblussers**" (Moondousers).

St-Romboutskathedraal

St-Romboutskathedraal (Mon–Sat 8.30am–5.30pm, Sun 2–5.30pm) dominates the town centre just as it was supposed to. It's the cathedral's mighty square **tower**

The bells, the bells

It was during the fourteenth century that **bells** were first used in Flemish cities as a means of regulating the working day, reflecting the development of a wage economy – employers were keen to keep tabs on their employees. Bells also served as a sort of public-address system: pealing bells, for example, announced good news, tolling summoned the citizens to the main square, and a rapid sequence of bells warned of danger. By the early fifteenth century, a short peal marked the hour, and from this developed the **carillon** (*beiaard*), in which the ringing of a set of bells is triggered by the rotation of a large drum with metal pegs; the pegs pull wires attached to the clappers in the bells, just like a giant music box. Later, the mechanics were developed so that the carillon could be played by means of a keyboard, giving the player (*beiaardier*) the chance to improvise.

Carillon playing almost died out in the nineteenth century, when it was dismissed as being too folksy for words, but now it's on the rebound, and several Flemish cities – including Bruges and Mechelen – have their own municipal carillon player. Belgium's finest carillon, a fifteenth-century affair of 49 bells, is housed in Mechelen's cathedral tower and resounds over the town on high days and holidays. There are also regular, hour-long **performances** on Saturdays (11am), Sundays (3pm), and from June through to mid-September on Monday evenings (8.30pm).

that takes the breath away, a wonderful, almost imperial Gothic structure with soaring, canopied pinnacles and extraordinarily long and slender windows. It's matched down below by heavy-duty buttressing, which supports a superb sequence of high-arched pointed windows that encircle the nave and the choir, rising up to the delicate fluting of a stone balustrade.

The construction of the church has not been without its problems. Work began with the draining of the marshes on which it was to be built in 1217, but the money ran out before the tower was erected, and the initial design had to be put on hold until the fifteenth century. In 1451, the Pope obligingly provided the extra funds when he put St Rombout's on a list of specified churches where pilgrims could seek absolution for their sins without visiting Rome. The money rolled in and the tower was completed by 1546 – just before the outbreak of the religious wars that would surely have stymied the whole project. In the last couple of years, this tower, the **St-Rombouttower** (Tues–Sun 10am–6pm, last entry 4.30pm; €7) has been opened to the public with an exhausting 500-step climb leading past assorted bell and carillon chambers to the observation platform right at the top; on a clear day, you can spy the Brussels Atomium (see p.96).

The nave and the transepts

The main **entrance** to the cathedral is just off the Grote Markt. Inside, the thirteenth-century **nave** has all the cloistered elegance of the Brabantine Gothic style, although the original lines are spoiled by an unfortunate series of seventeenth-century statues of the Apostles. Between the arches lurks an extraordinary Baroque **pulpit**, a playful mass of twisted and curled oak dotted with carefully camouflaged animal carvings – squirrels, frogs and snails, a salamander and a pelican. The main scene shows **St Norbert** being thrown from his horse, a narrow escape that convinced this twelfth-century German prince to give his possessions to the poor and dedicate his life to the church.

By the main entrance, the **south transept** displays the cathedral's most distinguished painting, **Anthony van Dyck**'s dramatic *Crucifixion*, which portrays the writhing, muscular bodies of the two thieves in the shadows to either side of the Christ, who is bathed in a white light of wonderful clarity. The painting now forms part of a heavy, marble Baroque altarpiece carved for the Guild of Masons, but it was only installed here after the French revolutionary army razed the church where it was originally displayed.

Across the church, in the chapel next to the **north transept**, is the tomb of Mechelen's **Cardinal Mercier** (1851–1926) plus a plaque, presented by the Church of England, commemorating his part in coordinating the Mechelen Conversations. These investigated the possibility of reuniting the two churches and ran from 1921 up to the time of Mercier's death in 1926, but with little result. In Belgium, Mercier is more often remembered for his staunch opposition to the German occupation of World War I. His pastoral letters, notably "Patriotism and Endurance", proclaimed loyalty to the Belgian king, paid tribute to the soldiers at the front and condemned the invasion as illegal and un-Christian.

Take a look also at the elaborate doors of the **high altar**, which hide the gilt casket containing the remains of St Rombout. They are only opened on major religious festivals, principally during the **Hanswijkprocessie**, held in May, when the reliquary is paraded through the town centre.

The ambulatory

Exhibited in the aisle of the ambulatory are twenty-five **panel paintings** relating the legend of St Rombout. Such devotional series were comparatively common in medieval Flanders, but this is one of the few to have survived, painted by several

The legend of St Rombout

Panel 1 Bishops and priests pray beside the tomb of the newly deceased Bishop of Dublin. Up above, an angel instructs them to select Rombout as his successor.
Panel 2 Rombout preaches to his Irish congregation. In the building in the background, an angel summons him to be a missionary.
Panel 3 Rombout crosses by boat to France, where he restores the sight of a blind man.
Panel 4 Rombout arranges an audience with the Pope so that he can surrender his bishop's ring of office.
Panel 5 Rome. Rombout receives the Pope's blessing for his mission to the heathens.
Panel 6 Back in France, Rombout exorcizes the devil from a madman.
Panel 7 Arriving in Mechelen, Rombout ticks off the locals for dancing on Good Friday – note the bagpipe player. A messenger arrives from the local lord, Count Ado, inviting him to his castle.
Panel 8 The count and countess receive Rombout. In the background, Rombout promises them a son, despite the countess's advanced years.
Panel 9 The countess's baby is christened.
Panel 10 In the background, St Rombout meets St Gommarus of Lier; in the foreground a messenger announces the death of Gommarus.
Panel 11 St Rombout's prayers revive Gommarus; Count Ado presents Rombout with a parcel of land; work begins on the construction of Rombout's first chapel.
Panel 12 Rombout admonishes an adulterous stonemason, whose face is a picture of guilt.
Panel 13 The mason kills Rombout, his workmate picks his pockets, and then they throw the body into the river.
Panel 14 Local Christians recover the body, guided by a celestial light.
Panel 15 St Rombout protects his chapel from Viking attack.
Panel 16 The Vikings are about to sail off, with Gerlindis, a devout nun, among their captives; St Rombout's prayers save her.
Panel 17 At Gerlindis's nunnery, a rooster crows the time for prayer, but one day a fox takes it. Rombout says a prayer and the fox returns the bird unharmed.
Panel 18 In St Rombout's chapel, a priest successfully prays for the return of his sight.
Panel 19 A knight wounded in a hunting-party is carried to St Rombout's chapel, where his health is restored.
Panel 20 As in Panel 19, but this time a knight has been attacked by devils.
Panel 21 Same again, though on this occasion healing comes to three possessed men and a woman with a lame hand.
Panel 22 A Flemish lord gives land to the chapel of St Rombout.
Panel 23 & 24 Battle scenes in which reliquaries of St Rombout bring victory to the Mechelaars.
Panel 25 The Brotherhood of St Rombout honours its patron saint.

unknown artists between 1480 and 1510. As individual works of art, the panel paintings are not perhaps of the highest order, but the cumulative attention to detail – in the true Flemish tradition – is quite remarkable, with all manner of folksy minutiae illuminating what would otherwise be a predictable tale of sacrifice and sanctity. The panels are exhibited in chronological order (from north to south), but they aren't labelled in English at present and neither is their meaning always obvious, hence the explanatory box above. Many of the panels carry a sombre-looking, kneeling man and woman – these were the donors.

As for the ambulatory itself, it's not quite all that it seems: many of the columns are made of wood painted as marble, a **trompe-l'oeil** technique for which Mechelen was once famous.

To St-Janskerk and the Koninklijke Beiaardschool

From the north side of the cathedral, Wollemarkt swerves its way past the refuge of the **Abdij van St-Truiden** (no public access), which sits prettily beside an old algae-covered canal, its picturesque gables once home to the destitute. Almost opposite, now on Goswin de Stassartstraat, an alley called Klapgat ("gossip") threads through to **St-Janskerk** (April–Oct Tues–Sun 1–5pm, Nov–March till 4pm), a fine illustration of the Gothic style dating from the fifteenth century. Inside, almost everything is on the grand scale, from the massive pulpit and the whopping organ through to two large and unusual canons' pews, but it's the Baroque high altarpiece that grabs the attention, a suitably flashy setting for a flashy but wonderful painting – **Rubens'** *Adoration of the Magi*. Painted in 1619, the central panel, after which the triptych is named, is an exquisite example of the artist's use of variegated lighting – and also features his first wife portrayed as the Virgin. The side panels are occasionally rotated, so on the left hand side you'll see either Jesus baptized by John the Baptist or John the Baptist's head on a platter; to the right it's St John on Patmos or the same saint being dipped in boiling oil.

Along the street from St Janskerk is Mechelen's internationally renowned **Koninklijke Beiaardschool** (Royal Carillon School; no public access; Ⓦwww.beiaardschool.be), which attracts students from right around the world. Playing the carillon is, by all accounts, extremely difficult and the diploma course offered here takes no less than six years to complete. Immediately behind the school is the city's main museum, the **Museum Hof van Busleyden**, though this is closed for refurbishment until 2015.

Joods Museum van Deportatie en Verzet

From St-Janskerk, it's a five-minute walk northwest to the **Joods Museum van Deportatie en Verzet**, at Goswin de Stassartstraat 153 (Jewish Museum of Deportation and Resistance; Sun–Thurs 10am–5pm, Fri 10am–1pm; closed Sat; free; Ⓦwww.cicb.be). During the German occupation, Nazi officials chose Mechelen as a staging point for Belgian Jews destined for the concentration camps of eastern Europe. Their reasoning was quite straightforward: most of Belgium's Jews were in either Antwerp or Brussels and Mechelen was halfway between the two.

Today's museum occupies one wing of the old barracks that were adapted by the Gestapo as their principal internment centre. Between 1942 and 1944 over 25,000 Jews passed through its doors; most ended up in Auschwitz and only 1200 survived the war. In a series of well-conceived multilingual displays, the museum tracks through this dreadful episode, beginning with Jewish life in Belgium before the war and continuing with sections on the rise of anti-Semitism, the occupation, the deportations, the concentration camps and liberation. It's designed with older Belgian schoolchildren in mind, so you may share the museum with one or more school parties, but it's still harrowing stuff and some of the exhibits bring a deep chill to the soul, none more so than the pleading postcard thrown from a deportation train. The final section, entitled "Personal Testimonies", is particularly affecting, comprising filmed interviews given by some of the survivors.

South of the Grote Markt

The innocuous **statue** of Margaret of Austria on the south side of the Grote Markt dates from 1849, but it was only moved here from the centre of the square a couple of years ago. Behind the statue stands the **Schepenhuis** (Aldermen's House), a good-looking Gothic structure of 1374 that marks the start of the **Ijzerenleen**, the focus of one of the region's best Saturday **food markets** (8am–1pm), which spreads over into the Grote Markt, Befferstraat and the Veemarkt.

At the far end of Ijzerenleen, turn right down Nauwstraat for the cluster of bars that are the heart of Mechelen's night-time action. Here also a footbridge spans the river, leading over to **Haverwerf** (Oats Wharf), where the old Lamot brewery has been turned into the architecturally unappetizing, very modern **Lamot Congres- en Erfgoedcentrum** (Lamot Conference & Heritage Centre; Ⓦwww.lamot-mechelen.be). Much more appealing are the three old and contrasting facades just a few metres away. On the right is **Het Paradijske** (The Little Paradise), a slender structure with fancy tracery and mullioned windows that takes its name from the Garden of Eden reliefs above the first-floor windows. Next door, the all-timber **De Duiveltjes** (The Little Devils), a rare survivor from the sixteenth century, is also named after its decoration, this time for the carved satyrs above the entrance. Finally, on the left and dating to 1669, is **St-Jozef**, a graceful example of the Baroque merchant's house, where the fluent scrollwork swirls over the top of the gable and camouflages the utilitarian, upper-storey door: trade goods were once pulled up the front of the house by pulley and shoved in here for safekeeping.

Kerk van Onze Lieve Vrouw over de Dijle

The pontoon walkway extending southeast along the river from Haverwerf makes for a pleasant stroll en route to the **Kerk van Onze Lieve Vrouw over de Dijle** (Church of Our Lady across the River Dijle; Tues–Sun 1–5pm, Nov–March till 4pm), a massive pinnacled and turreted affair that was begun in the fifteenth century and finally completed two hundred years later – hence the mix of late Gothic and Baroque features. Apart from its sheer size, the interior is really rather mundane, its mediocrity only redeemed by **Rubens**' *Miraculous Draught of Fishes*, an exquisite triptych painted for the Fishmongers' Guild in 1618 and displayed in the south transept. The central panel has all the usual hallmarks of Rubens in his pomp – note the thick, muscular arms of the fishermen – but it's the glistening and wriggling fish that inspire.

Five minutes' walk away, on the southern edge of the centre at the foot of Hoogstraat, stands the mighty **Brusselpoort**, the only survivor of Mechelen's twelve fourteenth-century gates, its striped brickwork and twin onion domes striking quite a pose.

Eating and drinking

Mechelen's **café** and **restaurant** scene has improved markedly in recent years and, although visitors are hardly overwhelmed with great choices, the town does have a couple of very good and distinctive places. Enjoyable **bars** are thinner on the ground, but there are certainly enough to be getting on with and, while you are here, be sure to try one particular local brew, **Gouden Carolus** (Golden Charles), a delicious dark-brown or blond barley beer once tippled by – or so they say – the Emperor Charles V. The town also boasts a bright new cultural centre, the **Cultuurcentrum Mechelen** (Ⓣ015 29 40 00, Ⓦwww.cultuurcentrummechelen.be), just off the Grote Markt on Minderbroedersgang, which offers a varied programme of theatre, dance and debate.

Cafés, restaurants and bars

Den Akker Nauwstraat 11. Laidback, vaguely New Age bar with an outside terrace overlooking the river. Mon–Sat from 11.30am, Sun from 3pm.

Brasserie de Margriet Bruul 52 Ⓣ015 21 00 17. Popular and very enjoyable brasserie in one wing of a former seminary, though this part of the building has been rehashed with standard-issue modern furnishings, so only the odd flourish – like the mullioned windows – gives a hint as to what went before. The menu covers all the Flemish bases, but there are a few surprises, notably a local delicacy, the *Mechelse Koekoek* (Mechelen cuckoo), a particularly succulent variety of chicken. The cuckoo costs €18, other mains about the same, but daily specials are as little as €10. Courtyard eating in the summertime, too. Mon–Sat 9am–10/11pm.

De Gouden Vis Nauwstraat 7. As for *Den Akker* (see above), but a couple of doors along and with ancient chandeliers and a slightly groovier clientele. Mon–Fri from noon, Sat from 10am, Sun from 3pm.

Lord Nelson Wollemarkt 8. One of several bars lining up beside the cathedral on Wollemarkt, this musters up a neat package of ersatz nautical decoration plus several fine beers – the dark and malty Corsendonk Pater is recommended.

De Met Grote Markt 29 ⓣ015 20 68 81. There are lots of restaurants on the Grote Markt, but this is the pick, a bright, modern place offering a good range of Flemish dishes geared to the seasons and using, as often as not, local produce. The daily specials are especially tasty. Main courses €18–23. Mon–Sat noon–10.30pm.

Den Stillen Genieter Nauwstraat 9. This curious bar, "The Silent Hedonist", is rather like a dusty, ramshackle cave, where the host presides over several hundred types of beer. No gentrification allowed. Daily from 2pm till late.

Around Mechelen: Fort Breendonk

Located about 12km west of Mechelen, **Fort Breendonk** (daily 9.30am–5.30pm; €7; ⓦwww.breendonk.be) was built as part of the circle of fortifications that ringed early twentieth-century Antwerp, but became notorious as a Gestapo interrogation centre during World War II. The fort's low concrete buildings were encased in a thick layer of sand until the Germans had this carted away by their prisoners in 1940. After the war, Breendonk was preserved as a national memorial in honour of the four thousand men and women who suffered or perished in its dark, dank tunnels and cells. As you might expect, it's a powerful, disturbing place to visit, with a clearly marked tour taking you through the SS tribunal room, poignantly graffitied cells, the prisoners' barrack room and the bunker that was used as a torture chamber. There's also a museum dealing with the German occupation of Belgium, prison life and the postwar trial of Breendonk SS criminals and their collaborators. Other displays explore the origins of Fascism and the development of the Nazi concentration camps.

By car, Fort Breendonk is a stone's throw from the A12 highway linking Antwerp and Brussels – just follow the signs. To get here from Mechelen **by public transport**, take the train to **Willebroek** (hourly; 10min) and the fort is on the edge of town, a 1500-metre walk west from the station along Dendermondsesteenweg.

Leuven

Less than half an hour by train from both Mechelen and Brussels, **LEUVEN** offers an easy and enjoyable day-trip from either. The town is the seat of Belgium's oldest university, whose students give the place a lively, informal air – and sustain lots of inexpensive bars and cafés. There are also a couple of notable medieval buildings, the splendid **Stadhuis** and the imposing **St-Pieterskerk**, which is home to three wonderful early Flemish paintings, and in the **Oude Markt** Leuven possesses one of the region's most personable squares. Otherwise, the centre is not much more than an undistinguished tangle of streets with a lot of the new and few remnants of the old. Then again, it's something of a miracle that any of Leuven's ancient buildings have survived at all, since the town suffered badly in both world wars: in 1914 much of Leuven was razed during the first German offensive and thirty years later the town was heavily bombed. If you stay a while, you may also pick up on the division between town and gown; some of the students see themselves as champions of the Flemish cause, but the locals seem largely unconvinced.

The history of the **university** isn't a particularly happy one, though everything began rosily enough. Founded in 1425, it soon became one of Europe's most prestigious educational establishments: the cartographer Mercator was a student here and it was here that the religious reformer Erasmus (1466–1536) founded the

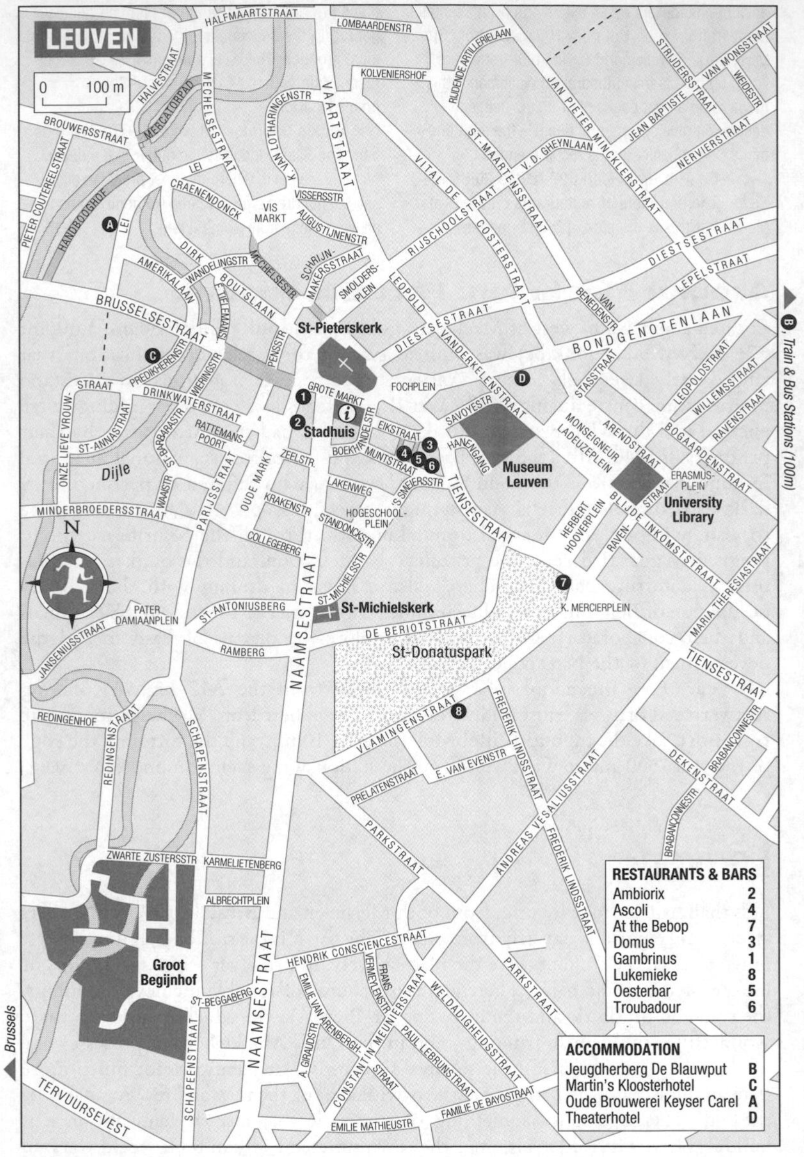

Collegium Trilingue for the study of Hebrew, Latin and Greek, as the basis of a liberal (rather than Catholic) education. However, in response to the rise of Lutheranism, the authorities changed tack, insisting on strict Catholic orthodoxy and driving the university into educational retreat. In 1797 the French suppressed the university, and then, after the defeat of Napoleon, when Belgium fell under Dutch rule, William I replaced it with a Philosophical College – one of many blatantly anti-Catholic measures which fuelled the Belgian revolution. Re-established after independence as a bilingual Catholic institution, the university became a hotbed of **Flemish Catholicism**, and for much of this century French and Flemish speakers were locked in a bitter nationalist dispute. In 1970 a separate, French-speaking university was founded at Louvain-la-Neuve, just south of Brussels – a decision that propelled Leuven into its present role as a bastion of Flemish thinking, wielding considerable influence over the region's political and economic elite.

Arrival, information and accommodation

It's an easy ten-minute walk west along Bondgenotenlaan from the **train** and adjacent **bus station** to the Grote Markt, the site of the Stadhuis and St-Pieterskerk. The **tourist office** is round the side of the Stadhuis at Naamsestraat 1 (Mon–Sat 10am–5pm; March–Oct also Sun 10am–5pm; ⓣ016/20 30 20, ⓦwww.visitleuven.be). Most of Leuven's **accommodation** is anchored at the cheaper end of the market, including a hostel and a number of very basic one-star hotels, but there are a few more pleasant places, too.

Hotels, hostel and a B&B

Jeugdherberg De Blauwput Martelarenlaan 11A ⓣ016 63 90 62, ⓦwww.leuven-hostel.com. A fair old hoof from the city centre – it's just on the far side of the train station – this HI hostel offers bunks in two- to six-bed en-suite rooms. There's a bar, café, internet access and a garden. Beds €20–25. ❶

Martin's Kloosterhotel Predikherenstraat 22 ⓣ016 21 31 41, ⓦwww.martins-hotels.com. Part of a medium-sized chain but the town's most distinctive hotel by a long chalk, this smooth and polished place occupies an immaculately renovated old mansion complete with mullioned windows and handsome brick gables. The forty-odd rooms are tastefully decorated, with beiges and creams predominant, and the location is central, too. ❻

Oude Brouwerei Keyser Carel Lei 15 ⓣ016 22 14 81, ⓦwww.keysercarel.be. Chichi B&B in a rambling old mansion, parts of which date back to the seventeenth century. Three neat and trim modern guest rooms, all en suite, plus an exercise area and relaxing views over the gardens. ❺

Theaterhotel Bondgenotenlaan 20 ⓣ016 22 28 19, ⓦwww.theaterhotel.be. In a grand nineteenth-century building, this agreeable three-star hotel has twenty-one large and pleasantly appointed modern guest rooms. ❼

The Town

The centre of Leuven is marked by two adjacent squares, the more easterly of which is the **Fochplein**, basically a road junction whose one noteworthy feature is the modern **Fons Sapientiae**, a wittily cynical fountain of a student literally being brainwashed by the book he is reading. Next door, the wedge-shaped **Grote Markt** is Leuven's architectural high spot, dominated by two notable late Gothic buildings – St-Pieterskerk and the Stadhuis. The **Stadhuis** is the more flamboyant of the two, an extraordinarily light and lacy confection, crowned by soaring pinnacles and a dainty, high-pitched roof studded with dormer windows. It's a beautiful building, though it is slightly spoiled by the clumsiness of its nineteenth century statues, representing everything from important citizens to virtues and vices. In contrast, the niche bases supporting the statues are exuberantly medieval, depicting biblical subjects in a free, colloquial style and adorned by a panoply of grotesques.

St-Pieterskerk

Across the square, **St-Pieterskerk** (Tues–Fri 10am–5pm, Sat 10am–4.30pm & Sun 2–5pm; mid-March to mid-Oct also Mon 10am–5pm) is a rambling, heavily buttressed late Gothic pile whose stumpy western facade defeated its architects. Work began on the present church in the 1420s and continued until the start of the sixteenth century when the Romanesque towers of the west facade, the last remaining part of the earlier church, were pulled down to make way for a grand design by Joos Matsys, the brother of the artist Quinten. It didn't work out – the foundations proved too weak – and finally, another hundred years on, the unfinished second-attempt towers were capped, creating the truncated, asymmetrical versions that rise above the front entrance today.

Inside, the church is distinguished by its soaring nave whose enormous composite pillars frame a fabulous **rood screen**, an intricately carved piece of stonework surmounted by a wooden Christ. The nave's Baroque **pulpit** is also striking, a weighty wooden extravagance which shows **St Norbert** being thrown off his horse by lightning, a dramatic scene set beneath spiky palm trees. It was this brush with death that persuaded Norbert, a twelfth-century German noble, to abandon his worldly ways and dedicate himself to the church, on whose behalf he founded a devout religious order, the Premonstratensian Canons, in 1120.

The ambulatory

The ambulatory accommodates the **Schatkamer** (Treasury; same times as church; €3), whose three key paintings date from the fifteenth century. There's a copy of Rogier van der Weyden's marvellous triptych, the *Descent from the Cross*, and two of the few surviving paintings by Weyden's apprentice **Dieric Bouts** (c.1415–75), who worked for most of his life in Leuven, ultimately becoming the city's official painter and an influential artist in his own right. Bouts' carefully contrived paintings are inhabited by stiff and slender figures in religious scenes that are almost totally devoid of action – a frozen narrative designed to stir contemplation rather than strong emotion. His use of colour and attention to detail are quite superb, especially in the exquisite landscapes that act as a backdrop to much of his work. Of the two **triptychs** on display here, the gruesome *Martyrdom of St Erasmus*, which has the executioners extracting the saint's entrails with a winch, is less interesting than the *Last Supper*, showing Christ and his disciples in a Flemish dining room, with the (half-built) Stadhuis just visible through the left-hand window; the two men standing up as well as the couple peeping through the service hatch are the rectors of the fraternity who commissioned the work. It was customary for Judas to be portrayed in a yellow robe, the colour of hate and cowardice, but Bouts broke with tradition and made him almost indistinguishable from the others – he's the one with his face in shadow and his hand on his left hip. The change of emphasis, away from the betrayal to the mystery of the Eucharist, is continued on the side panels: to the left Abraham is offered bread and wine above a Jewish Passover; to the right the Israelites gather manna and below the prophet Elijah receives angelic succour.

Museum Leuven

Big, flash and really rather groovy, the **Museum Leuven** occupies a striking modern building and the adjacent old mansion at Leopold Vanderkelenstraat 28 (Tues–Sun 11am–6pm, Thurs till 10pm; €7; Ⓦ www.mleuven.be). There are three main floors here, two devoted to temporary exhibitions, often of modern art, and one – Floor 0 – to the permanent collection, and the museum also hosts gigs and special events. The permanent collection includes piecemeal displays devoted to the likes of medieval sculpture, vestments, porcelain, silver and glassware, plus a good showing for Belgian nineteenth-century sculptors and painters, especially Constantin Meunier (for more on whom, see p.94). There's also a room full of medieval paintings, most memorably two works by **Rogier van der Weyden**, an exquisite *Seven Sacraments* and a *Holy Trinity*, though this has, at some point, actually been altered: if you look closely at Christ's shoulder, you'll spot a pair of bird's feet. Originally, these were the feet of the dove that represented the Holy Spirit, but somewhere along the line someone decided that God the Father and the Son would suffice.

To the Groot Begijnhof

The **Oude Markt**, a large cobblestoned square just to the south of the Grote Markt, is the boisterous core of Leuven's nightlife, its assorted bars and cafés occupying a handsome set of tall gabled houses that mostly date from the nineteenth century. To the immediate east of Oude Markt, Naamsestraat leads south to the **Groot Begijnhof**, a labyrinthine enclave of tall and rather austere red-brick houses tucked away beside the River Dijle. Once home to around three hundred *begijns* – women living as nuns without taking vows – the Begijnhof was bought by the university in 1962, since when its mostly seventeenth-century buildings have been painstakingly restored as student residences, and very nice they are too.

Eating and drinking

With all those students to feed and water, Leuven offers an almost bewildering range of cafés, restaurants and bars in which to exercise your stomach and test your liver – and there's a particular concentration among the old gabled houses of the **Oude Markt**, with a sea of people sitting out in the square when it's warm enough. Leuven is also just 15km south of the small town of **Werchter**, which plays host to Belgium's most famous open-air music event, the four-day **Rock Werchter** (Ⓦwww.rockwerchter.be), featuring top-ranking international stars. It's held over the last weekend of June or the first weekend of July, with special festival buses taking fans from Leuven train station straight to the site.

Restaurants and bars

Ambiorix Oude Markt 3. There was a time when all the bars on this square attracted students by the score, but today the scene is more varied – and this is one of the last student bars left. Rough-and-ready decor. Daily from noon.

Ascoli Muntstraat 17 Ⓣ016/23 93 64. Well-regarded Italian restaurant offering all the classics and then some. Mains from €12, pizzas from €8. Daily except Thurs noon–10.30pm.

At the Bebop Tiensestraat 82 Ⓣ016 20 86 04, Ⓦwww.atthebebop.be. Mixed bag of a place with a café, restaurant and a dancefloor. Frequent live gigs, mostly jazz and indie. Mon–Fri 4pm–4am, Sat 5pm–5am, Sun 8pm–2am.

Domus Tiensestraat 8. If not the best bar in town, then certainly the most distinctive, spread over two large floors with ancient beamed ceilings, old bygones on the walls and a small brewery out the back. Offers an excellent range of ales as well as a competent bar menu. Daily except Mon 9am–1am.

Gambrinus Grote Markt 13. The food may not be inspiring, but this handsome old café, with its 1890s leather banquettes, chandeliers and murals, beats all its rivals for decor. Mon–Sat from 10am.

Lukemieke Vlamingenstraat 55 Ⓣ016 22 97 05. Long-established vegetarian café with a good line in daily specials at around €9. Pleasant garden terrace for outside eating, too. Mon–Fri noon–2pm & 6–8.30pm.

Oesterbar Muntstraat 23 Ⓣ016 29 06 00. This smart place offers an international menu, but the big deal is seafood in general, and oysters in particular. Main courses hover around €30, oysters, in various formations, are €10–20. Mon, Tues & Fri noon–2.30pm & 6–10.30pm, Sat 6–10.30pm.

Troubadour Tiensestraat 32 Ⓣ016 22 50 65. Formal, even slightly old-fashioned restaurant, offering all the Belgian classics as well as an excellent range of seafood. Mussels, served every which way, are the house speciality. Mains from €15. Daily except Tues 11.30am–3pm & 5.30–11pm.

Hasselt

HASSELT, the capital of the province of **Limburg**, is a busy, modern town that acts as the administrative centre for the surrounding industrial region. A pleasant but unremarkable place, the roughly circular city centre fans out from a series of small interlocking squares, with surprisingly few old buildings as evidence of its medieval foundation. To compensate for this lack of obvious appeal, the local authority has spent millions of euros on lavish and imaginative prestige projects, from an excellent range of indoor and outdoor sports facilities to a cultural complex that aims to attract some of the world's finest performers. The best time to visit is in late August, when Hasselt hosts one of Belgium's biggest rock festivals, the three-day **Pukkelpop** (Ⓦwww.pukkelpop.be), which has something to suit just about everyone, from house and heavy metal to R&B.

There's nothing special to look at in Hasselt itself, though the **Gerechtshof** (Court of Justice) on Havermarkt, in between the train station and the Grote Markt, is housed in the town's one surprise – a handsome Art Deco building, whose elegant exterior is topped off by a delightful elliptical tower-cum-turret. In addition, Hasselt possesses no fewer than six **museums**, though ordinary mortals should settle – at most – for the best two. The most interesting is the **Nationaal Jenevermuseum**, at Witte Nonnenstraat 19 (Nov–March Tues–Fri 10am–5pm, Sat & Sun 1–5pm; April–Oct Tues–Sun 10am–5pm, plus Mon 10am–5pm in July & Aug; €3.50; Ⓦwww.jenevermuseum.be). Sited in a restored nineteenth-century distillery, it shows how jenever – a type of gin – is made and details the history of local production, with a free drink thrown in. To get here, head north from the Grote Markt down Hoogstraat/Demerstraat and watch for the turning on the right just before you reach the inner ring road. A left turn off Demerstraat opposite Witte Nonnenstraat brings you instead to the **Stedelijk Modemuseum**, Gasthuisstraat 11 (Nov–March Tues–Fri 10am–5pm, Sat & Sun 1–5pm; April–Oct Tues–Sun 10am–5pm; €5; Ⓦwww.modemuseumhasselt.be), with displays on the history of fashion from 1830 to the present.

Practicalities

From Hasselt's **train** and adjoining **bus station**, it's a ten-minute walk east to the Grote Markt: turn right out of the train station and proceed down Stationsplein/Bampslaan to the inner ring road; here, cross the road, veer to the right and follow Ridder Portmansstraat and its continuation, Havermarkt. The town's **tourist office** is about 150m north of the Grote Markt, located down a side street off Hoogstraat at Lombaardstraat 3 (Mon–Fri 9am–5pm, Sat 10am–5pm; April–Oct also Sun 10am–2pm; Ⓣ011 23 95 40, Ⓦwww.hasselt.eu).

Of the town's several **hotels**, two of the better choices are the *Hassotel*, St-Jozefsstraat 10 (Ⓣ011 23 06 55, Ⓦwww.hassotel.be; ④), a well-equipped modern place with Art Deco flourishes about five minutes' walk southeast from the Grote Markt – take Maastrichterstraat and turn first right; and *the Radisson Blu*, in a large tower block nearby at Torenplein 8 (Ⓣ011 77 00 00, Ⓦwww.radissonblu.com; ⑤).

Hasselt prides iteslf on its **restaurants**, with several of the best strung along **Zuivelmarkt**, a short walk from the Grote Markt: head north along Hoogstraat, hang a right on Botermarkt and Zuivelmarkt is on the left at the end. Options here include *De Goei Goesting*, Zuivelmarkt 18 (Ⓣ011 32 52 82; daily 8.30am–10.30pm), a chic little café-restaurant that serves Italian and Belgian dishes with élan (main courses from €16); and the cosy *De Karakol*, next door at Zuivelmarkt 16 (Ⓣ011 22 78 78; Tues–Sun noon–2pm & 6–11pm), where the main event is the seafood (from €20). Alternatively, there are lots of **café-bars** on the Grote Markt, notably the popular *Drugstore*, with a wide range of snacks served below a facade plastered with neon beer signs.

Tongeren and Zoutleeuw

Beginning south of Hasselt, the **Haspengouw** is an expanse of gently undulating land that fills out the southern part of the province of **Limburg**, its fertile soils especially suited to **fruit growing**. The area is at its prettiest during cherry-blossom time, but otherwise the scenery is really rather routine, a description that applies in equal measure to many of the Haspengouw's towns and villages. The main exceptions are **Tongeren**, whose small-town charms and enjoyable range of historic monuments make it well worth a detour, and pocket-sized **Zoutleeuw**, whose splendid, pre-Reformation St-Leonarduskerk somehow managed to avoid the attentions of both the Protestants and the Napoleonic army.

As regards public transport, there are regular **trains** from Hasselt to Tongeren, but to get to Zoutleeuw you'll need to catch a **bus** from Sint Truiden train station.

Tongeren

TONGEREN, about 20km southeast of Hasselt, is a small and amiable market town on the border of Belgium's language divide. It's also – and this is its main claim to fame – the oldest town in Belgium, built on the site of a Roman camp that guarded the road to Cologne. Its early history was plagued by misfortune – it was destroyed by the Franks and razed by the Vikings – but it did prosper during the Middle Ages in a modest sort of way as a dependency of the bishops of Liège. Nowadays, it's hard to imagine a more relaxing town, quiet for most of the week except on Sunday mornings (from 7am), when the area around Leopoldwal and the Veemarkt is taken over by the stalls of a vast **flea and antiques market**, one of the country's largest.

Arrival, information and accommodation

From Tongeren's **train** and adjoining **bus station**, it's a five- to ten-minute walk west to the Grote Markt. The town's **tourist office** is in the Julianus Shoppingcenter, off Maastrichterstraat (April–Sept Mon–Fri 8.30am–noon & 1–5pm, Sat & Sun 9.30am–5pm; Oct–March Mon–Fri 8.30am–noon & 1–5pm, Sat & Sun 10am–4pm; ⓣ012 39 02 55, ⓦwww.tongeren.be). They operate a free **bike rental** scheme for visitors who stay the night here – a network of cycle trails crisscrosses the surrounding countryside with the most rewarding target being St-Leonarduskerk in Zoutleeuw (see p.247), though this is a good couple of hours (30km) away. As for **accommodation**, Tongeren has two recommendable hotels and a hostel.

Hotels

Ambiotel Veemarkt 2 ⓣ012 26 29 50, ⓦwww.ambiotel.be. Modern, three-star hotel with twenty-two spacious rooms that somehow manages to be quite beguiling – it's not the decor, which is routine, but the small-town flavour of the place. ❹

Eburon de Schiervelstraat 10 ⓣ012 23 01 99, ⓦwww.eburonhotel.be. New kid on the accommodation block, this boutique hotel has lots of knicks and knacks, from flatscreen TVs to rainforest showers. The design is firmly modernist with acres of white and grey intercepted by streaks of lilac and mauve, all shoehorned into a medieval building that started out as a convent. ❹

Jeugdherberg Begeinhof St-Ursulastraat 1 ⓣ012 39 13 70, ⓦwww.vjh.be. Designed with groups in mind, this HI hostel has over seventy beds in four- to twelve-berth rooms, plus a communal lounge, a bar and internet access. Occupies a creatively modernized older building on the edge of the Begijnhof. Breakfast is included in the overnight rate with beds costing €15–16 per person. ❶

The Onze Lieve Vrouwebasiliek

Shadowing the Grote Markt, the mostly Gothic **Onze Lieve Vrouwebasiliek** (Basilica of Our Lady; daily 9am–5pm) towers over the town with an impressive, symmetrical elegance, its assorted gargoyles, elaborate pinnacles and intricate tracery belying its piecemeal construction: it's the eleventh- to sixteenth-century outcome of an original fourth-century foundation, which was the first church north of the Alps to be dedicated to the Virgin. Still very much in use, the yawning interior, with its high, vaulted nave, has preserved an element of Catholic mystery, its holiest object a bedecked, medieval, walnut statue of Our Lady of Tongeren – "**Mariabeeld**" – which stands in the transept surrounded by candles and overhung by a gaudy canopy.

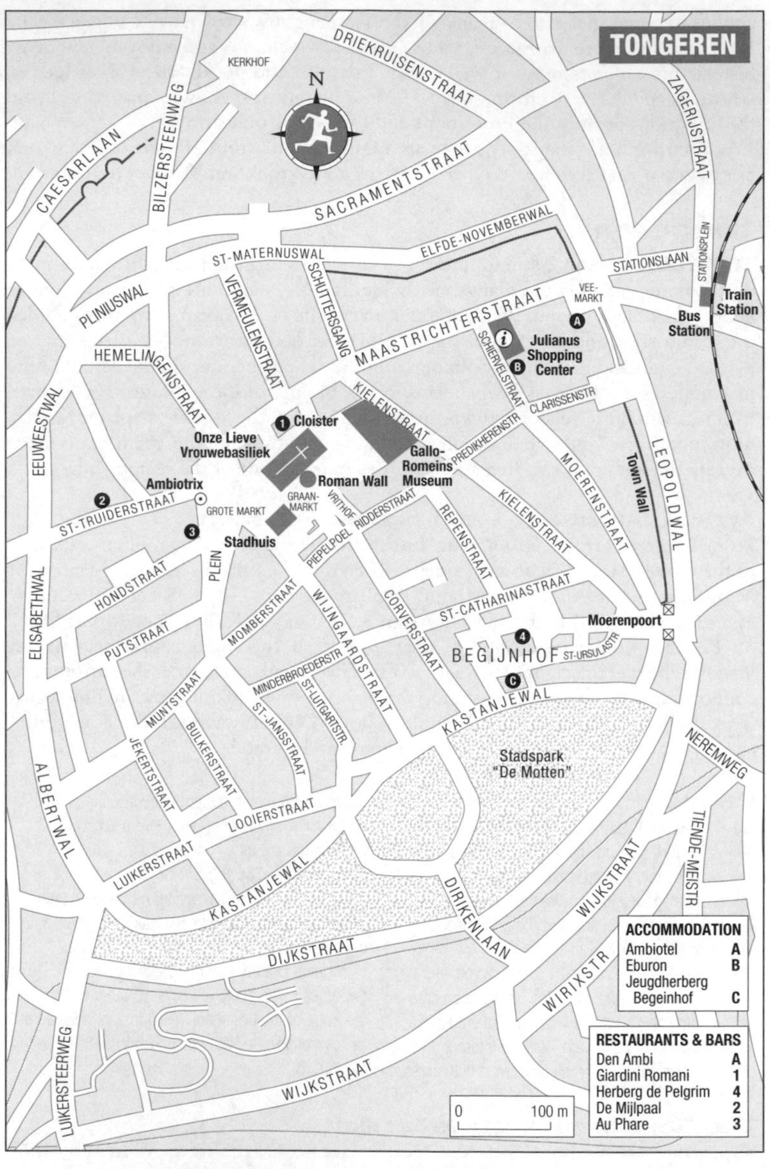

At the back of the church is the **Schatkamer** (Treasury; April–Sept Mon 1.30–5pm, Tues–Sun 10am–noon & 1.30–5pm; €2.50), one of the region's most interesting, crowded with reliquaries, monstrances and reliquary shrines from as early as the tenth century. Three artefacts stand out – a beautiful sixth-century Merovingian buckle; a pious, haunting eleventh-century *Head of Christ*; and an intricate, bejewelled, thirteenth-century *Reliquary Shrine of the Martyrs of Trier*, celebrating a large group of German Christians killed at the hands of the Romans in the third century AD.

The Gallo-Romeins Museum

Beside the church, in the middle of Graanmarkt, a small part of **Roman Tongeren** has been carefully excavated, principally the remains of a section of the fourth-century city wall: the masonry you can see actually covers the remains of a luxurious third-century villa, evidence that the city was shrinking – and its inhabitants becoming fearful – as the Roman Empire disintegrated. A few metres away, the **Gallo-Romeins Museum** (Tues–Fri 9am–5pm, Sat & Sun 10am–6pm; €7; Ⓦwww.gallo-romeinsmuseum.be) occupies a large, beetling concrete building, an imposing setting for an ambitious attempt to make the most of the town's Roman heritage. Inside, a series of well-considered displays track through Tongeren's early history, beginning with the region's prehistoric settlers and continuing with Rome's first attempts to subdue the area, and with substantial sections on life in Roman Tongeren.

The rest of the town

On the west side of the Grote Markt stands the haughty **statue of Ambiorix**, with his tumbling locks, bushy moustache and winged helmet. Erected in the middle of the nineteenth century, the statue commemorates a local chieftain who defeated the Romans here in 54 BC, but whatever he looked like, he didn't look much like this, his "noble savage" visage owing more to Belgian nationalism than historical accuracy.

Also on the Grote Markt is the eighteenth-century **Stadhuis**, whose graceful lines are nicely balanced by an external staircase, the whole caboodle imitative of the town hall in Liège. From here it's a five-minute walk to the pretty cottages and terraced houses of the **Begijnhof**. Finally, just to the east of the Begijnhof is the **Moerenpoort**, one of Tongeren's six medieval gates and now marking the southern limit of the town's popular Sunday antique and flea market.

Eating and drinking

For a small town, Tongeren does quite well for **restaurants**, though the **bar** scene is a bit limited.

Den Ambi Veemarkt 2 ⓣ012 26 29 50. Modern café-restaurant, where the home cooking is really very tasty, the seafood a treat; reckon on €18 for a main course. Part of the *Ambiotel* (see p.245). Daily 9am–11pm, kitchen till 10pm.

Giardini Romani Maastrichterstraat 17 ⓣ012 23 04 85. A traditional, even old-fashioned, Italian restaurant, which covers all the classics, though its forte is pizza; mains average €15, pizzas €12. Mon, Tues, Thurs, Fri & Sun noon–2.30pm & 5.30–10.30pm, Sat 5.30–10.30pm.

Herberg de Pelgrim Brouwersstraat 9. The best café-bar in town, this lovely old place occupies charmingly antique wood-beamed premises in the Begijnhof, and does a good line in pancakes. Wed–Sun 11am–11pm, kitchen closes 9.30pm.

De Mijlpaal St-Truiderstraat 25 ⓣ012 26 42 77. Smart and highly regarded restaurant where the menu is international, the tendency nouvelle. Particularly strong on seafood, with main courses averaging €25–30. Daily except Wed & Thurs noon–2pm & 7–9pm, closed Sat lunchtimes.

Au Phare Grote Markt 21. This old bar is something of an acquired taste: nothing seems to have changed here for decades – as of yore, there are ornamental plates on the pelmet and rugs on the tables. The beer menu is wide-ranging and, if you're really lucky, you'll get Jim Reeves on the sound system rather than Engelbert Humperdinck; who knows how much longer the place will survive.

Zoutleeuw

In a sleepy corner of Brabant, the hamlet of **ZOUTLEEUW**, some 30km west of Tongeren – and 7km west of Sint Truiden train station – was a busy and prosperous cloth town from the thirteenth to the fifteenth centuries. Thereafter, its economy slipped into a long, slow decline whose final act came three hundred years later when it was bypassed by the main Brussels–Liège road. The village has one claim to fame, the rambling, irregularly towered and turreted **St-Leonarduskerk** (April–Sept

Tues–Sun 2–5pm; Oct Sun 2–5pm; €2), whose magnificently intact Gothic interior is crammed with the accumulated treasures of several hundred years, being the only major church in the country to have escaped the attentions of both the Calvinists and the revolutionary French. The church is devoted to the French hermit St Leonard, whose medieval popularity was based upon the enthusiasm of returning Crusaders, who regarded him as the patron saint of prisoners.

The church's tall and slender, light and airy **nave** is dominated by a wrought-iron, sixteenth-century double-sided image of the Virgin, suspended from the ceiling, and by the huge fifteenth-century wooden cross hanging in the choir arch behind it. The side chapels are packed with works of religious art, including an intricate altar and retable of St Anna to the right of the entrance in the second chapel of the south side aisle, and a fearsome St George and the Dragon in the Chapel of Our Lady on the opposite side of the nave. The **north transept** is dominated by a huge stone sacramental tower, nine tiers of elaborate stonework stuffed with some two hundred statues and carved by Cornelis Floris, architect of Antwerp's town hall, between 1550 and 1552. The **ambulatory**, much darker and more intimate than the nave, is lined with an engaging series of medieval wooden sculptures, most notably a captive St Leonard with his hands chained. There's also a figure of St Florentius, the patron saint of tailors, holding an enormous pair of scissors; and a thirteenth-century statue of St Catherine of Alexandria, shown merrily stomping on the Roman Emperor Maxentius, who had her put to death.

Practicalities

Buses from Sint Truiden train station (Mon–Sat every 1–2hr; 20min) drop passengers in the centre of Zoutleeuw, metres from both St-Leonarduskerk and the sixteenth-century Stadhuis, which is home to the **tourist office** (April–Sept Tues–Fri 10am–noon & 1–4pm, Sat & Sun till 5pm; Oct–March Tues–Fri 10am–noon & 2–4pm; ⓣ011 78 12 88, ⓦwww.zoutleeuw.be). For something to **eat**, the *Restaurant Pannenhuis*, near the church at Grote Markt 25 (ⓣ011 78 50 02, ⓦwww.pannenhuiszoutleeuw.be; Thurs–Sat 6–9.30pm, Sun noon–2pm & 6–9pm), is a smart little place decorated in traditional style that does a good line in Flemish cuisine; mains start at €18.

Travel details

Trains

ⓦwww.b-rail.be

Antwerp to: Amsterdam (hourly; 2hr); Bruges (2 hourly; 1hr 20min); Brussels (every 20min; 40min); Ghent (every 20min; 50min); Hasselt (hourly, Sat & Sun every 2hr; 1hr 30min); Lier (every 15min; 15min); Mechelen (every 20min; 20min).

Hasselt to: Antwerp (hourly, Sat & Sun every 2hr; 1hr 30min); Leuven (2 hourly, Sat & Sun every hour; 50min); Liège (hourly; 1hr); Lier (hourly; 1hr 15min); Sint Truiden (hourly; 15min); Tongeren (hourly; 20min).

Leuven to: Brussels (every 30min, Sat & Sun hourly; 25min); Hasselt (2 hourly, Sat & Sun every hour; 50min); Mechelen (every 30min, Sat & Sun hourly; 25min).

Lier to: Antwerp (every 15min; 15min); Hasselt (hourly; 1hr 15min); Mechelen (hourly, Sat & Sun every 2hr; 15min).

Mechelen to: Antwerp (every 20min; 20min); Brussels (every 20min; 20min); Leuven (every 30min, Sat & Sun hourly; 25min); Lier (hourly, Sat & Sun every 2hr; 15min).

Tongeren to: Hasselt (hourly; 20min); Liège (hourly; 30min).

Buses

ⓦwww.delijn.be

Sint Truiden train station to: Zoutleeuw (Mon–Sat every 1–2hr; 20min).

Hainaut and Wallonian Brabant

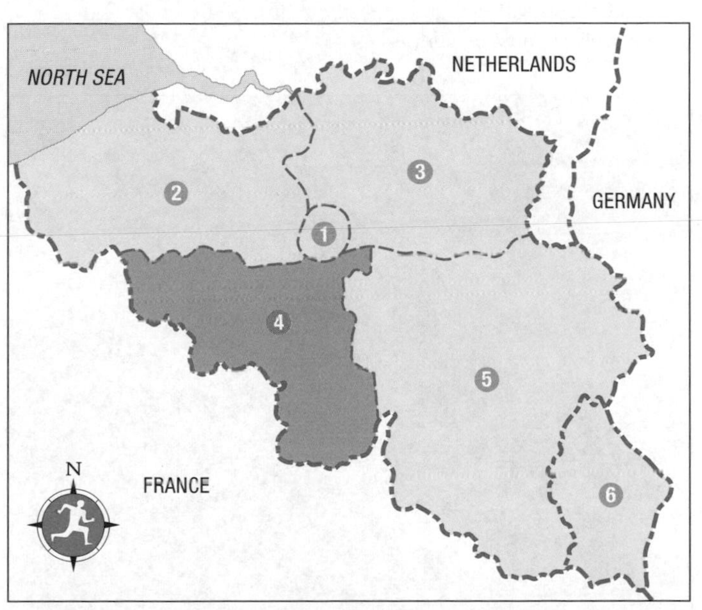

CHAPTER 4

Highlights

* **Cathédrale Notre-Dame, Tournai** One of the most stunning cathedrals in the whole of Belgium. See p.256
* **Grand Hornu – and Musée des Arts Contemporains** A converted mining complex whose industrial architecture frames a first-rate contemporary art museum. See p.263
* **Binche Carnival** Probably the liveliest, most colourful carnival in the country. See p.266
* **Abbaye de Villers** The ruins of this Cistercian abbey comprise one of the region's most evocative sights. See p.268
* **Chimay** A charming country town with a picture-postcard Grand-Place and enjoyable country walks. See p.275

▲ Abbaye de Villers

4

Hainaut and Wallonian Brabant

South of Brussels, the western reaches of **Wallonia** comprise the province of **Hainaut** and the French-speaking portion of Brabant, **Brabant Wallon**. The area has its beauty spots, with plenty of rolling farmland and wooded hills dotted across the entire region, but industry sets the general tone, especially between Mons and Charleroi, where the landscape is puckered with grassed-over slag heaps from the region's coal-mining heyday and the towns are for the most part functional and not very alluring. In the western part of the province, close to the French border, **Tournai** is something of a highlight – once part of France, and now a vibrant, unpretentious town with a number of decent museums, some good restaurants and a magnificent cathedral. East of Tournai, the town of **Mons** is also an agreeable place – and home to a fine church – but its appeal is more in its ebullient street life and hilltop setting, and its usefulness as a base for seeing some of the region's more scattered attractions. Within easy striking distance of both Mons and Tournai are several châteaux – of which **Beloeil** is the grandest and **Attre** the most elegant – and other more workaday leftovers form the area's industrial past. To the east, **Binche** is a humdrum place best known for its explosive February carnival (and its carnival museum, open all year). **Nivelles** is the principal town of Brabant Wallon, and boasts another Romanesque church in its abbey of Ste-Gertrude, while the elegiac ruins of the **Abbaye de Villers**, on the edge of the town of **Villers-la-Ville**, lie in a wooded valley just a few kilometres beyond.

To the south, the industrial and engineering centre of **Charleroi** is the biggest city in Hainaut by a long chalk, and few would call it pretty. But it is gallantly attempting to reinvent itself, and there are worse places to spend some time; it also has a couple of worthwhile attractions on its southern outskirts in its excellent museum of photography and the mining museum of Bois de Cazier. South of Charleroi, the rural **Botte du Hainaut** is actually an extension of the Ardennes and is named for its shape as it juts boot-like into France; most of the "boot" is part of Hainaut, but it also incorporates a narrow slice of Namur province, which for touring purposes we've included in this chapter. Largely bypassed by the Industrial Revolution, the area is a quiet corner of the country, its undulating farmland and forests dotted with the smallest of country towns. Among them, **Chimay**, with its castle and pretty old centre, is the most diverting, while **Couvin** is also fairly picturesque, and is well endowed with facilities for holidaymakers, since hundreds of vacationing Belgians

4

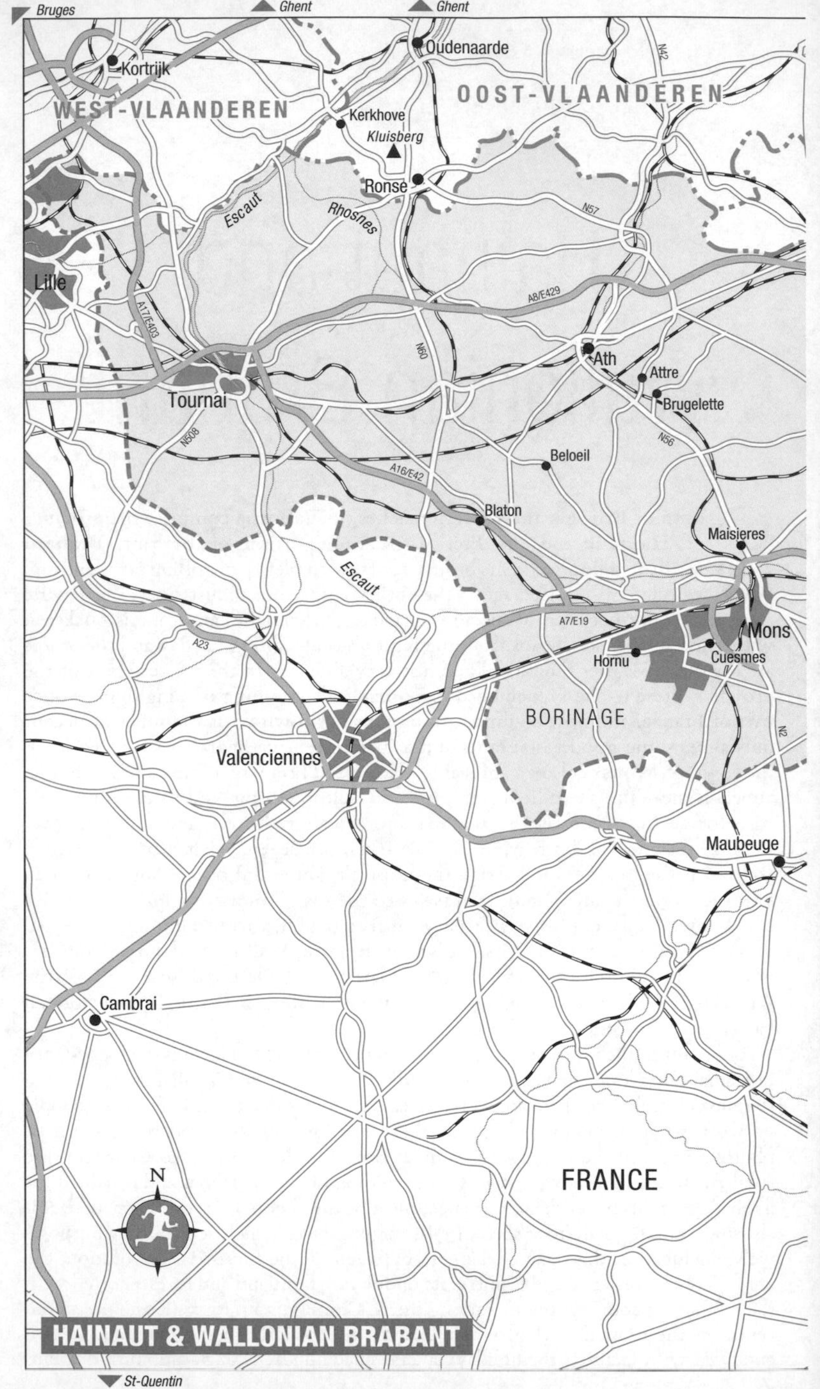
Bruges
Ghent
Ghent
Kortrijk
Oudenaarde
N42
WEST-VLAANDEREN
OOST-VLAANDEREN
Kerkhove
Kluisberg
Ronse
Escaut
Rhosnes
N57
Lille
A17/E403
A8/E429
N60
Ath
Attre
Brugelette
Tournai
N508
N56
Beloeil
A16/E42
Blaton
Maisieres
Escaut
A7/E19
Mons
A23
Hornu
Cuesmes
BORINAGE
N2
Valenciennes
Maubeuge
Cambrai
FRANCE
N
HAINAUT & WALLONIAN BRABANT
St-Quentin

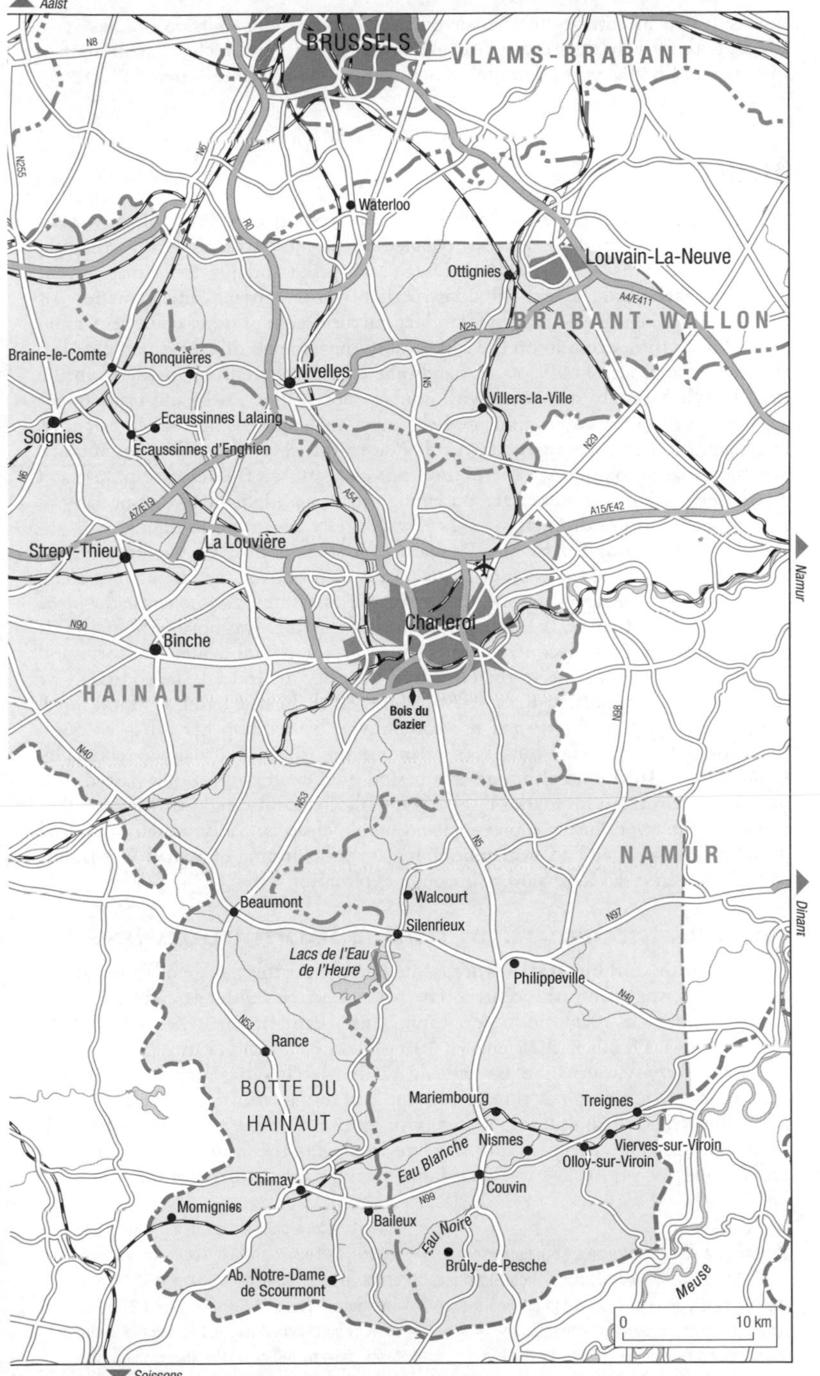
Aalst
BRUSSELS
VLAMS-BRABANT
N8
N6
N255
Waterloo
R0
Louvain-La-Neuve
Ottignies
A4/E411
BRABANT-WALLON
N25
Braine-le-Comte
Ronquières
Nivelles
N5
Villers-la-Ville
Soignies
Ecaussinnes Lalaing
Ecaussinnes d'Enghien
N29
N6
A7/E19
A54
A15/E42
Strepy-Thieu
La Louvière
Namur
Charleroi
N90
Binche
HAINAUT
Bois du Cazier
N98
N40
N53
N5
NAMUR
Beaumont
Walcourt
Dinant
Silenrieux
N97
Lacs de l'Eau de l'Heure
Philippeville
N40
N53
Rance
BOTTE DU HAINAUT
Mariembourg
Treignes
Nismes
Vierves-sur-Viroin
Olloy-sur-Viroin
Eau Blanche
Chimay
Couvin
N99
Momignies
Baileux
Eau Noire
Brûly-de-Pesche
Ab. Notre-Dame de Scourmont
Meuse
0
10 km
Soissons

hunker down in cottages in the surrounding countryside. Outside of these two towns, both of which are readily reached by public transport and have small supplies of hotels and B&Bs, you'll definitely need a car – and sometimes a tent.

Tournai

For many, **TOURNAI** is Wallonia's most interesting and enjoyable town, its ancient centre latticed by narrow cobbled streets and straddling the sluggish, canalized River Escaut (Scheldt in Dutch). Its pride and joy is its magnificent medieval **cathedral**, a seminal construction whose stirring amalgamation of Romanesque and early Gothic styles influenced the design of other churches far and wide. Most visitors zero in on the cathedral to the expense of everything else, but the town centre also holds lots of handsome eighteenth-century mansions in the French style – stately structures with double doors, stone lower and brick upper storeys, overhanging eaves, elongated chimneys and, often as not, fancy balconies and a central (horse-carriage) courtyard. Add to this several excellent restaurants, and the town's proximity to the extravagant châteaux of **Beloeil** (see p.264) and **Attre** (see p.264), and you've reason enough to stay a night or two, especially as tourism here remains distinctly low-key, with barely a tour bus in sight.

The city was founded by the Romans as a staging post on the trade route between Cologne and the coast of France. Later, it produced the French monarchy in the form of the **Merovingians**, a dynasty of Frankish kings who chose the place as their capital – **Clovis**, the most illustrious of the line, was born here in 465. It remained under French control for a large part of its subsequent history, and stayed loyal to its king during the **Hundred Years' War**. Indeed, the constancy of its citizens was legendary: Joan of Arc addressed them in a letter as "kind, loyal Frenchmen", and they returned the compliment by sending her a bag of gold. Incorporated into the Habsburg Netherlands in the 1520s, Tournai was retaken by Louis XIV in 1667, and although this period of French control only lasted fifty years or so, Louis left his mark on the town with the heavyweight stone quays that still flank the river, and in scores of handsome mansions. Sadly, much of central Tournai was damaged by German bombing at the beginning of World War II, but enough has survived to reward a thorough exploration.

Arrival, information and accommodation

Tournai's **train and bus stations** are located on the northern edge of town, about ten minutes' walk from the centre. The **tourist office** (Easter to Sept Mon–Fri 8.30am–6pm, Sat 10am–noon & 2–5pm, Sun 10am–noon & 2–5pm; Oct to Easter Mon–Fri 8.30am–5.30pm, Sat 10am–noon & 2–5pm, Sun 2–5pm; ⓣ069 22 20 45, ⓦwww.tournai.be) is at rue du Vieux Marché-aux-Poteries 14, just off the Grand-Place, though at time of writing was due to move to place E. Janson, just behind the cathedral. If you plan to visit a number of the town's museums, ask about the discount entry tickets that are available; the tourist office can also provide a list of Tournai's somewhat limited **accommodation** options.

Hotels

D'Alcantara rue des Bouchers St-Jacques 2 ⓣ069 21 26 48, ⓦwww.tournai.be/hotelalcantara. Friendly, family-run hotel located in an ingeniously converted Spanish mansion, with modern-style rooms behind its eighteenth-century brick and stone facade, a pleasant courtyard garden and terrace, and some parking. The most welcoming option in town, so book in advance. ❸

Cathédrale place St-Pierre 2 ⓣ069 21 50 77, ⓦwww.hotelcathedrale.be. Right in the centre of town, close by the cathedral, this modern,

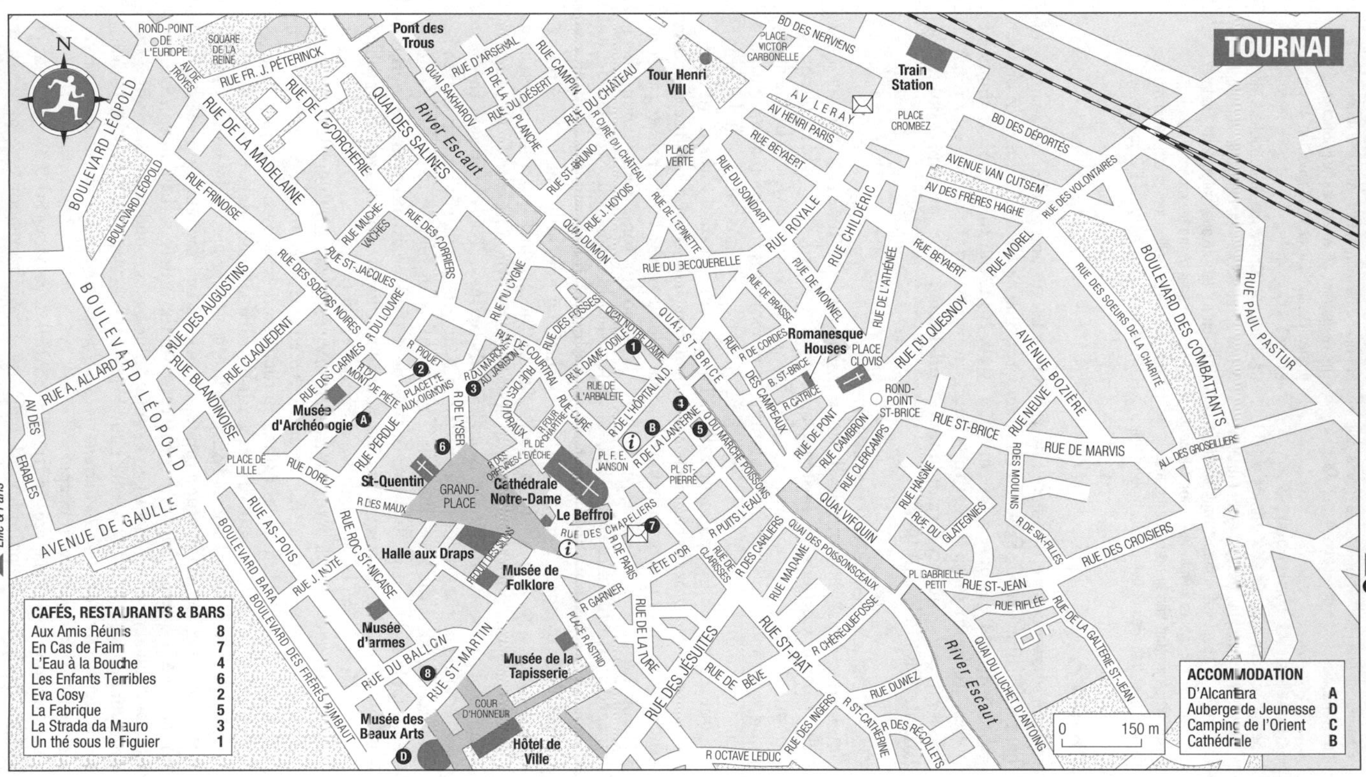
TOURNAI
CAFÉS, RESTAURANTS & BARS
Aux Amis Réunis 8
En Cas de Faim 7
L'Eau à la Bouche 4
Les Enfants Terribles 6
Eva Cosy 2
La Fabrique 5
La Strada da Mauro 3
Un thé sous le Figuier 1
ACCOMMODATION
D'Alcantara A
Auberge de Jeunesse D
Camping de l'Orient C
Cathédrale B
0 150 m
N
Train Station
Tour Henri VIII
Pont des Trous
Romanesque Houses
Cathédrale Notre-Dame
Le Beffroi
GRAND-PLACE
St-Quentin
Halle aux Draps
Musée de Folklore
Musée de la Tapisserie
Hôtel de Ville
Musée des Beaux Arts
Musée d'armes
Musée d'Archéologie
COUR D'HONNEUR
River Escaut
BOULEVARD DES COMBATTANTS
RUE PAUL PASTUR
BOULEVARD LÉOPOLD
AVENUE DE GAULLE
BOULEVARD BARA
BOULEVARD DES FRÈRES RIMBAUT
QUAI DES SALINES
QUAI VIFQUIN
QUAI ST-BRICE
QUAI NOTRE DAME
QUAI DU LUCHET D'ANTOING
RUE ROYALE
RUE DES JÉSUITES
RUE ST-PIAT
RUE DES CROISIERS
RUE DE LA MADELAINE
RUE DU QUESNOY
AVENUE BOZIÈRE
RUE DE MARVIS
RUE ST-BRICE
ROND-POINT ST-BRICE
PLACE CLOVIS
PLACE CROMBEZ
PLACE VERTE
ROND-POINT DE L'EUROPE
SQUARE DE LA REINE
PLACE DE LILLE
AV DES ERABLES
Lille & Paris

medium-sized hotel offers comfortable rooms with all conveniences, and a decent breakfast. ❸

Hostel and campsite

Auberge de Jeunesse rue St-Martin 64 ⓣ069 21 61 36, ⓦwww.laj.be. Occupying an attractive old mansion, a couple of minutes' walk south of the Grand-Place, this is a well-cared-for, friendly hostel. It has around one hundred beds, the majority in dormitories of five or six, though there are also a handful of two- and four-bunk rooms. The restaurant serves breakfast, lunch and dinner. Disabled access. Closed Jan. Dorm beds €17. ❶

Camping de l'Orient rue Jean-Baptiste Moens 8 ⓣ069 22 26 35. All-year campsite situated in the Aqua Tournai leisure and watersports complex, about 3km east of the town centre off the chaussée de Bruxelles: turn south down rue de l'Orient before you reach the E42 motorway.

The Town

Tournai's town **centre** is bisected by the River Escaut and girdled by a ring road that follows the course of the old city ramparts. The best way to explore is on foot – the town centre is only a few minutes' walk from end to end. Most things of interest are on the south side of the river, grouped around or within easy reach of the sprawling, roughly triangular **Grand-Place**. The principal sight, the **cathedral**, is just east of here.

The Cathédrale Notre-Dame

Dominating the skyline with its distinctive five towers is Tournai's Romanesque/early Gothic **Cathédrale Notre-Dame** (daily: April–Oct 9.15am–noon & 2–6pm; Nov–March 9.15am–noon & 2–5pm), built with the wealth of the flourishing wool and stone trades. Its mammoth proportions in combination with the local slate-coloured marble were much admired by contemporaries and the design was imitated all along the Escaut valley. The present cathedral is the third church on this site, most of it completed in the latter half of the twelfth century, although the choir was reconstructed in the middle of the thirteenth. It's a bit of building site at the moment, and likely to be so for some time, having been damaged by storms in the late 1990s, but you should inspect the west facade, on place de l'Evêché, with its three tiers of sculptures filling out the back of the medieval portico, before entering the church either here or by the main entrance on the south side. Inside, the **nave** is part of the original structure, erected in 1171, as are the intricately carved capitals that distinguish the lowest set of columns, but the vaulted roof is eighteenth-century. The **choir** was the first manifestation of the Gothic style in Belgium, and its too-slender pillars had to be reinforced later at the base: the whole choir still leans slightly to one side due to the unstable soil beneath. In front of the choir, the Renaissance **rood screen** is a flamboyant marble extravaganza by Cornelis Floris, embellished by biblical events such as Jonah being swallowed by the whale.

The ample and majestic late twelfth-century **transepts** are the cathedral's most impressive – and most beautiful – feature. Apsed and aisled to a very unusual plan, they impart a lovely diffuse light through their many windows, some of which (in the south transept) hold superb sixteenth-century **stained glass** depicting semi-mythical scenes from far back in Tournai's history. Opposite, in the north transept, is an intriguing twelfth-century mural, a pockmarked cartoon strip relating the story of St Margaret, a shepherdess martyred on the orders of the Emperor Diocletian. Its characters are set against an exquisite blue background reminiscent of – and clearly influenced by – Byzantine church paintings. Take a look, too, at Rubens' characteristically bold *The Deliverance of Souls from Purgatory*, which hangs, newly restored, beside the adjacent chapel.

Be sure also to see the **trésor** (treasury; April–Oct Mon–Fri 9.30am–noon & 2–6pm, Sat & Sun 2–6pm; Nov–March Mon–Fri 9.30am–noon & 2–5pm, Sat &

Sun 2–5pm; €2), whose three rooms kick off with a splendid wood-panelled, eighteenth-century meeting room and a chapel hung with a rare example of a medieval Arras tapestry, made up of fourteen panels depicting the lives of St Piat and of St Eleuthère, the first bishop of Tournai. Next door, have a look at the silver and gilded copper *châsse de Notre-Dame*, completed in 1205 by Nicolas de Verdun and festooned with relief figures clothed in fluidly carved robes, and a wonderful early sixteenth-century *Ecce Homo* by Quentin Matsys, showing Christ surrounded by monstrous faces. The treasury also once hosted a gem-studded Byzantine Cross, which was stolen in a high-profile armed raid a couple of years ago – hence the current heightened sense of security.

The Grand-Place

A short stroll from the cathedral's main entrance, virtually on the corner of the Grand-Place, **Le Beffroi** (belfry; April–Oct Tues–Sun 10am–1pm & 2–6.30pm; Nov–March Tues–Sat 10am–noon & 2–5pm, Sun 2–5pm; €3.50) is the oldest such structure in Belgium, its lower portion dating from 1200. The bottom level once held a prison cell, and the minuscule balcony immediately above was where public proclamations were announced. Climb the 257 steps to the top, where the carillon tower has been subjected to all sorts of architectural tinkering from the sixteenth through to the nineteenth century – hence its ungainly appearance.

A few steps west of the belfry, the **Grand-Place** is an open and airy piazza equipped with a modern water feature, whose automated jets do very nicely. The middle of the square is occupied by a **statue** of Christine de Lalaing, in heroic "to the ramparts" pose, clad in armour and holding a hatchet. A local aristocrat, Lalaing led the locals in a last-ditch stand against the Spanish Habsburg army in 1581, but to no avail. The south side of the Grand-Place holds the seventeenth-century **Halle aux Draps** (Cloth Hall), a crisply symmetrical edifice whose facade is graced by slender Renaissance pilasters and a row of miniature lions on the balustrade. Off the Grande-Place, via reduit des Sions, the amiably old-fashioned **Musée de Folklore** (April–Oct daily except Tues 9.30am–12.30pm & 2–5.30pm; Nov–March Mon & Wed–Sat 10am–noon & 2–5pm, Sun 10am–noon; €3.50) is one of the city centre's best museums, housed in an antique high-gabled brick mansion known as the Maison Tournaisienne and crammed with a treasure-trove of objects. There are reconstructions of various workshops and domestic rooms, a mock-up of a tavern with its old-fashioned *jeu de fer* game (a sort of cross between billiards and boules) and exhibits of Tournai's blue and white pottery. Look also at the replica cloister on the first floor, where one of the cells exhibits the pathetic tokens left by those impoverished parents forced to leave their children with the nuns; and a scale model of Tournai in 1701 on the top floor.

Musée de la Tapisserie

Just southeast of the Grand-Place on place Reine Astrid, the **Musée de la Tapisserie** (April–Oct daily except Tues 9.30am–12.30pm & 2–5.30pm; Nov–March Mon & Wed–Sat 10am–noon & 2–5pm, Sun 10am–noon; €3.50) features a small selection of old tapestries alongside modern work, temporary exhibitions and a restoration workshop. Tournai was among the most important pictorial tapestry centres in Belgium in the fifteenth and sixteenth centuries, producing characteristically huge works juxtaposing many characters and several episodes of history. The pick here are three tapestries recounting Homer's tale of Hercules and his dealings with Laomedon, the shifty king of Troy – still richly coloured, and crammed with detail and wry observation.

Pont des Trous and Mont St-Aubert

A ten-minute walk north of the town centre, the **Pont des Trous** still spans the River Escaut, and is the only surviving part of Tournai's medieval ramparts. It's the starting point for a walk out into the surrounding countryside to **Mont St-Aubert**, 6km or so to the north of town. There are smashing views from the top of this 149m hill, which was long the focus of all sorts of pagan shenanigans until the Catholic Church adopted it, naming it after St Aubert, an eighth-century French saint who founded France's hilltop Mont St-Michel. Free walking **maps** are available from Tournai tourist office, and the whole excursion takes about three hours.

Musée des Beaux Arts

On the southern edge of the town centre, behind the eighteenth-century Hôtel de Ville, the **Musée des Beaux Arts** (April–Oct daily except Tues 9.30am–12.30pm & 2–5.30pm; Nov–March Mon & Wed–Sat 10am–noon & 2–5pm, Sun 10am–noon; €3.50) occupies an elegant Art Nouveau edifice designed by Victor Horta, whose central hall and radiating rooms provide a suitably attractive setting for a small but enjoyable collection of mainly Belgian painting, from the Flemish primitives to the twentieth century. The works here are regularly rotated but the first room on the left is usually devoted to the nineteenth-century medievalist Louis Gallait (whose statue is in the gardens outside), two of whose vast and graphic historical canvases – of the *Plague of 1092* and the *Abdication of Charles V* – cover virtually a whole wall each. The next main room accommodates an exquisite *Virgin and Child* by Rogier van der Weyden, *St Donatius* by Jan Gossaert and a winter scene by Pieter Bruegel the Younger. Other rooms include Netherlandish still lifes, small studies by Jordaens and Van Dyck and a series of nineteenth-century paintings – Manet's romantic *Argenteuil* and the swirling colours of Monet's *Cap Martin,* as well as a final room of mainly Belgian works, with gritty working-class scenes by Constantin Meunier and a couple of canvases by James Ensor.

Musée d'Archéologie

The **Musée d'Archéologie** inhabits a rambling old brick building at rue des Carmes 8 (Nov–March Mon & Wed–Sat 10am–noon & 2–5pm, Sun 10am–noon; April–Oct daily except Tues 9.30am–12.30pm & 2–5.30pm; €3.50), and displays a hotchpotch of local archeological finds, including a heavy-duty Gallo-Roman lead sarcophagus downstairs and, upstairs, the skeleton of a horse and a smattering of rare Merovingian artefacts, from weapons to brooches and bee-shaped jewellery. The latter is thought to have come from the tomb of the Merovingian king Childeric, which was accidentally unearthed in 1653 on place Clovis, just north of the river. Interestingly, Napoleon adopted the Merovingian bee as his symbol in preference to the fleur-de-lys.

Eating and drinking

Tournai isn't stacked with gourmet **restaurants**, but there are one or two really good choices here, and the town centre is small enough to make everything easy to reach. There's also the odd **bar** that's worth seeking out, but otherwise the town centre is pretty quiet at night.

Aux Amis Réunis rue St-Martin 89. Dating back to 1911, this traditional Belgian bar has a good range of domestic beers, and its wood-panelled walls and antique feel make it one of the town's most agreeable watering holes. It also has a table for *jeu de fer* (a cross between billiards and boules).

En Cas de Faim rue des Chapeliers 50 ⓣ069 56 04 84. A Belgian restaurant with a Norwegian chef who specializes in Mediterranean cuisine. All the food is seasonal and freshly prepared, though the service can be somewhat haphazard. A two-course meal will set you back around €20. Mon–Sat noon–2.30pm; Fri & Sat only 7–9.30pm.

L'Eau à la Bouche quai du Marché Poissons 8 ⓣ069 22 77 20. French cuisine with an original flair served in a charming eighteenth-century house down by the riverside. Mains for €17.50, set menus €32–50, including wine. Booking recommended. Mon, Tues & Thurs noon–2pm, Fri–Sun noon–2pm & 7–9.30pm.

Les Enfants Terribles rue de l'Yser 35 ⓣ069 84 48 22. Just off the Grand-Place, with brasserie-style food – steaks, brochettes and salads – in a contemporary, minimalist setting. You can watch the chef at work on the television screen behind the bar. Starters €8–14, main course €12–18. Mon–Sat noon–3pm & 7–11pm.

Eva Cosy rue Piquet 6. Café-tearoom that's perfect for breakfast, lunch or afternoon tea, with home-made cakes, biscuits and bread. Try the maroccino – dark chocolate melted in an espresso. The decor is inviting, too, with lots of original touches. Tues–Fri 8.30am–6pm, Sat 9am–6pm, Sun 3–6pm.

La Fabrique quai du Marché Poissons 13b. This busy, boisterous bar is one of the town centre's best places for a drink, with a terrace where you can sip a beer by the river.

La Strada da Mauro rue de l'Yser 2. Brash, busy southern Italian that serves good pizzas cooked in a stone oven from €7 and giant bowls of pasta from €8.50. Extremely popular. Mon & Thurs–Sun noon–3pm & 7–11pm, Tues noon–3pm, closed Wed.

Un thé sous le Figuier quai Notre-Dame 26 ⓣ069 84 88 48. Riverfront Tunisian restaurant serving up couscous and tajines in dishes you can buy when you've finished, along with all the lamps, teapots and other bric-a-brac. Prices range from €13 to €23. Tues–Sat 7–10pm, Sun noon–3pm.

Mons and around

About forty minutes by train from Tournai, **MONS** may be familiar for its military associations. It was the site of battles that for Britain marked the beginning and end of World War I, and in 1944 the location of the first big American victory on Belgian soil in the liberation campaign. It has also been a key military base since 1967, when Charles de Gaulle expelled NATO – including SHAPE (Supreme Headquarters Allied Powers in Europe) – from Paris; SHAPE subsequently moved to Maisières, just outside Mons. Both continue to provide employment for hundreds of Americans and other NATO nationals – something which gives the town a bustling, cosmopolitan feel for somewhere so small. It's a pleasant place, with a good café society, spread over the hill that gave it its name.

Railways and roads radiate out from Mons in all directions, putting central Hainaut's key attractions within easy reach and making for several enjoyable day-trips; what's more, using Mons as a base avoids the difficulty of finding somewhere to stay – accommodation is thin on the ground hereabouts. The **Borinage**, a former coalfield southwest of the town, holds the most obvious sights: the **Vincent van Gogh house** and the former colliery complex of **Grand-Hornu**, which is given an extra edge by the addition of the **Musée des Arts Contemporains (MAC's)**. Elsewhere, to the northwest, lie two very visitable châteaux – imposing **Beloeil**, with its extensive grounds, and the enticing **Château d'Attre**, while to the east **Binche** boasts one of Belgium's most famous carnivals.

Arrival, information and accommodation

Mons' **train station** and the adjacent **bus station** are on the western edge of the town centre, on place Léopold. From here, there's a free bus shuttle to the Grand-Place, or it's a ten-minute walk up the hill. The **tourist office** is right in the centre at Grand-Place 22 (April–Sept daily 9am–7pm, Jan–March & Oct–Dec Mon–Sat 9am–6.30pm, Sun 9.30am–6pm; ⓣ065 33 55 80, ⓦwww.paysdemons.be).

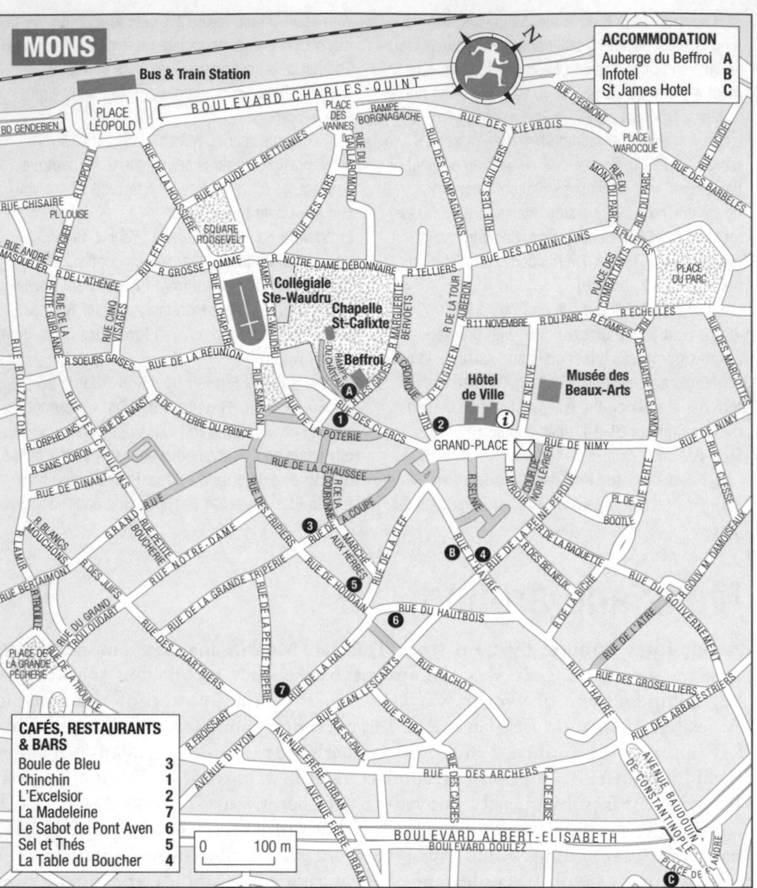

Hotels and hostel

Auberge du Beffroi rampe du Château 2 ⓣ065 87 55 70, ⓦwww.laj.be. Well-equipped, modern HI hostel in a great location, metres from the Grand-Place at the foot of the belfry. There's a bar, self-catering facilities, car parking and free wi-fi, and 115 beds in 29 one- to four-berth rooms. Dorm beds €17.50–19.50, doubles ❶

Infotel rue d'Havré 32 ⓣ065/40 18 30, ⓦwww.hotelinfotel.be. Set in a refurbished eighteenth-century house with a modern extension, this oddly named but very friendly hotel has nineteen pleasantly appointed rooms, all with free wi-fi. Great location too, just 100m from the Grand-Place, and free parking. ❸

St James Hotel place de Flandre 8 ⓣ065/72 48 24, ⓦwww.hotelstjames.be. This small hotel in a solid stone-and-brick nineteenth-century house, about ten minutes' walk east of the Grand-Place, is the closest Mons gets to a boutique hotel, with very comfortable rooms kitted out in contemporary-modernist style, either in the main building or an equally well-appointed garden annexe. Free parking, and wi-fi in the lobby. ❸

The Town

Mons zeroes in on its **Grand-Place**, a long, elegant square flanked by terrace cafés and framed by a medley of substantial stone merchants' houses and narrower brick buildings, both old and new. Presiding over the square is the fifteenth-century

Hôtel de Ville, a considerably altered building whose over-large tower was stuck on top in 1718. The tiny cast-iron **monkey** on the front wall is reputed to bring at least a year of happiness to all who stroke him with their left hand – hence his bald, polished crown – which is rather odd considering it was once part of the municipal pillory. Inside, some of the rooms are open for guided tours in July and August (more information at the tourist office), though the odd fancy fireplace, tapestry and painting are hardly essential viewing. The porch of the double-doored gateway on the front of the Hôtel de Ville carries several commemorative plaques. One is for the food sent to the town by the Americans at the end of World War II, another recalls the Canadian brigade who liberated Mons in 1918 and yet another – the most finely executed – honours the bravery of the Irish Lancers, who defended the town in 1914.

Musée des Beaux-Arts

Around the corner from the Hôtel de Ville, at rue Neuve 8, the **Musée des Beaux-Arts** (Fine Arts Museum; Tues–Sun noon–6pm; €4) occupies an impressive modern building and puts on regular contemporary shows alongside its permanent collection, which comprises mainly Belgian paintings from the sixteenth century onwards. High points of this regularly rotated collection include a striking *Ecce Homo* by the fifteenth-century artist Dieric Bouts, a *Virgin and Child* by Jan Gossaert, the mischievous *Soup Eater* by Frans Hals, and a selection of works by the local Expressionists Pierre Paulus, Arsene Detry and Fernand Gommaerts, who depicted Mons and its surrounding countryside and industrial landscapes in the 1920s and 1930s.

The belfry and park

To the southwest of the Grand-Place, **rue des Clercs** is one of the prettiest streets in town, shadowed by old mansions as it weaves around the hill that was once occupied by the medieval castle. At the end of a steep lane, the top of the hill now holds a miniature **park** (May to mid-Sept Tues–Sun 10am–8pm; mid-Sept to April Tues–Sun 10am–6pm; free) and the town's Baroque **beffroi** (belfry; no admission), from where there are fine views over the town and its surroundings. The park also incorporates a small tower that is pretty much all that remains of the medieval castle and the **Chapelle St-Calixte**, whose crypt was used as a

The Angels of Mons

Mons has figured prominently in both world wars. During **World War I**, in the latter part of August 1914, the British forces here found themselves outnumbered by the advancing Germans to the tune of about twenty to one. The subsequent Battle of Mons began on August 26, and the British – in spite of great heroics (the first two Victoria Crosses of the war were awarded here) – were inevitably forced to retreat. The casualties might have been greater, had the troops not been hard-bitten veterans. Meanwhile, back in England, the horror-story writer Arthur Machen wrote an avowedly fictional tale for the *Evening News* in which the retreating troops were assisted by a host of bowmen, the ghosts of Agincourt. Within weeks, rumour had transmogrified Machen's bowmen into the **Angels of Mons**, which had supposedly hovered overhead just at the point when the Germans were about to launch their final attack, causing them to fall back in fear and amazement. Machen himself was amazed at this turn of events, but the angel story was unstoppable, taking on the status of legend, and those soldiers lucky enough to return home obligingly reported similar tales of supernatural happenings on the battlefield. There's a painting of the angelic event, by one Marcel Gillis, in the Mons Hôtel de Ville.

bomb shelter in World War II and which has a handful of artefacts and some fresco fragments.

Collégiale Ste-Waudru

Below the belfry park, the **Collégiale Ste-Waudru** (Collegiate Church of St Waudru; daily 9am–6pm, 5pm on Sun) is a massive and majestic church which displays a striking uniformity in its architecture, most memorably in the long, sweeping lines of the windows and in its long, soaring Gothic nave. The church is named after a seventh-century aristocrat, who was faithful in marriage and obligingly bore her husband four children, raising them to be singularly virtuous before dedicating the rest of her life to the church and founding a small religious community here in Mons. There is much to see inside the church, not least the elaborate, eighteenth-century "Car d'Or" in the north aisle, used to transport the reliquary of Ste-Waudru around town on Trinity Sunday. More importantly, there's the work of the local sculptor, architect, builder and general factotum Jacques du Broeucq, whose alabaster rood loft (1535–39) was broken up by French Revolutionary soldiers in 1797, and is now spread around different parts of the church. These high-relief carvings are wonderful, designed to explain the story of Christ to a largely illiterate congregation. The north transept holds the reliefs of the *Resurrection*, the *Ascension* and the *Descent of the Holy Ghost*, while the south transept has the *Flagellation of Christ* and the *Bearing of the Cross*, as well as Broeucq's memorial plaque, while a chapel in the ambulatory displays *The Last Supper*. The church **trésor** (March–Nov Tues–Fri 1.30–6pm, Sat & Sun 1.30–5pm; €1.25) is also of some interest, with the usual reliquaries and statuettes alongside the shroud of Saint Waudru and the leather bag used to carry her body.

Eating and drinking

Like most provincial Belgian towns, Mons has an excellent variety of places to **eat** and **drink**: the cafés on the Grande-Place are perfect for nursing a beer, and are a short walk from one or two excellent town-centre restaurants.

Boule de Bleu rue de la Coupe 46 ☎065 84 58 19. Good organic soups, salads and filled focaccia alongside more substantial fare and a wide selection of teas and organic wines and beers. Coffee desserts served in glasses with ice cream and plenty of cream are especially popular. The interior is rustic and inviting, and there's a covered courtyard in the back. Mon–Thurs 11am–3pm, Fri & Sat 11am–11pm.

The Doudou

Every year, in late May or early June on the weekend before Trinity Sunday, Mons hosts the festival of the **Doudou**. Events kick off with a solemn ceremony on the Saturday, when the reliquary holding the remains of St Waudru is given to the city's mayor. Locals flock into the Collegiate Church to sing their version of the **Doudou folk song**, which will continue for the rest of the week. On Sunday morning, the reliquary is processed around the town in a golden carriage – the **Car d'Or** – accompanied by a thousand-odd costumed participants, with everyone joining in to push the carriage back up the hill to the church with one huge shove: failure to get it there in one go will bring bad luck to one and all.

After the relics are safely back in the church, chaos erupts on the Grand-Place, with a battle between **St George and the Dragon**, known here as "Lumeçon". St George and his thirty-eight helpers (all good men and true) slug it out with the dragon and his entourage (devils, the "Wild Men in the woods" and the "Men in White"). The crowd helps St George by pulling ribbons off the dragon's tail as it whips through the air just above their heads, and inevitably, George and crew emerge victorious.

Chinchin rue des Clercs 15. This buzzy cellar-bar pulls in a youthful crew, who knock back shot glasses of the sweet, citrus-based house cocktail at an alarming speed.

L'Excelsior Grand-Place 29. There is no shortage of bars on the main square, but the leather benches and wooden panelling of this one give it a warm and welcoming feel. Decent food and, like the rest, plenty of tables outside.

La Madeleine rue de la Halle 42 ⓣ065 35 13 70. Excellent fish and seafood restaurant where the house speciality is a plate of mixed shellfish and fish. The painted tiles on the walls are fishy too, and there's a good wine cellar. Main courses start at a fairly reasonable €20. Daily except Mon noon–3pm & 6.30–11pm.

Le Sabot de Pont Aven rue du Hautbois 8 ⓣ0496 17 13 61. This traditional Breton creperie is very popular with locals and has a really authentic feel, serving both savoury crepes from €6.50 and sweet ones from €2 – all washed down with Breton cider at €7 a bottle. Daily 11.30am–2.30pm & 6.30–10pm.

Sel et Thés rue de Houdain 6 ⓣ065 33 93 33. A great option for lunch, with salads and sandwiches, and presentation that matches the flair and flourishes of the decor. Starters around €10, main dishes €18. Tues–Sat noon–2.30pm & 6–10pm.

La Table du Boucher rue d'Havré 49 ⓣ065 31 68 38. There's nothing much for veggies, but this is a great little restaurant, serving perfectly cooked steaks, lamb and veal dishes from a blackboard menu from €9 for starters and €12 for mains. Good service, too, and a cosy interior with banquette seats and lots of bottles and wine cases. Daily noon–3pm & 6–11pm, Fri & Sat till midnight.

Southwest of Mons: the Borinage

The region immediately southwest of Mons is known as the **Borinage**, a poor, densely populated working-class area that, in the latter half of the nineteenth century, was one of Belgium's three main coalfields, an ugly jigsaw of slag heaps and mining villages. The mining is finished, but the cramped terraced housing remains, a postindustrial sprawl that extends toward the French frontier. There are, however, a couple of attractions that may tempt you out here, specifically a house that was once lived in by the painter **Vincent van Gogh**, and the **Grand Hornu**, a very real remnant of the region's industrial past.

The Vincent van Gogh house

In 1878, after a period in a Protestant school in Brussels, **Vincent van Gogh** was sent to the Borinage as a missionary, living in acute poverty and helping the villagers in their fight for social justice – behaviour which so appalled the church authorities that he was forced to leave. He came back the following year and lived in **Cuesmes**, on the southern outskirts of Mons, until his return to the Netherlands in 1881. It was in the Borinage that van Gogh first started drawing seriously, taking his inspiration from the hard life of the miners – "I dearly love this sad countryside of the Borinage and it will always live with me" – but although the connection was instrumental in the development of the painter's career, there's actually very little to recall his time here. Even the tidily restored two-storey brick **house**, at rue du Pavillon 3 (Tues–Sat 10.30am–noon & 1.30–6pm, Sun 10.30am–noon & 2–6pm; ⓣ065 35 56 11; €2.50), where van Gogh lodged, has merely a couple of period rooms and no original artwork. If you're determined to make a thankless pilgrimage, take bus #20 from outside Mons train station (every 30min; 10min) and ask the driver to put you off – the bus stop is 200m from the house.

Grand-Hornu

Between 1810 and 1830, in the village of **HORNU**, the French industrialist Henri De Gorge set about building the large complex of offices, stables, workshops, foundries and furnaces that comprises **Grand-Hornu** (Tues–Sun 10am–6pm; €6, including MAC's, audioguide €2 extra; ⓦwww.grand-hornu.be). De Gorge owned several collieries in the area, so the complex made economic sense, but he went much further, choosing to build in an elegant version of Neoclassical style and constructing more-than-adequate workers' houses just outside which survive to this day. This progressiveness did not necessarily win the affection of the workers – in 1830 the miners came within an inch of lynching him during an industrial dispute over wages – but De Gorge's mines, as well as Grand-Hornu, remained in operation until 1954. Thereafter, the complex fell into disrepair, but it was revived in the 1990s and, with its large elliptical courtyard and ruined workshops, it's a compelling slice of nineteenth-century industrial history. Furthermore, the old office buildings on one side now hold the **Musée des Arts Contemporain** (MAC's; same times; Ⓦwww.mac-s.be), which has already established a regional reputation for the quality of its temporary exhibitions of contemporary art. There's a bookshop and café, and a nice restaurant too, overlooking the large courtyard. To get to Grand-Hornu, take bus #7 or #9 from Mons train station (every 15min) and alight at place Verte, from where it's a five-minute walk.

Northwest of Mons: Beloeil

Roughly halfway between Mons and Tournai, the château of **BELOEIL** (April & mid-May Sat & Sun 1–6pm; mid-May to Oct daily 11am–6pm; €5; Ⓣ069 68 94 26) broods over the village that bears its name, its long brick and stone facades redolent of the enormous wealth and power of the Ligne family, regional bigwigs since the fourteenth century. This aristocratic clan began by strengthening the medieval fortress built here by their predecessors, subsequently turning it into a commodious moated castle that was later remodelled and refined on several occasions. The wings of the present structure date from the late seventeenth century, while the main body, though broadly compatible, was in fact rebuilt after a fire in 1900. Without question a stately building, it has a gloomy, rather despondent air – and the interior, though lavish enough, oozing with tapestries, paintings and furniture, is simply the collected indulgences – and endless portraits – of various generations of Lignes. Despite all this grandeur, only one member of the family cuts much historical ice. This is **Charles Joseph** (1735–1814), a diplomat, author and field marshal in the Austrian army, whose pithy comments were much admired by his fellow aristocrats: most famously, he suggested that the Congress of Vienna of 1814 "danse mais ne marche pas". Several of Beloeil's rooms contain paintings of Charles' life and times and there's also a small selection of his personal effects, including the malachite clock given to him by the Tsar of Russia. Otherwise, the best parts are the **library**, which contains twenty thousand volumes, many ancient and beautifully bound, and the eighteenth-century formal **gardens**, the largest in the country, whose lakes and flower beds stretch away from the house to a symmetrical design by Parisian architect and decorator Jean-Michel Chevotet.

To reach Beloeil by **public transport**, take the train from Mons or Tournai to **Blaton** (Mon–Fri every 30min, Sat & Sun hourly; 20min) and then take bus #81A from there; check bus times and routings at Tournai or Mons tourist office before you set out.

North of Mons: Château d'Attre

Completed in 1752, the elegant, Neoclassical **Château d'Attre** (April–June & Sept–Oct Sun 2–6pm; July & Aug Sat & Sun 1–6pm; park and castle €4.50; park only €3.50; Ⓣ068 45 44 60), just to the northeast of Beloeil, was built on the site of a distinctly less comfortable medieval fortress on the orders of the count of Gomegnies, chamberlain to emperor Joseph II. It soon became a favourite haunt of the ruling Habsburg elite – especially the archduchess Marie-Christine of Austria, the governor of the Southern Netherlands. The original, carefully selected furnishings and decoration have survived pretty much intact, providing an

The Ducasse

Just along the rail line from Attre, **Ath** is a run-of-the-mill industrial town that boasts a major claim to fame in its festival, the **Ducasse**, held on the fourth weekend in August and featuring the "Parade of the Giants", in which massive models, representing both folkloric and biblical figures, waggle their way round the town. If you're in the area around this time, don't miss it.

insight into the tastes of the time – from the sphinxes framing the doorway and the silk wrappings of the Chinese room through to the extravagant parquet floors, the ornate moulded plasterwork and the archducal room hung with the first hand-painted wallpaper ever to be imported into the country, in about 1760. There are also first-rate silver, ivory and porcelain pieces, as well as paintings by Frans Snyders, a friend of Rubens, and the Frenchman Jean-Antoine Watteau, whose romantic, idealized canvases epitomized early eighteenth-century aristocratic predilections. Neither is the castle simply a display case: it's well cared for and has a lived-in, human feel, in part created by the arrangements of freshly picked flowers chosen to enhance the character of each room. The surrounding **park** straddles the River Dendre and holds several curiosities, notably a 24m-high artificial rock with subterranean corridors and a chalet-cum-hunting lodge on top – all to tickle the fancy of the archduchess. The ruins of a tenth-century tower, also in the park, must have pleased her risqué sensibilities too; it was reputed to have been the hideaway of a local villain, a certain Vignon who, disguised as a monk, robbed and ravished passing travellers.

Getting to Attre by public transport isn't that easy. The nearest train station, **Mévergnies-Attre**, on the Mons–Ath line, is just over 1km from the château, but trains don't stop here at the weekend (when the château is open). The nearest alternative is **Brugelette**, 3km or so east of the château, again on the Mons–Ath line (Mon–Fri hourly, Sat & Sun every 2hr). The journey time from Mons to Brugelette is twenty minutes.

Binche

There's not much to bring you to **BINCHE**, a sleepy little town halfway between Mons and Charleroi, at the southern end of Hainaut's most decayed industrial region. However, it comes to life every year when it hosts one of the best and most renowned of the country's **carnivals**, and it's this that provides the main reason for a visit, not only when the carnival's on, but also to take in the town's **Musée International du Carnaval et du Masque** (Jan–Oct: Tues–Fri 9.30am–5pm, Sat & Sun 10.30am–5pm; €6; ⓦwww.museedumasque.be), which claims to have the largest assortment of carnival artefacts in the world. Whether or not this is an exaggeration, its collection of masks and fancy dress from carnivals throughout Europe, Africa, Asia and Latin America is certainly impressive, and it's complemented by an audiovisual presentation on the Binche carnival and temporary exhibitions on the same theme. Outside the museum, a statue of a Gille – one of the figures that dance through the city streets during carnival – is sandwiched between the big but undistinguished **Collégiale St-Ursmer** and the **Grand-Place**, a spacious square edged by the onion-domed **Hôtel de Ville**, built in 1555 by Jacques du Broeucq to replace a version destroyed by the French the previous year. A small **park** near the museum marks the site of the town's medieval citadel

Carnival in Binche

Carnival has been celebrated in Binche since the fourteenth century. The festivities last for several weeks, getting started in earnest on the Sunday before Shrove Tuesday, when thousands turn out in costume. During the main events on **Shrove Tuesday** itself, the traditional **Gilles** – males born and raised in Binche – appear in clogs and embroidered costumes from dawn onwards, banging drums and stamping on the ground. In the morning they wear "green-eyed" masks, dancing in the Grand-Place carrying bunches of sticks to ward off bad spirits. In the afternoon they don their plumes – a mammoth piece of headgear made of ostrich feathers – and throw oranges to the crowd as they pass through town in procession. The rituals of the carnival date back to pagan times, but the Gilles were probably inspired by the fancy dress worn by Mary of Hungary's court at a banquet held in honour of Charles V in 1549; Peru had recently been added to the Habsburg Empire, and the courtiers celebrated the conquest by dressing up in (their version of) Inca gear.

and contains what little remains of the former palace of Mary of Hungary. It's buttressed by the original **ramparts**, which date from the twelfth to the fourteenth centuries and curve impressively around most of the town centre, complete with 27 towers.

Practicalities

To get to Binche from Mons, take the hourly Charleroi **train** and change at La Louvière-Sud – allow forty to fifty minutes for the whole journey. Binche **tourist office** is located in the Hôtel de Ville on the Grand-Place (Mon–Fri 10am–noon & 1–5pm, Sat & Sun 2–6pm; ⓣ064 33 67 27, ⓦwww.binche.be), a ten-minute walk from the train station: take rue Gilles Binchois from the square in front of the station building and keep straight until you reach the end of rue de la Gaieté, where you turn left. There is very little **accommodation**; try the rooms at *Les Volet Verts*, rue de la Triperie 4 (ⓣ064 33 31 47, ⓦwww.lvv.net; ❷) For **food**, the unfussy, family-run *Restaurant Industrie*, tucked away in a corner of the Grand-Place near the tourist office, serves hearty Walloon dishes at very reasonable prices. The most amenable **bar** in town is the *Cote de Chez Boule*, around the corner from the carnival museum at rue St-Paul 13. They serve the favourite local **brew**, La Binchoise, produced at the brewery just down the hill.

Ronquières and the boat lifts

To the east of Mons lies one of the quietest corners of Hainaut, a pocket-sized district where drowsy little villages and whitewashed farmhouses dot a bumpy landscape patterned by a maze of narrow country lanes. It's perhaps best known for its **boat lifts** – part of the Canal du Centre, which has flowed through this region since its inception in 1888 to connect the rivers Meuse and Scheldt. Classified as a UNESCO world heritage site, the canal climbs over 20m overall by means of six locks. The so-called sloping lock of **Ronquières**, just off the N6 about 15km east of Soignies, is one of the most impressive of these, a massive transporter lock that's part of the Charleroi–Brussels canal; when completed in 1968, the lock cut the journey time between Charleroi and Brussels by around seven hours, a saving of around 25 percent. It's a gargantuan contraption, consisting of two huge water tanks, each 91m long, and a ramp, which together shift barges up or down

68m over a distance of 1500m. The main tower at the top (April–Oct daily 10am–7pm; €7; ⓣ067 64 66 80), 125m high, houses the winch room, runs a video describing how the whole thing works as well as life aboard the barges and, best of all, gives a bird's-eye view of proceedings. There are also hour-long **boat trips** downstream to Ittre (May–Aug Tues & Thurs–Sun 4 daily; €3.50, combined ticket with tower €8.50), though the tower should be quite sufficient for all but the most enthusiastic.

You can also visit some of the other locks along the canal, including the funicular lift at **Strepy-Thieu** (mid-March to Oct daily 9.30am–6.30pm; €5.50), where you can also watch a film showing how the lift was built as well as visiting the machine room and the rest of the contraption. Tourist boats also run between here and Ronquières once a month during summer, an all-day journey (€22 per person); see ⓦvoiesdeau.hainaut.be for more details.

Brabant Walloon

To the northeast of Mons you cross the border into **Brabant**, whose southern French-speaking districts – known as **Brabant Walloon** – form a band of countryside that rolls up to and around Waterloo, which is now pretty much a suburb of Brussels (and included in that chapter – see p.109). **Nivelles** is the obvious distraction en route, an amiable, workaday town worth a visit for its interesting church as well as its proximity to the beguiling ruins of the Cistercian abbey at **Villers-la-Ville**, a short car ride away (train travellers have to make the trip via Charleroi). The **Hergé museum**, meanwhile, is the highlight of the otherwise entirely missable new town of Louvain-la-Neuve.

Nivelles

NIVELLES grew up around its abbey, which was founded in the seventh century and became one of the most powerful religious houses in Brabant until its suppression by the French Revolutionary Army in 1798. Nowadays, the abbey is recalled by the town's one and only significant sight, the **Collégiale Ste-Gertrude** (daily 9am–5pm; free), a vast edifice that utterly dominates the Grande-Place at the heart of the town, and was erected as the abbey church in the tenth century. Little is known of Gertrude, but her cult was very popular on account of her supposed gentleness – her symbol is a pastoral staff with a mouse running along it. Built in the Ottonian style (the forerunner of Romanesque), with a transept and chancel at each end of the nave, the church itself is a beautiful and unusual construction, in better shape now than it has been for years following a long restoration. The west chancel represents imperial authority, the east papal – an architectural illustration of the tension between the pope and the emperor that defined much of Otto's reign. The interior is extremely simple, its long and lofty nave supported by sturdy pillars, between which sits a flashy oak and marble pulpit by the eighteenth-century Belgian artist Laurent Delvaux; the heavily restored, fifteenth-century wooden wagon kept at the western end of the church is used to carry the shrine of Ste Gertrude in procession through the fields once a year. Unfortunately, the original thirteenth-century shrine was destroyed in 1940, but a modern replacement has been made and the traditional autumn procession has recently been revived.

Outside, the cloisters are lovely, and you can see them and other parts of the church that are otherwise out of bounds on regular **guided tours** (Mon–Fri at 2pm, Sat & Sun 2pm & 3.30pm; 1hr 30min; €6; reservations on ⓣ067 84 08 64). Although usually in French, tours can be given in English if you book in advance, and take in the large Salle Impériale over the west choir, a copy of Ste Gertrude's shrine and what remains of the original and the large Romanesque crypt, where the foundations of a Merovingian chapel and church (seventh-century) and three Carolingian churches (ninth- and tenth-century) have been discovered, as well as the tombs of Ste Gertrude and some of her relations.

Practicalities

It's a ten-minute walk west down from Nivelles' **train station** along rue de Namur to the U-shaped Grand-Place. The **tourist office** is up the hill from here at rue des Saintes 48 (daily 8.30am–5pm; Ⓣ067 84 08 64, Ⓦwww.tourisme-nivelles.be). With Brussels so near (30min by train), there's no real reason to stay, but the medley of **cafés** edging the Grand-Place are fine for a coffee and a snack. Alternatively, if you're after something more substantial, head for the corner of the square and place Gabrielle Petit, where cosy *P'tit Gabriel* (Ⓣ067 44 36 16) serves fondues from €18 a head, and *Dis Moi Ou*, rue Ste-Anne 5 (Ⓣ067 64 64 64), has lunch menus for €12.50, mains €15–17.

The Abbaye de Villers

The ruined Cistercian **Abbaye de Villers**, at rue de l'Abbaye 55 (April–Oct daily 10am–6pm; Nov–March daily except Tues 10am–5pm; €5; Ⓦwww.villers.be), nestles in a lovely wooded dell on the edge of **VILLERS-LA-VILLE**, just off the N93 some 16km east of Nivelles, and is altogether one of the most haunting and evocative sights in the whole of Belgium. The first monastic community settled here in 1146, consisting of just one abbot and twelve monks. Subsequently the abbey became a wealthy local landowner, managing a domain of several thousand acres, with numbers that rose to about a hundred monks and three hundred lay brothers. A healthy annual income funded the construction of an extensive monastic complex, most of which was erected in the thirteenth century, though the less austere structures, such as the Abbot's Palace, went up in a second spurt of activity some four hundred years later. In 1794 French revolutionaries ransacked the monastery, and later a railway was ploughed through the grounds, but more than enough survives – albeit in various states of decay – to pick out Romanesque, Gothic and Renaissance features and to make some kind of mental reconstruction of abbey life possible.

From the entrance, a path crosses the courtyard in front of the Abbot's Palace to reach the **warming room** (*chauffoir*), the only place in the monastery where a fire would have been kept going all winter, and which still has its original chimney. The fire provided a little heat to the adjacent rooms: on one side the monks' **workroom** (*salle des moines*), used for reading and studying; on the other the large Romanesque-Gothic **refectory** (*réfectoire*), lit by ribbed twin windows topped with chunky rose windows. Next door is the **kitchen** (*cuisine*), which contains a few remnants of the drainage system which once piped waste to the river, and of a central hearth, whose chimney helped air the room. Just behind this lies the **pantry** (*salle des convers*), where a segment of the original vaulting has survived, supported by a single column, and beyond, on the northwestern edge of the complex, is the **guest house** (*brasserie*), one of the abbey's biggest and oldest buildings. The most spectacular building, however, is the **church** (*église*), which fills out the north corner of the complex. With pure lines and elegant proportions, it displays the change from Romanesque to Gothic – the transept and choir are the first known examples of Brabantine Gothic. The building has the dimensions of a cathedral, 90m long and 40m wide, with a majestic nave whose roof was supported on strong cylindrical columns. An unusual feature is the series of bull's-eye windows which light the transepts. Of the original twelfth-century **cloister** (*cloître*) adjoining the church, a pair of twin windows is pretty much all that remains, flanked by a two-storey section of the old monks' quarters.

Practicalities

There is no **public transport** direct from Nivelles to Villers-la-Ville, but you can still make the trip by **train**. Every half-hour (hourly at the weekend) a service links Nivelles with Charleroi, from where an hourly train goes to Villers-la-Ville; allow about an hour for the whole journey, twenty minutes more on the weekend. To get here from Brussels, catch a Namur train and change at Ottignies – reckon on an hour to an hour and a half depending on connections. The abbey is 1600m from Villers-la-Ville train station: follow the sign to Monticelli, head up and over a little slope until, after about 100m, you reach a T-junction; turn right and follow the road round until you see the ruins ahead. Right by the site, you can sit outside the *Moulin de Villers* restaurant which serves **lunch** every day and has €28.50 menus; it also has a small tavern for drinks and bar snacks.

The Musée Hergé

Established in the 1960s as a French-speaking rival to the ancient Flemish university town of Leuven, you wouldn't come to **LOUVAIN-LA-NEUVE** by choice. Like any new town, it's mostly a mixture of roundabouts and underpasses, with the university supplemented by a couple of shopping centres and arts complexes. But its most recent addition, the **Musée Hergé** (Tues–Sun 10am–6pm; €9.50, includes audioguide in English; Ⓦwww.museeherge.com), is perhaps Louvain's greatest achievement yet, and since it honours perhaps the most famous Belgian of them all, the creator of **Tintin**, it's likely to feature on anyone's itinerary. The brainchild of Hergé's second wife, Fanny Rodwell, the museum concentrates on his life and work, but his most celebrated creation inevitably figures extremely prominently. A couple of rooms take you through Hergé's "dreary but happy" childhood, his early cartoon creations and work in advertising and design, while later ones examine the inception of the Tintin stories in detail, with displays on each of the principal characters as well as Hergé's influences in creating them – foreign travel, science and cinema among them. It's all made accessible and entertaining by audioguides, which provide excellent commentary and background, though whether Hergé was quite the towering creative genius the museum makes him out to be is debatable. Nonetheless, it's all brilliantly done, and enjoyable whether you're a fan of the man – and his bequiffed reporter – or not.

Louvain-la-Neuve is relatively easy to get to from Brussels: there are two trains an hour to nearby Ottignies, which take around thirty minutes; from there, bus #20 runs every hour to Louvain-la-Neuve – a ten-minute journey.

Charleroi

Once the epicentre of one of Belgium's main industrial areas, home to glassworks, coal mines and iron foundries, the twentieth century wasn't kind to **CHARLEROI**, and its outskirts and, for that matter, its centre is not among the country's most alluring prospects. It's best known these days for being the home of Brussels' second airport, and with that impetus it's busy trying to re-invent itself – and although there's a long way yet to go, it hasn't done a bad job. Its centre is bustling and cosmopolitan, there are plenty of good places to eat and drink and, with three comfortable hotels, it's not a bad place to break your journey if you're travelling either to the Botte du Hainaut (see p.272) or east to the Ardennes (see Chapter 5).

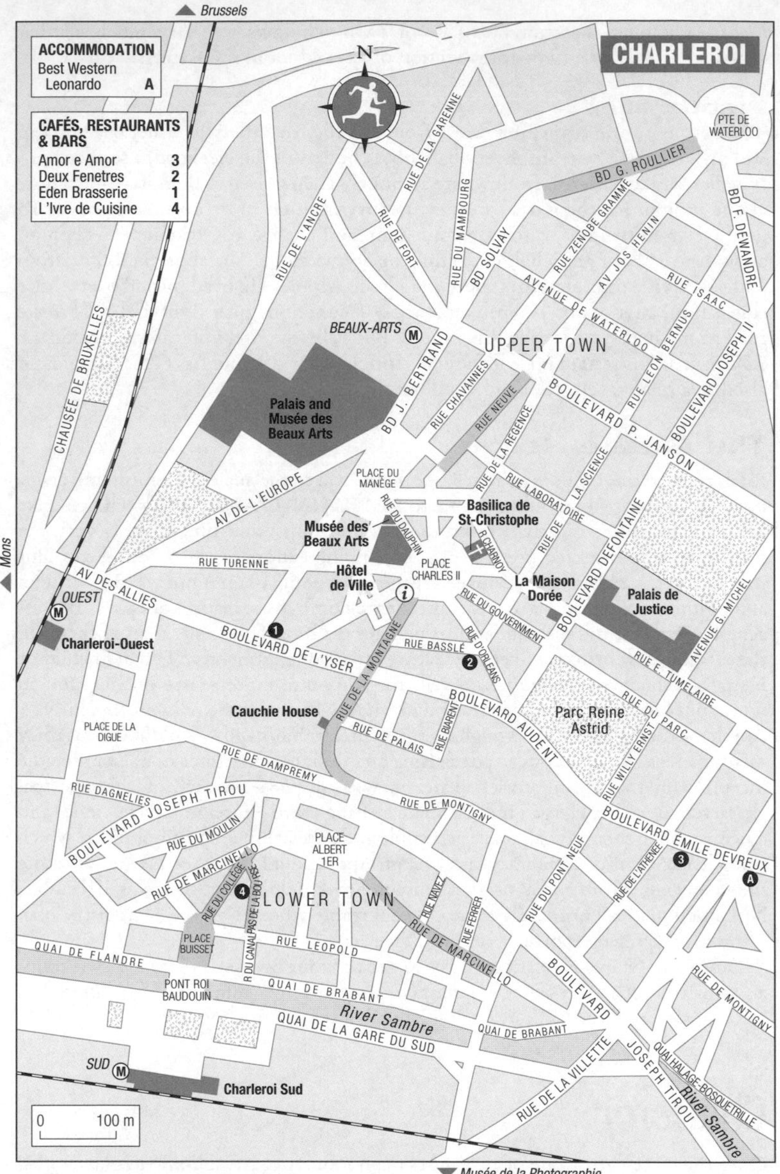

The Lower Town

Charleroi's **lower town** lies down by the River Sambre, recently cleaned up and spanned by the **Pont Roi Baudouin**, which sports two **statues** of workers by that champion of the working class, Constantin Meunier. Before the railways, the Sambre was crucial to the industrialization of the region, its dark waters crowded with coal and iron-ore barges; it was into this very same river, just 3km east of town in Châtelet, that René Magritte's mother, Régina, threw herself when she committed suicide in 1912. On the far side of the bridge lies the train station; on the other the riverside **quai de Brabant** and rue du Canal lead to the heart of the lower town, and to the **Passage de la Bourse** – an attractive covered arcade whose late nineteenth-century wooden-framed shops have survived in fine fettle. Beyond here, **place Albert 1er** is home to a daily morning market, beyond which busy **boulevard Tirou** leads to the cobbled shopping street of **rue de la Montagne**, which clambers toward the Upper Town. On the way, look out for the *sgraffiti* decorating the facade of rue de la Montagne 38, the work of one of Belgium's most talented Art Nouveau painters and architects, **Paul Cauchie** (1875–1952).

The Upper Town

Rue de la Montagne emerges into circular **place Charles II**, the centre of the **upper town** and formerly the site of a substantial fortress, built on the top of the hill in the 1660s. Nothing remains of the fortress today, but the area's gridiron street plan recalls its presence. Two fine Art Deco buildings flank place Charles II: one, the **Basilica de Saint Christophe** (daily 8am–9pm), has a stunning 200-metre-square gold-leaf apse mosaic illustrating the Book of Revelation, completed in 1957 to a design by local artist Jean Ransy; the other, the **Hôtel de Ville**, has a handsome period lobby and staircase and, around the back, a display on the life and times of one Jules Destrée (1863–1936), a local poet, lawyer and socialist politician who campaigned hard for improvements in working conditions in Wallonia during the early years of the twentieth century. Behind the Hôtel de Ville, busy **place du Manège** is overlooked by the striking Art Deco lines of the **Palais des Beaux Arts**, which is home to the **Musée des Beaux Arts** (Tues–Sat 10am–6pm; €1.50), whose entrance is round the back at the far end of rue du Dauphin, at the top of a handsome Art Deco staircase. The museum has a very good collection of Hainaut artists, supplemented by the work of other Belgian painters who lived or worked here. Highlights include the romantic Neoclassical paintings of Charleroi artist François Joseph Navez (1787–1869) as well as the contrasting naturalism of Constantin Meunier, whose grim vision of industrial life was balanced by the heroism he saw in the working class. There are also a number of canvases by the talented Pierre Paulus (1881–1959), whose oeuvre takes up where Meunier's leaves off – and arguably with greater panache.

The outskirts

Charleroi has another good museum in the inventive **Musée de la Photographie**, 5km southwest from the centre at ave Paul Pastur 11 (Tues–Sun 10am–6pm; €6; Ⓦwww.museephoto.be), housed in the imaginatively renovated neo-Gothic Carmelite monastery of Mont-sur-Marchienne. It's reachable on buses #70, #71 and #170, which depart from Charleroi-Sud train station; ask the driver to let you off. The museum holds a thought-provoking collection of nearly sixty thousand creative and documentary-style photographs, which are displayed in rotation, and a well organized and reasonably interesting permanent exhibition which takes you through the history of photography to the present day. Temporary exhibitions are held regularly, too.

Charleroi's other outlying attraction, the **Bois du Cazier**, rue du Cazier 80 (Tues–Fri 9am–5pm, Sat & Sun 10am–6pm; €6, free audioguides in English; Ⓦwww.leboisducazier.be), is similarly compelling, a former coal mine which gained a tragic notoriety in August 1956 when over 200 miners died in a fire here. Most of the mine buildings remain intact, and are both a memorial to those who died (more than half of whom were Italian immigrants) and a memorable piece of industrial heritage. There is lots of information in English, including a short film about the 1956 catastrophe, and the outbuildings hold a host of related objects and exhibitions, most interestingly a museum of industry full of fantastical heavy machinery from times gone by, although the most intriguing exhibits are those original to the mine: the showers where the miners ended their shift, or the punch clocks where they would begin.

Practicalities

Charleroi has two **train stations**, Charleroi-Sud by the River Sambre, where you're likely to arrive, and less important Charleroi-Ouest, a short walk west of the upper town. The city's **airport** – rather cheekily called Brussels South-Charleroi – is 6km north of town; Ryanair flies here from the UK and Ireland (see p.53). The city's main **tourist office** is at place Charles II 20 (Mon–Sat 9am–6pm; ⓣ071 86 14 14, ⓦwww.paysdecharleroi.be). Charleroi-Sud station also acts as the hub for local **buses**, most usefully a shuttle service to the upper town's place du Manège – a route that is followed by Charleroi's pocket-sized **métro**.

The most comfortable **hotel** is the *Best Western Leonardo*, which occupies a straightforward modern block to the east of the lower town at blvd Pierre Mayence 1 (ⓣ071 30 24 24, ⓦwww.leonardo-hotels.com; ❷); it has around fifty pleasantly appointed modern rooms, and those on the upper floors have views over town. For **food**, *Deux Fenetres*, rue Basslé 27 (ⓣ071 63 43 03; closed Sat lunch, Sun & Mon), is an excellent and authentic Italian restaurant in a converted garage, with a great selection of wine and appealing and fun decor. The tapas bar, *Amor e Amor*, blvd E Devreux 18 (ⓣ071 70 03 09; closed Sun–Tues), is good for a lighter bite at lunchtime or early evening, while in the lower town *L'Ivre de Cuisine*, rue du College 8, does snacks and sandwiches and has a restaurant out the back, with full meals for €10 and tables in the covered *passage*. Finally, the *Eden Brasserie* (ⓣ071 31 12 12) is a bar-cum-cultural centre at blvd Jacques Bertrand 1 that is open for lunch and dinner, after which it moves back the tables to make way for live music and other events.

The Botte de Hainaut

A tongue of land jutting south into France, the **Botte de Hainaut** (Boot of Hainaut) is a natural extension of the Ardennes range further east, if a little flatter and less wooded. It's mostly visited for its gentle scenery and country towns, among which **Walcourt** and **Chimay** are the most appealing – the former graced by a handsome basilica, the latter by a charming château and perhaps the prettiest main square in the whole of Wallonia. The Boot's one and only **train** line runs south from Charleroi to Walcourt, Philippeville and ultimately to Couvin; local **buses** fill in most of the gap, with a good service between Charleroi, Couvin and Chimay, but to tour beyond the towns you'll need a car. The other complication is that apart from campsites, **accommodation** is extremely thin on the ground. Chimay is your best bet, but consider making advance reservations in all cases, either direct or via the main regional websites: ⓦwww.botteduhainaut.com and the more comprehensive ⓦwww.paysdesvallees.be.

Walcourt and around

The straggling hillside settlement of **WALCOURT**, about 20km – and half an hour by train – from Charleroi, is a pleasant old town whose pride and joy is its medieval, artichoke-domed **Basilique St-Materne** (summer daily 8am–6pm, winter daily 8.30am–5pm). Dominating the town from its hilltop location at the top of the Grand-Place, it's imperious from the outside, while the interior is very dark and spiritual, distinguished by a marvellous Gothic rood screen, adorned by a flurry of Renaissance decoration, that was presented to the church by the emperor Charles V on the occasion of a pilgrimage he made to the Virgin of Walcourt – a silver-plated wooden statue that now stands in the north transept. An object of considerable veneration even today, the statue is believed to have been crafted in the tenth century, making it one of the oldest such figures in Belgium. Equally fascinating are the late medieval choir stalls, which sport a wealth of naturalistic detail, with centaurs and griffins, rams locking horns and acrobats alongside biblical scenes.

Practicalities

From Walcourt **train station**, it's a steep 1200m walk to the church – turn right outside the station building, hang a left down the short access road, turn right at the T-junction and then follow the road as it curves upwards. The **tourist office** is at the bottom of the wedge-shaped Grand-Place (Feb–June & Sept–Dec Tues–Fri 8.30am–noon & 12.30–5pm; July & Aug daily 10am–noon & 1–6pm; ⓣ071 61 25 26). There's only one recommendable **hotel**, the *Hôstellerie Dispa*, down a narrow side street near the station at rue du Jardinet 7 (ⓣ071 61 14 23; closed late Feb & early March; ❸). A tidy, well-cared-for place in a pretty old house with modern furnishings, the hotel also has the best **restaurant** in town, offering delicious seafood at reasonable prices.

The Lacs de l'Eau de l'Heure

A short way south of Walcourt, the main road bisects the **Lacs de l'Eau de l'Heure**, a series of lakes formed by the damming of the river here and which are now home to all kinds of leisure activities. There's a **Visitor Centre** just off the main road, before the bridge over the lakes, where you can hire bikes and canoes, and which also gives access to the **dam** itself, which is accessible via regular guided tours (July & Aug daily 10am–7pm; April–June & Sept Wed 10am–6pm; rest of year Wed 10am–5pm; €5.50); the visitor centre is also a pick-up point for the so-called **Crocodile Rouge**, a sort of bus-cum-boat which makes circuits of the main lake (€12 person).

Philippeville

It's a short hop southeast from Walcourt by train to unexciting **PHILIPPEVILLE**, whose gridiron street plan reflects its origins as a fortress town. Built to the latest star-shaped design by Charles V in 1555, the fortress has disappeared save for a couple of subterranean artillery galleries, the *souterrains*. Charles didn't actually intend to build the fort at all, but irritatingly the French had captured the emperor's neighbouring stronghold of Mariembourg, just 12km to the south, and Charles was obliged to respond. Philippeville is also home to a good and popular **restaurant** in *Les Armes de Philippeville*, place d'Armes 3 (ⓣ071 66 62 41; closed Tues & Wed), which serves excellent food in its restaurant and lighter fare in the bar.

Mariembourg

Ten kilometres south of Phillipeville, **MARIEMBOURG** is not any more interesting, and its fortress has sunk without trace. However, it is the base of the **Chemin de fer à vapeur des Trois Vallées**, a refurbished steam engine that puffs its way east across the surrounding countryside, from its terminus is 800m south of Mariembourg train station, to Treignes, near the French border, a two-hour journey (July & Aug daily 11.30am–6.30pm; rest of year Sat & Sun 11.30am–6.30pm; call ⓣ060 31 24 40 for times & tickets; €9, including museum). There's also a small museum of locomotives and other bits and pieces (March–Nov Tues–Fri 10am–5pm, Sat & Sun 10am–6pm; €5). You can combine a one-way train trip with a **bike ride**; cycles can be rented in Mariembourg from P. Caussin, at rue de la Gare 57 (ⓣ060 31 11 36), and you can take off along RAVeL 2, the disused railway line turned cycle path, which begins behind the train station, in the direction of **Hermeton-sur-Meuse**. Turn off towards **Treignes** at **Matagne-la-Petite** and you can jump on the steam train for the trip back to Mariembourg – bikes travel for free.

Couvin

COUVIN, just 5km south from Mariembourg, was one of the first settlements in Hainaut to be industrialized, its narrow streets choked by forges and smelting works as early as the eighteenth century. In the event, Couvin was soon marginalized by the big cities further north, but it has battled gainfully on as a pint-sized manufacturing centre. Tourism has also had an impact, as the town lies at the heart of a popular holiday area, a quiet rural district whose forests and farmland are liberally sprinkled with country cottages and second homes. Long and slim, and bisected by the River Eau Noire, Couvin is short on specific sights, but it does possess a good-looking if small **old quarter**, set on top of a rocky hill high above the river and main road, where you'll find the boringly modern main square, **place du Général Piron**. About 3km north of town, in a lovely spot that's difficult to reach without your own transport, tours of the **Grottes de Neptune** (April–June & Sept tours daily 11am–noon & 4pm; July & Aug 11am–5.30pm; Oct–March Sat & Sun 11am–4pm; €8; ⓦwww.grottesdeneptune.be) last an hour and take you part of the way by boat on an underground river, before wowing you with some typically dramatic music and light shows.

Practicalities

From Couvin **bus** and **train station**, it's a ten-minute walk south to the main square along rue de la Gare and its continuation, Faubourg St-Germain. The **tourist office** is on the way to the Cavernes de l'Abîme, at rue de la Falaise 3 (Mon–Sat 9am–5pm, Sun 10am–4pm; ⓣ060 34 01 40, ⓦwww.couvin.be). The best **place to eat** hereabouts is the fabled *Brasserie des Fagnes*, outside Couvin on the way to Mariembourg (ⓣ060 31 15 70; July & Aug daily 10am–9pm; rest of year Tues–Fri 11am–7.30pm, Sat & Sun 11am–9pm), which is very popular and does delicious, crispy pizza-breads topped with cheeses and ham, and serves them with its own beer, Super des Fagnes – of which there are no less than five hundred varieties, from the usual brown, blond and cherry brews to daily specials like a coriander and orange-flavoured ale.

Brûly-de-Pesche

South of Couvin on the N5, it's a couple of kilometres to the 5km-long turnoff that weaves its way up into the wooded hills to the small village of **BRÛLY-DE-PESCHE**, where Hitler had his advance headquarters during the invasion of 1940. At the beginning of the war, both the French and the British were convinced that Hitler would attack through northern Belgium. They concluded that the wooded hills of the Ardennes – and the Botte de Hainaut – would be impassable to the Germans, or at least they would take so much time to cross that the Allies would have plenty of time to prepare their response. It was a disastrous miscalculation: the Germans rushed through the hills and smashed the light French defences in just a few days; thereafter, the fall of France was inevitable. The Nazis commandeered the entire village, using the hotel as a press centre, and drew up the terms of the French surrender in the church. The so-called **Abri d'Hitler** is in a wooded park nearby (Easter to Sept daily 10.30am–5pm; €4), with a couple of rebuilt huts showing a film on the 1940 campaign, a display on the Resistance and a couple of decrepit concrete bunkers – the only survivors from the war.

Chimay

It's best known for the beer brewed by local Trappists, but the small and ancient town of **CHIMAY**, 14km west of Couvin, is a charming old place in its own right, governed for several centuries by the de Croy family, a clan of local bigwigs who continue to occupy the **Château des Princes de Chimay** in the centre of town (April to early Sept daily guided tours at 10am, 11am, 3pm & 4pm; €7). A considerably altered structure, it was originally built in the fifteenth century, but was reconstructed in the seventeenth, then badly damaged by fire and partly rebuilt to earlier plans in the 1930s. Today the main body of the building is fronted by a long series of rectangular windows, edged by a squat turreted tower. Tours are led by the elderly Princess Elizabeth de Croy herself, who is an engaging and personable guide and speaks excellent English. She'll show you the old chapel in one of the turrets, lots of family portraits (right up to the present day), a hotch-potch of period furniture and – the highlight – the carefully restored private theatre, modelled on the Louis XV theatre at Fontainebleau, where you can watch a short film on the family and the property. Many of the de Croy family were buried in the **Collégiale des Saints Pierre et Paul** (Mon–Fri 9am–noon & 2–4.30pm, Sat 9am–5pm, Sun 11am–5pm), a mostly sixteenth-century limestone pile with a high and austere vaulted nave. The church's walls crowd the town's slender **Grand-Place**, an eminently bourgeois and exceedingly pretty little square surrounding the dinky **Monument des Princes**, a water fountain erected in 1852 in honour of the de Croys.

Practicalities

With regular connections from Charleroi and Couvin, Chimay's **bus station** sits on the edge of the town centre, a five-minute walk from the Grand-Place. The **tourist office** is a few paces east of the Grand-Place at rue de Noailles (July–Aug daily 8.30am–6pm; rest of year Mon–Fri 8.30am–5pm, Sat & Sun 10am–5pm; ⓣ060 21 98 84, ⓦwww.botteduhainaut.com).

Chimay's Trappists

The **Trappist** monks of the Cistercian Order of the Strict Observance live outside Chimay in the **Abbaye Notre-Dame de Scourmont**, an architecturally dull complex dating from the 1850s near the French border, about 10km out of town. The monastery itself is out of bounds, but you can wander the grounds and visit the church, though frankly this is not exactly riveting stuff. The Trappists no longer brew **beer** at the abbey – the modern brewery is some way away and is also closed to the public – but you can sample their beers and cheeses at the nearby *L'Auberge de Poteaupré*, a restaurant-brasserie and shop in a converted school about 500m from the abbey on the main road (ⓣ060 21 14 33, ⓦwww.chimay.com, Easter to mid-June Tues–Thurs 11am–5pm, Fri–Sun 11am–10pm; mid-June to mid-Sept Tues–Sun 11am–10pm; mid-Sept to Easter Tues & Thurs 11am–5pm & Fri–Sun 11am–10pm).

There are no hotels in Chimay, but *Le Petit Chapitre* is a delightful **B&B** comprising a handful of period rooms in attractive old premises, metres from the Grand-Place at place du Chapitre 5 (ⓣ060 21 10 42 or 0477 76 70 60, ⓦusers.skynet.be/bs938209/lepetitchapitre; ❸). Alternatively, there's the six-room *Hostellerie du Gahy*, about 12km west of Chimay at rue de Gahy 2 in Momignies (ⓣ060 51 10 93; ❷), with stylish rooms in an imaginatively converted farmhouse, and there's also the *L'Auberge de Poteaupré* (see box, p.275). Chimay also has a rudimentary **campsite**, the *Camping Communale de Chimay*, just west of the centre at allée des Princes 1 (ⓣ060 51 12 57; April–Oct).

Among **places to eat**, one of the best is *La Chimassiette*, Grand Place 16 (ⓣ060 21 90 42), a small modern restaurant serving excellent home-cooked food including *escaveche*, a mix of either eel or trout with onions, white wine and vinegar that's a speciality of the Botte. If it's full, try the more old-fashioned *Brasserie du Casino*, place des Ormeaux 27 (ⓣ060 21 49 80; closed Mon), You can drink at the *Queen Mary*, rue St-Nicolas 22, a cosy and popular place with Chimay Tripel on tap, and the rather more original *Vieux Chimay*, Grand-Place 22 (closed Tues), whose interior also houses a tobacconist's; the beer menu here clocks up over forty brews, and there's an outside terrace. Finally another of the town's specialities are Bernadins de Chimay **biscuits**, made with almonds, honey and brown sugar, which you can buy at the Pâtisserie Hubert, Grand-Place 32.

Travel details

Trains

Charleroi-Sud to: Brussels (every 30–50min; 45min); Couvin (hourly; 1hr); Mariembourg (hourly, 1hr); Mons (every 30min; 35min); Namur (every 30min; 40min); Nivelles (every 30min; 20min); Ottignies (hourly; 40min–1hr); Villers-la-Ville (every 30min; 20min); Walcourt (hourly; 20min).
La Louvière-Sud to: Binche (hourly; 15min); Charleroi (every 30min; 30min); Mons (hourly; 15min).
Mons to: Ath (hourly; 30min); Brussels (every 30min; 45min); Charleroi-Sud (every 30min; 30min); La Louvière-Sud (hourly; 15min); Tournai (every 30min; 30–45min).
Ottignies to: Louvain-la-Neuve (every 30min; 10min).
Tournai to: Ath (every 30min; 20min); Brussels (every 30min; 1hr); Mons (every 30min; 30–45min).

Buses

Charleroi to: Binche (hourly; 40min); Chimay (hourly; 1hr 10min).
Chimay to: Binche (hourly; 30min); Charleroi (hourly; 1hr 10min); Couvin (every 2hr; 30min).
Couvin to: Chimay (every 2hr; 30min); Namur (hourly; 1hr 15min).

5

The Ardennes

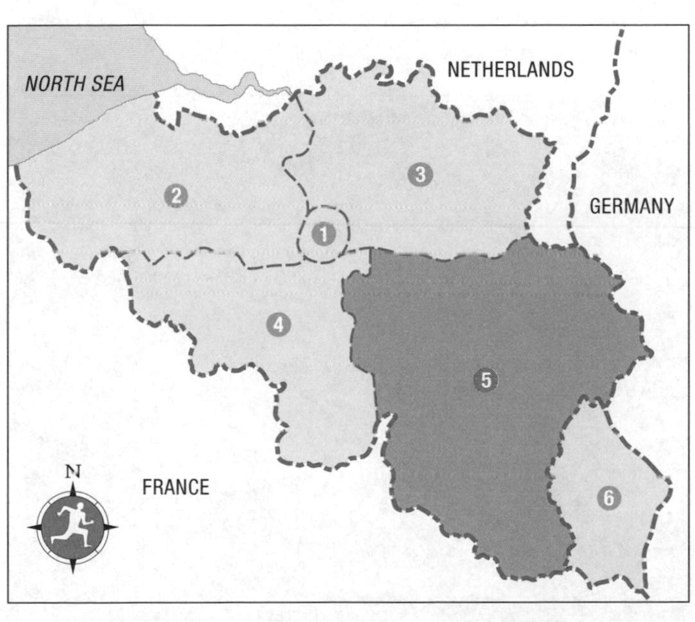

CHAPTER 5

Highlights

* **Trésor du Prieuré d'Oignies, Namur** A unique collection of exquisitely crafted, jewel-encrusted metalwork from the thirteenth century. See p.285
* **La Roche-en-Ardenne** This picture-postcard Ardennes resort is an ideal spot for some walking, camping or canoeing. See p.298
* **Bouillon's Château** The best preserved medieval castle in the country. See p.302
* **Stavelot's Carnival** One of Belgium's most flamboyant festivals – watch out for the Blancs Moussis, with their white hoods and long red noses. See p.318
* **Hautes Fagnes** Belgium's highest terrain, with genuinely wild walking through windy moorland and forest. See p.321

▲ La Roche-en-Ardenne

5

The Ardennes

Belgium's southern reaches are a striking contrast to the crowded, industrial north, for it's here in the south that the cities give way to the rugged wilderness landscapes of the **Ardennes**. Beginning in France, the Ardennes stretches east across Luxembourg and Belgium before continuing on into Germany, covering three Belgian provinces en route – Namur in the west, Luxembourg in the south and Liège in the east. The highest part, lying in the German-speaking east of the country, is the **Hautes Fagnes** (the High Fens), an expanse of windswept heathland that extends from Eupen to Malmédy. But this is not the Ardennes' most attractive or popular corner, which lies further west, its limits roughly marked by Dinant, La Roche-en-Ardenne and Bouillon. This region is given character and variety by its **river valleys**: deep, wooded canyons, at times sublimely and inspiringly beautiful, reaching up to high green peaks. The Ardennes' **cave systems** are also a major pull, especially those in the Meuse, Ourthe and Lesse valleys, carved out over the centuries by underground rivers that have cut through and dissolved the limestone hills, leaving stalagmites and stalactites in their wake.

The obvious gateway to the most scenic portion of the Ardennes is **Namur**, strategically sited at the junction of the Sambre and Meuse rivers, and well worth a visit in its own right. The town's pride and joy is its massive, mostly nineteenth-century citadel – once one of the mightiest fortresses in Europe – but it also musters a handful of decent museums, some good restaurants and (for the Ardennes) a lively bar scene. From Namur you can follow the Meuse by train down to **Dinant**, a pleasant – and very popular – journey, before going on to explore the **Meuse Valley** south of Dinant by boat or taking a canoe up the narrower and wilder **River Lesse**. From Dinant, routes lead east into the heart of the Ardennes – to workaday **Han-sur-Lesse**, surrounded by undulating hills riddled with caves, to prettier **Rochefort**, and to **St-Hubert**, with its splendid Italianate basilica. The most charming of the towns hereabouts, however, are **La Roche-en-Ardenne** to the northeast, a rustic, hardy kind of place, pushed in tight against the River Ourthe beneath wooded hills and renowned for its smoked ham and game; and **Bouillon**, a picturesque little place whose narrow streets trail alongside the River Semois beneath an ancient castle. Bouillon is situated close to the French frontier, on the southern periphery of the Belgian Ardennes and within easy striking distance of some of the region's most dramatic scenery, along the valley of the Semois. If you're visiting the eastern Ardennes, the handiest starting point is big and gritty **Liège**, an industrial sprawl from where it's a short hop south to the historic resort of **Spa** and the picturesque town of **Stavelot**, with its marvellous carnival. You can use Spa or Stavelot as bases for hiking or canoeing into the surrounding countryside and to venture into the **Hautes Fagnes**, though the attractive little town of **Malmédy** is slightly nearer.

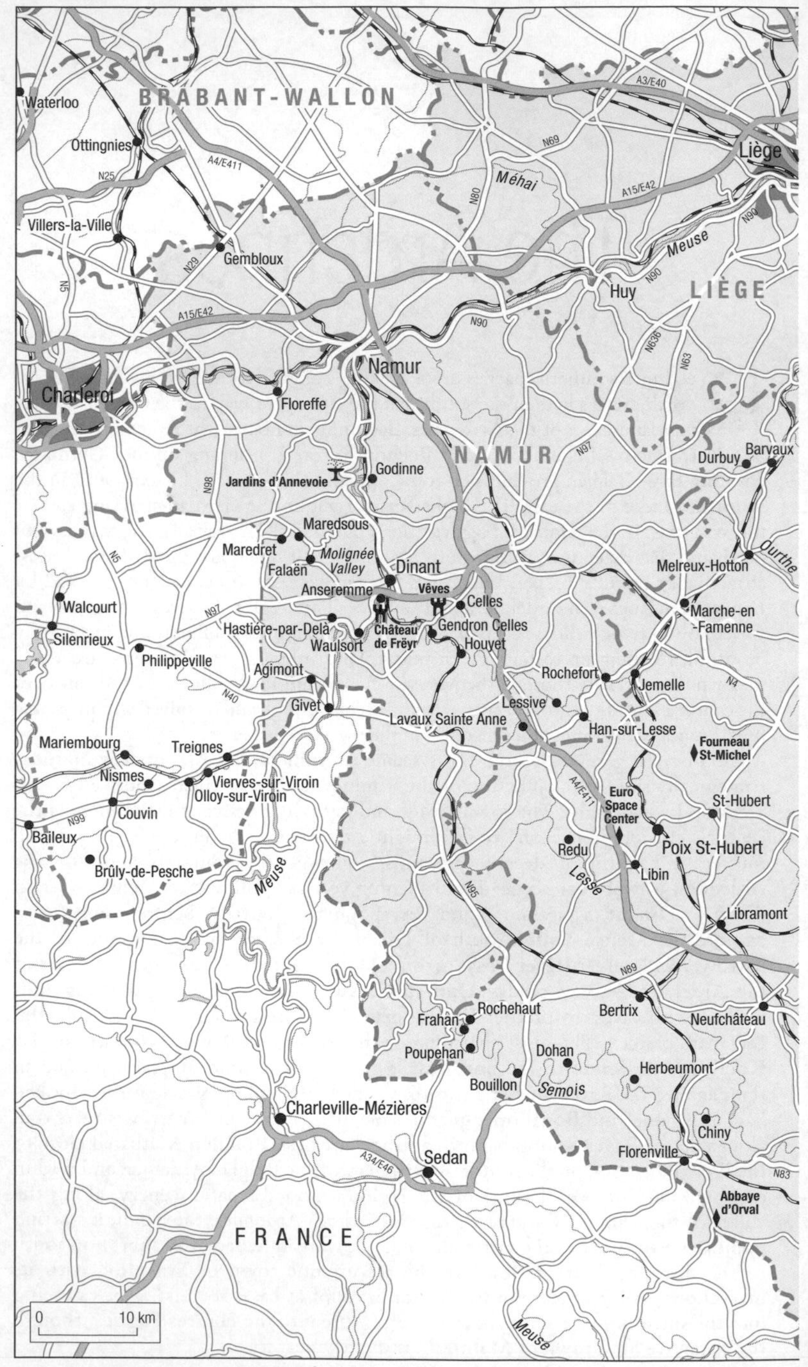
BRABANT-WALLON
Waterloo
Ottignies
A4/E411
N25
Villers-la-Ville
Gembloux
N29
N5
A15/E42
Charleroi
Floreffe
Namur
N90
Méhai
N80
N69
A3/E40
Liège
A15/E42
N90
Meuse
Huy
LIÈGE
N636
N63
NAMUR
N97
Durbuy
Barvaux
Jardins d'Annevoie
Godinne
N98
Maredsous
Maredret
Molignée Valley
Falaën
Dinant
N5
Anseremme
Vêves
Celles
Château de Frêyr
Gendron Celles
Houyet
Walcourt
N97
Hastière-par-Delà
Waulsort
Silenrieux
Philippeville
Agimont
N40
Givet
Ourthe
Melreux-Hotton
Marche-en -Famenne
N4
Rochefort
Jemelle
Lessive
Lavaux Sainte Anne
Han-sur-Lesse
Fourneau St-Michel
Mariembourg
Treignes
Nismes
Vierves-sur-Viroin
Olloy-sur-Viroin
Couvin
N99
Baileux
Brûly-de-Pesche
Meuse
A4/E411
Euro Space Center
Redu
St-Hubert
Poix St-Hubert
Libin
Lesse
N95
Libramont
N89
Bertrix
Neufchâteau
Rochehaut
Frahan
Poupehan
Dohan
Bouillon
Semois
Herbeumont
Chiny
Charleville-Mézières
Sedan
A34/E46
Florenville
N83
Abbaye d'Orval
FRANCE
0
10 km
Meuse

ARDENNES
N
N627
N3
A3/E40
Eupen
Verviers
Vesdre
HAUTES FAGNES
N67
Signal de
Botrange
(649m)
N62
Spa
Centre Nature
Botrange
Robertville
Aywaille
Remouchamps
Francorchamps
A27/E421
Malmédy
Race Circuit
N632
Stavelot
Amblève
Coo
Trois-Ponts
A26/E25
Lienne
N62
N89
N68
Samrée
La Roche-en-Ardenne
Maboge
Nadrin
Houffalize
Nisramont
GERMANY
A26/E25
LUXEMBOURG
Bastogne
Wiltz
Diekirch
Echternach
A11/E25
LUXEMBOURG
Arlon
LUXEMBOURG
CITY
Virton

Getting around the Ardennes is difficult – or at least time-consuming – without your own transport. The region is crossed by three main rail lines, but by and large they miss the main centres and to get to them you'll be reliant on connecting buses. Information on bus services is available through the regional bus provider **TEC** (see p.322), and local tourist offices will usually have a good set of timetables at hand. **Accommodation** is not always entirely straightforward either. **Hotels** are relatively thin on the ground given demand, and rooms are often in short supply in high season (late July and Aug) and at carnival time (Feb). There are plentiful self-catering alternatives, and of course the best way of appreciating the region is to **camp** at one of the many beautifully located sites. Wherever you end up, **walking** is the obvious pastime, rarely strenuous and often getting you out into some genuinely wild areas. **Canoes** and **kayaks** can be rented at most river settlements, and **mountain bikes** are often available too.

Namur and around

Just 60km southeast of Brussels, **NAMUR** is a logical first stop if you're heading into the Ardennes from the north or west, and is refreshingly clear of the industrial belts of Hainaut and Brabant. Many of Belgium's towns and cities have suffered at the hands of invading armies and the same is certainly true of Namur, so much so that from the sixteenth century up until 1978, when the Belgian army finally moved out, Namur remained the quintessential military town, its sole purpose being the control of the strategically important junction of the rivers Sambre and Meuse. Generations of military engineers have pondered how to make Namur's hilltop **citadel** impregnable – no one more so than Louis XIV's Vauban – and the substantial remains of these past efforts are now the town's main tourist attraction. Down below, the **centre** crowds the north bank of the River Sambre, its cramped squares and streets lined by big old mansions in the French style and sprinkled with several fine old churches and a handful of decent museums. There are some top-flight **restaurants** here too, but despite a substantial student presence, the **nightlife** is a little sedate, not that you'd guess if you visit during one of the town's main **festivals**: in particular, the four-day Namur en Mai (mid-May; Ⓦwww.namurenmai.be) packs the streets with jugglers, stilt-walkers and all sorts of spectaculars, and also showcases the talents of some internationally acclaimed performers.

Arrival and information

Namur's **train station** is on the northern edge of the town centre, on place de la Station. The square is also the terminus for local and regional buses, which stop outside the Maison du TEC, place de la Station 25 (Mon–Fri 7am–6pm, Sat 8.30am–5pm; Ⓣ081 25 35 55, Ⓦwww.infotec.be), which has lots of information about bus services across the whole of French-speaking Belgium. Two minutes' walk away is the main **tourist office**, on square Léopold (daily 9.30am–6pm; Ⓣ081 24 64 49, Ⓦwww.namurtourisme.be). Staff can help with accommodation, issue free town maps and brochures, give details of guided tours and provide information on what's on in the town and its environs.

From the train station, it takes about ten minutes to walk to the River Sambre via the **main street**, variously rue de Fer and rue de l'Ange. East of the foot of rue de l'Ange, the Pont de France spans the river to reach the tip of the "V" made by the confluence of the two rivers (the *grognon* or "pig's snout"). There's another tourist office by the river here, in the **Halle Al' Chair** (April–Oct daily

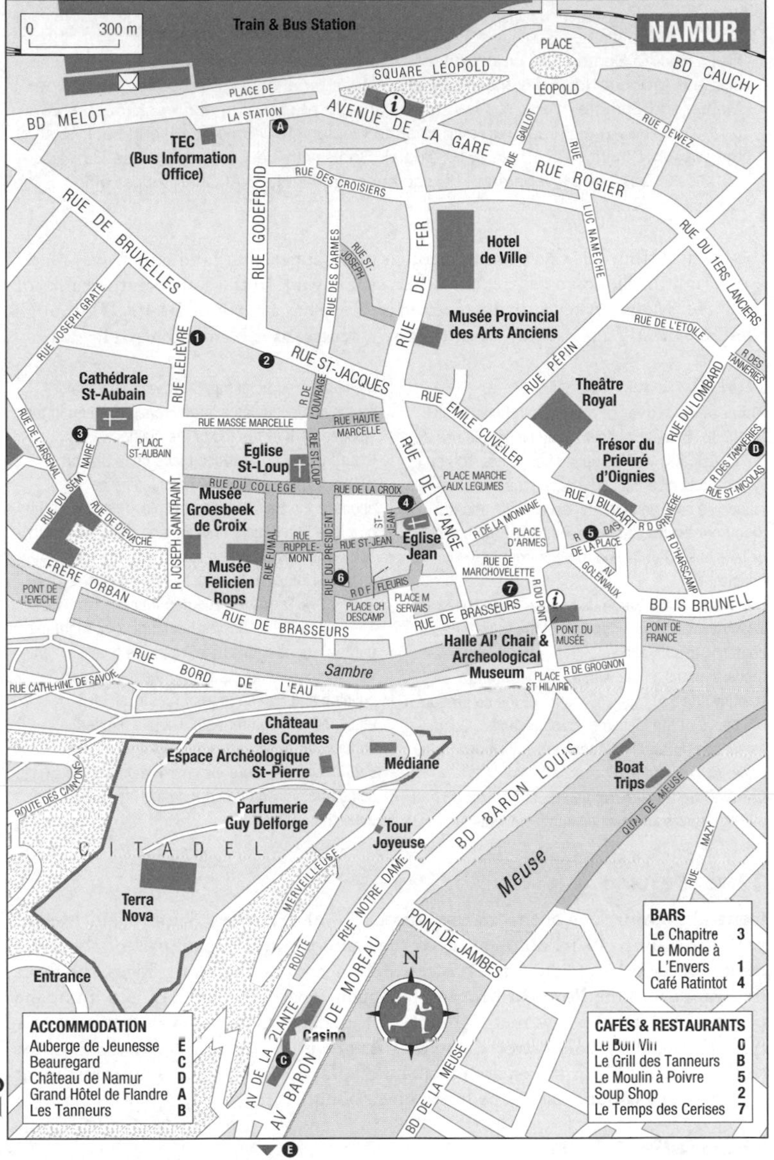

9.30am–6pm; ☎081 24 64 48), which offers the same services as the main office and sells tickets for river cruises.

Accommodation

Namur has relatively few hotels, and finding **accommodation** in high season can be a real pain if you haven't booked in advance. The cheapest **hotels** are close by

Boat trips

From April to September, **boat cruises** regularly sally forth from the quai de Meuse and the *grognon* to make the most of Namur's location at the confluence of the Meuse and Sambre rivers. You can take a short trip upstream and back (50min; €6) or, in July and August, make an excursion to Wepion (1hr 45min; €10) and back or all the way to Dinant (3hr 45min; €16 single). Book with La Compagnie des Bateaux (Ⓣ082 22 23 15, Ⓦwww.bateaux-meuse.be) or at the Halle Al'Chair tourist office.

the train station, but there are two much more appetizing (and expensive) places – one right in the town centre, the other a short walk to the south on the banks of the River Meuse. Alternatively, the tourist office has a stock of **B&Bs** (❶), though these are mostly a good way from the town centre, as is Namur's **hostel**.

Hotels and hostel

Auberge de Jeunesse ave Félicien Rops Ⓣ081 22 36 88, Ⓦwww.laj.be. In a big old house beside the Meuse, this well-equipped hostel has 100 beds in two- to twelve-bedded rooms, plus a kitchen, a laundry, a café and internet access. It's about 3km from the train station, south past the casino – or take bus #3 or #4. Dorm beds from €15, doubles. ❶

Beauregard ave Baron de Moreau 1 Ⓣ081 23 00 28, Ⓦwww.benotel.com. Part of the town's casino complex, this hotel has attractive, large and modern rooms, some with a river view and balcony. It's a 10min walk south of the centre, on the banks of the Meuse below the citadel. Good value, and an excellent breakfast is included in the price. ❸

Château de Namur ave de l'Ermitage 1 Ⓣ081 72 99 00, Ⓦwww.chateaudenamur.com. This medium-sized hotel has thirty well-appointed rooms and occupies a large French château in the wooded park at the top of the citadel. ❺

Grand Hôtel de Flandre place de la Station Ⓣ081 23 18 68, Ⓦwww.hotelflandre.be. Right opposite the train station, this place received a bit of a facelift a couple of years ago and now boasts spick-and-span modern rooms. Not the most characterful place to stay, but very convenient. ❸

Les Tanneurs rue des Tanneries 13 Ⓣ081 24 00 24, Ⓦwww.tanneurs.com. Right in the town centre, this hotel occupies a lavishly and imaginatively renovated seventeenth-century building and has a range of rooms, all well equipped and comfortable. There's (limited) parking, wi-fi and two good restaurants (see p.287), and the more expensive rooms are sometimes discounted during the off-season and weekends. ❺–❽

The Town

Central Namur fans out from the confluence of the rivers Sambre and Meuse, with the hilltop citadel on one side of the Sambre and the main part of the town centre on the other. Citadel and centre are connected by a pair of bridges, the **Pont de France** and the **Pont du Musée**. The main square, the modern and mundane **place d'Armes**, is a few metres north of these two bridges and a stone's throw from the main shopping streets, **rue de l'Ange** and its extension **rue de Fer**, just to the west of which the enclosed square of **place Marché aux Legumes** lies at the heart of Namur's mainly pedestrianized old quarter.

The Halle Al' Chair

Right on the river by the Pont du Musée, the red-brick **Halle Al' Chair** is one of the stand-out buildings of Namur's old town. Built by the Spanish in the sixteenth century, and originally a meat market, it now houses a branch of the tourist office (see p.282) and Namur's small **archeological museum** (Tues–Sun 10am–5pm; €2), with mosaics and other finds from the Roman era. Its most interesting exhibit is a scale model of Namur in the eighteenth century, a copy of the original in the Invalides museum in Paris.

The Trésor du Prieuré d'Oignies

The pick of the town's museums is also its smallest, the **Trésor du Prieuré d'Oignies**, housed in just one small room of a convent at rue Julie Billiart 17 (Tues–Sat 10am–noon & 2–5pm, Sun 2–5pm; €2). It's a unique collection that comprises examples of the exquisitely beautiful gold and silver work of **Brother Hugo d'Oignies**, one of the most gifted of the region's medieval metalworkers. From the eleventh to the thirteenth century, the Meuse valley was famous for the skill of its craftsmen, who worked in an essentially Romanesque style but evolved a more naturalistic and dynamic approach to their subject matter, a characteristic of early Gothic. Hugo was an innovator in the art of **filigree**, raising the decoration from the background so that the tiny human figures and animals seem to be suspended in space; and **niello**, in which a black mixture of sulphur or lead is used to incise lines into the gold. The pieces here are elaborately studded with precious and semiprecious stones and display an exquisite balance between ornament and function, depicting minute hunting scenes, with animals leaping convincingly through delicate foliage, engraved with a Christian dedication, or embossed with a tiny picture of the artist offering up his art to God in worship. In particular, look out for the intricately worked double-crosses, the dazzling reliquary cover for St Peter's rib, the charming songbird and goblet of St Marie of Oignies, and a magnificent cover for a Book of the Gospels. The free audio-guide in English helps to make sense of it all.

The Musée Provincial des Arts Anciens

The **Musée Provincial des Arts Anciens**, rue de Fer 24 (Tues–Sun 10am–6pm; €5) occupies one of the finest of Namur's eighteenth-century mansions, set back from the street behind a formal gateway and courtyard. The collection begins with an enjoyable sample of devotional metalwork from the Mosan, most memorably the dinky geometrics of the brass enamels, and moves on to medieval sculptures and painted wooden panels upstairs. Of the many paintings, the most distinguished are by Henri Bles, an early sixteenth-century, Antwerp-based artist who favoured panoramic landscapes populated by tiny figures. Look out also for the temporary exhibitions, most of which are displayed in the gatehouse.

The Église St-Loup and the Cathédrale St-Aubain

Perhaps the best of Namur's churches is the **Église St-Loup** on rue du Collège, a Baroque extravagance built for the Jesuits between 1621 and 1645, with a fluently carved facade and a sumptuous interior of marble walls and sandstone vaulting. The high altar is actually wood painted to look like marble – the ship carrying the last instalment of Italian marble sank and the Jesuits were obliged to finish the church off with this imitation.

At the far end of rue du Collège, place St-Aubain is home to the **Cathédrale St-Aubain**, a monstrous Neoclassical pile devoid of much charm, outside or in, with acres of creamy white paint and a choir decorated with melodramatic paintings by Jacques Nicolai, one of Rubens' less talented pupils. There's not much else to see, but the attached **Musée Diocésain** displays objects gathered from churches across Namur and Luxembourg provinces.

The Musée de Groesbeek de Croix and the Musée Felicien Rops

Just off place St-Aubain, the **Musée de Groesbeek de Croix**, rue Joseph Saintraint 3 (Tues–Sun 10am–12.30pm & 1.15–5pm; €3) is a large and rambling mansion that gives a fine impression of the lifestyle of a patrician family during the Enlightenment. It's an appealing mixture of the grand and the homely, with the dining table laid out for tea, a fabulously authentic eighteen-century kitchen and a delightful garden out the back. There's not much in the way of standout exhibits, but the feel of the place, as if the owners had just left the building, is satisfyingly authentic.

Around the corner from the Groesbeek, the **Musée Felicien Rops**, rue Fumal 12 (Jan–June & Sept–Dec Tues–Sun 10am–6pm; July & Aug daily 10am–6pm; €3), is devoted to the life and work of the eponymous painter, graphic artist and illustrator, Felicien Rops (1833–98), a native of Namur who settled in Paris in the 1870s and illustrated the works of Mallarmé and, in particular, Baudelaire. He had an interest in the occult and a reputation for a debauched lifestyle, but was also an accomplished artist, best known for his erotic and macabre drawings, of which there are a good selection on display here – skeletons, nuns and priests depicted in oddly compromising poses, or old men serviced by young, partially clad women. Some are just perverse, but the wit in his work is hard to deny: check out his famous *Pornocrates*, and his drawing of the *Apple Seller*.

The citadel

The result of centuries of military endeavour, Namur's **citadel** is an immense complex which clambers and crawls all over the steep and craggy hill that rises high above the confluence of the rivers Sambre and Meuse. It's a curious mixture of styles and periods: during the medieval period, a succession of local counts made elaborate additions to each other's fortifications, which were gradually abandoned when the section near the top of the hill – now loosely known as the **Château des Comtes** – was incorporated into a partly subterranean fortress, the **Médiane**, whose ramifications occupy the eastern portion of the present citadel. This part of the fortress was always the most vulnerable to attack and for the next two hundred years successive generations of military engineers, including Vauban and the Dutchman Von Coehoorn, tried to figure out the best way to protect it. The surviving structure reflects this preoccupation, with the lines of defence becoming more complex and extensive the further up you go. To further strengthen the defences, the Spanish completed the **Terra Nova** bastion at the west end of the citadel in the 1640s, separating the two with a wide moat; this made Namur one of the strongest fortresses in Europe, but didn't stop Louis XIV besieging the town in 1692. The Dutch rebuilt the citadel between 1816 and 1825, and much of today's remains date to this period.

Visiting the site

The plateau which comprises the top of the citadel can be reached by car and bike as well as on foot, and a **minibus** cruises the town centre and then travels up to the citadel at regular intervals every day during the summer months; one of its stops is at the tip of the *grognon*.

The citadel is open all year and there's no admission fee, though certain additional attractions are seasonal and impose charges. The views from the citadel, over the town and the surrounding countryside, are fantastic, and you could spend a happy half-day wandering around the complex, exploring its grassy spaces and ancient gates and bridges or ambling along one of the five colour-coded **walking routes**, detailed on a leaflet available from the tourist office or Terra Nova information office, best of which is the circular yellow walk, which lasts an hour and takes in most of the central area. If you don't want to walk, a mini-train does much the same route every hour or so for €5; you can also visit the underground casemates (€5), which stretch under Terra Nova and Mediane and are the largest such network in Europe, some 7km in total – a dank, 45-minute guided tour takes you through both the Dutch and Spanish tunnels, while another tour rambles around the medieval parts of the complex (€5), culminating with a visit to the so-called Château des Comtes, where a lower level displays swords, chain mail, cannonballs and the like from the Middle Ages – though you can visit this under your own steam, too. There's also the **Espace St-Pierre**, just below the Château des Comtes, which has displays on local archeological digs and discoveries, and for something completely different, the **Atelier de Parfumerie Guy Delforge**, just below Terra Nova, is a perfume shop and mini-factory (July & Aug daily 9.15am–5.30pm, Sun 2.15–5.30pm; rest of year closed Mon).

Eating and drinking

Namur has a first-rate selection of **cafés** and **restaurants** as well as a good supply of **bars**, many of them clustered on and around the quaint, pedestrianized squares just west of rue de l'Ange – place Marché-aux-Legumes and place Chanoine Descamps.

Cafés and restaurants

Le Bon Vin rue du Président 43 ⓣ081 22 28 08. Christiane and Willy Delcour have created a popular organic café here on the corner with rue des Fossés Fleuris. The food is freshly prepared and seasonal and, as the name suggests, there is a good selection of wine. Three courses and a *quart* of wine will set you back about €30. Tues–Sat lunchtime and Fri & Sat eve.

Le Grill des Tanneurs rue des Tanneries 13 ⓣ081 24 00 24. Situated on the first floor of the *Hôtel Les Tanneurs* (see p.284), this excellent restaurant features French-style cuisine in smooth (and convincing) repro-antique surroundings. Main courses start at a very reasonable €14. Mon–Sat noon–2.30pm & 7–11pm, Sun noon–2.30pm.

Le Moulin à Poivre rue Bas de la Place 19 ⓣ081 23 11 20. Cosy little restaurant offering tasty Franco-Belgian food, with mains from as little as €10. Mon–Sat noon–2.30pm & 6.30–10.30pm.

Soup Shop rue de Bruxelles 35. For a hearty and healthy lunch, this is the place to come. As you would expect from the name, soup is the main event, but the salads, quiches and desserts are delicious too – and great value, all at less than €10. Mon–Sat noon–6pm.

Le Temps des Cerises rue des Brasseurs 22 ⓣ081 22 53 26. Intimate, cherry-coloured and themed restaurant offering a quality menu of French and Basque dishes. Main courses average around €18. Tues–Sat from 6.30pm & Tues–Fri noon–3pm.

Bars

Le Chapitre rue du Séminaire 4. Unassuming bar tucked away behind the cathedral, with an extensive beer list. Popular with students and a very busy and convivial place for a drink late evening.

Le Monde à L'Envers rue Lelièvre 28. Lively bar just up from the cathedral. A favourite spot for university students.

Café Ratintot place Marché-aux-Legumes. With attractive antique decor, including an old French cockerel or two, this is one of central Namur's most original bars.

Around Namur

Namur is a pleasant place to spend two or three days, which gives you time to visit its leading local attractions: the splendid hilltop **L'Abbaye de Floreffe**, to the west of town; the classically landscaped **Jardins d'Annevoie**, set beside the Meuse about 18km south of town; and, south again, the abbey of **Maredsous** (good for beer and cheeses). A visit to the gardens is readily incorporated into a longer day-trip (by car or train) along this stretch of the **Meuse**. The river is too wide to be all that dramatic, but it's still an enjoyable journey as it passes through a varied landscape of gentle wooded slopes interrupted by steep escarpments capped by ruined castles. The Namur area has long been popular with rock-climbers, one of whom was King Albert I, who fell to his death in a climbing accident here in 1934.

L'Abbaye de Floreffe

Founded in 1121, **L'Abbaye de Floreffe** lies some 10km west of Namur towards Charleroi (French-language guided tours only: April–Sept daily at 1.30pm,

2.30pm, 3.30pm, 4.30pm & 5.30pm, plus July & Aug at 10.30am & 11.30am; 1hr; €2.50; Ⓦwww.abbaye-de-floreffe.be). The town of **Floreffe** is itself drab and dreary, but the abbey, with its well-kept grounds populated by a flock of peacocks, occupies a splendid hilltop location above the town with wide views over the River Sambre. Little remains of the original complex and the imposing brick buildings of today are mainly eighteenth-century, the main exception being the **abbey church**, a hotchpotch of architectural styles with Romanesque, Gothic and Baroque features. The interior is best known for its remarkable carved oak **choir stalls**, the work of one man, Pierre Enderlin, who took sixteen years (1632–48) to complete them. In a superb state of preservation and displaying a marvellous inventiveness and intricacy, the stalls are carved with a stunning variety of figures, including biblical characters, eminent and holy persons, and some 220 angels – each one of them unique. Many of the faces are obviously portraits, humorous, sometimes satirical in tone, and there's a self-portrait of the artist hidden among them. Below the main complex, the **Moulin Brasserie** (Ⓣ081 44 53 03; Mon–Fri 11am–6pm, Sat & Sun 11am–8pm), comprising the creatively refurbished old mill and brewery, showcases the abbey's products, principally beer and cheese. Amongst several brews, the most distinctive are Floreffe La Meilleure (8.5 percent), a strong, dark and tangy affair, and Temps des Cerises (3.5 percent), a cherry-flavoured beer; both are served from the barrel.

The abbey makes a comfortable half-day excursion by car from Namur, but getting there by **public transport** is a bit awkward. There are buses (#28) but they run infrequently – every two hours or so – and the Namur–Charleroi train, which is more frequent (hourly; 10min), drops passengers on the other side of the town from the abbey, a 1.5km walk away: turn right outside the station and keep going along the main street.

Les Jardins d'Annevoie

Les Jardins d'Annevoie (daily: April–June & Sept–Oct 9.30am–5.30pm; July & Aug daily 9.30am–6.30pm; €7.80; Ⓦwww.annevoie.be), in the wooded hills above the River Meuse about 18km south of Namur, is a highly recommended stop on the road between Namur and Dinant. The gardens are generally reckoned to be among the most appealing in the whole of the country, hence their popularity with day-trippers. The estate – both gardens and manor house – has been in the hands of the Montpelliers since 1675 and one of the clan, a certain Charles Alexis, turned his hand (or rather those of his gardeners) to garden design in the 1770s. Charles was inspired by his travels in France, Italy and England, picking up tips which he then rolled into one homogeneous creation. From the French came formal borders, from the Italians the romance of mossy banks and arbours, while the English influence is most obvious in the grotto of Neptune. They are architectural rather than flower gardens, and the common denominator is water – everywhere you look there are fountains, jets and mini-waterfalls, all worked from natural pressure from the tree-lined Grand Canal, immediately above the gardens. If you visit in July, you can also pick raspberries at the end of the walking circuit. Otherwise there is a pleasant café, the *Orangerie*, above the shop offering views over the garden and the local Maredsous beer on tap.

The nearest **train station** is Godinne, 2km east of the gardens and served by hourly trains on the Namur–Dinant line; to reach the gardens, walk up the ramp of the flyover from the station, turn right at the top and then hang a left to cross the bridge over the Meuse. It isn't a pleasant walk though – there's too much traffic. Alternatively, **bus** #21 Namur–Maredsous (4 daily; 30min) stops just outside the gardens, while the Namur–Dinant bus #34 (Mon–Fri 1 daily; 30min) stops on the main road, a ten-minute walk away.

Maredsous Abbey

Twelve kilometres west of Annevoie, the complex of the **Abbaye de Maredsous** (Ⓦwww.maredsous.be) sits high up among the trees, a popular place, and not necessarily as a religious institution. Founded in the 1870s, its neo-Gothic architecture is pretty routine, and most people head instead to the **St-Joseph visitor centre** (Mon–Fri 9am–6pm, Sat & Sun 9am–8pm), a complex of shops and cafes that does a roaring trade in Maredsous produce, selling, bread, butter, cheese, pâté and, of course, the abbey's various beers – they produce a blond, a bruin and a strong tripel. **Bus** #35 from Dinant train station (2–3 daily; 35min) and bus #21 from Namur bus station (2–4 daily; 50min) both stop at or near the Abbaye de Maredsous.

The Molignée Valley

Down below Maredsous, the beautiful **Molignée valley** winds it way towards the Meuse. With a good map you can explore on foot, but you might want to instead opt for a journey by **railbike** – adapted "bikes" which can carry up to four people along the disused railway tracks between Falaën, 4km south of Maredsous, and Warnant, about 10km to the northeast. You pick them up from the Railbike premises in Falaën at rue de la Gare 82 (daily 11am, 1pm, 3pm & 5pm; single person from €17 and groups of 2–4 people from €15 per person; Ⓣ082 69 90 79).

Dinant

Slung along the River Meuse beneath craggy green cliffs, **DINANT**, 30km from Namur, has a picture-postcard setting, its distinctive, onion-domed church of Notre-Dame lording it over the comings and goings of the barges and cruise boats. The Romans were the first to put the place on the map, occupying the town and naming it after Diana, the goddess of the hunt, but the town's heyday came much later, in the fourteenth century, when it boomed from the profits of the metal-working industry, turning copper, brass and bronze into ornate jewellery known as *dinanderie*. Dinant's prosperity turned rival cities, especially Namur, green with envy, and they watched with some satisfaction as local counts slugged it out for possession of the town. They may have been even happier when, in 1466, Charles the Bold decided to settle his Dinant account by simply razing the place to the ground. One result of all this medieval blood and thunder was the construction of an imposing **citadel** on the cliff immediately above the town, and, although Dinant was sacked on several subsequent occasions and badly damaged in both World Wars, the fortress has survived to become the town's principal attraction.

By boat from Dinant

Despite its serpentine profile, the River Meuse south of Dinant is not especially scenic, though the town's boat-tour operators still drum up lots of business for their **river cruises**. There are several different companies, but all boats depart from avenue Winston Churchill, one block from the main street, rue Grande; prices and itineraries are pretty standard whichever company you choose. Two good bets are the cruises to **Anseremme** (mid-March to Oct every 30min; €5; return trip 45min), where you can hike off into the surrounding countryside (see p.292); and **Freÿr** (May to mid-Sept 2.30pm; €9; return trip 1hr 45min). There are also boats north along the Meuse to Namur (see p.282) on Sundays from mid-July to late August (€14 single, €20 return).

Nowadays, Dinant makes a healthy living as a base for the tourist industry on the **rivers Meuse** and **Lesse** (see p.292), its cruise boats, canoes and kayaks providing watery fun and games for thousands of visitors – though frankly the scenery is not nearly as wild as you'll find deeper in the Ardennes, whilst the town itself is quickly exhausted.

Arrival, information and accommodation

Dinant's **train station** is about 300m from the bridge that spans the Meuse over to the church of Notre-Dame, next to what passes for the main square, place Reine Astrid. **Buses** arrive and leave from outside the train station. The **tourist office** is beside the west (train station) end of the bridge at ave Cadoux 8 (Mon–Fri 8.30am–7pm, Sat 9.30am–5pm, Sun 10am–4.30pm; ⓣ082 22 28 70, ⓦwww.dinant-tourisme.be).

Hotels are thin on the ground in Dinant and its immediate environs, though the tourist office does have the details of a few **B&Bs** (❶). There's no hostel, but there are plenty of **campsites**, one of the better being the well-appointed *Camping Villatoile* (ⓣ082 22 22 85, ⓦwww.villatoile.be; March–Oct), in a wooded setting beside the River Lesse in **Anseremme**, about 4km south of town.

Hotels

Aquatel rue du Vélodrôme 15, Anseremme ⓣ082 21 35 35, ⓦwww.ansiaux.be. Basic, one-star hotel with hostel-style rooms and kayak rental – it's beside the River Lesse, 4km or so south of Dinant. Rooms for two or five and a dormitory for eighteen. ❷

Le Freyr chaussée des Alpinistes 22, Anseremme ⓣ082 22 25 75, ⓦwww.lefreyr.be. Very comfortable hotel, with just six rooms and a first-rate restaurant. Set in a good-looking older building close to the Meuse about 4km south of Dinant. Closed Feb & March. ❷

Ibis Dinant Rempart d'Albeau 16 ⓣ082 21 15 00, ⓦwww.ibishotel.com. Chain hotel in a new and conspicuous brick block metres from the river, 1km or so south of the town bridge. No points for originality, but this *Ibis* does what it does proficiently enough, with most of its neat and trim, modern rooms looking out over the water. ❸

The Town

Dinant's long main street, **rue Grande**, follows the river one block inland from the town's most distinctive landmark, the originally Gothic **church of Notre-Dame** (daily 9am–6pm), on the main square of place Reine Astrid, topped with the bulbous spire that features on all the tourist brochures. Rebuilt on several occasions, there's actually not much of interest to see inside, but it's worth a quick look for its cavernous, high-vaulted interior and short nave. On the right of the ambulatory, there's an unfinished painting by one of Dinant's most famous sons, the nineteenth-century artist Antoine Wiertz (who has his own museum in Brussels; see p.86), a mawkish affair dedicated to his parents and entitled *We'll Meet Again in Heaven*.

The church is next to the entrance to Dinant's **citadel** (April–Sept daily 10am–6pm; Oct to mid-Dec & mid-Feb to March daily except Fri 10am–4.30pm; €7; ⓦwww.citadellededinant.be). You can either climb the 400-odd steps or save yourself the sweat by catching the cable car – the *téléphérique* (free, though open only on weekends out of season); you can see the various rooms of the citadel by joining one of the guided tours that leave from the castle keep every half-hour in summer. The French destroyed the medieval castle in 1703 and the present structure mostly dates from the Dutch occupation of the early nineteenth century. The citadel saw heavy **fighting** in both world wars. In 1914, the Germans struggled to dislodge French soldiers who had occupied the stronghold just before they could get here, and took a bitter revenge on the townsfolk, executing over six

Sax Appeal in Dinant

Dinant's most famous native is **Adolphe Sax** (1814–94), the inventor of the saxophone. Saxophiles will want to have a look at the musician's old home, at rue Adolphe Sax 35, marked by a commemorative **plaque** and a neat stained-glass mural of a man blowing his horn (sadly it's not open to the public), along with a statue of the king of cool reclining on a bench outside. For more sax appeal, take a left off Grand Rue onto rue en Rhée for the enjoyable **Maison de la Pataphonie**, at no. 51 (Wed 2.30pm & Sun 2pm & 4.30pm tours by reservation; 1hr 15min; €5; ☎082 21 39 39), which among other things supplies an interactive journey into the life and sounds of Sax but bear in mind it's popular and you need to book in advance.

hundred and deporting several hundred more before torching the town. The Germans took the citadel again in 1940, and it was the scene of more bitter fighting when the Allies captured Dinant in 1944. There's a memorial to those who gave their lives here and part of the interior has been turned into what is essentially a historical museum, with models recreating particular battles and the Dutch occupation, plus a modest military section with weapons from the Napoleonic era to the last war. You can also see the wooden beams which supported the first bridge in Dinant, built nine hundred years ago by monks and found again by accident in 1952, as well as prison cells and the kitchen and bakery of the Dutch fortress.

The final thing to see in Dinant is the **Grotte la Merveilleuse**, just outside town, on the far side of the river about 750m from the bridge at route de Philippeville 142 (hourly tours: July & Aug Mon–Fri 11am–5pm, Sat & Sun 10am–6pm; Sept & Oct & April–June 11am–5pm; Jan–Feb & Nov–Dec Sat & Sun 1–4pm; €8, €12 including a Dinant–Anseremme cruise), a cave system discovered in 1904 and opened as a tourist attraction shortly afterwards. It's not the largest or most impressive of the Ardennes cave complexes by any means, but its 45-minute tours take you some 40m below ground, and give a good grounding in the science of stalagmites and stalactites, rock formations and caves in general.

Eating and drinking

Catering for Dinant's passing tourist trade is big business, which means that run-of-the-mill **cafés and restaurants** are ten-a-penny, although quality places are thin on the ground. That said, there are still a couple worth mentioning, and several enjoyable **bars** too.

Les Amourettes place St-Nicolas 11 ☎082 22 57 36. Mid-range Franco-Italian restaurant at the end of rue Grande, with an inventive menu and a nice terrace on the square in the summer. Main courses around €15. Closed Mon.

La Broche rue Grande 22 ☎082 22 82 81. Smart and well-regarded French restaurant that does an excellent three-course menu for €26. Closed Tues & Wed lunch.

Patisserie Jacobs rue Grande 147. Patisserie with a small café section at the back that, among other things, sells *couques de Dinant*, a honey-flour combination that's better admired than consumed unless you have the teeth of a horse. Staff will assure you the harder they are, the fresher. Daily 9am–6pm.

Le Sax place Reine Astrid 13. Unpretentious bar with a good beer selection; sit outside when the traffic has calmed down and peer up at the flood-lit citadel.

Le Themis rue du Palais de Justice 26. Relaxed and easy-going neighbourhood bar with a better-than-average beer menu. A short walk south of the church along rue Grande – the third turning on the right.

A la Ville de Bruges rue Adolphe Sax 39 ☎082 224 155. Next door to the Adolphe Sax house, this is a friendly and unpretentious place, serving a safe but delicious menu of steaks and Belgian stapels for lunch and dinner. Most mains €10–12. Mon, Tues & Thurs–Sun 11.30am–3.30pm & 6–10.30pm.

South of Dinant: the Meuse and the Lesse river valleys

Beyond Dinant, the **River Meuse** loops its way south to Givet, across the border in France, and can be explored by cruise boat from Dinant. This stretch of the river is pleasant enough, but certainly not exciting – it's too wide and sluggish for that – and neither is the scenery more than mildly inviting, its best feature being the steep, wooded cliffs framing portions of the riverbank.

The tiny settlements lining up along the river are pretty bland too, the only real exception being **HASTIÈRE-PAR-DELÀ**, about 15km from Dinant, which is home to the fascinating **Église Notre Dame** (May–Sept daily 10am–5pm), a finely proportioned church built at the behest of a colony of Irish monks in the 1030s, although the Gothic choir was added two hundred years later. Subsequent architectural tinkering followed two attacks – one by Protestants in 1568, the

Walking, biking and canoeing along the River Lesse

The Dinant tourist office sells the Institut Géographique National's **map** *Dinant et ses Anciennes Communes*, which shows fifteen numbered **circular walks** in the Dinant area, each of which has a designated starting point at one of the district's hotels. Also shown on the map are one cycling circuit and five **mountain bike routes**, the latter ranging from five to forty kilometres in length; to see the most attractive scenery you need to get out on the longer routes 19 and 20. The 5km **Walk 5** takes in much of the locality's most pleasant scenery, weaving its way along and around the River Lesse between the hamlets of Anseremme and Pont à Lesse. It involves some reasonably testing ascents, whereas **GR route 126** offers about three hours of gentle walking along the Lesse between Houyet and Gendron-Celles, both of which have a train station. Take the train timetable along with your picnic and you can plan to arrive at Gendron-Celles in time for the return train to Dinant. The 8km **Walk 8** is not one of the more spectacular routes – much of it is over tarmac road – but it does allow you to visit a couple of places of some interest. From Gendron-Celles train station, the route leads about 2km northeast along a country road – and beside a small tributary of the Lesse – to **Vêves**, whose fifteenth-century château is perched on a grassy mound overlooking the surrounding countryside (April–Oct daily 10am–5.30pm; €6; ⓦwww.chateau-de-veves.be). With its spiky turrets and dinky towers, the château is inordinately picturesque, but the interior is disappointingly mundane – mostly eighteenth-century period rooms. A couple of kilometres further on, **Celles** is one of the prettier villages hereabouts, gently filing up the slope of a wooded hill, underneath the huge tower and Lombard arches of the Romanesque Église St-Hadelin (daily 9am–6pm; free). There's a sporadic bus service from here to Dinant, or you can return to Gendron-Celles train station via the Bois de Hubermont. If you're driving, note that Celles is on the N94, about 9km east of Dinant.

The standard itinerary for potential **canoeists and kayakers** begins at Anseremme, where most take the train (or special minibus) to either **Gendron-Celles** (for the 11km 3hr paddle back) or **Houyet** (21km; 5hr). If you're travelling by train to begin with, you can go straight to Gendron or Houyet from Dinant and pick up a boat there – but remember that advance reservations are well-nigh essential. The Lesse itself is wild and winding, with great scenery, though be warned that it sometimes gets so packed that there's a veritable canoe log jam. Consequently, it's a good idea to set out as early as possible to avoid some of the crush – though if you're paddling back from Houyet you really have to get going early anyway. Both Gendron-Celles and Houyet train stations are metres from the river – and the boats – and also make good starting points for hiking the surrounding countryside.

other by the French revolutionary army in the 1790s – but most of the medieval church has survived intact, with a flat wooden roof, plain square pillars and heavy round arches. The **triumphal arch** bears a faded painting dating from the original construction and is underpinned by gallows (wooden scaffolding), which in their turn support an unusual German fifteenth-century Calvary, depicting Christ, Mary and St John standing on a dragon. Close by, the wooden thirteenth-century **choir stalls** are among the oldest in Belgium, with unique misericord carvings – some allegorical, some satirical and some purely decorative. Curiously, a number of them were replaced with a plain triangle in 1443 on the grounds that they were blasphemous – or at least disrespectful. Finally, next to the baptismal font are two **statues** of the Virgin, one of which – the one on the left in the glass case – is an exquisite sixteenth-century carving, whose graceful posture has earned it a place in several national exhibitions. After you've explored the church, you can pop across the road to *Le Côté Meuse*, a pleasant **café** with a good line in crepes and waffles.

Wilder and prettier, the **River Lesse** spears off the Meuse in **ANSEREMME**, and although there's precious little point in hanging around here, it's a good starting point for both local hikes and canoe trips; by the river, Lesse Kayaks (Ⓣ082 22 43 97, Ⓦwww.lessekayaks.be) rents out one- and two-seater kayaks, three-person canoes and large piloted boats for up to twenty passengers. Reckon on paying €16–19 for a single kayak, €22–30 for a double, or around €30 for a three-person canoe.

Heading south from Anseremme, it's 2.5km to the solitary **Château de Freÿr**, a crisply symmetrical, largely eighteenth-century brick mansion pushed up against the main road and the river. The compulsory guided tour (April–June & Sept Sat & Sun 10.45am–12.45pm & 2–5.45pm; July & Aug Tues–Sun 10.30am–12.45pm & 2–5.45pm; Oct–March Sun 2–4.30pm; €7.50; 1hr 30min; Ⓦwww.freyr.be) traipses through a series of opulent rooms, distinguished by their period furniture and thundering fireplaces. Running parallel to the river are the adjoining **gardens**, laid out in the formal French style, spreading over three terraces and including a maze. A pavilion at the highest point provides a lovely view over the château and river.

Rochefort, Han and around

A few kilometres upstream from Houyet, to the southeast, lies one of the Ardennes' most beautiful regions, centring on the tourist resorts of **Han-sur-Lesse** and **Rochefort**. The district offers one or two specific sights, most notably the Han-sur-Lesse caves, as well as a scattering of castles, but the real magnet is the splendid countryside, a thickly wooded terrain of plateaux, gentle hills and valleys, and with quiet roads perfect for cycling. The best base for these rural wanderings is Rochefort, a middling sort of place with a good range of accommodation – and few of the crowds that swamp Han-sur-Lesse. By **public transport**, access is easiest from Namur; take the train to **Jemelle**, from where it's about 3km west to Rochefort, 6km more to Han; there is an hourly **bus** service linking all three.

Rochefort

A small, fairly undistinguished place, the pocket-sized town of **ROCHEFORT** is an excellent base for exploring the western reaches of the Ardennes, with a decent range of accommodation and other facilities. The town follows the contours of an irregularly shaped hill, with its long and pleasant main street, **rue de Behogne**, slicing through the centre from north to south. The ruins of the medieval **Château Comtal** perch atop a rocky outcrop off to the right of rue Jacquet, but were closed for renovation at the time of writing. In any case there's not much to see beyond the views – just the remains of the old walls, a couple of **wells** and, in the small **park** just below the entrance, the eighteenth-century arcades that were added to prop up the château's fashionable formal gardens.

Walking, cycling and canoeing around Rochefort

Crisscrossed by rivers, the handsome countryside around Rochefort provides lots of opportunities for walking, canoeing and mountain-biking. **Walkers** need the Institut Géographique National's map, *Rochefort et ses villages* (on sale at the tourist offices in Rochefort and Han), which lists almost thirty numbered walks, as well as eight routes for **mountain bikers** and three for **cyclists**. Kayaks Lesse et Lomme in Han (see below) rents out mountain bikes and regular bikes, and organizes excursions involving a combination of canoeing and cycling; mountain bikes can also be rented from the tourist office in Rochefort.

Walks from Rochefort

The Résurgence d'Eprave – **Walk 12** – is one of the most scenically varied, a 12km circular route. Take rue Jacquet out of town past the château and the route is signposted to the right, through **Hamerenne** with its tiny Romanesque chapel of St Odile, and across fields full of wild flowers, to the River Lomme. Follow the riverbank to the spot where the River Wamme emerges from underground to join the Lomme; don't try to cross the river but double back and turn right for the stiff climb uphill past the Eprave Grotto for grand views over the cornfields. Fifteen minutes' walk further on, the village of **Eprave** has a restored mill with a working water wheel and, opposite on rue de l'Aujoule, the *Auberge du Vieux Moulin*, an immaculate four-star hotel with ultramodern rooms, which makes a delightful place to stay or eat (Ⓣ084 37 73 18, Ⓦwww.eprave.com; ❺). The restaurant is open daily in July and August (noon–3pm & 7–9pm), but closes on Sunday and Tuesday evening as well as all of Monday at other times of the year; the menu is firmly nouveau, with main courses beginning at about €17. The walk back to Rochefort from here is rather dull, following the road, and you may want to retrace your steps, or join **Walk 4**, Grotte d'Eprave, to Han for the hourly bus back to Rochefort. A couple of good shorter walks around Rochefort include **Walk 7**, Lorette, a thirty-minute climb up through the woods above town, taking in the Lorette chapel and some decent views over the castle. Head up rue de Lorette towards the caves and turn left, keeping to the left where the track is signposted. The 6km **Walk 10**, Abbaye de Saint Rémy, goes the other way out of town, across the bridge and cutting north off the main road through some thickly wooded scenery as far as Abbaye de St Remy, where they produce Rochefort Trappist beer, before looping back to Rochefort.

Canoeing and kayaking on the River Lesse

To mess about on the river, **canoes and kayaks** can be rented from Kayaks Lesse et Lomme, near the bridge in Han (May to mid-Sept daily 9.30am–6pm; April, late Sept & Oct Sat & Sun 9.30am–6pm; Ⓣ082 22 43 97). They have a few canoes and pedal boats for splashing around town, but it's much more scenic and fun to join one of their **excursions**. The shortest (and least expensive) trip is the two-hour jaunt by kayak to Lessive, 6km away, and 4km back by bike (about €20 per person, €30 for two, all-inclusive). The longest is to Wanlin, 19km by kayak and 13km return by bike or bus. You can start the shortest trip anytime between 10am and 4pm; for Wanlin you have start between 10am and noon. Incidentally, in high summer the water level on the Lesse can drop low enough to make canoeing impossible; call ahead to confirm.

Practicalities

Buses to Rochefort pull in on the main street, rue de Behogne. The well-organized **tourist office** is at rue de Behogne 5 (Mon–Fri 8am–5pm, Sat & Sun 9.30am–5pm; ⓣ084 34 51 72, ⓦwww.valdelesse.be) and has the details of local **B&Bs** (❶–❷). Of a handful of **hotels**, there are two excellent central choices: *Le Vieux Logis*, rue Jacquet 71 (ⓣ084 21 10 24, ⓦwww.levieuxlogis.be; ❸), housed in a lovely old building with an immaculate, antique interior and attractive gardens; and *La Malle Poste*, rue de Behogne 46 (ⓣ084 21 09 86, ⓦwww.malleposte.be; ❺), a beautifully restored coaching inn with large, handsomely finished rooms and public spaces. Its rates are high for Rochefort but there are loads of facilities – an indoor pool, fitness centre and a beautiful garden and restaurant. *La Fayette*, at rue Jacquet 87 (ⓣ084 21 42 73, ⓦwww.hotellafayette.be; ❶), is the cheaper alternative, with a nice enough reception and restaurant downstairs but eight pretty plain rooms above. There's a convenient **campsite**, *Camping Les Roches* (ⓣ084 21 19 00, ⓦwww.lesroches.be; April–Oct), a ten-minute walk east of the centre of town; take Route de Marche from the crossroads and the first left after the river along rue du Hableau.

Rochefort isn't especially well provided for **food**. *La Gourmandise*, rue de Behogne 24 (ⓣ084 22 21 81; closed Mon, Fri & Sat lunch), opposite the tourist office, has a big menu of local dishes from around €12 and does excellent crepes too. *Le Limbourg*, place Albert 1er 21 (ⓣ084 21 10 36; closed Wed out of season), is a pleasant brasserie that does a good line in local specialities for lunch or dinner, with main courses averaging about €15. *Pizzeria Bella Italia*, rue de Behogne 50 (ⓣ084 22 15 20), is a good choice if you're after Italian food, offering substantial pizzas, pasta dishes and truly splendid calzone, as well as an extensive menu of good-value Belgian mains. Or try *La Caleche* (closed Wed & Thurs), the fancy French restaurant of *La Malle Poste*, where the €28 lunch menu is a bargain compared to the pricey à la carte mains for upwards of €26.

Han-sur-Lesse

Just 6km southwest of Rochefort, the busy village of **HAN-SUR-LESSE** has got one thing going for it, the **Grottes de Han**, rue J. Lamotte 2 (daily: April–June & Sept–Oct 10am–4.30pm; July & Aug 10am–5.30pm; €12.75, combined ticket with Grotte de Lorette €17.60; ⓦwww.grotte-de-han.be). Discovered at the beginning of the nineteenth century, the caves measure about 8km in length, a series of limestone galleries carved out of the hills by the River Lesse millions of years ago. The caves are actually just outside the village a little way downriver, but special **trams** (no extra charge) leave from a central ticket office in the heart of the village. Tours leave every half an hour during summer (hourly in April, Sept & Oct), last around an hour and are well worth it, although you visit only a small part of the cave system, taking in the so-called Salle du Trophée, the site of the largest stalagmite; the Salle d'Armes, where the Lesse reappears after travelling underground for 1km; and the massive Salle du Dôme – 129m high – which contains a small lake. After the tour, you make your own way back to the village on foot, which is a five- to ten-minute walk.

For an insight into how the caves were formed, head to the **Musée du Monde Souterrain**, at place Théo Lannoy 3 (daily: April, Sept & Oct 11am–4.30pm; May & June 11am–5pm; July & Aug 11am–5.30pm; €3.50); it's behind the tourist office and church, across the street from the caves' ticket office. A section of the museum explains the process, while others display the prehistoric artefacts unearthed during a series of archeological digs in and around the caves. Most were found where the Lesse surfaces again after travelling through the grottoes – among them flints, tools and bone ornaments from the Neolithic period, as well as weapons and jewellery from the Bronze Age.

Practicalities

Han's **tourist office** is right on the central square, place Theo Lannoy (daily 10am–5.30pm; ⓣ084 37 75 96, ⓦwww.valdelesse.be), and has a substantial list of local **B&Bs** (❶–❷). Han has several **hotels**, none of them particularly special, although the rooms at the *Stradella*, around the corner from the caves' ticket office at rue d'Hamptay 59 (ⓣ84 37 80 64; ❷) are nice enough; alternatively, there's the simple rooms of the *Auberge de Faule*, rue des Grottes 4–6 (ⓣ084 21 98 98; ❸), close by the caves' ticket office. There is also a nearby **campsite**, *Camping le Pirot*, by the river's edge on Route de Charleville, about 200m west of the tourist office (ⓣ084 37 72 90; April–Sept). You can't move for places to **eat** in Han, and prices are keen, though quality variable. The restaurant at *La Stradella*, rue d'Hamptay 59 (ⓣ084 37 80 64; closed Tues), is a proficient Italian serving pizzas and pastas from €9; you could also try the *Belle Vue Café*, right next to the caves at rue Lamotte 1 (closed Mon out of season), which offers good-quality, traditional Belgian cuisine at affordable prices, with main courses from around €14.

St-Hubert and around

ST-HUBERT, about 20km southeast of Rochefort, is another popular Ardennes resort, albeit one with an entirely different feel from its neighbours, largely on account of its solitary location, up on a plateau and surrounded by forest. A small town with just six thousand inhabitants, it's well worth a visit, though after you've explored its star turn, the **basilica**, and maybe hiked out into the surrounding woods, there's not much to detain you: the **town centre** is too dishevelled to be particularly endearing and the lack of quality accommodation may make you think twice about staying.

Basilique St-Hubert

The **Basilique St-Hubert** (daily: April–Oct 9am–6pm; Nov–March 9am–5pm; free) is easily the grandest religious edifice in the Ardennes and has been an important place of pilgrimage since the relics of the eponymous saint were moved here in the ninth century. A well-respected though shadowy figure, **St Hubert** (c.656–727 AD) was, according to legend, formerly Count Hubert, a Frankish noble whose love of hunting culminated in a vision of Christ between the antlers of a stag, after which he gave his money away and dedicated his life to the church, and was later canonized as the patron saint of hunters and trappers. The first abbey here predated the cult of St Hubert, but after the saint's relics arrived, the abbey – as well as the village that grew up in its shadow – was named in his honour. In medieval times, the abbey was one of the region's richest and a major landowner; it was suppressed by the French in the 1790s, but the abbey church – now the basilica – plus several of the old buildings survived, and flank the grand rectangular **piazza** that leads to the basilica's main entrance.

From the outside, the basilica's outstanding feature is the Baroque **west facade** of 1702, made of limestone and equipped with twin pepper-pot towers, a clock and a carving on the pediment depicting the miracle of St Hubert. Inside, the clear lines of the Gothic nave and aisles have taken an aesthetic hammering from both an extensive Baroque refurbishment and a heavy-handed neo-Gothic makeover in the 1840s. It's impressive more for its size rather than for any particular features, but do take a look at the **choir stalls**, typically Baroque and retelling the legend of St Hubert (on the right-hand side) and St Benedict (on the left), as well as the elaborate **tomb** of St Hubert, on the left at the beginning of the ambulatory, carved in the 1840s (King Léopold I, a keen huntsman, picked up the bill). Above the tomb is the only stained-glass **window** to have survived from the sixteenth century, a richly coloured, wonderfully executed work of art.

Practicalities

The nearest **train station** to St-Hubert is Poix St-Hubert, 7km away to the west on the Namur–Libramont/Arlon line. From here, there are regular **buses** to St-Hubert (Mon–Fri 12 daily, Sat & Sun 4 daily; 20min). The **tourist office** is at rue St-Gilles 12 (daily 9am–5.30pm; ⓣ061 61 30 10, ⓦwww.sthubert.be), just across the street from the basilica. Of the handful of **hotels** in the town centre, best is the nicely restored *Ancien Hopital*, just below the main square at rue de la Fontaine 23 (ⓣ061 41 69 65; ④), whose cool, well-appointed rooms have large bathrooms and feel quite out of step with the old-fashioned nature of the rest of St-Hubert – excellent value. Bang opposite the basilica, the *Hôtel de l'Abbaye*, place du Marché 18 (ⓣ061 61 10 23, ⓦwww.hoteldelabbaye.be; ②), has a claim to fame as the place where **Hemingway** hunkered down in 1944 as he advanced across Europe with the US army, though that aside, its twenty rooms – of which fourteen are en suite – are pretty ordinary. The *Cor de Chasse*, two minutes' walk away down rue St-Gilles at ave Nestor Martin 3 (ⓣ061 61 16 44, ⓦwww.lecordechassesainthubert.be; ②), is more enticing, with ten large, nicely kept rooms. The nearest **campsite** is the large, family-oriented *Europacamp* on route de Martelange, 2km southwest of town (ⓣ061 61 12 69; March–Dec).

For food, the **restaurant** of the *Ancien Hopital* (see above; daily except Tues & Wed noon–9.30pm) is the best option in town, with a menu of French and Belgian classics and tables set around an open wood fire and with tables in the garden in summer. Otherwise there's the slightly cheaper *St Gilles* (ⓣ061 23 28 94; closed Mon), rue St-Gilles 28, which has a good Belgian menu based around local and seasonal ingredients (mains from €15) and the more sedate restaurant of the *Cor de Chasse* (closed Mon eve and Tues), which again is mainly French.

Around St-Hubert

You could spend a few very happy days in St-Hubert, just hiking or cycling in the surrounding countryside, but there are a few worthwhile specific attractions to base your explorations around. One of the walks recommended by the St-Hubert tourist office is the 2–3hr trek up to **Fourneau St-Michel** (mid-Feb to April & Sept to mid-Nov Tues–Sun 10am–5pm; May & June daily 9.30am–6.30pm; July & Aug daily 9.30am–6.30pm; €7 for both sites; ⓦwww.fourneausaintmichel.be), about 8km north of town, an outdoor museum of rural life in Wallonia spread across a beautiful green valley in two main sites. It's typical of such places, its most important and interesting part made up of old buildings brought from all over the county – bakeries, farmhouses, forges, chapels, schools – reassembled here according to region and linked by paths that give the impression of strolling from one village to another. There are a couple of cafés but it's the perfect place for a picnic.

Euro Space Center

Some 12km west of St-Hubert, right by the E411 (Exit 24), the **Euro Space Center** (April–June & Sept–Oct Tues–Sun 10am–4pm; July & Aug daily 10am–5pm; €11; ⓦwww.eurospacecenter.be) is a hugely popular attraction, easily identified by the space rocket parked outside. Its hangar-like premises house a hi-tech museum telling you everything you ever wanted to know about space travel and the applications of space and satellite technology, with lots of buttons for kids to press in the many interactive displays, as well as full-scale models of the space shuttles and of the Mir space station.

Redu

Around 18km west of St-Hubert, across the E411, **REDU** is a small rather nondescript village, but one that reinvented itself several decades ago – à la the UK's Hay-on-Wye – as a bibliophile's paradise at the instigation of a local antiquarian bookseller, one Noel Anselot. The village now heaves with **bookstores**, selling new and used books, prints and pictures and offers a programme of literary events to match. Obviously most of the books are in French or Flemish, but several bookstores have a reasonable selection of English titles – try De Boekenwurm, at Voie d'Hurleau 51, for starters. There are a few arts and antiques shops nowadays, too. See Ⓦ www.redu-villagedulivre.be for more.

La Roche-en-Ardenne and around

About 30km northwest of Bastogne and 25km northeast of St-Hubert, **LA ROCHE-EN-ARDENNE** is amazingly picturesque, hidden by hills until you're right on top of it, and crowned by romantic castle ruins. It's a strange mixture: a hidden place, geographically cut off from the rest of the world and surrounded by some of the wildest scenery in the Ardennes, yet it teems with people during high summer (most of whom come to get out into the countryside on foot or by canoe). Near here too, is **Durbuy**, a pretty little place with excellent accommodation and great walking, and the **Grottes de Hotton**, one of the best of the many Ardennes cave complexes.

The Town

The grey-stone **centre** of La Roche squeezes into one small bend of the River L'Ourthe; winding between the two bridges, its main street is an unashamedly exploitative stretch of shops flogging Ardennes ham, knick-knacks and camping gear. That, however, is about it as far as development goes, and the streets around are unspoiled and quiet.

There are few tangible sights. The **château** (April–June, Sept & Oct daily 11am–5pm; July & Aug daily 10am–6.30pm; Nov–March Mon–Fri 1–4pm, Sat & Sun 11am–4.30pm; €4.50) was destroyed in the late eighteenth century on the orders of the Habsburgs – to stop it falling into the hands of the French – and today its ruins still command sweeping views over the valley and of the surviving fragments of the curtain wall that once enclosed the town. To get to the castle, take the steps that lead up from place du Marché, at the south end of the high street. On the high street itself, the **Musée Bataille des Ardennes**, rue Chamont 5 (July & Aug daily 10am–6pm; April–June & Sept–Dec Wed–Sun 10am–6pm; €6.40), is one of the best of the Ardennes battle museums, with a homespun but effective collection foraged from the surrounding hills that includes anti-tank guns and light weaponry, medical supplies and ancient unopened cigarette packs, all displayed by way of well-thought-out dioramas and tableaux. Curiously enough, the corner of the high street and rue de la Gare, a few metres to the north of the museum, is the spot where US and British soldiers met on January 11, 1945, as their respective armies converged on The Bulge; a commemorative **plaque** depicts the wintry scene.

Practicalities

La Roche is not on the rail network; the nearest **train station** is **Melreux-Hotton**, about 15km to the northwest, on the Jemelle–Liège line. From here, there are nine **buses** a day to La Roche during the week (four on Sat & Sun). The **tourist office** is at the south end of the main street, at place du Marché 15 (daily 9.30am–5pm; ⓣ084 36 77 36, ⓦwww.la-roche-tourisme.com). They have details of B&Bs in town and sell a combined walking and cycling map. Ardennes Aventures, on the main street at rue de l'Eglise 35 (ⓣ084 41 19 00, ⓦwww.ardenne-aventures.be), are a good first stop for canoes and kayaks (to Maboge and Nisramont), mountain bike hire and guided rafting trips.

Walking, cycling and canoeing in the Ourthe valley

The tourist office in **La Roche** sells a rather rudimentary **walking map** (*Carte de Promenades*), with a dozen circular walks marked in the vicinity. The longest and most attractive of these is the 13km **Walk 5**, which takes about six hours and is mildly strenuous. It starts on rue Bon Dieu du Maka, near place du Bronze, and rises steeply before levelling out through the woods above town and across fields of wildflowers. The walk follows GR route 57, dropping sharply to the river at **Maboge**, where several cafés offer lunch, then rejoining the main road for 500m until it turns left alongside a tributary of the Ourthe as far as the farm at Borzee. From here the route is easy to find, again heading through the woods with fabulous views, but when it descends towards the town keep your eyes peeled for a right and then an immediate left down an unpromising footpath that drops you onto the main road by the river. From here, take the second right for a final gentle stretch above the road, with good views over the town. Allow around three hours' walking time for the 13km; to extend the route by an hour or so, pick up **Walk 12** at Borzee, joining **Walk 11** as far as the small town of Samree and returning through the forest to La Roche.

If you're after a shorter hike, follow **Walk 4**, a 6km route that takes about two hours. From the tourist office, head for place du Bronze and before you cross the bridge turn left on rue Clerue, and sharp left again up rue St Quolin. Turn left at the top and follow the road round to **St Margaret's Chapel**, built in 1600 and once connected to the castle by an underground passageway. Just left of the chapel, a scramble up the steep slope leads up to a lookout point with views over La Roche, while continuing up the footpath brings you to the attractive but often crowded **Parc Forestier du Deister**. If you continue through the park you'll rejoin Walk 4, looping briefly north and then dropping back to town, all along the roadway. Alternatively, **GR route 57** provides a full half-day's walking between La Roche and the hamlet of Nadrin, a distance of around 15km. **Nadrin** is home to a belvedere – actually a high tower with a restaurant attached – from which you can see the River Ourthe at six different points on its meandering course in and out of the tightly packed hills. The return journey can be completed by bus, but this only runs twice daily, so be sure to check times with the tourist office before you leave.

Cycling, canoeing and other activities

Obviously enough, renting a **mountain bike** allows you to see more of the surrounding forests: eight circular routes are set out in the *Carte des Circuits Cyclotouristes*, on sale at the tourist office. Bikes can be rented from Ardennes Aventures by the north bridge (see above). They also organize **canoeing** trips on the Ourthe, bussing you (or letting you mountain bike) to Maboge for the 10km paddle downstream to La Roche (€15 per person, €30 with the bike ride), or to Nisramont for the strenuous 25km river trip (€20). They also organize **river rafting** and **cross-country skiing** in the winter.

The best budget **accommodation** is the *Moulin de la Strument*, Petit Strument 62 (ⓣ084/41 15 07; ❷), which has clean and cosy rooms in a very peaceful location about ten minutes' walk from the centre of town – take the first left after place du Bronze; it also has a campsite (see below). There's also the delightful, old-fashioned *Les Genets*, corniche de Deister 2 (ⓣ084 41 18 77, ⓦwww.lesgenetshotel.com; ❸), whose eight comfortable rooms provide superb views over the town from its lofty perch. It's a ten-minute climb up from the high street: take rue Clerue out of town from the bridge by place du Marché, and veer left again up rue St Quoilin. The *Clairefontaine*, about 2km outside La Roche on the road to Marche-en-Famenne (ⓣ084 41 24 70, ⓦwww.clairefontaine.be; ❹), is a decent second-best if *Les Genets* is full and you have a car; it's a lovely old lodge on the edge of the forest, strewn with antiques and offering large and extremely well appointed rooms.

There are no fewer than nine **campsites** in the vicinity. The closest are along rue de Harzé by the River Ourthe, within walking distance from the town centre: *Le Benelux* (ⓣ084 41 15 59, ⓦwww.campingbenelux.be; Easter to Sept), *Camping de l'Ourthe* (ⓣ084 41 14 59, ⓦwww.campingdelourthe.be; mid-March to Oct) and *Le Grillon* (ⓣ084 41 20 62, ⓦwww.campinglegrillon.be; April–Oct); to get to them, follow rue de la Gare from the north bridge. The *Moulin de la Strument* campsite is quieter and no further out, while *Lohan* (ⓣ084 41 15 45, ⓦwww.campinglohan.be), on the road to Houffalize, is a bit further but in a wonderfully tranquil riverside location.

La Roche boasts lots of **cafés** and **restaurants**, though standards are pretty variable. *L'Apero*, just off the main drag at rue Clerue 5 (ⓣ084 41 18 31; closed Sun), is a small, family-run restaurant with fine local cooking; the restaurant at *Les Genets* (see above; closed lunchtime and all day Thurs) isn't the cheapest, but the food is excellent and you can enjoy it in the hotel's marvellously old-fashioned dining room, which has lovely views over the town and valley.

Durbuy

A circuitous 25km northwest of La Roche, the tiny, inordinately pretty town of **DURBUY** is tucked into a narrow ravine beside the River L'Ourthe, below bulging wooded hills. Perhaps inevitably, Durbuy attracts far too many day-trippers for its own good, but out of season and late in the evening it remains a delightful spot, not because of any specific attractions but because its immaculately maintained huddle of seventeenth- and eighteenth-century **stone houses**, set around a cobweb of cobbled lanes, is a lovely spot for an idle wander; and you can always escape the crush by hiking up into the surrounding hills. You'll need your own transport to get here, however.

Durbuy's **tourist office** is on the main square, place aux Foires (Mon–Fri 9am–12.30pm & 1–5pm, Sat & Sun 10am–6pm; ⓣ086 21 24 28). There are several decent **hotels**, perhaps the best of which is the *Clos des Récollets*, rue de la Prevote 9 (ⓣ086 21 29 69, ⓦwww.closdesrecollets.be; ❹), a charming, partly whitewashed and half-timbered house right in the centre that has slick, modern and very comfortable rooms with large bathrooms. Close by, the ivy-clad *Victoria*, rue des Récollectines 4 (ⓣ086 21 23 00, ⓦwww.prevote.be; ❸), is also excellent, with slightly more rustic – and cheaper – rooms. For **food**, the *Clos des Récollets* restaurant (see above; closed Wed) does fancy French and is fairly traditional, with main courses for around €20, while the *Victoria*'s (see above; open daily) serves a more varied menu and is more relaxed, with a big open kitchen and mains from €16. Several less expensive places flank place aux Foires, of which *La Brasserie Ardennaise* (ⓣ086 21 47 44; daily 10am–midnight) is as good as any, offering soup and snacks from €3, or a wide range of meat and fish dishes from around €8. Or try the *Ferme au Chene*, rue Cote d'Ursel 36 (Ⓣ086 21 10 67), whose omelettes, salads and plates of ham and cheese are the perfect accompaniment to the excellent beer – Marckloff – brewed on the premises, which can also be enjoyed on an outside terrace overlooking the river.

The Grottes de Hotton

There's a touch of Jules Verne about the **Grottes de Hotton** (April–June & Sept–Oct daily 10am–5pm; July & Aug daily 10am–6pm; Nov–March Sat & Sun 2–3.30pm; €9). The deepest of the Ardennes cave systems, they're well worth the short trip from la Roche – and not just on a rainy day, either. **Tours** last an hour and take you 75m underground, where a fast-flowing river pours through a canyon almost 40m deep and just a few metres wide – an awesome sight. There are stalactites and stalagmites galore, again among the best you'll see in all of Belgium's caves, including patches of rare and peculiar specimens that grow horizontally from the rock.

The caves are about 2km from the centre of the sprawling village of Hotton – they're well signposted but only reachable on foot or by car; from the main riverside rue de la Roche, follow route de Speleo Club de Belgique.

Bouillon and around

Beguiling **BOUILLON**, close to the French border on the edge of the Ardennes, some 50km southwest of La Roche, is a well-known and quite handsome resort town, enclosed in a loop of the River Semois and crowned by an outstanding castle. It's a relaxed and amiable place, and an excellent base for exploring the wildly dramatic scenery of the countryside around, in particular the **Semois river valley**.

Arrival, information and accommodation

Bouillon isn't on the train network, but there are regular **buses** from the nearest main-line train station, **Libramont**, on the Namur–Luxembourg line 30km northeast (Mon–Fri 6 daily, Sat & Sun 1–2 daily; 50min). Some (but not all) of these buses call at **Bertrix train station**, a bit closer to Bouillon, and there are also branch-line trains to Bertrix from Libramont (every 2hr; 10min) and Dinant (Mon–Fri hourly, Sat & Sun every 2hr; 1hr). Though Bouillon is a small town, getting your bearings can be a little difficult. The main branch of the **tourist office** is by the river in the Archéoscope Godefroid de Bouillon (Mon–Sat 10am–6pm, Sun 10am–5pm; Ⓣ061 46 62 57, Ⓦwww.bouillon-sedan.com), and there's another small office in the castle (same times as castle; see p.302). Both have oodles of local information, book accommodation at no extra cost and sell local hiking maps. They also have details of a handful of **B&Bs** (❶–❷), both in town and on the outskirts, but Bouillon has a good range of **accommodation**, with around a dozen hotels, a hostel and a couple of campsites.

Hotels

Auberge d'Alsace Faubourg de France 3 Ⓣ061 46 65 88, Ⓦwww.aubergedalsace.be. Cosy and smart hotel at the east end of the Pont de France, with traditional decor and a sombre brown and beige exterior. Very comfortable rooms, most of which have pleasant river views, though these cost a bit more. The adjacent *Hotel de France* (same details) is part of the same complex. Closed Jan. ❷

Hostellerie Pommeraie rue de la Poste 2 Ⓣ061 46 90 17, Ⓦwww.hotelpommeraie.com. The rooms and service at this old château right in the centre of Bouillon can be a bit hit and miss, but it's a wonderful old building and they have a nice downstairs restaurant and garden – though you have to take half-board at €159 for two people. ❻

Hôtel de La Poste place St Arnould 1 ⓣ061 46 51 51, ⓦwww.hotelposte.be. There's been a hotel here, right by the Pont de Liège, since the 1730s. The present incarnation is nothing fancy, but it's pretty good value for what you get – and there's a nice, lively bar downstairs. There are great views of the castle from one side of the hotel, so be sure to get a room facing west, preferably high up in the hotel tower – worth the extra money. ❷

Hostel and campsites

Auberge de Jeunesse Route du Christ 16 ⓣ061 46 81 37, ⓦwww.laj.be. Large and well-equipped HI hostel with dorm beds and family rooms, plus kitchen, laundry and café. It's east across the river from the castle, on the hill opposite – a long walk by road, but there is a short cut via the steps leading up from rue des Hautes Voies, just above place St Arnould. Reservations advised. Closed Jan & early Feb. Dorm beds €17. ❶

Halliru route de Corbion 1 ⓣ061 46 60 09. Nicely situated and reasonably well-equipped riverside campsite, some 1500m southwest of the town centre on the road to Corbion. It's an easy walk – go through the tunnel by the Auberg d'Alsace, turn left and follow the path by the river. Open April–Sept.

Moulin de la Falize Vieille route de France 62, ⓣ061 46 62 00. Campsite with all the trimmings, including laundry, café, swimming pool and playground, about 1km south of town from the Auberge d'Alsace. Open April to mid-Nov.

The Town

Bouillon's pride and joy is its impossibly picturesque **Château**, set on a long and craggy ridge that runs high above town (April–June & Sept Mon–Fri 10am–6pm, Sat & Sun 10am–6.30pm; July & Aug daily 10am–6.30pm, plus Tues–Sun until 10pm; March, Oct & Nov daily 10am–5pm; Dec–Feb Mon–Fri 1–5pm, Sat & Sun 10am–5pm; €5.90, combined ticket with museum €8.60). The castle was originally held by a succession of independent dukes who controlled most of the land hereabouts. There were five of these, all called **Godfrey de Bouillon**, the fifth and last of whom left on the First Crusade in 1096, selling his dominions (partly to raise the cash for his trip) to the prince-bishop of Liège, and capturing Jerusalem three years later, when he was elected the Crusaders' king. However, he barely had time to settle himself before he became sick – either from disease or, as was suggested at the time, because his Muslim enemies poisoned him, and he died in Jerusalem in 1100. Later, Louis XIV got his hands on the old dukedom and promptly had the castle refortified to the design of his military architect **Vauban**, whose handiwork defines most of the fortress today.

It's an intriguing old place, with paths winding through most of its courtyards, along the battlements and towers, and through dungeons filled with weaponry and instruments of torture. Most visitors drive to the entrance, but walking there is easy enough too – either via rue du Château or, more strenuously, by a set of steep steps that climbs up from rue du Moulin, one street back from the river. Among the highlights, the **Salle de Godfrey**, hewn out of the rock, contains a large wooden cross sunk into the floor and sports carvings illustrating the castle's history; there's also the **Tour d'Autriche** (Austrian Tower) at the top of the castle, with fabulous views over the Semois valley.

Below from the castle, and accessible across the car park, the **Musée Ducal**, rue Petit (Easter to mid-Nov daily 10am–6pm; €4, combined ticket with castle €8.60) exhibits a wide-ranging collection in an attractive eighteenth-century mansion. As you'd expect, there are lots of artefacts relating to the fifth Godfrey, plus assorted weaponry, exhibits on medieval daily and religious life and a large-scale model of the town in 1690.

For yet more on Godfrey, head for the **Archéoscope Godefroid de Bouillon**, in an old convent across the river at Quai des Saulx 14 (Feb Tues–Fri 1–4pm, Sat & Sun 10am–4pm; March–April daily 10am–4pm; May–Sept daily 10am–5pm; Oct & Nov Tues–Sun 10am–4pm; Dec Tues–Fri 1–4pm, Sat & Sun 10am–4pm; €6.25, combined ticket with castle & museum €13.60; ⓦwww.archeoscopebouillon.be), whose exhibitions on the Crusades, Arab culture, castle building and so forth kick off with a multimedia show on the duke himself.

Eating and drinking

For a place of its size and popularity, Bouillon is surprisingly light on good places to eat – and its nightlife is more or less nonexistent. We've picked out the best from a rather uninspiring bunch.

Le Roy de la Moule quai du Rempart 42 ⓣ061 46 62 49. Mussels-every-which-way restaurant with a good choice of beers. Open daily for lunch and dinner.

Le Sawadie quai du Rempart 27 ⓣ061 46 67 92. Competent, straightforward and inexpensive Thai restaurant, which often stays open until late. Closed Mon & Tues.

La Vieille Ardenne Grand-rue 9 ⓣ061 46 62 77. Slightly old-fashioned restaurant near the Pont de Liège specializing in regional dishes, with main courses averaging around €18. Also has an extensive beer menu. Tues–Sun 10am–10pm.

Around Bouillon: the Semois valley

To the west of Bouillon, quiet country roads negotiate the **Semois river valley**, repeatedly climbing up into the wooded hills before careering down to the riverside. Holidaying Belgians descend on this beautiful area in their hundreds, and many of the old farmhouses here have been turned into myriad *gîtes*. Heading west from Bouillon along the N810, it's just 12km to **POUPEHAN**, an inconsequential village that straggles the banks of the River Semois. The target of the most popular canoe trips from Bouillon, Poupehan makes a healthy living from its many visitors, most of whom are here to enjoy the peace and quiet and to mess around in the river. The village has two **hotels**, the more appealing of which is the *Hôtel Chaire à Prêcher*, right by the bridge at Rue du Pont 1 (ⓣ061 46 61 54; ❷), and three **campsites**, including the well-equipped *Île de Faigneul*, on an island in the river ten minutes' walk from the centre of the village at rue de la Chérizelle 54 (ⓣ061 46 68 94, ⓦwww.camping-iledefaigneul.com; April–Oct).

From Poupehan, it's a steep 4km drive up through the woods to **ROCHEHAUT**, a beguiling hilltop village whose rustic stone cottages amble across a gentle dip between two sloping ridges. Nowadays, most visitors come here to **hike**, exploring the locality's steep forested hills and the valley down below by means of a network of marked trails. There are superb views over the Semois from the village, and it's here you'll also find the aptly named *La Pointe de Vue*, a plain and simple café-bar with a terrace that has a glorious vista back up the valley. There's a decent selection of places to stay too, among them the *Auberge de la Ferme*

Semois valley hikes

You can see the countryside around Rochehaut and Poupehan on foot by doing a **half-day's circular hike** from Rochehaut to Poupehan and back again. From Rochehaut, take the path out of the southern end of the village, which leads into thick forests high above the river, from where a series of fixed ladders help you to negotiate the steep slopes down to the water. This is by far the hardest part of the walk, and once you're at the bottom you can follow the easy path to Poupehan; from there, take the path that follows the river north back up to a quaint bridge over the river to the hamlet of **Frahan**, a huddle of stone houses draped over a steep hillock and surrounded by meadows. From here various paths will deliver you back up to Rochehaut on its perch high above.

Walking, cycling and canoeing around Bouillon

The **River Semois** snakes its way across much of southern Belgium, rising near Arlon and then meandering west until it finally flows into the Meuse in France. The most impressive part of the Semois **valley** lies just to the west of Bouillon, the river wriggling beneath steep wooded hills and ridges – altogether some of the most sumptuous scenery in the whole of the Ardennes.

Before setting out, **walkers** should get hold of the *Cartes des Promenades du Grand Bouillon* map (on sale at the tourist office), with nine "*grandes promenades*" marked and a further ninety circular walks that begin and end in Bouillon or one of the nearby villages. The routes are well marked, but you need to study the map carefully if you want to avoid having to walk on major or minor roads; the map also gives (pretty generous) suggested times for completing the walks. Note that the marked river crossings are not bridges, so you may well end up with wet feet. The tourist office also sells a map detailing suggested **cycling** routes, and **mountain bikes** can be rented from Semois Kayaks (see below).

Walks

From Bouillon's Pont de France, **Walk 11** (7km; 2hr) heads south to the French border, a pretty route through woods, although the return is mostly along a main road. A better option is to take **Walk 12** (4km; 1hr 30min) through the arboretum and down to the *Halliru* campsite by the river, joining **Walk 13** along the riverbank up to the Rocher du Pendu and as far as Moulin de l'Épine, where you can wade across the river to a superb restaurant-bar and the minor road that leads back to town above the Semois. More serious walkers can pick up **Walk 37** (7km; 3hr) or **Walk 72** (16km; 6hr) at Moulin de l'Épine for some fabulous views either side of the river; Walk 72 being particularly glorious as it heads around Le Tombeau du Géant. If you just want a brief walk around Bouillon, **Walk 16** (5km; 1hr 30min) is a good choice, climbing up out of town, with great views of the castle and surrounding countryside, and back through the outskirts of the Ferme de Buhan. In the other direction from Bouillon, the Semois twists its way to the resort-village of **Dohan**. The mammoth **Walk 19** (23km; 7hr) runs direct to Dohan from Bouillon, although it's more attractive to follow the river via **Walk 17** (11km; 3hr) as far as **Saty**, from where you can either canoe back to Bouillon (see p.301), or join Walk 19 towards Dohan. Finally, for an ambitious and varied day's walking, you can take **Walk 7** (21km; 6hr) from the Pont de France in Bouillon across the Ferme du Buhan and through Saty and Dohan as far as La Maka. Here you can pick up **Walk 45** (3.5km; 2hr), which incorporates the waterfalls at Saut de Sorcières and the lovely views over the river valley from Mont de Katron. From Les Hayons, **Walk 6** (23km; 7hr) runs directly back to Bouillon through Moulin Hideux.

Canoeing

As regards canoeing, the riverscape is gentle and sleepy, the Semois slow-moving and meandering – and the whole shebang is less oversubscribed than, say, Dinant. Bouillon has two main **canoe rental** companies, both of whom provide transport either to the departure point or from the destination. Les Epinoches, by the Pont de France (☎061 25 68 78, Ⓦwww.kayak-lesepinoches.be), rents kayaks and canoes to go down to Saty (7km; 2hr), Dohan (14km; 3hr) and Cugnon (28km; 5hr). Semois Kayaks (☎0475 24 74 23, Ⓦwww.semois-kayaks.be), on the other side of the town by the Pont de la Poulie, just below the road up to the castle, oversees routes in the other direction down to Poupehan (15km; 3hr) and from Poupehan to Frahan (5km; 1hr). Advance reservations are strongly advised. Single kayaks cost €18–20, doubles €30–36, depending on the distance. For a really active day out, you could canoe to Poupehan and either pick up walking routes back to Bouillon, or walk one of the circular routes around the village or up to Rochehaut and back (see p.303) If you do the latter, check when the last of the Semois's minibuses return to Bouillon.

Belgian food

Few people realise that Belgium has a significant culinary tradition, meaning that you can eat better here than almost anywhere in Europe. And it's not just mussels and chips either. There's a great deal more variety than you would expect for such a small country, with an emphasis on fresh, local produce and artisanal methods of preparation – much like neighbouring France, though with none of the pretentiousness that you sometimes find there. Food really is one of the joys of travelling in Belgium.

Frites ▲

Brussels waffle with fruit and cream ▼

Carbonnades à la flamande ▼

Street food and snacks

They may be known almost everywhere as French fries, but the fact is **frites** are a Belgian invention, and nowhere in the country are you far from a *frietkot* or *friture* stall. To be truly authentic, *frites* must be made with Belgian potatoes and parboiled before being deep-fried. They're also not quite the same unless eaten with a wooden fork out of a large paper cone, preferably with a large dollop of mayonnaise on top – or one of the many different toppings available, ranging from curry to goulash sauce.

The other ubiquitous street food – and one that's equally Belgian – is the **waffle** or *gaufre*, a mixture of butter, flour, eggs and sugar grilled on deep-ridged waffle irons and sold on the street in most cities. There are two types of waffle: you'll most likely come across the Brussels waffle, a gridlike slab of yeasty batter dusted with sugar and served with jam, honey, whipped cream, ice cream, chocolate or fruit. Its rival – the so-called Liège waffle – is a smaller and more intensely sweet affair, cooked with a sugar coating and more usually available from bakeries than street stands.

Main courses

The Belgian national dish is of course *moules frites* or **mussels and chips**, which can be found more or less everywhere when mussels are in season (ie when there is an "r" in the month – May to August is not mussels season and although you can find mussels during this time the most authentic places won't serve them). They're best eaten the traditional way, served in a vast pot with chips and mayonnaise on the side, either *à la marinière* (steamed with white wine, shallots and parsley or celery), or *à la crème* (steamed with the same ingredients but thickened with cream and flour). Discard the shells in the pot lid or scoop up the juices with them, and accompany the whole thing with lashings of crusty bread. The other way to eat mussels, though less fun and not nearly as satisfying, is baked, with a variety of sauces.

There are many other very **traditional Belgian dishes** worth trying, and what's on offer may vary depending on which part of the country you're in, although you can find most things in Brussels and there are some classic dishes you'll find pretty much everywhere. There's *carbonnades à la flamande* (*stoofvlees* in Flemish), a rich beef stew with beer that is often served with mashed potato (*stoemp*), with cabbage or other diced root vegetables; *waterzooi*, a creamy Flemish stew native to Ghent and around, made with chicken or white fish, leek and plain boiled potatoes; *anguilles au vert* (*paling in 't groen* in Flemish), or eels in green (parsley) sauce. On the vegetable front, try the chicory or endive, the Belgian variety of which is said to be the world's best; it's served most often *gratinée* (with

Cheese, please

Although it has nothing like the variety of France, Belgium boasts some decent **cheeses**, among which Herve, from the Liège province town of the same name, is one of the best and most common. It's a rind cheese, a bit like the French Pont l'Evêque, but stronger. Others, like Chimay, are made by monks in the Trappist monasteries, where the cheese-making tradition still exists alongside that of brewing. All provide proven ballast for beer drinking, and you'll often be served a small plate of cheese to accompany your chosen brew – one of Belgium's many civilized traditions.

▲ *Waterzooi*

▼ Cheeses at Abbaye d'Orval

▼ Endive *gratinée*

Moules frites ▲

Shrimp fisherman at Oostduinkerke ▼

cheese). *Lapin à la gueuze*, or rabbit cooked in the local beer of Brussels, is another favourite countrywide, as is *filet americain* – steak tartare or raw minced beef, highly seasoned and delicious with *frites*; and you'll usually find *tomates aux crevettes* on the menu wherever you are: tomatoes stuffed with tiny, deliciously sweet grey shrimps. Among other specialities, the Ardennes produces great cured hams – much like Parma ham – and good coarse liver pate; its restaurants often have game like wild boar on the menu, and there are any number of other delights to experience locally. Liege in particular has some robust and delicious culinary traditions, notably *boulettes Liegois*, meatballs doused in a sweet, syrupy sauce made with the local delicacy, *sirop de Liege* and served with (what else?) *frites*; and *salade Liegois*, with green beans, bacon and boiled potatoes.

Food events and festivals

Belgium's preoccupation with food is reflected in the many **food-related festivals** and events that take place annually all over the country, and there are more springing up all the time. Two of the most recent are Bruges's annual chocolate festival, held every April, and Antwerp's August *Bollekesfeest*, which displays the best of local produce in various open-air locations around the city, including the fish market and organized picnics. Oostduinkerke, on the Flemish coast, sees fishermen on horseback catch shrimps during the last weekend in June and then cook them up in the town; while in Malmédy, in the Ardennes, they make a giant omelette every August using ten thousand eggs and then distribute it among the keen and hungry.

(Ⓣ061 46 10 00, Ⓦwww.aubergedelaferme.be; ❷–❺; closed most of Jan), which offers a range of comfortable rooms in a tastefully modernized old stone inn with outbuildings and a modern annexe, and an excellent **restaurant** (although you can also eat more informally – and just as well – in the bar). The *Auberge de L'An* (Ⓣ061 46 40 60, Ⓦwww.an1600.be; ❺; closed Jan & late June to early July), is a first-rate alternative, with ten rooms and another top-quality restaurant in a charming whitewashed cottage; they also have chalets from €380 a week.

The Abbaye d'Orval

Around 30km southeast of Bouillon, the **Abbaye d'Orval** (daily 9.30am–6pm; €5.50; Ⓦwww.orval.be) is a place of legendary beginnings. It was founded, so the story goes, when Countess Mathilda of Tuscany lost a gold ring in a lake and a fish recovered it for her, prompting the countess to donate the surrounding land to God for the construction of a monastery. (A fish with a golden ring is still the emblem of the monastery, and can be seen gracing the bottles of **beer** for which Orval is most famous these days.) Most of the medieval abbey disappeared during an eighteenth-century revamp, but much of this was destroyed by the French Revolutionary army in 1793. Thereafter, the abbey lay abandoned until 1926, when the **Trappist** order acquired the property and built on the site to the eighteenth-century plans, creating an imposing new complex complete with a monumental statue of the Virgin.

The abbey has always been first and foremost a working community, making beer, cheese and bread (samples of which are on sale in the abbey shop), but sadly only the ruins remain and the main, modern part of the complex isn't open to the public. Of the original twelfth- and thirteenth-century buildings, you can see the ruins of the Romanesque-Gothic **church of Notre-Dame**, with the frame of the original rose window and Romanesque capitals in the nave and transept, and its attached cloister and surrounding buildings, including the almost-intact chapter house and the eighteenth-century **cellars**, which hold a small museum and models and photos of the abbey over the years.

Driving to the abbey is quick and easy, but getting there by **public transport** is difficult – there's an infrequent bus from Florenville, the nearest town on the train network. Not far from the abbey, on the main road, **accommodation** is available at the rusticated, half-timbered *Nouvelle Hostellerie d'Orval* (Ⓣ061 31 43 65; ❷; closed Mon). Besides six simple but comfortable rooms, it has a **restaurant** serving good-value Belgian fare, with three-course lunch menus and bar snacks, including large platters of Orval cheese.

Arlon

The capital of Luxembourg province, **ARLON** is one of the oldest towns in Belgium, a trading centre for the Romans as far back as the second century AD. These days it's an amiable country town, perhaps a little down on its luck, but with a relaxed and genial atmosphere that makes for a pleasant break in any journey – although there's not a lot to see. The modern centre is **place Léopold**, with the clumping Palais de Justice at one end and a World War II tank in the middle, commemorating the American liberation of Arlon in September 1944. Behind the Palais de Justice, to the left, the **Musée Archéologique**, at rue des Martyrs 13 (Tues–Sat 9am–noon & 1–5.30pm, Easter to early Sept also Sun 1.30–5pm; €4, €6 with Musée Gaspar), has a good collection of Roman finds from the surrounding area, many of which are evocative of daily life in Roman times. The associated

Musée Gaspar, rue des Martyrs 16 (Tues–Sun 9am–noon & 1.30–5pm; €4, €6 with Musée Archeologique), displays the works of nineteenth-century sculptor Jean-Marie Gaspar, who was a native of Arlon, along with a marvellously realistic sixteenth-century retable. A couple of minutes' walk from place Léopold, up a flight of steps, is Arlon's diminutive **Grand-Place**, where there are more fragments from Roman times, namely the **Tour Romaine** (no public access), formerly part of the third-century ramparts.

Arlon **train station** is five minutes' walk away from the south side of the town centre. The **tourist office** is just off the main square at rue des Faubourgs 2 (Mon–Fri 8.30am–5pm, Sat & Sun 9am–4pm; ⓣ063 21 63 60, ⓦwww.ot-arlon.be). For **food**, the *Maison Knopes*, rue de la Grand-Place 24 (ⓣ063 22 74 07) serves good coffee and tasty crepes as well as more substantial meals.

Bastogne

BASTOGNE, thirty-odd kilometres north of Arlon, is a brisk modern town and important road junction, whose strategic position has attracted the attentions of just about every invading army that has passed this way. Indeed, the town is probably best known for its role in World War II, when the Americans held it against a much larger German force in December 1944 – a key engagement of the Battle of the Ardennes, or Battle of the Bulge. The American commander's response to the German demand for surrender – "Nuts!" – is one of the more quotable, if apocryphal, of martial rallying cries. Nowadays, there's no strong reason to overnight here, but there are several sights, the more interesting of which are connected with the events of 1944.

As a token of its appreciation, the town renamed its main square **place McAuliffe**, after the American commander, and plonked an American **tank** here just to emphasize the point. Wide and breezy, the square is the most agreeable part of town and very much the social focus, flanked by a string of busy cafés. From its northeast corner, **Grand-rue** – the long main street – trails off to place St Pierre, a ten-minute walk away, where the **Église St-Pierre** sports a sturdy Romanesque tower topped by a timber gallery. Inside, and more unusually, the vaulting of the well-proportioned Gothic nave is decorated with splendid, brightly coloured frescoes, painted in the 1530s and depicting biblical scenes, saints, prophets and angels. Of note also are a finely carved Romanesque baptismal font and a flashy Baroque pulpit.

Close by, the chunky **Porte de Trèves** is the last vestige of the town's medieval walls – as illustrated in the nearby **Maison Mathelin**, at rue G. Delperdange 1 (July & Aug Tues–Sun 10am–noon & 1–5pm; €2), which has a model of the medieval town among a series of rooms tracking through Bastogne's history. Several rooms are devoted to the Battle of the Bulge, but the story is more fully told at the **American Memorial** (open access; free), situated 2km north of town on Mardasson hill; from place St Pierre, take rue G. Delperdange and keep going. This large, star-shaped memorial, inscribed with the names of all the American states, probably looks a great deal better from the air than it does from the ground, but the panels around the side do an excellent job of recounting different episodes from the battle, and the crypt, with its three altars, is suitably sombre. It's possible to climb up onto the roof for a windswept look back at Bastogne and the slag heaps and quarries of the surrounding countryside. Next door to the memorial, the **Bastogne Historical Center** (daily: March, April & Oct–Dec 10am–5.30pm; May–Sept 9.30am–6pm; €8.50; ⓦwww.bastognehistoricalcenter.be) collects together all manner of war-related artefacts – uniforms, vehicles and the like – in an impressive and imaginative series of displays, and shows a film of the battle compiled from live footage.

The Battle of the Ardennes

The Ardennes was the site of some of the fiercest fighting in the latter stages of World War II during the **Battle of the Ardennes** – sometimes known as the **Battle of the Bulge** – manifest everywhere in the various parked up tanks memorials, museums and, of course, cemeteries. The Allies liberated most of Belgium in September 1944, after which they concentrated on striking into Germany from Maastricht in the north and Alsace in the south, leaving a lightly defended central section whose front line extended across the Ardennes from Malmédy to Luxembourg's Echternach. In December 1944, Hitler embarked on a desperate plan to change the course of the war by breaking through this part of the front, his intention being to sweep north behind the Allies, capture Antwerp and force them to retreat. To all intents and purposes, it was the same plan Hitler had applied with such great success in 1940, but this time he had fewer resources – especially fuel oil – and the Allied air force ruled the skies. **Von Rundstedt**, the veteran German general who Hitler placed in command, was acutely aware of these weaknesses – indeed he was against the operation from the start – but he hoped to benefit from the wintry weather conditions which would limit Allied aircraft activity. Carefully prepared, Von Rundstedt's offensive began on December 16, 1944, and one week later had created a "bulge" in the Allied line that reached the outskirts of Dinant (the Germans famously reached the so-called Rocher de Bayard, which still marks the spot today), although the American 101st Airborne Division held firm around Bastogne. The success of the operation depended on rapid results, however, and Von Rundstedt's inability to reach Antwerp meant failure. Montgomery's forces from the north and Patton's from the south launched a counterattack, and by the end of January the Germans had been forced back to their original position. The loss of life was colossal, however: 75,000 Americans and over 100,000 Germans died in the battle.

Practicalities

Bastogne is not on the train network, but there are connecting **buses** from the nearest train station, at **Libramont**. The journey takes about forty minutes and buses stop at the main square, place McAuliffe. The **tourist office** is on place McAuliffe (mid-June to mid-Sept daily 8.30am–6.30pm; mid-Sept to mid-June daily 9.30am–12.30pm & 1–5.30pm; ⓣ061 21 27 11, ⓦwww.paysdebastogne.be) and has free town maps and a variety of brochures on the Battle of the Bulge, and will book accommodation on your behalf for free. Bastogne has five **hotels**, the most agreeable of which is the *Collin*, place McAuliffe 8–9 (ⓣ061 21 48 88, ⓦwww.hotel-collin.com; ❸), a smart and tasteful conversion of an older building, complete with Art Deco flourishes. For **food**, head for the cafés and restaurants on and around place McAuliffe. Among them, the best is the *Hotel Collin*'s *Café 1900* (see above), a smart and well-turned-out café that's good for snacks and light meals, and does great meatballs. Alternatively, try the bright and cheerful *Le Grill* (ⓣ061 21 49 07), at place McAuliffe 21, which does a tasty line in mussels, plus delicious meat and fish dishes from around €18.

Huy

Midway between Namur and Liège, and easily accessible by train from either, the bustling town of **HUY** – aside from Liège, the major centre of the northern Ardennes – spreads across both sides of the River Meuse. One of the oldest settlements in Belgium and for a long time a flourishing market town, the place was badly damaged by Louis XIV in the late seventeenth century and mauled by several passing armies thereafter. Consequently, little remains of the old town, but Huy is certainly worth a brief stop, mainly for its splendid church, the Collégiale Notre-Dame, and its dramatic citadel.

The Town

The centre of Huy is the **Grand-Place**, whose ornate bronze fountain of 1406 is decorated with a representation of the town walls interspersed with tiny statues of the same saints commemorated in the church; the wrought-iron and stone vats were added later, in the eighteenth century. The square is flanked by the **Hôtel de Ville**, a self-confident, château-style edifice dating from the 1760s, behind which is tiny **place Verte**, overlooked by an attractive Gothic church and at the start of a pretty maze of narrow lanes and alleys that stretch north to rue Vankeerberghen. Down by the river, the imposing Gothic bulk of the **Collégiale Notre-Dame** (Tues–Sun 9am–noon & 2–5pm) dominates the town, towering over the banks of the River Meuse with the high cliffs and walls of the citadel behind. Built between 1311 and 1536, the church's interior is decked out with fine stained glass, especially the magnificent **rose window**, a dazzling conglomeration of reds and blues. On the right side of the nave as you enter, stairs lead down to a Romanesque **crypt** and **trésor** (Tues–Sun 2–5pm; €3), where the relics of Huy's patron saint, St Domitian, were once venerated, and whose original twelfth-century shrine is on display, along with three other large shrines from the twelfth and thirteenth centuries, crafted by the Mosan gold- and silversmiths for which Huy was once famous. They're somewhat faded, but the beauty and skill of their execution shines through. Outside, on the side of the church facing the town centre, look out for the **Porte de Bethléem**, topped by a mid-fourteenth-century arch decorated with scenes of the nativity.

Huy's best-known sight however, is the **Fort de Huy** (April–June & Sept Mon–Fri 9am–12.30pm & 1–4.30pm, Sat & Sun 11am–6pm; July & Aug daily 11am–7pm; €4), which perches on top of a wooded outcrop high above the town; take the path up from Quai de Namur. There's been a fortress here since the ninth century, though the medieval castle that once occupied the site was demolished in 1717; the present structure, partly hewn out of solid rock, was erected by the Dutch in the early nineteenth century. The fort is a massive complex, and although much of it can be visited, the most compelling and coherent section is the dozen or so rooms used by the Germans as a prison during World War II, when no fewer than seven thousand prisoners passed through this bleak place. The cells, dormitories and interrogation chambers are grim enough, but the mountain of press cuttings, photos and personal effects pertaining to the Resistance and in particular concentration camps are harrowing indeed, and it's a relief to emerge into the daylight of the central courtyard, from where you can climb up onto the top for what are, predictably, stunning views over Huy and the countryside around.

There are two ways of getting to the fort: on foot, it's accessible from the quai de Namur by taking the path up to the left just beyond the tourist office; or you can use the **téléphérique** (cable car; June & Sept Sat & Sun 11am–12.15pm & 1–6.30pm; July & Aug daily 11am–12.15pm & 1–6.30pm; single €3.50, €4.50 return) from avenue De Batta on the other side of the river: cross over the Pont Roi Baudouin and turn left.

Practicalities

Huy's **train station** is on the opposite (west) side of the river from the town centre, a fifteen-minute walk: head straight out of the station down to the river, turn right and cross the Pont Roi Baudouin to reach the Collégiale Notre-Dame. The **tourist office** is right by the river and church at Quai de Namur 1 (Oct–March Mon–Fri 9am–4pm, Sat & Sun 10am–4pm; April–June & Sept Mon–Fri 8.30am–6pm, Sat & Sun 10am–6pm; July & Aug Mon–Fri 8.30am–6pm, Sat & Sun 10am–6pm; ⓣ085 21 29 15, ⓦwww.pays-de-huy.be). There's not much reason to stay, but if you need to the modern *Hôtel du Fort*, chaussée Napoleon 5 (ⓣ085 21 24 03, ⓦwww.hoteldufort.be; ❷), five minutes' walk along the river past the tourist office, has a range of variously sized and equipped rooms. Among **cafés** and **restaurants**, *Aromes et Volupthes*, rue Vierset Godin 3 (ⓣ085 240 433), has a huge array of great teas and coffees; *Le Central*, Grand-Place 25 (ⓣ085 51 47 82), has reasonably priced *plats du jour*; *Le 16.60*, rue Griange 16 (Tues–Sat 7–9pm, Sun noon–2pm & 7–9pm; ⓣ085 31 16 30), offers tasty French cuisine with main courses from €18; and *Villa Romana*, at rue des Brasseurs 21 (ⓣ085 31 01 10; daily noon–2.30pm & 6–11pm), does pizzas and good seafood dishes.

Liège

Though the effective capital of the Ardennes, and of its own province, **LIÈGE** isn't the most obvious stop on most travellers' itineraries. It's a large, grimy, industrial city, with few notable sights and little immediate appeal. However, it's somewhat hard to avoid if you're visiting the northern Ardennes and, once you've got to grips with the place, has a few pleasant surprises, not least the excellence of its restaurants. Certainly, if you're overnighting here, give yourself at least half a day to nose around.

For most of its history, Liège was an independent principality; from the tenth century onwards it was the seat of a long line of **prince-bishops**, who ruled over bodies and souls until 1794, when the French revolutionary army expelled the last prince-bishop, torching his cathedral to hammer home the point. Later, Liège was incorporated into the Belgian state, rising to prominence as an industrial city. The coal and steel industries hereabouts date back to the twelfth century, but it was only in the nineteenth century that real development of the city's position and natural resources took place, principally under one John Cockerill (1790–1840), a British entrepreneur whose family name you still see around town – though unfortunately for Liège and its workers, its industries are now in steep decline. Another name to conjure with is **Georges Simenon**, the famously priapic crime writer who spent his early life here – the tourist office has a leaflet describing a "Simenon Route".

Arrival, information and city transport

Liège has three **train stations**. All trains stop at the recently revamped main terminal, **Guillemins**, about 2km south of the centre. Most services also call at Liège's other two stations – **Jonfosse**, not far from boulevard de la Sauvenière just to the west of the centre, and **Palais**, near place St-Lambert in the city centre. Note, however, that express trains from Brussels and Luxembourg City only stop at Guillemins. To get to the centre of town from Guillemins station, either take the train to Palais or catch bus #1 or #4 to place St-Lambert; the taxi fare for the same journey is about €10.

The main city **tourist office** is located about 400m to the east of place St-Lambert at Féronstrée 92 (Mon–Fri 9am–5pm, Sat 10am–4.30pm, Sun 10am–2.30pm; ⓣ04 221 92 21, ⓦwww.liege.be). There's also a **provincial**

tourist office bang in the centre of town at place St-Lambert 35 (daily 9.30am–5.30pm; ⓣ04 237 92 92, ⓦwww.ftpl.be).

Accommodation

Most of Liège's cheaper **accommodation** options are out near the station, but you don't need to stay around there to save money; there are one or two excellent options in both the new and old parts of town.

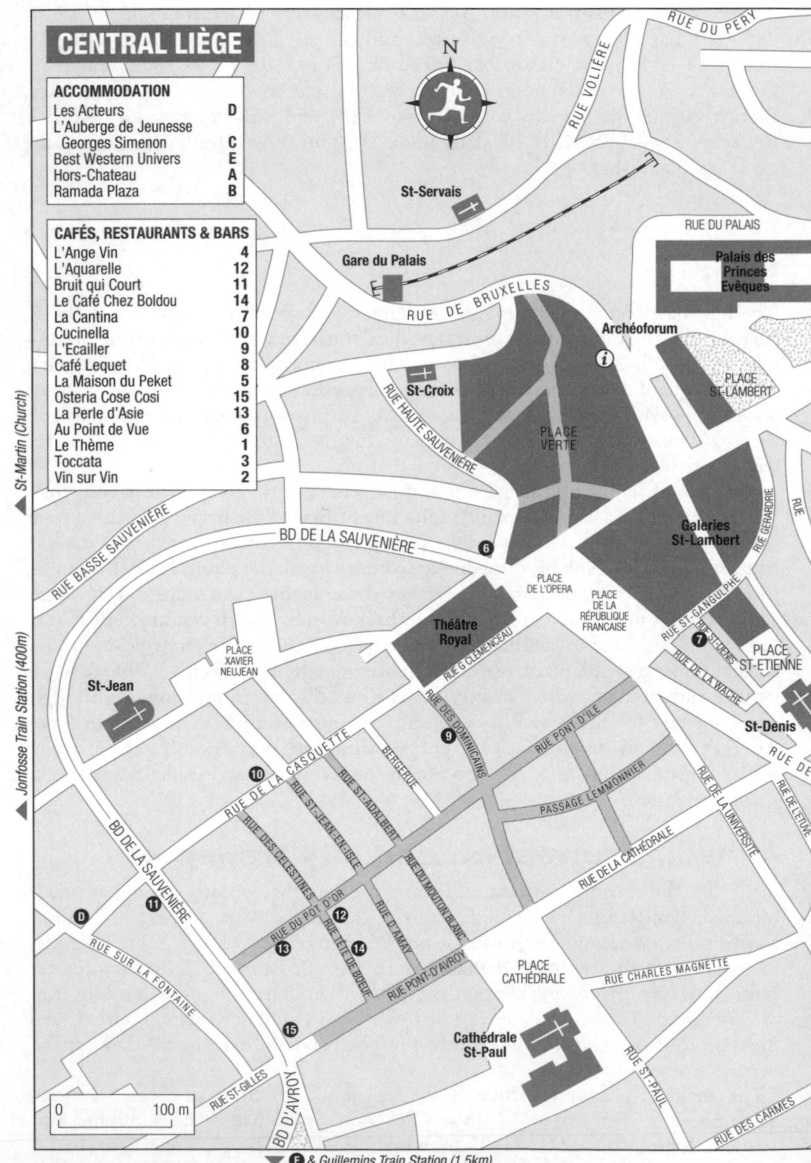

Les Acteurs rue des Urbanistes 10 ⓣ04 223 00 80. Handily – though not picturesquely – situated on a quiet street just outside central Liège's busiest quarter, this is decent value, with a friendly welcome and spick-and-span if not especially homely rooms. Small bathrooms too, but there's free wi-fi, and parking for €10 a night to make up for it. ❷

L'Auberge de Jeunesse Georges Simenon rue Georges Simenon 2 ⓣ04 344 56 89 ⓦwww.laj.be. Modern, well-equipped hostel in a pleasant old building with self-catering facilities, a café, internet access and a laundry. Two hundred beds in four- to sixteen-bed rooms, though doubles are available on request. In the heart of Outremeuse, 1km or so

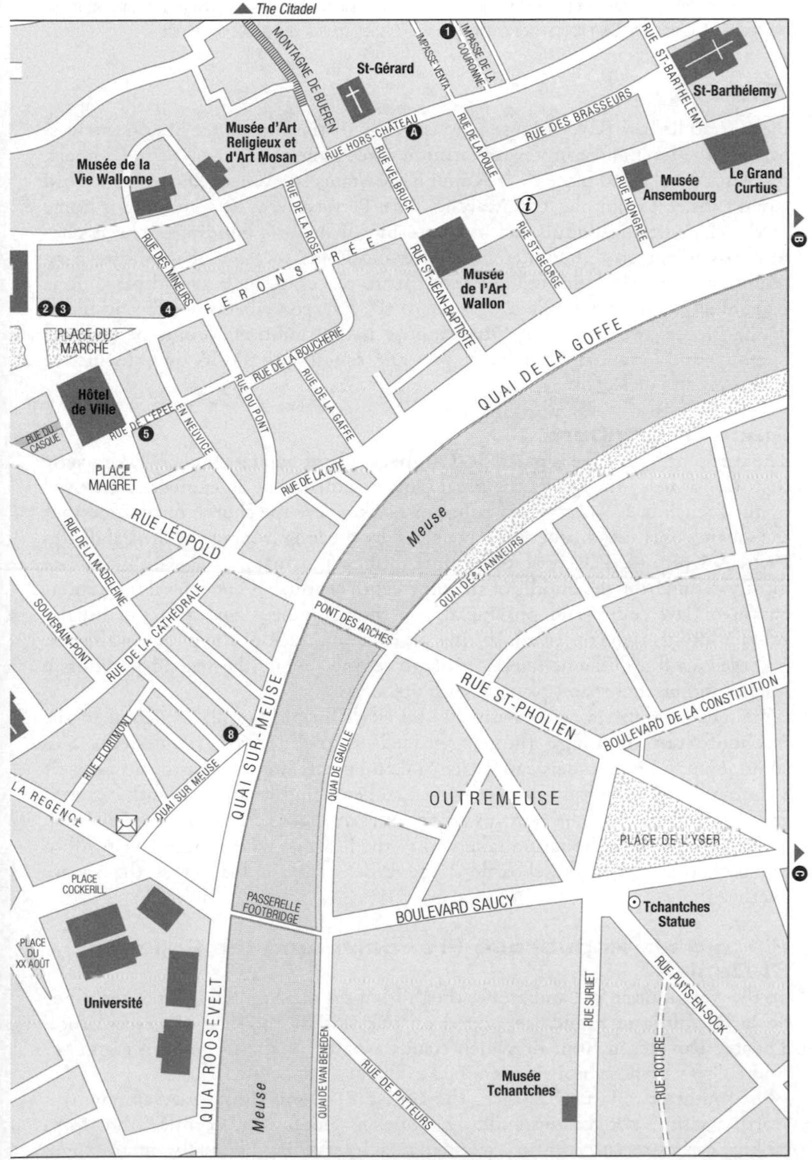

east of place St-Lambert. Closed most of Jan. Dorm beds €17, doubles ❶

Best Western Univers rue des Guillemins 116 ⓣ04 254 55 55, ⓦwww.univershotel.be. This comfortable, recently renovated three-star hotel opposite Guillemins train station is very convenient and very good value, too. ❷

Hors-Chateau rue Hors-Chateau 62 ⓣ04 250 60 68. In a great position right in the heart of Liège's old quarter, this ancient town house has smartly renovated rooms: not huge, but very comfy, with nice bathrooms and modern, minimalist decor. Good value, with wi-fi and parking too. ❸

Ramada Plaza quai St-Léonard 36 ⓣ04 228 81 11, ⓦwww.ramadaplaza-liege.com. Liège's most luxurious hotel, in a landmark 1960s building on the busy road which runs along the riverfront. Not in the best part of town, but perhaps the city's most luxurious option, with large, recently refurbished rooms and public areas. ❺

The City

Liège straddles the River Meuse, and the bulk of the city centre lies on the west bank of the river and congregates around three main squares: place St-Lambert, place du Marché and place de la République Française. What's known as the **old town** runs east from place du Marché, with Féronstrée as its spine, and is home to the city's best museums and a smattering of historic buildings. The livelier **new town**, the city's commercial centre and home to most of its shops, bars, restaurants and nightlife, nudges south from place St-Lambert and place de la République Française, while to the east of the river, on what is in effect an island in the Meuse, the district of **Outremeuse** is the traditional home of the true Liégoise, and harbours a cluster of bars and restaurants and its own distinctive traditions and dialect.

Place St-Lambert

The true centre of Liège is **place St-Lambert**, a large and rather cheerless expanse that was formerly the site of the great Gothic cathedral of St-Lambert, destroyed by the French in 1794. Ivy-clad columns mark where the church once stood, but the square's only real distinction is provided by the long frontage of the **Palais des Princes Evêques** (Palace of the Prince-Bishops), a mainly neo-Gothic edifice mostly dating from the middle of the nineteenth century. It's now used as a combination of law courts and provincial government offices, and you can usually wander into its two courtyards during office hours: each of the pillars in the first is carved with a different selection of grotesques, while the second harbours a smaller and prettier space, planted with greenery.

You can visit the excavated site of the city's former Gothic cathedral in the **Archéoforum of Liège** (hourly guided tours Tues–Sat 10am–6pm, Sun 11am–6pm; €5.50), underneath place St-Lambert. It was the fourth successor of a church that was built on the site of St Lambert's murder in the eighth century, and is mixed up with the remains of an extensive second-century Roman villa. Tours last around an hour and take you to the heart of where Liège began, all to the backdrop of the skateboarders and buses that rumble across the square overhead.

Place de la République Française and the Eglise St-Denis

To the west of place St-Lambert lies the third of the main central squares, the **place de la République Française**, edged on one side by the shed-like Neoclassical **Théâtre Royale**, in front of which stands a statue of the Liège-born composer André Grétry, whose heart is contained in the urn just below.

Just southeast, off rue Regence, the **Eglise St-Denis** (Mon–Sat 9am–5pm) is worth a visit – not for the building, which is gloomy and formless, but for a striking early sixteenth-century wooden retable, standing a good five metres high, which is displayed in the south transept, an amazing piece of work. The top – and principal – section has six panels showing the Passion of Christ, very Gothic in tone, full of drama and assertively carved. The bottom set of panels is later and gentler in style, with smaller figures telling the story of St Denis from baptism to decapitation.

Cathédrale St-Paul

From the Eglise St-Denis, rue de la Cathédrale leads down to tree-lined **place Cathédrale**, where the imposing grey steeple of the spartan **Cathédrale St-Paul** (daily 8am–5pm) makes a useful city landmark. The church was promoted to cathedral status in 1794, after the destruction of the city's former cathedral by the French. Inside are some swirling roof paintings of 1570 and a late thirteenth-century polychrome Madonna and Child at the base of the choir, although its **trésor** (Tues–Sun 2–5pm; €5.50), through the cloisters, is of most interest. The small collection features a mammoth 90kg bust reliquary of St Lambert, the work of a goldsmith from Aachen, dating from 1512, which contains the skull of the saint and depicts scenes from his life – the miracles he performed as a boy, his burial in Maastricht and the translation of his body from Maastricht to Liège by St Hubert, who succeeded him as bishop. There are also some lovely examples of ivory work from the eleventh century, and a similarly dated missal, stained by the waters of a 1920s flood that inundated the church.

Place du Marché, Féronstrée and the Montagne de Bueren

The eastern edge of place St-Lambert narrows into the smaller, tree-lined and more attractive **place du Marché**, whose northern side is flanked by a row of atmospheric bars and restaurants, behind which looms the curiously Russian-looking onion dome of the **Église Saint-André**. The south side of the square is occupied by the run-of-the-mill eighteenth-century **Hôtel de Ville**, while in the middle stands **Le Perron**, a grandiose symbol of civic independence, comprising a cumbersome water fountain of 1697 surmounted by a long and slender column.

From place du Marché, **Féronstrée** heads east to form the backbone of the old town, a historic but much quieter part of Liège – except on Sunday mornings, when the vigorous **La Batte market** takes over the nearby riverbank. For an impressive, panoramic view over the whole of Liège, make for **rue Hors-Château**, on the northern edge of the old town and just up from **Féronstrée**. From here, the 400-odd steps of the very steep **Montagne de Bueren** lead up to the **citadel**, which is now little more than a set of ramparts enclosing a modern hospital. Well worth the genuinely lung-wrenching trek, the views are superlative, looking right out over the city and the rolling countryside beyond.

Musée de la Vie Wallonne

The first turn off Féronstrée to the left, rue des Mineurs, leads up to the **Musée de la Vie Wallonne** (Tues–Sat 10am–5pm & Sun 10am–4pm; €5), the most impressive of the three old town museums devoted to Walloon culture. Housed in a beautifully restored former Franciscan friary, it's a nostalgic collection, with lots of assorted items from past eras. There are carnival masks and puppets, children's toys and old brands of soap and cigarettes, all displayed with a contemporary and serious approach. A series of room tableaux illustrate the changing fashions and technologies of the past century, and there are also displays examining Wallon militancy and separatism, and the decline of local industry (particularly the mines), and what has sprung up to take its place. It's an absorbing museum, though all the more enjoyable if you understand French.

Musée de l'Art Wallon

Further east along Féronstrée, the **Musée de l'Art Wallon**, Féronstreé 86 (Tues–Sat 1–6pm, Sun 11am–6pm; €5) comprises an attractive selection of works by French-speaking Belgian artists. The collection is arranged chronologically, starting at the top and leading down in a descending spiral. It begins with the wonderfully varied sixteenth-century paintings of Henri Bles, plus a few canvases by Liège's greatest artist, **Lambert Lombard** (1505–66), including the wonderfully irascible self-portrait that once adorned the nation's 100-franc note. It's the nineteenth- and early twentieth-century sections which are the strongest, however, ranging from the Manet-inspired portraits of Léon Philippet to the Seurat-like landscapes of Albert Lemaître, punctuated by moments of high pretension such as Antoine Wiertz's immense and wonderfully overblown *Greeks and Trojans in Dispute over the Body of Patrocles*. Look out too for the small group of works by Delvaux and Magritte, notably the former's wacky *L'Homme de la Rue*, showing a bowler-hatted businessman imperviously reading his newspaper amid a landscape of Classical ruins and cavorting nymphs.

The Musée d'Ansembourg and St-Barthélemy

Musée d'Ansembourg, Féronstrée 114 (Tues–Sat 1–6pm, Sun 11am–4.30pm; €5) occupies a grand, eighteenth-century mansion whose interior is distinguished by its sweeping wooden staircase, stucco ceilings and leather wallpaper. This provides a suitably lavish setting for a sumptuous collection of period furniture, Delftware, a selection of clocks (including a unique six-faced specimen by Hubert Sarton from 1795), and portraits of various local bigwigs – including several of Liège's prince-bishops – in various stages of self-importance.

The far end of Féronstrée is anchored by the square and church of **St-Barthélemy** (Mon–Sat 10am–noon & 2–5pm, Sun 2–5pm; €2), an originally Romanesque edifice dating back to the twelfth century. The interior, which was entirely re-equipped six centuries later, is large but not particularly special, but it does hold a supreme example of Mosan (Romanesque) sculpture in a magnificent bronze **baptismal font** of 1118. The work of a certain Renier de Huy, the font is decorated with a graceful, naturalistic relief depicting various baptisms in progress, and rests on ten oxen, who bend their heads and necks as if under the weight of the great bowl.

The Grand Curtius

The largest of the old town's museums, the **Grand Curtius**, Quai de Maastricht 13 (daily except Tues 10am–6pm; €5), is a museum of decorative and applied arts, originally housed in the seventeenth-century Curtius mansion and now swollen to occupy a spanking new wing next door. It's a bit of a romp through history, studiously covering all ages from the medieval period to Art Nouveau, and it's all beautifully displayed in a modern context, with some info in English. The Mosan metalwork is a standout, as is the religious woodcarving from the Middle Ages and the small collection of Flemish paintings. When you've had enough, check out the museum's ground-floor café, with its shady courtyard garden.

Outremeuse

Across from the centre of Liège, the bulbous island in the middle of the River Meuse holds **Outremeuse**, a working-class quarter that's said to be the home of the true Liégeois. The district's inhabitants were long known for their forthright radicalism, rioting against their masters on many occasions and refusing, during the German occupation of World War I, to keep the city's small-arms factories in production. Their appointed guardian was the folkloric figure known as **Tchantchès** (Liège slang for "Francis"), the so-called "Prince of Outremeuse", an earthy, independent-minded, brave but drunken fellow, who is said to have been born between two Outremeuse paving stones on August 25, 760. In later life, legend claims, he was instrumental in the campaigns of Charlemagne, thanks to the use of his enormous nose. Nowadays, Tchantchès can be seen in action in traditional Liège puppet shows; he's also represented in a **statue** on place l'Yser, the traditional place of his death, carried as a symbol of freedom by a woman dressed as a coal miner. Incidentally, one of Belgium's most acclaimed writers, **Georges Simenon** (1903–89), creator of Inspector Maigret, was a native of Outremeuse, and the "Simenon Route" walking-tour leaflet, available from the tourist office, will guide you around the areas where he misspent his youth.

Eating

Liège can be an excellent and often inexpensive place **to eat**. Hearty rather than refined, Liégoise cuisine is distinctive and delicious, and available at many places around town, while the city's ethnic mix means there are lots of non-Belgian choices too. The best restaurants are concentrated in the rectangle of streets northeast of the cathedral, but it's also worth a trip across the river to Outremeuse's **rue Roture**, a narrow alleyway which spears right off the main shopping thoroughfare of rue Puits-en-Sock, and which is thick with restaurants and bars.

Bruit qui Court blvd de la Sauvenière 142 ⓣ04 232 18 18. Trendy eatery serving simple and reasonably priced meals – and vegetarian friendly to boot. There's also a lively bar in the old converted bank vault downstairs. Mains average about €12. Mon–Sat 11am–midnight.

La Cantina rue St-Denis 2 ⓣ04 221 35 35. Excellent and authentic Italian restaurant, offering delicious food and friendly service. Good antipasti, menus for €30–45 and *plats du jour* for around €15. Tues–Sat noon–2pm & 7–9.30pm.

Cucinella rue de la Casquette 26 ⓣ04 222 36 52. Top-quality Italian restaurant providing an oasis of calm in a crazy area, with a garden in the back for summer evenings. Pasta dishes €12.50, osso bucco and other mains €16. Mon, Tues & Thurs–Sat noon–2.30pm & 6.30–11pm, Wed noon–2.30pm.

L'Ecailler rue des Dominicains 26 ⓣ04 222 17 49. Behind the Théâtre Royale, this old-fashioned and cosy joint is a long-term favourite and does great oysters and seafood platters. Main courses around €20. Daily 11.45am–2.30pm & 6.30–10.30pm.

Café Lequet quai sur-Meuse 17 ⓣ04 222 21 34. Basic and authentic restaurant that's perhaps the best place to sample traditional local grub. The *boulet-frites*, done Liégois-style with a sweet sauce made with sultanas and *sirop de Liège*, attracts people from miles around, but there is lots of other good stuff too, and changing daily specials. Daily except Tues & Sun noon–2.30pm & 6–9pm.

Osteria Cose Cosi blvd de la Sauvenière 153 ⓣ04 250 10 06. Simple and tasteful Italian cuisine, with home-made fresh pasta (from €10) served in a tasteful contemporary interior. Set menu on Fri and Sat for €25. Daily except Tues & Sun noon–2.15pm & 6–10.30pm.

La Perle d'Asie rue du Pot d'Or 49 ⓣ04 223 11 70. Excellent and authentic Vietnamese food, including good seafood choices, with set-lunch menus from €7.50 and dinner menus from €10.50 – prices that attract students by the score. Daily except Mon 11.30am–2pm & 6–11pm.

Au Point de Vue place Verte 10 ⓣ04 223 64 82. This cosy pub with an outside terrace right in the city centre has been going for years, and is good place to try traditional Liégoise food – meatballs, rabbit, veal kidneys and the like. Or just go for the simple salad Liégoise, with potatoes, green beans and bacon.

Le Thème Impasse de la Couronne 9 ⓣ04 222 02 02, ⓦwww.letheme.com. Excellent and quite reasonably priced French cuisine in an intimate setting on a tiny alleyway in the old town, with three-course (€32) and five-course (€38) menus. Great website, too. Reservations essential. Mon–Sat eves only from 7pm.

Toccata place du Marché 11 ⓣ04 222 31 00. Good spot for lunch with a selection of omelettes, *piadina* and tapas as well as fresh juices and an array of teas, though the main pull is the coffee.

Vin sur Vin place du Marché 9 ⓣ04 223 28 13. Mainly French cuisine, but with some highly original touches including fruit served every which way. A three-course meal will set you back about €40. Mon–Fri noon–2pm & 7–10pm & Sat noon–2pm.

Drinking and nightlife

The grid of streets in the new town running north from rue Pont d'Avroy to rue de la Casquette is the hub of the city's **nightlife**, with loads of good, largely student-oriented **bars** that can get very raucous later on. Rue Pont d'Avroy itself has lots of drinking haunts, but most of the best establishments are on the narrower streets behind, especially in the tiny alleyways of rue Tête de Boeuf and the parallel rue d'Amay. There's also a clutch of more sedate venues on and around the place du Marché.

L'Ange Vin place du Marché 43. A wine bar, as the name suggests, which gets pretty lively in the evenings and attracts a mixed gay and straight crowd.

L'Aquarelle Corner of rue Pot d'Or and rue Tête de Boeuf. Dim student hangout pumping out mainstream rock and pop.

Le Café Chez Boldou rue Tête de Boeuf 15. Entertainingly decorated bar full of eclectic bric-a-brac. It's popular with students and there's live music at weekends (no cover charge), as well as a nightclub, *En Bas* (Fri & Sat 11pm–8am; free), downstairs.

La Maison du Peket rue de l'Epée 4. The place to taste the local drink *peket* – a type of gin – in 250 varieties from guava and mango in the fruit section, to the aged dusty bottles of the vintage shelves.

Spa

SPA, about 30km southeast of Liège, was the world's first health resort, established way back in the sixteenth century: Pliny the Elder knew of the healing properties of the waters here and Henry VIII was an early visitor, but it was Peter the Great who clinched the town's fame, heralding it as "the best place to take the waters". Since then the town has given its name to thermal resorts worldwide, reaching a height of popularity in the eighteenth and nineteenth centuries, when it was known as the "Café of Europe", being graced by monarchs, statesmen, intellectuals and aristocrats from every corner of the continent. Later the town went into slow decline – when the poet Matthew Arnold visited in 1860, he claimed it "astonished us by its insignificance" – but Spa is now on the way back following the opening of a new thermal complex, **Les Thermes de Spa**, on the hill overlooking the resort. Furthermore, the town below still preserves an endearing sense of faded distinction and continues to draw a loyal clientele of elderly locals, whilst also making a good base for excursions into the Hautes Fagnes (see p.321), a short drive to the south and southeast.

Arrival, information and accommodation

Spa has two **train stations**, but the one you want for the town centre is **Spa-Géronstère**, a five-minute walk south of the casino. The large and well-stocked **tourist office** is at place Royale 41 (April–Sept Mon–Fri 9am–6pm, Sat & Sun 10am–6pm; Oct–March Mon–Fri 9am–5pm, Sat & Sun 10am–5pm; ⓣ087 79 53 53, ⓦwww.spa-info.be). The town also has a good **flea market** in the Leopold II Gallery just behind the tourist office on Sunday morning (8am–1pm).

There are no fewer than thirteen **hotels** dotted in and around Spa's centre and competition keeps prices down to manageable levels. There are also a couple of decent **campsites**, *Camping Spa d'Or*, 5km northeast of town at Stockay 17 (ⓣ087 47 44 00, ⓦwww.campingspador.be), and *Camping du Parc des Sources* at rue de la Sauvenière 141 (ⓣ087 77 23 11, ⓦwww.parcdessources.be).

Hotels

L'Auberge du Lac Lac de Warfaaz 2 ⓣ087 77 17 72, ⓦwww.lejardindeselfes.be. There are five recently modernized guest rooms at this semi-rusticated lakeside hotel, a couple of kilometres east of town. Parking and wi-fi too, and very peaceful after dark ❸

Best Western Hotel Villa des Fleurs rue Albin Body 31 ⓣ087 79 50 50 ⓦwww.villadesfleurs.be. Right in the centre of Spa, this is the town's most characterful and comfortable option, a handsome old town house dating from the 1880s with just twelve large guest rooms decorated in a modern version of period style – and with a nice private garden too. ❺

Radisson SAS Blue Palace place Royale 39 ⓣ087 27 97 00, ⓦwww.radissonblu.com. A great location right by the lift to the modern thermal spa, and decent standard-issue luxury at this smart, 120-room chain hotel. Discounts at the Spa, too. ❹–❺

Le Relais place du Monument 22 ⓣ087 77 11 08, ⓦwww.hotelrelais-spa.be. This small, well-cared-for hotel has eleven guest rooms, each kitted out in functional modern style, at a variety of prices. The town's best budget choice, in a great, central location. ❷

The Town

Spa's tidy **town centre** holds a striking cluster of grand Neoclassical buildings, presided over by the three towering steeples of the church of **Notre-Dame et St-Remacle**. Chief among these are the former **thermal baths**, no longer in use and still awaiting a new role. The neighbouring **casino**, the oldest in the world, was founded in 1763 under the improbable auspices of the prince-bishop of Liège, though the current building dates only from 1919. Curiously enough, it hosts the annual **Francofolies** festival, which plays tribute to the heady world of French *chanson* (ⓦwww.francofolies.be).

A little further along down rue Royale, the town's main mineral spring, **Pouhan-Pierre-le-Grand**, is currently undergoing a major restoration and is due to open again in 2012, when hopefully it will resume spouting a daily average of twenty-one thousand litres of cloudy water that is allegedly beneficial for lung and heart ailments as well as rheumatism. It's housed in a barnlike Neoclassical pavilion and named after Peter the Great, who appreciated the therapeutic effects of its waters and visited often. A number of Spa's other **springs** – notably Tonnelet, Barisart, Géronstère and Sauvenière – can be visited on a **mini-train**, which plies around the outskirts of town from outside the main baths (daily 11am–5pm; €5).

Five minutes' walk west of the town centre, situated in the former mansion of Queen Marie-Henriette, the **Musée de la Ville d'Eaux**, ave Reine Astrid 77, displays posters and objects relating to the resort and its waters (March–June & Oct–Nov Sat & Sun 2–6pm; July–Sept daily except Tues 2–6pm; €3 combined ticket with the Musée du Cheval). The stables next door have been turned into the **Musée du Cheval** (same times), exhibiting all things equine.

On the hill immediately above central Spa – and easily reached on the funicular from place Royale (€1 each way), or by following the path up through the woods just to the side – stands the town's pride and joy, **Les Thermes de Spa** (Mon–Thurs & Sat 9am–9pm, Fri 9am–10pm, Sun 9am–8pm; €17 for 3hr, €27 for the day; ⓣ087 77 25 60, ⓦwww.thermesdespa.com), a thermal complex offering a multitude of treatments. On arrival you can sample three different types of Spa spring water – Reine, Clementine and the iron-rich Marie-Henriette – and beyond there is both an outdoor and indoor pool with water-massage jets and jacuzzis galore. Upstairs is reserved for saunas, steam rooms and a relaxation area with chill-out music and a panoramic view of the valley below. For massage, mud wraps or water treatments in the famous retro copper baths, you need to book well in advance.

Lac de Warfaaz and around

Once you've seen the sights, two relatively undemanding **walks** can give you a taste of the countryside around Spa. One is the easy and pleasant stroll to **Lac de**

Warfaaz, about 2km east of the centre. To get there, leave Spa along rue du Marché and its continuation, boulevard des Anglais, then turn down avenue Amédée Hesse and keep going. The lake, which was created in 1880, is surrounded by wooded hills and a clear footpath circumnavigates it. The other option is a longer and slightly more challenging trek around the southerly outskirts of town, following the Francorchamps road out of town and taking a right up to connect with the so-called **Promenade des Artists**, which climbs up into the hills, criss-crossing a beautiful wooded stream by way of little wooden bridges before circling around past the Arboretum de Tahanfagne and back down into the town. It's a gentle 2–3hr walk, and the tourist office can provide you with more details.

Eating and drinking

There's plenty of choice when it comes to **eating out** in Spa. The restaurant of the *Hotel Le Relais* (Ⓣ087 77 11 08; daily from 6.30pm, plus Sat & Sun lunch), is a good choice – as is, a few doors along, the elegant *La Belle Époque*, at place du Monument 15 (Ⓣ087 77 54 03; closed Mon & Tues), which serves excellent fish mains from around €17 and three-course menus for €25. Or you might wander over to the *Brasserie des Thermes*, opposite the old baths at place Royale 25–27 (Ⓣ087 77 45 25), which is inexpensive if not terribly atmospheric, but with nice outdoor seating. Spa is never going to win any awards for nightlife, but if you fancy a late **drink**, *Bidul'*, rue Royale 49, is a decent local bar.

Stavelot

The small and tranquil town of **STAVELOT** rambles up the hill from the River Amblève. It grew up around its **abbey**, which ran the area as an independent principality until the French revolutionary army ended its privileges at the end of the eighteenth century. The town was also the scene of fierce fighting during the Ardennes campaign of the last war, and some of the Nazis' worst atrocities in Belgium were committed here.

These days it's a pleasant old place, the pretty streets of its tiny centre flanked by a battery of half-timbered houses that mostly date from the eighteenth century. The best time to be here is for its renowned annual **carnival**, the **Laetare**, first celebrated here in 1502 and held on the third weekend before Easter, from Saturday to Monday evening; the main protagonists are the **Blancs Moussis**, figures of which you'll see adorning various Stavelot houses. There are also

Spa-Francorchamps

Just outside Francorchamps, the race circuit of **Spa-Francorchamps** is renowned as one of the most scenic and historic venues in the motorsports world. Formerly a 14-km-long road circuit, races used to take in the whole of the surrounding area, to Malmédy and Stavelot and back, but now those towns serve as dormitories for the thousands who come here to enjoy the racing every year. The highlight by far is September's Belgian Grand Prix, but the circuit is busy almost every day between March and November, hosting all kinds of events, some of which are free. Anyone can visit, and most of the time there's free access to the paddock and pit lane, as well as the panoramic top-floor brasserie. It's also possible to see more of the circuit – the media centre and race control room, for example – by way of the regular guided tours that are run on the first and third Tuesdays of the month at 2pm (€9.50; Ⓣ087 29 37 00, Ⓦwww.spa-francorchamps.be).

The Deutschsprachige Gemeinschaft Belgiens

To the east of Spa, the pleasant but unexceptional little town of **Eupen** is the capital of the German-speaking region of Belgium, or **Deutschsprachige Gemeinschaft Belgiens**, a pint-sized area pushed tight against the German border that's home to around 75,000 people and enjoys the same federal status as the other two linguistic areas of the country. Once part of Prussia, the area was ceded to Belgium by the Treaty of Versailles at the end of World War I in 1919, but German remains the main language (and is still spoken somewhat in neighbouring Malmedy and other areas), and the area has its own tiny parliament and government. Eupen itself certainly has a distinctive Rhineland feel, but that aside there's precious little reason to visit.

festivals of theatre and music in July and August respectively, with performances in the abbey buildings.

The Town

There's an attractively cobbled main square, **place St-Remacle**, at the heart of Stavelot, but the town is really dominated by the **abbey**, a sprawling complex of mainly eighteenth-century buildings, in front of which the foundations of the former abbey are clearly visible, most notably the soaring Gothic arch on the right. The abbey buildings house the tourist office and three museums, the most notable of which is the **Musée Historique de la Principauté de Stavelot-Malmédy** (daily 10am–6pm; €7.50 for a combined ticket for all three museums; Ⓦwww.abbayedestavelot.be), which traces the history of the principality from the seventh century to the present day by means of religious artefacts, town crafts and folkloric exhibits alongside multimedia displays. In the vaulted cellars of the abbey, a second museum, the **Musée du Circuit de Spa-Francorchamps** (same times) contains a collection of racing cars and motorcycles from the nearby racetrack, home of the Belgium Formula 1 Grand Prix (see opposite), including the 1974 Lotus of Belgian ace Jackie Ickx, while on the second floor, the **Musée du Poete Guillaume Apollinaire** (same times), which was set up to commemorate the eponymous French writer, who spent the summer of 1899 in the town (he left without paying his bill, apparently) and wrote many poems about Stavelot and the Ardennes. The museum pays tribute to a man who – despite his early death in 1918 – was one of the most influential poets of his period.

Finally, the church of **St-Sebastien** on place du Vinâve (Mon–Sat 10am–12.30pm & 2–5pm) is home to the enormous thirteenth-century shrine of St Remacle, the seventh-century founder of Stavelot abbey, who is said to have built the abbey with the aid of a wolf he supposedly tamed for the purpose. Mosan in style, the shrine is of gilt and enamelled copper with filigree and silver statuettes, though you can normally view it only from a distance. A short walk downhill, the little **chapel of St-Laurent** was founded in 1030 by St Poppon, Abbot of Stavelot, and contains the sarcophagus that originally held his remains. To get there, turn left out of the abbey gateway, walk downhill across the bridge, and take the first left.

Practicalities

Stavelot's **tourist office** is in the abbey complex (daily 10am–1pm & 1.30–5pm; Ⓣ080 86 27 06, Ⓦwww.stavelot.be) and has maps and details of *chambres d'hôtes* (B&B) possibilities in the town. There are some good **places to stay** in Stavelot. Perhaps the most obvious choice is *La Maison*, in a handsome old town house at place St-Remacle 19 (Ⓣ080 88 08 91, Ⓦwww.hotel-la-maison.be; ❸–❺), whose large and comfortable rooms are excellent value. Its sister hotel next door, *L'Espion* (same details), has a handful of larger and more luxurious rooms and suites for slightly higher prices. The *Dufays*, at the far end of rue Neuve at no.115 (ⓣ080 54 80 08; ⓦwww.bbb-dufays.be; ④), is a very comfortable and welcoming alternative, while at the other end of the same street the arty *Mal Aimée*, rue Neuve 12 (ⓣ080 86 20 01; ⓦwww.omalaime.be; ③), has plain but stylish rooms (with wi-fi but no TV) for slightly lower prices, as well as an excellent **restaurant**, with seasonal three-course menus for €25–30. *La Maison* (see p.319) is perhaps the town's best fine-dining option, though *Pizzeria Figaro*, on place du Vinâve 4 (ⓣ080 86 42 86), is a popular and safe standby, with decent pizzas from €6, pasta from €7 and Italian and French main courses from €16. *Le Loup Gourmand*, ave Ferdinand Nicolay 19 (ⓣ080 86 29 95) serves a good selection of Belgian staples – plus couscous and pasta if that doesn't suit – in a relaxed environment.

Coo

Just under than 5km west of Stavelot, perched above the banks of the Amblève, **COO** is a nice enough village, but the real action is down by the river, where the modest waterfalls have given birth to a thriving resort area, made up of a cluster of hotels and restaurants in **Petit Coo** and, in **Grande Coo** on the other side of the river, the unfortunately named **Plopsa Coo**, an adventure and theme park aimed at families (see below). There are steps down to get up close to the falls, and Petit Coo also has a surprisingly peaceful riverside campsite, *Camping del la Cascade* (ⓣ0474 55 85 83, ⓦwww.camping-coo.be), as well as a small **tourist office** (July & Aug daily 11am–3pm; rest of year Sat & Sun 11am–3pm; ⓣ080 68 46 39) and **Coo Adventure** (ⓣ080 68 91 33, ⓦwww.coo-adventure.com), offering kayak and mountain bike hire among many other outdoor activities. **Plopsa Coo** (mid-May to mid-Sept daily 10am–5.30pm; rest of year hours vary; €28, children 85cm–1m €7.50, less than 85cm free; ⓦwww.plopsa.be) is worth a look whether or not you have kids: you can wander around for free, but you have to buy a ticket to try out any of the rides, which include the mildly terrifying two-person *télésiège* (cable car) up the mountain – an exhilarating experience, but not for those nervous of heights. You can also ride down a dry bobsleigh, go go-karting or any number of other activities. Parking costs €6, but it's possible to park in Petit Coo and walk across.

Remouchamps

About 25km down the Amblève valley from Coo, the village of **REMOUCHAMPS** is best known for the **Grottes de Remouchamps** (daily 10am–6pm; €9.50) the country's second largest caves after Han (see p.295) and, since the boat rides at Han ceased, the only ones with a navigable underground river. Tours last around ninety minutes and take you some 1200m through the heart of the cave system, which is 6km in length overall, before punting you back 700m to the entrance by river – a head-ducking and somewhat claustrophobic journey, but one not to be missed. Afterwards, take time off for **lunch** at the restaurant of the *Hotel Bonhomme*, almost next to the caves at rue de la Reffe 26 (ⓣ04 384 40 06; ③), a pleasantly old-fashioned affair which is also a nice place to **stay**.

Malmédy

About 8km northeast of Stavelot, and connected to it (and Trois Ponts) by regular buses, the bustling resort of **MALMÉDY** is a popular tourist destination, its attractive streets flanked by lively restaurants, smart shops and cheap hotels. There's not much to the town, but it's a pleasant place to spend a night or two and makes a relatively inexpensive base for the Hautes Fagnes (see p.321). Malmédy is also home to the **Cwarmê**, one of Belgium's most famous festivals, held over the four days leading up to Shrove Tuesday. The main knees-up is the Sunday, during which roving groups of masked figures in red robes and plumed hats – the so-called **Haguètes** – wander around town seizing people with long wooden pincers derived, it's thought, from the devices that were once used to give food to lepers. The **Musée du Cwarmê** on place de Rome has displays on the carnival, although at time of writing it was closed to visitors. The town's compact centre runs from **here to** the main square, **place Albert 1er**, off of which is the imposing but somewhat plain eighteenth-century **cathedral** (guided visits July & Aug 10am–noon & 2–5pm), surrounded by a clutch of fancy Germanic buildings.

Practicalities

The well-equipped **tourist office**, on place Albert 1er (Wed–Sat 10am–6pm; ⓣ080 33 02 50, ⓦwww.malmedy.be), has truckloads of information on the town and its environs. **Accommodation** is notable for its quantity rather than quality. The *Albert 1er*, place Albert 1er 40 (ⓣ080 77 03 93; ❸), is a good option, with six rooms that are nothing special but well looked after and right in the centre of the action. There's also the comparable *Saint-Géréon*, place St-Géréon 7–8 (ⓣ080 33 06 77, ⓦwww.saintgereon.be; ❷–❸), just off place Albert 1er, or the recently upgraded *L'Esprit Sain*, Chemin-rue 46 (ⓣ080 33 03 14, ⓦwww.espritsain.be; ❸), which has cool, modern rooms and public areas.

Malmédy's popularity means there are plenty of places to **eat**. The smart *Le Saint Célien*, Chemin-rue 21 (ⓣ080 33 78 74; Mon–Wed, Fri & Sun noon–2pm & 6–9pm, Sat 6–9pm) offers a seasonal menu for €25 and regional specialties à la carte at €17–25, while *A Vi Mam Di*, place Albert 1er 41 (ⓣ080 33 96 36), serves trout lots of ways plus a whole host of Belgian classics for €13–15.

The Hautes Fagnes

The high plateau that stretches north of Malmédy up as far as Eupen is known as the **Hautes Fagnes** (in German, the Hohes Venn or High Fens) and is now protected as a national park. This area marks the end of the Ardennes proper and has been twinned with the Eifel hills to form the sprawling Deutsch-Belgischer Naturpark. The Hautes Fagnes accommodates Belgium's highest peak, the Signal de Botrange (694m), but the rest of the area is boggy heath and woods, windswept and rather wild – excellent hiking country, though often fearsome in winter.

Some 7km north of Robertville, on the road to Eupen, the **Centre Nature Botrange** (daily 10am–6pm; €3; ⓣ080 44 03 00, ⓦwww.botrange.be) provides a focus for explorations of the national park. A **bus** runs to the centre from Eupen (7 daily; 20min), but otherwise you'll need your own car to get there. At the centre, multilingual audio-guides steer you around a permanent exhibition, Naturama, which describes the flora and fauna of the area and explains how the *fagnes* were created and how they've been exploited. The centre also rents out skis in winter and runs organized hikes (see box, p.322).

Walking the Hautes Fagnes

Large parts of the **Hautes Fagnes** are protected zones and are only open to walkers with a registered guide. Three- and six-hour walks in these areas are arranged by the **Centre Nature Botrange** (see p.321) on most weekends from March to November (€4–6). Each walk is organized around a feature of the local ecology, from medicinal plants to the endangered tetras lyre bird. In summer the walks can feel a bit crowded, and the guide's patter is normally in French or German, but they're a good way to see some genuinely wild country that would otherwise be off-limits.

To see some of the moorland on your own, ask staff at the centre for their free **map** (*Ronde de Botrange*) showing footpaths in the area. Many of them run along the edges of the protected areas, giving you a chance to see something of the *fagnes* even if you can't get on a guided walk. Dozens more local routes are marked on the *Promenades Malmédy* map, also available from the centre or from any local tourist office, though most are south of the Hautes Fagnes around Robertville, Xhoffraix and Malmédy. The varied 11km **route M6** can be picked up in Botrange, crossing the heath as far as the main road before dropping down through the woods and along the river to Bayhon, returning through some attractive, almost alpine scenery. From M6 you can take a detour north to incorporate the Fagne de la Poleur, or cross the main road and join **route M9**, which winds through the woods to Baraque Michel and then cuts south across the moors on the edge of the protected Grande Fagne.

Further up the main road is the **Signal de Botrange**, Belgium's highest point, though the high-plateau nature of the Hautes Fagnes means it doesn't feel very high at all. A tower marks the summit, offering a good panorama over the *fagnes*, and there's a restaurant that's ultra-popular with coach parties and walkers alike.

Travel details

Trains

Arlon to: Jemelle (hourly; 50min); Libramont (every 40min–1hr; 30min); Luxembourg City (hourly; 20min); Namur (hourly; 1hr 30min).
Dinant to: Anseremme (hourly; 5min); Bertrix (every 2hr; 1hr); Gendron-Celles (hourly; 10min); Houyet (hourly; 20min); Libramont (every 2hr; 1hr 20min); Namur (hourly; 30min).
Jemelle to: Brussels (hourly; 1hr 50min); Libramont (hourly; 25min); Luxembourg City (hourly; 1hr 20min); Namur (hourly; 40min).
Libramont to: Bastogne (hourly; 40min); Bertrix (hourly; 10min); Poix St-Hubert (every 2hr; 15min); Luxembourg City (hourly; 50min); Namur (hourly; 1hr).
Liège-Guillemins to: Brussels (hourly; 1hr); Coo (every 2hr; 50min); Eupen (hourly; 40min); Huy (every 20min; 20–30min); Jemelle (hourly; 1hr 30min); Leuven (hourly; 35min); Luxembourg City (hourly; 2hr 30min); Melreux-Hotton (hourly; 1hr); Namur (hourly; 45min); Trois Ponts (every 2hr; 55min); Spa, via Verviers (hourly; 55min).
Namur to: Arlon (hourly; 1hr 35min); Brussels (every 30min; 1hr); Charleroi (hourly; 30–40min); Dinant (hourly; 30min); Huy (every 30min; 20min); Jemelle (hourly; 40min); Libramont (hourly; 1hr); Liège (hourly; 45min); Luxembourg City (hourly; 2hr).

Buses

All buses are operated by **TEC** and bus timetables are detailed on its website Ⓦwww.tec-namur-luxembourg.be.
Bertrix train station to: Bouillon (2 daily; 50min).
Dinant to: Hastière (hourly; 20min).
Jemelle train station to: Han-sur-Lesse (4–6 daily; 15min); Rochefort (4–6 daily; 10min).
Libramont train station to: Bouillon (2 daily; 50min).
Melreux-Hotton train station to: La Roche-en-Ardenne (4–6 daily; 30min).
Namur to: Annevoie (1–4 daily; 40min).
Poix St-Hubert train station to: St-Hubert (3–6 daily; 15min).
Trois Ponts train station to: Malmédy (every 2hr; 25min); Stavelot (every 2hr; 10min).

Luxembourg

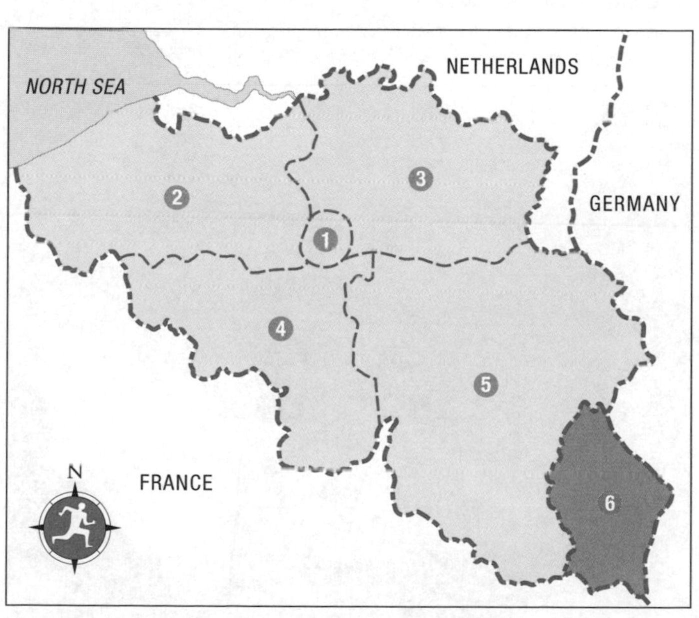

CHAPTER 6

Highlights

✱ **Chemin de la Corniche** This panoramic walkway offers some fabulous views over the capital's bastions and bulwarks. See p.336

✱ **The Schueberfouer** Luxembourg City's annual funfair, held over the last week in August and first two weeks of September. See p.340

✱ **Echternach** A lovely little town with a splendid abbey and an imposing basilica, not to mention some excellent hiking in the surrounding wooded hills and valleys. See p.343

✱ **Vianden** Luxembourg at its picture-postcard best, with the little town of Vianden set beneath an inordinately pretty castle, atop a steep, wooded hill. See p.349

▲ Echternach basilica

6

Luxembourg

Across the border from the Belgian province of Luxembourg (with which it has a closely entwined history), the **Grand Duchy of Luxembourg** is one of Europe's smallest sovereign states, a mere 85km from tip to toe. As a country it's relatively neglected by travellers, which is a pity considering its varied charms, not least some marvellous scenery: the rearing green hills and deep forested valleys that stretch along much of its eastern edge make for glorious **hiking**, and there's more of the same further to the west. The sharp, craggy hills that punctuate this dramatic landscape are crowned with handsome **châteaux** – around 130 altogether, some austere, fortified castles, others lavish country mansions. In other ways, Luxembourg lives up to its popular reputation: it's ultra-clean, efficient and well maintained, and its inhabitants are friendly though generally not very outgoing, which is perhaps why – Luxembourg City apart – many villages and towns seem almost eerily deserted at night and you're as likely to meet another tourist as you are a local.

The obvious place to start a visit is **Luxembourg City**, once the Habsburgs' strongest fortress, and now one of the best-looking capitals in Europe, home to a fifth of Luxembourg's population. Portions of its massive bastions and zigzag walls have survived in good order, while the broken terrain, with its deep winding valleys and steep hills, has restricted development, making the city feel more like a grouping of disparate villages than an administrative focus for the EU and a world financial centre. It's true that the city is not overly endowed with sights, but there's compensation in the excellence of its restaurants and the liveliness of its bar and club scene.

Within easy striking distance of the capital, in the southeast corner of the country, are the **vineyards** that string along the west bank of the **River Moselle**, the border with Germany. Tours and tastings of the wine cellars (*caves*) are the big deal here and, among a scattering of small riverside towns, the most appealing – in a low-key sort of way – are **Remich** and **Ehnen**. To the southwest of the capital

Luxembourg passes

Available from Easter to October, from tourist offices, hotels and campsites, the **Luxembourg Card** gives substantial discounts on a variety of attractions across the Grand Duchy as well as unlimited use of public transport. The cards are valid for one (€10), two (€17) or three days (€24); family cards cost €20 for one day, €34 for two days, €48 for three days. In terms of **public transport** alone, you can get a **day pass** which is valid for the whole of the Duchy's transport system – trains and buses; it costs €4 and is available from bus drivers and at bus and train stations.

is an industrial belt of little attraction – though you might consider a day-trip to the Duchy's second city, **Esch-sur-Alzette**. Further afield, the northeastern corner of the Duchy boasts spectacular scenery with rugged gorges gashing a high, partly wooded plateau, a beautiful district known as **La Petite Suisse Luxembourgeoise** – less fancifully Mullerthal in Luxembourgish. The inviting town of **Echternach**, which boasts a fine old abbey, is easily the best base hereabouts. Similarly delightful, further to the north in the **Luxembourg Ardennes**, is **Vianden**, a popular resort surrounded by craggy green hills and topped by a

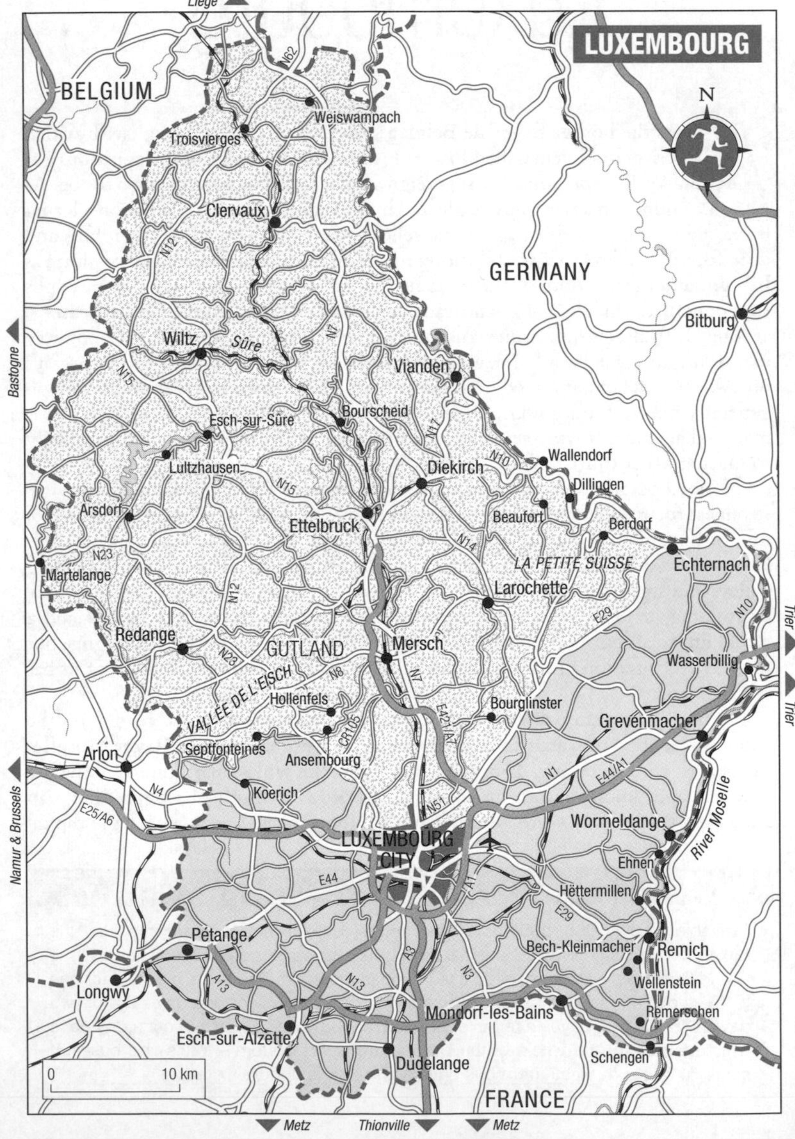

glistening and glowering castle. In between the two, more humdrum **Diekirch** boasts an extremely good museum dedicated to the Battle of the Bulge (much of which took place in the northern part of the country), and is also a handy base for venturing north into another beguiling part of the Luxembourg Ardennes, tracking along the valley of the **River Sûre** from the imposing castle of **Bourscheid** to the village of **Esch-sur-Sûre**, clasped in the horseshoe bend of its river.

Luxembourg has an excellent public transport system. With Luxembourg City as its hub, the **rail network** has four main lines. One reaches up through the centre of the country, connecting the capital with Ettelbruck, Clervaux and ultimately Liège in Belgium; a second runs west bound for Arlon, Namur and Brussels; a third heads east passing through Wasserbillig on the Moselle before going on into Germany; and a fourth links the city with Metz in France. Two branch lines respectively link Esch-sur-Alzette and Ettelbruck with Diekirch. **Buses** supplement the trains, with regular and reliable services to and from all the larger towns and villages not on the rail network, including Echternach and Vianden. The smaller villages can, however, be much more difficult to reach, especially as some local services are geared to the needs of commuters and schoolchildren rather than the tourist. **Free timetables** are available at train and bus stations, and at all but the smallest tourist office.

Some history

Before **Napoleon** rationalized much of western Europe, Luxembourg was just one of several hundred small kingdoms dating back to medieval times, and perhaps the most surprising thing about the modern state is that it exists at all: you'd certainly think that Luxembourg, perilously sandwiched between France and Germany, would have been gobbled up by one or the other, which is precisely what would have happened but for some strange quirks of history.

The **Romans** incorporated the region into their empire, colonizing Luxembourg City after the conquest of Gaul (including present-day Belgium) by Julius Caesar in 58–52 BC. Roman control lasted until the middle of the fifth century, when "Luxembourg" was overrun by the Franks, who had absorbed the area into their **Merovingian** empire by 511. Four hundred years later, with no dominant power, middle Europe had broken up into dozens of small principalities, and one of these was established by **Count Siegfried of Lorraine** when he fortified the site of what is now Luxembourg City in 963. Siegfried and his successors ensured that Luxembourg City remained – as it had been under the Romans – a major staging point on the trade route between German Trier and Paris, its strategic importance enhanced by its defensibility, perched high above the sheer gorges of the Pétrusse and Alzette rivers. These counts ruled the area first as independent princes and then as (nominal) vassals of the Holy Roman Emperor, but in the early fourteenth century, dynastic shenanigans united Luxembourg with Bohemia. In 1354 Luxembourg was independent again, this time as a **duchy**, and its first dukes – John the Blind and his son Wenceslas – extended their lands up to Limburg in the north and down to Metz in the south. This state of affairs was also short-lived; in 1443, Luxembourg passed to the dukes of Burgundy and then, forty years later, to the **Habsburgs**. Thereafter its history mirrors that of Belgium, successively becoming part of the Spanish and Austrian Netherlands before occupation by Napoleon.

Things got really complicated in the early nineteenth century. In 1814, the Congress of Vienna decided to create the **Grand Duchy of Luxembourg**, nominally independent but ruled by **William I** of Orange-Nassau, who doubled as the newly appointed king of the newly created united Kingdom of The Netherlands (including Belgium). This arrangement proved deeply unpopular in Luxembourg, and when the Belgians rebelled in 1830, the Luxembourgers joined in. It didn't do them much good. The Great Powers recognized an independent

Luxembourg's linguistic mix

Luxembourg has three **official languages**: French, German and **Luxembourgish** (Lëtzebuergesch), a Germanic language derived from the Rhineland. Most education is in **French** and **German**. French is the official language of the government and judiciary, but many Luxembourgers speak German with equal ease. **English** is widely understood and spoken by the younger generation, many of whom also speak Italian and Portuguese, a reflection of several decades of southern European immigration to the industrial districts of the south in particular. Nonetheless, there is a palpable sense of national identity, with one indication being the Duchy's motto, which can be seen engraved or painted on buildings around the country: *Mir Wöelle Bleiwe Wat Mir Sin* ("We want to remain what we are"). Attempts by visitors to speak Lëtzebuergesch are usually well received – though sometimes locals are too surprised to seem exactly pleased.

Moien	Good morning/hello
Äddi or *a'voir*	Goodbye
Merci (*villmols*)	Thank you (very much)
Pardon	Sorry
Entschëllegt	Excuse me
Wann-ech-glift (pronounced as one word)	Please
Ech verstin lech nët	I don't understand you
Ech versti kee Lëtzebuergesch	I don't understand any Luxembourgish

Belgium, but declined to do the same for Luxembourg, which remained in the clutches of William. Even worse, the Great Powers were irritated by William's inability to keep his kingdom in good nick, so they punished him by giving a chunk of Luxembourg's Ardennes to Belgium – now that country's *province* of Luxembourg. By these means, however, Luxembourg's survival was assured: neither France nor Germany could bear to let the Duchy pass to its rival and London made sure the Duchy was declared neutral. The city was demilitarized in 1867, when most of its fortifications were torn down, and the Duchy remained the property of the Dutch monarchy until 1890 when the ducal crown passed to another (separate) branch of the Orange-Nassaus.

In the **twentieth century**, the Germans overran Luxembourg in 1914 and again in 1940, when the royal family and government fled to Britain and the USA. The second occupation was predictably traumatic. At first, the Germans were comparatively benign, but later they banned the Luxembourgish language, dispatched conscripts to the Russian front and took savage reprisals against any acts of resistance. **Liberation** by US forces led by General Patton came in September 1944, but in December of that year, the Germans launched an offensive through the Ardennes between Malmédy in Belgium and Luxembourg's Echternach. The ensuing **Battle of the Bulge** (see p.307) engulfed northern Luxembourg: hundreds of civilians were killed and a great swathe of the country was devastated – events recalled today by several museums and many roadside monuments. In the **postwar period**, Luxembourg's shrewd policy of industrial diversification has made it one of the most prosperous parts of Europe. It has also discarded its prior habit of neutrality, joining NATO and becoming a founder member of the EU, and remains a **constitutional monarchy**, ruled by Grand Duke Henri (b.1955), who succeeded his long-serving father, Jean, in 2000. Luxembourg **politics** have a relaxed feel, with a number of green and special-interest parties vying with the more established centre-left and conservative parties – and the telephone directory lists direct lines for all ministers.

Luxembourg City

LUXEMBOURG CITY is one of the most spectacularly sited capitals in Europe. The valleys of the rivers Alzette and Pétrusse, which meet here, cut a green swath through the city, their deep canyons once key to the city's defences, but now providing a beautiful, leafy setting. These gorges have curtailed expansion and parcel the city up into clearly defined sections. There are four main districts (*quartiers*), beginning with the pint-sized **Old Town** (**La Vieille Ville**), the location of almost all the sights and most of the best restaurants, high up on a tiny plateau on the northern side of the Pétrusse valley. Today's Old Town dates from the late seventeenth century, by which time it had been rebuilt after a huge gunpowder explosion in 1554, though wholesale modifications were made a couple of hundred years later. Furthermore, over half of its encircling **bastions and ramparts** were knocked down when the city was demilitarized in 1867 – boulevards Royal and Roosevelt are built on their foundations – though the more easterly fortifications have survived pretty much intact. These give a clear sense of the city's once formidable defensive capabilities, and were sufficient to persuade UNESCO to designate the city a World Heritage Site in 1994.

Below the Old Town and its ramparts are the **river valleys**, a curious – and curiously engaging – mix of old stone houses, vegetable plots, medieval fortifications and parkland. They are well worth a leisurely exploration – allow an hour or two – unlike the mundane, early twentieth-century **modern quarter**, which trails south from the Pétrusse valley to the train station and beyond, and is home to many of the city's hotels alongside some of its more unsavoury bars and clubs. The fourth part of the city, the **Kirchberg plateau**, lies to the northeast of the Old Town, on the far side of the Alzette valley and reached by the imposing modern span of the Pont Grand-Duchesse Charlotte, usually known as the "Red Bridge" for reasons that will be immediately apparent. Kirchberg accommodates the **Centre Européen**, which is home to several EU institutions, including the European Investment Bank and the Court of Justice, while the new Musée d'Art Moderne Grand-Duc Jean (Mudam) and Philharmonie have made the area slightly more alluring to visitors.

Arrival

Findel, Luxembourg's **airport**, is situated 6km east of the city on the road to Grevenmacher. There are a number of ways of getting into town from here; the best is to take **bus** #16 (Mon–Sat every 15–20min, Sun every 30min) to the **bus station** in the Old Town on place E. Hamilius, or to the train station – a half-hour journey that costs a flat-rate €1.50, plus a small extra charge for any large items of luggage. Travelling by **taxi**, expect to pay €20–25 to get into the city centre.

The **train station** is in the modern quarter, a ten- to fifteen-minute walk from the Old Town. It has a left-luggage office and coin-operated luggage lockers and many of the city's cheaper hotels are located nearby. Most **long-distance buses** stop beside the train station. Almost all of the city's buses are routed via the train station, and the vast majority go on to (or come from) the bus station.

Information

The **Luxembourg National Tourist Office** is inside the train station concourse (July & Aug Mon–Sat 9am–6pm, Sun 9.30am–12.30pm & 1–5.30pm; rest of year daily 9.30am–12.30pm & 1–5.30pm; ⓣ42 82 82 20, ⓦwww.visitluxembourg.lu). It supplies free city maps, all manner of glossy leaflets and

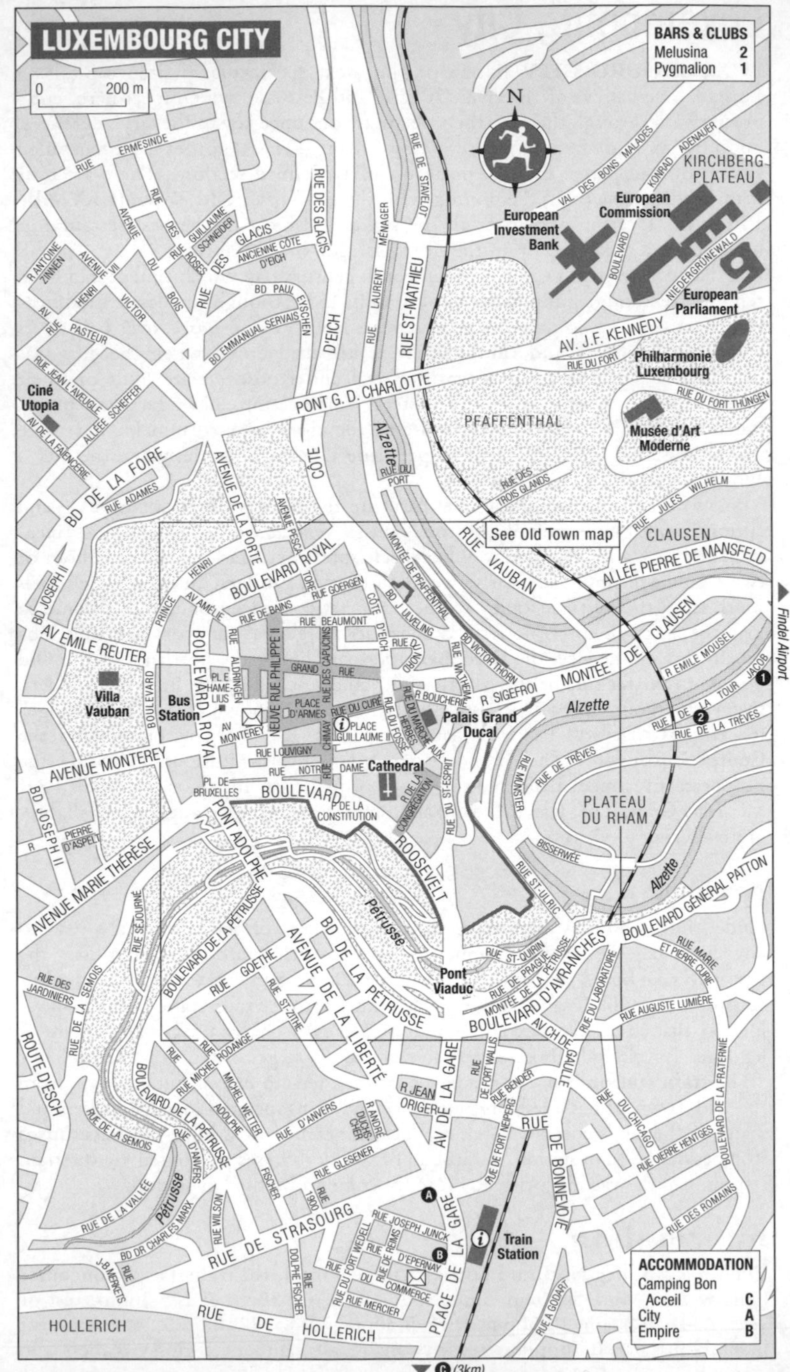

LUXEMBOURG CITY
0 200 m
BARS & CLUBS
Melusina 2
Pygmalion 1
N
KIRCHBERG PLATEAU
European Commission
European Investment Bank
European Parliament
Philharmonie Luxembourg
Musée d'Art Moderne
PFAFFENTHAL
CLAUSEN
PLATEAU DU RHAM
Alzette
Pétrusse
See Old Town map
Findel Airport
Ciné Utopia
Villa Vauban
Bus Station
Palais Grand Ducal
Cathedral
Pont Viaduc
Train Station
HOLLERICH
(3km)
AV. J.F. KENNEDY
PONT G. D. CHARLOTTE
BD DE LA FOIRE
BOULEVARD ROYAL
AVENUE DE LA PORTE
CÔTE D'EICH
RUE ST-MATHIEU
RUE VAUBAN
ALLÉE PIERRE DE MANSFELD
MONTÉE DE CLAUSEN
RUE DE TRÈVES
AV EMILE REUTER
AVENUE MONTEREY
AVENUE MARIE THÉRÈSE
BOULEVARD ROOSEVELT
PONT ADOLPHE
BOULEVARD DE LA PÉTRUSSE
AVENUE DE LA LIBERTÉ
BD DE LA PÉTRUSSE
BOULEVARD D'AVRANCHES
BOULEVARD GÉNÉRAL PATTON
AV DE LA GARE
RUE DE BONNEVOIE
RUE DE STRASOURG
RUE DE HOLLERICH
PLACE DE LA GARE
ROUTE D'ESCH
PLACE D'ARMES
PLACE GUILLAUME II
GRAND RUE
NEUVE RUE PHILIPPE II
RUE NOTRE DAME
PL. DE BRUXELLES
P DE LA CONSTITUTION
ACCOMMODATION
Camping Bon Acceil C
City A
Empire B

details of guided tours, and can advise on – and book – accommodation right across the Grand Duchy. There's also a busy **Luxembourg City Tourist Office**, in the middle of the Old Town on place Guillaume II (April–Sept Mon–Sat 9am–7pm, Sun 10am–6pm; Oct–March Mon–Sat 9am–6pm, Sun 10am–6pm; ⓣ22 28 09, ⓦwww.lcto.lu), which offers a similar service, though – as the name suggests – deals only with the city. There are also **tourist kiosks** set up on the streets of the Old Town from June to September (daily 10am–6pm) and out-of-hours **interactive computer terminals** at the airport, train station and on place Guillaume II.

City transport and bike rental

Luxembourg City has an excellent public-transport system, with **buses** from every part of the city and its surroundings converging on the **bus station** on place E. Hamilius in the Old Town, about ten minutes by foot from the train station. Usefully, most services are also routed via the train station. (Though the Old Town itself, where you're likely to spend most of your time, is very small and is most readily explored on foot.) **Tickets** cost a flat-rate €1.50 and are valid for two hours; a block of ten tickets costs €12 and you can also buy day-tickets for €4, or weekend tickets for €6. Public transport is free with the Luxembourg Card (see p.325). Before collapsing into a **taxi**, bear in mind that they are expensive in Luxembourg – during the day there's a pick-up charge of €2.50, plus over €1 per kilometre, with a ten percent surcharge at night and a whopping 25 percent supplement on Sunday.

Cycling is a good way to get around the city; there's a well-marked **cycle trail** and you can take advantage of it with the Veloh system (ⓣ800 61 10 00; ⓦwww.veloh.lu), whereby you pick up a bike at one location and drop it off at another. You pay a weekly fee of €1, the first half an hour is free and then it costs €1 per hour (up to a maximum of €5 per day). Alternatively you can just **rent a bike** from MTB Bikes, rue Bisserwe 8, Grund (April–Sept Mon–Fri 8am–noon & 1–8pm, Sat & Sun 10am–noon & 1–8pm; Oct–March Mon–Fri 7am–3pm; ⓣ47 96 23 83), which charges €5 an hour, €12.50 for a half-day, €20 a day, and €75 for a week, with twenty percent discounts available for groups of four or more and under-26s. They'll provide you with details of the cycle route (also available from the tourist office) and offer a repair service as well.

Guided tours

To orient yourself, you may want to take a **guided tour**. City Sightseeing Luxembourg run "hop-on-hop-off" **buses** (daily: April–Oct 9.40am–5.20pm every 20min; Nov–March 10.30am–4pm every 30min; ⓦwww.sightseeing.lu), charging €14 per person (€35 per family) to whisk you around the Old Town and out to the station and Kirchberg. Tickets are valid for 24 hours and can be purchased at the place de la Constitution, where tours start, at the city tourist office or on the bus itself. The same company runs a **miniature train** – the **Pétrusse Express** – which travels along the floor of the Pétrusse valley from Pont Adolphe to Grund and up to the plateau du Rham immediately to the east. This hour-long tour gives a good idea of the full extent of the city's fortifications and takes in some pleasant parkland too. The train leaves at regular intervals from place de la Constitution (April–Oct daily 10am–6pm; ⓦwww.sightseeing.lu); tickets cost €8.50 per person (families €27), or you can buy a combined ticket with the main tours for €19.

The tourist office also organizes a series of **guided walks**, starting from place Guillaume II, including a "City Promenade" tour of the Old Town (Easter–Oct daily at 2pm in English; Nov–Easter Mon, Wed, Sat & Sun at 1pm; €8; 2hr) and the excellent "Wenzel Walk" (Easter–Oct Sat 3pm; €9; 2hr), which takes you to the Casemates du Bock and right around the fortifications on the east side of the Old Town. It's advisable to make reservations in person at the city tourist office.

Accommodation

Many of the city's cheaper **hotels** are clustered near the train station, which is convenient but the least interesting part of town – and the side streets opposite the station are, at least by Luxembourg standards, a little seedy. It's better to try and find somewhere in the Old Town, where there are fewer alternatives but the prices aren't that much higher. Bear in mind also that rates are quite a lot cheaper nearly everywhere at weekends. The main budget alternative is the HI-affiliated **hostel**.

Unless otherwise stated, the places listed below are marked on the Old Town map, p.333.

Hotels

City Hotel place de la Gare 16 ⓣ29 11 22, ⓦwww.cityhotel.lu. Occupying an attractive Art Deco building, this hotel is handily situated right opposite the train station and has crisply decorated modern rooms that are a tad lacking in character but come down in price hugely on weekends. Parking (€12 for 24hr) is available. See map, p.330. ❻

Empire place de la Gare 34 ⓣ48 52 52, ⓦwww.empire.lu. This is a relatively modest choice, but its 35 brightly if simply furnished rooms are decent enough, have en-suite facilities and couldn't be closer to the station – and can be super-cheap at weekends. They also rent out self-catering apartments in separate buildings around town. See map, p.330. ❸

Français place d'Armes 14 ⓣ47 45 34, ⓦwww.hotelfrancais.lu. This attractive three-star has 24 smart and spotless rooms furnished in a crisp modern style. You couldn't be more central, and not surprisingly the rooms at the back are a lot quieter. Free wi-fi throughout, too. ❺

Grand Hôtel Cravat blvd Roosevelt 29 ⓣ22 19 75, ⓦwww.hotelcravat.lu. Charming, medium-sized four-star in the heart of the Old Town. The exterior is a little sombre, but the inside has oodles of atmosphere, and instead of a designer makeover the hotel has accumulated its furnishings and fittings over the years, from the antique lift, fresco and chandelier to the signed sepia photographs of distant celebrities and heroes. The well-proportioned rooms are in similar style, and those at the front have appealing views over place de la Constitution. ❾

Rix blvd Royal 20 ⓣ47 16 66, ⓦwww.hotelrix.lu. This smart, four-star hotel is conveniently situated just a couple of minutes' walk west of place d'Armes, just outside the Old Town on a road that's home to many of the city's offshore banking businesses. It has a pleasingly old-fashioned air, with cosy public rooms, a bar and 21 rooms that are, for the most part, tastefully decorated and have balconies. ❻

Simoncini rue Notre Dame 6 ⓣ22 28 44, ⓦwww.hotelsimoncini.lu. This sleek, contemporary choice is the city's first boutique hotel and has a great location bang in the centre of the Old Town, just off place Guillaume II. Rooms are cool, stylish and not over-priced, the service is good and there's free wi-fi throughout – though no parking or restaurant. Good weekend deals. ❺

Hostel and camping

L'Auberge de Jeunesse rue du Fort Olisy 2 ⓣ22 68 89 20, ⓦwww.youthhostels.lu. Modern, well-equipped, HI-affiliated hostel located down below the Bock fortifications in the Alzette valley. It has 240 beds in all: 30 four-bed rooms, all with shower and toilet, and 20 six-bed rooms, some with shower and toilet; plus a laundry, a café, internet access and 24hr reception. Dorm beds €19.80 per person, including breakfast. It's reachable from the airport on bus #9 and from the train station on bus #9, but ask the driver to put you off as otherwise you risk whistling by on the main road, about 300m from the hostel; on foot it takes about 30min to cover the 3km from the train station. ❶

Camping Bon Accueil rue du Camping 2 ⓣ36 70 69, ⓔmasp@pt.lu. This is the closest campsite to the centre, just 5km south of the city with a nice location on the banks of the River Alzette, off route d'Echternach in the village of Alzingen. See map, p.330. Open April to mid-Oct.

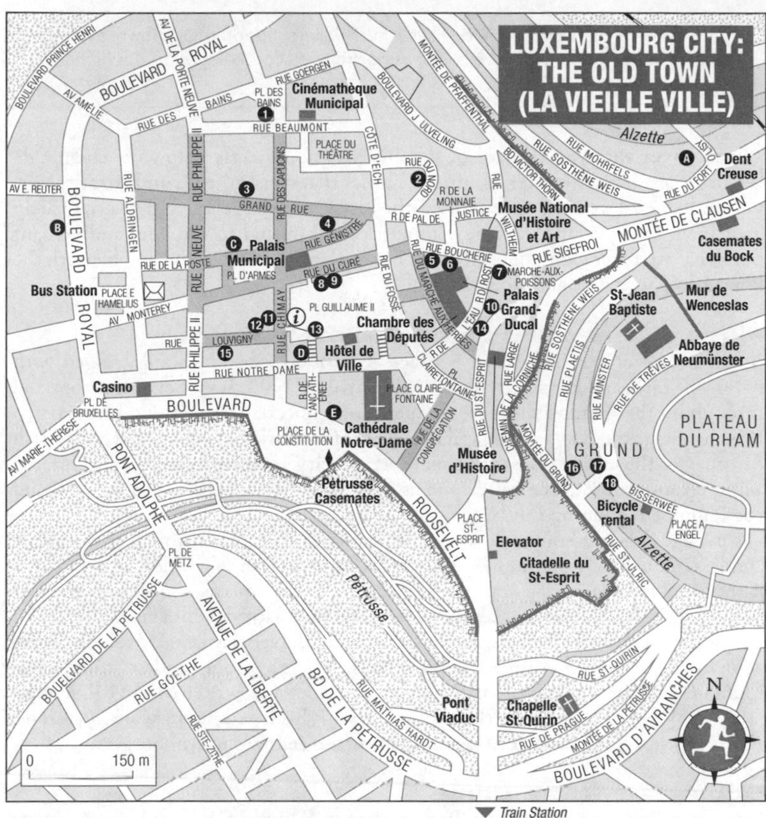

ACCOMMODATION		RESTAURANTS & CAFES				BARS & CLUBS	
L'Auberge de Jeunesse	A	Apoteca	6	Maison des Brasseurs	3	Café des Artistes	16
Français	C	Basta Cosi	12	Mosconi	17	Chiggeri	2
Grand Hôtel Cravat	E	Le Bouquet Garni	10	Oberweis	4	Scott's	18
Rix	B	Brasserie Guillaume	9	A la Soupe	13	The Tube	7
Simoncini	D	El Compañero	14	Speltz	11	Urban	5
		Français	C	Wengé	15	Vis à Vis	1
		Kaempf-Kohler	8				

The City

No more than a few hundred metres across, Luxembourg's **Old Town** (La Vieille Ville) is not actually very old; though the mazy street plan does date back to medieval times, its tight grid of streets are flanked by mostly eighteenth- and nineteenth-century buildings. It boasts a very good museum, the **Musée National d'Histoire et d'Art**, but the main pull is the old stone, rock and brick **fortifications** that anchor the east side of the centre. The earliest surviving portions flank the Montée de Clausen, linking the Old Town with Clausen in the valley below, but these medieval bits and pieces are really rather insignificant when compared with the mighty bastions and ramparts that are seen to best advantage along the scenic **chemin de la Corniche** walkway. These later works reflect the combined endeavours of generations of military engineers from the seventeenth to the nineteenth centuries, as does the honeycomb of subterranean artillery **casemates**, portions of which can be entered on both the Montée de Clausen and the place de la Constitution.

You can reach the Pétrusse and Alzette river valleys from the Old Town by road, steps or **elevator**: the main elevator runs from place St-Esprit to Grund (daily 6.30am–3.30am).

In the **river valley** to the east of the Old Town – directly below the chemin de la Corniche – lies the cluster of antique houses that constitute **Grund**, an attractive village-like enclave that once housed the city's working class, but is now partly gentrified. From Grund, it's a few minutes' walk round to the long and verdant **park** that stretches along the valley to the south of the Old Town and beneath the Pont Adolphe and Pont Viaduc bridges.

Place d'Armes and place Guillaume II

At the centre of the Old Town is **place d'Armes**, a shady oblong fringed with pavement cafés and the sturdy Palais Municipal of 1907. It's a delightful spot and throughout the summer there are frequent free concerts – everything from jazz to brass bands – as well as a small (and expensive) flea market every second and fourth Saturday of the month. Near the square are the city's principal shops, concentrated along **Grand-rue** and rue des Capucins to the north, rue du Fossé to the east, and rue Philippe II running south.

A passage from the southeast corner of place d'Armes leads through to the larger and less immediately picturesque **place Guillaume II**, in the middle of which is a jaunty-looking equestrian statue of William II. The square, the site of Luxembourg's main fresh-food market on Wednesday and Saturday mornings, is flanked by pleasant old town houses as well as the solid Neoclassical **Hôtel de Ville**, adorned by a pair of gormless copper lions. There's also a modest stone water fountain bearing a cameo of the Luxembourg poet and writer **Michel Rodange** (1827–76), who created something of a stir with his best-known work, *Rénert the Fox*, a satirical exploration of the character of his fellow Luxembourgers.

Cathédrale Notre-Dame

Steps lead down from place Guillaume II to rue Notre-Dame, where an ornate Baroque portico leads into the **Cathédrale Notre-Dame** (daily 7am–8pm), whose slender black spires dominate the city's puckered skyline. It is, however, a real mess of a building: the transepts and truncated choir, dating to the 1930s, are in a clumping Art Deco style and have been glued onto the (much more appealing) seventeenth-century nave. Items of interest are few and far between, but there is a **plaque** in the nave honouring those priests killed in World War II, and the Baroque **gallery** at the back of the nave is a likeable affair – graced by alabaster angels and garlands of flowers, it was carved by a certain Daniel Muller in 1622. In the apse is the country's most venerated **icon**, *The Comforter of the Afflicted*, a seventeenth-century, lime-wood effigy of the Madonna and Child which is frequently dressed up in all manner of lavish gear with crowns and sceptres, lace frills and gold brocade.

A door on the west side of the chancel leads through to the side entrance of the cathedral where stairs lead down to the **crypt**, and a barred chapel containing a number of ducal tombs. Here also is the Baroque **tomb** of John the Blind – Jean l'Aveugle – which depicts the Entombment of Christ in a mass of mawkish detail. John was one of the most successful of Luxembourg's medieval rulers, until he came a cropper at the Battle of Crécy in 1346.

Pétrusse Casemates and the Casino

Across from the side entrance to the cathedral, **place de la Constitution** sits on top of one of the old bastions, whose subterranean depths – the **Casemates de la**

Pétrusse (Easter, Whitsun & July–Aug guided tours daily 11am–4pm; €3) – are entered via a stone stairway. The Spaniards dug these artillery chambers in the 1640s and they make for a dark and dank visit. Place de la Constitution also acts as the starting point for the Pétrusse Express (see p.331).

A short walk away to the west, at rue Notre Dame 41, is the **Casino** – not a "Casino" in the sense of gaming, but an old bourgeois salon that has been turned into a gallery for **contemporary art** (Mon, Wed & Fri 11am–7pm, Thurs 11am–8pm, Sat & Sun 11am–6pm; €4, free Thurs 6–8pm; Ⓦwww.casino-luxembourg.lu), featuring exhibitions that are often challenging or downright obtuse.

The Palais Grand-Ducal and the Chambre des Députés

From place de la Constitution, pleasant **rue Chimay**, lined by shops and cafés, leads back towards place Guillaume II. Just to the east of the square, on rue du Marché aux Herbes, stands the **Palais Grand-Ducal** (guided tours mid-July to Aug daily except Wed; 4pm in English; €6; 45min), originally built as the town hall, but adopted by the Luxembourg royals as their winter residence in the nineteenth century. Remodelled on several occasions, the exterior, with its dinky dormer windows and spiky little spires, reveals a Moorish influence – though the end result looks more Ruritanian than anything else. The interior is, as you might expect, lavish in the extreme, with dazzling chandeliers, Brussels tapestries, frescoes and acres of richly carved wood panelling. Tours are very popular, so book at least a day in advance at the tourist office. To the right of the palace, an extension of 1859 houses the Luxembourg Parliament, the **Chambre des Députés**, in plainer but similarly opulent surroundings.

Musée d'Histoire de la Ville de Luxembourg

South of the Chambre des Députés, the **Musée d'Histoire de la Ville de Luxembourg**, rue du St-Esprit 14 (Tues–Sun 10am–6pm, Thurs till 8pm; €5; Ⓦwww.musee-hist.lu), is the last word on the development of Luxembourg and the city today. Converted from four historic houses (you can also access it from the chemin de la Corniche behind), it's an excellent museum with lots of English information and hi-tech interactive displays. As well as a series of wooden models of the city through the ages, and displays on the city's royal dynasty and government, industry and contemporary life for the Luxembourgeois, highlights include a 360-degree panorama painted by Antoine Fontaine showing city life in 1655 – it's a perfect example of a trompe-l'oeil, making you feel slightly giddy when you stand in the middle. In addition, a large part of the museum is dedicated to temporary exhibitions, mostly concerned with the city and its inhabitants.

Musée National d'Histoire et d'Art

The large and lavish **Musée National d'Histoire et d'Art**, situated on the pretty square of Marché aux Poissons (Tues–Sun 10am–5pm, Thurs until 8pm; €5; Ⓦwww.mnha.lu), occupies a brand-new building that provides a sleek frontage to the cluster of patrician mansions into which the museum was originally shoehorned. It has a wide-ranging permanent collection, beginning in the basement with a prehistoric section and then working its way up chronologically to the Middle Ages and Renaissance – above which are two floors devoted to fine art, mostly from Luxembourg and Belgium and stretching from medieval times to the early twentieth century; there's also a floor devoted to temporary exhibitions. The extensive **Gallo-Roman** section in the basement is a high point: southern Luxembourg has proved particularly rich in Roman artefacts with archeologists unearthing literally truckloads of bronzes and terracottas, glassware, funerary objects, busts and mosaics. In particular, look out for a fine – albeit weathered – marble bust of Septimius Severus and a magnificent mosaic from Vichten. Upstairs there are displays on the fortress and the **Middle Ages**, while the top-floor **fine art** galleries include an enjoyable sample of fifteenth- and sixteenth-century paintings, most memorably an exquisite *Pietà* by Adriaen Isenbrandt and a madly romantic *Bacchus, Venus and Love* by Rosso Fiorentino. Later works include the lively *Paysage de Cannes au Crépuscule* by Pablo Picasso, *La Montagna Sainte* by Paul Cézanne, and two paintings by Turner, who spent a lot of time in Luxembourg. You might also look out for the forceful Expressionism of Luxembourg's own Joseph Kutter (1894–1941).

The Bock

In 963 a powerful local lord, Count Siegfried of Lorraine, decided to build a castle on the **Rocher du Bock**, a sandstone outcrop rising high above the Alzette just to the east of today's Marché aux Poissons. The city of Luxembourg originated with this stronghold, but precious little survives of Siegfried's construction – it was incorporated into the much more impressive fortifications that were built round the city from the seventeenth century onwards. The only significant piece of masonry to survive is the so-called **Dent Creuse** (Hollow Tooth) stone tower on the north side of the rue Sigefroi/Montée de Clausen. This same road, linking the Old Town with the suburb of Clausen, makes it doubly difficult to appreciate the layout of the original castle, which was – in medieval times – linked to the Marché aux Poissons by a drawbridge. That said, the views looking out over the spires, outer fortifications and aqueducts of the Alzette valley are superb.

In 1745, the Spaniards began digging beneath the site of Siegfried's castle. Eventually, they honeycombed the Bock with around 20km of tunnels and galleries, within which they placed bakeries, kitchens, stables and all the other amenities necessary to support a garrison. Today a tiny portion of the tunnels can be visited on a guided tour of the **Casemates du Bock** (March–Oct daily 10am–5pm; €3). It's a rather damp and draughty way to spend half an hour, and there's nothing much to see beyond a few rusty old cannons, but it's good fun all the same; an audiovisual presentation gives the historical lowdown.

The chemin de la Corniche

From just above the Casemates du Bock on rue Sigefroi, you can follow the pedestrianized **chemin de la Corniche** along the ramparts that marked the eastern perimeter of the main fortress. The views are absolutely spectacular and there's no better way to get a sense of the strength of the city's fortifications, which several major European powers struggled to improve, no one more than the French who, after 1684, made Luxembourg into one of the continent's most strongly defended cities – the so-called "Gibraltar of the north". After a few minutes you emerge at place St-Esprit and more fortifications in the form of the **Citadelle du St-Esprit**, a colossal, stone-faced bastion built in 1685. On the far side you'll find the main **elevator** down to Grund and, beyond in a grassy little **park** that's also above the bastion, there are views over the Pétrusse valley and the Pont Viaduc, which leads south toward the train station.

The Alzette river valley

Below and to the east of the Old Town, the **Alzette river valley** is dotted with ancient, pastel-painted houses and the battered remains of the outer fortifications – with the walls of the main fortress rising steeply above. The best approach, down **Montée de Clausen**, brings you to the somewhat dishevelled district of **Clausen**. From here, rue de la Tour Jacob tracks along the riverside to reach the medieval curtain wall – the **Mur de Wenceslas** – which both spans the Alzette and served as a fortified footbridge leading back towards the Old Town.

Dead ahead, through the gate, is **Grund**, once a thriving working-class quarter but now an uneven mixture of fine old houses and dilapidation that strings along the river for a few hundred metres. Grund is wonderfully peaceful by day, dotted with cafés and art galleries, and centring on a chunky little **bridge** that spans the Alzette close by the elevator down from place St-Esprit and Montée du Grund. A left turn leads along **rue St-Ulric**, where the markers at no. 14 show how high the river has risen in flood years – the worst inundation was in 1756 – and beneath the massive walls of the Citadelle du St-Esprit before meeting rue St-Quirin at the east end of the Pétrusse valley. In the opposite direction, rue Münster follows the river to the church of **St-Jean Baptiste** (daily 10am–noon & 2–6pm), an imposing structure with a massive spire and a flashy Baroque portal. The interior boasts a whopping – and inordinately gaudy – high altar, whilst the side chapel holds a much-venerated black Madonna. Next to the church, the seventeenth-century **Abbaye de Neumünster** was used as a prison by the Nazis during World War II, but has since been entirely revamped and now houses the **Centre Culturel de Rencontre** (Mon–Fri 9am–7pm, Sat & Sun 10am–6pm; ⓣ26 20 52 1, ⓦwww.ccrn.lu) a cultural meeting centre with temporary exhibitions and a nice brasserie which features live jazz on Friday and Sunday.

Pétrusse river valley

The pathway of **Rue St-Quirin** threads its way west through the wooded parkland of the **Pétrusse river valley**. There's one specific sight here, the mostly fourteenth-century **Chapelle St-Quirin**, a tiny chapel chiselled out of – and projecting into – the rock-face and equipped with a dinky little spire. Further along the valley, paths clamber up to both ends of the **Pont Adolphe**, from where it's the briefest of walks back into the Old Town.

Villa Vauban

Just outside the Old Town, ten minutes' walk from place d'Armes at ave Emile Reuter 18 in the Parc Municipal, the nineteenth-century **Villa Vauban** (daily 10am–6pm, Fri until 9pm; €5; ⓦwww.villavauban.lu) is an elegant building that takes its name from the architect of the Luxembourg fortress, part of which served as the foundation of the building and can be seen in the basement. It's looking its best after a extensive restoration and makes a fitting backdrop for a small collection of eighteenth- and nineteenth-century paintings; it's also used to stage rotating exhibitions of like-minded visiting collections.

Kirchberg

For decades, the **Kirchberg** district, on a plateau a couple of kilometres to the northeast of the Old Town, was nothing more than an administrative centre for a battery of European institutions falling on either side of avenue John F. Kennedy. Today, however, the area is the site of the largest **urban development programme** in the country, with new office blocks designed by eminent architects appearing at breakneck speed, the overall aim being to consolidate and confirm the Duchy's leading role in the financial world. Capitalist eyecatchers include the **HypoVereinsbank Luxembourg**, designed by the American architect Richard Meier, who uses large white facades as his trademark, and the four-storey Cubist building housing the **Deutsche Bank**, designed by Gottfried Böhm. More than a dozen **sculptures** in public spaces enliven the area in between; look out for the cheerful *Grand Fleur Qui Marche* (Giant Walking Flower), a model based on a ceramic by Fernand Léger, and *Sarrequemines* by Frank Stella, inspired by floating smoke rings.

It's easy enough to get to Kirchberg from the Old Town by local **bus**, but – given that the district is about 3km long and 1.5km wide – it's perhaps best to drive, especially if you're set on a general exploration. The city tourist office issues a useful brochure detailing two Kirchberg **walks**.

Both of Kirchberg's prime attractions are on the south side of avenue John F. Kennedy, back towards the Old Town. At the northern tip of the place de l'Europe is the impressive **Philharmonie Luxembourg** (ⓣ26 32 26 32, ⓦwww.philharmonie.lu), designed by Christian de Portzamparc and strongly resembling an ancient Greek temple, with 823 shining columns rising 20m from the ground. There are guided tours of the building every Saturday at 10.30am (though not in English), and the Philharmonie offers regular classical concerts.

A short stroll southwest from here, a huge glass structure designed by the architect I.M. Pei (more famous for the Louvre pyramid) is the venue for spanking new **Musée d'Art Moderne Grand-Duc Jean** (Wed–Fri 11am–8pm, Sat–Mon 11am–6pm; €5; ⓦwww.mudam.lu), which has a far-reaching and wide-ranging collection of modern and contemporary art, exhibited in an ambitious programme of rotating temporary exhibitions on the first floor alongside regular visiting exhibitions. Displays from the museum's own collection mostly centre on envelope-pushing work by contemporary artists – think Gilbert and George, Cindy Sherman, Bruce Nauman alongside lots of more obscure names, including a fair sprinkling of Luxembourgisch folk.

Eating and drinking

Luxembourg City's Old Town is crowded with **cafés** and **restaurants**, from inexpensive places where a filling *plat du jour* can cost as little as €10, through to lavish establishments with main courses costing twice as much and more. French cuisine is popular, and traditional Luxembourgish dishes are found on many menus too, mostly meaty affairs such as neck of pork with broad beans (*judd mat gaardebounen*), black sausage (*blutwurst*) and chicken in Riesling (*hahnchen im Riesling*), not to mention freshwater fish from the River Moselle. Keep an eye out also for *gromperenkichelchen* – potato cakes, usually served with apple sauce – and in winter, stalls and cafés selling *glühwein*, hot wine mulled with cloves. One of the great Luxembourg traditions is **coffee and cakes** in a salon or one of the city's numerous patisseries, and here, as in Belgium, pavement cafés are thronged in the summertime, place d'Armes being the centre of the outdoor scene. Most visitors to the city are content to drink where they eat, but there is a lively **bar** and **club** scene spread around the various parts of town. Opening hours are fairly elastic, but bars usually stay open till around 1am, clubs till 3am. While you're out on the tiles, try one of the local **Luxembourg beers** – Mousel, Diekirch or Bofferding.

Unless otherwise stated, the places listed below are marked on the Old Town map, p.333.

Restaurants and cafés

Apoteca rue de la Boucherie 12 ⓣ26 73 77. Perhaps the most fashionable restaurant in town, solidly booked on the weekend, with a designer restaurant divided over two floors and a nightclub-like bar downstairs. The menu is wide-ranging and imaginative with good-value lunch menus and mains for around €16, €25 in the evening. If you ask for the wine list, you'll receive the key to the cellar where you can choose from wines ranging between €15 and €2000. Mon–Fri noon–2pm & 7.30–10.30pm, Sat & Sun 7.30–10.30pm. Bar Tues–Sat 5pm–1am, Fri & Sat till 6am.

Basta Cosi rue Louvigny 10 ⓣ26 26 85 85. Stylish restaurant with plasma screens and a huge bar with lots of dark wood. The menu is traditional with Italian old-timers like lasagne, saltimbocca and bruschetta dominating the list. Mains from €14. Open daily, kitchen till 10.30pm.

Le Bouquet Garni rue de l'Eau 32 ⓣ26 20 06 20. Polished restaurant with beamed ceilings and starched tablecloths, worthy of its Michelin star.

The French cuisine features local ingredients and is supplemented by an excellent wine cellar. Main courses from around €24. Closed Sat lunch & Sun.
Brasserie Guillaume place Guillaume II 14 ⓣ26 20 20 20. Bright, modern brasserie specializing in Luxembourgish dishes, and also boasting a fine line in mussels and carpaccio. A popular, fashionable spot and very affordable too, with *plats du jour* for €12.50 at lunchtime; otherwise it's €20 or so for a main course. Open daily, kitchen till midnight.
El Compañero rue de l'Eau 26. Fashionable place for Spanish tapas and wicked cocktails at a reasonable price; popular with the locals too. The bar, with funky bright pink walls, turns into a disco late at night.
Français place d'Armes 14. The pavement café of the *Hôtel Français* offers tasty salads and an extensive menu including several Luxembourgish standbys from €12.
Kaempf-Kohler rue du Curé 18 ⓣ26 86 86 1. This sumptuous deli is a nice place to shop, and also serves food (including delicious cheese platters accompanied by matching wines); all manner of takeaway sandwiches and other goodies are also available. Mon–Fri 8am–6.30pm, Sat 8am–6.30pm.
Maison des Brasseurs Grand-rue 48 ⓣ47 13 71. Modern Grand-rue, the city's main shopping strip, is also home to this long-established restaurant, which serves up delicious Luxembourgish dishes. *Plats du jour* from around €20. Mon–Sat 11am–10pm.
Mosconi rue Münster 13 ⓣ54 69 94. This smart Italian down by the river in Grund has two Michelin stars, and is a very sleek place with a waterside terrace. It's obviously not a budget option, but the set lunch menus can be a good deal, and it's a lovely place for a special night out. Closed Sun, Mon & Sat lunchtimes.
Oberweis Grand-rue 19 ⓣ40 31 40 1. There's a café-restaurant upstairs here, but the real deal is the cakes, chocolates and tarts – mouthwatering stuff and famous across the whole of the Duchy. Great sandwiches and wraps, too, and an outside terrace to enjoy it all from. Closed Sun.
A la Soupe rue Chimay 9 ⓣ26 20 20 47. Good for breakfast and lunch, with porridge in the morning and hearty bowls of soup with bread for €4.50 at lunchtime – all consumed from swish stools in a cool, modern environment. Mon–Sat 7am–8.45pm.
Speltz rue Chimay 8 ⓣ47 49 50. This busy brasserie has been going for two decades and serves excellent Luxembourgish food, from changing weekly menus. Great-value menus from €27, and *plats du jour* for €18. Mon–Sat 11.30am–4pm & 6–10pm.
Wengé rue Louvigny 15 ⓣ26 20 10 58. Delicious cakes, chocolates and quiches are on sale in the front (patisserie) part of *Wengé*, while the restaurant up the stairs offers a first-rate, French-style menu with mains starting at €15. Mon–Sat 8am–6.30pm, plus Wed & Fri eve.

Bars and clubs

Café des Artistes Montée du Grund 22. Charming café-bar close to the bridge in Grund. Piano accompaniment and *chanson* Wed–Sat – to a mixed and motley crew.
Chiggeri rue du Nord 15. Groovy, ground-floor bar in the Old Town, with a great atmosphere, funky decor and a mixed clientele. It also has a restaurant next door and an outside terrace, from where there are great views across the valley to Kirchberg.
Melusina rue de la Tour Jacob 145, Clausen ⓣ26 00 89 75 ⓦwww.melusina.lu. An expat favourite, with varied sounds Fri and Sat plus live jazz and folk music nights, as well as occasional theatrical performances. There's a restaurant (open daily) and outside terrace, too. See map, p.330.
Pygmalion rue de la Tour Jacob 19, Clausen. Busy Irish bar down in the depths of Clausen. Open till 1am weekdays and 3am weekends. See map, p.330.
Scott's Bisserwée. By the bridge in Grund, this pubby English bar is where expats congregate for draught Guinness and bitter. Daily 11am–1am.
The Tube rue Sigefroi 8, Old Town. Lively, youthful and earthy nightspot named after London's Underground – hence the Tube memorabilia. One of the city's more fashionable places; varied sounds from techno through to soul.
Urban rue Boucherie 6. This bar-restaurant is popular with expats and local business folk for its retro-chic interior and impressive cocktail list. Sun–Thurs 11am–1am, Fri & Sat 11am–2am.
Vis à Vis At the junction of rue des Capucins and rue Beaumont. Laidback, comfortable bar with old posters and a relaxed feel – good for a drink or a snack at any time of day. Closed Sun.

Listings

Airlines British Airways ⓣ34 20 80; Luxair ⓣ24 56 42 42.
Airport ⓣ24 64 0.
Bookshops Papeterie Ernster, rue du Fossé 21 (ⓣ22 50 77 270), has a reasonable range of English-language books and newspapers and is footsteps from place Guillaume II.
Car parks There are four underground car parks in the Old Town, though spaces can still be hard to find. One is off blvd Royale beside the bus station;

another beneath place du Théâtre; a third under place Guillaume; and a fourth is at the east end of blvd Roosevelt, near the Viaduc bridge. There's also an open-air car park just beyond the train station. All charge around €1.50 per hr during the day, with cheaper rates in the evening and on the weekend. There's some especially handy on-street parking on place de la Constitution, but spaces – and there aren't many – fill up fast. Ⓦwww.lcto.lu has regularly updated information on which car parks have spaces available.

Car rental Autolux ⓣ22 11 81; Avis ⓣ43 51 71; Europcar ⓣ40 42 28; Hertz ⓣ43 46 45.

Cinemas Cinemas show films in their original language, subtitled (rarely dubbed) as appropriate in French. A varied programme of art-house and classic films is screened in the Old Town at Cinémathèque Municipale, place du Théâtre 17 (ⓣ47 96 26 44). Mainstream films are on offer at, among a dozen other cinemas, the five-screen Ciné Utopia, north of the Old Town at ave de la Fiencerie 16 (ⓣ22 46 11, Ⓦwww.utopolis.lu) and at the ten-screen Utopolis, ave J.F. Kennedy 45, in Kirchberg (ⓣ42 95 11 1, Ⓦwww.utopolis.lu).

Embassies Belgium, rue des Girondins 4 ⓣ25 43 25 1; Ireland, route d'Arlon 28 ⓣ45 06 10 1; Netherlands, rue Ste-Zithe 6 ⓣ22 75 70; UK, blvd Joseph II ⓣ22 98 64; USA, blvd E. Servais 22 ⓣ46 01 23. For details of other embassies, see p.38.

Emergencies Fire and ambulance ⓣ112; police ⓣ113.

Festivals The Schueberfouer (Ⓦwww.fouer.lu), held over the last week in August and first two weeks of September, is the city's main knees-up, featuring one of the biggest mobile fairs in Europe. It started out as a medieval sheep market on the middle Sunday, in which shepherds bring their sheep to town, accompanied by a band, and work their way round the bars. The city also puts on an annual "Summer in the City" programme of free music concerts, fashion shows and parades, beginning in late June and ending in the middle of September; see Ⓦwww.summerinthecity.lu for more.

Left luggage There are coin-operated lockers and a luggage office at the train station.

Mail The main post office is by the bus station at rue Aldringen 25 (Mon–Fri 7am–7pm, Sat 7am–5pm).

Newspapers English-language newspapers are available from most newsagents from about 11am on the day of publication.

Pharmacies Central pharmacies include Goedert, place d'Armes 5. Duty rotas are displayed in pharmacy windows.

Police The main station is at rue Glesener 58–60 (ⓣ49 97 45 00).

Train enquiries The CFL office in the station is open daily 5am–9.30pm (ⓣ24 89 24 89, Ⓦwww.cfl.lu).

The Grand Duchy

There's much more to Luxembourg than its capital, and it's well worth spending some time discovering the rest of the **Grand Duchy** – although bear in mind that the areas close to the city are not perhaps the country's most appealing. Southwest of the capital is the most crowded part of the Grand Duchy; the red rock hereabouts produced the iron ore that transformed the country from a rural backwater into a modern, urban state in the early twentieth century. There's little on offer for the passing tourist, although brisk and modern **Esch-sur-Alzette**, Luxembourg's second largest city, does have its moments. East of Luxembourg City the landscape is flatter and duller, with little to detain you until you reach the gentle, sweeping scenery of the **River Moselle**, which, for 50km or so, forms the border with Germany. The river's west bank is lined with small towns and vineyards, whose grapes sustain Luxembourg's thriving **wine** industry. The towns themselves are rather mundane – the most agreeable targets are the pleasant town of **Remich** and the pretty village of **Ehnen** – but a number of wine producers run tours and tastings of their **wine cellars** (*caves*), making it a popular day-trip for Germans and Luxembourgers alike.

North of Luxembourg City, **Gutland** – literally "Good Land" – fills out much of the middle of the Duchy, rolling north to workaday **Mersch** and west to the Belgian border. To the northeast, cuddled up to a bend in the River Sûre on the German border, **Echternach** is one of Luxembourg's most beguiling towns, not least because of its splendid abbey; it also has the advantage of being at the heart of some wonderful scenery, comprising a parcel of land commonly called **La Petite Suisse Luxembourgeoise**, a beautiful area of steep wooded gorges gashing a rolling mountain plateau of open farmland and forest. The most enjoyable way to explore is on its excellent network of **hiking trails**, with Echternach as a base, perhaps targeting a couple of castles on the way, in the villages of **Larochette** and **Beaufort**. Northwest of Echternach, **Diekirch** is a busy little town, which – along with neighbouring **Ettelbruck** – has long been a major staging point on the highway north from Luxembourg City to Belgium's Liège. Both towns were badly mauled during the Battle of the Bulge (see p.307), but Diekirch – unlike its neighbour – has retained a modicum of charm and also possesses an interesting museum and a reasonable supply of hotels. It's a handy base for venturing out along the upper reaches of the **River Sûre**, through attractive scenery that accommodates both the impressive castle of **Bourscheid** and the picture-postcard hamlet of **Esch-sur-Sûre**.

Beyond Ettelbruck lies the narrowing neck of northern Luxembourg, where rolling forest sweeps over an undulating plateau. This is the **Luxembourg Ardennes** (D'Éisléck in Luxembourgish) – to all intents and purposes indistinguishable from much of its Belgian namesake (covered in Chapter 5), and at its most appealing around **Vianden**, whose castle and well-developed tourist industry are the major focus up here. The rest of the region is pleasant enough, especially the rearing, 20km country road (the CR324/CR326) connecting **Wiltz**, just off the N15 northwest of Esch-sur-Sûre, with **Clervaux**, a small town that is the last worthwhile stop before Belgium, whose border lies just a few kilometres to the north.

Esch-sur-Alzette

The district immediately to the southwest of Luxembourg City is a former iron-ore mining and steel-making region whose heavy industry and urban sprawls are, for the most part, best glimpsed from a train window on the way to somewhere else. Nowadays, much of the industry is gone, and the towns are being greened and cleaned, nowhere more so than **ESCH-SUR-ALZETTE**, whose population of around 27,000 includes a large number of Italians, whose forebears migrated here to work the foundries. Esch is at its most agreeable among the shops and cafés of its pedestrianized main street, **rue de l'Alzette**, and it also possesses one mildly enjoyable attraction, the **Musée Nationale de la Résistance**, at the west end of rue de l'Alzette in place de la Résistance (Wed–Sun 2–6pm; free), which tracks through the history of the Resistance in thorough detail. Esch is also home to the **Rockhal**, on the edge of town on ave du Rock'n'Roll 5 (Ⓣ24 55 51, Ⓦwww.rockhal.lu), a live music venue with two large halls and an impressive programme of international stars.

Esch is just 17km from Luxembourg City and its **train station** is on the south side of the town centre, about 300m from rue de l'Alzette along avenue de la Gare. The **tourist office** is at the east end of rue de l'Alzette on place de l'Hôtel de Ville (Mon–Fri 9am–5pm, summer also Sat 1am–5pm; Ⓣ54 16 37, Ⓦwww.esch-city.lu).

Remich and the Moselle valley

Around 25km east of Luxembourg City, **REMICH** is an amenable, modern place that slopes steeply up from the River Moselle. It's a major stop for the **cruise boats** that ply up and down the River Moselle from Easter to October, connecting Remich with Schengen to the south and Wormeldange, Grevenmacher and Wasserbillig to the north, and operated by **Entente Touristique de la Moselle**

Luxembourg's wineries

Whether or not the Romans introduced **wine** to the Luxembourg region is still the subject of much debate, but one thing is certain: the fertile banks of the River Moselle have been nourishing the vine for a very long time indeed. Rivaner and Elbling (one of the oldest wines in the world) used to dominate the area, but nowadays Riesling, Auxerrois, Pinot Gris and Pinot Blanc make a strong presence. Standards are generally very high, so it is perhaps surprising that Luxembourg wine is largely overshadowed by that of its neighbours, France and Germany. There are numerous small wineries in the area, and although many are not open to the public, we've picked out several that are.

Bernard Massard rue du Pont 8, Grevenmacher (April–Oct tours & tastings daily 9.30am–6pm; €4; ⓦwww.bernard-massard.lu). The most prominent among the wineries, on the southern side of Grevenmacher right next to the main street and river. Like the St-Martin *caves* in Remich (see below), Bernard Massard is known for its sparkling, *méthode champenoise* wine, but visitors usually see the modern production process, making it a less interesting – and shorter – tour. Included is a short introductory film and, at the end of a visit, a tasting in the slick hospitality suite.

Cep D'Or route du Vin 15, Hëttermillen (Mon–Fri 8am–noon & 2–7pm, Sat & Sun 3–7pm; ⓦwww.cepdor.lu). Designed by the Austrian architect François Valentiny, everything in this unusual, bunker-style *cave* is functional – even the artificial lake on top of the roof is there to keep the cellar cool. A family-owned winery, it's known for its Chardonnay and Gewürztraminer, and has a comfortable bar and terrace where you can sample them. No tours, though. Hëttermillen is between Remich and Ehnen.

Poll-Fabaire route du Vin 115, Wormeldange (May–Oct daily 10am–11.30am & 1.30–5pm; Nov–April by appointment only; €4.50; ⓦwww.vinsmoselle.lu). Part of the large Domaines de Vinsmoselle cooperative, this winery produces over a million litres a year and is best known for its sparkling *méthode champenoise*. Visitors can observe the modern production process, but things liven up on Sundays when a *vin dansant* with music adds to the atmosphere. Wormeldange is 12km north along the river from Remich.

St Martin route de Stadtbredimus 53, Remich (April–Oct daily 10am–noon & 1.30–5.30pm; €4; ⓦwww.cavesstmartin.lu). The house speciality here is sparkling wine and its tours are perhaps the pick of the bunch, showing the traditional *méthode champenoise* process in which the bottles are turned by hand every other day. The *caves* are located a fifteen-minute walk north along the river from the centre of Remich, on the left of the main road (the N10).

Wellenstein rue des Caves 13, Wellenstein (May–Oct daily 10am–6pm; other times by appointment; €2.75; ⓦwww.vinsmoselle.lu). Founded in 1930, this is Luxembourg's largest wine cellar, producing 3.5 million litres a year. Although their tour shows the modern production process, the explanation is very pleasantly done. Wellenstein is 4km or so south of Remich.

Luxembourgeoise about once a day (ⓣ75 82 75, ⓦwww.moselle-tourist.lu); as a sample fare, a single from Remich to Grevenmacher costs €8, €11 return. They also operate short cruises on the river from Remich (€3.50 per person; 30min). As well as the water, Remich's other main attraction is **wine**, with several local wineries offering tours and tastings – see box above.

There's no strong reason to stay overnight in Remich, but the town does have a couple of nice **hotels** – the two-star *Auberge des Cygnes*, in a comfortable 1950s building on the riverfront at Esplanade 11 (ⓣ23 69 88 52, ⓦwww.cygnes.lu; ❷), and the smart, four-star ★ *Hôtel St-Nicolas*, Esplanade 31 (ⓣ26 663, ⓦwww.saint-nicolas.lu; ❹), which occupies a distinguished old building dating back to the 1880s. Both have first-class **restaurants**, the first concentrating on Luxembourg dishes, the second French, although on a hot evening the terrace at the *Hôtel d'Esplanade*, Esplanade 5 (Ⓣ23 66 91 71), is *the* place to eat, with a menu of French classics starting at around €17 for a main course.

Ehnen

North of Remich along the Moselle, vineyards furrow the hillsides, intermittently interrupted by craggy bluffs – pretty scenery that heralds the hamlet of **EHNEN**, 10km from Remich (and accessible on bus #450), whose huddle of old and very quaint stone buildings is tucked away in a wooded dell just off the main road. There's a **Musée du Vin** here (April–Oct Tues–Sun 9.30–11.30am & 2–5pm; €3) – nothing very exciting, but with informative exhibits in the old fermenting cellar detailing various aspects of the wine-making process, past and present – as well as two **hotels**. Easily the pick of these is the neat and trim, three-star *Simmer*, route du Vin 117 (Ⓣ76 00 30; ❷), in a rambling, turreted brick mansion that dates back to the late nineteenth century; it has an excellent restaurant too, with a large terrace overlooking the Moselle.

Grevenmacher

With a population of just over four thousand, **GREVENMACHER**, about 20km upriver from Remich, and also accessible on bus #450, is the pint-sized capital of the Luxembourg Moselle. It possesses a pleasant old town, complete with a comely set of stone houses, but the main pull is the Bernard Massard **winery**, rue du Pont 8 (see box, p.342). For free town maps and other local gubbins, consult the **tourist office** at route du Vin 10 (Mon–Fri 8am–noon & 1–5pm, May–Aug also Sat 10am–3pm; Ⓣ75 82 75, Ⓦwww.grevenmacher.lu).

From Grevenmacher, there is an hourly **bus** service north along the river to Wasserbillig and Echternach (see p.343); at Wasserbillig, you can also pick up the **train** back to Luxembourg City.

Echternach and around

A town of around five thousand souls, **ECHTERNACH** grew up around an abbey that was founded here in 698 by **St Willibrord**, a Yorkshire missionary-monk who, according to legend, cured epilepsy and cattle diseases. Such finely balanced skills went down a treat with the locals, most of whom had been converted to Christianity long before his death here in 739 at the grand old age of 81. Nowadays, Willibrord is commemorated by a renowned day-long **dancing procession** in which the dancers cross the town centre in leaps and jumps – signifying epilepsy – to the accompaniment of the polka and holding white handkerchiefs. The procession, which first took place in 1533, is held annually on Whit Tuesday – two days after Whit Sunday – and begins at 9am.

Arrival, information and accommodation

With regular services from Luxembourg City, Diekirch and Ettelbruck, Echternach's **bus station** is 500m from the main square, place du Marché, straight down rue de la Gare. The **tourist office** is opposite the entrance to the basilica, just north of the main square at Parvis de la Basilique 9–10 (Mon–Fri 10am–5.30pm, Sat 10am–4pm, Sun 10am–noon; Ⓣ72 02 30, Ⓦwww.echternach.lu). It supplies free town maps, has lots of local information, sells hiking maps of the surrounding region and will book **accommodation** on your behalf at no extra cost – although you should have no problem finding somewhere: Echternach has quite a few hotels for a place of its size.

Hotels and hostels

L'Auberge de Jeunesse chemin vers Rodenhof ⓣ72 01 58, ⓦwww.youthhostels.lu. Echternach's sporty hostel – with professional climbing wall and artificial lake – is located about fifteen minutes' walk outside of the town centre on the road to Rodenhof. To get there, take bus #110 or #111 from Luxembourg City, get off at the Nonnemillen/Lac stop, and it's a 5min walk. There are 118 beds, in two- to six-bed rooms. Dorm beds €18.20, doubles ❶

Hostellerie de La Basilique place du Marché 7–8 ⓣ72 94 83, ⓦwww.hotel-basilique.lu. The priciest but probably the nicest hotel in the centre, a family-owned establishment with fourteen well-appointed, modern rooms, some of which overlook the main square. ❹

Le Petit Poète place du Marché 13 ⓣ72 00 72 ⓦwww.lepetitpoete.lu. Bang in the centre of town, and very cheap, with just twelve plain but perfectly adequate modern rooms above a café on the main square. Closed Dec & Jan. ❷

The Town

At the centre of Echternach is **place du Marché**, an airy, broadly rectangular piazza flanked by an elegant mix of old buildings. The most notable among them is the fifteenth-century **Palais de Justice** or Denzelt (Law Courts), a striking, turreted structure of roughly dressed stone held together by pinkish mortar and given poise by its Gothic arcade. The statues on the facade – of local, ecclesiastical and biblical figures – were, however, added in the 1890s. The Denzelt is now part of the **Hôtel de Ville**, the bulk of which was completed in a pleasing version of French Empire style, again in the nineteenth century.

The Basilique St-Willibrord

From place du Marché, it's a short stroll north to the **Basilique St-Willibrord** (daily 9.30am–6.30pm), a brooding, forceful edifice equipped with two sets of turreted towers. The church has had a long and chequered history. The first structure was a relatively modest affair, but as the Benedictine monastery grew richer, so the monks had it extended, stuffing it with all sorts of holy treasures. This made it a tempting target for the French Revolutionary army, who sacked the abbey and expelled the monks in 1797. Thereafter the monastery was turned into a pottery factory, but the Benedictines returned a few years later and promptly restored the abbey to an approximation of its medieval layout. There was yet more trouble during the Battle of the Bulge, when the abbey was heavily bombed, but the monks persevered, rebuilding the whole complex – again to the medieval plan – and reconsecrating the church in 1952. The postwar reconstruction was skilfully executed and today's basilica has all the feel of a medieval church, most notably in its yawning, dimly lit nave. That said, the furnishings are in themselves pretty pedestrian, and the only significant piece to have survived the bombing is a part of the exquisite **crucifix** on the nave's left-hand wall. Downstairs, the **crypt** is also a survivor, dating back to the original eighth-century foundation. The whitewashed walls are decorated by several faded frescoes and accommodate the primitive **coffin** of St Willibrord, though this is enclosed within a hideously sentimental marble canopy of 1906.

The Abbey

The huge **abbey complex** spreads out beyond the church, its crisply symmetrical, mainly eighteenth-century buildings now used as offices (including the tourist office) and a school. Next door to the church, the vaulted cellars of the former Abbot's Palace contain the **Musée de l'Abbaye** (daily: March–May & Oct 10am–noon & 2–5pm; June & Sept 10am–noon & 2–6pm; July–Aug 10am–6pm; €3), which has an excellent display on the medieval illuminated manuscripts for which Echternach once had an international reputation. Organized chronologically, the display explores the artistic development of these manuscripts, beginning in the eighth century, when Celtic and Anglo-Saxon influences are clearly discernible, and continuing through to the scriptorium's eleventh-century, German-influenced heyday. Among the exhibits, two of the finest are the tenth-century *Codex Caesareus Upsaliensis* and the book of pericopes (a selection of biblical texts) made for the Holy Roman Emperor Henry III (1017–56). Many of the manuscripts are illustrated and explained at some length (in French and German), though most are actually reproductions. The rest of the museum holds a few incidental bits and pieces, including a couple of seventh-century sarcophagi, a piece of mosaic flooring from a Roman villa discovered just outside town, and a modest display on St Willibrord's life and times. The formal beds of the old abbey gardens, by the river to the rear of the complex, have been turned into the very strollable **parc municipal**.

Eating and drinking

Most of Echternach's hotels have competent, occasionally very good **café-restaurants**, typically kitted out in a sort of semi-alpine style with oodles of wood. Many offer competitively priced *plats du jour*, others focus on Luxembourgish specialities – and some do both. *Giorgio's*, rue André Duchscher 4, serves excellent pizzas; *Le Petit Palais*, rue de la Gare 52, offers steaks, schnitzels and delicious crepes. As for **drinking**, there's a lively scene among the pavement cafés on and around the place du Marché, with the most inviting option here being the *Café De Philo'soff*, rue de la Gare 31, with French bygones on the wall and a leafy terrace.

Around Echternach: Larochette and Beaufort

Among the villages that dot the forested valleys and open uplands of La Petite Suisse, **LAROCHETTE**, a scenic 25km west of Echternach, is one of the most interesting, largely on account of its **château** (April–Oct daily 10am–6pm; €2), whose imposing ruins sprawl along a rocky ridge. There's been a fortress here since the tenth century, but the most significant remains date from the fourteenth century, when the local lords controlled a whole swath of Luxembourg. Allow a good thirty minutes to explore the fortress and then pop down to the village, which strings along the valley below, its attractive medley of old houses harbouring a fine old church and a couple of **hotels**, the pick of which is the *Grand Hôtel de la Poste*, at place Bleech 11 (Ⓣ87 81 78; ❸), which has comfy, spacious rooms and provides a warm welcome. There's also a **hostel**, in a well-kept older building on the edge of the village at Osterbour 45 (Ⓣ83 70 81, Ⓦwww.youthhostels.lu; dorm beds €18.20, doubles ❶), and a nice **campsite**, *Camping Birkelt*, at Um Birkelt 1 (Ⓣ87 90 40, Ⓦwww.camping-birkelt.lu; March–Oct). As for **eating**, there are half a dozen decent options on the main square, place Bleech.

Beaufort

From Larochette, it's about 15km northeast along pretty country roads to **BEAUFORT**, a humdrum agricultural village that straggles across a narrow, open plateau. In the wooded valley below is Beaufort's one and only claim to fame, its **château** (Easter–Oct 9am–6pm; €3), a rambling, mostly medieval stronghold whose stern walls and bleak towers roll down a steep escarpment. The most impressive part of a visit is the climb up the stone stairway into the fortress, past a series of well-preserved gateways. There's not too much to look at inside, though the old torture chamber is suitably grim and the stinky old well is a reminder that, by the fourteenth century, castles were as likely to surrender because of the stench of the sanitation as they were from enemy action.

Once you've seen the castle, there's no strong reason to hang around, but the village does have a pleasant, modern **hostel**, at rue de l'Auberge 6 (Ⓣ83 60 75, Ⓦwww.youthhostels.lu; dorm beds €16.20, doubles ❶; closed mid-Dec to

Walking, cycling and canoeing round Echternach

The tourist office sells a **hiking map** for the Echternach district entitled *La Petite Suisse Luxembourgeoise et Basse-Sûre*, detailing around fifty potential hikes, anywhere between 2km and 25km in length. The majority are clearly marked, however, so even without a map you can (usually) find your way around without too much difficulty. One popular route, taking in some fine rugged scenery, is the 6km walk west from Echternach to the plateau hamlet of **Berdorf**, up the dramatic **Gorge du Loup**. At the top of the gorge are an open-air theatre and grottoes, which may have been where the Romans cut mill stones. There's a fairly frequent bus service between Berdorf and Echternach, or you can extend the hike by returning down the next valley to the south, with the path weaving through the woods across the valley from the N11, the main road back into Echternach.

Cycling is another popular way of exploring the region. There are two official cycling routes departing from Echternach, the PC2 and PC3, both running along the old railway line. The **PC2** leads you to Luxembourg City on a 37km track, but note that this route is not for the faint-hearted as there are numerous stiff climbs. A bit longer but far less adventurous, the **PC3** runs along the rivers in the region, leading you on a 22km track to Wasserbillig or a 31km track to Vianden, with the more athletic able to take in Berdorf en route. Bicycles can be rented at The Outdoor Freizeit (see below) for €20 per day (€15 for half a day).

It's also possible to **kayak** down the River Sûre to Echternach from Dillingen, 12km north of Echternach, or Wallendorf, 16km north. Outdoor Freizeit, rue de la Sûre 10, Dillingen (Ⓣ86 91 39, Ⓦwww.outdoorfreizeit.lu), offers lots of advice – though the route is not especially difficult – and rents out single and double kayaks and canoes. Advance booking is essential, and costs vary from €12.50 to €17.50 per person for kayaks, or €30–40 for a Canadian canoe, which holds 2–3 adults or a family and young children.

mid-Jan) and a couple of reasonable **hotels**, best of which is the well-appointed *Meyer*, in a sprightly modern building with an indoor pool and sauna at Grand-rue 120 (Ⓣ83 62 62, Ⓦwww.hotelmeyer.lu; ❹). The *Meyer* has the village's best **restaurant**, too.

Ettelbruck

ETTELBRUCK, just 20km north of Luxembourg City, is a workaday cross-roads town at the confluence of the rivers Alzette and Sûre. Badly damaged in the fighting of 1944, the town is resolutely modern, the only significant sight being the **Musée Général Patton**, rue Dr Klein 5 (June to mid-Sept daily 10am–5pm; mid-Sept to May Sun 2–5pm; €5; Ⓦwww.patton.lu), which focuses on the eponymous general's involvement in the Battle of the Bulge (see p.307 & p.347). The museum is located a short walk north of the train station, just off avenue J.F. Kennedy. The **Patton memorial** is just outside of town on the N7 back towards Diekirch; it features a large statue of the general presented to the town by his son.

Free maps of Ettelbruck are available at the **tourist office**, rue Abbé Muller 5 (Mon & Tues 1.45–5.15pm, Wed–Sat 10am–12.15pm & & 1.15–5.15pm, plus July & Aug Sat 10am–noon & 2–4pm; Ⓣ81 20 68, Ⓦwww.ettelbruck-info.lu).

Bourscheid

North of Ettelbruck, two equally appealing country roads – the CR348 and the CR349 – worm their way through forested hills to the village of **BOURSCHEID**, a 10km journey. Bourscheid rambles along a bony ridge, down below which, on the steep and heavily wooded valley slopes, lurks a massive **château** (daily: April to mid-Oct 9.30am–6pm; mid-Oct to March 11am–4pm; €5). The first proper fortifications were erected here around 1000 AD, when stone walls were substituted for a previous wooden structure. Predictably, little of this original stronghold has survived and most of what you see today – most memorably the castle's mighty turrets and thick towers – dates from the fourteenth century. By comparison, the interior is something of a disappointment, with precious little to see, though the gabled **Stolzembourg house** gamely displays a ragbag of artefacts unearthed during several archeological digs, alongside occasional exhibitions featuring the work of local artists.

Down below Bourscheid castle, the CR348 plunges into the woods before emerging after about 1500m beside the River Sûre, where in pocket-sized **BOURSCHEID-MOULIN** you'll find the *Hôtel du Moulin* by the bridge (Ⓣ99 00 15, Ⓦwww.moulin.lu; ❹; closed mid-Nov to Feb), which occupies a large and expansive lodge-like mansion with lovely views along the valley and an indoor heated pool. Bourscheid-Moulin also has two riverside **campsites**, both open from mid-April to mid-October – *Um Gritt* (Ⓣ99 04 49, Ⓦwww.camp.lu), with chalet-style huts, and neighbouring *Du Moulin* (Ⓣ99 03 31, Ⓦwww. camp.lu).

General Patton

Loved and hated with equal passion, the redoubtable **General Patton** (1885–1945) was the American commander who, at the head of the US 3rd Army, drove the Germans out of Luxembourg in the later stages of the **Battle of the Bulge** (see p.307). It was a skilled operation that demonstrated Patton's military prowess to fine advantage, but as ever he muddied the waters by rashly remarking that the Allies "should let the sons of bitches go all the way to Paris, then we'll cut them off and round them up" – which is precisely what no one in newly liberated France wanted to hear.

Born in California to an affluent family with a strong military tradition, Patton entered the Virginia Military Institute at the age of 18, transferring to the United States Military Academy a year later. In **World War I**, he saw service in France, rising to the rank of lieutenant-colonel and taking a lead role in the Tank Corps before being badly wounded when a bullet ripped through his upper thigh. Forever after, he would joke about being a **"half-assed general"**, regularly dropping his pants to prove it.

In the interwar years, Patton campaigned long and hard for the development of a US **armoured corps**, but without much success until the Germans overran Poland in 1939. In a tizz, the US army hurriedly created an armoured force, making Patton one of its commanders. Three years later, Major-General Patton, as he now was, was dispatched to North Africa, the first of several campaigns in which he was involved. As a field commander, the charismatic, immaculately groomed Patton was among the best, but he was too impulsive to be a good strategist and he did not pay enough attention to organizational matters. **Eisenhower**, the Allied Commander in Chief, could probably have dealt with these military problems discreetly enough, but Patton had a habit of infuriating friend and foe alike. He repeatedly berated Montgomery for being too cautious and, worst of all, when he was visiting a hospital he slapped a battle-fatigued GI across the face, accusing him of cowardice. The ensuing furore almost wrecked his career for good.

By comparison with his tumultuous life, Patton's **death** can't help but seem anticlimactic – he died from injuries sustained in a car accident. It was perhaps a blessing in disguise: peace could hold little for a man who declared "Compared to war, all other forms of human endeavour shrink to insignificance…God how I love it".

Esch-sur-Sûre

From Bourscheid-Moulin, you can follow the River Sûre west along the N27 to reach, after about 15km, **ESCH-SUR-SÛRE**, a small village with a reputation out of all proportion to its size, mainly on account of its gorgeous situation, draped over a hill within an oxbow loop in the river. The village is short on specific sights, but wandering its old cobbled streets, lined with good-looking stone houses, is very enjoyable and you can scramble round the hilltop ruins of its medieval **château** (open access; free).

Accommodation includes the first-rate, four-star *Hôtel de la Sûre*, rue du Pont 1 (ⓣ83 91 10, ⓦwww.hotel-de-la-sure.lu; ❸; closed Jan), an immaculate modern hotel with all mod cons and facilities, including a good restaurant and bike rental. An equally inviting second choice is *Hôtel Beau-Site*, in a large old building on the other side of the river next to the town's main bridge at rue de Kaundorf 2 (ⓣ83 91 34, ⓦwww.beau-site.lu; ❸).

Diekirch

The compact centre of **DIEKIRCH** hugs the north bank of the River Sûre, its encircling boulevard marking the path of the long-demolished medieval walls. The town took a pounding in 1944 – hence the modern buildings that characterize the centre – but bits and pieces of the old have survived, and today Diekirch is a pleasant, small provincial town focused on the main pedestrianized shopping street, Grand-rue, and the main square of place de la Libération at its far end.

The main draw is the excellent **Musée National d'Histoire Militaire**, 200m north of the central place Guillaume at rue Bamertal 10 (daily: April–Oct 10am–6pm; Nov–March 2–6pm; €5; ⓦwww.nat-military-museum.lu), officially the Luxembourg military museum, but principally one of the best World War II museums in the region, providing an excellent historical survey of the Battle of the Bulge, with special emphasis on the US forces that liberated Diekirch. There's lots of equipment on display but the photographs are the real testimony, showing both sets of troops in action and at leisure, some recording the appalling freezing conditions of December 1944, others the horrific state of affairs inside the medics' tents. There's also a variety of dioramas, many modelled on actual photographs which are often displayed alongside (a particularly big display depicts a river crossing made on January 18, 1945), along with a hoard of military paraphernalia – explosives, shells, weapons, and personal effects of both American and German soldiers (prayer books, rations, novellas and the like). There's also a display entitled **Veiner Miliz**, detailing the activities of the Luxembourg resistance movement based in Vianden, and a room devoted to **Tambow**, the camp to which all the Luxembourgers captured by the Germans were sent – as well as the more recent peacekeeping activities of the Luxembourg army.

Practicalities

Diekirch's combined **bus** and **train station** is a five- to ten-minute walk southwest of the centre on avenue de la Gare; many buses also stop on or near place Guillaume. The **tourist office** is in the centre, on place de la Libération (July to mid-Aug Mon–Fri 9am–5pm, Sat & Sun 10am–4pm; mid-Aug to June Mon–Fri 9am–noon & 2–5pm, Sat 2–4pm; ⓣ80 30 23, ⓦwww.diekirch.lu). It issues free town maps and will book accommodation on your behalf without charge. It also rents out **bicycles** (city bike €7.50 a day, mountain bike €15 a day) and issues free foldouts detailing eight local **cycling** routes ranging between 35km and 88km.

Of the town's five **hotels**, the pick is the three-star *Hôtel Du Parc*, a spick-and-span, modern hotel facing the River Sûre at ave de la Gare 28 (ⓣ80 34 72,

Ⓦwww.hotel-du-parc.lu; ❸). A good alternative is the four-star *Beau Séjour*, on the encircling boulevard on the north side of the centre at rue de l'Esplanade 12 (Ⓣ26 80 47 15, Ⓦwww.hotel-beausejour.lu; ❷), which has bright and breezy modern rooms and a good restaurant, serving mainly French and seasonally inspired dishes. The town's two **campsites** – *de la Sûre* (Ⓣ80 94 25; April–Sept) and *Op de Sauer* (Ⓣ80 85 90, Ⓦwww.campsauer.lu; mid-April to mid-Oct) – are handily located a few minutes' walk from the old centre by the river on the route de Gilsdorf. To get there, cross the town's principal bridge and take the riverside path.

For **food**, the excellent *Restaurant du Commerce*, on place de la Libération, serves tasty, traditional Luxembourgish dishes at reasonable prices – mains for €17–20; otherwise, head for *Um Grill*, right in front of the church on rue de l'Esplanade, for grills, pastas and salads (closed Thurs).

Vianden

Hidden away in a deep fold in the landscape, beneath bulging forested hills and a mighty hilltop castle, tiny **VIANDEN**, just 30km or so northwest of Echternach, is undoubtedly the most strikingly sited of all Luxembourg's provincial towns. The setting, the castle and the magnificent scenery have long made it a popular tourist destination – and Vianden has the range of hotels and restaurants to prove it. Wherever else you go in Luxembourg, be sure to come here.

Arrival, information and getting around

With regular services from Diekirch and Ettelbruck, Vianden's tiny **bus station** is about five minutes' walk east of the town bridge along rue de la Gare and its continuation rue de la Frontière. The **tourist office** is at the west end of the bridge on the castle side of the river, on rue du Vieux Marché (Mon–Fri 8am–noon & 1–5pm, Sat & Sun 10am–2pm; Ⓣ83 42 57, Ⓦwww.vianden-info.lu). It has copious local information, issues hiking maps and sells a useful booklet describing around thirty **walks** in the vicinity of Vianden, ranging from a short ramble along the river to more energetic hauls up into the surrounding hills. **Cycling trails** link Vianden with both Diekirch and Echternach, and **mountain bikes** can be rented from the Pavillon de la Gare (mid-July to early Sept Mon–Sat 8am–noon & 1–5pm; Ⓣ26 87 41 57; advance booking recommended), beside the bus station, for €15 per day, €40 for three days. There's also a **tourist train**, which makes a forty-minute gambol round Vianden beginning at the town bridge (daily: April & Oct 1.30–5pm; May–Sept 11am–5pm; €6; Ⓦwww.benni-vianden.lu).

Accommodation

Accommodation isn't usually a problem in Vianden – virtually every other building seems to be a hotel – but you'd still be well advised to reserve in advance during the high season. There are also lots of **campsites** to choose from, the handiest of which is *Op dem Deich* (Ⓣ83 43 75, Ⓦwww.campingopdemdeich.lu; April to early Oct), by the river behind – and just along from – the bus station. In addition, there are two other campsites further along the road to Echternach. First up, about 1km from the bridge, is *De l'Our* (Ⓣ83 45 05, Ⓦwww.camping-our-vianden.lu; April to late Oct) and then, after another 400m or so, comes *Du Moulin* (Ⓣ83 45 01, Ⓦwww.campingdumoulin.lu; May–Sept). All three sites are reasonably well equipped – as is Vianden's **hostel**.

Hotels and hostel

Auberge de Jeunesse montée du Château 3 Ⓣ83 41 77, Ⓦwww.youthhostels.lu. Brisk, modern hostel in a nicely placed – but difficult to find – building at the top of Grand-rue, near the castle. Ten rooms, all with shared facilities, in two- to twelve-bedded rooms. Closed late Dec to Feb. Dorm beds €15.30, doubles ❶

Auberge du Château Grand-rue 74–80 ⓣ83 45 74, ⓦwww.auberge-du-chateau.lu. In a good-looking, three-storey town house on the castle side of the river, this well-kept hotel has forty revamped rooms, though they're not nearly as characterful as the rest of the building. Mid-Feb to mid-Nov. ❷

Hôtel Heintz Grand-rue 55 ⓣ83 41 55, ⓦwww.hotel-heintz.lu. Traditional, even old-fashioned, family-owned hotel, whose workaday facade belies its thoroughly alpine interior, with lots of wood panelling and oodles of local bygones. The rooms are comfortable and well appointed and some have private balconies with views over the river. April to early Nov. ❷

Hôtel Petry rue de la Gare 15 ⓣ83 41 22, ⓦwww.hotel-petry.com. In the centre of town and occupying a recently enlarged older building, this bright, modern, eco-friendly hotel has rainwater-flush toilets, a sauna and a fitness area. Late Feb to Dec. ❷

The Town

Some 500m from top to bottom, Vianden's main street – the **Grand-rue** – sweeps down a steep, wooded hill to the pint-sized **bridge** that both spans the River Our and serves as the centre of town. On the bridge there's a **statue** of St John Nepomuk, a fourteenth-century Bohemian priest who was thrown into the River Vltava for refusing to divulge the confessional secrets of his queen – an untimely end that was to make him the patron saint of bridges. Also on the bridge is a fine bust of **Victor Hugo** (1802–85), who was expelled from France for supporting the French revolutionaries of 1848. Hugo spent almost twenty years in exile, becoming a regular visitor to Vianden and living here in the summer of 1871. His former house, at the east end of the bridge, has been turned into a modest **museum** (Tues–Sun 11am–5pm; €4; ⓦwww.victor-hugo.lu) commemorating his stay here, with many letters and copies of poems and manuscripts, including his *Discourse on Vianden*. Here also are photographs of the town during the nineteenth century, and sketches by the great man of local places of interest – the castles at Beaufort and Larochette, for example. Sadly, few of Hugo's other possessions have survived, save for the bedroom furniture, complete with original bed.

Strolling up Grand-rue from the bridge, look out for the Gothic **Église des Trinitaires** on the left (daily 9am–6pm). The church's twin naves date back to the thirteenth century, as does the subtle, sinuous tracery of the adjoining **cloître** (cloister). Further up the street, the town's other museum, the **Veiner Musée**, occupies an old and distinguished-looking house at Grand-rue 96 (Easter–Oct daily 11am–5pm; €3). This holds an enjoyable hotchpotch of rural furniture, fancy firebacks and old clothes, plus a sprawling display of dolls and, on the top floor, a small room devoted to some fascinating historical documents and old photographs of the town and castle.

The castle

Vianden's principal sight is its inordinately picturesque **château** (daily: April–Sept 10am–6pm; March & Oct 10am–5pm; Nov–Feb 10am–4pm; €6; ⓦwww.castle-vianden.lu), perched high above the town. Originally a fifth-century structure, the castle you see today mostly dates from the eleventh century, though bits and pieces were added much later – hence the mixture of Romanesque, Gothic and Renaissance features. The castle was the home of the counts of Vianden, who ruled the town and much of the area during the twelfth and thirteenth centuries – until they fell under the sway of the House of Luxembourg in 1264. Later, in 1417, the Luxembourg family took over the building, and it remained the property of the grand dukes until 1977 when it was handed over to the state.

A very large complex, the castle is now open in its entirety following a very thorough and sensitive restoration (previously much of it was in ruins), though the crowds trooping through the pristine halls and galleries on the self-guided tour can't help but spoil the atmosphere. Some rooms have been furnished in an approximation of period style – the **Salle des Banquets** (Banqueting Hall) being a case in point – while others display suits of armour and suchlike. Of particular architectural merit are the long **Galerie Byzantine** (Byzantine Room), with its high trefoil windows, and the **Chapelle Supérieure** (Upper Chapel) next door, surrounded by a narrow defensive walkway. There are, furthermore, exhibits on the development of the building, detailing its restoration, and on the history of the town. For a bit of authentic mustiness, peek down the **well** just off the Grand Kitchen, its murky darkness lit to reveal profound depths in which, legend maintains, a former count can be heard frantically playing dice to keep the devil at bay and avoid being dragged off to hell.

The obvious **approach** to the castle is along the short access road at the top of Vianden's main street. More interestingly, a fairly easy **footpath** leads round to the castle from one of the hills immediately to the north. Even better, it's possible to reach this hilltop, 450m above the river, without breaking sweat by means of a **télésiège** or chairlift. This departs from rue du Sanatorium, a five-minute walk from the town bridge – just follow the signs. The upper terminal of the *télésiège* also has a café and offers extravagant views over Vianden, and is just five minutes' walk from the castle.

Eating and drinking

Almost all of the town's hotels have **restaurants** – in fact there's barely a restaurant which isn't part of a hotel. The restaurant of the *Hôtel Heintz* is especially good, serving an excellent line in Luxembourgish dishes at reasonable prices, a description which applies in equal measure to the restaurant of the *Auberge du Château*. At both, main courses start at €18, Another – more casual – alternative is the café-restaurant of the *Hôtel Auberge de l'Our*, by the bridge, whose restaurant has a more varied menu and is a bit more contemporary than its intensely traditional rivals. The riverside terrace **bar** here is one of the most convivial places in town, though it gets jam-packed on summer weekends.

Clervaux

In the far north of Luxembourg, **CLERVAUX** is an ancient place, with its jumble of slate roofs in a tight loop of the River Clerve. At the centre of things is the **château**, dating from the twelfth century but rebuilt in the seventeenth and again after considerable damage in the last war. This later episode is recounted in the **Battle of the Bulge Museum**, beside the central courtyard (March–May & Oct to mid-Sept Sat & Sun 1–5pm; June Mon–Sat 1–5pm, Sun 11am–6pm; July to mid-Sept Tues–Sun 11am–6pm; €2.50). Another part of the castle holds a **museum of models** (same times and price), incorporating miniature mock-ups of several of the country's castles, but this pales when compared with the castle's prime exhibit, the **Family of Man** (March–Dec Tues–Sun 10am–6pm; €4.50, combined ticket €7), a remarkable collection of over five hundred photographs compiled by Edward Steichen (1879–1973), a former director of photography at the Museum of Modern Art in New York. The Steichen family migrated to the States from Luxembourg when Edward was two years old, but clearly he maintained an attachment to the country of his birth, bequeathing the collection to the Grand Duchy in his will. First exhibited in 1955, Steichen's photographs were selected from no less than two million pictures by nearly three hundred photographers and they depict life, love and death in 68 countries, a truly international collaboration that Steichen called the "culmination of his career" and classified by UNESCO as a memory of the world.

Practicalities

Clervaux is on the Luxembourg City–Liège **train line**, which bisects northern Luxembourg. From Clervaux **train station**, it's a good ten-minute walk south into the town centre, straight down rue de la Gare and its continuation, Grand-rue. The **tourist office** is at place de la Libération 2 (April–June Mon–Sat 2–5pm; July & Aug daily 9.45–11.45am & 2–6pm; Sept Mon–Sat 9.45–11.45am & 1.30–5.30pm; Oct Mon–Sat 9.45–11.45am & 1–5pm; ⓣ92 00 72, ⓦwww.tourisme-clervaux.lu); it has details of local accommodation and issues free town maps.

Accommodation options aren't great in Clervaux. The most central hotels are the modern, cosy and well-kept *Hôtel du Commerce*, just below the chateau at rue de Marnach 2 (ⓣ92 91 81, ⓦwww.hotelducommerce.lu; ❸), which has an indoor pool, and the *Koener*, Grand-rue 14 (ⓣ92 10 02; ❷–❸), whose rooms are variable but mostly large and comfortable. There are also a couple of **campsites**, the better one being *Camping Reilerweier* (ⓣ92 01 60; April–Oct), about 2km out of town on the Vianden road, beside the river. For **food**, the *Koener* has a decent restaurant and brasserie and its terrace is the nicest place in town to nurse a **drink**.

Travel details

Trains

Luxembourg City to: Arlon (every 30min; 20min); Brussels (hourly; 3hr); Clervaux (hourly; 50min); Diekirch (hourly; 30–40min); Ettelbruck (every 20min; 20–25min); Liège (hourly; 2hr 30min); Namur (hourly; 2hr); Wasserbillig (every 30min; 30–40min).

Buses

Diekirch to: Echternach (hourly; 35min); Vianden (every 30min; 20min).
Echternach to: Beaufort (9 daily; 20min); Diekirch (hourly; 35min); Ettelbruck (16 daily; 45min); Grevenmacher (hourly; 40min); Larochette (every 1–2 hr; 1hr); Luxembourg City (hourly; 1hr); Wasserbillig (hourly; 30min).
Ettelbruck to: Diekirch (hourly; 10min); Echternach (15 daily; 45min); Esch-sur-Sûre (hourly; 25min); Vianden (hourly; 25min).
Grevenmacher to: Echternach (hourly; 40min); Wasserbillig (hourly; 10min).
Luxembourg City to: Diekirch (hourly; 1hr 20min); Echternach (hourly; 50min); Mondorf-les-Bains (hourly; 25min); Remich (hourly; 45min).
Remich to: Ehnen (hourly; 15min); Grevenmacher (hourly; 30min).
Wasserbillig to: Echternach (hourly; 20min); Grevenmacher (hourly; 10min).

Contexts

Contexts

History

Jumbled together throughout most of their history, the countries now known as **Belgium**, **Luxembourg** and the **Netherlands** didn't define their present frontiers until 1830. Before then, their borders were continually being redrawn following battles, treaties and alliances, a shifting pattern that makes it impossible to provide a history of one without frequent reference to the others. To make matters more involved, these same three countries were – and still are – commonly lumped together as the "**Low Countries**" on account of their topography, though given the valleys and hills of southern Belgium and Luxembourg, this is more than a little unfair. Even more confusing is the fact that the Netherlands is frequently called "Holland", when Holland is actually a province in the Netherlands. In the account that follows we've used "Low Countries" to cover all three countries and "Holland" to refer to the province. In addition, we've termed the language of the northern part of Belgium "Flemish" to save confusion, though "Dutch" or even "**Netherlandish**" are sometimes the preferred options among Belgians themselves.

Beginnings

Little is known of the **prehistoric** peoples of the Low Countries, whose various tribes only begin to emerge from the prehistoric soup after Julius Caesar's conquest of Gaul (broadly France) in 57–50 BC. The **Romans** found three tribal groupings living in the region: the mainly Celtic **Belgae** (hence the nineteenth-century term "Belgium") settled by the rivers Rhine, Meuse and Waal to the south and, further north, two Germanic peoples, the **Frisians** and the **Batavi**. The Romans conquered the Belgae and incorporated their lands into the imperial province of **Gallia Belgica**, but the territory of the Batavi and Frisians was not considered worthy of colonization. Instead, these tribes were granted the status of allies, a source of recruitment for the Roman legions and curiosity for imperial travellers. In 50 AD Pliny observed, "Here a wretched race is found, inhabiting either the more elevated spots or artificial mounds…When the waves cover the surrounding area they are like so many mariners on board a ship, and when again the tide recedes their condition is that of so many shipwrecked men."

The **Roman occupation** continued for nigh on five hundred years until the legions were pulled back to protect the heartland of the crumbling empire. Yet, despite the length of their stay, there's a notable lack of material evidence to indicate their presence, an important exception being the odd stretch of city wall in Tongeren (see p.245), one of the principal Roman settlements.

The Merovingians

As the Roman Empire collapsed in chaos and confusion, the Germanic **Franks**, who had been settling within Gallia Belgica from the third century, filled the power vacuum to the south, and, along with their allies the Belgae, established a **Merovingian** kingdom based around their capital in Tournai. A great swath of forest extending from the Scheldt to the Ardennes separated this predominantly Frankish kingdom from the more confused situation to the north and east, where other tribes of Franks settled along the Scheldt and Leie – a separation which came to delineate the ethnic and linguistic division that survives in Belgium to this day. North of the Franks of the Scheldt were the **Saxons**, and finally the north coast of the Netherlands was settled by the **Frisians**.

Towards the end of the fifth century, the Merovingians extended their control over much of what is now north and central France. In 496 their king, **Clovis**, was converted to **Christianity**, a faith which slowly filtered north, spread by energetic missionaries like St Willibrord, first bishop of Utrecht from about 710, and St Boniface, who was killed by the Frisians in 754 in a final act of pagan resistance before they too were converted. Meanwhile, after the death of the last distinguished Merovingian king, Dagobert, in 638, power passed increasingly to the so-called "mayors of the palace", a hereditary position whose most outstanding occupant was **Charles Martel** (c.690–741). Martel ruled a large but all too obviously shambolic kingdom whose military weakness he determined to remedy. Traditionally, the Merovingian (Frankish) army was comprised of a body of infantry led by a small group of cavalry. Martel replaced this with a largely mounted force of trained knights, who bore their own military expenses in return for land – the beginnings of the **feudal system**.

The Carolingians

Ten years after Martel's death, his son, Pepin the Short, formally usurped the Merovingian throne with the blessing of the pope, becoming the first of the **Carolingian** dynasty, whose most famous member was **Charlemagne**, king of the west Franks from 768. In a dazzling series of campaigns, Charlemagne extended his empire south into Italy, west to the Pyrenees, north to Denmark and east to the Oder, his secular authority bolstered by his coronation as the first **Holy Roman Emperor** in 800. The pope bestowed this title on him to legitimize the king's claim to be the successor of the emperors of imperial Rome – and it worked a treat. Based in Aachen, Charlemagne stabilized his kingdom and the Low Countries benefited from a trading boom that utilized the region's principal rivers. However, unlike his Roman predecessors, Charlemagne was subject to the divisive inheritance laws of the **Salian** tribe of Franks, and after his death in 814, his kingdom was divided between his grandsons into three roughly parallel strips of territory, the precursors of France, the Low Countries and Germany.

The growth of the towns

The **tripartite division** of Charlemagne's empire put the Low Countries between the emergent French- and German-speaking nations, a particularly dangerous place to be – and one that has defined much of its history. This was not, however, apparent amid the cobweb of local alliances that made up early feudal western Europe in the ninth and tenth centuries. During this period, French kings and German emperors exercised a general authority over the Low Countries, but power was effectively in the hands of **local lords** who, remote from central control, brought a degree of local stability. From the twelfth century, feudalism slipped into a gradual decline, the intricate pattern of localized allegiances undermined by the increasing strength of certain lords, whose power and wealth often exceeded that of their nominal sovereign. Preoccupied by territorial squabbles,

The béguinages

One corollary of the urbanization of the Low Countries from the twelfth century onwards was the establishment of **béguinages** (*begijnhoven* in Flemish) in almost every city and town. These were semi-secluded communities, where widows and unmarried women – the **béguines** (*begijns*) – lived together, the better to do pious acts, especially caring for the sick. In **construction**, *béguinages* follow the same general plan, with several streets of whitewashed, brick terraced cottages hidden away behind walls and gates, and surrounding a central garden and chapel. The **origins** of the *béguine* movement are somewhat obscure, but it would seem that the initial impetus came from a twelfth-century Liège priest, a certain Lambert le Bègue (the Stammerer). The main period of growth came a little later when several important female nobles established new *béguinages*, like the ones in Kortrijk, Ghent and Bruges.

Béguine communities were different from convents in so far as the inhabitants did not have to take vows and had the right to return to the secular world if they wished. At a time when hundreds of women were forcibly shut away in convents for all sorts of reasons (primarily financial), this element of choice was crucial.

this streamlined nobility was usually willing to assist the growth of towns by granting charters, which permitted a certain amount of autonomy in exchange for tax revenues, and military and labour services. The first major cities were the **cloth towns of Flanders**, notably Ghent, Bruges and Ieper, which grew rich from the manufacture of cloth, their garments exported far and wide and their economies dependent on a continuous supply of good-quality wool from England. Meanwhile, the smaller towns north of the Scheldt concentrated on trade, exploiting their strategic position at the junction of several of the major waterborne trade routes of the day.

The **economic interests** of the urbanized merchants and guildsmen often conflicted with those of the local lord. This was especially true in **Flanders**, where the towns were anxious to preserve a good relationship with the king of England, who controlled the wool supply, whereas their count was a vassal of the king of France, whose dynastic aspirations clashed with those of his English rival. As a result, the history of thirteenth- and fourteenth-century Flanders is punctuated by endemic conflict, as the two kings and the guildsmen slugged it out, but though the fortunes of war oscillated between the parties, the underlying class conflict was never resolved.

The Burgundians

By the late fourteenth century the political situation in the Low Countries was fairly clear: five lords controlled most of the region, paying only nominal homage to their French or German overlords. Yet things began to change in 1419, when **Philip the Good**, Duke of Burgundy, succeeded to the countship of Flanders and by a series of adroit political moves gained control over the southern Netherlands, Brabant and Limburg to the north, and Antwerp, Namur and Luxembourg to the south. Philip consolidated his power by establishing a strong central administration based in Bruges and by curtailing the privileges granted in the towns' charters. Less independent it may have been, but **Bruges** benefited greatly from the duke's presence, becoming an emporium for the **Hanseatic League**, a mainly German association of towns which acted as a trading group and protected its interests by an exclusive system of trading tariffs.

Philip died in 1467 to be succeeded by his son, **Charles the Bold**, who was killed in battle ten years later, plunging his father's carefully crafted domain into turmoil. The French took the opportunity to occupy Arras and Burgundy and, before the people of Flanders would agree to fight the invading French, they kidnapped Charles's successor, his daughter **Mary**, and forced her to sign a charter that restored the civic privileges removed by her grandfather.

The Habsburgs

After her release, Mary married the Habsburg **Maximilian of Austria**, who assumed sole authority when Mary was killed in a riding accident in 1482. A sharp operator, Maximilian continued where the Burgundians had left off, whittling away at the power of the cities with considerable success. When Maximilian became Holy Roman Emperor in 1494, he transferred control of the Low Countries to his son, **Philip the Handsome**, and then – after Philip's early death – to his grandson **Charles V**, who then became king of Spain and Holy Roman Emperor in 1516 and 1519 respectively. Charles ruled his vast kingdom with skill and energy but, born in Ghent, he was very suspicious of the turbulent Flemish burghers. Consequently, he favoured **Antwerp** at their expense and this city now became the greatest port in the Habsburg Empire, part of a general movement of trade and prosperity away from Flanders to the cities further north. As part of the process, the Flemish cloth industry had, by the 1480s, begun its long decline, undermined by England's new-found cloth-manufacturing success.

By sheer might, Charles systematically bent the merchant cities of the Low Countries to his will, but regardless of this display of force, a spiritual trend was emerging that would soon question the rights of the Emperor and rock the power of the Catholic Church.

The Reformation

An alliance of church and state had dominated the medieval world: pope and bishops, kings and counts were supposedly the representatives of God on earth, and they worked together to crush religious dissent wherever it appeared. Much of their authority depended on the ignorance of the population, who were entirely dependent on their priests for the interpretation of the scriptures, their view of the world carefully controlled. The **Reformation** was a religious revolt that stood sixteenth-century Europe on its head. There were many complex reasons for it, but certainly the development of **typography** was a crucial element. For the first time, printers were able to produce relatively cheap Bibles in quantity, and the religious texts were no longer the exclusive property of the priesthood. The first stirrings of the Reformation were in the welter of debate that spread across much of western Europe under the auspices of theologians like **Erasmus of Rotterdam** (1465–1536; see box opposite), who wished to cleanse the Catholic Church of its corruptions, superstitions and extravagant ceremony; only later did many of these same thinkers – principally **Martin Luther** – decide to support a breakaway Church. In 1517, Luther produced his 95 theses against indulgences, rejecting – among other things – Christ's presence in the sacrament of the Eucharist, and denying the Church's monopoly on the interpretation of the Bible. There was no way back, and when Luther's works were disseminated his ideas gained a European following among

Erasmus

By any measure, **Desiderius Erasmus** (1466–1536) was a remarkable man. Born in Rotterdam, the illegitimate son of a priest, he was orphaned at the age of 13 and defrauded of his inheritance by his guardians, who forced him to become a monk. He hated monastic life and seized the first opportunity to leave, becoming a student at the University of Paris in 1491. Throughout the rest of his life Erasmus kept on the move, travelling between the Low Countries, England, Italy and Switzerland, and everywhere he went his rigorous scholarship, sharp humour and strong moral sense made a tremendous impact. He attacked the abuses and corruptions of the Church, publishing scores of polemical and satirical **essays** which were read all over western Europe. He argued that most monks had "no other calling than stupidity, ignorance . . . and the hope of being fed". These attacks reflected Erasmus's determination to reform the Church from within, both by rationalizing its doctrine and rooting out hypocrisy, ignorance and superstition. He employed other methods too, producing **translations** of the New Testament to make the scriptures more widely accessible, and co-ordinating the efforts of like-minded Christian humanists. The Church authorities periodically harassed Erasmus but generally he was tolerated, not least for his insistence on the importance of Christian unity. Luther was less indulgent, bitterly denouncing Erasmus for "making fun of the faults and miseries of the Church of Christ instead of bewailing them before God". The quarrel between the two reflected a growing schism among the reformers that led directly to the Reformation.

reforming groups branded as **Lutheran** by the Church, whilst other reformers were drawn to the doctrines of **John Calvin** (1509–64). Luther asserted that the Church's political power was subservient to that of the state; Calvin emphasized the importance of individual conscience and the need for redemption through the grace of Christ rather than the confessional.

These **Protestant** seeds fell on fertile ground among the merchants of the Low Countries, whose wealth and independence had never been easy to accommodate within a rigid caste society. Similarly, their employees, the guildsmen and their apprentices, had a long history of opposing arbitrary authority, and were easily convinced of the need to reform an autocratic, venal Church. In 1555, **Charles V abdicated**, possibly on account of poor health, transferring his German lands to his brother Ferdinand, and his Italian, Spanish and Low Countries territories to his son, the fanatically Catholic **Philip II**. In the short term, the scene was set for a bitter confrontation, while the dynastic ramifications of the division of the Habsburg Empire were to complicate European affairs for centuries.

The revolt of the Netherlands

After his father's abdication, **Philip II** decided to teach his heretical subjects a lesson they wouldn't forget. He garrisoned the towns of the Low Countries with Spanish mercenaries, imported the **Inquisition** and passed a series of anti-Protestant edicts. However, other pressures on the Habsburg Empire forced him into a tactical withdrawal and he transferred control to his sister **Margaret of Parma** in 1559. Based in Brussels, the equally resolute Margaret implemented the policies of her brother with gusto. In 1561 she reorganized the Church and created fourteen new bishoprics, a move that was construed as a wresting of power from civil authority, and an attempt to destroy the local aristocracy's powers of religious patronage. Protestantism – and Protestant sympathies – spread among the nobility, who now formed the "**League of the Nobility**" to counter Habsburg policy. The League petitioned Philip for moderation but was dismissed out of hand by one of Margaret's Walloon advisers, who called them "*ces geux*" (those beggars), an epithet that was to be enthusiastically adopted by the rebels. In 1565 a harvest failure caused a winter famine among the urban workers across the region and, after years of repression, they finally struck back. The following year, a Protestant sermon in the tiny Flemish textile town of Steenvoorde incited the congregation to purge the local church of its papist idolatry. The crowd smashed up the church's reliquaries and shrines, broke the stained-glass windows and terrorized the priests, thereby launching the **Iconoclastic Fury**. The rioting spread like wildfire and within ten days churches had been ransacked from one end of the Low Countries to the other, nowhere more so than in Antwerp. The ferocity of this outbreak shocked the upper classes into renewed support for Spain, and Margaret regained the allegiance of most nobles – with the principal exception of the country's greatest landowner, Prince William of Orange-Nassau, known as **William the Silent**. Of Germanic descent, he was raised a Catholic, but the excesses and rigidity of Philip had caused him to side with the Protestant movement. A firm believer in individual freedom and religious tolerance, William became a symbol of liberty for many, but after the Fury had revitalized the pro-Spanish party, he prudently slipped away to his estates in Germany.

The Duke of Alva and the sea-beggars

Philip II was keen to capitalize on the increase in support for Margaret following the Iconoclastic Fury, and in 1567 he dispatched the **Duke of Alva** (and an army of ten thousand men) to the Low Countries to suppress his religious opponents absolutely. Margaret was not at all pleased by Philip's decision and, when Alva arrived in Brussels, she resigned in a huff, initiating what was, in effect, military rule. One of Alva's first acts was to set up the Commission of Civil Unrest, which was soon nicknamed the "**Council of Blood**", after its habit of executing those it examined. No fewer than twelve thousand citizens were polished off, mostly for taking part in the Fury.

Initially the repression worked: in 1568, when William attempted an invasion from Germany, the towns, garrisoned by the Spanish, offered no support. William waited and conceived other means of defeating Alva. In April 1572 a band of privateers entered Brielle on the Meuse and captured it from the Spanish. This was one of several commando-style attacks by the so-called **Waterguezen** or **sea-beggars**, who were at first obliged to operate from England, although it was soon possible for them to secure bases in the Netherlands, whose citizens had grown to loathe Alva and his Spaniards.

Luis de Resquesens, the Spanish Fury and the Union of Brussels

After the success at Brielle, the revolt spread rapidly: by June the rebels controlled the province of Holland and William was able to take command of his troops in Delft. Alva and his son Frederick fought back, but William's superior naval power frustrated him and a mightily irritated Philip replaced Alva with **Luis de Resquesens**. Initially, Resquesens had some success in the south, where the Catholic majority were more willing to compromise with Spanish rule than their northern neighbours, but the tide of war was against him – most pointedly in William's triumphant relief of Leiden in 1574. Two years later, Resquesens died and the (unpaid) Habsburg garrison in Antwerp mutinied and attacked the town, slaughtering some eight thousand of its people in what was known as the **Spanish Fury**. Though the Habsburgs still held several towns, the massacre alienated the south and pushed its inhabitants into the arms of William, whose troops now swept into Brussels, the heart of imperial power. Momentarily, it seemed possible for the whole region to unite behind William and all signed the **Union of Brussels**, which demanded the departure of foreign troops as a condition for accepting a diluted Habsburg sovereignty. This was followed, in 1576, by the **Pacification of Ghent**, a regional agreement that guaranteed freedom of religious belief, a necessary precondition for any union between the largely Protestant north (the Netherlands) and Catholic south (Belgium and Luxembourg).

The United Provinces break free

Despite the precariousness of his position, Philip was not inclined to compromise, especially after he realized that William's Calvinist sympathies were giving his new-found Walloon and Flemish allies the jitters. The king bided his time until 1578 when, with his enemies arguing among themselves, he sent another army from Spain to the Low Countries under the command of Alessandro Farnese, the **Duke of Parma**. Events played into Parma's hands. In 1579, tiring of all the wrangling, seven northern provinces agreed to sign the **Union of Utrecht**, an alliance against Spain that was to be the first unification of the Netherlands as an identifiable country – as the **United Provinces**. The assembly of these United Provinces was known as the **States General** and it met at The Hague. The role of **Stadholder** was the most important in each province, roughly equivalent to that of governor, though the same person could occupy this position in any number of provinces. Meanwhile, in the south – and also in 1579 – representatives of the southern provinces signed the **Union of Arras**, a Catholic-led agreement that declared loyalty to Philip II and counter-balanced the Union of Utrecht in the north. Parma used this area as a base to recapture Flanders and Antwerp, which fell after a long and cruel siege in 1585. But Parma was unable to advance any further north and the Low Countries were, de facto, divided into two – the Spanish Netherlands and the United Provinces – beginning a separation that would lead, after many changes, to the creation of three modern countries.

The Spanish Netherlands (1579–1713)

With his army firmly entrenched in the south, Philip was now prepared to permit some degree of economic and political autonomy, exercising control over the **Spanish Netherlands** through a governor in Brussels, but he was not inclined to tolerate his newly recovered Protestant subjects. As a result, thousands of weavers, apprentices and skilled workers – the bedrock of Calvinism – fled north to escape the new Catholic regime, thereby fuelling an economic boom in Holland. It took a while for this migration to take effect, and for several years the Spanish Netherlands had all the trappings – if not the substance – of success, its mini-economy sustained by the conspicuous consumption of the Habsburg elite. Silk weaving, diamond processing and tapestry- and lacemaking were particular beneficiaries and a new canal was cut linking Ghent and Bruges to the sea at Ostend. This commercial restructuring underpinned a brief flourishing of artistic life centred on **Rubens** and his circle of friends – including Anthony van Dyck and Jacob Jordaens – in Antwerp during the first decades of the seventeenth century.

Habsburg failure

Months before his death in 1598, Philip II had granted control of the Spanish Netherlands to his daughter and her husband, appointing them the **Archdukes Isabella and Albert**. Failing to learn from experience, the ducal couple continued to prosecute the war against the Protestant north, but with so little success that they were obliged to make peace – the **Twelve-Year Truce** – in 1609. When the truce ended, the new Spanish king **Philip IV** proved equally foolhardy, bypassing Isabella – Albert was dead – to launch his own campaign against the Protestant Dutch. This was part of the **Thirty Years' War** (1618–48), a devastating conflict that spread across most of western Europe in a mix of dynastic rivalry and religious (Catholic against Protestant) hatred. The Spanish were initially successful, but they were weakened by war with France and Dutch sea-power. Thereafter, from 1625 onwards, the Spaniards suffered a series of defeats on land and sea and in 1648 they were compelled to accept the humiliating terms of the **Peace of Westphalia**. This was a general treaty that ended the Thirty Years' War, and its terms both recognized the independence of the United Provinces and closed the Scheldt estuary, an action designed to destroy the trade and prosperity of Antwerp. By these means, the commercial pre-eminence of Amsterdam was assured.

The Spanish Netherlands paid dearly for its adherence to the Habsburg cause. In the course of the Thirty Years' War, it had teetered on the edge of chaos – highwaymen infested the roads, trade had almost disappeared, the population had been halved in Brabant, and acres of fertile farmland lay uncultivated – but the peace was perhaps as bad. Denied access to the sea, Antwerp was ruined and simply withered away, while the southern provinces as a whole spiralled into an economic decline that pauperized its population. Yet the country's ruling families seemed proud to appear to the world as the defenders and martyrs of the Catholic faith; those who disagreed left.

The Counter-Reformation

Politically dependent on a decaying Spain, economically ruined and deprived of most of its more independent-minded citizens, the Spanish Netherlands turned in on itself, sustained by the fanatical Catholicism of the **Counter-Reformation**. Religious worship became strict and magnificent, medieval carnivals were transformed into exercises in piety, and penitential flagellation became popular, all under the approving eyes of the **Jesuits**. Indeed, the number of Jesuits was quite extraordinary: in the whole of France, there were only two thousand, but the Spanish Netherlands had no fewer than 1600. It was here that they wrote their most important works, exercised their greatest influence and owned vast tracts of land. Supported by draconian laws that barred known Protestants from public appointments, declared their marriages illegal and forbade them municipal assistance, the Jesuits and their fellow Catholic priests simply overwhelmed the religious opposition; in the space of fifty years, they transformed this part of the Low Countries into an introverted world shaped by a mystical faith, where Christians were redeemed by the ecstasy of suffering.

The visible signs of the change were all around, from extravagant Baroque churches to Crosses, Calvaries and shrines scattered across the countryside. Literature disappeared, the sciences vegetated and religious orders multiplied. In **painting**, artists – principally Rubens – were used to confirm the ecclesiastical orthodoxies, their canvases full of muscular saints and angels, reflecting a religious faith of mystery and hierarchy; others, such as David Teniers and the later Bruegels, retreated into minutely observed realism.

French interference

In 1648, the **Peace of Westphalia** freed the king of France from his fear of Germany, and the political and military history of the Spanish Netherlands thereafter was dominated by **Louis XIV**'s efforts to add the country to his territories. Fearful of an over-powerful France, the United Provinces, England and Sweden, among others, determinedly resisted French designs and, to preserve the balance of power, fought a long series of campaigns beginning with the **War of Devolution** in 1667 and ending in the **War of the Spanish Succession**. The latter was sparked by the death in 1700 of **Charles II**, the last of the Spanish Habsburgs, who had willed his territories to the grandson of Louis XIV of France. An anti-French coalition refused to accept the settlement and there ensued a haphazard series of campaigns that dragged on for eleven years, marked by the spectacular victories of the **Duke of Marlborough** – Blenheim, Ramillies, Malplaquet and Oudenaarde. Many of the region's cities were besieged and badly damaged during these wars, and only with the **Treaty of Utrecht** of 1713 did the French abandon their attempt to conquer the Spanish Netherlands. The latter were now passed to the Austrian Habsburgs in the figure of the Emperor Charles VI.

The Austrian Netherlands (1713–94)

The transfer of the country from Spanish to **Austrian control** made little appreciable difference: there were more wars and more invasions, and a remote central authority continued to operate through Brussels. In particular, the **War of the Austrian Succession**, fought over the right of Maria Theresa to assume the Austrian Habsburg throne, prompted the French to invade and occupy much of the country in 1744, though imperial control was restored four years later by the **Treaty of Aix-la-Chapelle**. Perhaps surprisingly, these dynastic shenanigans had little effect on the country's agriculture, which survived the various campaigns and actually became more productive, leading to a marked increase in the rural population, especially after the introduction of the **potato**. But intellectually the country remained vitrified and stagnant – only three percent of the population were literate, workers were forbidden to change towns or jobs without obtaining permission from the municipal authorities, and skills and crafts were tied to particular families.

This sorry state of affairs began to change in the middle of the eighteenth century as the Austrian oligarchy came under the influence of the **Enlightenment**, that belief in reason and progress – as against authority and tradition – that had first been proselytized by French philosophers. In 1753, the arrival of a progressive governor, the **Count of Cobenzl**, signified a transformation of Habsburg policy. Eager to shake the country from its torpor, Cobenzl initiated an ambitious programme of public works. New canals were dug, old canals deepened, new industries were encouraged and public health was at least discussed, the main result being regulations forbidding burial inside churches and the creation of new cemeteries outside the city walls. Cobenzl also took a firm line with his clerical opponents, who took a dim view of all this modernizing and tried to encourage the population to thwart him in his aims.

The Brabant Revolution

In 1780, the **Emperor Joseph II** came to the throne, determined, as he put it, to "root out silly old prejudices" by imperial decree. His reforming zeal was not, however, matched by any political nous and the deluge of edicts that he promulgated managed to offend all of the country's major groups – from peasants, clerics and merchants right through to the nobility. Opposition crystallized around two groups – the liberal-minded **Vonckists**, who demanded a radical, republican constitution, and the conservative **Statists**, whose prime aim was the maintenance of the Catholic status quo. Pandemonium ensued and, in 1789, the Habsburgs dispatched an army to restore order. Against all expectations, the two political groups swallowed their differences to combine and then defeat the Austrians near Antwerp, in what became known as the **Brabant Revolution**. The rebels promptly announced the formation of the United States of Belgium, but the uneasy alliance between the Vonckists and Statists soon broke down, not least because the latter were terrified by the course of the revolution which had erupted across the border in France. Determined to keep the radicals at bay, the Statists raised the peasantry to arms and, with the assistance of the priests, encouraged them to attack the Vonckists, who were killed in their hundreds. The Statists now had the upper hand, but the country remained in turmoil and when Emperor Joseph died in 1790, his successor, **Léopold**, was quick to withdraw many of the reforming acts and send in his troops to restore imperial authority.

French rule and its aftermath (1794–1830)

The new and repressive Habsburg regime was short-lived. French Republican armies brushed the imperial forces aside in 1794, and the Austrian Netherlands was annexed the following year, an annexation that was to last until 1814. The **French** imposed radical reforms: the Catholic Church was stripped of much of its worldly wealth, feudal privileges and the guilds were abolished, and a consistent legal system was formulated. **Napoleon**, in control from 1799, carried on the work of modernization, rebuilding the docks of Antwerp and forcing the Netherlanders, whose country the French had also occupied, to accept the reopening of the Scheldt. Unrestricted access to French markets boosted the local economy, kick-starting the mechanization of the textile industry in Ghent and Verviers and encouraging the growth of the coal and metal industries in Hainaut, but with the exception of a radical minority, the French occupation remained unpopular with most of the populace. Looting by French soldiers was commonplace, especially in the early years, but it was the introduction of **conscription** which stirred the most resistance, provoking a series of (brutally repressed) peasant insurrections.

The United Kingdom of the Netherlands (1815–1830)

French rule in the Low Countries began to evaporate after Napoleon's disastrous retreat from Moscow in 1812, and had all but disappeared long before

Napoleon's final defeat just outside Brussels at the **Battle of Waterloo** in June 1815. At the **Congress of Vienna**, called to settle Europe at the end of the Napoleonic Wars, the main concern of the Great Powers – including Great Britain and Russia – was to create a buffer state against any possible future plans the French might have to expand to the north. With scant regard to the feelings of those affected, they decided to establish the **United Kingdom of the Netherlands**, which incorporated both the old United Provinces and the Spanish (Austrian) Netherlands. On the throne they placed Frederick William of Orange, crowned **King William I**. The Great Powers also decided to give Frederick William's German estates to Prussia and in return presented him with the newly independent **Grand Duchy of Luxembourg**. This was a somewhat confused arrangement. The duchy had previously been part of both the Spanish and Austrian Netherlands, but now it was detached from the rest of the Low Countries constitutionally and pushed into the German Confederation at the same time as it shared the same king with the old United Provinces and Austrian Netherlands.

Given the imperious way the new Kingdom of the Netherlands had been established, it required considerable royal tact to make things work. William lacked this in abundance and indeed some of his measures seemed designed to inflame his French-speaking (Belgian) subjects. He made Dutch the official language of the whole kingdom and, in a move against the Catholics, he tried to secularize all Church-controlled schools. Furthermore, each of the two former countries had the same number of representatives at the States General despite the fact that the population of the old United Provinces was half that of its neighbour. There were **competing economic interests** too. The north was reliant on commerce and sought free trade without international tariffs; the industrialized south wanted a degree of protectionism. William's refusal to address any of these concerns united his opponents in the south, where both industrialists and clerics now clamoured for change.

Independent Belgium: 1830–1900

The **revolution** against King William began in the Brussels opera house on August 25, 1830, when the singing of a duet, *Amour Sacré de la Patrie*, hit a nationalist nerve and the audience poured out onto the streets to raise the flag of Brabant in defiance of the king. At first the revolutionaries only demanded a scaling down of royal power and a separate "Belgian" administration, but negotiations soon broke down and in late September the insurrectionists proclaimed the **Kingdom of Belgium**. William prepared for war, but the liberal governments of Great Britain and France intervened to stop hostilities and, in January of the following year, they recognized an independent Belgian state at the **Conference of London**. The caveat – and this was crucial to the Great Powers given the trouble the region had caused for centuries – was that Belgium be classified a "**neutral**" state, that is one outside any other's sphere of influence. To bolster this new nation, they ceded to it the western segments of the Grand Duchy of Luxembourg and dug out Prince Léopold of Saxe-Coburg to present with the crown. William retained the northern part of his kingdom and even received the remainder of Luxembourg as his personal possession, but he still hated the settlement and there was a further bout of sabre-rattling before he finally caved in and accepted the new arrangements in 1839.

Léopold I

Shrewd and capable, **Léopold I** (1830–65) was careful to maintain his country's neutrality and encouraged an industrial boom that saw coal mines developed, iron foundries established and the rapid expansion of the railway system. One casualty, however, was the traditional linen-making industry of rural Flanders. The cottagers who spun and wove the linen could not compete with the mechanized mills, and their pauperization was compounded by the poor grain harvests and potato blight of 1844–46. Their sufferings were, however, of only mild concern to the country's political representatives, who were elected on a strictly limited franchise, which ensured the domination of the middle classes. The latter divided into two loose groups, the one attempting to undermine Catholic influence and control over such areas as education, the other profoundly conservative in its desire to maintain the status quo. Progressive elements within the bourgeoisie coalesced in the **Liberal party**, which was free trade and urban in outlook, whereas their opponents, the **Catholic party**, promised to protect Belgian agriculture with tariffs. The political twist was that the Catholic party, in its retreat from the industrialized and radicalized cities, began to identify with the plight of rural Dutch-speaking Belgians – as against the French-speaking ruling and managerial classes.

Léopold II

Léopold II's long reign (1865–1909) saw the emergence of Belgium as a major industrial power. The 1860s and 1870s also witnessed the first significant stirrings of a type of **Flemish nationalism** which felt little enthusiasm for the unitary status of Belgium, divided as it was between a French-speaking majority in the south – the Walloons – and the minority Dutch-speakers of the north. There was also industrial unrest towards the end of the century, the end results being a body of legislation improving working conditions and, in 1893, the extension of the **franchise** to all men over the age of 25. The Catholic party also ensured that, under the Equality Law of 1898, Dutch was ratified as an official language, equal in status to French – the forerunner of many long and difficult debates. Another matter of concern was the **Belgian Congo**. Determined to cut an international figure, Léopold II had decided to build up a colonial empire. The unfortunate recipients of his ambition were the Africans of the Congo River basin, who were effectively given to him by a conference of European powers in 1885. Ruling the Congo as a personal fiefdom, Léopold established an extraordinarily cruel colonial regime – so cruel in fact that even the other colonial powers were appalled and the Belgian state was obliged to end the embarrassment by taking over the region – as the Belgian Congo – in 1908.

The twentieth century to 1939

At the beginning of the twentieth century, Belgium was an industrial powerhouse with a booming economy and a rapidly increasing workforce – 934,000 in 1896, 1,176,000 in 1910. It was also determined to keep on good terms with all the Great Powers, but could not prevent getting caught up in **World War I**. Indifferent to Belgium's proclaimed neutrality, the Germans had decided as early as 1908 that the best way to attack France was via Belgium, and this is precisely what they did in 1914. They captured almost all of the country, the exception being a

Belgium's kings

Léopold I (1831–65). Foisted on Belgium by the Great Powers, Léopold, the first king of the Belgians, was imported from Germany, where he was the prince of Saxe-Coburg – and the uncle of Queen Victoria. Despite lacking a popular mandate, Léopold made a fairly good fist of things, keeping the country neutral as the Great Powers had ordained.

Léopold II (1865–1909). Energetic and forceful, Léopold II – son of Léopold I – encouraged the urbanization of his country and promoted its importance as a major industrial power. He was also the man responsible for landing Brussels with such pompous monuments as the Palais de Justice and for the imposition of a particularly barbaric colonial regime on the peoples of the Belgian Congo (now the Republic of Congo).

Albert I (1909–34). Easily the most popular of the dynasty, Albert's determined resistance to the German invasion of World War I, when the Germans occupied almost all of the country, made the king a national hero whose untimely death, in a climbing accident, traumatized the nation. Albert was the nephew of Léopold II and the father of Léopold III.

Léopold III (1934–51). In contrast to his father, Léopold III had the dubious honour of becoming one of Europe's least popular monarchs. His first wife died in a suspicious car crash; he nearly lost his kingdom by remarrying (then anathema in a Roman Catholic country); and he was badly compromised during the German occupation of World War II. During the war, Léopold remained in Belgium rather than face exile, fuelling rumours that he was a Nazi collaborator – though his supporters maintained that he prevented thousands of Belgians from being deported. After several years of heated postwar debate, during which the king remained in exile, the issue of Léopold's return was finally put to a referendum in 1950. Just over half the population voted in his favour, but there was a clear French/Flemish divide, with opposition to the king concentrated in French-speaking Wallonia. Fortunately for Belgium, Léopold abdicated in 1951 in favour of his son, Baudouin.

Baudouin I (1951–93). A softly spoken family man, Baudouin did much to restore the popularity of the monarchy, not least because he was generally thought to be even-handed in his treatment of the French- and Flemish-speaking communities. He also hit the headlines in April 1990 by standing down for a day so that an abortion bill (which he as a Catholic had refused to sign) could be passed. Childless, he was succeeded by his brother.

Albert II (1993–). Born in 1934, the present king (Baudouin's younger brother) is impeccably royal, from his Swiss finishing school to his aristocratic Italian wife, Queen Paola. Albert, a steady chap who looks distinctly avuncular, has proved a safe pair of hands, becoming a national figurehead in the manner of his predecessor and steering a diplomatic course through the shoals of Flemish–Wallonian antagonisms. Scandalously, though, Queen Paola was the first Belgian royal to be photographed in a swimming costume – and a bikini at that

narrow strip of territory around De Panne. Undaunted, **King Albert I** (1909–34) and the Belgian army bravely manned the northern part of the Allied line, and it made the king a national hero. The trenches ran through western Flanders and all the towns and villages lying close to them – principally Ieper (Ypres) and Diksmuide – were simply obliterated by artillery fire. Belgium also witnessed some of the worst of the slaughter in and around a bulge in the line, which became known as the **Ypres Salient** (see pp.137–141). The destruction was, however, confined to a narrow strip of Flanders and most of Belgium was practically untouched, though the local population did suffer during the occupation from lack of food, and hundreds of men were forced to work in German factories.

Political change in the 1920s and 1930s

After the war, under the terms of the **Treaty of Versailles**, Belgium was granted extensive reparations from Germany as well as some German territory – the slice of land around Eupen and Malmédy and, in Africa, Rwanda and Burundi. Domestically, the Belgian government extended the franchise to all men over the age of 21, a measure that subsequently ended several decades of **political control** by the Catholic party. The latter was now only able to keep power in coalition with the Liberals – usually with the Socialists, the third major party, forming the backbone of the opposition. The political lines were, however, increasingly fudged as the Catholic party moved left, becoming a Christian Democrat movement that was keen to cooperate with the Socialists on such matters as social legislation. The political parties may have been partly reconciled, but the **economy** staggered from crisis to crisis even before the effects of the Great Depression hit Belgium in 1929.

The political class also failed to placate those **Flemings** who felt discriminated against. There had been a widespread feeling among the Flemish soldiers of World War I that they had borne the brunt of the fighting and now an increasing number of Flemings came to believe – not without justification – that the Belgian government was overly Walloon in its sympathies. Only reluctantly did the government make Flanders and Wallonia legally unilingual regions in 1930, and even then the linguistic boundary was left unspecified in the hope that French-speakers would come to dominate central Belgium. Furthermore, changing expectations fuelled these **communal tensions**. The Flemings had accepted the domination of the French-speakers without much protest for several centuries, but as their region became more prosperous and as their numbers increased in relation to the Walloons, so they grew in self-confidence, becoming increasingly unhappy with their social and political subordination. Inevitably, some of this discontent was sucked into **Fascist** movements, which drew some ten percent of the vote in both the Walloon and Flemish communities, though for very different reasons: the former for its appeal to a nationalist bourgeoisie, the latter for its assertion of "racial" pride among an oppressed group.

World War II

The Germans invaded again in **May 1940**, launching a blitzkrieg that overwhelmed both Belgium and the Netherlands in short order. This time there was no heroic resistance by the Belgian king, now **Léopold III** (1934–51), who ignored the advice of his government and surrendered unconditionally and in such great haste that the British and French armies were, as their Commander-in-Chief put it, "suddenly faced with an open gap of twenty miles between Ypres and the sea through which enemy forces might reach the beaches". It is true that the Belgian army had been badly mauled and that a German victory was inevitable, but the manner of the surrender infuriated many Belgians, as did the king's refusal to form a government in exile. At first the occupation was relatively benign and most of the population waited apprehensively to see just what would happen. The main exception – setting aside the king, who at best played an ambivalent role – was the right-wing edge of the **Flemish Nationalist movement**, which cooperated with the Germans and (unsuccessfully) sought to negotiate the creation of a separate Flemish state. Popular opinion hardened against the Germans in 1942 as the occupation became more oppressive. The Germans stepped up the requisitioning of Belgian equipment, expanded its forced labour schemes, obliging thousands of Belgians to work in Germany, and cracked down hard on any sign of opposition. By the end of the year, a **Resistance** movement was mounting acts of sabotage against the occupying forces and this, in turn, prompted more summary executions of both Resistance fighters and hostages.

The summer of 1942 witnessed the first roundups of the country's **Jews**. In 1940, there were approximately 50,000 Jews in Belgium, mostly newly arrived refugees from Hitler's Germany. Much to their credit, many Belgians did their best to frustrate German efforts to transport the Jews out of the country, usually to Auschwitz: the Belgian police did not cooperate, Belgian railway workers left carriages unlocked and/or sidelined trains, and many other Belgians hid Jews in their homes for the duration. The result was that the Germans had, by 1944, killed about half the country's Jewish population, a much lower proportion than in other parts of occupied Europe. With the occupation hardening, the vast majority of Belgians were delighted to hear of the D-Day landings in June 1944. The **liberation** of Belgium began in September with the American troops in the south and the British and Canadian divisions sweeping across Flanders in the north.

1945–2005

After the war, the Belgians set about the task of economic **reconstruction**, helped by aid from the United States, but hindered by a divisive controversy over the wartime activities of **King Léopold**. Inevitably, the complex shadings of collaboration and forced cooperation were hard to disentangle, and the debate continued until 1950 when a **referendum** narrowly recommended his return as king from exile. Léopold's return was, however, marked by rioting across Wallonia, where the king's opponents were concentrated, and Léopold **abdicated** in favour of his son, **Baudouin**.

Otherwise, the development of the **postwar** Belgian economy followed the pattern of most of western Europe – boom in the 1960s; recession in the 1970s; and retrenchment in the 1980s and 1990s. Significant events included the belated extension of the franchise to women in 1948; an ugly, disorganized and hasty evacuation of the Belgian Congo in 1960 and of Rwanda and Burundi in 1962; and the transformation of Brussels from one of the lesser European capitals into a major player when it became the home of the EU and NATO (the latter organization was ejected from France on the orders of de Gaulle in 1967). There was also acute **labour unrest** in the Limburg coalfield in the early 1980s, following plans to close most of the remaining pits; a right royal pantomime when Catholic King Baudouin abdicated for the day while the law legalizing **abortion** was ratified in 1990; and public outrage in 1996 when the Belgian police proved itself at best hopelessly inefficient, at worst complicit, in the gruesome activities of the child murderer and pornographer **Marc Dutroux**. The Euro currency was introduced in January 2002; the legalization of same-sex marriages came in 2003 and the same year saw the government formally opposing the invasion of Iraq.

Communal tensions take centre stage

Above all, the postwar period was dominated by increasing **tension** between the Walloon and Flemish communities, a state of affairs that was entangled with the economic decline of Wallonia, formerly the home of most of the country's heavy industry, as compared with burgeoning Flanders. One result of the tension was that every **national institution** became dogged by the prerequisites of bilingualism and at the same time all the main political parties created separate Flemish- and French-speaking sections. Bogged down by these inter-communal preoccupations, the federal government often appeared extraordinarily cumbersome, but there again much of the political class came to be at least partly reliant on the linguistic divide for their jobs and, institutionally speaking, had little incentive to see the antagonisms resolved. **Regional government** was also transformed by this communal rivalry. The country had long been divided into provinces, but superimposed on this, in 1962, was the **Language Divide** (see box opposite), which recognized three linguistic communities – French-, Flemish- and German-speaking. This was supplemented, in 1980, by the division of the country into three **regions**, one each for the French and Flemish, with Brussels, the third, designated a bilingual region. The transfer of major areas of administration from the centre to the regions followed.

Belgium today

In 1999, **Guy Verhofstadt**, the leader of the Liberal VLD, cobbled together a centre-left coalition and repeated this political feat after the federal elections of 2003. Matters might then have proceeded fairly smoothly had it not been for a bitter conflict between French- and Flemish-speaking politicians over the electoral arrangements pertaining to **Brussels-Halle-Vilvoorde** (BHV for short). This extraordinarily complex dispute sapped the strength of the national government and, after the **federal elections of 2007**, no politician was able to construct a ruling coalition and the country was left rudderless for several months. Eventually, a government was formed, but the new Prime Minister – **Yves Leterme** – was soon struggling to keep his coalition afloat and as a result he tendered his resignation to the king in July 2008. It was rejected and Leterme soldiered on, but the instability at the heart of the national government remained, with a political carousel of resignations and changing party alliances. There were new federal elections in June 2010,

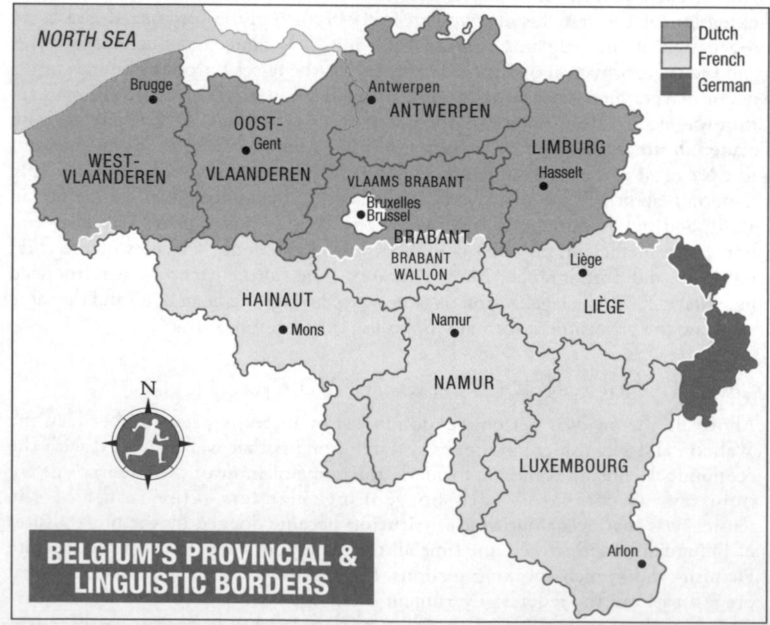

The Belgian Language Divide

There are almost eleven million Belgians, divided between two main groups. The **Flemings**, Dutch- or Flemish- speakers, are concentrated in the north of the country, and form about sixty percent of the population; to the south are the **Walloons**, French-speakers, who account for around forty percent. There are also, in the far east of the country, a few pockets of **German**-speakers around the towns of Eupen and Malmédy.

The Flemish–French **language divide** has troubled the country for decades, its significance rooted in deep class and economic divisions. When the Belgian state was founded in 1830, its ruling and middle classes were predominantly French-speaking, and they created the new state in their linguistic image: French was the official language and Flemish was banned in schools. This Francophone domination was subsequently reinforced by the way the economy developed, with Wallonia becoming a major coal mining and steel-producing area, whilst Flanders remained a predominantly agricultural, rural backwater. There were nationalist stirrings among the Flemings from the 1880s onwards, but it was only after World War II – when Flanders became the country's economic powerhouse as Wallonia declined – that the demand for linguistic and cultural parity became irresistible. In the way of such things, the Walloons read Flemish "parity" as "domination", setting the scene for all sorts of inter-communal hassle.

As a response to this burgeoning animosity, the **Language Frontier** was formally drawn across the country in 1962, cutting the country in half from west to east. The aim was to distinguish between the French- and Flemish-speaking communities and thereby defuse tensions, but it didn't work. In 1980, this failure prompted another attempt to rectify matters with the redrafting of the constitution and the creation of a federal system, with three separate **communities** – the Flemish North, the Walloon South and the German-speaking east – responsible for their own cultural and social affairs and education. At the same time, Belgium was divided into three **regions** — the Flemish North, the Walloon South and bilingual Brussels, with each regional authority dealing with matters like economic development, the environment and employment.

In hindsight, the niceties of this partition have done little to calm troubled waters, and right across Belgium discontent on almost any matter – but especially immigration and unemployment – smoulders within (or seeks an outlet through) the framework of this linguistic division; even individual neighbourhoods can be paralyzed by language disputes, with **Brussels-Halle-Vilvoorde** (BHV; see opposite) being a case in point.

All this said, it would be wrong to assume that Belgium's language differences have gone beyond the level of personal animosity and institutionalized mutual suspicion. Belgian **language extremists** have been imprisoned over the years, but very few, if any, have died in the fight for supremacy. Indeed, some might see a bilingual nation as a positive thing in a Europe where trading – and national – barriers are being increasingly broken down. Suggesting this to a Belgian, however, is normally useless, but there again the casual visitor will rarely get a sniff of these tensions. It's probably better to speak English rather than Flemish or French in the "wrong" part of Belgium, but if you make a mistake, the worst you'll get is a look of glazed indifference.

but the results did nothing to hold the centre: the largest party in Flanders was the right-wing, separatist **Nieuw-Vlaamse Alliantie** (NVA; New Flemish Alliance), under the controversial leadership of Bart de Wever, while Wallonia went left with the winners being the **Parti Socialiste** (PS; Socialist Party) led by Elio Di Rupo. At time of writing, no ruling coalition had emerged from the 2010 elections and a caretaker government under Yves Leterme had taken over as the political horse-trading continued. Not for the first time, the breakup of Belgium seems a distinct possibility, but there is one intractable problem: who gets Brussels – and this may in itself be enough to hold things together.

These political difficulties reflect deep inter-communal tensions. In essence, the **Walloons** fear that the wealthier and more numerous Flemings will come to dominate the state, and indeed they may make this a self-fulfilling prophecy with their reluctance to learn Flemish – bilingualism being a prerequisite for any national job. The **Flemings**, on the other hand, want political and cultural recognition, and many bristle at what they perceive as Wallonian cultural and linguistic arrogance. These tensions can, however, be exaggerated. In 2006, a Belgian TV station, RTBF, mounted an elaborate spoof, saying that the Dutch-speaking half of the country had declared independence. There were pictures of cheering crowds waving the Flemish flag and of trams stuck at the new international border, but few Belgians were jubilant and instead there was widespread alarm, bordering on horror. Polls indicate that a clear majority of Belgians want their country to survive, though few would give the same reason as the country's most popular writer, the recently deceased **Hugo Claus**, who wrote "I insist on being Belgian. I want to be a member of the pariah nationality, the laughing stock of the French and the object of contempt of the Dutch. It's the ideal situation for a writer."

The Grand Duchy of Luxembourg from 1830

At the Congress of Vienna in 1815, Luxembourg had been designated a **Grand Duchy** by the Great Powers and given (as personal property) to King William I of Orange-Nassau, the ruler of the United Kingdom of the Netherlands (see p.364). After Belgium broke away from William's kingdom in 1830, Luxembourg remained the property of the Dutch monarchy until 1890 when the ducal crown passed to another (independent) branch of the Nassau family, who have ruled there ever since. In 1867, the Great Powers made further decisions about Luxembourg: the **Treaty of London** reaffirmed the duchy's territorial integrity and declared it neutral in perpetuity, thereby – it was hoped – protecting it from the clutches of both Germany and France. Following this declaration, Luxembourg City's fortifications were largely demolished.

The second half of the nineteenth century saw Luxembourg's agricultural economy transformed by the discovery, and then the mining, of **iron ore deposits**, which led to the foundation of what was soon one of Europe's largest steel industries. In 1914, the Grand Duchy confirmed its neutrality, but was still occupied by the Germans – as it was again in **World War II** when the Luxembourgers put up a stubborn resistance, leading to many brave acts of defiance and considerable loss of life. In particular, the Battle of the Bulge (see p.307) was a major disaster for Luxembourg – and as the war ended in 1945, one-third of the country's farmland lay uncultivated, the public transportation system was in ruins, and some sixty thousand people were homeless.

In the **postwar years**, reconstruction was rapid, though there was a major crisis in the mid-1970s when the iron and steel industry hit the economic buffers, obliging the government to pursue a policy of industrial diversification, with the main area of growth being the **financial sector**, which now accounts for one third of the duchy's tax revenues. Luxembourg also forsook its policy of neutrality, opting to join both NATO and the EC (EU), where it has often played a conciliatory role between the larger countries. In striking contrast to its neighbour, the duchy has also been extremely stable politically: the **Christian Social People's Party** (CSV) has been in power almost continuously since 1945, and the present Prime Minister, **Jean-Claude Juncker**, has been in office since 1995.

Belgian art

From medieval times, the Low Countries and its successor states – the Netherlands, Belgium and Luxembourg – have produced some of Europe's finest **artists**, whose work has been digested and analysed in countless art books, some of which are reviewed in the "Books" section on p.377. This book doesn't have the space to cover the subject in any great detail, but the text below provides some background on ten of the country's most important **painters**. You'll see their work in museums across Belgium, but especially in Antwerp, Brussels and Bruges. The one major omission here is **René Magritte** – for more on whom, see the box on p.80.

Jan van Eyck

Medieval Flanders was one of the most artistically productive parts of Europe with each of the cloth towns, especially Bruges and Ghent, trying to outdo its rivals with the quality of its religious art. Today, the works of these early Flemish painters, known as the **Flemish Primitives**, are highly prized and an excellent sample is displayed in Ghent, Bruges and Brussels. **Jan van Eyck** (1385–1441) is generally regarded as the first of the Flemish Primitives, and has even been credited with the invention of oil painting itself – though it seems more likely that he simply perfected a new technique by thinning his paint with (the newly discovered) turpentine, thus making it more flexible. His fame partially stems from the fact that he was one of the first artists to sign his work – an indication of how highly his talent was regarded by his contemporaries. Van Eyck's most celebrated work is the *Adoration of the Mystic Lamb*, a stunningly beautiful altarpiece displayed in St-Baafskathedraal in Ghent (see p.183). The painting was revolutionary in its realism, for the first time using elements of native landscape in depicting biblical themes, and was underpinned by a complex symbolism which has generated analysis and discussion ever since.

Rogier van der Weyden

Apprenticed in Tournai and the one-time official painter to the city of Brussels, **Rogier van der Weyden** (1400–64) turned his hand to both secular and religious subjects with equal facility. His serene portraits of the bigwigs of his day were much admired across a large swathe of western Europe, their popularity enabling him to set up a workshop manned by apprentices and assistants, who helped him with his work (and have often made authentication of his paintings problematic). In 1450, Weyden seems to have undertaken a pilgrimage to Rome and although contact with his Italian contemporaries does not appear to have had much effect on his paintings, it did bring him several rewarding commissions. Perhaps, above all, it's his religious works that are of special appeal: warm and emotional, sensitive and dramatic, as in *St Luke painting the Portrait of Our Lady*, now displayed in Bruges (see p.160).

Hans Memling

Born near Frankfurt, but active in Bruges, **Hans Memling** (1440–94) was almost certainly a pupil of van der Weyden (see above), from whom he learnt an exquisite attention to detail. Memling is best remembered for the pastoral charm of his landscapes and the quality of his **portraiture**, producing restrained and impeccably crafted works that often survive on the rescued side-panels of triptychs. His **religious paintings** are similarly delightful, formal compositions that still pack an emotional punch – as exemplified by his *Moreel Triptych* (see p.161). The Memling collection in Bruges (see p.165) has a wonderful sample of his work.

Hieronymus Bosch

One of the most distinctive of the early Netherlandish painters, **Hieronymus Bosch** (1450–1516) lived in the southern Netherlands for most of his life, though his style is linked to that of his Flemish contemporaries. About forty examples of his work survive, but none is dated and no accurate chronology can be made. Nonetheless, it seems likely that his more conventional religious paintings, like *The Crucifixion* in the Musées Royaux in Brussels (see pp.76–81), were completed early on. Bosch is, however, much more famous for his **religious allegories**: frantic, frenetic paintings filled with macabre visions of tortured souls and grotesque beasts. At first glance, these works seem almost unhinged, but it's now thought that they are visual representations of contemporary sayings, idioms and parables. While their interpretation is far from resolved, Bosch's paintings draw strongly on subconscious fears and archetypes, giving them a lasting, haunting fascination.

Quinten Matsys

Following Flanders' decline at the end of the fifteenth century, the leading artists of the day migrated to the booming port of Antwerp, where they began to integrate the finely observed detail that characterized the Flemish tradition with the style of the Italian painters of the Renaissance in what is sometimes called the **Antwerp School**. A leading light of this school was **Quinten Matsys** (1464–1530), who was born in Leuven but spent most of his working life in Antwerp. Matsys introduced florid classical architectural details and intricate landscapes to his work, influenced perhaps by Leonardo da Vinci. As well as religious pieces, he also painted portraits and **genre scenes**, all of which have recognizably Italian facets and features, thereby paving the way for the Dutch genre painters of later years.

Pieter Bruegel the Elder

The greatest Netherlandish painter of the sixteenth century, **Pieter Bruegel the Elder** (c.1525–69) remains a shadowy figure, but it seems probable he was born in Breda in the Netherlands, and he certainly travelled widely, visiting France and Italy (where he was impressed by the Alps rather than the Italian painters) and working in both Antwerp and Brussels. Many of his early works were landscapes, but in the 1560s he turned his skills to the gruesome **allegories** and innovative interpretations of religious subjects for which he is now most famous – as in *The Fall of the Rebel Angels* and *The Fall of Icarus* (see p.78). Pieter also turned out a number of finely observed **peasant scenes**, genre paintings that influenced generations of Low Country artists. Bruegel's two sons, **Pieter Bruegel the Younger**

(1564–1638) and **Jan Bruegel** (1568–1625) were lesser painters: the former produced fairly insipid copies of his father's work, though Jan developed a style of his own, producing delicately rendered flower paintings and genre pieces that earned him the nickname "Velvet".

Pieter Paul Rubens

Easily the most important exponent of the Baroque in northern Europe, **Rubens** (1577–1640) was born in Siegen, Westphalia, but raised in Antwerp, where he entered the painters' guild in 1598. He became court painter to the Duke of Mantua in 1600, and until 1608 travelled extensively in Italy, absorbing the classical architecture and the art of the High Renaissance. By the time of his return to Antwerp he had acquired an enormous artistic vocabulary: the paintings of **Caravaggio** in particular were to influence his work strongly. His first major success was *The Raising of the Cross*, painted in 1610 and displayed today in Antwerp cathedral (see p.212). A large, dynamic work, it caused a sensation at the time, establishing Rubens' reputation and leading to a string of commissions. *The Descent from the Cross*, his next major work (also in the cathedral), consolidated this success; equally Baroque, it is nevertheless quieter and more restrained. Thereafter, he was able to set up his own **studio**, where he gathered a team of talented artists (among them Anthony van Dyck and Jacob Jordaens). The subsequent division of labour ensured a high rate of productivity and a degree of personal flexibility; the degree to which Rubens personally worked on a canvas would vary – and would determine its price. From the early 1620s onwards Rubens turned his hand to a plethora of themes and subjects – religious works, portraits, tapestry designs, landscapes, mythological scenes, ceiling paintings – each of which was handled with supreme vitality and virtuosity. From his Flemish antecedents he inherited an acute sense of light, using it not to dramatize his subjects (a technique favoured by Caravaggio and other Italian artists), but in association with colour and form. The drama in his works comes from the vigorous animation of his characters. His **large-scale allegorical works**, especially, are packed with heaving, writhing figures that appear to tumble out from the canvas. The energy of Rubens' paintings was reflected in his **private life**. In addition to his career as an artist, he also undertook diplomatic missions to Spain and England, and used these opportunities to study the works of other artists and – as in the case of Velázquez – to meet them personally. In the 1630s, gout began to hamper his activities, and from this time his painting became more domestic and meditative. **Hélène Fourment**, his second wife, was the subject of many portraits and served as a model for characters in his allegorical paintings, her figure epitomizing the buxom, well-rounded women found throughout his work.

Anthony van Dyck

Anthony van Dyck (1599–1641) worked in Rubens' studio for two years from 1618, often taking on the depiction of religious figures in his master's works that required particular sensitivity and pathos. Like Rubens, van Dyck was born in Antwerp and travelled widely in Italy, though Rubens influenced his initial work much more than his Italian contemporaries. Eventually, van Dyck developed his own distinct style and technique, establishing himself as court painter to Charles I in England from 1632, and creating **portraits** of a nervous elegance that would influence portraiture there for the next hundred and fifty years. Most of his great portrait paintings remain in England, but his best religious works – such as the *Crucifixion* in Mechelen's cathedral (see p.234) – can be found in Belgium.

James Ensor

Born to an English father and a Belgian mother, **James Ensor** (1860–1949) lived in Ostend for almost all of his long life, and was one of Belgium's most original artists. His early works were bourgeois in tone and content, a mixed bag of portraits and domestic interiors that gave little hint as to what was to follow. In the 1880s, he was snubbed by the artistic elite in Brussels and this seems to have prompted a major rethink, for shortly afterwards he picked up on the subject matter which was to dominate his paintings thereafter: macabre, disturbing works of skeletons, grotesques and horrid **carnival masks**, whose haunted style can be traced back to Bosch and Bruegel. As such, Ensor was a formative influence on the Expressionists and was claimed as a forerunner by several leading Surrealists.

Marcel Broodthaers

Born in Brussels, **Marcel Broodthaers** (1924–76) is one of Belgium's most celebrated modern artists, a witty and multi-talented man who doubled as a film-maker and journalist. He also tried his hand as a poet, but in 1964, after twenty largely unsuccessful years, he gave up, symbolically encasing fifty unsold copies of his poetry in plaster and thereby, somewhat accidentally, launching himself as an artist. Initially, Broodthaers worked in the Surrealist manner with found objects and collage, but he soon branched out, graduating from cut-paper geometric shapes into both the plastic arts and the sharp and brightly coloured **paintings** of everyday artefacts, especially casseroles brimming with mussels, for which he became famous. Broodthaers summed himself up like this: "I wondered whether I could not sell something and succeed in life . . . Finally the idea of inventing something insincere crossed my mind and I set to work straight away".

Books

Most of the **books** listed below are in print and in paperback, and those that are out of print (o/p) should be easy to track down either in secondhand bookshops or online. Titles marked with the ★ symbol are especially recommended. Popular Belgian authors in print, but not in English, include Serge Delaive, Stefan Hertmans and Caroline Lamarche.

Travel and general

Charlotte and Emily Brontë (ed. Sue Lonoff) *The Belgian Essays*. The Brontë sisters left their native Yorkshire for the first time in 1842 to make a trip to Brussels; and Charlotte returned to Brussels the following year. This handsome volume, published by Yale in 1997, reproduces the twenty-eight essays they penned (in French) during their journey and provides the English translation opposite. A delightful read with particular highlights being *The Butterfly*, *The Caterpillar* and *The Death of Napoleon*.

Hilde Deweer *All Belgian Beers*. This is the most comprehensive guide on the market, with 1568 pages covering its subject in extravagant detail. Everything you ever wanted to know about Belgian beer and then some.

Michael Farr *Tintin: The Complete Companion*. This immaculately illustrated book – written by one of the world's leading Tintinologists – explores every aspect of Hergé's remarkably popular creation. It's particularly strong on the real-life stories that inspired Hergé, but you do have to be seriously interested in Tintin to really enjoy it. Farr has written a string of books on Tintin, and this was published in 2002; the latest is the comparable *Tintin & Co* of 2007.

Hergé *The Calculus Affair* and *Tintin: Explorers on the Moon*. Tintin comic strips come in and out of print at a rapid rate, usually in anthologies; there's a wide selection of audio cassettes too. The two anthologies listed here are as good a place as any to start.

Bruce McCall *Sit!: The Dog Portraits of Thierry Poncelet* (o/p). This weird and wonderful book features the work of Belgian Thierry Poncelet, who raids flea markets and antique shops for ancestral portraits, then restores them and paints dogs' heads over the original faces.

Benoit Peeters *Tintin and the World of Hergé: an Illustrated History* (o/p). Examines the life and career of Hergé, particularly the development of Tintin, and the influences on his work, with no fewer than three hundred illustrations.

★ **Luc Sante** *The Factory of Facts*. Born in Belgium but raised in the US, Sante returned to his native land for an extended visit in 1989, at the age of 35. His book is primarily a personal reflection, but he also uses this as a base for a thoughtful exploration of Belgium and the Belgians – from art to food and beyond.

Marianne Thys *Filmography of Belgian Movies, 1896–1996*. This authoritative hardback volume has reviews of every Belgian film ever made. Published in 2000, it's 992 pages long, as is reflected in the cost.

★ **Tim Webb** *Good Beer Guide to Belgium*. Belgium produces the best beers in the world; Webb is one of the best beer writers in the world – and the result is the best book on its subject on the market: cheeky, palatable and sinewy, with just a hint of fruitiness. Belgium's best bars, beers and breweries are covered in loving, liver-drowning detail. Webb's *100 Belgian Beers to Try Before You Die!* is similarly excellent.

History and politics

Neal Ascherson *The King Incorporated: Leopold the Second and the Congo*. Belgium's King Léopold II was responsible for one of the cruellest of colonial regimes, a savage system of repression and exploitation that devastated the Belgian Congo. Ascherson details it all.

Malcolm Balen *A Model Victory: Waterloo and the Battle for History*. Some twenty years after Waterloo, the British government asked Lieutenant William Siborne, a great fan of the Duke of Wellington, to prepare a scale model of the battle. They assumed that he would depict the start of the engagement, but he chose the crisis instead – and this is where he came unstuck. Based on interviews with scores of Waterloo veterans, Siborne's model had the Prussian army arriving on the battlefield earlier than the duke claimed, thereby taking some of the glory from the British army. Siborne felt the full fury of Wellington's ire – and this much-praised book details it all.

J.C.H. Blom (ed.) *History of the Low Countries* (o/p). Belgian history books are thin on the ground, so this incisive, well-balanced volume is very welcome. A series of historians weigh in with their specialities to build a comprehensive picture of the region from the Celts and Romans through to the 1980s. Hardly deckchair reading, but highly recommended nonetheless.

Nicholas Crane *Mercator*. Arguably the most important map-maker of all time, Gerard Mercator was born in Rupelmonde near Antwerp in 1512. This book details every twist and turn of his life and provides oodles – perhaps too many oodles – of background material on the Flanders of his time.

Paul Fussell *The Boys' Crusade*. This concise and well-written book zeroes in on the experience of the (very youthful) American troops who fought in Europe in World War II, and includes an especially revealing section on the Battle of the Bulge.

Galbert of Bruges *The Murder of Charles the Good*. A contemporaneous chronicle of the tempestuous events that rattled early twelfth-century Bruges, this detailed yarn gives all sorts of insights into medieval Flanders.

Pieter Geyl *The Revolt of The Netherlands 1555–1609*. Geyl presents a detailed account of the Netherlands during its formative years, chronicling the uprising against the Spanish and both the formation of the United Provinces and the creation of the Spanish Netherlands (the Belgium of today). First published in 1932, it has long been regarded as the classic text on the subject, though it's a hard and ponderous read.

Craig Harline and Eddy Put *A Bishop's Tale*. An unusual book based on the journals of Mathias Hovius, who was Archbishop of Mechelen in the early seventeenth century. It is, perhaps, a little too detailed to enthral the average reader, but it does provide a real insight into the period – its preoccupations and problems.

Christopher Hibbert *Waterloo*. For many years, Hibbert (who died in 2008) was one of Britain's leading historians, an astute commentator who wrote in a fluent and easily accessible style. This three-part book examines Napoleon's rise to power; Wellington and his allies; and the battle itself. Hibbert was also responsible for editing *The Wheatley Diary*, the journal and sketchbook of a young English officer who fought his way across Europe during the Napoleonic Wars.

Adam Hochschild *King Leopold's Ghost*. Harrowing

account of King Léopold's savage colonial regime in the Congo, explaining, exploring and assessing all its gruesome workings. Particularly good on Roger Casement, the one-time British consul to the Congo, who publicized the cruelty and helped bring it to an end. Hochschild's last chapter, *The Great Forgetting*, is a stern criticism of the Belgians for their failure to acknowledge their brutal colonial history.

Lisa Jardine *The Awful End of Prince William the Silent*. Great title for an intriguing book on the premature demise of one of the Low Countries' most acclaimed Protestant heroes, who led the revolt against Habsburg Spain and was assassinated in 1584 for his pains. The tale is told succinctly, but – unless you have a particular interest in early firearms – there is a bit too much information on guns.

B.H. Liddell Hart (ed.) *The Letters of Private Wheeler 1809–1828*. A veteran of World War I, Liddell Hart writes with panache and clarity, marshalling the letters penned by the eponymous private as he fought Napoleon and the French across a fair slice of Europe. Wheeler fought at Waterloo, but the section on the battle is surprisingly brief. As a whole, the letters are a delight, a witty insight into the living conditions and attitudes of Wellington's infantry. In similar vein, his *History of the Second World War* (o/p) is an excellent introduction to military strategy and tactics. Hart always claimed (with some justification) that he foresaw the potential importance of tanks – a voice crying in the British military wilderness before Hitler unveiled his blitzkrieg on, among many others, the poor old Belgian army.

Philip Mansel *Prince of Europe: the Life of Charles Joseph de Ligne (1735–1814)*. The Habsburg aristocracy, which dominated the Austrian Netherlands (Belgium) in the eighteenth century, has rarely come under the historical spotlight, but this weighty tome partly remedies the situation. This particular aristocrat, the priapic Charles Joseph, was a multifaceted man, a gardener and a general, a curious traveller and a diplomat and the owner of the château of Beloeil (see p.264). Mansel explores his life and milieu thoroughly and entertainingly.

Jules Marchal *Lord Leverhulme's Ghosts: Colonial Exploitation in the Congo*. In his later years, Jules Marchal, who had been a Belgian diplomat in the Congo, became incensed by the suppression of information on the cruelties inflicted by his countrymen on the Congolese. After he retired in 1989, he spent fourteen years researching this same colonial history, producing seven extremely detailed books on the subject, four on the Léopold regime and three on forced labour from 1910 to 1945. Only one has been translated into English, and this is it, with the spotlight falling on the British entrepreneur Lord Leverhulme, who came to the Congo to exploit its rubber and was perfectly happy to take advantage of King Léopold's system of forced labour.

Janet Morgan *The Secrets of Rue St Roch*. Intriguing account of British spy operations in occupied Luxembourg during World War I. Drawn from the assorted documents of a certain Captain George Wellington, a Paris-based intelligence officer who ran several agents, including a Belgian soldier who began by landing behind enemy lines in a balloon.

Geoffrey Parker *The Dutch Revolt*. Compelling account of the struggle between the Netherlands and Spain. Quite the best thing you can read on the period, even if it is out of print. Parker's *The Army of Flanders and the Spanish Road 1567–1659* may sound academic, but gives a fascinating insight into the Habsburg army that occupied the

Low Countries for well over a hundred years – how it functioned, was fed and moved from Spain to the Low Countries along the so-called Spanish Road.

Andrew Wheatcroft *The Habsburgs*. An excellent and well-researched trawl through the dynasty's history, from its eleventh-century beginnings to its eclipse at the end of World War I. Enjoyable background reading.

Geoffrey Wootten *Waterloo 1815*. About one-third of the length of Hibbert's *Waterloo* (see p.378), this 96-page book focuses on the battle, providing a clear, thorough and interesting account.

World War I

William Allison & John Fairley *The Monocled Mutineer* (o/p). An antidote to all those tales of soldiers dying for their country in World War I, this little book recounts the story of one Percy Toplis, a Nottinghamshire lad turned soldier, mutineer, racketeer and conman who was finally shot by the police in 1920. Includes an intriguing account of the large-scale mutiny that broke out along the British line in 1917.

Paul Fussell *The Great War and Modern Memory*. Intriguing take on World War I, giving prominence to the rants, epistles, poems and letters of those British soldiers who were caught up in it – and, by implication, the effect it had on British society as a whole.

Robert Graves *Goodbye To All That*. Written in 1929, this is the classic story of life in the trenches. Bleak and painful memories of World War I army service written by Graves, a wounded survivor.

Martin Gilbert *First World War*. Highly regarded account of the war focused on the battles and experiences of the British army. Very thorough – at 680 pages.

Siegfried Sassoon *The Memoirs of an Infantry Officer*. Sassoon's moving and painfully honest account of his experiences in the trenches of the World War I. A classic, and infinitely readable.

A.J.P. Taylor *The First World War: An Illustrated History*. First published in 1963, this superbly written and pertinently illustrated history offers a penetrating analysis of how the war started and why it went on for so long, plus a fine section on events in the Ypres Salient. Many of Taylor's deductions were controversial at the time, but such was the power of his arguments that much of what he said is now mainstream history.

Art and architecture

Ulrike Becks-Malorny *Ensor*. Eminently readable and extensively illustrated account of the life and art of the often neglected James Ensor, one of the country's finest painters.

Kristin Lohse Belkin *Rubens*. Too long for its own good, this book details Rubens' spectacularly successful career both as artist and diplomat. Belkin is particularly thorough in her discussions of technique and the workings of his workshop, while extensive reference is made to Rubens' letters. Excellent illustrations.

Robin Blake *Anthony van Dyck*. Whether or not van Dyck justifies a book of this considerable length is a moot point, but he did have an interesting life and certainly thumped out a fair few paintings. This volume explores every artistic nook and cranny.

Till-Holger Borchert *Jan van Eyck*. Not much is known about van Eyck, but Borchert has done his best to root out every detail in this nicely balanced and attractively illustrated 100-page Taschen book. Borchert has also written *Van Eyck to Dürer: The Influence of Early Netherlandish Painting on European Art, 1430–1530*, beautifully illustrated and covering its subject with academic rigour (it's 432 pages long). Similarly detailed is Borchert's *Bruegel: The Complete Paintings, Drawings and Prints*, which he co-authored with Manfred Sellink.

Walter Bosing *Bosch: The Complete Paintings*. Attractive little book in the Taschen art series that covers its subject in just the right amount of detail (it's 96 pages long). Well conceived and well illustrated.

Aurora Cuito (ed) *Victor Horta*. Concise and readily digestible guide to the work of Victor Horta, Belgium's leading exponent of Art Nouveau (see p.91). Since its publication in 2002, the book has become something of a collector's item, so unless you have a special interest – or lots of money – you'll probably want to settle for a secondhand copy.

Rudi H. Fuchs *Dutch Painting*. As complete an introduction to the subject as you could wish for, in just a couple of hundred pages. Particularly good on the early Flemish masters. Published in the 1970s, so an update would be welcome.

Suzi Gablik *Magritte*. Gablik lived in Magritte's house for six months in the 1960s and this personal contact informs the text, which is lucid, perceptive and thoughtful. Most of the illustrations are, however, black and white. At 208 pages, it's also much longer than the Hammacher version (see below).

Walter S. Gibson *Hieronymus Bosch* and *Bruegel*. Two wonderfully illustrated titles on these two exquisite allegorical painters. The former contains everything you wanted to know about Bosch, his paintings and his late fifteenth-century environment, while the latter takes a detailed look at Pieter Bruegel the Elder's art, with nine well-argued chapters investigating its various components.

Rachel Haidu *Absence of Work*. Haidu, an American art professor, clearly has a real respect for the Belgian artist Marcel Broodthaers, and it shows in this detailed exploration of his life and times, work and philosophy.

A.M. Hammacher *René Magritte* (o/p). This well-written and beautifully illustrated book provides a detailed examination of Magritte's life, times and artistic output. At just 128 pages, it's concise, too.

Stephan Kemperdick *Rogier van der Weyden*. Van der Weyden is something of a shadowy figure, but Kemperdick does well to muster what information there is – and the analysis of the paintings is first-rate.

Mark Lamster *Master of Shadows: The Secret Diplomatic Career of Peter Paul Rubens*. Detailed investigation of Rubens' work as a spy and diplomat it's a wonder he ever got round to the painting.

Alfred Michiels *Hans Memling* Thorough and very workmanlike investigation of the life and times of Hans Memling with a particularly good chapter on his major works. Extensively illustrated.

Gilles Neret *Rubens*. This Taschen art book is a well-composed and concise introduction to the great man, his times and his art.

Literature

Mark Bles *A Child at War* (o/p). This powerful book describes the tribulations of Hortense Daman, a Belgian girl who joined the Resistance at the tender age of fifteen. Betrayed to the Gestapo, Daman was sent to the Ravensbruck concentration camp, where she was used in medical experiments, but remarkably survived. This is her story, though the book would have benefited from some editorial pruning.

Hugo Claus *The Sorrow of Belgium.* Claus was generally regarded as Belgium's foremost Flemish-language novelist, and this was his finest novel, charting the growing maturity of a young boy living in Flanders under the Nazi occupation. Claus' style is dense to say the least, but the book gets to grips with the guilt, bigotry and mistrust of the period, and caused a minor uproar when it was first published in the early 1980s. His *Swordfish* is a story of an isolated village rife with ethnic and religious tensions which precipitate a boy's descent into madness, while *Desire* is a strange and disconcerting tale of two drinking buddies who, on an impulse, abandon small-town Belgium for Las Vegas, where both of them start to unravel.

Alan Hollinghurst *The Folding Star.* Not a Belgian novel, but a British writer's evocation of a thinly disguised Bruges, in a compelling novel of sex, mystery and obsession. The enthusiastic descriptions of gay male sexual encounters make this a climactic book in more ways than one.

Barbara Kingsolver *The Poisonwood Bible: A Novel.* In 1959, an American Baptist missionary and his family set out to convert souls in the jungly depths of the Belgian Congo. They are unprepared for the multiple disasters that befall them – from great, stinging ants to irregular Congolese soldiers.

Amelie Nothomb *Hygiene and the Assassin.* English-language translations of modern Belgian books are a rarity, but Nothomb, one of Belgium's most popular novelists, has made the linguistic leap. This particular novel deals with a terminally ill prizewinning author, who grants deathbed interviews to five journalists. A deeply unpleasant man, the protagonist is only unpicked by his last interviewer – to stunning effect. Other Nothomb novels in translation include *The Stranger Next Door*, featuring weird and disconcerting happenings in the Belgian countryside, and the controversial *Sulphuric Acid*, where a Big Brother-style show turns into a blood-fest in the manner of a concentration camp – hence the furore.

Jean Ray *Malpertuis.* This spine-chilling Gothic novel was written in 1943 by Ghent's own Raymundus de Kremer, who adopted the pen name Jean Ray for his novels – he also turned out comic strips under the guise of John Flanders. The novel is set in Flanders, where the suffocating Catholicism of the Inquisition provides a suitably atmospheric backdrop.

Georges Rodenbach *Bruges la Morte.* First published in 1892, this slim and subtly evocative novel is all about love and obsession – or rather a highly stylized, decadent view of it. It's credited with starting the craze for visiting Bruges, the "dead city" where the action unfolds.

Georges Simenon *Maigret Loses His Temper* and *Maigret And The Killer.* There can be no dispute that Simenon was Belgium's most famous crime writer, his main creation being the Parisian detective Maigret. There are dozens of books to choose from – these two ripping yarns can get you started.

Emile Zola *Germinal.* First published in 1885, and the inspiration for a whole generation of Belgian radicals, *Germinal* exposed the harsh conditions of the coal mines of northeast France. It was also a rallying call to action with the protagonist, Etienne Lantier, organizing a strike. A vivid, powerful work, Zola had a detailed knowledge of the mines – how they were run and worked – and makes passing reference to the coalfields of southern Belgium, where conditions and working practices were identical.

Language

Language

Flemish and French

Throughout the **northern part of Belgium**, in the provinces of East and West Flanders, Antwerp, Limburg and Flemish Brabant, the principal language is **Dutch**, which is spoken in a variety of distinctive dialects commonly (if inaccurately) lumped together as **Flemish**. Flemish-speakers have equal language rights in the capital, Brussels, where the majority of Belgians speak a dialect of **French** known as **Walloon**, as they do in the country's southern provinces, known logically enough as **Wallonia**. Walloon is almost identical to **French**, and if you've any knowledge of the language, you'll be readily understood. French is also the most widely spoken language in **Luxembourg**, along with German – although most Luxembourgers also speak a local and distinctive German dialect, **Lëtzebuergesch** (see p.328).

Flemish

Flemish, or Dutch, is a Germanic language and although Dutch-speakers are at pains to stress the differences between the two, if you know any German you'll spot many similarities. Many Flemish-speakers also speak English to varying degrees of excellence, especially in the larger cities, and partly as a result any attempt you make to speak Flemish may be met with bewilderment – though this can have as much to do with pronunciation (Dutch is very difficult to get right) as their surprise that you're making an effort. The following words and phrases serve as an introduction to the language, and we've included a basic **food and drink glossary** too, though menus are often multilingual and where they aren't, ask and one will almost invariably appear.

As for **phrasebooks**, the *Rough Guide to Dutch* is pocket-sized, and has a good dictionary section (English–Dutch and Dutch–English) as well as a menu reader; it also provides a useful introduction to grammar and pronunciation.

Pronunciation

Flemish is **pronounced** much the same as English. However, there are a few Dutch sounds that don't exist in English, which can be difficult to get right without practice.

Consonants

Double-consonant combinations generally keep their separate sounds in Flemish: **kn**, for example, is never like the English "knight". Note also the following consonants and consonant combinations:

j is an English y, as in yellow

ch and **g** indicate a throaty sound, as at the end of the Scottish word loch. The Dutch word for canal – gracht – is especially tricky, since it has two of these sounds – it comes out along the lines of khrakht. A common word for hello is Dag! – pronounced like daakh

ng as in bri**ng**

nj as in o**nion**

y is not a consonant, but another way of writing **ij**

Vowels and diphthongs

A good rule of thumb is that doubling the letter lengthens the vowel sound.

a is like the English **a**pple

aa like c**ar**t

e like l**e**t

ee like l**a**te

o as in p**o**p

oo in p**o**pe

u is like the French **tu** if preceded by a consonant; it's like w**oo**d if followed by a consonant

uu is the French **tu**

au and **ou** like h**ow**

ei and **ij** as in f**i**ne, though this varies strongly from region to region; sometimes it can sound more like l**a**ne

oe as in s**oo**n

eu is like the diphthong in the French l**eu**r

ui is the hardest Dutch diphthong of all, pronounced like h**ow** but much further forward in the mouth, with lips pursed (as if to say "oo").

Words and phrases

The basics

yes	ja
no	nee
please	alstublieft
(no) thank you	(nee) dank u or bedankt
hello	hallo, dag or hoi
good morning	goedemorgen
good afternoon	goedemiddag
good evening	goedenavond
goodbye	tot ziens
see you later	tot straks
Do you speak English?	Spreekt u Engels?
I don't understand	Ik begrijp het niet
women/men	vrouwen/mannen
children	kinderen
men's/women's toilets	heren/dames
I want…	Ik wil…
I don't want to…	Ik wil niet… (+verb)
sorry	Sorry

Travel, directions and shopping

How do I get to…?	Hoe kom ik in…?
Where is…?	Waar is…?
How far is it to…?	Hoe ver is het naar…?
How much is…?	Wat kost…?
far/near	ver/dichtbij
left/right	links/rechts
airport	luchthaven
post office	postkantoor
postbox	postbus
money exchange	geldwisselkantoor
cash desk	kassa
railway platform	spoor or perron
ticket office	loket
here/there	hier/daar
good/bad	goed/slecht
big/small	groot/klein
open/closed	open/gesloten
push/pull	duwen/trekken
new/old	nieuw/oud
cheap/expensive	goedkoop/duur
hot/cold	heet or warm/koud
with/without	met/zonder
north	noord
south	zuid
east	oost
west	west

Signs and abbreviations

alle richtingen	all directions (road sign)
A.U.B.	*Alstublieft*: please (also shown as S.V.P., from French)
BG	*Begane grond*: ground floor
geen toegang	no entry
gesloten	closed
ingang	entrance
K	*kelder*: basement
let op!	attention!
heren/dames	men's/women's toilets
open	open

rechtdoor	straight ahead
T/M	*Tot en met*: up to and including
toegang	entrance
uitgang	exit
V.A.	*vanaf*: from
Z.O.Z.	please turn over (page, leaflet, etc)

Useful cycling terms

tyre	band
cycle	fiets
cycle path	fietspad
broken	kapot
chain	ketting
puncture	lek
pump	pomp
brake	rem
handlebars	stuur
pedal	trapper
wheel	wiel

Days of the week

Sunday	zondag
Monday	maandag
Tuesday	dinsdag
Wednesday	woensdag
Thursday	donderdag
Friday	vrijdag
Saturday	zaterdag
yesterday	gisteren
today	vandaag
tomorrow	morgen
tomorrow morning	morgenochtend
week	week
day	dag

Months

year	jaar
month	maand
January	januari
February	februari
March	maart
April	april
May	mei
June	juni
July	juli
August	augustus
September	september
October	oktober
November	november
December	december

Time

hour	uur
minute	minuut
What time is it?	Hoe laat is het?

Numbers

When saying a number, Dutch speakers generally transpose the last two digits: for example, €3.25 is drie euro vijf en twintig.

0	nul
1	een
2	twee
3	drie
4	vier
5	vijf
6	zes
7	zeven
8	acht
9	negen
10	tien
11	elf
12	twaalf
13	dertien
14	veertien
15	vijftien
16	zestien
17	zeventien
18	achttien
19	negentien
20	twintig
21	een en twintig
22	twee en twintig
30	dertig
40	veertig
50	vijftig
60	zestig
70	zeventig
80	tachtig
90	negentig
100	honderd
101	honderd een

200	twee honderd
201	twee honderd een
500	vijf honderd
525	vijf honderd vijf en twintig
1000	duizend

A Flemish menu reader

Basic terms and ingredients

belegd	filled or topped, as in **belegde broodjes** (bread rolls topped with cheese, etc)
boter	butter
boterham/broodje	sandwich/roll
brood	bread
dranken	drinks
eieren	eggs
gerst	barley
groenten	vegetables
honing	honey
hoofdgerechten	main courses
kaas	cheese
koud	cold
nagerechten	desserts
peper	pepper
sla/salade	salad
stokbrood	french bread
suiker	sugar
vegetarisch	vegetarian
vis	fish
vlees	meat
voorgerechten	starters/hors d'oeuvres
vruchten	fruit
warm	hot
zout	salt

Cooking terms

doorbakken	well-done
gebakken	fried/baked
gebraden	roasted
gegrild	grilled
gekookt	boiled
geraspt	grated
gerookt	smoked
gestoofd	stewed
half doorbakken	medium-done
rood	rare

Starters and snacks

erwtensoep/snert	thick pea soup with bacon or sausage
huzarensalade	potato salad with pickles
koffietafel	light midday meal of cold meats, cheese, bread, and perhaps soup
patat/friet	chips/French fries
soep	soup
uitsmijter	ham or cheese with eggs on bread

Meat and poultry

biefstuk (hollandse)	steak
biefstuk (duitse)	hamburger
eend	duck
fricandeau	roast pork
fricandel	frankfurter-like sausage
gehakt	mince
ham	ham
kalfsvlees	veal
kalkoen	turkey
karbonade	a chop
kip	chicken
kroket	spiced veal or beef in hash, coated in breadcrumbs
lamsvlees	lamb
lever	liver
ossenhaas	beef tenderloin
rookvlees	smoked beef
spek	bacon
worst	sausages

Fish and seafood

forel	trout
garnalen	prawns
haring	herring
kabeljauw	cod
makreel	mackerel

Flemish specialities

hutsepot – a winter-warmer consisting of various bits of beef and pork (including pigs' trotters and ears) casseroled with turnips, celery, leeks and parsnips

konijn met pruimen – rabbit with prunes

paling in 't groen – eel braised in a green (usually spinach) sauce with herbs

stoemp – mashed potato mixed with vegetable and/or meat purée

stoofvlees – cubes of beef marinated in beer and cooked with herbs and onions

stoverij – stewed beef and offal (especially liver and kidneys), slowly tenderized in dark beer and served with a slice of bread covered in mustard

waterzooi – a delicious, filling soup-cum-stew, made with either chicken (*van kip*) or fish (*van riviervis*)

mosselen	mussels
oesters	oysters
paling	eel
schelvis	haddock
schol	plaice
tong	sole
zalm	salmon
zeeduivel	monkfish

Vegetables

aardappelen	potatoes
bloemkool	cauliflower
bonen	beans
champignons	mushrooms
erwten	peas
hutspot	mashed potatoes and carrots
knoflook	garlic
komkommer	cucumber
prei	leek
rijst	rice
sla	salad, lettuce
stampot andijvie	mashed potato and endive
stampot boerenkool	mashed potato and cabbage
uien	onions
wortelen	carrots
zuurkool	sauerkraut

Sweets and desserts

appeltaart/ appelgebak	apple tart or cake
gebak	pastry
ijs	ice cream
koekjes	biscuits
pannenkoeken	pancakes
pepernoten	Dutch biscuits
poffertjes	small pancakes/fritters
(slag) room	(whipped) cream
speculaas	spice- and cinnamon-flavoured biscuit
stroopwafels	waffles
taai-taai	spicy Dutch cake
vla	custard

Fruits and nuts

aardbei	strawberry
amandel	almond
appel	apple
appelmoes	apple purée
citroen	lemon
druiven	grape
framboos	raspberry
hazelnoot	hazelnut
kers	cherry
kokosnoot	coconut
peer	pear
perzik	peach
pinda	peanut
pruim	plum/prune

Drinks

anijsmelk	aniseed-flavoured warm milk
appelsap	apple juice
bessenjenever	blackcurrant gin
chocomel	chocolate milk

warme chocolade melk	hot chocolate
citroenjenever	lemon gin
droog	dry
frisdranken	soft drinks
jenever	Dutch gin
karnemelk	buttermilk
koffie	coffee
koffie verkeerd	coffee with warm milk
kopstoot	beer with a jenever chaser
melk	milk
met ijs	with ice
met slagroom	with whipped cream
pils	Dutch beer
proost!	cheers!
sinaasappelsap	orange juice
thee	tea
tomatensap	tomato juice
vruchtensap	fruit juice
wijn (wit/rood/rosé)	wine (white/red/rosé)
vieux	Dutch brandy

French

Most **Walloons** (French-speaking Belgians) working in the business and tourist industries have at least some knowledge of English, but beyond that, and especially in Wallonia's small towns and villages, you'll need at least a modicum of **French** to have any sort of conversation at all. Differentiating words is the initial problem in understanding **spoken Walloon** – it's very hard to get people to slow down. If, as a last resort, you get them to write it down, you'll probably find you know half the words anyway – French and English share many words. Of the available **phrasebooks**, Rough Guides' own *French Phrasebook* should sort you out better than most.

Pronunciation

Consonants

Consonants are pronounced much as in English, except:

c is softened to the **s** sound when followed by an "e" or "i", or when it has a cedilla (ç) below it

ch is always **sh**

g is softened to a French **j** sound when followed by e or i (eg gendarme)

h is silent

j is like the s sound in "measure" or "treasure"

ll is like the **y** in **y**es

qu is normally pronounced like a **k** as in **k**ey (eg quatre)

r is growled (or rolled).

th is the same as **t**

w is **v**

Vowels

These are the hardest sounds to get right. Roughly:

a as in h**a**t

e as in g**e**t

é between g**e**t and g**a**te

è between g**e**t and g**u**t

eu like the **u** in h**u**rt

i as in machi**n**e

o as in h**o**t

o, **au** as in **o**ver

ou as in f**oo**d

u as in a pursed-lip version of **u**se

More awkward are the combinations below when they occur at the ends of words, or are followed by consonants other than *n* or *m*:

in/im like the an in **an**xious

an/am, **en/em** as in d**on** when said with a nasal accent

on/om like the d**on** in D**on**caster said by someone with a heavy cold

un/um like the u in **u**nderstand.

Words and phrases

Basics

yes	oui
no	non
please	s'il vous plaît
(no) thank you	(non) merci
hello	bonjour
how are you?	comment allez-vous?/ ça va?
good morning	bonjour
good afternoon	bonjour
good evening	bonsoir
good night	bonne nuit
goodbye	au revoir
see you later	à bientôt
now/later	maintenant/plus tard
sorry	pardon, Madame, Monsieur/je m'excuse
do you speak English?	parlez-vous anglais?
I (don't) understand	je (ne) comprends (pas)
women	femmes
men	hommes
children	enfants
I want…	je veux…
I don't want	je ne veux pas
OK/agreed	d'accord

Travel, directions and shopping

how do I get to…?	comment est-ce que je peux arriver à…?
where is…?	où est…?
how far is it to…?	combien y a-t-il jusqu'à…?
how much is…?	c'est combien…?
when?	quand?
far/near	loin/près
left/ right	à gauche/à droite
straight ahead	tout droit
through traffic only	voie de traversée
airport.	aéroport
post office	la poste
stamp(s)	timbre(s)
money exchange	bureau de change
cashier	la caisse
quay, or (railway) platform	quai
railway station	gare
ticket office	le guichet
here/there	ici/là
behind	derrière
good/bad	bon/mauvais
big/small	grand/petit
push/pull	pousser/tirer
new/old	nouveau/vieux
cheap/expensive	bon marché/cher
hot/cold	chaud/froid
with/without	avec/sans
a lot/a little	beaucoup/peu
East	est
North	nord
West	occidental/ouest
South	sud

Signs and abbreviations

S.V.P.	*S'il vous plaît*: please
acces interdit	no entry
Attention!	attention!
entrée	entrance
étage	floor (of a museum, etc).
fermé	closed
fermeture	closing period.
hommes/femmes	men's/women's toilets
ouvert	open
sortie	exit

Useful cycling terms

cycle	bicyclette
broken	cassé
chain	chaîne
brake	frein
handlebars	guidon
pedal	pédale
puncture	pneu crevé
tyre	pneu
pump	pompe
wheel	roue

Days of the week

Monday	lundi
Tuesday	mardi

Wednesday	mercredi
Thursday	jeudi
Friday	vendredi
Saturday	samedi
Sunday	dimanche
morning	matin
afternoon	après-midi
evening	soir
night	nuit
yesterday	hier
today	aujourd'hui
tomorrow	demain
tomorrow morning	demain matin
day	jour
week	semaine

Months

month	mois
year	année
January	janvier
February	février
March	mars
April	avril
May	mai
June	juin
July	juillet
August	août
September	septembre
October	octobre
November	novembre
December	décembre

Time

minute	minute
hour	heure
What time is it...?	Quelle heure est-il...?

Numbers

0	zéro
1	un
2	deux
3	trois
4	quatre
5	cinq
6	six
7	sept
8	huit
9	neuf
10	dix
11	onze
12	douze
13	treize
14	quatorze
15	quinze
16	seize
17	dix-sept
18	dix-huit
19	dix-neuf
20	vingt
21	vingt-et-un
30	trente
40	quarante
50	cinquante
60	soixante
70	soixante-dix (local usage is septante)
80	quatre-vingts
90	quatre-vingt-dix (local usage is nonante)
100	cent
101	cent-et-un
200	deux cents
500	cinq cents
1000	mille

A French menu reader

Basic terms and ingredients

beurre	butter
chaud	hot
crème fraîche	sour cream
dessert	dessert
dégustation	tasting (wine or food).
escargots	snails
frappé	iced
fromage	cheese
froid	cold
gibier	game
hors d'oeuvres	starters

légumes	vegetables
oeufs	eggs
pain	bread
poisson	fish
poivre	pepper
riz	rice
salade	salad
sel	salt
sucre/sucré	sugar/sweet (taste)
tourte	tart or pie
tranche	slice
viande	meat

Cooking terms

à point	medium done
au four	baked
bien cuit	well done
bouilli	boiled
frit/friture	fried/deep fried
fumé	smoked
grillé	grilled
mijoté	stewed
pané	breaded
rôti	roast
saignant	rare (meat)
sauté	lightly cooked in butter

Starters and snacks

assiette anglaise	plate of cold meats
bisque	shellfish soup
bouillabaisse	fish soup from Marseilles
bouillon	broth or stock
consommé	clear soup
croque-monsieur	grilled cheese and ham sandwich
crudités	raw vegetables with dressing
potage	thick soup, usually vegetable
un sandwich/une baguette…	a sandwich…
de jambon	with ham
de fromage	with cheese
de saucisson	with sausage
à l'aïl	with garlic
au poivre	with pepper
oeufs…	eggs…
au plat	fried eggs
à la coque	boiled eggs
durs	hard-boiled eggs
brouillés	scrambled eggs
omelette…	omelette…
nature	plain
au fromage	with cheese
salade de…	salad of…
tomates	tomatoes
concombres	cucumbers
crêpes…	pancakes…
au sucre	with sugar
au citron	with lemon
au miel	with honey
à la confiture	with jam

Meat and poultry

agneau	lamb
bifteck	steak
boeuf	beef
canard	duck
cheval	horsemeat
cuisson	leg of lamb
côtelettes	cutlets
dindon	turkey
foie	liver
gigot	leg of venison
jambon	ham
lard	bacon
porc	pork
poulet	chicken
saucisse	sausage
veau	veal

Fish and seafood

anchois	anchovies
anguilles	eels
carrelet	plaice
crevettes roses	prawns
hareng	herring
lotte de mer	monkfish
maquereau	mackerel
morue	cod
moules	mussels
saumon	salmon

Some Walloon and Brussels specialities

carbonnades de porc Bruxelloise – pork with a tarragon and tomato sauce
chicorées gratinées au four – chicory baked with ham and cheese
fricadelles à la bière – meatballs in beer
fricassée Liégois – fried eggs, bacon and sausage or blood pudding
le marcassin – young wild boar, served either cold and sliced or hot with vegetables
pâté de faisan – pheasant pâté
truite à l'Ardennaise – trout cooked in a wine sauce

sole	sole
truite	trout

Vegetables

aïl	garlic
asperges	asparagus
carottes	carrots
champignons	mushrooms
choufleur	cauliflower
concombre	cucumber
genièvre	juniper
laitue	lettuce
oignons	onions
petits pois	peas
poireau	leek
pommes (de terre)	potatoes
tomate	tomato

Sweets and desserts

crêpes	pancakes
crêpes suzettes	thin pancakes with orange juice and liqueur
glace	ice cream
madeleine	small, shell-shaped sponge cake
parfait	frozen mousse, sometimes ice cream
petits fours	bite-sized cakes or pastries

Fruits and nuts

amandes	almonds
ananas	pineapple
cacahouète	peanut
cerises	cherries
citron	lemon
fraises	strawberries
framboises	raspberries
marrons	chestnuts
noisette	hazelnut
pamplemousse	grapefruit
poire	pear
pomme	apple
prune	plum
pruneau	prune
raisins	grapes

Drinks

bière	beer
café	coffee
eaux de vie	spirits distilled from various fruits
jenever	Dutch/Flemish gin
lait	milk
orange/citron pressé	fresh orange/lemon juice
thé	tea
vin…	wine…
rouge	red
blanc	white
brut	very dry
sec	dry
demi-sec	sweet
doux	very sweet

Glossary

Flemish terms

Abdij Abbey.

Begijnhof Convent occupied by beguines (*begijns*), ie members of a sisterhood living as nuns but without vows, retaining the right of return to the secular world. See box, p.357.

Beiaard Carillon (ie a set of tuned church bells, either operated by an automatic mechanism or played by a keyboard).

Belfort Belfry.

Beurs Stock exchange.

Botermarkt Butter market.

Brug Bridge.

Burgher Member of the upper or mercantile classes of a town, usually with certain civic powers.

Gemeente Municipal, as in *Gemeentehuis* (town hall).

Gerechtshof Law Courts.

Gilde Guild.

Gracht Canal.

Groentenmarkt Vegetable market.

(Grote) Markt Central town square and the heart of most Flemish communities.

Hal Hall.

Hof Courtyard.

Huis House.

Jeugdherberg Youth hostel.

Kaai Quay or wharf.

Kapel Chapel.

Kasteel Castle.

Kerk Church; eg Grote Kerk – the principal church of the town.

Koning King.

Koningin Queen.

Koninklijk Royal.

Korenmarkt Corn market.

Kunst Art.

Lakenhal Cloth hall: the building in medieval weaving towns where cloth would be weighed, graded and sold.

Molen Windmill.

Onze Lieve Vrouwekerk or **OLV** Church of Our Lady.

Paleis Palace.

Plaats A square or open space.

Plein A square or open space.

Polder An area of land reclaimed from the sea.

Poort Gate.

Raadhuis Town hall.

Rijk State.

Schatkamer Treasury.

Schepenzaal Alderman's Hall.

Schone kunsten Fine arts.

Schouwburg Theatre.

Sierkunst Decorative arts.

Stadhuis The most common word for a town hall.

Stedelijk Civic, municipal.

Steeg Alley.

Stichting Institute or foundation.

Straat Street.

Toren Tower.

Tuin Garden.

Vleeshuis Meat market.

Volkskunde Folklore.

Weg Way.

French terms

Abbaye Abbey.

Auberge de jeunesse Youth hostel.

Beaux arts Fine arts.

Beffroi Belfry.

Béguinage Convent occupied by beguines, ie members of a sisterhood living as nuns but without vows and with the right of return to the secular world (see box, p.357).

Bourse Stock exchange.

Chapelle Chapel.

Château Mansion, country house, or castle.

Cour Court(yard).

Couvent Convent, monastery.

Église Church.

Fouilles Archeological excavations.

Gîte d'étape Dormitory-style lodgings situated in relatively remote parts of the country, which can house anywhere between ten and one hundred people per establishment.

Grand-place Central town square and the heart of most Walloon communities.

Halle aux draps Cloth hall. The building in medieval weaving towns where cloth would be weighed, graded, stored and sold.

Halle aux viandes Meat market.

Halles Covered, central food market.

Hôpital Hospital.

Hôtel Hotel or mansion.

Hôtel de ville Town hall.

Jardin Garden.

Jours feriés Public holidays.

Maison House.

Marché Market.

Moulin Windmill.

Municipal Civic, municipal.

Musée Museum.

Notre Dame Our Lady.

Palais Palace.

Place Square, marketplace.

Pont Bridge.

Porte Gateway.

Quartier District of a town.

Roi King.

Reine Queen.

Rue Street.

Syndicat d'initiative Tourist office.

Tour Tower.

Trésor Treasury.

Art and architectural terms

Ambulatory Covered passage around the outer edge of the choir of a church.

Apse Semicircular protrusion (usually) at the east end of a church.

Art Deco Geometrical style of art and architecture popular in the 1930s.

Art Nouveau Style of art, architecture and design based on highly stylized vegetal forms. Especially popular in the early part of the twentieth century.

Balustrade An ornamental rail, running, almost invariably, along the top of a building.

Baroque The art and architecture of the Counter-Reformation, dating from around 1600 onwards. Distinguished by extreme ornateness, exuberance and by the complex but harmonious spatial arrangement of interiors.

Basilica Catholic church with honorific privileges.

Carillon A set of tuned church bells, either operated by an automatic mechanism or played on a keyboard.

Carolingian Dynasty founded by Charlemagne; mid-eighth to early tenth century. Also refers to art, etc, of the period.

Caryatid A sculptured female figure used as a column.

Chancel The eastern part of a church, often separated from the nave by a screen (see "rood screen", p.398). Contains the choir and ambulatory.

Classical Architectural style incorporating Greek and Roman elements – pillars, domes, colonnades etc – at its height in the seventeenth century and revived, as Neoclassical (see below), in the nineteenth.

Clerestory Upper storey of a church with windows.

Diptych Carved or painted work on two panels. Often used as an altarpiece – both static and, more occasionally, portable.

Expressionism Artistic style popular at the beginning of the twentieth century, characterized by the exaggeration of shape or colour; often accompanied by the extensive use of symbolism.

Flamboyant Florid form of Gothic (see "Gothic" below).

Fresco Wall painting – durable through application to wet plaster.

Gable The triangular upper portion of a wall – decorative or supporting a roof – which is a feature of many canal houses.

Gallo-Roman Period of Roman occupation of Gaul (including much of present-day Belgium), from the first to the fourth century AD.

Genre painting In the seventeenth century the term "genre painting" applied to everything from animal paintings and still lifes through to historical works and landscapes. In the eighteenth century, the term came only to be applied to scenes of everyday life.

Gobelin A rich French tapestry, named after the most famous of all tapestry manufacturers, based in Paris, whose most renowned period was during the reign of Louis XIV; also loosely applied to tapestries of similar style made in Belgium.

Gothic Architectural style of the thirteenth to sixteenth centuries, characterized by pointed arches, rib vaulting, flying buttresses and a general emphasis on verticality.

Grisaille A technique of monochrome painting in shades of grey.

Merovingian Dynasty ruling France and parts of "Belgium" from the sixth to the middle of the eighth century. Refers also to art, etc, of the period.

Misericord Ledge on choir stall on which the occupant can be supported while standing; often carved with secular subjects (bottoms were not thought worthy of religious subject matter – quite right too).

Mosan Adjective applied to the lands bordering the River Meuse – hence Mosan metalwork.

Nave Main body of a church.

Neoclassical A style of classical architecture (see above) revived in the nineteenth century, popular in the Low Countries during and after French rule in the early nineteenth century.

Neo-Gothic Revived Gothic style of architecture popular in the late eighteenth and nineteenth centuries.

Pediment Feature of a gable, usually triangular and often sporting a relief.

Pilaster A shallow rectangular column projecting, but only slightly, from a wall.

Renaissance The period of European history marking the end of the medieval period and the rise of the modern world. Defined, among many criteria, by an increase in classical scholarship, geographical discovery, the rise of secular values and the growth of individualism. Began in Italy in the fourteenth century. Also refers to the art and architecture of the period.

Retable Altarpiece.

Rococo Highly florid, light and intricate eighteenth-century style of architecture, painting and interior design, forming the last phase of Baroque.

Romanesque Early medieval architecture distinguished by squat, heavy forms, rounded arches and naive sculpture.

Rood loft Gallery (or space) on top of a rood screen.

Rood screen Decorative screen separating the nave from the chancel.

Stucco Marble-based plaster used to embellish ceilings, etc.

Transept Arms of a cross-shaped church, placed at ninety degrees to nave and chancel.

Triptych Carved or painted work on three panels. Often used as an altarpiece.

Tympanum Sculpted, usually triangular and recessed, panel above a door.

Vauban Seventeenth-century French military architect whose fortresses still stand all over Europe and the Low Countries; hence the adjective Vaubanesque.

Vault An arched ceiling or roof.

Travel store

Travel

Andorra The Pyrenees, Pyrenees & Andorra Map, Spain
Antigua The Caribbean
Argentina Argentina, Argentina Map, Buenos Aires, South America on a Budget
Aruba The Caribbean
Australia Australia, Australia Map, East Coast Australia, Melbourne, Sydney, Tasmania
Austria Austria, Europe on a Budget, Vienna
Bahamas The Bahamas, The Caribbean
Barbados Barbados DIR, The Caribbean
Belgium Belgium & Luxembourg, Bruges DIR, Brussels, Brussels Map, Europe on a Budget
Belize Belize, Central America on a Budget, Guatemala & Belize Map
Benin West Africa
Bolivia Bolivia, South America on a Budget
Brazil Brazil, Rio, South America on a Budget
British Virgin Islands The Caribbean
Brunei Malaysia, Singapore & Brunei [1 title], Southeast Asia on a Budget
Bulgaria Bulgaria, Europe on a Budget
Burkina Faso West Africa
Cambodia Cambodia, Southeast Asia on a Budget, Vietnam, Laos & Cambodia Map [1 Map]
Cameroon West Africa
Canada Canada, Pacific Northwest, Toronto, Toronto Map, Vancouver
Cape Verde West Africa
Cayman Islands The Caribbean
Chile Chile, Chile Map, South America on a Budget
China Beijing, China, Hong Kong & Macau, Hong Kong & Macau DIR, Shanghai
Colombia South America on a Budget
Costa Rica Central America on a Budget, Costa Rica, Costa Rica & Panama Map
Croatia Croatia, Croatia Map, Europe on a Budget
Cuba Cuba, Cuba Map, The Caribbean, Havana
Cyprus Cyprus, Cyprus Map
Czech Republic The Czech Republic, Czech & Slovak Republics, Europe on a Budget, Prague, Prague DIR, Prague Map
Denmark Copenhagen, Denmark, Europe on a Budget, Scandinavia
Dominica The Caribbean
Dominican Republic Dominican Republic, The Caribbean
Ecuador Ecuador, South America on a Budget
Egypt Egypt, Egypt Map
El Salvador Central America on a Budget
England Britain, Camping in Britain, Devon & Cornwall, Dorset, Hampshire and The Isle of Wight [1 title], England, Europe on a Budget, The Lake District, London, London DIR, London Map, London Mini Guide, Walks In London & Southeast England
Estonia The Baltic States, Europe on a Budget
Fiji Fiji
Finland Europe on a Budget, Finland, Scandinavia
France Brittany & Normandy, Corsica, Corsica Map, The Dordogne & the Lot, Europe on a Budget, France, France Map, Languedoc & Roussillon, The Loire, Paris, Paris DIR, Paris Map, Paris Mini Guide, Provence & the Côte d'Azur, The Pyrenees, Pyrenees & Andorra Map
French Guiana South America on a Budget
Gambia The Gambia, West Africa
Germany Berlin, Berlin Map, Europe on a Budget, Germany, Germany Map
Ghana West Africa
Gibraltar Spain
Greece Athens Map, Crete, Crete Map, Europe on a Budget, Greece, Greece Map, Greek Islands, Ionian Islands
Guadeloupe The Caribbean
Guatemala Central America on a Budget, Guatemala, Guatemala & Belize Map
Guinea West Africa
Guinea-Bissau West Africa
Guyana South America on a Budget
Holland see The Netherlands
Honduras Central America on a Budget
Hungary Budapest, Europe on a Budget, Hungary
Iceland Iceland, Iceland Map
India Goa, India, India Map, Kerala, Rajasthan, Delhi & Agra [1 title], South India, South India Map
Indonesia Bali & Lombok, Southeast Asia on a Budget
Ireland Dublin DIR, Dublin Map, Europe on a Budget, Ireland, Ireland Map
Israel Jerusalem
Italy Europe on a Budget, Florence DIR, Florence & Siena Map, Florence & the best of Tuscany, Italy, The Italian Lakes, Naples & the Amalfi Coast, Rome, Rome DIR, Rome Map, Sardinia, Sicily, Sicily Map, Tuscany & Umbria, Tuscany Map, Venice, Venice DIR, Venice Map
Jamaica Jamaica, The Caribbean
Japan Japan, Tokyo
Jordan Jordan
Kenya Kenya, Kenya Map
Korea Korea
Laos Laos, Southeast Asia on a Budget, Vietnam, Laos & Cambodia Map [1 Map]
Latvia The Baltic States, Europe on a Budget
Lithuania The Baltic States, Europe on a Budget
Luxembourg Belgium & Luxembourg, Europe on a Budget
Malaysia Malaysia Map, Malaysia, Singapore & Brunei [1 title], Southeast Asia on a Budget
Mali West Africa
Malta Malta & Gozo DIR
Martinique The Caribbean
Mauritania West Africa
Mexico Baja California, Baja California, Cancún & Cozumel DIR, Mexico, Mexico Map, Yucatán, Yucatán Peninsula Map
Monaco France, Provence & the Côte d'Azur
Montenegro Montenegro
Morocco Europe on a Budget, Marrakesh DIR, Marrakesh Map, Morocco, Morocco Map,
Nepal Nepal
Netherlands Amsterdam, Amsterdam DIR, Amsterdam Map, Europe on a Budget, The Netherlands
Netherlands Antilles The Caribbean
New Zealand New Zealand, New Zealand Map

DIR: Rough Guide **DIRECTIONS** for short breaks

Small print and Index

A Rough Guide to Rough Guides

Published in 1982, the first Rough Guide – to Greece – was a student scheme that became a publishing phenomenon. Mark Ellingham, a recent graduate in English from Bristol University, had been travelling in Greece the previous summer and couldn't find the right guidebook. With a small group of friends he wrote his own guide, combining a highly contemporary, journalistic style with a thoroughly practical approach to travellers' needs.

The immediate success of the book spawned a series that rapidly covered dozens of destinations. And, in addition to impecunious backpackers, Rough Guides soon acquired a much broader and older readership that relished the guides' wit and inquisitiveness as much as their enthusiastic, critical approach and value-for-money ethos.

These days, Rough Guides include recommendations from shoestring to luxury and cover more than 200 destinations around the globe, including almost every country in the Americas and Europe, more than half of Africa and most of Asia and Australasia. Our ever-growing team of authors and photographers is spread all over the world, particularly in Europe, the US and Australia.

In the early 1990s, Rough Guides branched out of travel, with the publication of Rough Guides to World Music, Classical Music and the Internet. All three have become benchmark titles in their fields, spearheading the publication of a wide range of books under the Rough Guide name.

Including the travel series, Rough Guides now number more than 350 titles, covering: phrasebooks, waterproof maps, music guides from Opera to Heavy Metal, reference works as diverse as Conspiracy Theories and Shakespeare, and popular culture books from iPods to Poker. Rough Guides also produce a series of more than 120 World Music CDs in partnership with World Music Network.

Visit www.roughguides.com to see our latest publications.

Rough Guide credits

Text editor: Polly Thomas
Layout: Umesh Aggarwal
Cartography: Animesh Pathak
Picture editor: Chloë Roberts
Production: Erika Pepe
Proofreader: Karen Parker
Cover design: Nicole Newman, Dan May,
Photographers: Roger Mapp and Jean-Christophe Godet
Editorial: **London** Andy Turner, Keith Drew, Edward Aves, Alice Park, Lucy White, Jo Kirby, James Smart, Natasha Foges, James Rice, Emma Beatson, Emma Gibbs, Kathryn Lane, Monica Woods, Mani Ramaswamy, Harry Wilson, Lucy Cowie, Alison Roberts, Lara Kavanagh, Eleanor Aldridge, Ian Blenkinsop, Charlotte Melville, Joe Staines, Matthew Milton, Tracy Hopkins; **Delhi** Madhavi Singh, Jalpreen Kaur Chhatwal, Jubbi Francis
Design & Pictures: **London** Scott Stickland, Dan May, Diana Jarvis, Mark Thomas, Nicole Newman, Sarah Cummins; **Delhi** Ajay Verma, Jessica Subramanian, Ankur Guha, Pradeep Thapliyal, Sachin Tanwar, Anita Singh, Nikhil Agarwal, Sachin Gupta
Production: Rebecca Short, Liz Cherry, Louise Daly
Cartography: **London** Ed Wright, Katie Lloyd-Jones; **Delhi** Rajesh Chhibber, Ashutosh Bharti, Rajesh Mishra, Jasbir Sandhu, Swati Handoo, Deshpal Dabas, Lokamata Sahu
Marketing, Publicity & roughguides.com: Liz Statham
Digital Travel Publisher: Peter Buckley
Reference Director: Andrew Lockett
Operations Coordinator: Becky Doyle
Operations Assistant: Johanna Wurm
Publishing Director (Travel): Clare Currie
Commercial Manager: Gino Magnotta
Managing Director: John Duhigg

Publishing information

This fifth edition published June 2011 by
Rough Guides Ltd,
80 Strand, London WC2R 0RL
11, Community Centre, Panchsheel Park,
New Delhi 110017, India

Distributed by the Penguin Group

Penguin Books Ltd,
80 Strand, London WC2R 0RL

Penguin Group (USA)
375 Hudson Street, NY 10014, USA

Penguin Group (Australia)
250 Camberwell Road, Camberwell,
Victoria 3124, Australia

Penguin Group (NZ)
67 Apollo Drive, Mairangi Bay, Auckland 1310,
New Zealand

Rough Guides is represented in Canada by Tourmaline Editions Inc. 662 King Street West, Suite 304, Toronto, Ontario M5V 1M7

Cover concept by Peter Dyer.

Typeset in Bembo and Helvetica to an original design by Henry Iles.

Printed in Singapore

416pp includes index
A catalogue record for this book is available from the British Library
ISBN: 978-1-84836-720-3
The publishers and authors have done their best to ensure the accuracy and currency of all the information in **The Rough Guide to Belgium and Luxembourg**, however, they can accept no responsibility for any loss, injury, or inconvenience sustained by any traveller as a result of information or advice contained in the guide.
1 3 5 7 9 8 6 4 2

Help us update

We've gone to a lot of effort to ensure that the fifth edition of **The Rough Guide to Belgium and Luxembourg** is accurate and up-to-date. However, things change – places get "discovered", opening hours are notoriously fickle, restaurants and rooms raise prices or lower standards. If you feel we've got it wrong or left something out, we'd like to know, and if you can remember the address, the price, the hours, the phone number, so much the better.

Please send your comments with the subject line "**Rough Guide Belgium and Luxembourg Update**" to ⓔ mail@uk.roughguides.com. We'll credit all contributions and send a copy of the next edition (or any other Rough Guide if you prefer) for the very best emails.

Find more travel information, connect with fellow travellers and book your trip on ⓦ www.roughguides.com

Acknowledgements

Martin Dunford A big thank you to my co-authors, Suzy and Phil; to Polly for seamless editing; and to everyone else who helped me along the way.

Phil Lee would like to thank his editor, Polly Thomas, for her exemplary attention to detail during the preparation of this new edition of the Rough Guide to Belgium and Luxembourg. Special thanks also to Anita Rampall of Visit Flanders; Pieter Van der Gheynst from the Conseil Bruxellois des Musées; Nathalie Standaert from the *Hotel Adornes*, Bruges; Florie Wilberts of Toerisme Mechelen; Ellen Hubert of Antwerpen Toerisme; Veronique De Muynck from the *Alegria Hotel*, Bruges; Mia Ackaert of Chambreplus in Ghent; and Freya Sackx and Erwin Van de Wiele from Ghent tourist office. Thanks also to my co-authors, Martin Dunford, Suzy Sumner and Loïk Dal Molin.

Readers' letters

Thanks to all the readers who have taken the time to write in with comments and suggestions (and apologies if we've inadvertently omitted or misspelt anyone's name):

John Akhurst; John Allen; Rob Andrews; Anthony Neil Ashworth; Richard Barker; Tom Baxter; Johan Bergstromallen-Allen; Otto Beuchner; Alexsandra Bilos; Lianne Bissell; Julia Bomken; Nawal Boulyou; Chris Burin; Piroja Bustani; Dick Butler; Richard Butler; Martin Connors; David Cox; Emmanuel David; John & Frances Davies; Nele Depoorter; Mike Dobson; Simon Evans; Franck Faraday; Anthea Finlayson; Sheina Foulkes; Catherine Froidebise; Patrick Gardinal; Eric Van Geertruyden; Johan De Geyndt; Pieter Van der Gheynst; Mike Gingell; Kareen Goldfeder; J. Goodfellow; Sally Gritten; David Gruccio; Katrien Gysen; Tony Hallas; John Hammond; Helen Harjanto; Lucy Hartiss; Pat Hindley; Herman Hindricks; Nick Howard; Jay Jones; Adam Kramer; John & Angela Lansley; Peter & Vivien Lee; Simon Loveitt; Heather McCann; Richard Madge; Fab Marsani; Loes Maveau; Claudia Merges; Slávi Metz; Deirdre & David Mills; William Milne; Paul Mitchell; Bernadette & Michael Mossley; Ros Murphy; Mary Murray; B.E. Neale; Stuart Newman; Barry Newsome; Delphine Nizet; Adolphe Nzeza; Maureen O'Keefe; Marc Oris; Isabel Payno; Melissa Perry; Susan Plowden; Johnny Pring; David Reeves; Barbara Reid; Kiron Reid; Greg Richardson; John A. Rosenhof; Chris Serle; Tiana Sidey; Silke; Ed Silverman; Pascale Slagmulders; Roel Smeyers; Christine Smith; Tim Smith; William Smith; Phyllis Snyder; Zoe Spyvee; K. Tan; Alan Tanner; Colin Tattersall; Warren Thomas; Christina Thyssen; Robin Tilston; Elisabeth Timenchik; David Trussler; Frederik Vlieghe; Mary Whitham; Brian & Suzanne Williams; James Williams; Jim Williams; Steve Willis; Stephen Wills; Melanie Winterbotham; Glenda Young.

Photo credits

All photos © Rough Guides except the following:

Introduction

Grot Markt and Stadhuis, Antwerp © Travel Ink/Getty
Chocolate *Mannekin Pis* statues, Brussels © Steve Vidler/Superstock
Luxembourg City © Craig Aurness/Corbis
Beach near Ostend © Lisa Valder/Getty
Sandcastle Festival, Zeebrugge © Mark Renders/Getty

Things not to miss

02 The beach north of Ostend, Flanders © Rieger Bertrand/Superstock
03 Kayaking on the Lesse, Ardennes © Pattyn Wouter/Arterra Picture Library/Alamy
04 Jan van Eyck's God, St-Baafskathedraal, Ghent © Superstock
06 Steamed mussels © Ben Fink/Getty
07 Grund lower town, Luxembourg City © Walter Bibikow/Corbis
08 Hergé Museum, Louvain-la-Neuve © Wu Wei/Corbis
09 Onze Lieve Vrouwekathedraal, Antwerp © Shaun Egan/Getty
11 Djiver Canal, Bruges © Paul Hardy/Corbis
12 Hautes Fagnes © Horst Jegen/Superstock
13 Blancs Moussis, Stavelot © Francois Lenoir/Corbis
16 Magritte Museum © Eric Vidal/Corbis

Belgian beer colour section

Westmalle beer © Pictures Colour Library/Alamy
Glass of Brugse Zot © Cephas Picture Library/Alamy
Chimay's Abbaye Notre-Dame de Scourmon © David Kleyn/Alamy
Beer drinkers, Bruges © John Warburton-Lee Photography/Alamy
Hoegaarden and dark Leffe beer, Bruges © Lee Martin/Alamy
Abbaye d'Orval © Ronnie McMillan/Alamy
Logo of the lambic brewery, Cantillon © BigTom/Alamy
Gueuze beer production © SUDRES Jean-Daniel/hemis.fr/Alamy
A la Mort Subite café, Brussels © Colin Matthieu/Superstock

Food and drink colour section

Belgian chocolate truffles © Francis Hammond/Getty
A cone of Belgian *frites* © Francis Hammond/Getty
Brussels waffle with strawberries and cream © David Gee 5/Alamy
Carbonnades à la flamande © Simon Reddy/ALamy
Cheese display, Bruges © Gary Yeowell/Getty
Endive gratin © Jean Cazals/Alamy
Leon de Brussels restaurant, rue des Bouchers © Colin Matthieu/Hemis.fr/Alamy
Shrimper, Oostduinkerke festival © Clément Philippe/Alamy

Black and whites

p.48 Jacques Brel © Pictorial Press/Alamy
p.116 *Adoration of the Mystic Lamb* © The Gallery Collection/Corbis
p.200 Rubenshuis © Renault Philippe/Hemis.fr/Superstock
p.250 Abbaye de Villers © Abbaye de Villers-la-Ville ASBL
p.278 La-Roche-en-Ardenne © Starfoto/CORBIS
p.324 Echternach basilica, Luxembourg © Thomas Stankiewicz/Alamy

Index

Map entries are in colour.

INDEX

C

D

INDEX

INDEX

H

I

J

K

L

M

INDEX

N

O

P

R

S

T

U

V

W

X

Y

Z

INDEX

Map symbols

maps are listed in the full index using coloured text

	International boundary		Museum
	Regional boundary		Memorial/monument
	Chapter division boundary		Castle
	Motorway		Fountain/gardens
	Road		Restaurant
	Pedestrianized road	P	Parking
	Steps	Ⓜ	Metro station
	Tunnel	Ⓟ	Prémétro station
	Footpath		Race circuit
	Railway	★	Bus/tram stop
	Ferry route	(i)	Information office
	River		Post office
	Wall		Statue
	Bridge		Building
▲	Mountain peak		Church
	Point of interest		Cemetery
	Airport		Park
	Gate		Beach
	Abbey		